THE CLOSED
ENTERPRISE SYSTEM

This book is printed on one hundred percent recycled paper

Also available:

ACTION FOR A CHANGE: *A Student's Guide to Public Interest Organizing*, by Ralph Nader and Donald Ross

THE CHEMICAL FEAST: *Ralph Nader's Study Group Report on the Food and Drug Administration*, by James S. Turner

THE INTERSTATE COMMERCE OMISSION: *Ralph Nader's Study Group Report on the Interstate Commerce Commission and Transportation*, by Robert C. Fellmeth

OLD AGE: THE LAST SEGREGATION: *Ralph Nader's Study Group Report on Nursing Homes*, Claire Townsend, Project Director

SOWING THE WIND: *Ralph Nader's Study Group Report on Agribusiness and the Public Interest*, by Harrison Wellford

UNSAFE AT ANY SPEED: *The Designed-in Dangers of the American Automobile* (expanded and updated, 1972) by Ralph Nader

VANISHING AIR: *Ralph Nader's Study Group Report on Air Pollution*, by John C. Esposito

THE WATER LORDS: *Ralph Nader's Study Group Report on Industry and Environmental Crisis in Savannah, Georgia*, by James M. Fallows

WATER WASTELAND: *Ralph Nader's Study Group Report on Water Pollution*, by David Zwick and Marcy Benstock

WHAT TO DO WITH YOUR BAD CAR: *An Action Manual for Lemon Owners*, by Ralph Nader, Lowell Dodge, and Ralf Hotchkiss

WHISTLE BLOWING: *The Report on the Conference on Professional Responsibility*, edited by Ralph Nader and Peter Petkas

THE WORKERS: *Portraits of Nine American Jobholders*, by Kenneth Lasson

THE CLOSED

Ralph Nader's Study Group Report
on Antitrust Enforcement

ENTERPRISE SYSTEM

by Mark J. Green
with Beverly C. Moore, Jr.,
and Bruce Wasserstein

Grossman Publishers
New York   1972

All royalties from the sale of this book will be given to The Center
for Study of Responsive Law, the organization established by Ralph
Nader to conduct research into abuses of the public interest by business and governmental groups. Contributions to further this work are
tax-deductible and may be sent to the Center at P.O. Box 19367,
Washington, D.C. 20036.

THE STUDY GROUP

MARK J. GREEN, Project Director and Editor
A.B. Cornell University, 1967
J.D. Harvard Law School, 1970
Member, District of Columbia Bar

BEVERLY C. MOORE, JR., Associate Director
A.B. University of North Carolina, 1967
J.D. Harvard Law School, 1970
Member, District of Columbia Bar

BRUCE WASSERSTEIN, Associate Director
A.B. University of Michigan, 1967
M.B.A. Harvard Business School, 1971
J.D. Harvard Law School, 1971

MARSHALL BEIL
B.A. Swarthmore College, 1967
J.D. Harvard Law School, 1971

LARRY P. ELLSWORTH
B.A. Michigan State University, 1969
Third-year student, Harvard Law School

DAVID HEMENWAY
B.A. Harvard College, 1966
M.A. University of Michigan, 1967
Ph.D. Candidate in Economics, Harvard University

ARTHUR KAPLAN
B.A. University of Pennsylvania, 1967
J.D. Harvard Law School, 1970
Member, Pennsylvania Bar

RICHARD LASTER
A.B. University of Virginia, 1966
LL.B. University of Richmond, 1969
LL.M. Harvard Law School, 1970
Member, Virginia Bar

TOM SEARS
B.A. Rice University, 1964
Ph.D. in Economics, Harvard University, 1970
Assistant Professor of Economics, Amherst College

Introduction by Ralph Nader

This is a report on crime in the suites. It is a report on the closed enterprise system and its human, political, and economic costs to Americans. It is most intensively a report on the federal antitrust enforcement effort—terribly lagging, sometimes aiding and abetting, though, on occasion, dedicated enough to illuminate how the proper workings of a safeguarded market system can give just power to the consumer. It is finally a study of corporate radicalism so deeply insinuated into the politico-economic fabric of the society that a veritable revolution against citizens has occurred. Competition, free enterprise, and an open market were never meant to be symbolic fig leaves for corporate socialism and monopolistic capitalism. The outright disregard of market principles and antitrust laws has become too institutionalized and too costly to be considered any longer a mere deviation from the norm.

But the rebuttal: Isn't this the most productive economy the world has witnessed and the highest standard of living? Certainly it is among them and certainly the largest among them. But does this mean that economic crime, armaments, poverty, waste, pollution, disease, bureaucracy's invisible chains, and a deteriorating quality of life have to be the price of progress? Why compare our Gross National Product to other nations' when we should be comparing it to our own unrealized potential? And why do the victims always pay the price rather than the perpetrators? And what of the future with the trends pointing sharply away from brightness for the young and unborn? What, indeed, do such esoterica as antitrust laws, monopolization, anticompetitive practices, price-fixing, product-fixing, tying arrangements, and oligopoly have to do with these dichotomies between our nation's wealth and its deepening problems? This book answers—Plenty!

What people are charged; what kind of goods and services are they offered; what level of product hazards and pollution prevail; what value do government contracts and purchases receive; what important innovations are permitted; what are the sources of potential power; what amount of power is unaccountable; what chance is there for small business; what is the response of the professions; what is the choice for the consumer? These and many other questions, which affect the daily well-being and freedom of 200 million Americans, are what antitrust policy and violations are all about.

There are enormously recidivist patterns to antitrust violations which cost consumers billions yearly, as the book shows. Price-fixing is rampant, and as price-fixing and concentration in an industry or market increase, less and less overt behavior is required to achieve the objectives of the price-fix. A lawyer for the plumbing-fixtures conspiracy once yearned to a confidant that things would go so much smoother if his client companies engaged in "price leadership" instead. The words of criminogenic behavior—conscious parallelism, protective imitation, and anticipatory inaction—now replace the more finely etched description of the executive-suite conspiracy. The steel companies and the banks, for example, have an elaborate cue system for prices and interest rates which do not require meetings that conclude after third-decimal-point agreements. Many government procurement bids are socialized into a finely orchestrated response pattern by the few firms who divide up the business. What begins with conspiracy frequently develops into conditioned response, with only occasional explicit coordination required.

The ultimate overthrow of the market and antitrust occurs when legal loopholes develop for antitrust illegality. Quotas, exemptions, *ad hoc* waivers perforate antitrust for some industries, such as petroleum, like so much Swiss cheese. Then there is the peculiar phenomenon where antitrust crime becomes more entrenched with age, as if the law is supposed to recognize a corporate age of consent in reverse. General Motors is considered by many leading antitrust economists and lawyers to have been in continual violation of the Sherman Act for years. The perceived crime however, has been just too big to tackle, in the opinion of those who decide such matters in the federal administration. Above all, antitrust violations are part of a phenomenon which, to the public, is too complex, too abstract, and supremely dull. The specialized legal and economics professions, rigorous in their myopia, have done little to relate antitrust policy to any audience beyond their tightly knit fraternities.

It may not be too sanguine to say that from the present on, antitrust and its brace of phrases will start to become household words; that the prices people pay for their bread, gasoline, auto parts, prescription drugs, and houses will be more and more related to antitrust violations and the costs of concentration; that the air they breathe and the consumer hazards they suffer will be increasingly connected to industrial collusion and controlled markets; that those aggrieved by antitrust violations will more and more directly reach toward the companies and their executives for suitable redress and other sanctions through the courts. Contrary to Richard Hofstadter's comment on the antitrust movement as "one of the faded passions of American reform," antitrust enforcement—private and public—will make a comeback to show the modern relevance of this traditional wisdom first formulated into law by a conservative Republican Congress in 1890.

The momentum toward a vigorous antitrust impact on anticompetitive and collusive business behavior depends on the following series of developments:

1. The growth of a professional antitrust constituency outside the federal government. This would include state attorneys general and city corporation counsel, private antitrust plaintiffs' bar, and public-interest lawyers. Recent settlements in the tetracycline and other price conspiracies,

and actions by state attorneys general in the "smog" conspiracy case involving the auto industry, augur a quickened pace here.

2. Popularizing the contempt which many large corporations have for competitive capitalism and their relentless drive to secure government guarantees and subsidies against the rigors of competition. Growing by buying or creating their own parents (holding companies) is not exactly a reflection of classical economics or the productive work ethic.

3. The congruence of common interest between the consumer and environmental movements, on the one hand, and antitrust remedies on the other. There is the growing consciousness by consumers of the amount of their incomes which goes into involuntary expenditures; for example, the auto aftermarket is generated by collusive industry-wide deficiencies in the original automobile, like the fragile ornamental bumpers requiring purchase of major parts after a four-mile-per-hour collision.

4. The rapid growth of the United States multinational corporations with even lesser loyalties to the American economy and its workers, thereby losing further claim to patriotism and the loyalty of organized labor. Union Carbide's arrogant boast in advertisements which say to Americans: "Overseas, we're you" will not be swallowed by workers and their families who watch Carbide build abroad to sell back to the United States.

5. The wider exposure of the weak, politicized, and fractionated antitrust enforcement effort by the Antitrust Division in the Justice Department and the Federal Trade Commission. The elaborate analysis of such official pretense in this report and the concrete recommendations for changes in organization, personnel, budget, and sanctions should launch these agencies into arenas of visibility which will commence significant changes. The posture of two agencies with a combined budget of $20 million and 550 lawyers and economists trying to deal with anticompetitive abuses in a trillion-dollar economy, not to mention an economy where the 200 largest corporations control two-thirds of all manufacturing assets, is truly a charade. Neither Congress nor the White House presently desires otherwise, but their political antennae will be sensitive to any of the foregoing trends. Once antitrust enforcement becomes part of the formal political process, as is true now

of antitrust suppression, the forces unleashed will accelerate one another.

6. Large areas of economic activity will raise antitrust issues in ways of direct interest to citizens, community, and professional groups. The flexible tools of antitrust law—with its common-law capacity for growth—will be pressed into service on such abuses as relate to:

- Standards-setting organizations
- Government procurement (to recoup losses)
- Multinational corporations
- Foreign export conspiracies vis-à-vis the United States market
- One-bank holding companies
- Computer languages and programs
- Conglomerate tie-ins
- Company towns
- Product-fixing
- Concentration of land ownership (a major scandal soon to erupt)
- Professional or occupational abuses (minimum-fee schedules and local trades price-fixing).

Basic to the speed and depth of these trends is a deployment of lawyers and economists to work systematically for operational strategies in antitrust application. There is at present an imbalance of legal manpower in antitrust enforcement—private and public—that has no comparative analogy in any other major field of the law. Remedying this paucity of lawyers and economists working full time for competition by breaking up shared monopolies and challenging the many other anticompetitive abuses should not be insurmountable tasks. Too much is at stake for this catalytic agent to remain so small in numbers when so large a constituency of Americans awaits the benefits of savings, safety, and quality from a competitive market system.

June, 1971
Washington, D.C.

CONTENTS

PREFACE

The prejudices encountered were fairly predictable. Government antitrust enforcers warned that there was nothing to uncover, that all was well—at least relatively well—with the antitrust agencies. Then personal friends and Washington *apparatchik* generally just wondered whether antitrust was all that important, a view I shared upon first meeting an antitrust lawyer in the summer of 1967. By late 1969, when Ralph Nader asked me to head a study of antitrust enforcement, I would have been as eager to delve into the Bureau of Commercial Fisheries. At the time civil rights and poverty law, consumer and environmental law, urban law, and drug, juvenile, and military law were the relevant fields. But antitrust?

Yes, antitrust. Five man-years of research and 500 interviews later, it is my judgment that the record of antitrust enforcement has a clear and present impact on our politics, our society, and our economic system. The concentration of industrial assets, the distribution and extent of our wealth, productivity, innovation, pollution, employment, racism, political contributions, and lobbying—all are issues of national pitch and moment, all are touched by antitrust policy. As our competitive economy goes, so goes our polity; the two are inseparable. At a time of increasing concern with "corporate accountability"—to consumers, to shareholders, to employees, and to distributors—accountability to the market mechanism and antitrust laws must be stressed. For if corporations obeyed the "laws" of competition so righteously espoused at annual meetings, they would go a long way toward fulfilling their economic and political obligations to society.

Eight professionals and graduate students, blending legal, economic, and business disciplines, began this study in June, 1970. First, the vast literature on antitrust was surveyed and outlined; various themes were tentatively developed and questions prepared. Second, and most significantly, field interviews were intensively conducted— with present and past enforcers, with Congressmen, Senators, and their staffs, with defense and plaintiffs' counsel, and with businessmen and economists. The original report, released in June 1971, therefore employs the often ignored oral tradition in the law. This mix of oral/investigative and library research provides a way of unraveling the workings of a government which often strays far from standard political science and econometric models.

Gunnar Myrdal has eloquently argued that, despite the claims of many self-proclaimed purists, no social science can be entirely disinterested. "All scientific work has to be based on value premises," he said. "There is no view without a viewpoint, no answers except to questions." Rather than deny this obvious truth, it is crucial to articulate one's operating premises. Ours were fourfold. The maximization of consumer welfare was our talisman—not the value of small or big enterprise for their own sakes, not the balance of payments nor needs of today's money managers or collective bargainers. Before all else, the economic system must deliver a diversity of quality goods at low prices. It is an idea as old as Adam Smith: "Consumption is the sole end and purpose of all production; and the interest of the producer ought to be attended to, only so far as it may be necessary for promoting that of the consumer." Second, we opted for the private, competitive economy and against public ownership as the most efficient and equitable mechanism to serve consumer welfare. When a capitalist society nationalizes, as Michael Harrington has pointed out, it takes over the corporate lemons and leaves untouched the corporate fruit. Envisioning a Spiro Agnew or Maurice Stans running the railroads—for they, not a Jean Monnet, not a John Gardner, would be at the helm—and anticipating problems of excessive bureaucratization, derogation of democracy, and suffocation of initiative militate against socialism. Third, although both will be discussed, it is anticompetitive *structure* more than *conduct* which cripples industrial performance and which should be the emphasis of rational antitrust policy. By structuring industry so as to be competitive, not monopolistic, the needs of the consumer are best served. And fourth, there was the suspicion of excessive economic power, *either* public or private. Conservatives conveniently chastise the former and neglect the latter. Given the historic mis-emphasis on this issue, we focus on private economic power and government attempts to control it.

This book is divided into three general sections. "The Matrix" describes in nontechnical language the setting in which antitrust enforcement occurs—both economic and political. While much has been written on industrial concentration and antitrust, it has mostly been by economists for economists; nothing has been written about political interventions into the enforcement process. "The Department of Justice" and "The Federal Trade Commission" discuss the performances of these separate agencies whose antitrust jurisdictions largely overlap; the FTC section concludes with a summary and suggestion which integrate points made in both.

It is necessary to stress what this book is *not* about. It is not about labor monopolies; it is not about state antitrust enforcement; it is not about government regulation.* No doubt, for example, an important book awaits writing on the extent and impact of our huge labor unions, on how they relate to industrial monopolies on the one hand and consumers on the other. But this is not that book. Nor is it intended as an antitrust textbook. There are good ones around, from Philip Areeda's *Antitrust Analysis* (1967) in

* A follow-up book, also based on our two-volume antitrust report of June, 1971, will be released later this year. It will concentrate on Uncle Sam as monopoly man, as the official policies of our regulatory and legislative bodies either ignore or create monopoly-like conditions.

law to Joseph Bain's *Industrial Organization* (1959) in industrial economics. Rather, *The Closed Enterprise System* focuses on the policies and procedures, the politics and personalities comprising the empirical reality of antitrust enforcement. How does government enforcement actually work—or not? And if not, why not?

Since the release of our report a half-year ago, a number of key events affecting antitrust policy and enforcement have occurred. In August and October 1971, President Nixon announced his New Economic Plan, an advanced form of managed capitalism to combat the tandem evils of inflation and unemployment. It is premature to predict now whether this move is a temporary palliative to cure an economic aberration or whether it is the precursor of a state capitalism that will render the free market antique. At a minimum, antitrust enforcement must be especially alert to detect the kind of inter-firm collaboration, also occurring during and after the OPA years, which arises in the congenial atmosphere of common price ceiling determinations. In October, during his short-lived presidential campaign, Senator Fred Harris offered his cure to our industrial affliction of rapidly and ever-increasing prices: a deconcentration bill to break up our biggest monopolies. This was the first serious antimonopoly legislation submitted to Congress in two decades; Senator Philip Hart, Chairman of the Senate Antitrust and Monopoly Subcommittee, will shortly introduce his own version of such legislation.

In December Congressman Emanuel Celler, head of the House Judiciary Committee and Antitrust Subcommittee, proposed a centralizing of the functions of the Antitrust Division of the Justice Department and the Federal Trade Commission; he also proposed a statutory presumption against major mergers. Both proposals were contained in our report. Finally, the Assistant Attorney General in charge of Antitrust, Richard McLaren, resigned in December to become a District Court judge in Chicago. Although he served nearly three years, it was not entirely clear whether his nomination to the court was a promotion or an eviction. Staffers and superiors spoke highly of his tenure; but one White House aide, according to *Newsweek,* thought his record a bit too activist for this administration: "McLaren inflicted us with a lot of battle damage. He didn't pick up signals well."

The Study Group would like to thank Senator Philip Hart and Representative Benjamin Rosenthal, who urged Antitrust Division Chief Richard McLaren to cooperate with this project at a time when he seemed less than enthusiastic at the idea. We must also express appreciation to Attorney General John Mitchell, who overruled McLaren's initial refusal to cooperate with our study. Mitchell made the point during Justice Department deliberations—which occurred after the Cambodian invasion and Kent State killings, both igniting student uprisings—that an administration professing open-mindedness with the young could ill afford not to cooperate with a student *study* of the workings of government. We would also like to thank several Antitrust Division, FTC, and Senatorial staffers for their valuable comments on the manuscript, as well as the comments of Gordon Spivack, Robert L. Wright, Paul Mac-Avoy, Roger Sherman, Marc Roberts, and William Long. They are, of course, in no way responsible for the final content of the report. But one who is responsible—at least for the good parts—is our editor, Tom Stewart, who throughout retained patience, humor, and (happily) a talented editorial eye. Finally, we must acknowledge the valuable cooperation of many interviewees who requested anonymity, a condition carefully observed. This modesty was prevalent among lawyers, trained by temperament and the canons to shun publicity or be professionally hazed. Ideally, "citizen professionals" will begin to realize that peer pressure and retainer interests should not mute their public contributions on major issues.

Americans have often set up models which do not exist, which have never existed, and which they may never permit to exist, yet which assuage our frontieristic, democratic spirit. Equal justice, economic opportunity, racial freeedom, a peace-loving nation—our list of unachieved hyperboles is long. Among them must be included our faith in "the free enterprise system" and in the antitrust laws which supposedly maintain it. This phrase and these laws are of such vintage, and have been so repeated into catechism, that they are accepted on faith as part of the great American tradition. Yet, as with many of our democratic models, the reality is more apparent than actual. This book looks hard at the ideal of competition and antitrust, and concludes that it is time to state that the emperor has no clothes. Many in the antitrust court will not like to hear this opinion, but a problem which goes unexposed goes unanswered. "Sunlight," Louis D. Brandeis observed, "is said to be the best of disinfectants."

Mark J. Green
January, 1972
Washington, D.C.

PART I

The Matrix

It exists; it is pervasive; it is dangerous. It poses what I con-
sider the No. 1 domestic problem of our time—the prevalence
of private socialism in what we like to think of as a free
enterprise economy.

—Professor Walter Adams

1

The Economics of Antitrust

—An international quinine cartel cornered the world market in the early 1960s, then raised the price of quinine
from 37¢ an ounce to $2.13. The drug, taken mostly by
the elderly to restore natural heart rhythm, became priced
beyond many patients' means. "I cannot continue to pay
these high prices," complained one older citizen, "yet my
doctor tells me I cannot live without it." [1]

—Between 1953 and 1961, 100 tablets of the antibiotic
tetracycline retailed for about $51. This price had been set
by an illegal conspiracy among some of the nation's largest
drug houses. Ten years later, after the exposure of Congressional hearings and indictment, the price for the same
quantity was approximately $5, a 90% decrease.

—Due to a conspiracy among nearly all the country's
manufacturers of plumbing fixtures, homeowners and apart-
ment dwellers overpaid for their sinks and toilets in the
early Sixties. The firms had met secretly and decided to

produce only the most expensive fixture models and charge a uniformly high price.

—In 1964 all Americans paid about 20¢ for a loaf of bread. But in Seattle they paid 24¢, or 20% more, due to a local price-fixing conspiracy. After a Federal Trade Commission ruling ended the conspiracy, the Seattle price began to fall, reaching the national average by 1966. In its 10-year life, the conspiracy robbed consumers in the Seattle-Tacoma area of some $35 million.[2]

—Minneapolis-St. Paul had many competing milk firms. In Duluth-Superior, however, three big firms accounted for more than 90% of all milk sold. Although production and distribution costs for milk were similar in each market, the wholesale price for a half-gallon in 1967 was 33.8¢ in Minneapolis-St. Paul and 45¢ in Duluth-Superior,[3] a 33% difference.

—Most estimates of the consumer cost of our oil-import quota system range from $5–$7 billion per year. This is because the oil giants can price their product far above competitive levels since foreign competition is restricted. For the motorist it means about $1.45 extra every time he says, "Fill it up." [4] For the family of four in New York State it means an average of $102.32 added to gasoline and home-heating bills every year.[5]

—Federal Trade Commission economists estimate that cold-cereal prices are inflated 15 to 20% because three giant firms (Kellogg, General Mills, and General Foods) control 82% of the market and their high advertising expenditures (some 20% of sales) intimidate potential competitors.

—While there once were as many as 88 American auto manufacturers, today GM, Ford, and Chrysler make 83% of all cars sold in the country and 97% of all domestic models. Economist Leonard Weiss of the University of Wisconsin estimates that the noncompetitive state of the industry costs consumers $1.6 billion a year.

OF MODELS AND PREMISES

Antitrust and *monopoly:* the words typically project antique images on our memory screens—a combative Teddy Roosevelt, industrial tycoons, corporate empires, victimized farmers. The old robber barons are gone, replaced by Harvard Business School types with forgettable names. (Who today would have the public nerve or unwisdom to utter, as did J. P. Morgan, "I owe the public nothing"?) The old trusts and monopolies themselves have largely disappeared, with more subtle variations—oligopolies and conglomerates—arising instead. And monopoly costs usually go unperceived by victims due to their remote and technical nature.

"Antitrust is dead; long live antitrust," says the *Wall Street Journal* half-jokingly. It explains, "The British are not about to restore their monarchy to its former glory, but neither are they ready to depose their queen. Ditto, Americans and their antitrust law." [6]

But, like Mark Twain's death, the unimportance of antitrust is greatly exaggerated. In fact, if the consumer movement wanted to focus on the issue with the most impact on the purchasing public, it would choose the failure of antitrust enforcement. Paying a $100 auto-repair bill when only $50 worth of work was done is painful. So is repairing $125 worth of damage because a bumper is so fragile that it surrenders in a four-mile-an-hour collision. But paying hundreds of dollars more when you first purchase the car —since the industry is dominated by a noncompeting "Big Three"—is the supreme bilk, no less distressing because the cost is invisible. When supposed competitors get together to fix the price of their products, or when an industry becomes controlled by so few big firms that price competition ceases, the consumer pays more. All the opening vignettes showed pocketbook losses by consumers because the model of our economic system, the free enterprise model, failed. The antitrust issue then becomes radically modern: Can a competitive marketplace give consumers their money's worth? Or will collusion and bigness continue to infect industry, reducing the purchasing power of the dollar and increasing corporate inefficiency and profits?

The above examples argue the latter. At times the economic malfunctioning involved illegal business *conduct,* like price-fixing in the cases of quinine, antibiotics, plumbing fixtures, and bread. *Structural* problems—when an industry is dominated by a few large sellers able to exact excessive profits—were evident in the milk, oil, cereal, and auto examples. Both defects mar our system of "competitive capitalism," an economy supposedly decentralized and self-regulated. Many sellers compete for the consumer's dollar, and consumers, in turn, buy the best products at the lowest prices. By "voting" with his dollars, the consumer determines the types, quantities, and prices of goods to be produced. The result is that economic resources are allocated among users to maximize consumer satisfaction. Sellers who want to survive the competitive struggle must constantly increase their efficiency and seek out product innovations. "The unrestrained interaction of competitive forces," summarized the Supreme Court as early as 1904, "will yield the best allocation of our economic resources, the lowest prices, the highest quality, and the greatest material progress." [7]

That, at least, is the theory. There are many deviations from it. Government antitrust policy then attempts to correct the misfiring system. Antitrust is an umpire in the competitive game, permitting all to fight for the purchasers' dollar, within certain rules prohibiting illegal behavior. Thus, price-fixing, monopolization, and below-cost pricing are all considered out-of-bounds. We allow the business unit great freedom to pursue its own economic gain, but we arrange the system so that in obtaining his own ends he also serves the economic needs of society.*

But if this competitive system fails to assure livable wages, or permits pollution, or produces dangerous products, or discriminates racially, corrective laws are passed: minimum-wage and social-security laws, air- and water-quality acts, product-safety bills, and antidiscrimination laws. And if the industry is a "natural monopoly," where only one firm can be efficient and profitable, as with public utilities, then the government regulates that industry in the public interest. In all other areas not in need of remedial legislation, competition, promoted by antitrust enforcement, continues as the production and delivery system. This blend of competition and occasional regulation properly allows for the fact that while the competitive marketplace is our wisest allocator of goods, it is far from omniscient or comprehensive.

* This economic structure has been confused with the justifiably abused laissez-faire model, although clearly they are opposites. Too often laissez-faire meant not that all were free to compete but that the big firms were free to devour the small ones; any government interference was shunned, even when the model was breaking down. The frequent result, as Marx predicted, was monopoly capitalism, where ownership by one had replaced control by the many. And as will shortly be shown, monopoly denotes high profits, low efficiency, and laggard innovation.

THE EXTENT OF CONCENTRATION

"An industry which does not have a competitive structure," said former Chief Justice Earl Warren, "will not have competitive behavior." [8] As defined by its structure, much of the American economy is neither monopolistic (like Xerox, Western Electric, or IBM) nor competitive (like wheat, fashion, and furniture). In the twilight between is *shared monopoly* or *oligopoly*—a form of imperfect competition where the firms producing and selling a particular product are few in number and often large in size. Because there are few firms, the actions of one are noticed by the rest; each realizes that any move on its part—a price increase, for example—will generate a reaction by the other firms. Since the best way to maximize profits is to act as a monopolist would, the oligopolistic firms begin to march to the same corporate drummer. Such joint behavior has been described as "parallel pricing," "conscious parallelism," and "price leadership"—or what one former antitrust official has called "conspiracy through newspaper pronouncements." [9] The technique is simple: U.S. Steel announces a price increase of 6% on many major products; within two days all other firms increase their prices by an identical amount. No formal price-fixing conspiracy has occurred—yet the effect is the same.

What is the extent of industrial monopoly in America today? One widely used measure of the existence of monopoly and oligopoly is concentration ratios—the percentage of shipments produced by a certain number of the leading firms in an industry. When four or fewer firms supply 50% or more of a particular market, a shared monopoly results, one which performs much as a monopoly or cartel would. Most economists agree that above this level of industrial concentration—a "four-firm ratio of 50%"—the economic costs of shared monopoly are most manifest. Familiar examples of such oligopolistic industries are automobiles (GM, Ford, and Chrysler), aluminum (Alcoa, Kaiser, and Reynolds), rubber tires (Goodyear, Firestone, U.S. Rubber, and Goodrich), soaps and detergents (Procter & Gamble, Colgate, and Lever Brothers), cigarettes (Reynolds, American, Philip Morris, L & M), and electric bulbs (GE, Westinghouse, Sylvania).

The extent of shared monopoly can modestly be called

staggering. In 1959 Professors Carl Kaysen and Donald Turner concluded in their now classic *Antitrust Policy* that "There are more concentrated than unconcentrated industries in manufacturing and mining, they are larger in aggregate size, and they tend to occupy a more important position in the economy." [10] Over a decade later two other authors on corporate America corroborated this estimate. Professors William Shepherd and Richard Barber both calculate that shared monopolies control about two-thirds of our manufacturing sector.[11]

Data conflict on how much worse this already high level of concentration is getting. Based on *market concentration* —the share of business held by the leading firms in a particular industry—there has been a slight increase over the past two decades. The average four-firm industry ratio went from 35.3% in 1947 to 39.0% in 1966. As judged by eight-firm concentration ratios, a somewhat finer gauge, 50 industries experienced increasing concentration between 1958 and 1966, says a study by the Cabinet Committee on Price Stability, while only 15 had decreases.[12]

Another measurement is *aggregate concentration*—the concentration of all manufacturing assets or sales. Here the increase has been dramatic, as is evident from the following table:

CORPORATE SIZE GROUP	PERCENT OF TOTAL ASSETS [13] 1950	1965
20 largest	14.5%	18.0%
50 largest	30.2%	35.2%
100 largest	38.6%	45.4%
200 largest	46.7%	55.4%

Dr. Willard Mueller, the former chief economist of the FTC, who compiled this data in 1965, returned to the Senate Subcommittee on Antitrust and Monopoly to testify in November, 1969:

> You may recall that I testified before this Committee in 1965 that, should post-war trends in aggregate concentration continue, by 1975 the 200 largest manufacturing corporations would control ⅔ of all manufacturing assets. *Unhappily, we have reached this level ahead of schedule. Today the top 200 manufacturing corporations already control about ⅔ of all assets held by corporations engaged primarily in manufacturing.* [Emphasis added] [14]

It is difficult to comprehend the meaning of this fact. Imagine a room seating 200 people, not much larger than a college classroom. There could sit the men who control two-thirds of American industry and approximately one-third of all *world* manufacturing. Pharaohs and emperors would gaze in envy.

In sum, the 100 largest corporations today have a greater share of all manufacturing assets than the 200 largest did in 1950, the year Congress enacted the Celler-Kefauver Act to stop the trend toward concentration. And the top 200 today control the same share of assets the *1,000* largest held in 1941, the year the Temporary National Economic Committee submitted its final report to Congress recommending an "Investigation of Concentration of Economic Power."

Yet even the asset size of our largest corporations understates the extent of industrial concentration. Three additional factors decrease the vigor of competition and contribute to our closed enterprise system. First, joint ventures are common forms of business. And "businesses that are partners in one market," says the Cabinet Committee on Price Stability, "may be disinclined to behave independently when they meet as rivals in others." [15] One study reported that in 1962 the 100 largest manufacturing corporations appeared in 210 joint ventures, over half involving firms who were direct competitors in closely related products.[16] Second, interlocking management and directors are prevalent. In 1962, for example, the 29 largest manufacturing firms alone had interlocks with 745 industrial and commercial corporations, 330 banks, and 51 other corporations.[17] Third, by 1967, 49 banks were trustees of $135 billion in assets. These banks held 5% or more of the outstanding shares of one or more classes of stock in 5,270 companies (many being direct competitors), or 108 per bank; they had interlocking directorates with 6,591 companies, an average of 164 per bank.[18] The late Professor A. A. Berle's concern over the control of bank trust funds is applicable to the marketplace in general: "We thus dimly discern the outline of a permanently concentrated group of officials, holding a paramount and virtually unchallenged power position over the American industrial economy." [19]

THE CREATION OF CONCENTRATION

The route to this industrial concentration was via mergers and acquisitions, when one firm combined with another.

In the 1960s, for example, approximately 75% of corporate growth was due to mergers, not internal firm growth.[20] Oddly, the three great merger waves of the past 80 years have each followed the passage of antitrust legislation aimed at slowing them down.

The early merger movement, culminating in a flurry of consolidations between 1898 and 1902, left a permanent imprint on the American economy. During these years the pattern of concentration characteristic of 20th Century American business formed and matured. In this four-year period 2,653 important industrial consolidations occurred, an average of 531 a year, against an average of 46 a year for the previous three years.[21] By 1904, when the Supreme Court finally forbade monopoly by merger in the *Northern Securities* case, the trusts controlled fully 40% of the manufacturing capital of the country. [22] U.S. Steel was formed in this period, as well as U.S. Rubber, the Tobacco Trust, American Can, U.S. Gypsum, General Electric, International Nickel, International Paper, United Fruit, National Lead, National Biscuit Company, International Salt —and many others.

Between 1925 and 1929 the country wallowed in a second merger wave. In these five years there were 4,583 mergers, with a peak of 1,245 in 1929. Although the average size of the mergers was smaller than before, the total number nearly doubled its turn-of-the-century predecessor. Like the first wave, it was propelled by a buoyant, promotionally minded stock market (until the crash); in addition, it followed the 1914 Clayton and Federal Trade Commission Acts.

Beginning slowly in 1955 (after the 1950 Celler-Kefauver Act), a third merger wave gained force before peaking in 1969. From 1955 to 1959 there was an annual average of 1,162 mergers; in 1960–66 there were 1,664 mergers annually. By 1967 through 1969 there was an average of *3,605* mergers, more per year than had occurred in the entire first merger wave. The wave was 80% "conglomerate"—when the firms merging are neither direct competitors (horizontal merger) or in a supplier-distributor relationship (vertical merger). Behemoths like Ling-Temco-Vought, International Telephone and Telegraph, Litton Industries, and Gulf and Western were conglomerated in this period.

Not only were there many acquisitions, but they were

big. Between 1962 and 1968, 110 of *Fortune*'s 500 largest industrials disappeared by merger. Moreover, between 1948 and 1968 over 1,200 manufacturing companies with assets of $10 million or more were merged with other firms. Such companies are the type expected to grow and challenge entrenched oligopolies; their disappearance negated whatever competitive potential they possessed. In all, between 1948 and 1968 the 200 top firms acquired assets in excess of $50 billion. American industry in these two decades underwent a face-lift unmatched in its history.

A number of independent factors account for these periods of merger intensity. Some mergers, no doubt, are propelled by the belief that efficiencies will be realized by the final combination; * perhaps the plant sizes of each are less than efficient scale, or perhaps one lacks the managerial ability that the other has. Mergers can also be procompetitive, as when a failing company is resuscitated and made productive again, or when a stodgy, non-innovative management is taken over by those more eager to reap profits, not relaxation. Yet many, probably most, mergers are motivated by a variety of financial and psychological impulses.

Tax and accounting rules underwrite the financial incentive to merge. Although in most mergers significant premiums are paid over the market value and certainly over the basis of stock, there is generally no taxation on the transfer of stock. Under the provisions of the Internal Revenue Code, for example, 14 of the largest 18 mergers in 1967–68 were tax free. The FTC estimates that in 1968 alone "taxes uncollected on the capital gains from these mergers amounted to at least several hundred million dollars." [24] Although the 1969 Tax Reform Act limited the deductibility of interest on debt instruments used in acquisitions, the tax structure still fuels the merger movement.

Of the accounting rules spurring mergers, "pooling" is the most important. Essentially, "pooling" results in higher earnings for acquiring companies because the full cost of

---

* Advocates of the giantism and concentration resulting from these merger waves often cite the efficiencies realized when two firms merge, a claim unsupported by the evidence. One out of every six mergers involving manufacturing firms ended in complete failure, with the consolidated firm going out of business.[23] The Cabinet Committee on Price Stability concluded that the merger booms were "not rooted in technological imperatives."

the merger is not reflected on their books. Thus, pooling allows a company to reflect the full earnings of an acquisition without reflecting the full cost. The larger the difference between the full cost and the book cost, the greater the incentive to pool—and merge.

Finally, aside from companies seeking to boost earnings and stock prices, there are institutions with a vested interest in the merger movement. For example, Lazard Freres, New York City investment bankers, received over $16 million in merger fees alone between January, 1964, and September, 1969; their income from merger and acquisition services increased 584% in this period. Thus the banks and arbitrage and investment houses that finance these programs become merger brokers in a gigantic corporate dating game, resulting in many financial marriages.

The psychological incentive to merge is also prevalent. In a country where size often equals status—in homes, in cars, in income—it is not surprising that some firms take over others just to be bigger, just to be kingpins. Harold Geneen, the ambitious chief of the ITT conglomerate, has power over 279,601 employees in 27 countries and over $5.24 billion in sales. Others—Henry Ford of Ford, David Rockefeller of Chase Manhattan—possess similar power. For lesser titans, pride and power are evident from huge advertising accounts, company jets, fat expense accounts and salaries, all accouterments of the corporate estate. An unofficial Treasury Department estimate in 1957 placed corporate expense account outlays at between $5 and $10 billion annually.[25] The unnecessary part of such expenditures can be considerable. In one study, reducing discretionary spending more than doubled the firm's return on investment.[26] These outlays can be self-serving. Two recent studies argue that merging firms are oriented more toward the interests of managers than toward profit maximization for shareholders.[27] The *Wall Street Journal* recently complained in a headline, "Some Officials Scored for Personal Bargaining When Companies Join." [28]

Wrapped up in such a personal impetus is, of course, the urge to monopolize, not only to be big but to dominate a particular industry. "The history of corporations," wrote Professor Eugene Rostow more than two decades ago, "is the best evidence of the motivation for their growth. In instance after instance [it] appears to have been the quest for monopoly power, not the technological advantages of scale." [29] This goal is sought regardless of inefficiency or losses in the merger itself. In tandem, a potentially damaging competitor is eliminated and the resulting corporation is better able to set monopoly prices, either alone or in a shared monopoly.

Mergers were the way our economy grew so concentrated; "high entry barriers," in the language of the economist, are why it remains so. An entry barrier is an obstacle confronting a potentially new competitor into an industry. The threat of a new entrant can discourage existing firms from raising prices so high as to induce new competitors to enter the market. But various "barriers" can make entry into an industry difficult: the large capital outlay initially required, given an imperfect capital market, discriminates against the new firm; due to superior production techniques, managerial talent, control over special resources or special patents, established firms may be able to maintain an absolute cost advantage; existing firms may have all distribution outlets tied up by "exclusive dealing" contracts, requiring a new firm to enter both on a production *and* a distribution level.

Another important entry barrier is "product differentiation"—excessive, non-informational advertising. For example, soap and detergent firms spend some 20% of all sales revenues on ads, and drug houses spend *four times* more on advertising than on research. Once the product is made to seem sexier or faster or groovier, the seller can price it above the other brands, confident that consumers will continue to buy from him because a sense of "brand name" loyalty has been developed. "Competition" in gadgetry, trading stamps, style, and clever ads replaces price competition. Haven't we all pulled into an Esso station, bypassing something called Red Sky Gas, or bought Noxema Shave Cream rather than the drab A&P brand? After all, Esso puts a "tiger in your tank" and Noxema promises to "take it off, take it all off."

Besides appealing to our glandular instincts, such advertising tugs at our purse strings as well. If both Esso and Red Sky have the same 100-octane gasoline, and if Esso charges 44¢ per gallon and the nonmajor brand charges 33¢, the consumer pays 30% more for nothing; the same is true for many products. For example, while Bayer "works wonders" at 69¢ per 100 tablets, the Safeway Stores brand costs 19¢ per 100 (and clears up your headache as well, since aspirin is aspirin, a basic chemical compound).

"Industries with high advertising outlay," said Professor Donald Turner while he was head of the Antitrust Division of the Justice Department, "tended to earn profit rates which were about 50% higher than those which did not undertake a significant effort. . . . It is likely that these additional returns represent monopoly rewards." [30]

THE COSTS OF CONCENTRATION

The structural defects in our closed enterprise economy take a severe toll. First, there is overpricing. Twenty-seven of 28 econometric studies have found a significant correlation between monopoly market power and high prices.[31] An internal Federal Trade Commission report notes that "if highly concentrated industries were deconcentrated to the point where the four largest firms control 40% or less of an industry's sales, prices would fall by 25% or more." Price is supposed to be the "invisible hand" of the marketplace, determining supply and demand. But monopoly pricing upsets the market mechanism, restricting output, diverting resources to less pressing needs, and producing a smaller Gross National Product than is our national potential. Two recent studies by industrial economists have attempted to quantify this "lost GNP." While Minnesota Professor D. R. Kamerschen estimated it as 6% of national income,[32] F. M. Scherer of Michigan State calculated it at 6.2% of GNP.[33] Translating these estimates into dollar amounts, and based on 1970 national income and GNP, *the overall cost of monopoly and shared monopoly in terms of lost production is somewhere between $48 billion and $60 billion annually.*

Aside from *lost output,* there is the *transfer cost* of monopoly. When consumers pay excessive prices, income from the consuming public is redistributed to the shareholders of particular corporations. Professor William Shepherd, of the University of Michigan, has estimated this transfer of wealth at $23 billion annually.[34] "Shareholder Democracy"—that "the people" own our corporations—is a frequent rebuttal. But although millions own *some* stock, only a handful get the lion's share of corporate dividends. In a 1963 study Robert J. Lampmann of Princeton pointed out that 1.6%

of the adult population of the United States owned 82.4% of all publicly held stock.[35] This redistribution of wealth— exacerbating the disparity of a society where the richest 1% of U.S. families receive more income than the bottom 20% and the top 5% more than the bottom 40%—can eventually have serious political consequences. "A man who thinks that economics is only a matter for professors," author-economist Robert L. Heilbroner once wrote, "forgets that this is the science that has sent men to the barricades." [36]

Lost output and inequitable income transfer are not the only ill effects of monopolies. Other dynamic effects are less measurable but still severely damaging to our industrial and social health.

(1) Inflation and Unemployment

Senator Philip Hart stated in 1967 that we were in the midst of a profit inflation, not the cost-push inflation cited by many economists. After-tax corporate profits had increased by $20 billion annually, said Hart, or 88% over the base years 1957–1959; manufacturing labor costs had gone up less than 2.5%,[37] taking productivity into account. Therefore, to the extent that labor's demands in the past three years *have* greatly exceeded their productivity, they are clamoring for their "take" of the monopoly profit being earned.

Even when labor is successful in bargaining, management often merely passes on the added costs to consumers, there being little market sanction to force them to keep prices down. GM, for example, announced frequent price increases before and after their strike settlement in 1970, attempting to maintain their target price and their anticipated 20% return (on net worth after taxes) rather than suffer a less than monopoly-like return. Such target prices are maintained regardless of the economic environment. They are high to begin with, and they do not go down in a sluggish economy. Economist John Blair studied 16 pairs of products, one from a concentrated industry, the other from a more competitive one (*e.g.,* steel building materials vs. lumber; pig iron vs. steel scraps). During the two recessions of the 1950s, the price of every unconcentrated product fell, while the price of 13 of the 16 concentrated products actually rose.[38]

Traditionalists continue to associate inflation only with excess demand, big labor contracts, and an adjustable interest rate. Others, however, understand the structural triggering of inflation, especially in light of the phenomenon of an inflation wrapped inside a recession. The eminent Gardiner Means estimated that up to 90% of our inflation is due to giant firms' market power. "At unemployment rates of 4 percent, we may expect an annual inflation rate of 1 percent when manufacturing profits average 10.1 percent of net worth," said a 1969 White House economic staff report as reported in the *Washington Post*. "But with profit rates of 14.6 percent [which the report associated with concentrated industries] we may expect an annual inflation rate of 3 percent." In the same year the FTC's Bureau of Economics pointed out that "major concentrated industries, through the exercise of discretionary pricing power, contribute to both inflation and unemployment." Caspar Weinberger, former FTC Chairman and now Deputy Director of the Office of Management and Budget, agreed that the higher profits in concentrated industries induced big wage settlements which then set the pattern for other industries.

As such views mount, relief could be sought in antitrust enforcement. The *Washington Post* editorialized that "In a free economy the discipline of competition is the chief weapon against inflation." Summarizing this approach was Senator Hart:

> There are many methods, of course, for dealing with inflation, but certainly any long-term solution requires attention to antitrust factors. It is significant of current attitude, I think, that recent attempts by government to hold down specific price rises have involved many agencies—but apparently not the Antitrust Division of the Department of Justice.[39]

Clearly not the Department of Justice—especially since the then Antitrust Division head, Richard McLaren, told the Congressional Joint Economic Committee that inflation was dealt with best by means other than antitrust.

Unemployment results in two ways from monopoly power. Shared monopolies artifically restrict output, which in turn reduces the number of workers who would otherwise be producing. Some percentage of our 27% unused industrial capacity, therefore, is idle because of this market power. If monopoly disruption accounts for only a fifth of all our unemployed, this translates into over a million unemployed workers. In addition, prior to his "New Economic Policy" of August 15, 1971, President Nixon chose to tolerate high unemployment levels as a technique to fight inflation. Consequently, two million workers were laid off between 1969 and 1971 to cool off the economy—in a gigantic misinterpretation of a "market power" inflation for one caused by "excessive consumer demand."

(2) Political and Social Effects

Before correlating the political power of corporations with increasing economic concentration, the predicate for such an analysis must be laid; *i.e.,* corporations do in fact exercise political power.

Their control over the independent agencies has been documented in prior Nader reports. The "regulatory-industrial complex" is an environment where one can look at the regulators and then at the regulatees and be unable to distinguish them. A second manifestation of corporate power is the network of business advisory councils in the Executive Branch. About 1,500 such groups are appended to various agencies, helping to shape policies that affect them. Third is the army of lobbyists who cover the Senate and House, tax deductible courtesy of the IRS. Finally, the most powerful lever which business firms pull on Capitol Hill is the one controlling campaign financing. Although a Congressman is elected by voters in his district, he often accepts campaign contributions from businesses and businessmen anywhere. Consequently, money from corporations and corporate officials pours into electoral politics. Senator Russell Long (D.-La.), who as Chairman of the Senate Finance Committee should know, estimated that about 95% of Congressional campaign funds derived from businessmen, with 80% of it donated by individuals worth over 250,000 dollars.[40]

Thus the Corporate Estate has political power; what, then, are the costs? As economic diversity decreases, the number of contributors to the political process decreases accordingly. So does democracy. In the *Federalist Papers* James Madison argued that the only way to guarantee political freedom in America was to create many "factions," setting faction against faction until a political equipoise resulted. But as business gets bigger and many independent firms are swallowed up, we accelerate toward "America, Inc." in Morton Mintz's and Jerry Cohen's phrase, "one gigantic industrial and financial complex functioning much like a separate government." The Founding Fathers were loath to repose this kind of power in one entity, and it is the kind of centralized power that both radicals and rightists abhor.

The effects are both social and political. Socially, not only are people increasingly governed by distant operatives, but overall economic mobility is reduced as the number of important independent firms dwindles. He who was tarred by McCarthy's brush found it difficult to get a job in or out of government; until the Wagner Act, it was nearly impossible for a union organizer to work in a company town in Pennsylvania or West Virginia. As we approach being a "company" country, job mobility declines and employees are compelled to embrace job security more than ever. "Free enterprise" converts itself into a paternal and threatening relationship between management and employee, the kind of dependence found in both the cartelized Japanese economy and the communized Soviet one. General Robert E. Wood, former chairman of the Board at Sears, Roebuck, once observed, "We complain about government and business, we stress the advantages of the free enterprise system, we complain about the totalitarian state, but in our individual organizations . . . we have created more or less of a totalitarian system in industry, particularly in large industry."

There are other untoward social effects. As firms grow bigger, "shareholder democracy" becomes even more of a farce. When a national company picks up a local firm, bank deposits abandon the localities for New York City, leaving less for local investment and use.* And racial discrimination is facilitated as firms grow big. William Shepherd studied racial patterns in white-collar jobs, concluding that firms with market power could afford the luxury of discriminat-

---

* In 1946 Professor C. Wright Mills studied three pairs of cities; in each pair was one city dominated by a few large firms and one characterized by many independent small firms. After factoring out other variables, Mills found that the level of civic welfare was substantially higher in the cities where local proprietors were personally concerned about the quality of life. For example, the small-business cities had a lower percentage of slum dwellings, a lower infant death rate, and a lower frequency of school dropouts; *per capita* expenditures for community cultural and recreational services were higher, as were home ownership and the installation of telephones.[41]

ing against blacks—and they did. Competitive firms, who had to hire the best employees—white or black—were found to discriminate less.[42]

Politically, when a conglomerate like ITT, with employees in all 50 states, has a problem on Capitol Hill, it can command a new kind of attention. "When a major corporation from a state wants to discuss something with its political representatives," Senator Hart has said, "you can be sure he will be heard. When that same company operates in 30 states, it will be heard by 30 times as many representatives." [43] This technique was employed by ITT in its effort to merge with the ABC network in 1968. It enlisted 300 Congressmen and Senators to complain to the Antitrust Division about its intervention at the FCC in opposition to the merger. Since ITT has substantial holdings as well as 1,600 employees in Louisiana, it also convinced Senator Russell Long, usually found in the populist opposition to such big consolidations, to read a speech into the *Congressional Record* supporting the merger.

Ling-Temco-Vought, another huge conglomerate, understands the tactic. An internal Ling-Temco management document in 1962 gave the following justification for its then pending merger with Chance-Vought, another large Texas defense contractor.

It is tacitly recognized in the industry that a depressed labor area with a large, capable, highly qualified defense contractor backed by purposeful and dedicated congressmen represents a significant additional factor considered by the government in awarding new contracts.

A Ling-Temco backed by Congressman X or a Chance-Vought backed by Congressman Y is not so powerful an applicant for a government contract as the combined companies backed by *both* X and Y.

In 1968 Representative Henry Reuss urged the FTC to include a study of the link between economic concentration and political power in its upcoming probe of conglomerates. One suggested approach was to determine how many corporations had significant holdings in more than 35–40% of the Congressional districts in the country. Legislation of direct interest to these corporations could then be scrutinized to determine the extent of correlation between a Congressman's favorable vote and the corporate holdings in his dis-

trict. Chairman Paul Rand Dixon of the FTC rejected the
Reuss suggestion, acknowledging its value but blaming "very
limited resources."

As big firms push out or buy out the small, another political
cost is suffered: the "mavericks" of industry disappear. A
maverick firm is one which is innovative when others are
complacent, cuts prices when others follow-the-pricing-
leader, refuses an invitation to price-fix or tells the government about it. Its disappearance reduces a source of political options. Professor Milton Friedman, leader of the
conservative Chicago School of Economics, has argued that
a great benefit of the competitive system is the capitalistic
patron, that wealthy eccentric who will donate to some public cause or legislative candidate which others shun. If General Motors is unlikely to donate money to the programs of
Saul Alinsky, Gordon Sherman of the Midas Muffler Foundation will. If Douglas Dillon of Dillon & Read won't
donate to Eugene McCarthy, Howard Stein of the Dreyfus
Fund will. As the number of private sources for funds is
reduced, the unpopular or new cause finds it more difficult
to get backing.

The loss of similar independent contributors can only
accentuate the present imbalance in our system of competing factions. The Liberty Lobby spends millions while Welfare Rights Groups cannot afford subsistence salaries. The
Nixon-Agnew ticket spent $25 million, Humphrey-Muskie
$10.6 million. The expenditure ratio in 1970 was 5 to 1 for
the Republicans. Lawrence O'Brien, chairman of the Democratic National Committee, complained that he expected
the 1972 elections to be the same. "Outspent 5 to 1. Is that
a two-party system? . . . The question is a basic one—do
we have to abide by the decisions of the private sector as
to whether we have a chance to present the views of our
candidates effectively to the public?" [44] The answer must be
yes, until the law adequately controls the sources and
spending of campaign money (which is presently under
consideration).

The connection between economic diversity and political
freedom has at times been recognized. Justice William O.
Douglas is especially sensitive to it.[45] Also, Judge Learned
Hand, in his famous *Alcoa* decision of 1945, said, "We have
been speaking only of the economic reasons which forbid
monopoly, as we have already implied there are others,
based upon the belief that *great industrial consolidations are*

inherently undesirable, regardless of their economic re-sults." [46] (Emphasis added.) William Orrick, head of the Antitrust Division from 1963 to 1965, made more specific such sentiments in Senate Hearings: "Concentration of industrial power may lead to the police state. Can anyone doubt that the pre-war experiences of Germany, Japan, and Italy have proven the wisdom of the nation's concern over concentration of economic power?" [47]

In sum, there is a political and social price to pay for corporate bigness, and this price must be considered in any sensible antitrust policy. "There is room in the antitrust law," Senator Hart has argued, "both for the political scientist and the sociologist in addition to the economist. Certainly antitrust enforcement needs to rest on something more than economic gamesmanship." Absolute corporate size, it must be stressed, is dangerous because it connotes both an uncompetitive market structure and a homogenized political structure. Some current antitrust theoreticians deride such views, saying that it favors "Ma & Pa" stores over technology and "competitors over competition." Efficient production and distribution—not the local farmer, local druggist, or local grocer—remain primary assumptions of antitrust enforcement and of this book. Only when the marketplace exploits actual efficiencies can the consumer get the most goods at the lowest cost. The charge of "bad economics" and "irrational populism" is misplaced, therefore, when the point made is not that there should be more small, inefficient units, but that General Motors, with $24 billion in sales in 1969, could profitably be split into three to nine companies, or that LTV, with 87 subsidiaries, is neither efficient nor interested in the communities in which it invests.

Proponents of Big Business, on the other hand, argue that there are alternative benefits in our present state of super-concentration. The two they stress are the efficiencies of large size and the innovation encouraged by it; on close examination, however, their verbal arrows boomerang.

(3) Efficiencies

Competition is the whip of efficiency, driving firms to produce better goods at lower costs to maximize profits. Monopoly and oligopoly lead to "the quiet life," in Learned Hand's phrase, a state of mind and economy where there is no need to seek efficiency since the targeted return is fixed and the market percentage is predictable. This environment leads not to price competition, which benefits the consumer, but to gratuitous spending—large salaries, expense accounts, thick rugs, etc.—which proliferates with market power. On study found, in each of 30 industries studied, a significant correlation between top executives' salaries and both concentration ratios and entry barriers.[48]

The most significant work in the area of size vs. efficiency is *Barriers to New Competition* by Dr. Joe Bain of the University of California. He found that efficiency increases and unit cost declines as plants become larger—*up to a point.* Beyond that point bigness either does not generate efficiency or breeds actual dis-economies of scale, usually due to unwieldy management.* "Referring to the first 4 firms in each of our industries," Bain concluded in an intensive study of 20 industries, "it appears that concentration by the large firms is in every case but one greater than required by single plant economies, and in more than half of the cases very substantially greater." [49] Robert Townsend, former head of Avis and author of *Up the Organization,* put it more bluntly: "Excellence and bigness are incompatible." The collapse of the Penn Central and the near-collapse of LTV make it clear that efficiency may not be the inevitable child of bigness.

(4) Innovation

What about bigness benefiting invention (the idea) and innovation (the application)? According to the renowned Joseph Schumpeter and his disciple John Kenneth Galbraith, big firms can innovate better because they are able to risk huge investments in Research and Development (R&D). "A benign providence," Galbraith has intoned, "has made the modern industry of a few large firms an almost perfect instrument for inducing technical change." Again the weight of evidence refutes this theory, indicating that while large firms are important for significant research undertakings, the present Brobdingnagian size of many corporations is unnecessary.

---

* Kenneth Boulding, addressing the American Economic Association, said: "There is a great deal of evidence that almost all organizational structures tend to produce false images in the decision maker, and that the larger and more authoritarian the organization, the better the chance that its top decision makers will be operating in purely imaginary worlds. This perhaps is the most fundamental reason for supposing that there are ultimately diminishing returns to scale."

It is difficult to relate innovation to firm size or market structure. Research and development expenditures, the "input" for innovation, are often employed as one measuring device. Leonard Weiss examined a great many such expenditure reanalyses and concluded: "Most studies show that within their range of observation, size adds little to research intensity and may actually detract from it in some industries." [50] Not only do R&D *expenditures* not increase proportionally with size, neither does inventive *output*. Scherer, using patent statistics as a proxy for inventive output, looked at the nation's 500 largest corporations and found, among other things, that the "smaller" of the 500 accounted for a slightly higher share of inventive activity than of sales. He summarized:

These findings . . . raise doubts whether big, monopolistic conglomerate corporation is as efficient an engine of technological change as disciples of Schumpeter (including myself) have supposed it to be. . . . Perhaps a bevy of fact-mechanics can still rescue the Schumpeterian engine from disgrace, but at present the outlook seems pessimistic. [51] *

Specific industry probes reinforce these conclusions. For example, a study of the highly concentrated steel industry revealed that of 13 major inventions between 1940 and 1955, *none* was made by American steel companies. [52] Not only did the largest American steel companies play no role in the discovery and initial development of the revolutionary oxygen steelmaking process, they lagged badly in introducing it. A small Austrian company, one-third the size of a single U.S. Steel *plant,* perfected and introduced the process. The first American company to adopt it was McLouth Steel, which had less than 1% of industry capacity. Although other small companies followed the lead, it was fully 10 years before Bethlehem and U.S. Steel introduced this method.

What of a large corporation commonly thought to be a major innovator, like General Electric, where "progress is our most important product"? In the household-appliance field alone, the late T. K. Quinn, a former vice president of GE, credits small companies with the discovery and initial

---

* The "Schumpeterian" thesis is further undermined by two facts. Two-thirds of all research is financed by the government anyway, not huge corporations; second, there is little trend toward concentration in producer-goods industries, where technology is very important, and much new concentration in consumer goods, where it is not.

production of: electric toasters, electric ranges, electric refrigerators, electric dryers, electric dishwashers, vacuum cleaners, clothes-washing machines, deep freezers, electric hot irons, and electric steam irons. Quinn summarized his own experiences at GE:

> I know of no original product invention, not even electric shavers or hearing aids, made by any of the giant laboratories or corporations, with the possible exception of the household garbage grinder, developed not by the research laboratory but by the enginering department of General Electric. But the basic idea of this machine came from a smaller concern producing commercial grinders. . . . [T]he record of the giants is one of moving in, buying out, and absorbing the smaller concerns.[53]

Nor was industrial bigness involved in the development of stainless-steel razor blades, transistor radios, photocopying machines, or the "quick" photograph; Wilkinson, Sony, Xerox, and Polaroid were all small and unknown when they introduced these inventions.

In their book *America, Inc.,* Jerry Cohen and Morton Mintz, former staff director of the Senate Antitrust Subcommittee and *Washington Post* reporter respectively, emphasize how innovation retardation is inherent in the very structure of concentrated industries:

> With millions of dollars invested in open-hearth furnaces the steel industry hardly can be condemned for not wishing to change over to the oxygen converter until it became absolutely necessary. An auto industry with millions of dollars invested in great stamping dies to turn out steel bodies has no incentive to embrace the new technologies of plastics.

Virginia Knauer, consumer advisor to President Nixon, gave some specific examples in the auto industry of this tendency by big oligopolists not to rock the boat. American inventors of a nonpolluting Freon-powered engine, an exhaust-reduction system, and a hydraulic bumper attachment absorbing collisions up to 30 mph excited no interest among the Big Four American auto companies. Inventors then turned abroad, where all their discoveries were quickly picked up by Japanese and German auto manufacturers.

High industrial concentration also encourages the continued indifference of the corporate sector to antipollution innovation. It was not difficult for the auto companies to agree to research commonly on antipollution exhaust devices, a "sharing" which turned into "suppressing." In 1953 GM, Ford, Chrysler, and American Motors agreed that no one firm could publicize or develop a device until they all could—the antithesis of the competitive, innovative model. Specifically, as alleged by the Antitrust Division, in 1961 and in 1962–63 they agreed to delay installation of improved antipollution devices. Chapter VIII documents this "product-fixing" conspiracy step by step, exposing the intimacy between oligopoly and innovation retardation.

Chrysler, in the early 1960s, seemed to be heading toward development of a relatively low-pollution gas turbine engine. This engine was lighter, quieter, cooler, cheaper to run, and produced more mileage and similar efficiency than the piston engine, according to industry experts in *Automotive News* and Congressional hearings.[54] Yet it was never marketed. The massive investment required would have disrupted the capital structure of the industry, and a tight oligopoly highly values stability. Recently a Chrysler executive candidly admitted to a newspaper reporter that "We can't go into turbine engines without GM"—and so it was not done. This cost of market concentration, it must be emphasized, is vast and personal: auto exhaust accounts for 60% of air pollution, and air pollution exacts an enormous toll of disease, premature death, and property damage. Physical damage alone caused by air pollution costs $11–$13 billion annually.[55]

Concentration, anti-innovation, and pollution have further interrelationships. The airlines' trade association, the Air Transport Association, has instructed its members to tell states which demand cleaner engines that "retrofitting" is a long and difficult process and that retrofitting devices are available only for the JT8D engine. Neither is true.*

* A memorandum of February 27, 1970, "To: Airline Attorneys/From: John E. Stephen [General Counsel]/Subject: *Pending State Jet Air Pollution Proceedings*" contained the following incriminating paragraph:
We should appreciate your sending us a copy of any responses filed [with state agencies] on behalf of your company. We would hope that any such responses are consistent with the basic undertakings of the "Finch Agreement," as reflected in the New Jersey Stipulation sent to you with our Memorandum of February 17, 1970. In particular, it is hoped that there will be no discrepancies of the kind referred to in the last two paragraphs of page 1 of that Memorandum. A *Washington Post* news story on February 22 indicates that "major airlines" have responded to the Maryland inquiry by stating that they will complete a retrofit program earlier than the December 31, 1972 date in the Finch Agreement. A copy is attached. If most carriers have actually made such statements to the Maryland Department of Health, it is likely that such a commitment will be demanded elsewhere.

Common to these examples is the simple fact that the few huge firms in concentrated industries can resist governmental and public pressure to reform their dirty habits. In a competitive industry it is easier for government to regulate pollution levels and more likely that a small firm might present the public with a radically "cleaner" product. Such innovations do not readily grow in the stifled atmosphere of oligopoly.

THE CONGLOMERATE THREAT

The superconcentration caused by the recent conglomerate explosion also inflicts economic costs, though of a different and more subtle nature. While an oligopolist is a huge firm in an industry with a few big firms, a conglomerate is a huge firm with holdings and subsidiaries in *many* industries. It is the modern form of the old trust and holding company, only instead of securing controlling shares in many companies, they own the companies outright. Textron, with 1970 sales of $1.6 billion, is a fast-growing new conglomerate with octopal interests: textiles, aircraft and parts, electronic equipment, iron and steel castings, bathroom fixtures, machine tools, plastic products, car parts, boat building, agrochemicals, pharmaceuticals, shoes, zippers, and golf carts. Ling-Temco-Vought, with sales of $3.7 billion in 1970, is into aerospace and missiles, sporting equipment, telephone and power cables, pharmaceuticals and chemicals, processed foods, electronic equipment, steel, domestic airplane service, and meats. Consequently, while oligopolies involve concentration in one industry, conglomerates affect overall, economy-wide concentration.

With little antitrust law established to contest this growth —most cases and statutes aim at actual horizontal or vertical competitors—the conglomerate boom took off in the late 1960s. As noted, 80% of the recent merger wave was conglomerate; and high frequency combined with large size. Of 698 manufacturing and mining firms acquired in 1965–69 with assets over $10 million, 561 were conglomerate.[56] The assets involved in manufacturing and mining mergers jumped from an average of $2.8 billion a year in 1960–66 to $10.8 billion per year in 1967–69.

Conglomerates have little redeeming competitive value. They are fueled by and exploit financial gimmicks, leading even *Forbes* magazine to complain that for some "the corporation was no longer primarily a vehicle for conducting business; it had become a machine for compiling an earning record." [57] They are classic examples of empire-building by aggressive managers, indifferent to the inefficiencies of too-large scale, as sprawling, diverse companies are "connected by a common financial heart and a common financial brain." [58] Five separate economic studies have all concluded that there was no relationship between conglomeration and efficiency.[59]

It is true that a conglomerate merger *can* help generate competition. When a conglomerate acquires a small company in a sluggish, concentrated industry, called a "toehold acquisition," and infuses new capital and an innovative energy, the oligopoly can be shaken up into a state of competition. Although by definition conglomerates do not involve direct competitors, they are anticompetitive in several ways. First, since a Procter & Gamble might have gone into bleach production via internal expansion, there is a loss of *potential competition* when it merges with Clorox; such a threat of potential entry can be a significant check on the abuse of monopoly power by the dominant firms in an industry. Second, there is a heightened danger of *reciprocity*, when a firm takes its business to firms who buy from it. Such interrelationships foreclose the market to more efficient competitors, who lose out not to a superior product but to a back-scratching relationship. Oligopoly would be magnified by a kind of circular integration, and "the U.S. economy might end up completely dominated by conglomerates," complained *Fortune*, "happily trading with each other in a new kind of cartel system." Third, when a conglomerate buys a leading firm, it can *entrench* the firm's dominant position; conglomerate backing, plus large advertising outlays, can intimidate small competitors and potential entrants. Finally, there is, in the words of Willard Mueller, "conglomerate interdependence and forbearance." A conglomerate merger, greatly increasing size and diversification, concomitantly increases the number of contact points shared with competitors, suppliers, and customers. While competition in any one line of commerce is not severely diminished, "aggregate" competition can be. Communities of interest among major industrial decision-makers arise, and a situation of cartel-like deferral, or soft competition, replaces real competition. "Management difficulties with newly acquired companies," concluded the *Celler Conglomerate Report* in September, 1971, "indicate that combination frequently had an injurious effect on efficiency, on productivity and upon corporate values." [60]

Conglomerates seem to be falling of their own weight. The "high flyers," as they were called in 1967 and 1968, saw their glamour-stock reputation wane as their stock prices tumbled. By mid-1969 the average price of conglomerate stocks had fallen 40–60%, while the composite market index itself was down only about 10%; there was some recovery through early 1971, but it was far from complete. The political and social power held by conglomerates, however, will not wither away as easily as its dividends.

A combination of mismanagement, a depressed stock market, tight money, and government lawsuits brought these trendy consolidations down, one hopes disproving the frank prediction of one conglomerate president that in 10 years there would be only 200 industrial companies left in the United States. By 1970 no less than eight agencies and Congressional committees were studying the conglomerate meteor, the proper initial response to a phenomenon of such widespread impact. Yet when this problem and response are compared to the more continuous and generic costs of shared monopoly, and the official indifference expressed toward it, the policy mispriority becomes evident. If LTV or ITT creates economic and political problems by concentration of assets, what of AT&T and Standard Oil (N.J.), both of which are bigger? "I suggest it is bizarre," said Edwin Zimmerman, a recent Antitrust Assistant Attorney General, "to concoct a particular antitrust doctrine in order to contain the emerging political power or social impact of a Northwest Industries but not a General Motors. . . ." [61]

There are large blocks of our industrial economy which are characterized by "workable competition," where firms follow the laws of supply and demand to compete for the sovereign consumer's dollar. Given the earlier data on market concentration, one feels about these competitive sectors as Dr. Samuel Johnson did of the dog who could walk on his hind legs: marveling not that he could do it well but that he could do it at all.

What of the monopolized sectors of our economy? In

the name of free enterprise, up to two-thirds of American manufacturing has been metamorphosed into a closed enterprise system. While businessmen spoke the language of competitive capitalism, each sought refuge for himself. Price-fixing, parallel pricing, mergers, excessive and deceptive advertising, tariffs, quotas, subsidies, loan guarantees, political favoritism, and preferential tax treatment—all have created a system of what Senator Estes Kefauver aptly labeled "corporate socialism—a collective run by business, not government." It is a business collective with staggering consumer and public costs: lost GNP *alone* of $60 billion is enough to cover our annual crime bill ($32 billion), the removal of major sources of pollution ($15 billion) and the elimination of poverty ($11 billion for a $3,000 minimum income).[62] The reality of Big Business is—like sex in Victorian England—our big dirty secret. Occasional reference is made to the obvious pretense. As Michael Harrington ironically states in his *Accidental Century,* "Adam Smith has been stood on his head. . . . The capitalist destruction of the capitalist ethic took place primarily through the private collectivization of the Western economy for minority profit." [63] The dominance over large blocks of industrial production by huge enterprises free from the restraints of the competitive marketplace presents the challenge to the antitrust agencies: enforcement must confront the competitive and consumer costs of this giantism, to avoid the charge it is a "charade" (J. K. Galbraith) or mere "folklore" (Thurman Arnold).

Suppose you go to Washington and try to get at your government. You will always find that while you are politely listened to, the men really consulted are the men who have the biggest stake—the big bankers, the big manufacturers, the big masters of commerce. . . . The government of the United States at present is a foster child of special interests.

—Woodrow Wilson, 1914

2

The Politics of Antitrust

If there was one chorus repeatedly sung by most of the 500 people interviewed for this study, it was: "There is very little politics involved in antitrust enforcement." Yet politics and economics cannot be easily segregated. The relationship between economic power and political power, described in the opening chapter, the fact that legislators, executive officials and businessmen politick to shape and distort antitrust enforcement for special interests, and the fact that the laws which give antitrust enforcement definition and jurisdiction are created on Capitol Hill—all guarantee that politics will enter in.

REALPOLITIK

"Policy based on power rather than on ideals" is the *American College Dictionary*'s definition of "realpolitik." Contrary to the protestations of nearly all enforcement officials, it is not a phenomenon unknown to antitrust enforcement. Too much rides on the filing of a case, and elected officials are too dependent on business in a network of ways, for it to be otherwise. Power politics gets into antitrust enforcement in two forms. First, and more rarely, antitrust law is used for politically affirmative or "offensive" reasons. In 1948 two sets of civil suits were filed, against manufacturers of farm implements and against meat packers. The underlying purpose of the case, noted a former Division official in an interview, was to attract farm votes. The cases lost in court, after the election. In the early 1950s a possible monopoly suit against the *Kansas City Star* was kicking around the lower staff levels, unable to get clearance from above. What untracked it and led to its filing, according to a former and experienced section chief at the Division, was the *Star*'s consistently anti-administration position; President Truman personally ordered the suit filed. The steel industry deserved a good probe into its pricing policies, and politics gave such an investigation a shove in 1962. Led by U.S. Steel, the industry raised its prices in April, 1962. The annoyed Kennedy administration launched a massive counter-offensive, which included calling a grand jury to study the possibility of issuing criminal antitrust indictments. "There is no doubt," said one Division attorney, reflecting the prevailing view, "that the grand jury was, in part, called by Robert Kennedy to pressure the industry into capitulation."

More pervasive and troublesome, however, is "defensive" politicking—trying to quash a good case, efforts usually undertaken by (1) Congress or (2) an Executive Branch–Big Business alliance.*

(1) In 1952 RCA and most of the major oil firms were under grand-jury investigation for allegedly criminal activities. Senator Pat McCarran, Chairman of the Senate Judiciary Committee and ally of business, telephoned Graham Morison, the Antitrust Division head, to urge that both grand juries be dismissed. Morison refused. "I'm *telling* you what to do," the Senator shouted in reply; "dismiss those cases." Morison—whose year-and-a-half tenure was later cut short because of poor relations with Capitol Hill—told McCarran where to go, and stood fast.

* This section only considers Department of Justice cases. Politics at FTC will be discussed generally throughout the chapters on that Agency.

Other Congressional interferences have involved the media—a politically powerful industry, since adverse press coverage can be as fatal to a politician as a well dry of campaign funds. Pressure over newspapers is decidedly two-sided. The *Kansas City Star* example shows one side. The other was evident in the Antitrust Division's 1956 attempt to block a joint operating agreement between the *Deseret News* (owned by the Mormon Church) and the *Salt Lake City Tribune*. Attorney General Herbert Brownell signed the complaint and sent it to the Division's San Francisco office for filing. The chief of that office, however, got an 11th-hour telegram *not* to file. Senator Wallace Bennett (R.-Utah) and Ezra Taft Benson, a devout Mormon and Eisenhower's Secretary of Agriculture, had pressured Brownell against bringing suit. The combined powers of press and church convinced the Attorney General of his folly. The Justice Department later attempted to negotiate a compromise settlement, but the two newspapers, confident of their political muscle, refused to negotiate, and the case was never filed.*

This precedent blocked similar valid cases against various joint operating ventures over the next few years. But in 1964 the log jam created by the episode was broken when Representative Morris Udall (D.-Ariz.) complained to his neighbor, Attorney General Nicholas Katzenbach, that a Republican-oriented newspaper chain was about to swallow up the last large Arizona paper with a Democratic editorial voice. A case against the takeover, which had an aspect of a joint operating venture, had been stalled at the staff level of the Division. Katzenbach's encouragement got it in gear.

The merger of two rice-milling companies in Louisiana, International Rice Milling Company and Associated Rice Products, also involved Katzenbach. Senator Allen Ellender —Louisiana Democrat and Chairman of the Senate Agriculture Committee—became personally concerned that the Justice Department would try to block the merger. He asked President Johnson to ensure that no case would be brought. Johnson referred him to Katzenbach, but not before the documents formally announcing the merger were

---

* For documentation of this episode, we refer to the Antitrust Division file of the case, which contains a coded memorandum with such cryptic passages as "stop order" and "your people in the field still harassing us." While the memo was not to be signed, the secretary who took the notes initialed it: ETB, WB and HB.

sent in a White House envelope to the Assistant Attorney General for Antitrust, William Orrick. Ellender then met with Katzenbach. At the meeting Katzenbach indicated that, based on the evidence before him, the merger would be legal. The Attorney General recalled to the Study Group that, based on later evidence, "Ellender's representations were inaccurate and so were those of the companies." Yet at that time the Antitrust Division had data of its own, from a disgruntled competitor, showing the merger to be clearly above the permissible market percentages.

The rice-milling companies, assured by Ellender that no suit would be forthcoming, then asked Justice for a Business Review Letter, which is a statement of intent to move or not to move against a merger. Orrick drafted a strong letter stating that it would. Katzenbach watered it down with so many qualifiers that the companies could not understand if it granted them a release or not. When they asked Orrick what it meant, he replied that, based on the present evidence, the merger would be attacked. Orrick then sent Katzenbach a proposed complaint to block the merger. Senator Ellender complained that he had been deceived. He was considerably embarrassed and agitated, since he had guaranteed his constituent companies that the deal was on. Yet his pressure ultimately succeeded: no case was brought and the merger went through.

When Katzenbach was asked why he initially approved the merger, he mentioned a call from Secretary of Agriculture Orville Freeman urging him to go easy on Ellender since a key administration bill was pending before Ellender's Agriculture Committee. "Since I thought a case shouldn't be brought based on the statistics [later shown false] which Ellender gave me," Katzenbach confessed, "I reasoned: 'Why not get a political benefit from what you are going to do anyway?' " Why not? Because it encourages others to make similar political efforts and perverts law enforcement; because it is highly irregular and foolish to accept the statistics of an interested party without independent investigation.

Even so, why didn't Katzenbach sign a complaint once the true facts were known? "The problem became saving my face with the Senator and saving his face with his constituents, neither of which was easy," Katzenbach told the Study Group.

Katzenbach began to get a reputation for realpolitik. Politicians—all Democrats—began a steady procession to his office to urge that cases not be brought, or that divestiture relief not be pursued, because plants might close down or employees become unemployed. In Lyndon Johnson's Great Society, such "antipoverty" arguments had appeal to Katzenbach, who was not very sympathetic to antitrust anyway. The *Wall Street Journal* reported that "to hardened government antitrust prosecutors the smell of contrivances is in the air." [1] The self-serving assertion by interested companies that workers would be laid off or plants closed if a merger were not permitted was not provable, yet was often successful. Senators Ribicoff (D.-Conn.) and McClellan (D.-Ark.) urged Justice not to sue, as the Antitrust Division intended, against General Electric's takeover of a household-appliance company, Lander, Frary, and Clark, because plants employing 1,000 in New Britain, Connecticut, and 600 in Fort Smith, Arkansas, would shut down if there were no merger. No case was filed. Ribicoff also blocked a suit against the merger of General Electric and Universal Electric, based on the same arguments.

Worst of all was the Kaiser case. Kaiser Aluminum Company bought a wire-and-cable plant in Bristol, Rhode Island, from U.S. Rubber in 1957. Four years later the government successfully filed suit to undo the acquisition. In 1964 Senator Pastore (D.-R.I.) appealed to Katzenbach that divestiture would close down the Bristol plant, costing 700 jobs in an area officially designated a "labor-surplus area." So an agreement was reached between the Justice Department and Kaiser in January, 1964, that the Bristol plant would be offered for sale at a very high price for nine months; if there were no takers, Kaiser could keep the plant. There were, predictably, no buyers. One government antitrust official called the settlement "the closest thing to hogwash I've seen." [2]

Of such cases generally, Professor Corwin Edwards has written that if "the collapse of a great concern injures so many people that it cannot be tolerated . . . [then] the concern's activities are no longer private in character and therefore should no longer be determined privately. The logic of the argument implies a need for public regulation, of which prevention of bankruptcy would be only a small part." [3] What antitrust enforcers like Katzenbach do not realize is that competitive capitalism presupposes that inefficient firms may fail, with the released capital and labor being reallocated to a more efficient and rational use. The solution for any unemployment is vigorous relief and job-corps measures by government—not the scuttling of anti-trust.

There were other, less successful attempts. The late Senator Everett Dirksen sent Katzenbach a letter, at a time when the 1964 Civil Rights Act was pending and his support was being solicited, asking the Attorney General to check into the Antitrust Division's investigation of United Fruit Company. Dirksen was not merely asking on behalf of an interested constituent; he represented the president of the company, Thomas Sunderland, in his private capacity as an attorney. By representing the company head rather than the company itself, Dirksen presumably thought he got around the federal prohibition against taking clients with an interest against the government. But he also was trading on his official prestige and power for private gain. The *Chicago Daily News* said of his private practice in general that "Dirksen insists he does not see any possible conflict of interest in sending 'non-Federal' clients to [his firm]. ('And if they want to remunerate me for it, why not?')" [4] Katzenbach was unaffected by this pressure. "It was too flagrant," confided a Division official in an interview.

Senator James Eastland (D.-Miss.) also made a blatantly self-interested pitch to Attorney General Ramsey Clark, in 1968, when three Mississippi banks planned to merge. The merger seemed illegal, as the memorandum from Assistant Attorney General Turner to Clark explained: "The present Mississippi mergers represent the clearest examples of . . . anticompetitive market extension mergers which have come to our attention to date." Nevertheless, Eastland tried to get the case killed, both because Mississippi banks were involved and because his wife had financial interests in one of them. His interference so irritated the staff on the case that they pushed the case through faster than usual. The case was filed and lost in a typically poor district-court opinion.

Antitrust arm-twisting is not limited to conservative Congressional chieftains. In 1961, Lee Loevinger, head of the Antitrust Division and a former Minnesota lawyer and judge, empaneled a grand jury to investigate certain Minnesota banks and bank officials for alleged Sherman Act violations. "Clean" Gene McCarthy (D.-Minn.) protested

violently, giving speeches in his home state and calling
Loevinger into his Senatorial office to complain. "[He] did
everything but break Lee's arm," a Division official noted.
A criminal case was eventually brought against the banks
but not against the bank officials.

The most spectacular politicking by a Congressional liberal involves Representative Emanuel Celler (D.-N.Y.),
Chairman of both the House Judiciary Committee and the
House Antitrust Subcommittee. Celler is a near legendary
figure on antitrust, co-author of the Celler-Kefauver Act;
so his transgressions are all the more inexcusable.

—In the *Burlington Watch* case of the mid-Fifties, Celler's
New York law firm represented Benrus, a competitor of the
defendant. Benrus was unhappy with the practice of importers bringing in low-jeweled (lower-duty) watches and "up-
jeweling" them here. They wanted this practice included in
the complaint, but Mary Gardiner Jones, then an attorney
in the Antitrust Division and now an FTC Commissioner,
did not. The Division received an official letter from Celler
asking why this count was not included. Jones drafted a
scathing reply, which Antitrust Chief Stanley Barnes chose
not to send; instead no reply at all was sent and no follow-
up was received from Celler. Later Commissioner Jones
stated that this official silence was the best way of letting
Celler know that he had stepped out of line.

—A case was proposed by the Division against Schenley
Industries, Inc., producer of liquors, which was being defended by Celler's firm. Celler lobbied Katzenbach about it,
opening the conversation by commenting on his labors for
the Administration's then-pending Civil Rights Bill. He
argued that the case should not be brought because the Division was in error over the issue involved—whether a
license to import Cutty Sark was an asset within the meaning of the 1950 Act. He claimed that, as one of the authors
of the Act, he was well qualified to interpret the law in this
situation. His arguments were ultimately ignored.

—Later, Schenley found itself in the opposite situation,
urging the Antitrust Division to investigate its competitor
Seagram's for an alleged conspiracy in restraint of trade.
The Division considered the evidence insufficient to call a
grand jury. Celler demanded an explanation, and a high
antitrust official had to be dispatched to explain the issue to
him. How did the courier feel? "Rotten," he told the Study
Group.

—A decade ago Celler's Antitrust Subcommittee staff pushed for a strong bill against interlocking directorships to close some loopholes in the Clayton Act. Significant resources were devoted to a study of interlocking ties. between corporations and between banks. Yet when the study was presented to Celler's chief of staff, Bess Dick, she noted that the time, 1963, was inappropriate for its release or for legislative proposals. Attention would undoubtedly focus on the fact that Celler himself was a director of a New York City mutual fund, at a time when newspapers had recently uncovered and criticized his private law-firm arrangement. A year later the interlock study was assigned to a new staff member, who worked on it alone. "The eventual result was a shadow of the original study," complained the staffer who first proposed the interlock idea to Celler; "I therefore refused to sign it."

Celler has a so-called "two-door" arrangement with his law firm. Clients with business against the federal government enter through one door, which lacks Celler's name; other clients enter through a door *with* Celler's name on it. No one is fooled. Robert Sherrill, writing in the *New York Times Magazine,* notes that the Celler arrangement is "one of the longest-standing and most notorious embarrassments to Congress." [5] A former top official at the Antitrust Division confirms that the word has gone out: "If you want Celler's support, hire his law firm."

Celler, nevertheless, at times exerts an innovative voice on antitrust. In August, 1970, the *Wall Street Journal* quoted him as suggesting that a super-agency be created to pass on all mergers in the regulated industries. The article urged that the Penn-Central debacle be probed as a case study—which might prove embarrassing since the New York Central was a client of Celler's firm. In 1968, according to ICC records, the law firm of "Weisman, Celler, Allan, Spett & Sheinberg" received $51,664 in legal fees from Penn-Central, which had picked up its predecessor's tab.*

When asked about these conflicts in a Study Group interview, Celler denied any knowledge of them. "Your constituents are the final arbiter of any conflicts," he added, "and I'm always re-elected."

---

* Representative Celler is not entirely alone in his compromising status. In May, 1969, 56 Congressmen reported that their names were still on the doors of the law firms where they practiced upon entering Congress. Another 19 admitted to practicing law while in office, according to a *Washington Post* report.

(2) Congress is not alone in tampering with antitrust; the Executive Branch in conjunction with the Corporate Estate often tries its hand.

President Truman's role in generating a case against a bothersome newspaper has already been noted. During Eisenhower's Presidency the Radio Corporation of America was indicted for criminal antitrust violations. The four-count indictment, charging conspiracy and the attempt to monopolize radio fixtures and patents, brought no-contest pleas and $50,000 fines for each count. The fines imposed were the maximum permissible under the Sherman Antitrust Act. It was a spectacular case—but less spectacular than it could have been. Attorney General Brownell, under orders from the White House, had struck off the proposed indictment the name of a suggested criminal defendant: General David Sarnoff, founder and chairman of RCA.

The paradigm of political intrigue in antitrust remains the story behind the 1956 consent decree with AT&T, then and now the largest company in the world. It was here that the Eisenhower Administration's tenderness toward business was most clearly manifest.

In 1949 the Department of Justice filed suit against AT&T to divest itself of Western Electric, charging that the two companies monopolized the telephone market in violation of the Sherman Act. While AT&T may be a "natural monopoly," since only one company can efficiently lay down telephone wires, the government argued that telephone manufacturing was decidedly not a "natural monopoly." If Western Electric were split into three separate companies, then competition in telephone production would occur, lowering prices for telephone servicing and calls and stimulating innovation.

But AT&T liked its dual monopoly. First it conscripted the Secretary of Defense, Robert Lovett, to claim that its contribution to the Korean War effort would be diminished if key personnel had to be taken off military projects to prepare an adequate defense. Lovett accepted their claims *prima facie,* urging that Justice postpone the case and (in a memorandum to the files) that his successor take the same view.*

By 1953 little had been done on the case. The advent of

---

* The material for this case study was mostly drawn from Joseph Goulden's *Monopoly* (1968) and from hearings held by Representative Celler in 1959.

a Republican administration, which had criticized the Democrats for their "prosecution of business," interested H. S. Dumas, an AT&T vice president and its lead attorney on the suit. He arranged to meet the new Attorney General, Herbert Brownell, in the Washington hotel suite of a mutual friend, New York banker Bayard Pope. Dumas told Brownell that the case was weak and should be dismissed; Brownell made no promises. A second meeting was soon arranged between Brownell and T. Brook Price, AT&T general counsel. The conference took place at a private cottage Brownell was occupying in White Sulphur Springs, West Virginia. Price's memorandum from the AT&T files, obtained by an investigator from Celler's committee, lucidly described the event:

> [Brownell] reflected a moment and said in substance that a way ought to be found to get rid of the case. He asked me whether, if we reviewed our practices, we would be able to find things we are doing which were once considered entirely legal, but might now be in violation of the antitrust laws or questionable in that respect. . . . Consequently, he thought that we could readily find practices that we might agree to have enjoined with no real injury to our business.
>
> . . . I [Price] said that our management had not been willing to so admit that any injunction ought to be entered against the company, but they felt that the case ought to be dropped. He said, "I don't think that's a very sensible attitude for them to take." I said, "They are sensible people, and they will give this matter further consideration. . . ."
>
> As I got up to go he walked down the steps with me and repeated his statement that it was important to get this case disposed of. He said the President would understand this also and that if a settlement was worked out he could get the President's approval in five minutes. . . .

Price later said that he doubted Brownell knew much about the details of the case, and that he thought Brownell was "giving us a little friendly tip" on how to approach the Antitrust Division with a settlement. The Celler committee concluded that Brownell's actions revealed

> partiality towards the defendants incompatible with the duties of his public office. It may be added that it hardly is in keeping with the ethics of the legal profession for an Attorney General . . . to give his adversary a "friendly little tip" to approach the Justice Department with a proposal whose acceptance would prove harmless to its clients.

And as it turned out, the "tip" was most valuable. At least an outright dismissal, which AT&T initially wanted, would have permitted some later, more antitrust-minded administration to move against AT&T. A consent-decree settlement, however, protected the firm from further attack.

To help obtain a settlement, Brownell transferred the experienced Division staff off the AT&T case and gave it to Edward Foote, a special assistant to Stanley Barnes, the Assistant Attorney General for Antitrust. Foote had never tried an antitrust case and his expertise in the complicated communications field was "not very much," according to his own assessment. In January, 1956, Foote invited AT&T General Counsel Price to his Washington home for dinner, where he told Price that he thought it "silly" to go to trial and that Division attorney Victor Kramer was pressing for a dismissal rather than "take a weak decree." Celler's committee dealt harshly with Foote's disclosures:

> [They] had the effect of seriously undermining the government's bargaining position at the negotiating table. It stands to reason that when the chief government negotiator tells the other side that he has no sympathy with the case, and that from his standpoint it is silly to consider trial, most unusual would be the counsel who so forewarned did not hold out for a more favorable settlement than he might otherwise be willing to accept.

After a fourth meeting with Brownell, a consent decree was prepared. It did not order the divestiture of Western Electric from AT&T, which was the main purpose of the suit; it did not order AT&T and its operating companies to buy telephone equipment by competitive bidding; it did not require Western Electric to sell back to AT&T its 50% stock ownership in the Bell Telephone Laboratories; it did not enjoin arrangements between the two making Western Electric the exclusive purchaser, supplier, developer, installer, and repairer for the Bell System. All such relief had been sought in the original complaint.

The most affirmative provision required that AT&T license existing and future patents to all applicants at reasonable royalties; yet with AT&T a "natural monopoly" and buying telephones *only* from Western Electric, how could any potential competitor, even with patents, get a foothold against Western Electric? Victor Kramer refused to sign the decree because he considered it would be inconsistent with his oath of office. Brownell later said that "everybody" who worked on the case recommended the consent decree. Yet virtually the entire pre-Foote staff strenuously opposed the settlement, a point Foote admitted he told Brownell.

The decree was formally filed with the district court on January 12, 1956. Brownell and other Justice Department spokesmen called the decree a "major victory" and "miraculous" for the government. But it was not so simple to pass off baloney as filet. *Business Week* commented that the "antitrust consent decree against AT&T hailed last week as a 'major victory' turned out on second look to be hardly more than a slap on the wrist for the biggest corporation in the world." [6] Frederick R. Kappel, then president of Western Electric and later to be head of AT&T, understood the decree better, it appeared, than Brownell did. In an outline of a talk to other Western Electric officials, he wrote: "Use discretion. . . . Don't brag about having won victory or getting everything we wanted. . . . Antitrust suit disposed of, but still have politicians, etc., to think of." [7]

President John Kennedy basically left antitrust cases to his brother, although on one case—the divestiture action against Alcoa for acquiring Rome Cable—the President personally called a Division official to judge whether the case had merit. The lawyer, First Assistant Robert Wright, number-two man in the Division, said, "I was amazed to find the President on the phone. Someone from the industry must have asked him to check into the suit." (Katzenbach later acknowledged that business pressure on this case was intense.) On another case, the Schlitz Beer Company tried to quash the suit against its mergers with John Labatt, Ltd., and Burgermeister Brewing Corporation by sending a former general and former JFK campaign director to lobby the President. When it failed, they obtained a second audience, *sans* general, but again without success. Yet the firm had been so confident of the outcome of these meetings that they found themselves unprepared for trial when it was scheduled a year and a half after the complaint had been filed. They sought a court extension—and failed once more.

As already noted, the calling of the grand jury to look into the steel industry's 1962 price increase was partly rooted in the motive of political intimidation. By the time the grand jury had been empaneled and witnesses were being called, however, the battle was over and the administration was in a different mood. When Gordon Spivack, the Division attorney on the case, began to call witnesses, he was told by an opposing lawyer that his clients would not produce subpoenaed documents, because a Cabinet official had told them that the documents did not have to be delivered. Spivack, furious, threatened to bring criminal contempt charges against those who failed to produce the documents. They were produced.

Lyndon Johnson also supposedly kept out of antitrust enforcement, according to his former advisor, Joseph Califano, because he was sensitive to the "wheeler-dealer" label pinned on him by critics. Johnson did "clear" the filing of at least two cases while at the White House: the *BMI* case, where his own station was involved, and the *Scripps-Howard* case. That newspaper chain, already owning one of the two Cincinnati newspapers, attempted to control the other by acquiring a voting trust. The violation was too clear to ignore and the case was filed. Yet the White House was not merely President Johnson. When ABC president Leonard Goldenson sought assurances that the government would not move against ABC's acquisition by the ITT conglomerate, he got them from a prominent Presidential aide; but word never filtered down to Antitrust Chief Donald Turner, who fought the merger both at the FCC and in court, a move which surprised the network.

Federal authorities are not alone in lobbying for their sectional interests. State politicians also enter the act. One curious episode involved Claude Kirk, then Governor of Florida, who visited Turner aide Edwin Zimmerman while Turner, was away from Washington. Kirk pushed the proposed North American–Rockwell merger, which would supposedly result in a new Florida plant. Kirk asked Zimmerman, "Did you ever practice law? Do you know about the real world?" The ex-Governor answered himself by dismissing Zimmerman as "just an academic." During this harangue, Kirk stationed two of his Florida state troopers in the Antitrust Division hallway by Zimmerman's door. The attempted intimidation failed to persuade Zimmerman of anything (except Kirk's eccentricities), although the Division later decided to permit the merger to go through.

Governors were also quite interested in the Penn-Central merger. President Johnson even took Attorney General

Ramsey Clark to meet with five New England governors and the vice chairman of the ICC on the then-pending merger. "They yelled at me for opposing the merger before the ICC, citing the argument that the New Haven [railroad] had to be saved," observed Clark, whose ethical sensitivities were upset at the presence of an ICC commissioner on an issue awaiting adjudication.

The Executive Branch was more significantly involved in the Penn-Central merger case than this one meeting. The importance of merging two of the largest railroad systems in the Northeast led President Kennedy to establish the Interagency Committee on Transportation Mergers to pass on the merits of the Penn-Central merger. Focusing the decision-making power in one body aided the strenuous lobbying of Stuart Saunders, Chairman of the Pennsylvania Board. He saw all the committee members, to the extent that Katzenbach, then Deputy Attorney General under Robert Kennedy, complained that "I hardly ever went to any office during that time without expecting to see Mr. Saunders sitting there." The Committee eventually decided to permit the Antitrust Division to appear at the ICC hearing, not to oppose the merger outright but to emphasize that certain procompetitive conditions must be attached to it. But antitruster Joseph Saunders (no relation), who argued the case, stressed the Division's opposition to the merger, listing some procompetitive conditions at the tail end of his argument. Stuart Saunders called up Katzenbach immediately afterward to protest he'd been "double-crossed."

Saunders exacted his pound of flesh in another way. It was 1964 and Robert Kennedy had decided to run for the Senate from New York. Although he opposed the Penn-Central merger as Attorney General, he wanted a free hand to *favor* it, if necessary, as a Senator from an interested state. The Penn Railroad chief and Katzenbach urged Kennedy to write a memorandum to the files which would suggest that his successor not contest the Penn-Central merger if approved by the ICC. Saunders liked the idea as a way of exerting pressure on the next Attorney General. Katzenbach (who did not expect to be Kennedy's successor) convinced a reluctant Kennedy for the same reason he would not later stop the rice-milling merger: why not get a political benefit if it costs you nothing? There would be no cost, he candidly told the Study Group, because no memo to the files could really bind a later Attorney General. This Machiavellian move, however, was not costless. It was logical that Saunders would not forget Katzenbach's role when it came time for Katzenbach to make decisions as Attorney General. Thus when the Antitrust Division recommended to Katzenbach that it wanted to oppose the merger outright and "confess error" at the ICC, the new Attorney General never even replied to the request. One knowledgeable Division attorney on the case thought that "Katzenbach's" memo had "immobilized him." Saunders later admitted to the press that "I could not have gotten the merger through without help from members of the Administration." [8]

In 1969 the Nixon administration's vigorous moves against conglomerates, and non-moves against existing oligopolies, struck some observers as political discrimination —suing new-money Democrats and leaving old-money Republicans alone. Two specific cases, however, began to give support to those who feared that this Republican administration might be as partial toward business as its 1950s predecessor.

In early 1969 ITT attempted to acquire the Canteen Corporation, the leading vending-machine producer. Such a merger would have, in the eyes of Division lawyers on the case, foreclosed markets due to reciprocity and foreclosure (ITT puts Canteen vending machines in all its plants), entrenched a leading firm, raised entry barriers, and triggered similar mergers. The memorandum from Antitrust Chief Richard McLaren to John Mitchell said: "We believe that *a preliminary injunction is particularly necessary here.* If we allow Canteen's public ownership to be bought out another corporation will likely be the eventual purchaser of Canteen." (Emphasis added.)

Attorney General Mitchell withdrew from consideration of the case due to a conflict of interest. It fell to Richard Kleindienst, Deputy Attorney General and a former Goldwater assistant, to decide what to do. Two weeks before the merger was to be completed, ITT counsel requested, and received, a two-week period during which the Department would not file suit and ITT would reconsider the merger. During this supposed respite, ITT, aided by New York investment houses which would greatly profit if the merger were completed, lobbied White House staff close to

Nixon to get the case dropped. ITT's importunings were relayed, with approval, to Kleindienst, who promptly refused to file the complaint.

Since the suit was important to his anti-conglomerate enforcement program, McLaren was furious. He went to the White House and announced that he would resign if the case were not brought. Negotiations then occurred between White House staff, McLaren, and Kleindienst. The final resolution was a compromise. The case was filed, but *after* the merger had been consummated. There was no chance for a preliminary injunction.

In July, 1970, Warner-Lambert Pharmaceutical Company announced plans to merge with Parke Davis & Company. According to the *Wall Street Journal,* the merged firm would have sales of more than $1.1 billion and would be the fifth largest drug firm. There were submarkets between the firms where competitive overlap existed. Representative Celler considered the merger illegal in a letter to McLaren, and FTC staffers agreed.[9] Furthermore, there were strong elements of potential competition present, especially in areas of mutual firm interest like oral contraceptives and antibiotics. McLaren approved a suit against the merger.

Again Mitchell had to take himself off the case because Warner-Lambert had been a client of his (and Nixon's) former law firm—Mudge, Rose, Guthrie & Alexander. And again Kleindienst refused to file the case. The political context of this case is even more suspect than in ITT-Canteen. The honorary Chairman of Warner-Lambert, Elmer Bobst, is known to be a close friend of President Nixon. It was Mr. Bobst who encouraged Nixon to move from California to join the Mudge, Rose firm. Bobst also has been a frequent and heavy contributor to Nixon's campaigns, giving at least $55,000 in 1968 alone.

A large number of attorneys interviewed both within and without the Antitrust Division attribute Kleindienst's refusal to file to political, not legal, considerations. An assistant section chief at the Division said of the case, "It's a fix." Another staff attorney noted that "There won't be any proof of what really happened since there was a fix on." And a third similar view was offered by one of the highest officials at the FTC in response to the question why the case was eventually transferred to the FTC: "I suppose the reason is that it is harder to fix a case with five commissioners." Congressman Celler told the Study Group in an interview, "It was a straight political move." How did he know? "You don't have to rub it under your nose to know it's cologne." A final dissident was Richard McLaren, who considered resigning if the case were not transferred to the FTC for further investigation. McLaren even went so far as drafting a letter of resignation, according to a Division official who read it, but put it away when the case was sent to the FTC.

Incriminating stock dealings point out one very likely motivation behind the unusual actions of the Department. A Wall Street client of a prominent Washington law firm has said that the Mudge, Rose law firm sent a message reading "All contingencies are met" when discussing the merger with a block of investors. Our source, a former Antitrust Division official who wishes to remain anonymous, said that "They never would have sent such an encouraging message unless they had inside information." In fact, there was heavy trading both in Warner-Lambert and Parke Davis stock just *before* as well as after the Justice Department announced its withdrawal from the case. This information was corroborated by a Jack Anderson column, which covered the same ground and acknowledged the difficulty of proof:

> Sources with excellent Wall Street pipelines have told us that a small, select financial group seemed to have advance knowledge that Justice wouldn't seek an injunction against the merger. This apparent assurance permitted the insiders to clean up $135 million on quick profits, our sources allege. . . . They claim a prominent Wall Street financier advised his special clients to buy up all the stock they could get in the two pharmaceutical firms. "It's a cinch," he is quoted as telling them. . . . This sort of inside dealing is almost impossible for a newsman without subpoena power to prove.[10]

After the merger was completed, the case was referred to the FTC for reconsideration. The reasons initially given for the switch were spurious. If there was FTC expertise in such drug mergers, as claimed, why wasn't the case given to the FTC in the first instance, which is the usual procedure? It seems that the case was intentionally channeled to the Division, presumably because of its preliminary-injunction powers, which the FTC lacks except in unusual situations. One staff attorney at Antitrust emphasized that "We fought to get the Warner-Lambert case." In addition, the fact that Mitchell takes himself off a case has never been a cause to destroy all the staff work below; the established procedure is simply to have the Deputy decide to file or not.

Another reason for refusing to block the merger, offered by Kleindienst, was that one of the companies, presumably Parke Davis, was "failing." Yet in 1969 Parke Davis made a profit of $20.7 million on sales of $273.5 million. In a November 12, 1970, memorandum to McLaren, Kleindienst reported that FDA Commissioner Charles Edwards thought that the merger would revive the research program of Parke Davis, a program the Deputy represented as being "further cut back." Yet Commissioner Edwards has denied making such a statement and Parke Davis has reported their research spending is going *up,* not down.

The Department's refusal to file and the transfer to the FTC did accomplish something ITT sought: as in Canteen, no preliminary injunction was secured to block the merger. An FDA publication, *FDA Reports,* was quick to point out: "But even if the FTC attacks the merger with some novel economic-legal theory of antitrust law, it is now too late to completely unscramble the marriage." [11] On April 20, 1971, the FTC *did* attack the merger, alleging competitive injury for 52 specified kinds of drugs, thereby giving its sister agency a lesson in antitrust enforcement.

THE CONGRESSIONAL CONTEXT

To a large extent, the above political maneuverings occurred unconnected to the specific substance of the antitrust laws. Yet even nonpolitical, "normalized" antitrust enforcement is politically rooted, the result of legislative and executive forces. Bills which Congress passes, as well as those they will *not* pass, all have a direct impact on cases brought and not brought.

Antitrust legislation was born in the late 1800s just as the American economy seemed to be moving toward Karl Marx's predicted last stage of capitalism—monopolistic capitalism. A national railroad network led to cheaper transportation costs and nationwide firms. These new firms, seeking larger economies of scale, were serviced by equally new industrial banking houses able to supply vast venture capital to a single firm. Liberal state incorporation laws permitted easy acquisitions and the delegation of decision-making power from shareholders to full-time managers. The great trusts arose, in turn changing the rules of the free enterprise game. John D. Rockefeller, creator of the Standard Oil empire, proclaimed in 1882 that "The day of combinations is here to stay. Individualism is gone, never to return." Others disagreed. An antimonopoly coalition formed, composed of farmers, labor organizations, and small businesses. Their complaints found a voice in the Populist Party:

We meet in the midst of a country brought to the verge of moral, political and material ruin. . . . The fruits of the toil of millions are boldly stolen to build up colossal fortunes for a few. . . . From the same prolific womb of governmental injustice we breed the two great classes—tramps and millionaires.

The public demanded action. Democrats favored controlling trusts through the competition of foreign goods resulting from lowered tariffs. Republicans were dedicated to high tariffs and so sought solutions elsewhere. Since President Benjamin Harrison and the majority party in Congress were Republicans, the Sherman Act was that solution. The Congress and President readily accepted it, because, according to historian Richard Hofstadter, "it was recognized by most of the astute politicians of that hour as a gesture, a ceremonial concession to an overwhelming public demand for some kind of reassuring action against the trusts." [12] Senator Orville Platt at its passage candidly observed that the bill resulted from a desire "to get some bill headed: 'A Bill to Punish Trusts' with which to go to the country." [13]

The Sherman Act followed well-known common-law principles which condemned both undue restraints and the monopolization of trade, applying these principles to the new trusts. Section 1 made illegal "every contract, combination . . . or conspiracy, in restraint of trade"; Section 2 forbade monopolizing or attempting to monopolize trade. Violation of either was a criminal offense, a misdemeanor, punishable by a fine not exceeding $5,000 or by imprisonment up to a year, or both. Any person injured by another's antitrust violation could recover treble damages—that is, three times the actual amount of damages suffered.

Some thought the Act an heroic effort. An economist writing decades later observed that "For the first time in history, a government faced with growing monopoly power chose to fight the power itself rather than concede the inevitability of concentration and regulate its effects." [14] Others were less charitable. Justice Oliver Wendell Holmes called it "a humbug based on economic ignorance and incompetence." Yet most view the Sherman Act as part of the great common-law tradition—a general principle capable of growth with changing times. In its flexibility, generality, and principled nature, the Sherman Act is our Economic Constitution.

By 1912, however, the Sherman Act's growth had been severely stunted. It was not used to stop the greatest merger movement in American history, which occurred during 1898–1902. When the Act was finally given form by the 1911 *Standard Oil* and *American Tobacco* cases, the Supreme Court limited its scope by invoking the "Rule of Reason": only "bad" trusts, those that abused their power by predatory conduct, were illegal, but "good" trusts were legal. Critics of lax enforcement and judicial emasculation demanded a newer and tougher act. These critics were largely the Progressives, an urban middle-class successor to the rural Populists. At the same time Congress realized that corporations were expanding through stock acquisitions at a rate which threatened to re-create the old trusts in the form of new holding companies.

The result was the Clayton Act of 1914. It did not include any provision aimed at circumventing the Supreme Court's antitrust approach, but did prohibit any stock acquisition by a corporation where its effect "may be substantially to lessen competition," certain interlocking directorates, and price discrimination and sales on condition that the buyer cease dealing with the seller's competitors. It also exempted farmer and labor organizations from the reach of antitrust laws.

Although the Sherman Act failed in its initial enforcement efforts, at least it had significant potential. The Clayton Act had neither. The proscription that a *director* of one corporation could not be a director of a competing corporation did not include interlocking *management* of the competitors; the prohibition of *stock* acquisitions leading to a Sherman Act violation did not include *asset* acquisitions, which soon began to proliferate; as the FTC subsequently reported, corporations thereby continued to grow alarmingly.[15] *

---

* The Federal Trade Commission Act, also passed in 1914, which established the FTC, will be discussed in Chapter 10.

Two New Deal Acts, aimed largely at protecting small businessmen from the vicissitudes of competitive combat, were passed. The 1936 Robinson-Patman Act forbade price discrimination—but in language so turgid as to discourage the lowering of one's prices, which is the goal of antitrust. The Miller-Tydings Act the next year legalized price-fixing between manufacturers and dealers in order to protect inefficient small dealers. The bill was introduced by the first Senator Tydings; he attached it as a rider to the District of Columbia appropriations bill, where it could not be discussed on its merits. A law partner of Senator Tydings, who was also an attorney for the National Association of Retail Druggists, prepared the bill.

By the late 1940s the failure of the antimerger section of the 1914 Clayton Act was evident. Congress responded with the Celler-Kefauver Act of 1950. Its most momentous provision was the new Section 7, amending its 1914 predecessor by adding the italicized language: "No corporation engaged in commerce shall acquire . . . the stock . . . or any part of the *assets* of another corporation engaged also in commerce, where *in any line of commerce in any section of the country,* the effect of such acquisition may be substantially to lessen competition, or to tend to create a monopoly . . ."; the "may be" language permitted suits against asset acquisitions whose dangers were more incipient than actual.

The clear impetus for the legislation was concern over the political and economic effects of concentration. Senator Estes Kefauver, one of its authors, said during the debates:

> The control of American business is steadily being transferred . . . from local communities to a few large cities in which central managers decide the policies and the fate of the far-flung enterprises they control. Millions of people depend helplessly on their judgment. Through monopolistic mergers the people are losing power to direct their own economic welfare. When they lose the power to direct their economic welfare they also lose the means to direct their political future.[16]

In the first Supreme Court decision construing the Celler-Kefauver Act, *Brown Shoe* in 1962, the Court corroborated this view: "The dominant theme pervading congressional consideration of the 1950 amendments was a fear of what was considered to be a rising tide of economic concentration in the American economy." [17]

The *House Report* explained how the new Act was to apply to mergers. Proscribed acquisitions were listed:

[Horizontal]: elimination in whole or in material part of the competitive activity of an enterprise which has been a substantial factor in competition . . .

[Vertical]: establishment of relationships between buyers and sellers which deprive their rivals of a fair opportunity to compete . . .

[Conglomerate]: increase in the relative size of the enterprise making the acquisition to such a point that its advantage over its competitors threatens to be decisive.[18]

Charts in the *Report* illustrated the three types of mergers, and a comment stressed that the "same principles" would apply equally to horizontal, vertical, and conglomerate transactions.[19] Nevertheless, for the third time in as many attempts, major antitrust legislation did not stop an impending merger wave, a conglomerate one which peaked in 1967–69.

Yet as Congress giveth, Congress taketh away. Capitol Hill not only writes antitrust legislation, it also divests the courts of jurisdiction when they support antitrust enforcement too militantly, and it stifles efforts to pass additional, necessary legislation. The prior pattern began with the Clayton Act, which exempted farm and labor organizations from the reach of the Sherman Act and itself. Once it was seen what political power could reap, other groups began lobbying to obtain the special privilege of being free from antitrust prosecution. For example, the Webb-Pomerene Act of 1916 permitted businessmen to act together in export trade; by the Shipping Act of 1916, common-carrier rate agreements approved by the Maritime Commission were exempted from the antitrust laws; exemptions for agricultural seller cooperatives were passed in 1922, 1926, and 1937. Of these efforts,. Professor Corwin Edwards has complained that the "administrative technique is to entrust exercise of public power to persons who are privately interested, without adequate provision for public surveillance." [20] In more recent history:

—The Supreme Court upheld, in the 1944 *South-Eastern Underwriters* case, a Sherman Act indictment against a group of insurance companies which had fixed prices and employed various coercions to eliminate competition. The insurance industry was shocked, having assumed for many

years that they were under the antitrust exemption umbrella.
They descended on Congress to obtain immunization. In
1945, one year later, the McCarran-Ferguson Act exempted
insurance companies from the antitrust laws until 1948,
and thereafter the exemption would extend *if* such activities were regulated by state law.

—The Miller-Tydings amendment to the Sherman Act
exempted resale price contracts between producer and dis-
tributor when such agreements are lawful in the state of
resale ("fair-trade state"). It encouraged artificially high
prices by discouraging competition at the retail level. One
issue not covered in the 1937 legislation was the status of
the nonsigner, the retailer who had not specifically con-
tracted to sell the commodity at a certain price. Was he
bound by other agreements between other producers and
distributors? The Supreme Court said "No" in the 1951
decision of *Schwegmann Bros.* v. *Calvert Distillers Corp.*
The next year Congress reversed the Court and said "Yes"
in the McGuire Act. Thus, if *any* manufacturer in a fair-
trade state set the price of his product, *all* retailers in that
state were bound.

—Under the threat of a pending antitrust action, Congress passed the 1948 Reed-Bulwinkle Act, amending the
Interstate Commerce Commission Act to legalize the price-
fixing activities of "rate bureaus"—organizations of either
rail, water, or motor carriers which set common tariffs. The
Act adds that any carrier who so desires has "the free and
unrestrained right to take independent action." Professor
Walter Adams comments that "in practice, this right is little
more than a sterile gesture. To the rate bureaus, it represents a minor annoyance which cannot break down the self-
imposed restraints 'born of history, habit and strong mutual
self-interest.' " [21]

—The Bank Merger Act of 1960 directed the three banking-regulatory agencies to consider, among other factors,
the competitive effects of a proposed merger before approving it. In 1963 the Supreme Court surprised the banking
and regulatory community in its *Philadelphia Bank* decision,
which held that banking was included in the coverage of
Section 7 of the 1950 Act and that the 1960 Bank Merger
Act did not immunize from antitrust prosecution agency-
approved mergers. Whatever the benefits to the community,
the Court reasoned, Section 7 proscribed all anticompeti-

tive mergers. This case, plus the then-pending suit against the Manufacturers-Hanover merger and "the prospect of splitting that $6 billion institution in two . . . led to the passage of the Bank Merger Act of 1966," according to *Antitrust Developments 1955–1968*. Kenneth Elzinga, recently the resident economist at the Antitrust Division, criticized the political maneuverings behind this exemption:

This bill was in direct response to antimerger activity directed against banking—and specifically nullified three court divestiture orders! Even those who have resigned themselves to the role of strong lobbies and powerful special interest groups in a democracy cannot help but be somewhat disturbed by the determined and successful efforts of the banking interests to ram this bill through Congress.[22]

In the legislative history, Congress "forgave" bank mergers (other than those "attempting to monopolize") consummated prior to June 17, 1963, the date of the *Philadelphia Bank* decision.* The Act permitted the regulatory agencies to condone mergers which might lessen competition *if* "the anticompetitive effects . . . are clearly outweighed . . . [by] meeting the convenience and needs of the community to be served." At first six district courts held that the burden was on the Antitrust Division to prove the anticompetitive effects were *not* outweighed. The Supreme Court, as it has done so many times, then came to the rescue of antitrust enforcement and reversed these rulings. The Court held it was up to the banks to prove their merger fell within the "convenience and needs" exception rather than for the government to prove the negative. In addition, the Court would review the facts *de novo* (anew) rather than accord any presumptive validity to the opinion of any banking-regulatory agency. The scope of the Act was thus severely narrowed.

—Many of us are sports fans, which partially accounts for the soft treatment professional sports has been accorded by the antitrust laws. In 1953 the Supreme Court declared baseball exempt from the antitrust laws because, *mirabile dictu,* it was not "interstate commerce"—as if Yogi Berra

* Senator Robertson (D.-Va.) managed the bill in the Senate. In 1966 he faced a difficult primary race, so Manufacturers Hanover Trust, the consolidation that his bill exonerated, sent letters to 44,000 stockholders declaring, "We believe that Senator Robertson, Senate Office Building, Washington, D.C., would like to know you appreciated his attitude and efforts."

suddenly appeared in Chicago without having traveled there from New York. Professional football, wary of such thin analysis, chose instead to lobby for a specific statutory exemption for the planned merger of the NFL and AFL leagues. In the House, Emanuel Celler held the bill up with hearings, due to his unhappiness with the whole antitrust treatment of sports. It went to the Senate, where Russell Long—promised a New Orleans franchise for his home state by the AFL—got the exemption attached as a rider to the Investment Tax Credit Suspension Act. ("Now, *that* shows power," proclaimed a staffer on the Senate Antitrust Subcommittee.) This procedural coup got it sent to the House Ways and Means Committee, bypassing Celler's Antitrust Committee. It quickly and easily passed.

—The most recent and spectacular example of the Congressional vetoing of a Supreme Court antitrust ruling involved one of the most powerful political constituencies in the country—the media.

By 1969 the number of cities with two or more independently owned daily newspapers had dwindled to 61, but in 22 of these cities the competing papers had entered into agreements to fix advertising rates and pool their profits. And there were plenty of profits to be pooled. Advertising rates per inch in Tucson, Arizona, rose from 55¢ in 1940, when the *Star-Citizen* joint agreement was born, to $1.82 in 1964. During the same period the papers' combined pretax profits went from $28,000 to $1,725,000. Twenty-five years after its creation, the *Tucson Star-Citizen* merger was finally attacked by the Justice Department. When the case reached the Supreme Court in 1969, an 8–1 majority held that the 1940 price-fixing agreement was a *per se* violation of the Sherman Act.

So, apparently, were the agreements in the 21 other cities, but the newspaper publishers had contingency plans. Soon after the Department had filed the Tucson suit, Senator Carl Hayden of Arizona introduced the "Failing Newspaper Act." The bill in effect exempted all 22 newspaper price-fixing agreements from antitrust purview and opened the door to similar agreements by making it easy to establish the "failing company" defense which the Supreme Court rejected in the *Tucson* case.

Was it really necessary for major metropolitan dailies in 22 cities to fix prices in order to avoid bankruptcy? The public record cannot answer that question—despite seven

large volumes of Senate hearings on the various bills—
because the publishers refused to give profit and loss figures
to Senator Hart's Antitrust Subcommittee without a promise
of secrecy. They claimed that disclosure might compromise
them in negotiating with future competitors and labor
unions and in defending future antitrust suits. The publishers were requesting an exemption based on financial need,
but refused to document that need. Representative Abner
Mikva (D.-Ill.), who did see the confidential financial data
as a member of the House Judiciary Committee, said that
it "shows more black figures than red." [23]

The passage of this "poverty program for the rich," in
Senator Hart's words, was achieved by active lobbying. Led
by the American Newspaper Publishers Association (ANPA)
on the outside, and by Senator Dirksen on the inside, Congress was made to realize the intimate relationship between
politics and publishing. "Lobbying overwhelms opponents
of Newspaper Preservation Act," read a headline in the
National Journal; legislators wanted to "collect IOU's,"
according to Mikva, to exchange for future endorsements
from local publishers; Representative Brown of Ohio complained he had received considerable pressure from "reporters acting on behalf of their chains." [24] At times, however, the squeeze backfired. One California Congressman
is quoted as saying that the large vote against the bill was
partly due to "the way the *San Francisco Chronicle* treated
Jeff Cohelan." Representative Cohelan, who did not support the bill, was defeated in his Democratic primary.
"[H]e didn't get a word in the *Chronicle* all through his
campaign," said the above California Congressman, "and
they had supported him editorially and covered his other
campaigns. So some of the guys just decided if it was that
kind of operation, they didn't want any part of it." [25] Senator Gaylord Nelson, who also opposed the bill, invited
cascades of criticism from his Madison, Wisconsin, newspapers, a "joint-agreement" city.

The political action, however, generally succeeded. The
National Journal studied the votes of Congressmen and
Senators from districts and states with joint agreements. Of
38 such Senators, only two voted against the bill: Nelson
and Byrd of West Virginia. Districts with joint ventures
have 32 members in Congress. Of the 27 who did vote on
the newspaper bill, *all* voted in favor of it.

And the Newspaper Act was not unique. For Congress

is a political body more sensitive to the needs of powerful business than to the principles of competition. The more recent Lockheed "bail-out" bill, exempting one of our biggest corporations from the rigors of competition, is yet another example. Of such favoritism in general, Senator Hart has aptly noted:

When the Poor People's Campaign comes to Washington, disorganized and hesitant, it is regarded as asking for special treatment, for handouts, for subsidies. The Congressional welcome is not enthusiastic.

But when some large industrial segment loses an antitrust case, there is no hesitancy to ask antitrust amendments to take care of its special problems. The needs of industry—its special treatment—as it outlines them as necessary for its vigor and health gets general acceptance. It does not have the bad flavor of the poor, non-corporate petitioner.

In addition to granting exemptions outright, Congress's antipathy to antitrust can be seen in its failure to pass needed legislation. The present chairman of the Senate Antitrust and Monopoly Subcommittee, Philip Hart—himself a champion of antitrust—presides over a den of *anti*-anti-trusters. The three Republicans on the Committee, Roman Hruska, Strom Thurmond, and Hiram Fong, have joined two of the four Democrats, John McClellan and Sam Ervin, to form a consistent majority opposed to expansion of antitrust. (The other two Democrats have been Hart and Edward Kennedy. At the beginning of the new session of Congress in January, 1971, Senators John Tunney [D.-Calif.] and Dan Gurney [D.-Fla.] were added to the Subcommittee.) Most observers agree that Senator Eastland, chairman of the full Judiciary Committee, stacked the Subcommittee with antitrust opponents after the death in 1963 of Senator Estes Kefauver, former head of the Subcommittee and an independent Senatorial power. Now, with rare exceptions, only legislation which erodes antitrust can get by the Subcommittee. And for the Congress as a whole in the 20 years since the Celler-Kefauver Act, the record is identical: there has been *no* legislation broadening the substantive scope of the antitrust laws.

Although the second largest subcommittee on Capitol Hill in terms of its budget ($643,500 for 31 staff positions in 1970), the Antitrust Subcommittee's record of recommended legislation which became law is minuscule. Its 20-year tally is:

—increased fines for Sherman Act violations, from $5,000 in 1890 to $50,000 in 1955. Few could contest this legislative effort, since as matched against corporate assets and the possible benefits of a price-fixing scheme, the $50,000 could be viewed as a trivial cost of doing business. When a proposal to increase the fine to $500,000 passed the Subcommittee in 1970, it languished and died in the full Judiciary Committee.

—orders issued by the Federal Trade Commission under Section 11 of the Clayton Act became final, if not appealed, relieving the FTC of its burden of having to go into court to enforce their decrees (1959).

—a bill permitting the Antitrust Division to subpoena business records of companies "under investigation" pursuant to civil proceedings. But not permitted by the bill were "oral" subpoenas (depositions), the right to subpoena other companies to aid in the case against another and the right to make the information later available to private litigants.

Aside from nonpassage of legislation, the Subcommittee has also blocked affirmative efforts. The subpoena difficulty, among others, in the Newspaper Act hearings is not a singular example. Subpoenas to the steel industry, necessary to probe that sluggish oligopoly, were voted down 11–4 by the full Judiciary Committee in 1962. Senator Hart was aware that the Subcommittee and full Committee would not approve of subpoenas being sent to American drug companies regarding their alleged suppression in the early 1960s of low-cost drugs to South American peasants. The investigation, therefore, died stillborn. Even when subpoenas do get out, success is far from guaranteed. Massive studies of the drug industry by Senator Kefauver documented extreme exploitation in that "ethical industry." Yet the provisions concerning the structure and patent rights of the industry, aimed at lowering prices, were stripped from the Drug Amendments bill of 1962 by the combined backstage machinations of Senators Dirksen, Hruska, and Eastland. Richard Harris's *The Real Voice* documents how they accomplished their feat—without Kefauver's knowledge and with the help of drug-industry lawyer-lobbyists Lloyd Cutler and Thomas Corcoran.

One member of the Subcommittee's majority staff, speaking of the pro-trusters on the Committee, exclaimed that "Those guys may stop us from getting legislation, but they can't stop us from holding hearings." [26] And hearings are something the Subcommittee does well. In the last 15 years it has published well over 200 volumes totaling more than

100,000 pages. Some are aimed at specific consumer antitrust problems, like automobile insurance, diet pills, and
hospital costs, while others are more conceptual and structural, such as the recent eight-volume work on "Economic
Concentration." (Nevertheless, these uniquely valuable
"Concentration" hearings resulted in *no* Subcommittee Report and not *one* piece of recommended legislation.)

All these hearings, however, do at least account for the
little good Congress has produced on antitrust. First, investigative hearings have significantly contributed to some of
the most important cases of the past decade. These include
the electrical price-fixing cases, the antibiotics conspiracy,
the price-fixing of children's books and the international
quinine conspiracy. Secondly, the hearings and the very
able majority staff seek to emphasize the consumer aspect
of antitrust, aware that an interested constituency is essential for any active antitrust program to succed.

The House Antitrust Subcommittee, under the Chairmanship of Representative Celler, is far less productive than
even its troubled Senate partner. In the Fifties it held numerous and valuable hearings, with subjects ranging from
the Clayton Act amendment to General Motors to the Antitrust Division's consent-decree program. The past decade,
however, has seen legislative arteriosclerosis.

Vigorous procompetition speeches by Celler are rarely
delivered. Hearings have declined in frequency and impact.
In 1965 a probe on interlocking directorates uncovered new
data and recent and valuable conglomerate hearings produced an able report in September 1971. Oddly, while the
report was critical of conglomerates, Celler was lavish in
praise of conglomerate chief executives in his accompanying
press release. And it, not the report's indictment, is what
many newspapers pick up. Otherwise, the record is sparse.
So is the Committee's output of suggested legislation. The
budget and staff of the Antitrust Subcommittee have declined; only two full-time professionals remain. Celler has
even been criticized by Chairman Wayne Hays of the
House Administration Committee, according to Representative Robert Kastenmeier (D.-Wisc.), for requesting
such a small appropriation for the Judiciary Committee;
the *full* Committee gets about $350,000 or one-half as
much as the Senate Antitrust Subcommittee. (Celler is the
Chairman of Judiciary, which disburses money to its sub-

committees.) And the little the Antitrust Subcommittee
gets is not entirely devoted to antitrust. It has also dealt
with civil rights and liberties, the administration of the
Federal Judiciary, and redistricting, all of personal interest
to Celler.

"There were months when we had absolutely nothing to
do," grumbled a former Subcommittee staffer in an interview. "For some reason Celler went backwards on antitrust."
Actually, the reasons are multiple: Celler's time is limited,
and most of it has been devoted to civil-rights issues and
to the administration of his Judiciary Committee; his energy
is naturally diminishing—Celler is 83 years old—but he will
not relinquish his Subcommittee post; and ideologically
Celler seems to have mellowed on antitrust, due either to
decades of lost battles or to the erosion of faith created by
his conflicts of interest.

The Congressional committees, however, are no better
and no worse than Congress as a whole. It is a body uninterested in the policy of competition, or "free enterprise"
as they like to brag on the hustings. Such a policy needs
adequate legislation, which is lacking; adequate financing,
which is deficient; and adequate industrial information,
which is sparse. In 1963 the Bureau of Economics of the
FTC, realizing the critical need for corporate data, proposed a massive 1,000-firm study of the economy. The
purpose of the study was to determine the extent of merger
activity and the web of intercorporate relations between
large firms. But "the influence of powerful special-interest
groups and the problem of Congressional appropriations,"
said one economist, "were responsible for the fact that what
promised to be one of the most important and revealing
studies ever attempted concerning American business was
never completed." [27] Not only did the Appropriations Committees of the two Houses delete the money for the study
from the FTC budget, but they went on to attach a special
rider to the FTC appropriation specifying that no money
could be used for this purpose. When the choice came between protecting business or opening it up to active antitrust scrutiny, Congress capitulated to the former.

The Capitol Hill problem has two basic sources. Many
supposed liberals sacrifice antitrust to higher interests. Senator Hartke is for steel quotas, Senator McCarthy supported
the oil and drug industries, Senator Muskie favors shoe

quotas, and Senator Javits, self-proclaimed representative of Wall Street, wants to disembowel our foreign antitrust efforts. In addition, many conservative legislators are unwilling to rock the business boat that carries them to office. Bobby Baker is quoted as saying of his former boss, Senator Robert Kerr, that "Bob Kerr used to say that he was opposed to all monopolies—unless he had a piece of them." As one assesses the Congressional antitrust ledger, the debits far exceed the credits.

CONCLUSIONS

The second half of this chapter portrays Congress as a body undevoted to the policy of economic competition. There is no easy corrective for this omission. Congress is largely propelled by pressure, not principle, and until enough people tell it that antitrust is important, until a political coalition coalesces which actively lobbies for consumer antitrust, Congress will continue its energetic indifference.

Despite official denials of political influence, at least the business sector understands its existence. In a questionnaire sent by the Study Group to the presidents of *Fortune*'s 1,000 top industrial firms of 1969, the following question was asked: "Do you think political considerations are ever involved when the Government decides whom to sue and whom not to sue?" Of the 100 chief executives replying to this question, 77 said "Yes." *

What, if anything, is exactly wrong with the petitioning of one's Government, some might ask? That it were so neutral. First, a major corporation can get special access to special people, obtaining the unique services of an Everett Dirksen or Albert Ellender to see a Nicholas Katzenbach. Second, they can throw extraordinary resources into an issue—which is different from you and me. Third, the effect can be momentous, not just another anti- or pro-war letter to a Congressman; *i.e.*, GM cannot *really* hide behind the fiction that it is just another person playing pluralistic politics. "[C]orporate institutions are not voluntary associations with individuals as members," Cornell Professor Andrew Hacker has observed, "but rather associations of assets, and no theory yet propounded has declared that machines

* The complete results of the Businessmen's Questionnaire can be found in Appendix B.

are entitled to a voice in the democratic process." [28] Fourth, to the extent antitrust enforcement is obstructed, competition and its benefits for consumers go unachieved—and the $60 billion lost GNP, and the $23 billion transfer loss, begin accumulating. And enforcement is affected not only by direct political thrusts but also by *anticipatory* politics. Many Justice Department staff think it unwise to suggest certain big cases, like one to break up General Motors, either because they know it will not get by the Attorney General or because, even if it is successful, Congress they suspect will overrule it. All of which begins to give shape to the populist lament of FCC Commissioner Nicholas Johnson: "I think basically you have to start with a realization that the country is principally run by big business for the rich . . . [A] government of the people, by the people, and for the people, has become, I think, a government of the people, certainly, but by the corporations and for the rich."

While the tactics and costs of corporate lobbying are clear, its impact is not. Why do some efforts fail while others succeed? There is no sure touchstone for success, or litmus test for failure. Several factors affect every lobbying foray. Who is the official lobbied? It makes a difference whether the subject is Nicholas Katzenbach, whose philosophy of "political benefit" repudiated his oath of office, or whether it is Ramsey Clark, who made it clear that attempts to influence antitrust enforcement were "corrupt." Who is the person doing the lobbying? Ezra Taft Benson is not just your average Cabinet Secretary, Arthur Dean (as will be seen) is not on "Storefront Lawyers," and Elmer Bobst is only one of President Nixon's closest friends. How controversial is the public issue? Few care about a potential suit against rice-milling firms, so secretive efforts in the bowels of the Antitrust Division can achieve successful leverage; but when a merger reaches the FTC after a public controversy over its handling by Justice —as was true in the Warner-Lambert–Parke-Davis case— it cannot be closeted gracefully. Finally, how much is at stake? Divesting assets from AT&T, the world's largest corporation, is different from suing Schenley Industries, Inc.

What remedies are there for the perversion of corporate law enforcement by politics? Appeals to Congressmen, Sen-

ators, Attorneys General, and Presidents to ignore importunings and permit unimpeded enforcement are necessary
but insufficient. More important is the creation of a consumer-antitrust constituency. Then politicians like Mc-
Carthy and Katzenbach will have a political incentive to
urge that antitrust cases be filed, not filed away. But at the
least, participants in such politicking—people like Brownell,
Katzenbach, and Kleindienst, and the Cellers, Dirksens,
and Ellenders—must be exposed and publicized, hopefully
as a deterrent to those later tempted.

One further procedural sanitizer would be to require
that *all* meetings between businessmen and enforcement
officials from the level of Assistant Attorney General on
up be made public by those petitioning. This new lobbying
act would require the listing of every visit with, and the
purpose for every visit with, the Assistant Atttorney General, the Deputy Attorney General, Attorney General, or
anyone in the White House, including the President. The
public officials involved would be under an affirmative
obligation to match up their calendars with the filed reports to ensure that none were omitted. The filings would
be kept open for perusal by interested parties. Any meeting unreported by businessmen would be a federal offense,
as is now the case with the existent Federal Lobbying Act
(a law loopholed to futility). Any meeting knowingly un-
confirmed by the public official involved would be mal-
feasance of office, making him subject to removal.

While antitrust politics is *a* problem, it is not the *only*
problem. Influence-peddling, corruption, and politicking
occur, often on important cases, but in sum they occur
on only a minority of cases. The real erosion of enforcement is a process at once more subtle and pervasive. Congress passes inadequate or conflicting legislation; the Executive Branch requests few funds, and Congress, in turn,
underfinances it; the Attorney General stresses opposing
interests; Antitrust Division chiefs lack the resources and
vigor to file against the many violations which occur, and
they lack the courage and creativity to formulate new
cases to cope with new problems. Big business and big
labor support this somnambulism, and the public doesn't
seem to care—as everybody pays homage to antitrust but
not very much attention to it.

PART II

The Department of Justice

Attorneys General don't have antitrust programs. If they do anything, it's to say "no" to a specific case. Their function is to be a brake on antitrust activity. They are political representatives whose function is to temper justice with politics.
                    —*Justice Department attorney, quoted
                    in* Fortune, *1961*

3

A History of Personality on Policy

THE EARLY YEARS

In March, 1903, President Roosevelt and Attorney General Knox gave William A. Day five lawyers and four stenographers to begin an antitrust section of the Department of Justice. It was not an auspicious birth, but then, neither was the Sherman Act's. The initial excitement had given way to non-enforcement: the 1895 *Sugar Trust* case upheld a combination controlling 98% of all sugar production because, said the Supreme Court, "manufacturing" was not "interstate commerce" within the scope of the Act; Richard Olney, the Attorney General for two years prior to this decision, applauded the result. He considered the Sherman Act "an experimental piece of legislation," and therefore did not file a single antitrust case during his term in office.[1]

To overcome such resistance, Roosevelt and Knox established the Antitrust Division. One success of William Day's two-year tenure was his prosecution of the *Northern Securities* case of 1904, which narrowed the *Sugar Trust* rule and broke up a holding company of competing railroads. The dissent of Justice Holmes in this case provoked Teddy Roosevelt's famous gibe that he could "carve more spine out of a banana." Such dicta, and frequent preachings against the "malefactors of great wealth," earned Roosevelt his nickname, the Great Trustbuster. Yet Roosevelt's reputation far exceeds his contributions. He devoted few resources to enforcement and filed very few cases against the trusts. "The man who advocates destroying the trusts," he said in 1902, "by measures which would paralyze the industries of this country is at least a quack and at worst an enemy to the Republic." [2] * Other speeches carrying the opposite message, plus a sense of timing and public relations, assured his reputation as an antitrust hero.

Occasional rhetoric proved inadequate to stop the galloping concentration of the day. Resources devoted to the antitrust effort remained slim; the Antitrust Division averaged only 18 lawyers between 1914 and 1923. Presidents Wilson, Harding, and Coolidge lacked the arousing powers of a Teddy Roosevelt on antitrust, and their Attorneys General (AG) and Assistant Attorneys General (AAG) —Moody, Bonaparte, Gregory, Daugherty, Purdy, Ellis, Fowler, and Todd—did not become household words. Between the two Roosevelts, however, was one notable and surprising exception: the regime of Republican William Howard Taft and his Attorney General, George Wickersham. Despite heavy criticism from their own political constituency, they indicted the Morgan Partners and the Eastern Republican Finance Committee for attempting to monopolize the railroads. The late Richard Hofstadter wrote that "it was characteristic of the age that Taft, who started twice as many antitrust actions as TR, but had not half his gift for dramatization, was not thought of as a trustbuster." [3]

At the beginning of Franklin Roosevelt's first term, the

---

* During Roosevelt's own time, Finley Peter Dunne's Mr. Dooley accurately lampooned the trustbuster: "Th' trusts," says he, "are heejous monsthers built up be th' inlightened intherprise in th' men that have done so much to advance progress in our beloved country," he says. "On won hand, I wud stamp thim undher fut, on th' other hand not so fast." And three decades later another well-known trustbuster, Thurman Arnold, saw Roosevelt as the man "with his big stick that never hit anybody."

Antitrust Division still had only 18 lawyers. Enforcement was random at best, a farce at worst—a point repeatedly made in the late 1930s by a Yale Law professor named Thurman Arnold. "The competitive struggle without effective antitrust enforcement is like a fight without a referee," said Arnold. "In such a contest, the man who puts on brass knuckles will win. This situation will not be solved by hanging mottos of fair play on the four posts of the ring." [4] The answer, obviously, was a vigorous referee. FDR agreed and appointed Arnold the head of the Antitrust Division in 1938. Under Arnold the present contours of the Division were shaped in two significant ways: first, a verbal commitment was made to vigorous and pervasive enforcement; second, the personnel of the Division leapt from a few dozen in the mid-1930s to 190 by 1940.

Thurman Arnold was a publicist, but a more consistent one than Teddy Roosevelt. He spoke, wrote, and issued press releases with frequency and gusto, denouncing the predatory practices of his business defendants. His propaganda was eventually *too* successful. Attorney General Francis Biddle finally tired of reading Arnold's press releases in the newspapers, attracting headlines and followers. According to confidants of Arnold, Biddle told him, "There is only one Attorney General in this Department and that's me!" He then instituted new rules which are accepted practice today: the Department of Justice, rather than the Antitrust Division, would issue press releases, beginning a tradition of dully factual legal statements; and, most significantly, Arnold would no longer file his own cases but would refer them, both civil and criminal, to AG Biddle, who would file them—or not.

The intention of the resuscitated Division was to police price and competitive practices, not to attack existing concentration. AAG Arnold combined this enforcement emphasis with his desire to educate the consumer public about the evils of restrictive trade practices. He therefore chose to concentrate his resources on the food, clothing, and construction industries, those with direct impact on the consumer. Eighty men alone were committed to the construction industry in 26 cities, a project that resulted in many criminal prosecutions and civil suits.

Arnold's reign was not an unmitigated success. He was so fascinated with the publicity-generating criminal indictment that he slighted significant structural cases. Even his criminal program ultimately fell flat, as not one defendant ever went to prison as a result of Arnold's prosecutions. But "Arnold didn't care about sending anyone to jail," observed Antitrust Division veteran Victor Kramer. "He just wanted to keep a lot of them under indictment, since businessmen under indictment behave better." Decrees entered against oil pipelines and ASCAP (American Society of Composers, Authors and Publishers) were shadows of the original complaints: the major oil companies were not divested of their common ownership of pipelines and were permitted to continue anticompetitive activities; and instead of abolishing ASCAP, the eventual decree created continuous regulation over it.

By 1943 Arnold had created enemies. Biddle disliked him personally for his presumptuousness; and business disliked the way he popularized their exploits and the frequency with which he filed criminal prosecutions. His vigor in general—filing a record 97 cases in fiscal 1942, a mark which still stands—was viewed as antibusiness. Critics got Roosevelt's ear, at a time when the President needed business cooperation in the war effort, and Arnold was nudged out into a circuit-court judgeship in 1943.

ANTITRUST UNDER EISENHOWER *

During Eisenhower's Presidency the size of the Division remained the same; but the number of cases filed, and their significance, dwindled, and scandal and politics tainted some enforcement efforts.

Attorney General Herbert Brownell, Jr., at least began with a procedural bang, weeding out many inept legal staffers in the Department, the political appointees of earlier eras. Brownell began the so-called "Honors Program," under which only top law-school graduates would be considered for employment by the Justice Department (although by 1960, some Division staff told us, the Senate Republican Campaign Committee still "cleared" a few job applicants). Also, upset at the way Herbert Bergson, antitrust AAG under Truman, allegedly represented former Division defendants when he left government,† Brownell

---

* Many cases and industries mentioned in this chapter will be discussed at length in later chapters on criminal prosecutions, consent decrees, deconcentration suits, oil, automobiles, and professional societies.

† A grand jury was called in the Bergson situation, but no indictment was handed down, the Democrats claiming it was all a Republican ploy for publicity.

established a firm rule: for two years after leaving the Division you could not privately represent anyone against whom the Division had moved while you were there; in addition, you could never privately represent a firm on whose case you had actually worked.

But Brownell himself took a political approach to enforcement. The system of Attorney General review, which Biddle had initiated, now began to realize its damaging potential.

The AT&T consent decree, discussed in Chapter 2, was a sell-out affecting the pocketbook interest of every phone user. It blemished the integrity of the Antitrust Division in the eyes of the public, the bar, and the government. We also discussed the civil case not brought against the Salt Lake City newspapers due to the suasion of Republicans Wallace Bennett and Ezra Taft Benson, and the dropped criminal case against General David Sarnoff, Chairman of RCA.

As soon as the Republican administration took over in 1953, Brownell dismissed the grand jury studying the world oil cartel. An FTC report the year before had uncovered many collusive practices in the industry, from price-fixing to boycotts to territorial division of markets. Brownell replaced the criminal case with a civil one based on the same allegations. The oil lobby—here represented by an armada of lawyers headed by Arthur Dean from the Wall Street law firm of Sullivan and Cromwell, whose senior partner was incoming Secretary of State John Foster Dulles—was pleased. An oil representative expressed appreciation of the "broader approach" of the new administration, noting that "we are undoubtedly going to work together for a long time." [5] Leon Emmerglick, who headed up the trial staff working on the case, quit over the political cave-ins.

Division attorneys had developed an antitrust case against the New York Medical Society for refusing to let its doctors work in prepayment medical groups. The four lawyers working full-time on this case investigated conditions in 12 states, coming up with six suits. After a small one in Oregon was filed, Brownell was told that the New York case was the best and biggest complaint, and if that were not filed, none of the others should be either. Brownell then vetoed the New York case. "The colorable argument against filing," one of the four lawyers told the Study

Group, "was that there was not enough interstate commerce. The real reason was that it was politically upopular for that administration to challenge medical societies in New York State. In those years it was afraid of being accused of fomenting socialized medicine."

The first AAG under Brownell, Stanley Barnes, was a man with no prior antitrust experience, yet his effort to meet every attorney in the Division and a generally genial style soon won the staff's confidence. The vigor of his program, however, was undermined by Brownell, who gave him two top assistants to "watchdog" his activities. This move was initiated by business friends of Eisenhower, who convinced the President that the Division staff had brainwashed Barnes. The first of this duo, J. Thomas Schneider, labeled a "political czar" by an attorney still at the Division, screened job applicants for their antitrust and political views, occasionally rejecting those who did not fit the Republican mold. The second assistant, Edward Foote of AT&T fame, resigned in 1957 when a Congressional delegation presented him with evidence that he had been speculating, in his wife's name, in the stock of companies then under antitrust prosecution.[6] * But before this exposé Barnes had delegated much power to Foote. As Foote, who was incompetent as well as unscrupulous, exercised more and more daily control over the Division, the staff became increasingly discouraged and productivity suffered.

Barnes's biggest failing was the inattention paid to Section 7 of the 1950 Celler-Kefauver Act. Here, finally, was a law to prevent merger by acquisition as well as by stock, yet the Antitrust Division did not file a *single* case under it for the first half of the 1950s. Barnes finally did file *Brown Shoe* in November, 1955, which became a cornerstone for Section 7 enforcement once it was decided by the Supreme Court in 1962, but it was far too late in coming.

In 1956 Barnes, eager to retire from the Division, was appointed to the Ninth Circuit Court in California; he was replaced by another California judge, Victor Hansen. An honest public servant, Hansen was intellectually and emo-

* It was discovered after Barnes left office that he had purchased $12,000 of Warren Petroleum stock for speculative purposes in November, 1955, immediately after the Department decided that there were no grounds to block Warren's merger with Gulf Oil.[7] Most observers credited this indiscretion to the product of a bad memory by the usually ethical Barnes.

tionally unequipped for this important post. Like Barnes, he knew no antitrust law at the beginning, but, unlike Barnes, he did not learn any. Hansen enjoyed both a light schedule and California, to which he escaped for sizable chunks of his three-year term. At times Hansen would first find out about a case when he read about it in the newspapers. He left the running of the Division to Robert Bicks—fortunately—who occasionally decided on his own which cases to file, affixing Hansen's signature to the complaint.

Bicks succeeded Hansen in 1959. His two-year leadership of the Division is revered by Democrats and Republicans alike for its energy and productivity. Bicks was brilliant, tireless, mercurial, and egotistical. He took over the Division at the tender age of 31, a fact that, with his brashness, upset many career attorneys. Consequently, the most typical reminiscence of Bicks among our interviewees was expressed by one former Division attorney: "We never knew if it was antitrust or Bicks he was interested in, but he really got us to produce."

Bicks was an antitrust lawyer, not a politician, and his Division reflected it. William Rogers, who followed Brownell as Attorney General and who is presently Secretary of State, got along well with the young AAG and usually gave him control over the cases filed. The only Bicks case Rogers vetoed was one against the National Football League for attempting to bully the American Football Conference out of existence. Rogers felt that if there was merit to the case, Texas millionaire Lamar Hunt should bring it, since he was the major complainant and was rich enough to finance the litigation. It was a case in which Vice President Richard Nixon, a rabid fan, called Rogers to urge that the NFL not be sued.

Bicks's vigor made enemies on Capitol Hill, and he was never confirmed by the Senate in his appointment. In fact, Eisenhower did not even formally nominate Bicks during his first years as chief of the Division. *The New York Times* credited the omission partly to business complaints about Bicks to Eisenhower, and the paper editorially compared the President's timidity with Bicks's courage.[8] President Eisenhower finally and formally made him an Assistant Attorney General in a recess appointment on July 12, 1960.

AAG Bicks filed 86 cases in fiscal 1960, the largest

number of cases since Arnold's days. Thirty-five dealt with the infamous *Electrical Conspiracy* cases—18 criminal and 17 civil; thus his oft-cited prolific record was inflated by a large body of cases which were not difficult to file once the basic conspiracy was established.

Bicks reorganized the Division to give priority to merger suits under Section 7 of the Celler-Kefauver Act. The 13 antimerger cases filed in 1960 more than doubled those of the previous year, partially overcoming the laggard policy of his predecessors. As *New York Times* analyst Anthony Lewis wrote, "Mr. Bicks put Section 7 on the map." 9 * Some of the significant merger cases included: *United States* v. *Von's Grocery Company*, where the Supreme Court held in 1966 that a merger of two stores with 7.5% of the grocery sales in a market with a trend toward concentration violated Section 7; *United States* v. *Aluminum Company of America*, where the Supreme Court held in 1964 that an addition of 1.3% of the relevant market to the leading producer, where concentration was already great and increasing, violated Section 7; *United States* v. *Penn-Olin Chemical Company*, where the Supreme Court held in 1964 that a joint venture into a related field, when one or both of the firms may have entered independently or remained a potential entrant, violated Section 7; and *United States* v. *General Motors*, challenging the acquisition by the leading automobile manufacturer of Euclid, the dominant producer of off-highway earthmoving equipment. (A consent decree in 1968 divested GM of Euclid.)

If antimerger law was Bicks's strong suit, antimonopoly enforcement was his weak one. He often stated that big monopoly and oligopoly cases were simply not worth the Division's time. This prejudice seemed to keep him from filing a major deconcentration case in the copper industry. A November 7, 1957, "MEMORANDUM FOR THE ATTORNEY GENERAL. RE: Recommendation for Filing a Copper Suit" was written by staff attorneys. The 41-page document began, "Few, if any segments of American industry have been pointed out so often, and by so many, as anticompetitive, monopolistic and tainted with restraints of trade, as the copper industry." It then showed that three inte-

---

* One exception was Bicks's stated belief that Section 7 did not apply to bank mergers. This view retarded antitrust efforts in banking until the 1963 Supreme Court decision in the *Philadelphia Bank* case, which held that banking *was* controlled by antitrust laws.

grated copper firms (Kennecott, Phelps-Dodge, and Ana-conda) owned 83.6% of copper ore reserves, and that four firms (these three plus American Smelting) controlled 90.9% of all smelting and 81.5% of all refining. Prices were high and maintained over time despite important changes in supply and demand; profits, unsurprisingly, were exorbitant. The staff on the study, and their immediate superiors, therefore urged a Section 2 monopolization case as well as a Section 7 Clayton Act charge.

Hansen, who had first been presented with the case, could not make up his mind, reassigning it for continued study. By the time Bicks was given the memorandum, a study by the Division's Economic Section and the FBI (which at times collected industry data for the Division) had affirmed its conclusion. Bicks, however, was unimpressed by the crushing weight of the evidence. He refused to urge the Attorney General to file a complaint.

ANTITRUST UNDER THE DEMOCRATS

When Attorney General Rogers resigned in January, 1961, he left a pen and a bottle of aspirin for his successor, along with a note saying that the pen was for judgeships and the aspirin for antitrust problems. Bicks, too, resigned with the advent of the Kennedy administration, despite hints from Byron White that Robert Kennedy might keep him on as AAG. Instead Attorney General Kennedy chose Lee Loevinger, a Minnesota Supreme Court judge. Loevinger had all the correct credentials: scholar and judge, prolific writer and speaker, antitrust practitioner (usually for plaintiffs), and former Antitrust Division attorney—one who had quit the Division largely over the refusal of the then AG, Tom Clark, to ask for a grand-jury indictment in the *Mortgage Conference* case. "I believe in antitrust almost as a secular religion," Loevinger told AG Kennedy.[10]

The Kennedy-Loevinger combination suggested a period of energetic enforcement was at hand. As Attorney General, Robert Kennedy had, and more importantly was *known* to have, the full confidence and support of the President. The kind of constraints apparent in Eisenhower's business-oriented White House were absent. Yet, whatever the potential, antitrust enforcement lagged in the early 1960s.

The problem was threefold. First, Loevinger was painfully arrogant, a terrible administrator, prone to snap emotional decisions.* These traits led to sloppy, shotgun enforcement and open resentment by his staff. Second, AG Kennedy was sensitive to his "antibusiness" label. The *Wall Street Journal* reported that "It's no secret that the Administration has been trying to convince the business community it has nothing to fear from Washington." [11] The AG viewed the large number of suits Loevinger filed as too prosecutorial-minded, according to Kennedy's personal assistant, Andrew Oehman. This fear of business criticism merely grew after the administration's confrontation with the steel industry in 1962.

The third major factor, a partial result of the prior two, was that Kennedy lost confidence in Loevinger's judgment. To repair this rift, Kennedy took the unusual step of subjecting many of the cases Loevinger recommended to a review by three officials: Burke Marshall, who headed the Civil Rights Division; Byron White, Deputy Attorney General; and Archibald Cox, Solicitor General. For all these reasons, a number of significant cases were not brought by the Department.

—The Division produced compelling evidence of a criminal conspiracy between the Hearst and Chandler newspapers in Los Angeles, a violation which personally involved both Norman and Otis Chandler and William Randolph Hearst II. The alleged conspiracy involved a division of the newspaper market to permit Hearst's *Herald-Examiner* to monopolize the afternoon market and Chandler's *Los Angeles Times* the morning one; and a set of three "codes" covering advertising, production, and ethics which fixed prices and practices between the two publishing groups. The codes were signed by Otis Chandler and William Randolph Hearst II, and constituted a *per se* criminal violation in the eyes of four antitrust attorneys familiar with the case.

But no grand jury was empaneled. The reasons for this failure—what one experienced Senate observer called "the worst antitrust scandal I've ever seen"—are complex. A

---

* For example, he told a Congressional committee that the Department might sue to divest AT&T of its international activities; no decision on this had been reached by Justice, and AT&T stock dropped six points. He also threatened General Electric officials in a private meeting with dismemberment of their corporation. Such braggadocio angered Kennedy.

Hearst lawyer, James McInerney, sought a clearance from Loevinger for Hearst and Chandler to stop publishing their competing newspapers. Loevinger later claimed that no oral permission for the market division was granted; McInerney claimed otherwise. The situation became complicated when McInerney died in a car accident. Kennedy supposedly saw the word of the Justice Department at stake, especially since McInerney could no longer represent his version. He therefore refused to bring either criminal or civil charges against the newspapers.

Yet this explanation, derived largely from sources close to Kennedy, omits painful but contradictory evidence. Loevinger disclaims any uncertainty about his conversation with the Hearst lawyer. And even if the "word" of the Department was important, so was enforcing the law. Moreover, while there may have been confusion over the newspaper market division, what of the "codes" and the price-fix? Why weren't cases brought against them? The broader context of this incident also cannot be ignored. McInerney had been a lawyer for the Kennedy family; when McInerney was AAG in charge of the Criminal Division, he gave Robert Kennedy his first job with the Justice Department. Finally, late 1963 was encroaching on the then expected Presidential race, and few Attorneys General, especially former campaign managers of their brother's Presidential races, would be eager to sue criminally two of the biggest newspaper chains in the country.

Circumstantial evidence of a whitewash was also evident on Capitol Hill. In March of 1963 Celler's Antitrust Subcommittee began to investigate the Los Angeles newspaper market. After four days of hearings, as Celler's staff were preparing to cross-examine the implicated executives, Celler suddenly halted the proceedings. He said that civil-rights legislation was more urgent and that his subcommittee sought to avoid covering the same ground as a Justice Department suit or investigation.

Again, more questions than answers are raised. The Justice Department had sent out civil subpoenas on the case before the hearings began; therefore, anxiety about overlapping jurisdiction could have been raised at any time, not just as the price-fix was to be exposed. And if Celler did not want to interfere with the Department's investigation, why weren't the hearings resumed after Justice decided not to move? Even more troublesome, the House Subcommittee never printed the four days of hearings which occurred; their existence is nowhere evident in the *Index of Antitrust Subcommittee Publications*. It devolved to the Senate Antitrust Subcommittee to print the transcript five years later, much to the consternation of Celler's committee. Celler claimed in an interview with the Study Group that the hearings were not published because they were never completed; but they were incomplete because Celler called them off. Catch 22.

—In 1961 and 1962 *and* 1963 Loevinger sought to file a case to bypass the 1956 AT&T consent decree, one charging AT&T with monopolizing both telephone service and telephone equipment. The five-count complaint was never brought.

—Loevinger had a grand jury called to study some Minnesota banks and some dozen of their officers. When Kennedy later asked Loevinger about the extent of his evidence against such a large number of possible defendants, Loevinger quickly suggested lopping off eight names. Kennedy, appalled, dropped all the rest because of Loevinger's seeming sloppiness. Two other reasons enter in dismissing the individual names: it seemed unfair to the AG's office to file *criminal* charges in an area, banking, where it was questionable whether the antitrust laws fully applied; and Senator Eugene McCarthy exerted considerable pressure on Justice against filing the case—with some apparent success. The refusal by Kennedy and Katzenbach to seek individual indictments is surprising in light of the evidence the grand jury produced. Detailed minutes of "Bank Correspondents Meeting[s]" were uncovered for the 1956–59 period. One document, dated January 20, 1956, described one aspect of that day's meeting:

1. Rate of interest charged correspondent bankers on loans collateraled by bank stock. On this subject after the hottest debate I have ever sat in on, and after some name-calling, a vote was taken, and all at the meeting agreed that loans to bankers collateraled by bank stock should be made at no less than 4% and any renewals should be increased to 6%. . . .

Another document dated April 19, 1956, began by noting that "This memorandum is merely for your information and is intended as confidential insofar as the agreements are concerned. My copy will not go into our bank's file and I suggest your copy be destroyed after reading it." The "agreements" which followed covered items ranging from the rates of interest charged correspondent bankers on loans collateraled by bank stock to the bankers' mutual attendance at various meetings, conventions, and funerals.

Loevinger did in fact file many suits, 73 his first fiscal year and 62 his second. But, sensitive to comparisons between himself and Bicks, in which Loevinger was the numerical loser, he frequently played statistics, matching his 135 cases filed against the 64 filed in the *first* two years of the Eisenhower regime. The enforcement emphasis of this period was criminal price-fixing, a seemingly natural result of the convictions of the electrical-manufacturing defendants. Robert Kennedy, who had a deep Catholic moralistic streak in him, had strongly castigated such conduct as "economic racketeering." Of the cases filed in this period, 40% were aimed at criminal activity, as compared to 25% for the remainder of the decade. Yet it was an enforcement policy with noticeable costs. Although Loevinger was critical of his predecessor Republicans for filing many small violations to create a good track record, he was guilty of the same offense. His price-fixing suits against Venetian blinds, kosher hotdog rolls, and touring ice shows did not solve the central antitrust problems of the nation.

This record contrasts with Loevinger's tirades against big business and concentration when he entered office, which had led *Fortune* magazine to predict: "When the Loevinger record in office is added up and placed on top of his pre-appointment career, he emerges as a man who intends to use his job to go after the biggest suits in U.S. business." [12] Instead, Anthony Lewis ended up criticizing the Division for "putting its antitrust effort into trivial cases of no great economic significance." [13] *Business Week* agreed that "in terms of economic impact such suits are piddling." [14] Nicholas Katzenbach in an interview complained that the emphasis on price-fixing "produced more cats and dogs of cases." Loevinger himself agreed, blaming the Division's limited resources (which were approximately the same from 1948 to 1971) and the uncertain economic climate of the early Sixties.

In his two years Loevinger did institute some novel cases against banks, did bring two criminal suits against GM, did

convince Kennedy to permit public comment for 30 days
after the negotiation of a consent decree, and did help ease
a bill through Congress that gave the Division limited subpoena power in civil cases. But the conflicts with the AG
were too great. One day in June, 1963, he got a phone call
from the White House, informing him that within two
hours he was going to be appointed a Commissioner of the
FCC. "Loevinger was shocked," recalls a high staff official;
"he fussed and fumed, trying to call Bobby, who wouldn't
answer his phone. He tried to call the White House, but
couldn't get through." Later, at a departure party at the
Division, he blamed his exit on "fighting the good fight."
To other attorneys he has cited his unwillingness to work
on Kennedy's civil-rights cases. To the Study Group he
said, "President Kennedy wanted someone of stature to go
to the FCC."

Replacing Loevinger was William Orrick, whose strong
traits were his predecessor's weak ones. A proven administrator with an ability to stimulate a staff, he had been
chairman of the Northern California Kennedy Campaign
Committee, chief of the Civil Division of Justice, and
Deputy Undersecretary of State for Administration. Most
significantly, he got along well with Robert Kennedy. He
knew no antitrust law, but, aware of his inexperience, had
an economist in the Economics Section make up an antitrust reading list, which he studied diligently. The staff was
wary of him at first, but his admitted ignorance, his open-
ness, and frequent meetings with the lawyers in the Division soon lifted their morale.

When Orrick attempted to learn the *policy* of the Antitrust Division, he found there was none. The agency was
a "reactive" one, with more than 95% of its cases begun
by a letter of complaint from outside.[15] Little initiative
investigation occurred, and there was no real planned enforcement. Seventy percent of pending matters (cases,
grand juries, civil subpoenas, investigations) concerned
price-fixing and behavioral problems; only 30% dealt with
structural problems like mergers and monopolization.[16]
To remedy this mis-emphasis, Orrick created a new Policy
Planning section in the Division with an "evaluations"
sub-unit, to review Division priorities and resources. As
conceived—although its four-man staff was much too
small—it was a major contribution to the Division. Policy

had been haphazard at best. Law professor Richard Posner has written: "It would be only a slight exaggeration to say that, in the early Sixties, the only real coordination of antitrust policy took place in the Solicitor General's office, where coherent theories were formulated for the antitrust cases bound for the Supreme Court." [17] A career attorney and present high staff official at the Antitrust Division also confirmed the prevailing view:

> Even when we brought the big cases like *Von's, Lever Bros., El Paso, Pabst,* and *Continental Can,* it was a poorly organized effort, with much confusion. The trial staff theories were not centrally coordinated. They tried a hodgepodge of theories and lost at the trial level as a result. Luckily, the Supreme Court did bail them out.

Orrick expended considerable Division resources studying the industries where past cases had been brought and studying where future cases should be brought. He had a team probe the dozen most concentrated industries in the country, with an eye toward bringing monopolization and divestiture suits. On April 17, 1964, Orrick delivered a major address, threatening to use the *GM-DuPont* precedent of 1957 to undo past mergers which had *grown* anticompetitive. Noble sentiments, but nothing happened. No big cases were brought, and the overall number of cases filed dropped precipitously under Orrick, to 43 in 1965 after an average of 69 for the prior six years. It was especially disappointing compared to Orrick's own projection, given to a House Appropriations Subcommittee, that he would file 70 cases in 1964 and 75 in 1965.

Ironically, part of the slowdown was attributable to Policy Planning. Part was also attributable to a declining interest in antitrust due to the death of Estes Kefauver, the major publicist of consumer antitrust, in 1963. Yet much of the problem lay with the new Attorney General, Nicholas Katzenbach, who succeeded Robert Kennedy following the assassination of President Kennedy in November, 1963.* While acknowledged to be brilliant— a former Rhodes Scholar and Yale law professor—Katzenbach didn't believe in antitrust and was easily swayed by political considerations. These two failings led to facile exercising of the AG veto, with rejections often simply

---

* Although Kennedy did not officially leave the Justice Department until September, 1964, he left the running of the Department mostly to others, especially Katzenbach, after the assassination.

reading "The Attorney General does not wish to bring this case at this time."

—Katzenbach's damaging compromises in the rice-milling company and Penn-Central mergers, and his acceptance of "unemployment" arguments in a number of cases were documented in the prior chapter.

—An AT&T case again was sent to the AG for approval, again sought the divestiture of Western Electric from AT&T, and again was not filed.

—A major suit was recommended which would have barred the three television networks from producing programs, based on the 1948 *Paramount* case, which forbids the great movie producers from also being exhibitors. CBS, NBC, and ABC would have been limited to "exhibiting" shows, not making, owning, and selecting them. Katzenbach would not sign the complaint, citing the fact that the FCC had been looking at the problem since 1955.

—One case involved the Oregon swimwear firm Rose Marie Reid and its agreement to maintain retail prices. Katzenbach knocked off the individual names in the criminal suit, wondering how the potential defendants could know what they did was illegal—"which has a ring of truth to it since the Attorney General of the United States didn't know it was illegal," in the view of a high official of the Division who once before had had to explain to a surprised AG why vertical price-fixing had been held to be *per se* illegal by the Supreme Court for decades. At court in the Rose Marie Reid suit, the judge dismissed the government opposition to entrance of a *nolo contendere* plea, arguing that if the Department of Justice thought the case important, it would have named individual defendants.

—In 1964 the Columbia Broadcasting System announced plans to purchase 80% of the New York Yankees for $11.2 million. In reporting the event, the opposition of the *New York Times* was obvious. On August 14, 1964, it reported:

With control of the Yankees, CBS will have a strong voice in American League's future television and radio commitments. . . .

For a long-range standpoint, the major leagues must consider the uses of pay-television. CBS, in company with the National and American Broadcasting Companies, have been staunch opponents of pay-television. CBS now will be in a position to carry its opposition into the inner sanctums of baseball.

Jack Gould, the *Times* TV critic, warned that "in some TV quarters there were dark hints that CBS might gain an educated edge in knowing how much to bid for a World Series or an All-Star game." The Division staff drew up a complaint to block the merger, based on arguments novel then but now being used against other conglomerate mergers: entrenchment, vertical foreclosure, and destruction of a possible competitor; in addition, there was some horizontal competitive overlap (the Yankees were appearing occasionally on CBS and on a CBS competitor, WPIX television in New York City). The problems were more than hypothetical. A 1968 issue of the *Columbia Journalism Review* reported that a WCBS radio executive in New York City had criticized the news staff for their late reporting of Yankee scores, saying, "If I have to spell it out for you I will: CBS *owns* the New York Yankees."

Katzenbach could not understand the argument at first. When he did, he asked incredulously: Aren't you really saying that all such big conglomerate mergers are illegal? When told yes by Division official Gordon Spivack, he got cold feet, especially since CBS had told him that if the Department challenged the merger, it would be abandoned. He refused to block the merger merely by filing suit, and so permitted it to go through merely by *not* filing suit.* An excellent chance was thereby lost to make anticonglomerate law two years before the huge conglomerate merger wave in the second half of the 1960s.

Largely as a result of such cases, tensions and conflicts between the AG and the AAG grew severe, and Orrick retired to private practice in June, 1965. Katzenbach had blamed his problems with the Antitrust Division on the inept quality of work and memoranda written under Loevinger and Orrick; in turn, Orrick was upset at the AG's insensitivity to antitrust and, as an Orrick staff official put it, "the slew of cases Katzenbach killed." Yet perhaps there was a higher reason, for President Johnson needed all the business support he could get for his Great Society programs. Antitrust, moreover, was simply not a part of Lyndon Johnson's ideological baggage, as an attorney in Katzenbach's office attested to the Study Group: "The Johnson Administration saw no need to push antitrust

---

* Katzenbach later told the Study Group that no formal complaint was drawn up for this merger, "but I sure would have liked to have stopped that combination."

enforcement; we were not aggressive here, and this tone filtered down and across the government."

As Kennedy turned to Orrick to repair Loevinger's sins, so Katzenbach turned to Donald Turner to repair Orrick's alleged failures. A Harvard law professor with a doctorate in economics, co-author of the famous Kaysen and Turner *Antitrust Policy,* Turner was "far and away the most eminent expert in this field" according to Derek Bok, now president of Harvard. He was also hard for President Johnson to swallow when Katzenbach proposed him as the new AAG of Antitrust. When Katzenbach was asked in an interview whether Johnson's hesitance was based on his Texas disdain for Harvard elitism or his anxiety over the *professor* in politics and as enforcer, he replied, "Both."

Why Donald Turner? Katzenbach was still concerned with scattergun enforcement, especially in light of the huge powers the Supreme Court had given the Antitrust Division by its recent rulings in *Philadelphia Bank, Alcoa-Rome, Continental Can, Brown Shoe,* and *Penn-Olin (Procter & Gamble, Von's Grocery,* and *Pabst-Blatz* were soon to come). All, in various ways, greatly expanded the scope of Section 7 to attack mergers. The AG stated in 1965 that "It may be that we have, from the point of view of business, more power than is necessary or essential to the carrying out of an intelligent merger policy. I am inclined to believe that we may be able to block more mergers than it makes economic sense to block." [18] Katzenbach felt a "breathing spell" was needed. His concern seemed to be exagggerated, since of the 1,797 mergers that past year, the Division had attempted to block 17, or a mere 1%; nevertheless, his concern was serious, and relayed to Turner.

Professor Turner, therefore, was appointed to "rational[ize] policy and articulat[e] it in terms the business community can understand." [19] Toward these ends, Turner began a series of thoughtful lecture-speeches whose main theme was the statement that "It is the duty of the Department of Justice not to bring a case simply on the basis that it thinks it *can* win, but to bring only those cases it *should* win." [20] He also promised to produce published "guidelines" to explain just what was legal and illegal. The business media were perplexed. *Business Week* wrote that "he may yet turn out to be one of the strongest [Division chiefs]"; but the *Wall Street Journal* thought Turner's anti-trust policies would be even weaker than those of his predecessor.

To "rationalize antitrust," Turner upgraded Policy Planning and the Evaluations Section, which had dwindled to a handful of people by June of 1965. Turner beefed it up to a staff of 15–20 bright young law-school graduates, with Robert Hammond, brought over from the FTC Merger Section, as the Policy Planning Director and with Lionel Kestenbaum, a very competent Division attorney, as chief of Evaluations. By reviewing all civil subpoenas (called CIDs, Civil Investigative Demands), complaints, and briefs sent up by the trial staff, Evaluations could formulate a unified Division policy, something essential to an agency with meager resources and wide discretion.

That was the idea. In practice Evaluations was a bureaucratic boondoggle unparalleled in decades of Division enforcement. First, it was a waste of resources. Any case, including the most pedestrian, had to run an 11-man gamut of review, from the trial attorney to his assistant section chief and section chief, to the Director of Operations, Gordon Spivack, then to Evaluations for review, to Kestenbaum and Hammond to be worked over, and to the desk of Edwin Zimmerman, Turner's First Assistant, who microscopically scrutinized it and passed it to Turner's legal assistant; and, of course, Turner provided his close and expert reading. If approved, it went to the Deputy Attorney General's office and then, finally, to the Attorney General for his signature—that is, after *his* legal aide looked at it.

It was foolish extravagance. A section chief had earned his station by upwards of 10 years on the firing line; all acknowledged that Kestenbaum, Hammond, Spivack, Zimmerman, and Turner were as brilliant a core of officials as ever headed the Division. Must *every* complaint be read by *all* of them? Resources were already inadequate. Furthermore, this hierarchy had a built-in bias toward criticism and censure, since to justify one's function, one felt obliged to reformulate, sanitize, and at times veto a case. At any rung on this 11-man ladder a case could be stopped.

Second, Evaluations created a bottleneck. Recommended complaints were backed up for months. CIDs were not acted on for an average of two months, according to the best estimates, and at times up to a year. This problem was exacerbated by the perfectionist instincts of Hammond and Zimmerman, who became convinced that in Professor Turner's regime every complaint and brief should be publishable. Hammond was perhaps the worst offender, with eight in-boxes piled high with staff recommendations. Meanwhile the staff waited, lost interest and momentum, and moved to other cases—all of which took a massive toll on efficiency.

Third, as a result of this bottleneck, morale at the Division collapsed. Trial attorneys—the bulk of the Division, the lawyers who investigated the cases, tried them, and wrote the complaints and briefs—saw two Antitrust Divisions: Turner's and theirs. Delays on their major cases, with the review level and reviewer often impossible to locate, discouraged them. That the reviewers were inexperienced young attorneys, often brash and disdainful of the "zealots" below (a view Turner nurtured), embittered them further. The hostility was reflected in their epithets for Evaluations: "the Harvard-Stanford axis," "the Gold Coast," "a tribe of pencil pushers." Alan Ward, a former Division section chief who is presently Director of the Bureau of Competition at the FTC, called it "a layer of fat."

The flaw in the operation of Policy Planning and Evaluation was emphasized by Gordon Spivack, widely considered one of the most talented lawyers the Division had produced in the last decade, in a Study Group interview:

> I would say, "Don—what do you need policy planning for? What do you think the section chiefs and I [as Director of Operations] do all day when we review briefs? *We're* your policy planning." Yet we used to fight over the definition of a word in a CID. Ridiculous. . . . I never thought that Policy Planning and Evaluations was worth the cost of delay and morale.

The unsurprising result was a severe loss of productivity. The number of CIDs sent out by the Division fell from an average of 272 for fiscal 1964–65 to an average of 109 for fiscal 1966–67, Turner's first two years. The number of cases filed fell from an average of 65 under Bicks, Loevinger, and Orrick to an average of 49 for Turner's three years. Turner's predictions to Congress about the number of cases he expected to file fell as flat as Orrick's. While he projected 72 in 1966 and 70 in 1967, the actual numbers were 44 and 53. And if the 18 vertical price-fixing cases brought against the publishers of children's books count as one horizontal-conspiracy suit, which they really were, a total of only 36 cases were filed in his second full year. Enforcement was grinding to a near halt.

The conclusion is *not* that there should be no policy planning. Trial attorneys are often too addicted to the trivial and simple price-fixing case to generate suits of great impact; their case theories at times conflict. Clearly, there has to be some coordination of Division enforcement; more clearly, there should be a group brainstorming on new theories, planning where to devote Division resources in the long run. The irony is that Policy Planning—with a handful of exceptions—did neither. It was so consumed by its review function and putting out daily fires that it never really planned policy. There was no attempt to compute the input on a case or a group of similar cases and then match it against the "output" of a case or cases—*i.e.,* the extent to which competition resulted and prices declined. Lionel Kestenbaum, later to be the head of Policy Planning, acknowledged that lack of input-output data hurt rational planning. "It is one of the great failings of antitrust enforcement," he said. Lacking such vital data, policy remained *ad hoc.*

Richard Posner concluded his lengthy statistical study of Antitrust Division enforcement with a criticism of its efforts at policy planning. His views warrant expanded quotation:

> So far as I am able to determine, the Department of Justice . . . makes little effort to identify those markets in which serious problems of monopoly are likely to arise; except in the merger area, does not act save on complaint; makes no systematic effort to see whether its decrees are being complied with; keeps few worthwhile statistics on its own activities— and none on those of other components of the enforcement system; does not have adequate records of the criminal and civil penalties imposed on the defendants in its cases; makes no systematic effort to identify repeated violators of the antitrust laws . . . and is, in short, inappropriately run as a law firm, where the workload is determined by the wishes of the clients (in this case mostly unhappy competitors, aggrieved purchasers, and disgruntled employees), and where the social product of the legal services undertaken is not measured.[21]

The second significant attempt to rationalize enforcement was the Merger Guidelines. Katzenbach had announced in the spring of 1965 that they would be written to further President Johnson's intention that the government explain to business the public policies which might affect it. And when the *New York Times* reported that their formulation occurred "under instructions from LBJ"—a President who wanted to "help, not harass business"—critics already wary of an enforcement agency announcing in advance when it would *not* sue were further disquieted. The Guidelines, first promised for 1966, finally came out on May 28, 1968, Turner's last day in office. Basing the legality of mergers almost wholly on market structure, they detail the market percentages below which a merger is legal and above which it is illegal.*

The elephantine gestation of the Guidelines embarrassed AAG Turner, but the fact that they were issued at all angered many trustbusters on six counts: (a) The Guidelines hurt enforcement by telling savvy businessmen and their lawyers how close they can get to the line of illegality; such help will encourage brinksmanship, line-crossing, and quibbling over percentage points. Three prominent attorneys in the Division, Stan Disney, Charles Mahaffie, and Robert Hummel, argued this point in an internal memorandum: "The Justice Department, as an enforcement agency, should not seem to give clearance to transactions that are not squarely covered by the guidelines." (b) There were no public discussions or hearings to refine or criticize the cut-off statistics. (c) The Guidelines freeze antitrust law, inhibit-

---

* For horizontal mergers, if the market is "highly concentrated"—*i.e.,* the four largest firms have approximately 75% of the market—the following percentages are the maximum permissible:

Acquiring Firm	Acquired Firm
4%	4% or more
10%	2% or more
15%	1% or more

If the market is less highly concentrated than a four-firm concentration ratio of 75%, the following cut-offs apply:

Acquiring Firm	Acquired Firm
5%	5% or more
10%	4% or more
15%	3% or more
20%	2% or more
25% or more	1% or more

The Guidelines go on to prohibit vertical mergers between a supplying firm accounting for 10% or more of market sales, and one or more purchasing firms accounting for 6% or more of the total market purchases. Finally, the Guidelines discuss conglomerate mergers and the theories of potential entry, reciprocal buying, and entrenchment which could prohibit them, admitting that conglomerate law is too new for definitive guidelines.

ing flexibility as situations change. Of all our jurisprudence, antitrust law is most like common law, evolving with every court opinion, and many feared that the Guidelines would inhibit future and progressive Division or court judgments. If there had been Guidelines 10 years ago, would the major Supreme Court decisions of the past decade have occurred? (d) Certain passages are less restrictive than Supreme Court rulings. For example, the Supreme Court had already disposed of the "economies argument" in the *Philadelphia Bank* case: "Congress determined to preserve our traditionally competitive economy. It therefore proscribed anticompetitive mergers, the benign and malignant alike, fully aware, we must assume, that some price might have to be paid." [22] But the Guidelines said that in "exceptional circumstances" the economies defense was admissible, thus encouraging AGs like Katzenbach (who proved especially amenable to the argument) to avoid filing a good suit. (e) The horizontal and vertical merger provisions are more strict than the conglomerate provisions. The result, according to a study by the National Economic Research Associates of New York, has been that businessmen rechanneled their merger propensities into the conglomerate realm, accelerating the already growing conglomerate merger wave. (f) Finally, critics argue that the Guidelines are simply unnecessary, since the relevant percentages and rulings could be culled from court decisions, which has always been the way corporations and lawyers have known what was legal and illegal.

Turner partisans emphasized that their percentages were as strict as those in *Von's Grocery,* which they were, and that it was equitable for a prosecutor to limit his discretion, which is true (but somewhat questionable in this context, since Turner abused discretion by refusing to give the judiciary close cases). Finally, they argue that, given the Antitrust Division's limited resources, guidelines to encourage voluntary compliance by businessmen were necessary. By the time the Guidelines were published, they contained a disclaimer to the effect that they were not binding on this or any administration, and "were subject to change at any time without prior notice." So were they worth all the effort?

Certainly rational antitrust enforcement should issue general policy statements—under certain conditions. They must be strict, formulated after an open proceeding, and capable of amendment; they must not encourage voluntary compliance at the expense of tough enforcement, as was evidently so with Turner. The thrust must be deterrence, not counseling; therefore, certain activities should be clearly marked off as illegal while others are left neither *per se* legal or illegal. Finally, they should be aimed at specific industries rather than all industry. Turner's Guidelines may make sense as applied to grocery-store chains but not oil firms. For these reasons the FTC Guidelines (discussed in Chapter 12) more closely approximate what is necessary.

Even more troublesome than Turner's Policy Planning and Guidelines were his administrative abilities—or lack thereof. Although a pleasant and kind person personally, to the Division staff he was intellectually arrogant, politically naive, and bureaucratically unaggressive. Many of the staff never met him, as Turner seemed loath to rub elbows with the lower echelon. To compound the problem, the young evaluators Turner installed between the staff and their chief were intolerant toward the trial lawyers. Lawyers who made inquiries could not always find out where their cases were in the hierarchy. At times a case would be shelved, or filed, without even informing the staff attorney. Cases would be settled by Turner, in private meetings with defense counsel but *without* trial staff, over the heads of those negotiating below.

Moreover, Turner was not an aggressive leader, and to unclog the bottleneck, to hurry review along by probing phone calls, required a dynamic AAG. Turner's style was low-key and indecisive. Like the proverbial Harvard law professor, he would rarely decide, only discuss. There were no solutions, only problems, as Turner and his circle probed all sides of all questions.* The result was a paralysis of decision-making and a thin enforcement record, with cases dying by inaction.

When a reporter asked a Turner aide why his chief failed as an enforcer, the aide attributed it to Turner's inability

---

* This professorial habit, as well as his general naiveté, caused Turner some chagrin. In a meeting with an attorney for a Tucson, Arizona, newspaper which was about to be sued for a joint operating venture, Turner reflected on the merits of both sides of the dispute. Academic integrity led him into a dialectic on the weaknesses of the Division position according to a Division official who was present. Later in court the attorney quoted Turner's comments to discredit the argument of the Division lawyer.

to decide without a deadline, while he did well in the regulatory agencies just because they gave him fixed deadlines. Turner's brilliance offered no relief; it was part of the trouble—like Hamlet's.

Turner de-emphasized criminal cases in favor of horizontal-merger cases. He refused to bring a criminal action against the automobile manufacturers for conspiring to suppress the development of smog-control devices, although three of the four attorneys who worked 18 months on it thought it should be filed, although a grand jury, including the foreman, wanted to return an indictment regardless of what Turner did, and although Turner admitted in an interview that he could have gotten a conviction out of a Los Angeles jury. Another example of weak criminal enforcement involved eight of the largest steel manufacturers, indicted for an alleged conspiracy to eliminate price competition in the carbon-sheet industry—which represented an annual volume of business of $3.6 billion, or *double* the amount involved in the great electrical-conspiracy cases. A *Yale Law Journal* article described its importance:

> The investigation process lasted nearly two years and cost the Government hundreds of thousands of dollars. The case was considered among the most important of recent antitrust prosecutions; the Government was particularly interested in establishing price-fixing in order to discredit the theory that fluctuations in steel prices were the natural by-products of price leadership unaffected by agreements among the members of the industry. And, according to a Government attorney, the activities of the defendants had "one of the greatest impacts [on the economy] in recent antitrust history." [23]

The defendants pleaded no contest, and Turner acquiesced. He did not press for a guilty plea or trial, despite a Division tradition of opposing no-contest pleas in criminal cases because they encourage insignificant penalties and lessen public exposure. Turner said he wasn't sure the government would win, but that argument holds true for every case. More relevant was the *New York Times* comment that "he was not inclined to see the point to jail sentences." [24] Jail sentences simply did not fit into his stylistic or intellectual view of antitrust, which he thought more a discipline of economics than law.

Good antitrust now became good economics and vice versa. "I do not think it is possible," Turner stressed, "to bring very much order into antitrust law unless we can succeed in disentangling it from many policy considerations having little or nothing to do with the protection of competition." His "policy considerations" excluded the antipathy to bigness which forged the Sherman and Celler-Kefauver Acts. He was not very sensitive to the political and social costs of economic concentration (see Chapter I). His aversion to "silly cases" with negligible economic impact included *Von's Grocery* and *Brown Shoe,* both of which were upheld by the Supreme Court, both of which form cornerstones for Section 7 enforcement and the Guidelines, and both of which Turner said he would not have filed.

Not only did Turner disdain the view that bigness alone is evil, but he ignored the actual competitive costs of bigness. Civil antitrust cases involve future economic consequences which can only be stated as probabilities. In close cases Turner often decided in industry's favor and against the government, contrary to a series of Supreme Court decisions urging the exact opposite presumption; as a result, major cases which would have restructured many industries were never filed. In the oil industry, for example, Turner approved a series of mergers which were of huge absolute size *and* possessed obvious economic harms: increased market concentration, entrenched vertical integration, reduced potential competition, and inter-energy competition dwindling in a merger wave. These situations involve Pure Oil and Union Oil (with assets, at that time, of $193 million and $261 million, respectively), Atlantic and Richfield (with assets of $184 million and $159 million), and Continental Oil and Consolidation Coal (with assets of $1.67 billion and $446 million). In a reversal of antitrust form, the Federal Power Commission urged the Antitrust Division to block the latter merger, but without success.

Indifference to the real competitive costs of bigness stopped Turner from filing two of the most important cases of his term: a complaint to split GM into three divisions, due to its earlier illegal mergers and coercive restraints, and a suit in the vertically concentrated copper industry, to spin off fabricators from producers. In addition, there was the Colonial Pipeline draft complaint, aiming to break up this joint venture of nine major oil firms. Colonial, the largest petroleum-products pipeline in the country, was built under an agreement which effectively excluded competing refiners from use of the pipeline and which stabilized the regional market shares of the member firms. Lower and upper staff recommended a suit, but Turner refused to bring it. (But in the tradition of triviality exemplified by Loevinger's suits against ice-skating shows and hot-dog rolls was a civil case which Turner *did* file in the bull-semen "industry.")

Two of Turner's decisions in the automobile market made his predecessors bridle. Bicks was upset at the settlement of the *GM Bus* case, which he had worked on in the Fifties and which documented the predatory ways GM had built up its monopoly in this market. The decree, which Turner personally negotiated, permitted GM to retain its 85% monopoly of the intercity bus market. It contained a provision which required compulsory, and at times royalty-free, licensing to competitors, although at the time they barely existed and despite the fact that there was no real expectation that new firms would enter the market.

The court case pending against GM's monopoly of the locomotive market met a more severe fate: it was dropped outright. Turner and staff claimed that the monopoly simply resulted from GM making a better locomotive. Bicks and Loevinger sharply disagreed, thinking the evidence sufficient to prove that the dominance was due either to earlier mergers or to actual reciprocity (railroads buying GM's locomotives to get its shipping business). Even if it was not, however, the danger that the railroad believed that it had to buy GM to keep GM's business was anticompetitive, regardless of what GM did. These two cases were planned peripheral attacks on GM's basic monopoly, which was (and is) in cars. Not only did Turner have that chance to file against GM's car monopoly and did not, but in the bus and locomotive cases "Turner was sold a bill of goods and gutted the hell out of our plan," according to one of the Division architects of that plan.

The greatest cost of Turner's sublime economics was the conglomerate merger movement. As mentioned before, Turner rode the crest of a merger wave in his term as AAG (1965–68). In 1948–54 the assets involved in acquisitions of firms of more than $10 million in assets averaged less than $1 billion a year; in 1955–62 it averaged $2 billion; 1963–64 it averaged $3 billion; 1965–66, $4 billion; 1967,

$9 billion; and by 1968 it was up to $13 billion. Thus, the amount of assets acquired more than tripled in Turner's term alone, from $4 to $13 billion.[25] Yet throughout this crisis Turner coolly clung to his view that conglomerates were not an antitrust problem. Meanwhile a counterpart at the FTC, Dr. Willard Mueller, head of the Bureau of Economics, was predicting that if the merger wave were not stopped, the 200 top corporations would own two-thirds of all manufacturing assets by 1975. It was a prediction, as discussed, which came true five years ahead of schedule— due in some measure to Turner's policies.*

Turner, of course, had the right to file or not to file cases as he wished. Paternalistically, Turner thought that judges should not even be given conglomerate and other cases for fear they might mistakenly approve them. By individually deciding that conglomerates were legal, the prosecutor became judge, depriving the courts of the chance to determine what was the intent of the 1950 bill, which, based on the legislative history, seemed to make conglomerate mergers also illegal. Indeed, as Turner told one staff meeting, in discussing the *El Paso* decision, he and the Division knew antitrust better than the Supreme Court. Donald Turner may know more antitrust law than William Douglas, but there is a Constitutional presumption that Douglas should make the decision. On close questions of law, especially those defining the boundaries of a law for the first time, the intelligent prosecutor should rise above his own prejudices and permit the courts to judge. The Sherman and Clayton Acts are our economic common law. They depend on case-by-case court development. If the courts cannot hear the important and close cases, the Acts are drained of their vitality.

Even on cases where Turner expressed a personal and intellectual interest, little was done. He was sincerely concerned about patent abuses, began some studies, and filed

* Ed Zimmerman bravely defends the Turner record on conglomerates by stressing that "we *did* file conglomerate suits." He cites cases brought or threatened against Bethlehem Steel–Cerro (copper), International Minerals–Morton Salt, and Caterpiller–Chicago Pneumatic. All involved "conglomerate" arguments like potential entry and entrenchment. Yet all involved firms in directly related fields, and at times with some competitive overlap. None involved such unrelated firms and "pure" conglomerate mergers as LTV–Jones & Laughlin and ITT–Canteen, cases brought by Zimmerman's successor, Richard McLaren. Finally, it is inferentially difficult to argue that the Turner regime did move against conglomerates while Turner himself delivered speeches for three years saying he would *not* move against conglomerates.

a few cases. But many important patent cases were not filed until an aggressive Patent Unit was set up in the Division after he had left. "Don thought that if he gave a speech against some practice," reflected one high staff official, in only half-exaggeration, "that practice would stop. But the only way to stop illegal practices is to file tough cases." "Tough" cases were likewise not filed against *shared monopolies*, a concept Turner helped originate and develop. A shared monopoly was another name for an oligopoly, emphasizing the fact that *de facto* monopolies exist in industries where three or four firms dominate and where there is a high degree of interdependence and parallel pricing. As early as April, 1966, Turner discussed with his staff the possibility of testing the limits of monopoly suits brought under Section 2 of the Sherman Act. Wording from cases like *American Tobacco* and *Standard Stations* would support an attack on "collective, even though not collusive" action. By August of 1967 five of his staff had produced an internal memorandum listing 12 industries which were rated "promising shared-monopoly cases." Furthermore, a separate team of lawyers and economists studied the soap market and a possible shared-monopoly suit against Procter & Gamble, Lever Brothers, and Colgate based on their huge advertising expenditures. This study buttressed Turner's view, widely reported after a June, 1966, speech, that excessive advertising was anticompetitive since it raised entry barriers and entrenched existing oligopolists. Columnist David Lawrence fumed that such efforts at advertising "equalization" were not unlike "the main objective of Communism," [26] and *Business Week* headlined, "Justice in a lather over soap and outlays."

They needn't have worried. No shared-monopoly suit was ever filed by Turner or his successors, and another effort —a major one—to revive our competitive economy died on the drawing board. Turner did, however, write an article for the *Harvard Law Review* after his departure which urged that the Antitrust Division bring some shared-monopoly suits. "This raises the question of his intellectual integrity," complained one of a large number of disappointed Division attorneys; "why didn't *he* attack oligopolies under his own theory while he was there?" Turner claims that he fully developed and refined this theory only after he resigned as AAG; but by 1966, his group of evaluators were digging into the problem with a detailed list of conditions

which were thought to comprise a "shared monopoly."
Robert Wright's view seems apt: "Don Turner talked innovation, but just never filed innovative suits."

Most of the potential but unfiled cases died by Turner's
self-censorship. Some, however, despite his good relations
with Attorneys General, were squelched by the higher echelon.

—As if AT&T had not inflicted enough *déjà vu* on Division AAGs, Turner tried his hand at undoing the 1956
settlement. After hiring an economic consultant to confirm
what all already knew, Turner sent a proposed complaint
to the AG on July 29, 1966. It charged monopolization of
telephone equipment *since* the entry of the 1956 decree, an
argument which cleverly avoided the *res judicata* problems
(when an earlier case controls a later case) of attempting
to challenge the earlier decree. The proposed complaint
was simply ignored. Again on August 18, 1967, Turner
recommended that a suit be brought. And again "nothing
happened," according to a Division official close to Turner;
"no reasons were given and it never came back down."
When Katzenbach was asked why he did not bring this
case, he cryptically said, "We had problems with it." He
then elaborated what the "problems" were in an interview:
"It's just easy to keep putting off a case like that. We never
really decided a definite 'no' on that, and it just kept sitting
around. The daily cases got more of our attention." Even
more incredible, Ramsey Clark, who became AG after
Turner sent it up the second time, never even *knew* such a
case had been recommended for him to act on.

—A grand jury was convened to investigate alleged price-
fixing in the aircraft-tire market. The Division attorney on
the case was convinced that a violation had occurred, but
Katzenbach refused to ask for a grand-jury indictment. The
stated reason was that although a violation probably *had*
occurred, and although the statute of limitations had not
yet run, the violation had last occurred nearly five years
before.

—As the *Tucson* case against joint-operating newspaper
agreements was working its way to the Supreme Court
(where such agreements were finally found unlawful),
Turner sought to file a similar suit against two San Francisco newspapers, including the *San Francisco Chronicle*.
Katzenbach was upset to find out *after* filing the *Tucson*
case that 21 other joint-operating agreements existed. (He

denied knowledge of the others, although Division attorneys on the cases say he was informed upon filing *Tucson;* furthermore, Ramsey Clark, then Deputy Attorney General, confirmed that much political pressure was exerted against the suit.) Katzenbach refused to file against the San Francisco papers, arguing that he would wait until the Supreme Court first decided the *Tucson* case. Based on such reasoning, the following Section 7 cases would not have been filed until the first significant one, *Brown Shoe,* was decided in 1962: *Continental Can, Bethlehem-Youngstown, El Paso Natural Gas, Pabst-Blatz, Von's Grocery,* and *Alcoa-Rome.*

—Finally, Ramsey Clark, when Attorney General, refused to block the merger between the McDonnell and Douglas aircraft companies. McDonnell produced military aircraft and Douglas domestic, but since Douglas could easily tool up to produce military aircraft also, the antitrust problem became one of obvious potential competition. Douglas claimed that it was a "failing company," one of the few established defenses to a Section 7 suit. The Division contested this claim. Evaluations chief Donald Baker suspected that this argument was fabricated by bankers financing the merger as a way to "bluff" Clark into permitting the merger. The staff argued that Douglas was composed of two parts, aerospace and aircraft, and that even if the aircraft division was losing money, it was no justification to permit McDonnell to acquire the healthy aerospace division. Some pressure was exerted on Clark by Senator Stuart Symington and by the Pentagon, both solicitous of Douglas's well-being. The AG agonized over this massive merger, deciding in its favor because the possible benefit in stopping it was not worth the possible risks of bankruptcy, shareholder pain, and cancellation of orders. He also feared that if Douglas went under, Boeing would remain as the only producer of domestic aircraft in the United States. As later revealed by *Fortune,* there *were* possible alternative buyers that Douglas had considered besides McDonnell. Some of these companies, like General Dynamics and Signal Oil, would have created less antitrust problems than did McDonnell.[27]

Donald Turner's term at the Antitrust Division did have some noble moments. Interventions against the ABC-ITT merger at the FCC and in court, and against the Stock Exchange for its fixed minimum commissions before the SEC, were both significant and successful. They inaugurated an era of greater Division scrutiny of actions by regulatory agencies. Turner kept up the pace against bank mergers, despite the inhibitory effect of the 1966 Bank Merger Act. The post of Special Economic Assistant, which has attracted a top economist to the Division for one-year stays, began during his tenure. And he infused a sense of craftsmanship and doctrine at the Division which is still reflected in its work. Gordon Spivack thought that "No man has done more to rationalize antitrust doctrine in the long run [than Turner]." "Those briefs are beautiful," commented one Wall Street lawyer of the Supreme Court briefs under Turner. And in fiscal 1967, 47 civil cases and nine criminal cases were terminated without one being lost in court.

Yet the cost of such success came high. The parameters of the law were not probed, and both the number and the impact of cases fell drastically. The Division staff knew it, the antitrust bar knew it, and, worst of all, business knew it. Calling Turner a "Gentle Trustbuster," Louis Kohlmeier wrote in the *Wall Street Journal:* "Psst! Want to merge? Go ahead. Chances are better than they've been in years that the Government's antitrusters will not try to block a corporate marriage." [28] Arnold Lehrman, a Washington antitrust lawyer writing in *Dun's Review,* catalogued the failure: "A key ingredient for compliance was often missing —the conviction of businessmen that the Antitrust Division would *act.* . . . As time passed, a growing suspicion spread among the business community that the Antitrust Division was a paper tiger." [29] Yes, Katzenbach got his "breathing spell."

Turner was succeeded by his First Assistant, Edwin Zimmerman, who served for six months until the Republicans took over. Zimmerman had been a Stanford law professor, felt comfortable with Turner's program, and continued in much the same vein. While he was friendlier toward the staff than Turner, he was as much a perfectionist, to the extent that he spent some of his time correcting the wording and grammar of letters sent to Congressmen. Yet Zimmerman had a deadline to hasten his decision-making: Jaunary 20, 1969. In his seven-and-a-half-month stay, he filed 33 cases, a somewhat better pace than his predecessor's. In his last week in office, civil suits were filed against the automobile firms for their alleged smog conspiracy and against IBM for its alleged monopolization of the computer industry. While some viewers, like the *Economist,* thought the lateness of the suits showed they were intended as a political albatross around the Republicans' neck, it is far more likely their lateness stemmed from Zimmerman's procrastination. Toward the end of Zimmerman's term, some former Division lawyers, with the blessing of present personnel, leaked word of the IBM case to the press in an effort to make sure the case got filed. Their anxiety was understandable, given Turner's track record, but in this case misplaced, since Zimmerman had sent the case to Ramsey Clark before the leak occurred.

Ramsey Clark, who was very unlike his predecessor, helped the IBM case along. His father had once headed the Antitrust Division, and Clark had practiced some antitrust law before he arrived at Justice. These facts combined with a populist zeal against business illegality to shape his sensitivity to antitrust. Rather than ignore or suppress a big controversial case like IBM, he urged his subordinates to bring it. According to Clark, he was even "brokenhearted" that it was not filed a year earlier.

Clark also attempted to interest U.S. Attorneys, who are under the aegis of the Justice Department, in local price-fixing cases. He helped obtain a 10% increase in Antitrust Division manpower, the first such increase in authorized strength in a decade. Finally, Clark wanted conglomerate cases brought, but the arm of Justice which would have had to develop such cases did not. As a result of a number of such experiences, he grew disappointed with the Turner-Zimmerman regime. In an interview with the Study Group, Clark stressed that if he had to do it again, "I would not select a professor to run the Antitrust Division."

ANTITRUST UNDER NIXON

Richard Nixon and John Mitchell did not select a professor. Instead they turned to a practitioner, Richard McLaren. It was an obvious choice. McLaren had been a partner in a Chicago law firm—Chadwell, Keck, Kayser, Ruggles & McLaren—specializing in counseling antitrust defendants. In addition, he had been the widely respected chairman of the Antitrust Section of the ABA and the editor of *Antitrust Developments 1955–1968.* And McLaren was Republican, cautious, and committed to antitrust as a bulwark of "free enterprise."

His own appointments, however, were disappointing. McLaren at first wanted an acadamic as his First Assistant, but his superiors discouraged him. He then asked Lionel Kestenbaum, the talented head of Evaluations under Turner. Kestenbaum had already committed himself to private practice, yet when the AG's office found out about the offer to a Democrat, it was vocally upset. At this point McLaren safely turned to another Republican ABA notable, Walker Comegys. "Dick thought he was good when he chose him," notes a former evaluator, "but he knows better now." Comegys does what he thinks McLaren will want, and no more. This assessment is widely held, even to an extent by Comegys himself. In response to a request for an interview, he wrote, "In the light of my close association with the Assistant Attorney General, Antitrust Division, I do not feel that it would be appropriate for me to grant such an interview. As you have noted, you have interviewed a great many of our attorneys, and I do not feel that this omission [he is the number-two man in the Division] will hamper your study." In sum, he has not brought an independent review to his crucial office.

Nor has Roland Donnem, chief of Policy Planning. Donnem even more than Comegys is a political appointment. The administration owed Taggert Whipple—a prominent Wall Street lawyer with the firm of Davis, Polk —a favor. He cashed in his chips by sending Donnem, a permanent associate of the firm, to Washington.* Given the pivotal and crucial position of Policy Planner, Donnem's credentials and competence are seriously suspect. Finally, McLaren kept on Baddia Rashid as Director of Operations; Rashid is a career Division attorney, acknowledged to be efficient although not innovative.

McLaren's top staff is neither as brilliant nor as dilatory as Turner's. He has deployed it in a more productive way than his Democratic predecessors. Evaluations has been intentionally downplayed, as a memorandum to all trial staff emphasized. The only items routed to Policy Planning and Evaluations are cases with new or difficult theories; routine matters are no longer sent to the former bottleneck. This new routing system has encouraged Policy Planning to plan rather than merely review, although Donnem's time

---

* In March, 1971, Donnem resigned to become vice president and general counsel of Standard Brands, Inc., New York.

was still split about 50–50 between his two roles, according to his own estimate. Furthermore, McLaren has created, with the luxury of added personnel, two new units: a patent section to concentrate on creative patent suits and a judgments-enforcement section to review past judgments to see if they are being obeyed. Previously the over 1,000 outstanding judgments were not monitored at all. The most significant improvement has been in staff morale, which had dimmed during the Turner and Zimmerman regimes. Despite the very conservative business-orientation of Nixon and Mitchell, attorneys felt they had a decisive and vigorous chief.

McLaren began impressively, with the help of leftovers from former AAGs. Sitting on his desk at his arrival were the U.S. Steel reciprocity case, the Cleveland Trust interlock case, a series of patent cases, and the basic investigation of the Ling-Temco-Vought conglomerate. The emphasis of his enforcement program has been twofold, reflected by the number of suits filed in each area: reciprocity and conglomerates.

Reciprocity occurs when a company uses its purchasing power and economic muscle to sell its own products to suppliers. Essentially it means that company X buys from company Y only if Y buys from X in return. Such a practice forecloses competitors from a market, with sales made not on the basis of price, quality, or service. In 1961 *Purchasing Magazine* published a poll of 300 purchasing agents showing that reciprocity was a significant factor in the buyer-seller relations of 51% of the companies surveyed and of 78% of companies with a sales volume of more than $50 million. Though reciprocity has been forbidden since the 1930s,[30] it was ignored by the enforcement agencies for more than 30 years, until a couple of cases in the mid-1960s and until McLaren's systematic attack.

In January, 1968, U.S. Steel was charged with reciprocal purchasing agreements in violation of Sections 1 and 2 of the Sherman Act. A consent decree six months later settled the case, prohibiting the company from purchasing products on the condition that the supplier buy from it and abolishing its "Commercial Relations Service," which ran the reciprocity program. Between June and November, 1970, four more steel companies were sued for reciprocity —Inland, Republic, Armco, and Bethlehem; in February,

1971, a similar case was filed against National Steel. In each case a consent order settling the case was filed simultaneously with the complaint.

Important questions remain for McLaren. It is likely that reciprocity remains prevalent. Months after the U.S. Steel suit was filed, the president of one company told the *Wall Street Journal:*

> I don't call it reciprocity. I call it corporate friendliness. We'd be pretty sorry salesmen if we didn't point out to our suppliers that they can buy from us as well as sell to us. . . . We keep track of every ton of steel we buy. And we're just narrow-minded enough to remind the steel companies every now and then just how little they are buying from us. We make no bones about it.[31]

Consent decrees do not make law, and it is doubtful that filing a settlement simultaneously with filing the suit—settlements which only prohibit but in no way punish—will deter other offenders. Unless McLaren plans on filing reciprocity suits *cum* decree forever, he must litigate a case to judgment, then file and win a criminal prosecution, and then announce that the practice is either illegal *per se* or illegal above a certain volume of commerce. Criminal indictments, if necessary, must then follow to end this built-in business coziness.

Clearly, McLaren's most controversial and significant moves have been against conglomerates. He deserves credit not so much for filing the cases as for the fact that he did not neglect to file them. Based on the legislative history in the 1950 Act, it would have been dereliction of office to decline to prosecute these cases. In all, it has taken more than *20 years* for the definition of conglomerate law under the Celler-Kefauver Act to be first tested by the Antitrust Division.

McLaren has been fully supported by Mitchell in this campaign. Most notably, the AG delivered a widely reported speech that the Department "will probably oppose any merger by one of the top 200 manufacturing firms with any leading producer in any concentrated industry." McLaren's specific cases seek to block the following acquisitions:

(a) *LTV of Jones & Laughlin.* LTV—at the time of suit the 14th largest corporation in the United States, managing 80 companies with annual sales of $2.75 billion—sought to acquire Jones & Laughlin [J&L], the sixth largest steel corporation with annual sales over $900 million. The basis of the suit was the fear of reciprocity between LTV's subsidiaries and J&L, and the fact that LTV was a "potential competitor" of J&L, via either a new entry or the acquisition of a less dominant steel firm than J&L.

LTV already had 63% of J&L by the time the suit was announced on March 23, 1969. Three days later LTV and Justice negotiated an unprecedented agreement: the firm could buy up to 81% of J&L's stock, promising to divest itself fully of J&L if the Justice Department later won its suit.* Negotiations continued through the fall and winter with the Division hurried along by the pressure of James Ling, chairman of LTV, who was frustrated because part of the interim agreement forbade him any voting power or management control in J&L; "Ling and Arnold & Porter [LTV counsel] were there nearly every day pushing us along and complaining," recalls one attorney on the case.

By February a consent decree had been reached, again of an unprecedented species. It gave LTV the choice of divesting itself of its 80.44% of J&L stock *or* divesting itself of two companies it already owned, Braniff Airwaves and the Okonite Company. (LTV has since opted to keep J&L.) Also, LTV would have to obtain Justice Department approval for any acquisition within the next 10 years of any company with assets of more than $100 million. The *Wall Street Journal* doubted the agreement would slow down the company's merger hunger, although the prediction has not yet come true. And others wondered why the case was settled—again a procedure which breaks no new ground on merger law—after so much publicity was given to the conglomerate suits. When it had been filed, Louis Kohlmeier had written that "it's a test case carefully picked for maximum chance of victory in court." [32] Division lawyers on the case confided that they had to settle because LTV, with all its subsidiaries, workers, and shareholders, was close to bankruptcy. If that was the case, "why have filed the suit at all?" asked a former Division official. Finally, in May, 1971, District Judge Louis Rosenberg, who presided over the *LTV-J&L* case, sharply criticized Justice for allowing the sale of Okonite to Omega-Alpha, Inc.; the latter is

---

* The agreement was concluded because LTV was in trouble with its cash flow, and stood to gain a $20 million tax benefit since once a company owns 80% or more of another company, dividends are freely transferable from one to the other on a tax-free basis.

headed by none other than James Ling, who had been ousted by LTV for mismanagement.

(b) *ITT of Canteen Corporation, Hartford Fire Insurance, and Grinnell Company*. ITT is America's largest "pure" conglomerate corporation, with 1969 sales of $5.24 billion and assets of $2.31 billion. Canteen is largely a producer of vending machines, Grinnell makes burglar and fire alarms, and Hartford Fire Insurance, with annual premiums of about $1 billion, is the nation's fourth largest property-casualty insurer. The Canteen case was typical of the three suits. The fact memorandum sent to the AG read:

> We contend that through vertical integration and reciprocity this acquisition will foreclose a substantial portion of the relevant markets from competition, entrench a leading firm, raise barriers to entry and very likely trigger similar mergers by other leading food and vending firms.

McLaren's conglomerate program has suffered two initial, though far from fatal, blows in these cases. District Court Judge William Timbers refused a preliminary injunction which would have prevented ITT from acquiring Hartford and Grinnell before the case was finally decided; he doubted that the mergers would "substantially lessen competition." And in *Grinnell* he has ruled against the Division on the actual merits of the case.

On July 30, 1971, the Antitrust Division and ITT announced a package settlement to all three cases. ITT gave up Canteen, Grinnell, and four other holdings, and in return was permitted to keep Hartford. ITT was also prohibited from acquiring any domestic concern with assets of more than $100 million, or from acquiring leading concerns in concentrated domestic markets without prior approval from the Justice Department or courts. The terms and context of the settlement are ambiguous. On paper, the Justice Department has obtained the largest divestiture ever accomplished in an antitrust case—and this after two district court losses. Yet, when combined with the LTV settlement, it lost the opportunity to make conglomerate law by a Supreme Court decision; the Department sanctioned the Hartford acquisition, which was allegedly illegal; further, ITT was not forced to disgorge the profits made between acquisition and divestiture, a retention which can only induce others to try for short-run profits.

The financial gaming and political dealings behind the

settlement cannot be ignored. The SEC was known to be investigating ITT's Hartford acquisition for alleged insider trading and fraud. Some observers speculated that the shelving of this probe was a tacit *quid pro quo* in the settlement. Then, after the settlement was announced, the *St. Louis Post Dispatch* uncovered the fact that five vice presidents of ITT, as well as its secretary and chairman of its new Hartford subsidiary, had sold ITT stock *after* negotiations had begun but *before* the settlement was announced. Since ITT stock, as would be expected, dropped after the settlement, substantial losses, estimated as high as $300,000, were avoided. Finally, another *St. Louis Post Dispatch* column reported on August 1 that Rep. Robert Wilson of California, chairman of the Republican National Congressional Campaign Chest, had met privately with Deputy Attorney General Richard Kleindienst on the case, shortly after conversing with ITT chairman Geneen. As later reported in *The New York Times,* Wilson was instrumental in finding a guarantor of up to $400,000 for San Diego's bid for the Republican National Convention in 1972. The source of the guarantee: the Sheraton Corporation, a subsidiary of ITT.

(c) Northwest Industries of B. F. Goodrich. Northwest, which is basically a holding company of the Chicago and Northwestern Railroads, is a growing conglomerate. It had 1969 sales of $721 million and assets of $1.41 billion. Goodrich, producer of tires, had sales of $1.23 billion and assets of $1.25 billion the same year. The combined firm would be 38th in revenues and 24th in assets among U.S. firms. The Division was concerned with potential competition in a number of chemical markets where there was already some overlap, and with reciprocity resulting from increasing the size and scope of the firms by merger.

(d) The First National City Corporation of the Chubb Corporation. First National is the nation's second largest, and New York City's largest, commercial bank; Chubb was the nation's 14th largest property and casualty-insurance company. The fact memorandum sent to the AG's office said, "The primary danger is the creation of the power of the merged firms to tie insurance to bank loans and thereby to foreclose marketing opportunities to competing insurance companies." Especially in times of tight money, a bank enjoys significant market power and leverage over a borrower. This danger was not remote, since

Percy Chubb II told McLaren personally that a Chubb insurance agent might be placed in every Citibank office, an obviously illegal tie-in. The Division feared this merger would trigger others between banks and insurance companies to counter Chubb's competitive edge. When the Department made its objections known, the merger was abandoned.

The legal theories behind these cases were couched in terms of a "tendency to substantially lessen competition," by reciprocity, entrenchment, and heightened entry barriers, and loss of potential competition. Yet the underlying motive for the suits seems to be the growing state of superconcentration of wealth, which has political implications, too. McLaren's memorandum in Northwest–Goodrich stressed that "The effect of the merger movement (90% conglomerate in 1968) has been to place a steadily increasing percentage of the nation's industrial wealth in the hands of a few giant corporations." In testimony before Congress he noted the "human dislocalities" which occur when a person's job, town, and industry are run by distant corporate managers. And McLaren has emphasized that competition is needed because "it protects our political system by promoting a broad dispersion of economic power among the many, rather than concentration in the hands of the few." [33]

There was expected criticism from politicians (Senator John Tower of Texas attacked the move against Texas-based LTV as an enforcement agency "legislating" new law), businessmen (Ling protested, "LTV is not a raider. LTV is not a liquidator"), the press (the *Economist* called McLaren a "trigger-happy trustbuster"), and economists (some, like Robert Bork of Yale Law School, complained that conglomerates were pro-, not anti-competitive).

One recurring charge, grounded only in logic and circumstance, is that the conglomerate suits were politically motivated. The theory is that they were aimed at "new money," often Democratic firms, rather than at Establishment, Republican firms like GM and U.S. Steel. John Westerguard, president of Equity Research Associates, has made this charge; [34] a number of Democrats,[35] including two high officials in the Johnson administration, are convinced of it. Forty-six percent of the respondents to the Businessmen's Questionnaire thought there was a "political motivation behind the current suits against conglomerates." One New

York consulting-firm study, never released, showed that, unlike older, mostly nondiversified firms, the more pure conglomerates were run by non-Easterners, non-Republicans, non-WASP wealth, non-Ivy Leaguers, foreigners, and Jews. The president of the National Economic Research Associates, Dr. Irwin Stelzer, has written:

> And, when *Business Week* reported that Leasco's chairman [the takeover firm] was, in the eyes of Chemical Bank and its customers, an "outsider"—"young, sometimes brash, a Johnny-come-lately, and Jewish to boot"—many began to wonder about the nature of the sudden opposition to conglomerates by a Republican business-oriented administration.* [36]

Furthermore, it has been widely reported that older Establishment firms have been vigorously lobbying on Capitol Hill and in the Executive Branch for legislation to restrict the growth of conglomerates. Kohlmeier thought that the suits were to dissuade Congress from passing antimerger law which might be too inclusive, including blue-chip oligopolies as well as the new conglomerates. And there are, after all, "close to a dozen apparently traditional U.S. corporations . . . which possess a breadth of unrelated diversification at least as great as that of the so-called conglomerates," according to *Forbes*.[37] The Antitrust Division denies all such charges of political motivation.

McLaren's moves against conglomerates are as new as his failure to move against oligopolies is old. If superconcentration is what concerns McLaren, General Motors, among others, has a large concentration of wealth. Yet he has ignored a series of staff recommendations to break up the auto giant. He told the *Washington Evening Star* soon after his term began that he would not attack past mergers "because we're so busy with the current crop we're not looking backward." [38] Eight months later, when asked by a reporter what he intended to do about GM's 50–60% share of the market, McLaren replied, "I haven't focused on the auto industry." [39] In July of 1970, he told a Congressional hearing that "one thing . . . not feasible under

---

* James Ling of LTV and Ben Heineman of Northwest were both members of President Johnson's Business Council and were both personally close to the former Democratic President. But ITT's Chairman Harold Geneen, the object of three suits, is a big Republican. Also, the participants in the aborted First National City–Chubb merger were as establishment and Republican as corporations can get. In this latter case, AG Mitchell knew the area of law involved, finance, and knew the people from these firms personally. It took McLaren a few trips to his office to convince Mitchell to file the suit, but suit *was* filed.

present law is the wholesale dissolution of oligopolistic firms." [40] Suddenly, two months later, he delivered an address to the District of Columbia Federal Bar Association criticizing the lack of innovation and inefficiency of huge corporations, hinting that the Division might soon move against some existing oligopolies. Yet, in the unanimous view of present Division staff we interviewed, McLaren is *not* eager to break up concentrated industries, believing that new technology will erode the positions of the old oligopolies. His speech seems more bravado than a genuine threat.

Some of McLaren's imperfect record arises from cases *not* filed or pursued, as opposed to the small ones prosecuted. Honeywell, number three in the computer hardware industry, was allowed to acquire General Electric's division, number five; the combined annual revenues of $351 million and $412 million respectively make it the number-two company worldwide, with 10% of the market. Although still far behind IBM's 70% monopoly, the merger clearly falls within the Guidelines for concentrated industries, which McLaren stated he would observe. It has never been accepted as sensible antitrust policy to permit two firms to merge in order to countervail the power of an existing monopolist; if so, all industries would logically devolve into duopolies. In fact, GE chairman Fred Borch, pleased with the merger, opined that "you'll see a lot more mergers in the computer industry." [41]

The Antitrust Division under McLaren has shown considerably more timidity toward banking mergers than his Democratic forerunners. One front-office lawyer, usually an admirer, criticized McLaren: "He has one fatal flaw; he's chicken on appeals." The examples cited involved banking cases. He has had a chance to appeal four district-court losses, all dealing with market-extension and potential-competition mergers, in Mississippi (2), Maryland, and Idaho.* At least one of the cases should be appealed for several reasons: all agree the market-extension and potential-competition issues were important ones; district-court judges traditionally hold against innovative antitrust cases; there was no guarantee that better test cases would come along

---

* Formally, the Solicitor General files an appeal for the United States, and McLaren must convince him that the appeal is necessary; "but if he [the AAG] wants a case appealed," said a Division lawyer on the Idaho case, "he can get it appealed."

soon; the longer the delays, the more counterprecedent would be built up and the harder it would be to overturn; the only *possible* way to win on the merits was to appeal, not vacillate. McLaren has vacillated. The Division softly urged that one of the Mississippi cases be appealed, and decided against review on the other three; when the Solicitor's office indicated problems with the one recommended, McLaren withdrew his request. The staffer on the Idaho case acknowledged to the Study Group in April, 1971, that "Policy Planning now admits it was a mistake not to appeal."

The *O. M. Scott* case was also not appealed from a loss in district court. O. M. Scott was the dominant firm in the lawn-seed and fertilizer market, which maintained its prices by pressuring dealers and by "preticketing," a device where the manufacturer puts a "suggested" price label on the product. The retailer then cannot charge more than the stamped price without incurring consumer hostility, or charge less without deceiving the consumer into thinking he is getting a discount. The original purpose of the *O. M. Scott* case was to test the legality of preticketing *per se*. McLaren at first agreed to appeal it. The Solicitor General's office sent it back for more work and comments. McLaren temporized, and then dropped it, deciding that the key element had been *actual coercion* and *not* preticketing. "He was afraid of losing and he was afraid of winning," commented one evaluator involved; "he didn't like to lose appeals. And he was afraid that winning would mean preticketing was illegal, which would hurt all his former dairy clients to whom he would be returning. These firms rely on a high level of product differentiation, by advertising and preticketing, which is the way to exclude people from competing or entering."

Many of McLaren's difficulties have arisen because he is part of a conservative Republican administration. Some errors have been partially self-inflicted. The Nixon administration wanted to take a hard line against a bill to open the federal courts to a broad range of consumer class-action suits, the kind which help cheated consumers get their money back and, therefore, the kind businessmen detest. Chosen to denounce a measure strongly advocated by consumer spokesmen was Richard McLaren, a government official with his own "consumer" jurisdiction. He executed his obligation with conservative ease. The two

FTC chairmen who spoke on the issue, Caspar Weinberger
and Miles Kirkpatrick, favored the legislation.

He also seemed to compromise the vigor of the Division
move challenging the minimum brokerage fees of the New
York Stock Exchange before the SEC. When McLaren delivered a speech on the issue on June 26, 1969, in Chicago,
he was concerned that local newspapers had interpreted his
remarks as more militant than he had desired. Four days
later he wrote a letter to Bernard Lasker and Robert Haack
—chairman and president, respectively, of the New York
Stock Exchange—clarifying his comments. He expressed
concern over any interpretation of "a renewal of the effort
by the Antitrust Division to eliminate fixed broker commission rates," and assured Lasker and Haack that his emphasis "was upon the fact that the matter is now in the
hands of the Securities and Exchange Commission." The
letter implied that the decision was the SEC's, hinting that
no appeal would follow if the SEC turned the Division
down. The letter becomes suspect against the political
background of this battle: Lasker and Haack had been to
the White House while Johnson was President to restrain
the Division from filing its case. Nixon's now famous and
intended secret campaign letter to businessmen, denouncing
the strictness of regulatory agencies, specifically mentioned
the SEC *and* the move to end brokerage price-fixing. In
addition, Lasker was a major fund-raiser for Nixon-Agnew
in 1968 and is personally close to Nixon, being the recipient
of a White House birthday party in August of 1970. The
McLaren letter dismayed the SEC staff who favored the
Division's intervention, and deeply upset one well-known
Washington antitrust observer, long a McLaren partisan:
"He's no longer Mr. Pure to my eyes."

McLaren and the Attorney General's office get along
well. Richard Kleindienst has remarked that the AG's
office regards the Antitrust Division as the "Cadillac Division" in the Department. Of Mitchell, McLaren has
effused in an address: "I met John Mitchell in January,
and I think he's terrific. . . . [H]e's the kind of fellow I
think any one of you would thoroughly enjoy having as a
law partner." In return, Mitchell has confidence in Mc-
Laren, which is important, since Mitchell and Kleindienst
know little about antitrust and usually let McLaren run his
own program. Usually, but not always.

—McLaren has lost at least three inter-agency disputes.

He sat for a time on the President's Task Force on Oil Imports, opposing, as any sane consumer-antitruster must, the quota program which costs the purchasing public an estimated $5–$7 billion a year. His position was undermined by the appearance of AG Mitchell at some of the meetings, who was more sympathetic to the President's political needs. Mitchell told George Shultz, Chairman of the Task Force and critic of the oil import program, "Don't box the President in." Shultz's group recommended the moderate measure of gradually replacing the quota system with a tariff. Nixon now established the Oil Policy Committee, with John Mitchell as a member but lacking George Shultz, to study the recommendations. At this point McLaren contributed a move in the oil game. Division attorney John Lamont had been the Justice Department's staff representative on inter-agency oil committees, also doing work on the Shultz study. McLaren removed him from future inter-agency oil work, a move which the staff familiar with the problem attribute to Lamont's persuasiveness and hostility to such giveaways as the oil import quota. With Lamont out of the way, the Oil Policy Committee decided in February, 1970, to discontinue "consideration of moving to a tariff system of control." Although McLaren had been delegated the job of representing the Department on the Committee, Mitchell attended in his stead on the day the import quotas were upheld.

Second, McLaren vigorously opposed the Failing Newspaper Act as an antitrust travesty that gave newspapers a loophole based on their political power. McLaren testified before the Senate Antitrust and Monopoly Subcommittee that "We do not think that a newspaper or any other unregulated business enterprise should be saved from failure at the expense of price-fixing or profit-pooling arrangements." Yet in late 1969, a few days after Richard Berlin, president of the Hearst Corporation, visited President Nixon at the White House on the issue, Nixon authorized the Commerce Department, not the Antitrust Division, to speak for the administration on this antitrust issue. Commerce favored the bill.

Finally, in a January 5, 1971, letter to Senator Mike Gravel (D.-Alaska), McLaren criticized the extensive and anticompetitive role AT&T played in Comsat, favoring new legislation to correct this abuse. (McLaren was replying to a Gravel inquiry received 11 months earlier.) McLaren had cleared his letter with the Office of Management and Budget and the Office of Telecommunications Policy at the White House. Nevertheless, Clay Whitehead, director of the latter office, quickly told the press that McLaren had *not* been speaking for the administration. "A few more of these and he'll just quit," fretted a Division staffer.

—McLaren wanted to launch a Division investigation into reciprocal dealings in the oil industry. Attorney General Mitchell rejected the idea because there were already a number of outstanding suits against oil companies and because the administration wanted to stay politically friendly with the industry, as Nixon's oil-import decision above indicates. McLaren then tried without success to get the FTC interested.

—Mitchell also refused McLaren's request to investigate the controversial Alaskan pipeline. The pipeline poses antitrust problems since it is a joint venture among major oil firms; such an arrangement could favor the venturers over independent firms who might want to use the pipeline. To avoid this potential for discrimination, the pipeline's common-carrier status must be guaranteed, but since no antitrust investigation was permitted, this solution was not reached.

—On August 16, 1971, National Steel, the nation's fourth-ranked steelmaker, merged with Granite City Steel, ranked 11th, to form the third largest firm in this already concentrated industry. It was a relatively simple case to the Division staff on it: a *per se* horizontal-merger violation, exceeding the permissible market percentages in the Department's Merger Guidelines. The proposed complaint alleged no less than 70 combined markets of illegal overlap; the firms themselves conceded six lines of commerce where they were direct competitors above the Guidelines (which permitted a combined 10% market share). The failing-company exemption was unavailable: National had earned $59 million the previous year and Granite City $3.6 million. When presented with these facts, and since the Department had opposed a steel merger in 1969 involving only the 18th and 17th largest firms which aimed to become the 11th largest, McLaren had no difficulty in signing the complaint and recommending it to Mitchell.

But the Attorney General refused to file the case. McLaren tried a second time, again without success. Although no explanation was given the Division—or the public—it was well known that the steel firms and some administration spokesmen, like Commerce Secretary Maurice Stans, had been urging a relaxed antitrust policy toward mergers in the steel industry to permit it to better meet foreign competition. The merger was allowed the day after President Nixon's "new economic policy" speech, one heavy with protectionist emphasis. Finally, the chairman of National is Gilbert W. Humphrey, Republican notable and contributor, and the brother of Eisenhower's powerful Treasury Secretary, George Humphrey.

The Division staff were outraged at the failure to sue. One attorney on the case accepted the decision with flip equanimity: "Well, there were 25 states where the competitive overlap didn't exceed 30 percent."

—Chapter II has detailed the political interference practiced by Kleindienst in the ITT-Canteen and Warner-Lambert–Parke-Davis mergers. During both incidents McLaren came close to resigning. After the Warner-Lambert case, *Newsweek* did report that "he [was] fed up with Kleindienst's interference," and planned to quit if Mitchell ever left and Kleindienst became the Attorney General. McLaren, proving himself at once disingenuous and a good member of the Administration team, protested to *Newsweek* in a letter:

> Deputy Attorney General Kleindienst has been an effective advocate and enthusiastic supporter of this Administration's vigorous antitrust enforcement program. Indeed, as Acting Attorney General, he signed the complaints in some of our most important conglomerate merger cases (e.g., ITT-Hartford, ITT-Canteen, ITT-Grinnell).

Since Kleindienst signed the Canteen complaint only because McLaren went to the White House threatening to quit if he did not, and given McLaren's well-known consternation over the treatment of his Warner-Lambert–Parke-Davis case by the Deputy Attorney General, Mr. McLaren, we think, protests too much.

CONCLUSIONS

A number of conclusions emerge from this personality and policy cataloguing of AGs and AAGs. All of the AAGs of the past decade have been men of competence and caution, none of whom could actually master "policy planning" and none of whom ever did anything about existing concentration. The specific differences in temperament, ability to arouse morale, and enforcement priorities were evident. They were largely immune to political pressures, unlike the Attorneys General above them.

Two basic conclusions remain. Attorney General Review was instituted to filter out politically troublesome antitrust cases and should be changed. Former AG Ramsey Clark complained about the procedure to the Study Group:

> The review given a case is usually brief and *ad hoc*. Yet why do antitrust cases go up at all? Neither tax nor civil nor criminal cases routinely need Attorney General approval. Why just antitrust? Because it's sensitive. But what kind of reason is that? And what expertise is there in the Attorney General's office to justify it? The other reason for it is that it acts as a control mechanism. At the same time an Assistant Attorney General, on his own authority, can dismiss a case. Thus the whole setup is structured against filing cases.

The Tax and Civil Divisions can file their own cases, having been delegated the authority by the Attorney General. A lawyer in the office of the Civil Division AAG said that in his 25 years there only *one* case had ever been brought to the attention of the Attorney General before filing. If cases can be filed by Tax and Civil Division AAGs, they can be filed by Antitrust AAGs. The present seven-tier review a case undergoes at the Antitrust Division is as good a guarantee as feasible that a case deserves to be brought. The rare times that this collective judgment is incorrect, a court can dismiss it. But the problem is not that bad cases are filed. It is that not *enough* cases are filed, especially not enough innovative ones.

To avoid the involvement of politics in antitrust enforcement, and to place enforcement in the hands of those who know it best, a Departmental regulation should permit the AAG of Antitrust to file cases and to call grand juries on his own. His status would then equal that of his Tax and Civil Division counterparts. Since he is a Presidential appointee and removable from office, he would remain ultimately accountable to his President and Attorney General. Some could argue that this scheme logically leads to a separate agency for antitrust; while not an inevitable conclusion, it is surely a possible one, and is discussed in detail subsequently in Chapter XV.

Since it is unlikely that this recommendation will be

eagerly embraced by the present AG's office, an alternative and compromise Departmental regulation can be proposed: the only cases to be referred to the AG's office for his signature are (1) any civil case where the amount of commerce allegedly foreclosed exceeds $100 million; (2) any merger case where the assets of the acquiring company exceed $500 million; (3) any civil or criminal case where a substantial departure from past policy occurs; and (4) for those cases which the AG reviews and rejects, he should respectfully answer the Division's memorandum of the case with his own written opinion explaining why the case was not filed. Since any such exercise of this AG veto power would likely involve a major policy position of that Administration, it should be made a matter of public record (except where criminal cases with individual defendants were involved).

Under this plan, the AG would retain his right of review in major civil cases—such as AT&T, ITT–Canteen, Warner-Lambert–Parke-Davis—but stipulation (4), providing a written rationale for non-action, will help guarantee that cases would not be lost or wither away (*e.g.*, AT&T) in his office. The purpose of these guidelines would be to remove from possible AG tampering civil cases like the rice-milling companies' merger, as well as criminal cases like those of the Los Angeles newspapers, RCA, and aircraft tires.

The second basic conclusion deals with an old antitrust chestnut: Republicans are more dedicated to antitrust than are Democrats. Four reasons are offered: (a) Republicans embrace the free enterprise system antitrust seeks to establish; (b) Republicans are afraid to appear too "soft" on business; (c) Democrats are afraid to be too "tough" on business; (d) Democrats prefer regulation to enforcement. The theorem has validity if one narrows his universe of relevant fact. It seems evident that Bicks, who has reiterated point (a) in public speeches, was more aggressive than Turner, whose economic metaphysics exemplified (d). AG Rogers at one point reportedly told Bicks he approved of his antitrust program because the Republicans could not afford to be timid toward business, thereby supporting (b); and the *New York Times* reported that AG Kennedy feared being considered too rough on business, which is evidence for (c). Going further back, *Fortune* magazine concluded in 1957 that "twenty years of Democratic rhetoric left 'big business' almost completely intact," attributing this inaction to the power that large labor unions had over Democratic administrations; big labor, *Fortune* argued, liked fewness in the market, making collective bargaining easier and more stable.[42]

Q.E.D.? Not quite. Richard Posner studied the number of cases brought by Democratic and Republican administrations in the modern era of antitrust enforcement, Franklin Roosevelt's second term to the present. Taking into account the number of years each occupied the White House, he could find no difference between Democrats and Republicans in either the number of cases filed or the number of "landmark" cases filed.[43] It should be asked: If Republicans are proud of Robert Bicks (1959–61), what of Victor Hansen (1956–59)? In addition, whatever the current vitality of antitrust enforcement, Thurman Arnold, a Democrat, has a large degree of responsibility. Whatever the success antitrust has had in the courts, much of the credit is due Justices Black and Douglas, Democratic populists. And whatever the adequacy of antitrust legislation, Representative Celler and Senators Kefauver and O'Mahoney in the 1950s, and Senators Hart and Metcalf more recently deserve acknowledgment—*not* Senator Javits, who wants to emasculate antitrust for his Wall Street constituency, and *not* Senator Dirksen, who thwarted enforcement efforts at vested-interest opportunities. Finally, President Eisenhower, AG Brownell, and Deputy AG Kleindienst, attentive to their corporate constituencies, have shown more political astuteness than antitrust sympathy.

Antitrust enforcement is largely a bipartisan affair, with the vigor of enforcement turning on the personal attributes of the Attorney General or the Assistant Attorney General. A few like Arnold and Bicks won glamourous trustbusting reputations. Some enforcers from both parties, from Barnes to Turner, have felt that tilting at business simply wasn't worth it. While still other Democrats and Republicans, like Katzenbach and Brownell, have followed the siren that antitrust just was not all that important. Any differences have been individual, not ideological. Yet the actual differences have been minor: a few from each party were equally good; most were equally bad.

Even if the Antitrust Division and the Federal Trade Commission enjoyed appropriations five times as large as they now have, they could not conceivably bring a tenth of the cases it would be possible to bring.
— *Professor Edward S. Mason, 1949*

4

Management, Resources, Process

STRUCTURE OF THE DIVISION

Richard Nixon would seem to have little in common with Sir Henry Maine, the great English legal scholar at the turn of the century, but each in his way has stressed that form precedes policy. The President, announcing his proposed reorganization of the federal government, noted that responsive government depends on a well-organized government. And legal scholar Maine uttered the famous dictum that "substantive law [is] . . . gradually secreted from the interstices of procedure." Likewise, antitrust policy and practice are first shaped by the structure and process of the enforcement institution.

The Antitrust Division is headquartered in the Justice Department building on Pennsylvania Avenue, and has seven field offices throughout the country. About 60% of

STRUCTURE OF THE ANTITRUST DIVISION

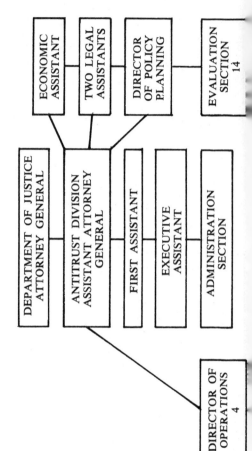

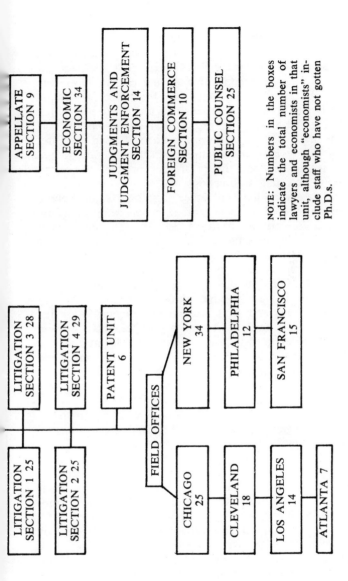

APPELLATE SECTION 9

ECONOMIC SECTION 34

JUDGMENTS AND JUDGMENT ENFORCEMENT SECTION 14

FOREIGN COMMERCE SECTION 10

PUBLIC COUNSEL SECTION 25

LITIGATION SECTION 1 25

LITIGATION SECTION 2 25

LITIGATION SECTION 3 28

LITIGATION SECTION 4 29

PATENT UNIT 6

FIELD OFFICES

CHICAGO 25

CLEVELAND 18

LOS ANGELES 14

ATLANTA 7

NEW YORK 34

PHILADELPHIA 12

SAN FRANCISCO 15

NOTE: Numbers in the boxes indicate the total number of lawyers and economists in that unit, although "economists" include staff who have not gotten Ph.D.s.

all manpower, including all the top officials, is located in the Washington office. It is headed by the Assistant Attorney General for Antitrust, a Presidential appointee who must be confirmed by the Senate. His First Assistant substitutes during the AAG's absence and reviews most items before the AAG sees them; the Director of Operations supervises the four litigating sections and seven field offices, requiring that he study all proposed investigations and complaints that percolate up from the trial staff; and the Director of Policy Planning complements the Operations head by reviewing the legal theory of cases brought and recommending new policy directions.

The theory of the field office, first used extensively by Thurman Arnold, is to encourage people with complaints to come forward by having offices conveniently located. In addition, a permanent field office can develop better relations with local judges than the distant Washington office. But the concept creates problems. Tom Huyak, an attorney formerly in the Chicago office, complained that "the morale is zero in those offices. You investigate, prepare the papers and send them to Washington for review, but you hardly ever get to try a case." In his five years there he never tried a case. (While the field attorneys try especially few cases, their comrades in the main office don't often get to court either.) "There is a feeling in the field offices," said one Division lawyer in Washington, "that the big cases are kept away from them." This is undoubtedly true, since the main purpose of these offices is to spot local and regional cases, important in their vicinities but neither of national import nor of precedential value.

The field offices—far from the center of power and excitement—also tend to take things slower. Staff caliber is often below that of Washington. Work output—especially since price-fixing cases, their specialty, are relatively simple to try—is anemic. Chicago, with a 1970 budget of $748,-000, filed just three cases that year; Los Angeles and Philadelphia, each with over $330,000 appropriated, brought two actions each; and San Francisco filed three suits based on a $476,000 budget. The New York and Cleveland offices did somewhat better, each filing seven cases on budgets of $909,000 and $403,000.

Cases come to Washington and to the field offices in similar ways. Basically, the Antitrust Division usually moves when a complaint is brought to its attention rather than generating the complaint itself. An internal memorandum summarizing a July 15, 1969, meeting between Division and FTC officials said: "Mr. Donnem [Director of Policy Planning] observed that about 95% of all matters initiated by the Antitrust Division arises as the result of complaints. We operate out of the mailbox, he said. Sometimes, as at present, the Division is operating substantially 100% out of the mailbox." Such "mailbox" complaints come overwhelmingly from businessmen who compete with the alleged offender. When a complaint arrives, a preliminary and then a full investigation will occur if the trial attorney, his section chief, or the Director of Operations sees any potential for a case. After the investigation, the senior trial attorney on the case either writes up a proposed complaint supported by a fact memorandum or recommends closing the case. Before the complaint is actually filed, it and the fact memo wind through the many levels of the Division and Department described in the previous chapter.

While filing cases is the Division's main business, is has other responsibilities. It is the antitrust advocate in proceedings before the Interstate Commerce Commission, Federal Communications Commission, Federal Power Commission, and other agencies. It reports to the President and Congress on anticompetitive developments connected with the Defense Production Act, Interstate Oil Compact, Small Business Administration, and Identical Bid Program. The Division also answers Congressional correspondence, some 650 letters per year. "It's a lot of wasted energy," complains Joe Saunders, chief of the public-counsel section. Nevertheless, such mail has a high priority. The official Office Manual stresses that "All Congressional correspondence must be acknowledged or answered in full within 48 hours." Policy Planning Director Donnem explains why: "They can destroy us with the stroke of a pen."

Finally, the Division has a Business Clearance Program whereby corporations divulge their future plans, hoping to obtain advance antitrust clearance. The scheme was explained to Congress as follows: "Although the Department of Justice is not authorized to give advisory opinions to private parties, for several decades the Antitrust Division has been willing in certain circumstances to review proposed business conduct and state its enforcement intentions." [1]

Theoretically, it creates certainty for the firm while saving the Division the resources it might later expend on an investigation and suit. Multiple problems, however, have outweighed the benefit: corporations do not like to divulge much information to the government; the Division itself is wary of relying on their antagonists' data; and since a clearance invariably becomes a permanent immunity, many staffers dislike restricting their future action. (For example, in the early Sixties Goodyear got a clearance to merge with another tire maker; when later staff sought to sue Goodyear for monopolization—because it had intentionally lowered its prices to weaken smaller competitors and then buy them out—they were told that the clearance letter had prohibited further action.) Due to such problems, only 16 business-review requests were received in fiscal 1970, and 20 in 1969. Those who avail themselves of this mechanism, according to one staff lawyer, are "firms who have gotten burned in the past and who want to avoid the same hassle."

There is, however, a more chronic defect in the business-clearance procedure: it is entirely secret. Not even the existence of a clearance attempt is made public. The GE–Honeywell merger, which was above the Guidelines, was condoned by this method, and in January, 1971, 15 international oil companies, mostly American, were granted antitrust immunity to bargain with the Arab oil-producing states. The common bargaining of competitors with a supplier is a *per se* Sherman Act offense. If an exemption from the antitrust laws is to be granted for so classic an illegality, it should be done by Congress, not by a government prosecutor on his own and entirely *ex parte*. At the very least, the letter of release and the justifications for it should be made public.

The basic structure and operations of the Division have remained remarkably fixed over time. AAG William Orrick initiated an evaluations section in 1964, and Richard McLaren started a new patent unit, but the basic framework remains. When AG Ramsey Clark attempted some major alterations, the immutability became especially apparent. In 1967 Clark directed all U.S. Attorneys to begin handling local price-fixing cases, to free Division field personnel for more difficult antitrust cases. "If they could get on the side of antitrust," Clark explained, "it would be better than setting up six more field offices. Price-fixing in localities is *per se* illegal and a discernible fact question for them to handle.

And they're better equipped than the Antitrust Division to convince local juries of such practices." The plan failed. U.S. Attorneys lacked interest in antitrust and were pressured by heavy caseloads in other areas. Worse, the Antitrust Division balked at helping out its supposed allies in the Justice Department, because price-fixing cases are both simple and "sexy." Over a year after this abortive effort, a disillusioned Clark said, "The Antitrust Division lawyers are captive of the legend that antitrust is special and that only the expert is competent to handle antitrust cases."

The Division's structure could be altered. One particularly bad suggestion, in our view, was offered by Professor Turner after he left the Division. Turner disliked the built-in bias of the present trial attorney, who invariably wants "his" case filed so he can try it. So he envisioned something like a law firm, with one unit of lawyers investigating the cases, another one reviewing, theorizing, and writing briefs, and a final group arguing in court. "I don't think the function of the Antitrust Division is to strain to find cases. Our outlook should have been more neutral: is there a case or isn't there?" Turner told the Study Group.

We strongly disagree. First, the proposed corps of reviewers would merely duplicate the inefficiencies of Turner's evaluation unit. Second, it should be obvious that the segregation of the fact-finders and the theorizers is not productive of creative cases. "Theories are modified by execution and experience," emphasized Richard Stern, a former evaluator and now head of the patent unit; therefore, there has to be a constant interreaction between fact and theory, between investigators and reviewers. They should not be isolated from each other. Moreover, given the caution which afflicts the Division hierarchy, agitation from below is a creative and stimulating force. Letting the investigator litigate his case is precisely the kind of incentive that should be encouraged. Perhaps a special corps of top litigators could be set up for big cases, to form a litigating team with the investigating attorneys, combining experience on the case with experience in court. Anything more, however, would discourage the staff from aggressively hunting out corporate illegality.

Based on the present management and structure, other proposals for reform seem more productive. There should be more special units focusing on particular problems. The new patent unit, under Stern's energetic leadership, has six lawyers and seven cases, obviously far above the usual Division ratio. Small and directed units on shared-monopoly suits, advertising-as-entry-barrier cases, or the automobile, oil, or communications industries, for example, could produce a series of coordinated and innovative actions. Responsiblity and accountability for work done and undone would be clear and would spur productivity.

In addition, as people retire from the larger field offices, their slots should be eliminated and new personnel deployed to Washington or new field offices. The basic functions of the field offices—as a contact point for local complaints and to gain a familiarity with the local judicial structure—would remain unimpaired, while staffing would be reduced to a point commensurate with the number of cases filed. Again, staff could be held more accountable for their performance; and by giving the same responsibility to fewer men, the chronic problem of under-utilization of field-office staff would be eliminated.

Top Division officials—the AAG, his aides, and the Directors of Operations and Policy Planning—and the attorneys in the field offices should speak to consumer groups as well as business and legal gatherings. Until the Division begins to cultivate a constituency and explore the intimate connection between antitrust and consumerism, antitrust enforcement will be treated as an historical oddity. By outlining the dangers of which local consumers should be aware, more complaints would be generated for the field offices to handle.

Our overview of Antitrust Division structure and performance leads to a conclusion that a new Department should be created for antitrust enforcement, combining the Antitrust Division and the FTC. This new department will be described in Chapter XV.

BUDGET AND PERSONNEL

The proposed fiscal 1972 budget for the Antitrust Division is $11,417,000; while Justice as a whole is seeking a 24% increase over 1971, only a 6% increase is sought for antitrust. This total of $11.4 million is one-twentieth Procter & Gamble's advertising budget, one-tenth the cost of one C-5A cargo plane, and one-fifth the appropriation of the

Bureau of Commercial Fisheries. Although the present request is an increase of about 200% since 1950, the vast bulk of the difference has gone toward higher salaries required by statutory pay increases, not more manpower.

In 1950 the Antitrust Division had 314 professional staff lawyers and economists. Today it has 354 professional personnel (316 lawyers and 38 economists and statisticians), a mere 12% increase in over two decades. In these years the 200 top industrial corporations increased their control over manufacturing assets from approximately 46% to 66%. For a trillion-dollar economy, with 245 firms having assets over a billion dollars, with 85,000 firms over one million dollars in assets, and with 1.5 million corporations in all, 354 policemen are not enough.

The Division's budget is determined by a triumvirate. The Division initially has to clear any requested increases with the Attorney General. The budget request then goes to the Office of Management and Budget (OMB), which holds hearings on the request and sets the amount the Division can request from Capitol Hill. Armed with this budgetary ceiling, the Antitrust Chief and his Executive Assistant then bravely journey to Representative John Rooney's House Appropriations Subcommittee. Rooney, a former district attorney, prides himself on rigorous and humiliating cross-examination. Philip Bassford, Executive Director from 1960 to 1965, recalls these annual jousts: "The hearings bore no relationship to our need for money. He just wanted to make us look like fools. . . . He once told us that he performs as he does because he needed a record on which to campaign!"

Rooney likes the "numbers game." He always asks how many executives went to jail (knowing that usually none do), and probes how many cases were won and lost and how many cases were brought. He never asks about the impact of selective cases, why certain mergers and practices were not attacked, or why specific innovative cases are not brought. The resulting emphasis on trivia has negative results. Cases are settled, not litigated, to ensure a good won/ lost record; there is also a tendency to bring small price-fixing cases so that the statistics look good; and the temptation exists to make multiple cases out of one fact situation in order to pad the record.

In 1952 Rooney slashed the budget 25%. The Brooklyn

Congressman was angry at the way Graham Morison, the Division head, had run Justice's Claims Division prior to his Antitrust tenure. He was also critical of the Division's "won/lost" record (15 cases won, five lost), the 50% decline in fines collected, and the way the Division filed suit whenever it had evidence of a violation rather than "handling this in a more informal manner." [2] As a result of the budget cut, three of 11 field offices were closed, 85 professionals were released, and 125 pending investigations were terminated.

Since that time, however, every budget presented to Rooney has been accepted. At best, Rooney makes AAGs defend their record—the *only* time the Division is ever held publicly accountable for its performance. But he discourages the Division from asking for manpower increases, as they fear his possible wrath and rejection. For Rooney has made it clear that the FBI can get whatever it requests, but not the Antitrust Division. Ramsey Clark once complained, speaking of the Justice Department in general, that Rooney "had us so cowed that if we needed 100 lawyers, we'd ask for 20 and hope to get five." [3]

The three-tier budget system hides the responsibility for the meager increase in Division legal staff over the decades. Senator Kefauver claimed that for years he tried to get the Division to ask for additional funds, but that successive AAGs said they had enough. When William Orrick was asked in an interview why more staff were not requested, he claimed that they were and that OMB quashed the idea. Most observers, however, blame Sal Andretta, Assistant Attorney General in charge of Administration from 1945 to 1965. He exercised dictatorial and tight-fisted control of all budgets in the Department. Single-handedly he was able to block many requests to the Attorney General for larger outlays. The combined forces of Andretta, OMB, Rooney, and timid AAGs have kept Division staff largely fixed for the past decade.

Two generic problems become immediately obvious when one studies Division personnel: *quantity* and *quality*.

Lack of enough personnel, traceable to the inadequate budget just discussed, has numerous adverse effects on antitrust enforcement. Fewer investigations are launched, and those that are have insufficient manpower and take longer to complete. Far fewer cases are brought to court than would be if the Division had more attorneys, as over 80% of all cases are settled before trial. When Division officials are asked why so many cases end in consent judgments, one answer is *always:* "We lack the resources to take them all to trial." And the cases that are tried witness batteries of corporate lawyers opposing a slender Division trial staff. For example, in the pending IBM suit, three Division attorneys are confronting 30 Cravath, Swaine & Moore lawyers, some of whom are going to a special computer school to comprehend the complex issues. (One Cravath attorney confided that his firm had considered setting up a satellite law firm to handle just the IBM litigation.) Most Division staff said in interviews that they felt overwhelmed by the sheer number of their legal adversaries. Finally, the big and innovative cases, which require a large staff to investigate and prosecute, are the earliest casualties of inadequate personnel. AAG Bicks said that many Section 2 cases were simply too big and costly to be worth the effort. The result is an over-emphasis on trivial "conduct" cases instead of significant "structural" complaints, a priority which deals a lethal blow to effective enforcement.

The quality of Antitrust Division lawyers is mixed. Division staff believe their overall caliber is as high as in any large government agency. Many of the trial staff are indeed extremely able, drawn to the Antitrust Division by its history of famous chiefs (Thurman Arnold, Robert Jackson, Thomas Clark), by the excitement of working on big cases of national impact, and by potentially high-paying jobs when they leave government. On the other hand, Robert Kennedy always turned to other Justice staff for his favored cases. Nicholas Katzenbach told the Study Group that the Tax and Civil Rights Divisions had far better attorneys, and Donald Turner always believed that the trial staff were generally incompetent.

There certainly is a layer of "deadwood" or "fat" in the legal staff. Many interviewees estimated that "30% do 90% of the work." Some of the incompetence traces to political appointments. Other attorneys, happily homeostatic in a government sinecure, have lost their zeal for public service or the law. One veteran complained that "the workload for many is nil," adding that the inactivity of older attorneys discouraged the younger staff. A former evaluator, Jonathan DuBois, said that "the judgments people were especially appalling, and it became a dumping ground. One judgments man whom I shared an office with would come to work late, leave early, take a morning coffee break, two-hour lunch breaks, and would leave every two hours to move his car so it wouldn't get a ticket." Another attorney with similar roommate problems reported them to a top Division official. He was told that fully "one in five" did very little work, but the Justice Department's dismissal procedures,* requiring a difficult burden of proof, left the Division no alternative but to tolerate them.

This response is inexcusable. A public-service job creates an obligation, and both employers and employees must realize the fact. Failure affects not merely the employee but others in society, victims of illegal schemes as well as the taxpayer whose money is wasted. If the public employee does not fulfill his obligation, the public treasury should be released from its obligation. This view accords with the Code of Ethics for Government Service, promulgated by Congress: ". . . 3. Give a full day's labor for a full day's pay; giving to the performance of his duties his earnest effort and best thought."

But firings for incompetence are extremely rare. Jerry Pruzan, formerly with the Division and now an FTC official, noted that "no one ever fails; you have to shoot your section chief to be ousted." Years ago it was different. Truman's outgoing Attorney General gave incoming Herbert Brownell a list of 100 lawyers in the Department, including some in the Antitrust Division, for whom he recommended release. All were called in and asked to resign; if they refused, they were told, charges of incompetence would be brought. All resigned. When Robert Kennedy asked Antitrust Chief Lee Loevinger for such a list, the AAG would not produce one. "Lee knew he'd only be there a few years and didn't want to be a son-of-a-bitch," according to a Division official. Orrick, too, was timid, especially since he had once, when he headed the Civil Division at Justice, been forced to go to court to remove his

---

* The legal staff at the Division are not Civil Service employees. Their grievance procedure is governed by Department of Justice regulations. Lawyers who are military veterans, however, do count as civil servants and can invoke the similar procedures of the Civil Service.

First Assistant. In the first five years of the Sixties there were two dismissals for incompetence. Each person left voluntarily. It has averaged less than one a year since then, according to Jack O'Donnell, former Executive Assistant at the Division.

If the employee does demand a hearing, it can be a lengthy process. In the interests of fairness to the employee, the Division must be prepared to pursue such a hearing. But in most cases, as the record shows, the employee will leave voluntarily, unwilling to endure hearings which air his ineptitude. Such charges must be carefully and selectively brought, and the hearing process vigorously retained, to avoid political purges or retaliatory firings. Judicious use of this penalty can arrest the trend of bureaucracy existing for its own sake, rather than for a public purpose.

Magnifying the problem of staff inefficiency is the under-utilization of staff by the Division hierarchy. Many of the lawyers interviewed simply had little to do. Thus, the Division is inefficient for what it *is* doing at the same time that it is too small for what it *should be* doing. A seven-year veteran at the Division believes that "Many of the staff, especially the younger staff—regardless of all the hand-wringing over 'lack of resources'—don't have enough work. And I hope you print that, since McLaren won't find out about it any other way." He went on to complain that this under-employment is bad for staff morale. "It's somewhat professionally degrading not to be kept busy, and the tone is set for less work per man hour throughout the Division." The plight of Tom Huyak, the trial attorney who never got to try a case in five years, is not unique. When an agency ends up trying an average of only 12.7 cases a year, it is difficult for over 200 litigating attorneys to gain trial experience or to maintain a full agenda.

Other attorney-personnel problems reduce enforcement productivity. "Working conditions are a disgrace," says the Deputy Director of Operations, Robert Hummel, noting that at times three or even four lawyers share one office and that secretarial support is very slim. Second, the size and delay of the cases severely sap an attorney's emotional energy. When a case is not brought after a year or two of investigation, or when a case is settled just prior to a scheduled trial, there is a severe psychological letdown. Leonard Henske, with the Division from 1965 to

1969, cites such frustration as the reason for his departure. He thinks that much of the deadwood problem is due not to incompetent but to "broken" men who have seen years of their professional lives wasted. Third, the annual turnover rate for attorneys is high, averaging 14.5% over the past six years. An attorney usually leaves after three to six years, just as he accumulates sufficient experience to begin making his most valuable contributions to the Division. He then earns between $17,761 (GS-13) and $24,251 (GS-15), when former law-school classmates in private firms are moving into the $30,000 bracket. William McManus, a veteran of 23 years, studied the Division personnel list and estimated that at least one-quarter of the legal staff will be eligible to retire within five years. Already there is a severe shortage of experienced trial attorneys, mostly due to the scarcity of trials and the three-to-six-year turnover period. Any acceleration of this loss of experience would seriously disrupt enforcement.

Finally, although some view Division lawyers as tigers who have to be held back, "they are quite traditional in the use of legal theory," says Robert Hammond, former First Assistant at the Division. The lawyers are attracted to the conceptually simple price-fixing and merger cases. They often resist the "new economics"—that structure predicts conduct and that product differentiation can be as important as price-fixing. Their orientation has a crucial bearing on enforcement, since approximately 90% of all investigations are started by the trial attorneys. It would be worthwhile to require that all staff unschooled in industrial economics take the equivalent of six semester hours in it. If it requires 1500 hours flight time to be a jet pilot and 300 training hours to be a competent bartender, 90 does not seem excessive when billions of dollars of commerce are involved.[4]

There is another kind of professional at the Division: economists. They are second-class citizens. They have little or no say in the type of cases brought, the legal theories used, or the relief sought. In general, they neither conduct long-range studies nor work closely with the policy-planning staff. Mostly they aid attorneys in the preparation of statistical data for trial, and they occasionally testify. They are technicians—"statisticians," as nearly all the lawyers call them—and act like it. One broke off an interview with us because, he explained as he hurried off to confer with an attorney, "my master called."

The competence of "economists," as compared to their counterparts at the FTC's Bureau of Economics or to the Division lawyers, is quite low. There are few Ph.D.s, and most have an economics background consisting of a number of courses in college. They do not publish, nor do they keep abreast of the current economic literature. (One candidly told us, "I'm from the old school; I don't understand it anyway.") Many of the economists are old, and one of the unit's own members characterized the economics section as a "home for the aged."

The insignificant work and poor personnel quality cripple recruitment efforts. Because the work is trivial, talented economists do not come; in turn, because the section lacks talented economists, it is not entrusted with important work. Harvard Professor William Comanor, for example, former special assistant to Donald Turner, told us that he would never advise any of his students to work in the economics section. Not even Donald Turner, a lawyer-economist who wanted to infuse antitrust with an economic emphasis, upgraded this section. Turner was dismayed by its low quality. "The introduction of this economics orientation," observed Professor Charles Havighurst, who did some consulting work for the Division, "has coincided with the virtual exclusion of the Division's Economic Section from the decision-making process." [5]

To arrest this trend, good young economists must be recruited by promising them a chance to conduct basic industry studies and to confer on major policy decisions. If the promise is kept, good people will arrive and antitrust enforcement will become sophisticated. Furthermore, more economists should be hired, improving on the present 9:1 ratio of lawyers to economists. It is irrational to have the structural economic policy of the country run by an agency top-heavy with non-economists.

There is one inescapable conclusion to be drawn from the Antitrust Division's budget and personnel levels: they are absurdly low. The remedy cannot be some slight incremental increase in appropriations, as now occurs, which merely enables antitrust enforcement not to fall even further behind in its task. As long as antitrust resources remain trivial, enforcement must be trivial and major anti-oligopoly suits are *per se* discouraged. If enforcement is to be more than a bipartisan homily, a commitment must be made to budget at least $100 million a year to antitrust efforts.

For many this will seem too much, but only because comparison is made to the existing budget rather than to what the Division budget ought to be or to other federal budgets. The country now spends over $30 billion a year —local, state, and federal—to combat street crime, surely one of our most serious social problems. The FBI is appropriated $257 million, largely in the same effort. But what of business crime, which in terms of net financial theft is more costly than all street crime? The electrical-conspiracy defendants alone in 1961 stole more money from overcharged consumers than the total of all "conventional" robberies in that year. And Chapter I emphasizes that the cost of the lost production of our structurally noncompetitive economy is between $48 and $60 billion. While no amount of money will enable us to attain perfect competition, $100 million will go a long way toward retiring our debt of billlions in corporate theft and monopoly/oligopoly. Twenty million (the combined Justice and FTC antitrust budgets) will not. Such a budgetary increase is a *sine qua non* for this payoff and for all the recommendations which follow: studying more mergers, filing more innovative and anti-oligopoly cases, litigating more cases, lessening delays, obtaining adequate relief, and increasing surveillance of and prosecution of price-fixers.

INFORMATION-GATHERING AND DELAY

Unlike murder or rape, an antitrust violation leaves no *corpus delicti*. Ferreting out the facts is an art and a chore. In order of their effectiveness, there are five basic ways of compelling disclosure of corporate information prior to filing a case:

(1) A grand jury can be empaneled when the Division has cause to believe a crime has been committed. It is by far the best investigatory tool the Division possesses. The grand jury can demand documents, and subpoena witnesses for cross-examination without their lawyers present. Because of the adverse connotations of being the subject of a

grand-jury inquiry, and because the Division fears calling too many grand juries which do not return indictments, not many grand juries are actually called. There were 26 in fiscal 1970 and 22 in 1969.

(2) Prior to 1962 there were three logically possible, but actually unproductive, ways to obtain information in civil cases: one could ask the firms to disclose information voluntarily, but, to no one's surprise, violators did not confess; the use of FTC investigatory powers for the benefit of the Attorney General, permitted by statute, was never attempted, "presumably because of the budgetary problems involved in making the FTC the investigative arm of the Department of Justice"; [6] or, lacking the necessary evidence, a suit could be filed in the hope that discovery proceedings would turn it up—the worst form of prosecutorial brinksmanship.

By the early 1960s many firms under investigation were refusing to supply any requested data to the Division. "The situation is getting steadily worse," Attorney General Robert Kennedy protested. "We are just not getting cooperation from the business community of the United States." [7] In 1962, and after several attempts, Congress finally passed a Civil Investigative Demand Act, which stated: "Whenever the Attorney General or Assistant Attorney General . . . has reason to believe that any person under investigation may be in . . . control of any documentary material relevant to a civil antitrust investigation, he may . . . issue . . . a civil investigative demand [CID] requiring such person to produce such material for examination." Violation of a CID request incurred a fine up to $5,000 or imprisonment up to five years, or both. As drafted and passed, however, the bill had grievous omissions: information could be obtained only from a firm "under investigation," not other parties or potential witnesses; the later release of information to private plaintiffs was forbidden; and there was no provision for "oral" CIDs—"deposing" the potential defendants and cross-examining them. While some Congressmen inveighed against "the prying eyes of a powerful bureaucracy," [8] the statute was needed to keep antitrust from going the way of the buffalo.

(3) Despite the availability of CIDs, the voluntary request for information has again become the primary way of uncovering information in civil cases. The use of CIDs,

after an energetic start, has drastically declined: in 1963 there were 127; in 1964, 254; 1965, 290; 1966, 97; 1967, 120; 1968, 105; 1969, 74; and 1970, 123. Voluntary requests are less formal and easier to draw up, do not need to be reviewed by the Director of Operations and the AAG, and hence can be sent out faster than CIDs. In that crucial Division parlance, "It saves resources." One staff attorney summarized the basis of this trend: "The goal is to make antitrust enforcement the least burdensome to defendants and to conserve our own resources."

This crippling attitude allows all kinds of toothless informal procedures to flower while stronger mechanisms wilt: consent decrees, no-contest pleas, and voluntary requests are preferred over litigation, guilty pleas, and CIDs. In each the sting of antitrust is cushioned, making enforcement less "burdensome" to defendants. Business likes voluntary requests, too, because they need not be complied with as rigorously as CIDs (there being no felony penalty for failure to cooperate) and because the destruction of incriminating documents is easier without the deterrence of a possible felony charge.

(4) The FBI often acts as an investigating arm of the Division when many people have to be interviewed in a short period of time—*e.g.,* 100 dealers on a pattern of manufacturer discrimination. A staff attorney lists the precise questions to be asked, and the FBI agent asks them. While a large volume of information can be obtained by this means, agents lack the background and expertise to pursue answers with appropriate follow-up questions.

(5) Finally, there are a number of ways a violation is initially uncovered. Complaints from consumers, competitors, or informers usually give the Division its first lead. Newspapers, trade journals, and reports of identical bidding are also reviewed for indications of illegal conduct and mergers. Very rarely, the policy-planning staff undertakes industry-wide studies.

Mechanisms (1) to (5) consume varying resources and produce varying results. But, taken together, it becomes clear that *it is extremely difficult, time-consuming, and costly to uncover even the most basic industrial information.* Even such a basic fact as the market share of the investigated firm—often the key determinant of a violation —is difficult to determine. Sometimes studying *Moody's* and annual reports will produce the data. Other times, however, due often to lack of division-by-division sales reports by corporations, the only way to get market-share data is to ask competitors *their* sales and profits. But there is no legal way to compel such information from firms not "under investigation."

The Executive Branch of government compounds the problem. Census Bureau figures, a potentially valuable source of information, consist of aggregations of *accounting* data which are not broken down into the relevant *economic* markets which are being sought. (For example, they may have a category called "drills," when the Division lawyer is studying the competitive submarket called "twist drills.") Also, census data per firm are not made available to sister agencies of government, because the Census Bureau claims that otherwise it would be too difficult to obtain any information. An internal Division report to AAG Lee Loevinger in 1961 explained the issue:

> Fundamentally, the Bureau appears to take the position that it is primarily, if not almost entirely, an organization set up for the benefit of businessmen, and that Government agencies are low on the totem pole insofar as cooperating with respect to furnishing information. . . . This is not a minor matter. Upon our ability to secure such information will often depend the success or failure of cases we bring involving the Sherman and Clayton Acts.

When the Supreme Court in late 1961 ruled that the FTC could see manufacturing data per firm, the Census Bureau and industry lobbyists euchred a bill through Congress overruling that decision. The Bureau argued that this restriction was needed to encourage disclosure of confidential information. Deference to business firms continues, therefore, for its own sake, not for any higher purpose. To make this data available to the Division, corrective legislation should be passed.

The lack of product-line or divisional data particularly impedes antitrust and competition. As conglomerates grew more numerous and big, it became important for antitrust agencies to know the sales and profits of the different prodducts of a firm. Hypothetically, it did the Division little good to know ITT's net profits if it studied the predatory pricing in the Rent-a-Car market (ITT owned Avis) or in the bread market (ITT owns Continental Baking Company). Furthermore, the economy itself requires such data, since the rise and fall of industries in a competitive economy occur in response to profit opportunities. Increasingly, potential entrants must make marketing decisions in total ignorance of the profit experience of firms already in the industry.

For years neither Congress nor the FTC nor the SEC did anything about this knowledge gap, although each had the power to act. Finally, at the urging of Senator Philip Hart, the SEC issued an order, effective in January, 1971, requiring companies to break down their pretax earnings by "lines of business" in their annual reports. While the direction of this reform is commendable, there are problems, as described by the *Wall Street Journal:*

> One catch is that the SEC allows companies considerable latitude in defining "lines of business," and unless a particular product line accounts total sales or pretax earnings, (15% in the case of companies with less than $50 million annual sales), it doesn't have to be reported separately. . . . And if you think General Motors is going to provide the pretax earnings of its Chevrolet, Pontiac, Cadillac, or Frigidaire divisions, forget it. It isn't likely that any of the Big Three—GM, Ford, or Chrysler—will break its earnings down further than "automotive and nonautomotive," which for analysis purposes will be practically useless since 90% or more of the three companies' business is automotive.[9]

In addition, the opposition of many businessmen to such a reporting requirement has generated a feeling that they will try to avoid cooperating with it. Some have said: "I'm dead opposed to all the burden of it"; "Why are you stirring this up?;" "If competitors know all about you, they can pick out your weakness . . ."; it will only "confuse" stockholders; and some want to "see what other companies are doing." [10]

An April, 1971, study by the FTC's Bureau of Economics, not as yet made public, documents the actual inadequacy of this reporting requirement. Sixty percent of the largest firms, those over $1.5 billion annual sales, are still able to report profit data based on a so-called "2-digit SIC Code"—a very vague industrial classification, like automotive and non-automotive. But only 23% of firms with $200–$500 million in sales were able to practice this corporate camouflage. Furthermore, 43% of small firms, those with $5 million in sales, reported their data in "7-digit classifications"—an extremely detailed category which goes beyond even divisional reporting. The SEC "lines of business" requirement, therefore, favors the large, diversified firms who are big enough to hide their divisional profits—precisely the firms most likely to be involved in antitrust actions.

But antitrust enforcement cannot act as the referee of our competitive economy if it does not know what the players are doing. This statistical ignorance is owed to two of our sillier economic shibboleths: America's aversion to socialism foments a distrust of any economic "planning," so that proposals to enlighten government about business activities invariably invite "Big Brother" responses; corporations have been able to transform the rights of personal privacy and trade secrets into a shield against the dissemination of "private" information. But does a GM or IBM, with larger gross revenues than most countries and having enormous impact on millions of people, have a right to "privacy"?

In any rational regime of economic competition, the opposite of corporate privacy and privilege must be true: divisional and profit data, and premerger information, should be freely available so that enforcement efforts are efficient and prompt. Support for such disclosure is as old as Theodore Roosevelt, who said in his first Inaugural Address: "Artificial bodies such as corporations depending upon statutory law for their existence or privileges should be subject to proper governmental supervision, and full and accurate information as to their operations should be made public at reasonable levels."

Consequently, we strongly recommend the creation of an Economic Information Center, so that intelligent "planning for competition" can occur. All publicly and privately held corporations would report sales and profit along divisional lines, as well as general data ranging from their investment accounts to advertising expenditures, to one computerized central information-storage system. Disappointingly, the FTC and SEC have had something resembling this power for years, but it has gone unused. The kind of data now reported to the SEC, Census, Bureau of Labor Statistics, IRS, and Commerce would be all housed under one roof. Government agencies would then be able at the push of a button to obtain a print-out of the data necessary for intelligent decision-making. Quickly, and with far less expenditure of resources, the Antitrust Division could tell what the market shares are, what an industry's concentration ratio is, what the actual economic effect of past cases has been, and, partly as a result, could decide what future cases should be filed. The need here is obvious. *"Antitrust inaction,"* italicized one writer, *"stems in large measure from precisely this lack of data."* [11]

Protracted proceedings also drain meager antitrust resources. This is a problem not only of antitrust today, but of legal justice traditionally. Dickens memorialized court delays in *Bleak House*. Further back, a lawsuit between Nuremberg and the electorate of Brandenberg began in 1526 and was undecided when the German court was dissolved in 1805. Although the Division is somewhat more expeditious, delayed proceedings are a widely acknowledged problem. It permeates all enforcement: Section 2 antimonopoly cases are avoided because of their anticipated length; consent decrees reflect the fear of time-consuming litigation; resources which could be deployed on creative case-making are devoted to the few cases which are brought; AAGs are discouraged from filing creative and difficult cases, knowing that any possible reward will occur years after their departure; and, paraphrasing Justice Brandeis, relief delayed becomes justice denied.

By excluding all cases settled within six months of filing, Richard Posner found that it took an average of 33 months during 1955–59 and 38 months during 1960–64 between the filing of a complaint and its resolution.[12] These statistics exclude the investigation time expended before the filing of a complaint. Based on the common estimate of one year investigating time before a complaint is filed, and on the more recent average of 29.5 months from complaint to disposition between 1965 and 1970,[13] *the average Division case takes about three and a half years from start to finish.* Merger and monopoly cases take quite a bit longer.

Examples of horribly unwieldy and protracted cases are easy to find. The present IBM case, already mentioned, is one. The 1945 *Alcoa* case had 15,000 pages of documentary evidence and took 20 years to resolve, although at issue was a firm with 100% of the market. *National Lead* two years later had 1,400 exhibits to be identified and authenticated. *Ferguson* v. *Ford Motor Company,* a private suit filed in 1948, entailed 100,000 pages of depositions from 173 witnesses, with some 700,000 pages of documents in all. The oil-cartel case of 1953 against the five biggest integrated oil companies accumulated 100,000 documents and took 13 years to decide—by a combination of ineffective decrees and dismissals; the case never did get out of pretrial proceedings. Longer yet is *El Paso Natural Gas:* filed in 1957, it has been to the Supreme Court four times and is still unresolved. Suits against GM for its bus monopoly and its acquisition of Euclid each took a decade to settle, without any litigation. While these are extreme examples, no comfort can be taken from the *average* merger or monopolization case. Kenneth Elzinga found that it took an average of 63.8 months—or over five years—from the time of an illegal merger to a final divestiture order. Richard Posner found the average length of a monopolization suit to be about eight years.

The causes of protracted proceedings are many. The various sectors involved—businessmen, lawyers, government attorneys, and judges—tend to blame each other, while the reality is that all combine to create the phenomenon.

First, time is money to the businesses charged. Every day that an illegal scheme or merger can be continued means additional profits to that firm, since there is no retroactive sanction. According to a *Fortune* reporter, renowned antitrust counsel Hugh Cox told his client DuPont to divest itself of its GM stock voluntarily in 1949 since he predicted, accurately, that they would lose the case. DuPont refused, proposing a full legal battle since there were many profits to be made in the interim. Interim profits plus inadequate enforcement personnel have an obvious result, as a *Newsweek* interview revealed: " 'The government can't hit everyone,' says a San Francisco executive, 'so a business goes ahead and does what it wants, if it isn't obviously crooked, and gambles that it won't get caught. There is no moral dimension to it. The odds are in your favor.' " Slowing down the proceedings has other benefits for defendants. Witnesses die, evidence and memory grow stale, markets change, and new administrations take over Washington—all of which can moot any relief or lead to a dismissal. Delay pays.

Second, defense counsel have made a legal art out of

delay, as their clients benefit by the profits of time and as they reap huge fees on a per-hour basis. The purpose and extent of intentionally dilatory tactics by defense counsel were discussed by many interviewees, none of whom desired to be quoted by name for their corroborating views:

> Antitrust is a game to private counsel. They think they can milk a client since they know it can take eight years for a resolution. They know no one will push them, so they take a free ride and travel around the country getting admissions and taking depositions—which alone can take three years.
> —Former Antitrust Division lawyer

> Delay—that's what they get paid for.
> —Antitrust Division trial lawyer

> Defense counsel tell their clients: if the Antitrust Division sues, you will lose, but you can still gain three to five years to make your profit or acquire know-how from the illegal merger. Delaying a government prosecution is justified on the theory of maybe getting a better deal next year. In private treble-damage suits the philosophy is consciously or semiconsciously to wear out the plaintiff.
> —Former Division lawyer, New York City defense attorney

> Delay? It's the greatest disgrace of the antitrust bar.
> —Wall Street antitrust lawyer

> Law firms do feel free to delay when it is in the best interests of their clients—which includes attacking everything with motions of very little factual basis. For example, one judge for all aspects of the case speeds it up, so you challenge such form of assignment. You will certainly lose, but will certainly add a month and a half to the litigation. Discovery and depositions are a rich field ("sorry, he's away; sorry, wrong man, etc.").
> —Former Division attorney, New York City defense attorney

These assessments were confirmed some years back by former judge and defense counsel Bruce Bromley, who in a burst of candor admitted what most of his colleagues disingenuously deny:

> Now I was born, I think, to be a protractor. . . . I quickly realized in my early days at the bar that I could take the simplest antitrust case that Judge Hansen could think of and protract it for the defense almost to infinity. . . . If you will look at that record [*United States* v. *Bethlehem Steel*], you will see immediately the Bromley protractor touch in the third line. Promptly after the answer was filed I served quite a comprehensive set of interrogatories on the Government. I said to

myself, "That'll tie brother Hansen up for a while," and I went about other business.[14]

Lawyers can also obstruct antitrust justice by developing so-called "document retention systems" which involve the burning of past corporate records to discourage investigations, by counseling clients to attempt schemes of doubtful legality, and even by aiding clients in overt antitrust violations. Case examples for all exist, to the extent that the respected District Court Judge John P. Fullam was prompted to tell an antitrust lawyers' convention:

> The antitrust field I think is an area where lawyers, perhaps without realizing it, come closest to the very limits of what is ethically proper. . . . On the defendant's side they are closer to the line in actually advising clients to cover up criminal activity. Some of the essays I have read in the *Antitrust Law Journal,* if you took out the word "antitrust" and substituted "prostitution" or "narcotics" you would think that the lawyer would be disbarred if he put into practice the views expressed.

Third, the Division staff on a case are usually undermanned and often lethargic. There is no real pressure on them to hurry a case along. Thus, when defense counsel request extensions of deadlines and postponements, as they frequently do, the trial staff usually comply. One young Division attorney was bitter at the mutual slowdown: "The Antitrust Division is lazy, with a tendency not to push things along. And defense counsel, of course, plays on this." In addition, the Division has a tendency to expand a case as it slows it down. The former veteran trial attorney Victor Kramer has blamed the government for "overtrying" cases, throwing everything possible into the complaint.[15]

Fourth, many judges are inept on antitrust cases.* The complex issues control them rather than vice versa, and a variety of expeditious pretrial procedures are often not exploited. In addition, judges are often indecisive with the

---

* A questionnaire was sent by the Study Group to all district-court judges in the United States; 43 replied wholly or in part. Thirty of 42 answered "no" to the question "Did you practice any antitrust law before your appointment to the bench?" Only eight out of 40 admitted to "any background in economics" prior to their appointments (one college course not counted as constituting "background"). When asked "Given the complexity and size of some antitrust cases, do you ever find yourself ill-equipped to deal with a large antitrust case?"—15 said "yes" while 20 said "no." The complete results of this questionnaire can be found in the Appendix.

difficult issues presented them, "afraid to make a damn fool of themselves" says a former staff attorney. According to the estimates of Baddia Rashid, present Director of Operations at the Division, most rulings come down six to eight months after trial, and he recalls cases which took over two years and pretrial motions which consumed over a year. Division trial attorney Sinclair Gearing mused in an interview, "If a jury is expected to render a verdict immediately after the trial has ended, why can't a federal judge do likewise?"

Finally, there is the inherent difficulty of the case itself. The controlling legislation, the Sherman and Clayton Acts, and legal concepts like "relevant market" and "conspiracy" are intentionally broad. When this generality is combined with the complexity of the issues, each side is insecure about what must be proven and how much is needed to prevail. As a result, both prosecution and defense tend toward a full soup-to-nuts case, with truckloads of statistics, witnesses, and documents. This tendency, however, overleaps necessity. All are conditioned to expect big cases when big money is at stake. The historical expectation that antitrust trials are lengthy thus becomes self-fulfilling.*

There has been much professional writing on possible solutions. From the *Prettyman Report* to the Judicial Conference in 1951 to the recent *Manual for Complex and Multidistrict Litigation*—whose epigraph reads, "There are no inherently protracted cases, only . . . inefficient procedures and management"—a number of worthwhile procedural suggestions have been made and attempted: pretrial conferences should be frequent, stipulating facts, eliminating false issues, dispensing with motions, and authenticating exhibits; all documents should be logically labeled and kept in a "documents depository"; the usually liberal discovery rules should be severely limited at the discretion of the judge; special "masters" should be utilized to handle special and extensive problems, such as fielding all the objections to motions and depositions; both pretrial and trial stages should be assigned to a single judge; strict deadlines should be imposed at every stage of the

* The Judges' Questionnaire asked judges to rank five factors in order of their responsibility "for delays involved in antitrust cases." Consolidating the 25 replies, the following order, most responsible to least, resulted: (1) defense counsel; (2) inherent in the case; (3) plaintiff counsel; (4) Antitrust Division; (5) judges.

pretrial meetings; multiple cases based on the same factual situation should be tried together. All these reforms stress that a judge should administer a big case as well as decide it.

Finally, more judges must be appointed to our district courts to remove the backlog of cases and expedite difficult cases. A more specific, far-reaching, and important judicial proposal was suggested by Victor Kramer.[16] He recommended the establishment of a National Antitrust Court to hear the more difficult and important antitrust cases. The Chief Justice of the Supreme Court, with the advice of the Judicial Conference, would appoint a panel of district-court judges who have shown themselves most capable at handling big antitrust cases. Along with their regular district-court duties, they would occasionally be assigned a selected antitrust case, either when a district-court judge certifies that the case is of nationwide importance, or when the Attorney General, with supporting memorandum, so certifies it. The Judicial Conference would then decide whether, and to whom, to assign the case. The plan has the virtue of sending the most important antitrust cases to those best equipped to deal with them. By rotating assignments among a number of judges who handle other litigation as well, it also avoids the defects which throttled the Commerce Court of 60 years ago. Those judges, dealing only with large commercial and regulatory cases, became coopted by those who constantly appeared before that court—which ignited a successful demand for its abolition. It is far less likely that a strict and able judge on the antitrust panel would be as obsequious to business interests as a Commerce Court judge or even as an average district-court judge today. And why a judicial rather than an administrative court? "That is because there is a judge in a robe sitting over it" was Thurman Arnold's reply to the same question in 1949; "an administrative tribunal taking drastic action against a powerful political group cannot survive." [17]

PRIORITIES

Having examined the Division's resource problems, what are its enforcement priorities—*i.e.*, where does it devote its limited resources? In its first year and a half, the staff of the Mitchell-Kleindienst Justice Department filled out time sheets gradated to every 10 minutes. When and if these are analyzed, they may tell Antitrust Division officials just how and where their resources are expended. Right now, however, the Division can neither gauge the empirical results of their lawsuits nor compute the precise input of their resources into different enforcement areas. In this respect, rational policy planning is far off.

Yet certain estimates are available. Baddia Rashid, Director of Operations, estimates that 30–40% of the Division's time is spent on anticompetitive conduct, 30–40% on mergers, 10% on monopoly cases, and some 10% on agency work. This breakdown is partially confirmed by the cases actually filed in the past six years (1965–70). There have been 149 cases involving price-fixing, 99 merger cases, and 38 monopolization cases.[18] Approximately half the cases dealt with conduct cases and half with structural cases.

This summary contrasts sharply with the five years 1960–64. Then there were 206 price-fixing cases (civil and criminal), 62 merger cases, and 45 monopolization cases—or approximately two-thirds conduct and one-third structure. The change may be partly due to AAG William Orrick, who in 1964 criticized the fact that fully 70% of pending matters concerned behavioral problems, such as price-fixing, while only 30% dealt with structural issues, such as mergers and monopolization. Part of his purpose in creating the Policy Planning section was to reverse this trend.

A more recent measure of Antitrust Division enforcement priorities can be made by matching antitrust cases brought between 1945 and 1970 against manufacturing industries as presented in Table A. Over this period 464 cases were brought against manufacturing firms, ranging from 66 cases against food and beverage companies to zero cases against tobacco firms. If the number of cases brought against an industry is a reasonable measure of the Division's concern about monopoly activities within that industry, the ranking of industries in Table A represents a rough picture of antitrust priorities since World War II.

Several ways to measure the costs of monopoly power have been put forward in economic literature. One commonly used measure, popularized by Arnold Harberger, is an estimate of the net dollar loss ("welfare loss") resulting from monopoly, without considering the difficult problem of comparing the utility of capital holders and consumers.

Management, Resources, Process   143

TABLE A * 19

INDUSTRY	RANK			
	1945–1970 Cases Brought	Welfare Loss	Excess Profits	Total Assets
1 Food & Kindred Products	66	12	7	6
2 Non-Electrical Machinery	53	3	4	4
3 Chemicals & Allied Products	41	2	2	5
4 Fabricated Metal Products	35	10	9	8
5 Electrical Machinery	28	11	11	7
6 Instruments & Related Equipment	28	9	12	16
7 Petroleum & Coal Products	26	1	1	1
8 Primary Metal Industries	26	4	3	3
9 Miscellaneous Manufacturing Industries	26	17	16	14
10 Printing & Publishing	25	8	10	12
11 Transportation Equipment	25	6	5	2
12 Stone, Clay & Glass Products	24	7	8	11
13 Apparel & Other Textile Products	16	20	20	15
14 Rubber & Plastic Products	16	14	13	17
15 Paper & Allied Products	10	5	6	10
16 Furniture & Fixtures	8	16	17	19
17 Lumber & Wood Products	5	15	15	13
18 Leather & Leather Products	5	19	19	20
19 Textile Mill Products	1	18	18	9
20 Tobacco Manufacturers	0	13	14	18

* These are two-digit Standard Industrial Classification Categories.

Table A presents a ranking of industries using the Harberger measure of welfare loss based on data from 1956.* This ranking provides a rough index of the priorities that economists might establish for antitrust action against different manufacturing industries. A ranking based solely on excess profits (using the value of profits which produce rates of return on capital investment above the minimum rate of return in manufacturing) is also shown in Table A; for the most part, it parallels the ranking derived from the Harberger measure.

Examination of Table A indicates some important differences between antitrust and economic rankings. It suggests that the Division has underprosecuted paper, tobacco, petroleum, transportation equipment, stone, clay and glass, and primary metals, in that order; and has overprosecuted

* This year was chosen because it was roughly midway between 1945 and 1970 *and* because it was neither a peak nor a trough of the business cycle.

food, apparel, miscellaneous manufacturing industries, fabricated metals, electrical machinery, and instruments, again in that order. Bringing most of its cases (about 15%) against the food industry, which ranks 12th in estimated welfare gains, strikes us as a misallocation. At the same time, bringing only 10 cases (2%) against the paper industry, which ranks fifth in welfare-gain possibilities, also seems a misuse of scarce resources.

In considering why the Antitrust Division's priorities seem to differ from those suggested by economics, Table A provides one important clue. Industries are ranked in the last column according to the value of their total assets in 1956. In all cases the underprosecuted industries listed above (paper, tobacco, etc.) rank *higher* according to total assets than their rank according to cases brought; all industries listed as relatively overprosecuted by the Division (food, apparel, etc.) are ranked *lower* according to total assets than their rank according to cases brought. This suggests that the total capitalization of an industry deters antitrust activity against that industry. Thus, for example, while the welfare-gains and excess-profits measures mark the petroleum industry as a prime candidate for antitrust enforcement, its top-ranking asset position may explain why it ranks eighth in terms of cases brought against it.

Until our suggested $100 million budget becomes a reality, the Division must refocus its enforcement aim away from "conduct" problems in local markets and toward the market "structure" of our most concentrated industries; this includes the regulated monopolies and appearances before regulatory agencies. Chapter 9 articulates the basis for the general campaign against monopoly and oligopoly. Offhandedly but only half humorously, the idea was well expressed by Vic Kramer in a recent public address. All Division lawyers should have a list of the 200 top industrial corporations by their desk, Kramer said. If a suggested case would lessen the market power of one of these 200, he said, it should be filed. But if it does not, forget it.

As through this world I've rambled, I've seen lots of funny men. Some rob you with a six-gun and some with a fountain pen.

—*Woody Guthrie, Pretty Boy Floyd*

5

Criminal Law and Corporate Disorder

Home-improvement and auto-repair frauds, supermarket underweighting and mislabeling, embezzlement and securities thefts, tax evasion and price-fixing—all comprise the world of the white-collar criminal. Coined and defined by sociologist Edwin Sutherland in the 1940s, white-collar crime is crime committed by businessmen, government officials, and professionals in their occupational roles. Rather than triggering visions of Richard Speck or Danny Escobedo, the culprits look like us, which is partly why the concept is difficult for many to digest. For example, white-collar crime never made it into Richard Nixon's "law and order" campaign. But Lyndon Johnson, to his credit, recognized it in 1967. Addressing Congress on the occasion of the release of his Commission on Law Enforcement and the Administration of Justice, he announced that "the economic cost of white-collar crime . . . dwarfs that of all crimes of violence."

This assessment should hardly be surprising. Millions of dollars are involved in antitrust crime, government kickbacks, and securities frauds, but how many million-dollar bank robberies are there? Still, white-collar crime is largely ignored by a populace conditioned to imagine a rapist or rioter when the word "crime" is uttered. Especially difficult to establish is the fact of *corporate antitrust crime,* a subcategory of white-collar crime which involves premeditated business practice. Having shucked off its robber-baron image of 75 years ago—"You don't suppose you can run a railroad in accordance with the statutes, do you?" Arthur Vanderbilt had said—the corporate community today commands respect as concerned, hard-working, and law-abiding "pillars of the community." Business statesmen populate urban task forces, churches, and charitable boards; they initiate job training for minorities and decry pollution with the rest of us.

Yet how are we to distinguish between the pillars and pillagers of the community? For the reality of antitrust crime can be as hidden as a card-up-the-sleeve. After relieving Colonel Vanderbilt of much money by business chicane some decades back, businessman Daniel Drew vowed that he would never again defraud a powerful victim. Instead Drew declared that henceforth he would confine himself to those consumers scattered throughout the community, those who could neither recognize their plight, organize, nor fight back. This vow, anecdotally, explains both the prevalence and invisibility of corporate economic crime. When one person is robbed face to face, the injustice and indignity are obvious. But when millions are deceived in a complex economic structure, when pinpointing blame is difficult if not impossible, when crime grows so impersonal that it becomes "technical"—then we lose our perception of the criminal act.

The moral and legal content of an act, however, should not depend on our distance from the victim. The plotter of a kidnapping who stays in his retreat is as guilty as he who commits the actual act. So too with businessmen who knowingly raise prices or divide markets to pocket extra income at the expense of everyone else. The impact of the scheme is the thing—*e.g.,* a kidnapping or price-hike—not how complex the perpetrators can make it.

When recognized for what it is, corporate crime is more costly in both economic and social terms than street crime. The street criminal dents our pocketbooks and security. The business criminal, however, sabotages our body politic, social ideals, and economic structure. For, unlike his street equivalent, he violates our trust and, consequently, inspires mistrust. If nothing else, the street robber usually robs from necessity and promises us nothing. The suite robber robs from want, after taking us into respectable confidence. "If the word 'subversive' refers to efforts to make fundamental changes in a social system," Edwin Sutherland once noted, "the business leaders are the most subversive influence in the United States."

It has been said that one can tell how civilized a society is by the way it treats its criminal defendants. Such a sentiment, no doubt, envisioned a street criminal in the defendant's chair. The adage, for different reasons, is equally applicable when corporate defendants are on trial. For once institutionalized favoritism affects law enforcement, once the wealthy are treated differently because they are considered a different class of citizens, a cornerstone of our system—equal justice under law—is yanked out from under the legal edifice. It is a situation engendering cynicism and disrespect in those less able to fend. "The law," muttered a Blackstone Ranger recently. "When last you hear of a millionaire going to the electric chair? When last you hear of the president of one of those big old corporations going to jail for fixing prices or selling people rotten meat or even for income-tax evasion. When you hear anything like that?"

BUSINESS ETHICS

Not very often, although the old-style businessmen in the Upton Sinclair and Ida Tarbell critiques have not entirely disappeared. In 1949 Edwin Sutherland published his now classic *White Collar Crime,* a study of crime committed by "persons of respectability and high social status," for whom "a violation of the legal code is not necessarily a violation of the business code." Sutherland found such crime and

attitudes prevalent. He considered 60% of the 70 corporations he studied in depth "habitual criminals"—*i.e.,* those
having four convictions or more, with most of them coming
in the 10 years before his study. Slightly over 97% of the
corporations were "recidivists," with at least two convictions. He went on to conclude that "practically all large
corporations engage in illegal restraint of trade, and . . .
from half to three-fourths of them engage in such practices
so continuously that they may properly be called 'habitual
criminals.' " [1]

This view of business ethics was reaffirmed by a 1961
Harvard Business Review survey. Seventeen hundred executive readers, 34% of the magazine's 5,000 circulation,
replied to the questionnaire. About four out of seven respondents to one question believed that businessmen "would
violate a code of ethics whenever they thought they could
avoid detection." One-half of the respondents agreed that
"the American business executive tends to ignore the great
ethical laws as they apply immediately to his work. He is
preoccupied chiefly with gain." [2] And when asked, "In your
industry are there any [accepted business] practices which
you regard as unethical?" four-fifths responded affirmatively.
That same year a corporate executive convicted of an antitrust violation told the *Wall Street Journal* in an interview,
"One of the problems of business is what is normal practice,
not what is the law. If it is normal practice, it's ethical—
not legal, but ethical.[3] Finally, the Businessmen's Questionnaire sent by the Study Group asked recipients if they
agreed with a statement by a GE executive that price-fixing
is illegal but *not* immoral: Over a quarter agreed. "At Car-
thage," Greek historian Polybius noted two millennia ago,
"nothing which results in profits is regarded as disgrace-
ful." [4]

While the corporate sector is far from ethically pure, the
precise amount of criminal antitrust activity is difficult to
gauge. One empirical fact is that some five to 25 criminal
antitrust indictments are filed each year, but that tells little.
Educated speculation must substitute for prevalency studies,
which have never been attempted.

First, many consider industrial collaboration to be the
inevitable result of competitive capitalism. One businessman testifying before the FTC candidly confessed the prevailing situation:

When two businessmen get together, whether it is a chain institute meeting or a bible class meeting, if they happen to belong to the same industry, just as soon as the prayers have been said, they start talking about the conditions in the industry, and it is bound definitely to gravitate, that talk, to the price structure in the industry. What else is there to talk about? [5]

After the electrical manufacturers were convicted, the president of Allen Bradley, Inc., one of those involved, said: "No one attending the gatherings was so stupid he didn't know the meetings were in violation of the law. But it is the only way business can be run. It is free enterprise." [6]

The encouragement at trade-association meetings for all to raise their prices, camouflaged in speeches on poor profit margins of all the members, is legion. And many firms oxymoronically believe, as did the Allen Bradley president, that price-setting is essential to competition: In 1959 the Antitrust Division actually got a letter from a group of businessmen who had gotten together to set prices and who wanted to know what action could be taken against a participating member who was not living up to the agreement! [7] A book entitled *Profitable Oil Jobbing,* written for petroleum marketers, unabashedly notes that:

The jobber who is engaged in community affairs will have opportunities to become better acquainted with his competitors. Such friendly contacts can help avoid bitter misunderstandings. A disastrous price war can be avoided by friendly competitors who are willing to discuss a situation instead of taking angry reprisals for real or fancied wrongs.[8]

Finally, in utter naiveté, one trade association wrote to its members: "We are advised by our attorneys that it is all right for us to set uniform prices as long as we don't put the agreement in writing." [9]

The vast scale of the electrical-manufacturing conspiracy of 1961, involving nearly every firm in that industry, startled many complacent antitrust watchers who had intoned that price-fixing was non-existent, even unnecessary, in an oligopolistic industry. One defendant in the case commented, "Conspiracy is just as much 'a way of life' in other fields as it was in electrical equipment." When businessmen were asked in our questionnaire if they agreed with this assertion, 46.8% of the replies from the 500 top industrials agreed, while a huge 70.5% of the second-500-firm respondents agreed. Due to the increased number of informers and co-conspirators who came forward to the Antitrust Division, spurred on by the publicity over the electrical case, First Assistant Bob Wright reasoned that price-fixing was far more frequent than government enforcers had imagined. The only scholarly attempt to estimate the extent of price-fixing concluded—based on the electrical-manufacturing situation, an analysis of state and federal enforcement, and scrutiny of TNEC (Temporary National Economic Committee, 1940) records—that "it is apparent that price-fixing is quite prevalent in American business." [10]

Federal enforcement each year attacks only a small number of antitrust criminal activities. The pattern and consistency of violations, when combined with the inadequate budget of the Antitrust Division, has led two well-placed observers 20 years apart to come to identical conclusions: Attorney General Tom Clark said in 1949 that "the effectiveness of the enforcement of the antitrust laws is sort of like an iceberg . . . about 96% under water"; [11] and in 1970 Harold Kohn, a noted plaintiff's antitrust counsel, told a Senate subcommittee that, based on the number of violations which are discovered, "I would suspect what we unearth is like the tip of the iceberg and the rest is below the surface." [12]

Although the number of cases prosecuted each year is actually small—averaging 25 a year from 1960 to 1964, and 11 a year from 1965 to 1970—the total number of industries involved in criminal antitrust acts in the past 30 years is quite large. Nearly every conceivable industry has been affected, from milk and bread to heavy electrical equipment, from lobster fishing, shrimping, and the cranberry and chrysanthemum industries to steel sheets and plumbing fixtures. This large volume, plus the fact that the industries implicated are in no significant way unlike many others, suggest that their illegal acts are practiced elsewhere—without detection.

The business community takes umbrage at such estimates. They often see antitrust as antibusiness (one-half of the respondents to the Businessmen's Questionnaire did) and are dismayed by laws which make some of their clan out to be criminals. John T. Cahill, well-known Wall Street lawyer, protested in 1952 against the bringing of *any* criminal cases, giving as one reason that they aided Communist propaganda.[13] More recently the president of Morton Salt told a business group what many of their ilk feel: that all businessmen should band together to support any of their number accused of an antitrust violation, and that any successful defense of an antitrust suit is a victory for business as a whole.[14] The general complaints of businessmen against criminal antitrust suits follow:

(1) "The law is so complex that an innocent businessman could be indicted." This canard is contradicted by actual enforcement. Cases are filed only against clearly established violations (the so-called *per se* cases like price-fixing, market divisions, and boycotts), and only against individuals who broke the law knowingly. Furthermore, one suspects that a large reason for the very high percentage of no-contest pleas in criminal cases is that the defendants were caught and knew it.[15]

(2) "There is no moral wrongdoing to justify criminal sanctions." When labor leaders violate the trust of their union members by appropriating funds, all would agree that a criminal and immoral breach has occurred. Breach of consumer trust, by corporations who appropriate additional profits by means of price-fixing, is equally blameworthy. The nature of the crime is complex, the harm vast but diffuse, and the victim not readily apparent. But the damage is real, often involving millions and billions of dollars transferred from consumer pocketbooks into corporate coffers. And, regardless of the collar color of the perpetrator, antitrust violations do involve "moral turpitude." Lee Loevinger, during his term of office, expressed this view well:

> It should now be clear that a deliberate or conscious violation of the antitrust laws is not a mere personal peccadillo or economic eccentricity, but a serious offense against society which is as immoral as any other act that injures many in order to profit a few. Conspiracy to violate the antitrust laws is economic racketeering which gains no respectability by virtue of the fact that the loot is secured by stealth rather than by force.[16]

(3) "The defendants are not criminals but respected citizens." So were Bobby Baker and Billy Sol Estes, until caught. To the extent that many businessmen and much of the public holds this view, the Justice Department and the media have failed to communicate the pervasiveness and

impact of corporate crime. Justice Department press releases luridly describe names and individual charges against organized-crime defendants—but not against antitrust indictees; and there is often lavish pretrial publicity in the political-dissident cases—but not in antitrust cases. Coverage of white-collar crime is constantly underplayed by the media as compared to the street crimes—murder, rape, drugs, and demonstrations—which dramatically grab the headlines. For example, in 1961 the *New Republic* discovered that of 22 large newspapers surveyed the day after the 29 electrical-conspiracy defendants had pleaded *nolo contendere* or guilty, only four put the story on their front pages, four had one column of type on it in the inside pages, 10 had less than a column on the inside, and four well-known newspapers entirely failed to cover the story—the *Boston Globe*, the *New York Daily News*, the *Christian Science Monitor*, and the *Kansas City Times*. *Newsweek* gave it six inches of space, *Time* four inches, and *U.S. News and World Report* gave it none at all.[17] Five days later, after sentencing had occurred and seven executives were sent to jail, 20 newspapers, with one-fifth of all the newspaper circulation in the United States, were surveyed: 45% kept the sentencing off the front page, and, according to a comment in the *Yale Law Journal*, "None of the newspapers emphasized that the corporations were actually guilty of committing crimes." [18] Why the muted coverage? Sutherland once answered that the media is an industry too. "Public opinion in regard to pickpockets would not be well organized," he said, "if most of the information regarding this crime came to the public directly from the pickpockets themselves." [19]

(4) "The spectacle of a trial is severely damaging to a defendant, even if later acquitted." However true, it is an ancillary cost of all criminal enforcement. The only way to avoid it is not to indict anyone, or guarantee that only the guilty are indicated—which is the purpose of a trial. Yet even the extent of this complaint is slim: in the past two decades fully 88% of those indicted were convicted.

While many corporations complain about antitrust laws and/or criminally violate them, many others (there is some overlap) institute intrafirm programs aimed at wiping out antitrust illegality. According to the replies from our Businessmen's Questionnaire, for example, 43 of 51 firms listed in *Fortune*'s top 500 had such programs, and 30 of 56 in the second 500 did. Effective programs can include the following: a written statement of corporate antitrust policy; pamphlets explaining the operations of, and importance of, the antitrust laws; warnings about the legal consequences and firm disciplinary measures to be taken if a violator is found out; a procedure for contacting the firm's legal-counsel section if a question should arise concerning certain practices; and workshops and seminars. Unfortunately, some programs include document destruction—the burning of old and unnecessary files which might contain evidence of some antitrust indiscretion.

Even more unfortunately, such programs often exist without any behavioral effect. General Electric had Policy Directive 20.5 since 1946, forbidding illegal antitrust activities through all levels of the corporate hierarchy. Thus, either the directive was flagrantly disobeyed or it was never meant to be followed. After the convictions in 1961, the *Wall Street Journal* noted that "the violations were known and condoned at the highest echelons of the companies, or else the top officials were not acquainted with important aspects of their business." [20]

CASE STUDIES

Based on Richard Posner's statistics, of the 1,551 separate cases brought by the Antitrust Division between 1890 and 1969, 694 have been criminal cases, 45% of the total.[21] The trend has been toward fewer criminal prosecutions in recent times: in 1940–49, 58% of the cases were criminal; in 1950–59, 48% were criminal; and in 1960–69, 31% were criminal. In fiscal 1970, Richard McLaren and John Mitchell filed a total of five criminal cases, a mere 9% of the 59 total cases brought. Of the criminal cases filed and disposed of from 1890 to 1969, 57% have been settled by acceptance of a *nolo contendere* (no-contest) plea, 21% by a guilty plea or conviction, and 22% by acquittals and dismissals. Adding the first two statistics, there has been a 78% conviction rate in all criminal antitrust cases brought in the 80 years of antitrust history. While the number of criminal cases brought has recently decreased, the conviction percentage has gone up: from 78% in the 1940s, to 89% in the 1950s and 88% in the 1960s.

154

Although the absolute level of criminal enforcement is dwindling, and although the extent of punishment, as discussed later, is feeble, there have been some significant criminal cases in the last decade. Three of the more notorious cases follow.

(1) Electrical Equipment Manufacturing Cases

The conspiracy began sometime in the mid-1940s, when various electrical manufacturers met at the annual meeting of the National Electrical Manufacturers' Association. These meetings traced back to the New Deal–OPA days, "but instead of discussing pricing under government controls," noted one commentator, "the conspirators turned to fixing prices among themselves." [22] By the 1950s there were some 19 little cartels fixing prices and allocating markets in numerous products, from $2 insulators to multimillion-dollar turbine generators. Nearly every firm in the industry participated at one time or another, with General Electric and Westinghouse being the most prominent conspirators. During the period of the conspiracy, some $7 billion of equipment sales were implicated.

Meetings to coordinate the conspiracy took place in a variety of obscure bars and expensive hotels on the Eastern Seaboard.* Many of the conspirators aped the intelligence establishment by their clandestine techniques: they would never list their employer when registering at hotels; they would never breakfast with another conspirator; only pay phones would be used; all communications would be sent in plain envelopes to home addresses, to avoid unreliable secretaries; and they would never tell their lawyers anything. When someone in the GE organization would worry about Chairman Ralph Cordiner's Directive 20.5, which strongly forbade antitrust violations, "They would be told it doesn't apply now," said one conspirator; "we understood this was what the company wanted us to do." [23] One GE executive later explained that "the boys could resist everything but temptation."

The conspiracies were of two types—open bids and sealed bids. Open bids were sales to the private sector, ac-

---

* In 1957 a major meeting, apportioning the TVA 500,000-kilowatt contract to GE, occurred at the Barclay Hotel in New York. Three years later this hotel suavely advertised itself in *The New York Times;* "Antitrust-corporation secrets are best discussed in the privacy of an executive suite at the Barclay."

counting for $55–$60 million per year. They were based on classic price-fixing, with frequent meetings (35 in 1959 alone) to set the price. Sealed bids involved the submission of bids for jobs to public agencies, which the member firms divided up among themselves according to what they called the "phase of the moon system." All the companies would submit very high bids; but one firm, chosen in advance by a schedule based on the lunar cycle, would submit a slightly lower bid and obtain the commission. When each firm's "phase" arrived, it reaped the illegal returns. The spoils were divided according to a strict formula: in switchgears, for example, involving $650 million in sales during 1951–58, GE got 45%, Westinghouse 35%, Allis-Chalmers 10%.

The result of these machinations was grossly inflated prices. Generator prices rose 50% from 1951 to 1959, while wholesale prices on all commodities rose only 5%. The Senate Small Business Committee later asserted that Westinghouse had bilked the Navy by a 900% overcharge on certain gear assemblies, and that GE had charged 446% too much on another contract.

The Antitrust Division first became interested in the situation when the TVA complained to Senator Estes Kefauver about the frequent submission of identical bids by American companies. Although the Division had investigated various aspects of the electrical-equipment industry in 1949–50 and again in 1952–53 without any results, they convened a grand jury in Philadelphia on the suspect pricing patterns. A general probe to the I-T-C Circuit Breaker Company firm arrived at the desk of Nye Spencer, a local sales manager and, as it turned out, secretary for the switchgear conspiracy. Spencer, incredibly, had kept memoranda of the meetings to train his assistant. When the subpoena arrived, he turned over all the incriminating evidence rather than multiply his crimes by document destruction. Then, in late 1959, Paul Hartig of GE, a lower-level executive, admitted his role in the insulator price-fix to the grand jury. His testimony implicated Ray Smith, a GE vice president, in the far bigger transformer cartel. After Smith was fired by GE, he fingered William Ginn, his boss and head of GE's turbine division. With these two leads, the case clicked open like a safe.

Indictments began to be handed down in February, 1960, and by the end of the summer 29 corporations and 45 executives had been charged with price-fixing, bid-rigging, and market-splitting. Many observers, despite the magnitude of the crime, expected the court to accept no-contest pleas from the defendants, but Division Chief Robert Bicks and Attorney General Rogers made unique appeals to ward it off. Bicks personally went to Philadelphia to oppose acceptance of the no-contest pleas and Rogers sent a letter to the judge arguing that enforcement would suffer if guilty pleas were not demanded. Judge J. Cullen Ganey agreed. Division and defendant lawyers then negotiated a settlement: of the 20 total indictments (involving multiple defendants), defendants would plead guilty in seven cases while they could plead no contest in the remaining 13 cases.

On February 6, 1961, sentencing began. Judge Ganey's review of the case chilled the courtroom:

> This is a shocking indictment of a vast section of our economy, for what is really at stake here is the survival of the kind of economy under which America has grown to greatness, the free enterprise system. The conduct of the corporate and individual defendants alike . . . flagrantly rocked the image of [this] economic system . . . and destroyed the model which we offer today as a free world alternative to state control and eventual dictatorship.

First to step forward was John H. Chiles, 57, a vice president and division manager of Westinghouse, a senior warden of St. John's Episcopal Church in Sharon, Pennsylvania, vice president of his United Fund drive, and "the benefactor of charities for crippled children and cancer victims," according to his lawyer. Judge Ganey sentenced him to 30 days in the Montgomery County Jail. Despite attorney protestations against sending their clients to jail with the likes of embezzlers and thieves, Judge Ganey sentenced six more individuals to 30-day jail terms. Twenty others received suspended sentences. In all, $1,954,000 in fines was assessed. GE paid out $437,500, Westinghouse $372,500, while the individual defendants were fined only $1,000 to $12,500 apiece. It was the first time in the 70-year history of the Sherman Act that officials of "big business" had been sent to prison.

The indicted had been convicted. Yet what of the top management of the corporations, like GE's Cordiner? In court, GE counsel Gerhard Gesell stressed that the case involved derelictions of individuals, not of the company.

The next defense lawyer, however, in pleading for clemency for his individual client, said the defendant "only followed long-established company policy by getting together with supposed competitors, to arrange their business." He added that "there is such a thing as business compulsion, as corporate coercion. . . . There is such a thing as atmosphere, there is such a thing as knowing acquiescence in a situation." [28] Judge Ganey affirmed this assessment:

> In a broader sense, [the companies] bear a grave responsibility for the present situation, for one would be most naive indeed to believe that these violations of the law, so long persisted in, affecting so large a segment of industry and, finally, involving so many millions upon millions of dollars, were facts unknown to those responsible for the conduct of the organization.[29]

It was about this time—December 10, 1960, exactly— that the National Association of Manufacturers proclaimed Ralph Cordiner its man of the year.

(2) The Quinine Cartel

The basic facts of this international cartel were broken open by the Senate Antitrust Subcommittee in 1967 after it had managed to obtain secret minutes of 17 meetings held by the conspirators. The product involved was quinidine, a chemical derivative of quinine. The Subcommittee estimated that it was used by a quarter-million people in this country, most by the elderly in order to maintain normal heart rhythm. Therefore, when the retail price of quinidine jumped 300 to 600% in 1964–65, it was cause for alarm.

The cartel traces back to an 1892 agreement between Dutch and German quinine processors. By 1913 the European quinine manufacturers and the producers of Javanese bark (from which quinine comes) had divided the world markets among themselves. Fifteen years later the international and American conspirators were indicted for antitrust transgressions, which had a complete lockhold on world quinine. The case was settled by a companion consent decree, which, as it turned out, did little to arrest the cartel's activities.

It became reactivated in 1959–62 when the 17 meetings were held by the conspirators in Paris, London, Hamburg, and Brussels. According to John Blair in the Subcommittee report, the cartelists "entered into a series of restrictive agreements designed to control prices, distribution, and production in every aspect of the quinine industry," with a key objective being "the elimination of competition among the various producers in securing the U.S. stockpile." The stockpile was 13.8 million ounces of quinine which the United States declared as surplus in 1955 and which the General Services Administration (GSA) planned to dispose of to private firms. Between 1958 and 1962 secret negotiations occurred among the GSA, the State Department, and the Dutch Embassy, with the last acting for the cartel. The Dutch Embassy asked for the entire quantity, and the State Department was not averse because, according to the GSA Administrator at the meetings, "[it] has indicated that it would strenuously oppose domestic sales of the stockpile as this would seriously disturb relations with the Netherlands and with the Government of the Republic of Indonesia."

As a result of the complicity of GSA and State, the cartel was able to corner about 90% of the surplus quinine —despite the fact that the Small Business Administration and the Comptroller General had committed GSA to sell half the surplus to small business. The result: Nedchem, the Dutch firm acting for the conspiracy, bought the quinine for 21¢ per ounce, although the GSA listed its book value as 63¢; by the end of 1964 the cartel was reselling the 21¢ quinine at more than $2 per ounce; by the end of 1966 it was more than $3. After obtaining the quinine for the cartel, Nedchem then double-crossed its co-conspirators and dissolved the cartel which it had created. This Dutch firm shared its world monopoly only with a German firm, leaving the French and British members of the cartel with no quinine and without legal redress, for one cannot enforce an illegal agreement.

"Where does the blame lie?" asked Senator Hart, who ran the hearings which uncovered this evidence. "Principally," he said, "in the operations of an international cartel, with the Dutch firm in the driver's seat . . . [and] in the State Department, [which] rendered valuable assistance to the cartel."

(3) Plumbing Fixtures

"A trail of deceit, blackmail, and stupidity led some of them to jail," [26] read the sub-headline to the *Fortune* magazine article on this most recent and momentous price-fixing conspiracy. It involved 15 manufacturers of plumbing fixtures, from the 76-employee Georgia Sanitary Pottery firm to American Standard, with more than $1 billion in sales a year. In all, bathtubs, sinks, and toilets worth more than $1 billion were affected by the illegal activity. The plumbing-fixture industry had actually been fixing prices since the 1920s, with two major interruptions. A 1940 case against some of their members shattered the organization, and a slumping market for housing construction in the late 1950s led to a break-up of the cartel. As one conspirator later confided in an interview to the Study Group, "From 1957 to 1961 was the only period that you had what you could call really American-style competition. . . . That was the only time that there was any significant improvement in the product and product methods."

In late 1961 the industry reverted to its mood of cooperation. The first meeting was held a mere six months after the seven electrical executives had earned their convict status. Meetings occurred under the auspices of the Plumbing Fixtures Manufacturing Association (PFMA); after the legitimate business had been dispatched, the conspiracy reconvened at rump sessions. The first meetings in 1961 and 1962 were held without the bigger firms in attendance. *Fortune* described their caper:

> The conspirators were like members of Alcoholics Anonymous, Pope [a conspirator] remarked. They had to meet repeatedly to "reassure" themselves. As the meeting broke up, Oscar Gerber warned the others not to allow incriminating memoranda to creep into their files, and Stan Backner cautioned a colleague not to throw votes in the wastebasket. They departed in a jovial mood.[27]

By late 1962 the major companies, which produced both the high-quality enamel and lower-quality china fixtures, had joined in. There were two rapid and profitable results: prices on enameled cast-iron bathtubs increased 7%; then the united industry convinced the Bureau of Standards in the Commerce Department to change its "bathtub standard" so that only the more expensive acid-resistant enamel tubs, not regular enamel tubs, could be produced. This action, successful in July, 1963, reduced consumer choice and compelled purchase of the higher-priced model, thereby making the conspiracy easier to manage and the illegal profits even more lucrative.

William Kramer, the executive secretary of PFMA, was centrally involved in uncovering the conspiracy. Kramer bugged some of the conspirators' meetings for self-serving purposes. When the PFMA threatened to fire and expose Kramer, he in turn threatened to release his tapes. Having failed to browbeat him, the Association tried to bribe him with a 10-year $50,000-per-year contract if he would keep quiet. Kramer instead resigned his position and left the country.

Meanwhile the IRS was investigating him and came to his former office to locate canceled salary checks. As they were leaving, Stan Backner, the new executive secretary and an active conspiracy member, made a friendly gesture. "By the way," he said, pointing to Kramer's old desk, "I'm throwing out a bunch of Kramer's stuff. Want to take a look at it?" [28] They did and, to Backner's dismay, found three of Kramer's secret tape recordings. With these as leads, the Justice Department empaneled a grand jury. Kramer, tired of lamming and hopeful of official leniency, sent in 16 more tapes and surrendered. In the summer of 1966 the grand jury returned 18 indictments.

All entered guilty pleas except for three corporations— American Standard, Borg-Warner, and Kohler Company —and three individuals, who pleaded not guilty and who went on trial in 1969. The jury found all guilty. The three convicted individuals and five other individual defendants who had pleaded no contest served jail sentences up to 30 days. Fines totaling $752,500 were paid by the firms, with five of them paying the $50,000 maximum.

From this partial list of antitrust criminality, conclusions of general applicability emerge. In each, the ethic of the unfettered marketplace quashed all notions of legal and public respectability. The everyday consumer was cheated. He paid more for such necessities as bathroom fixtures, electrical bills, and medical supplies. All involved government complicity prior to government crackdown: price paternalism in the OPA led to price-fixing in the electrical industry; the State Department and GSA willfully aided the Dutch quinine cartel; and the Bureau of Standards formalized the plumbing price-fix by its helpful bathtub standard.

Two cases prominently featured trade associations as

vehicles for the conspiracy. Bringing together all members of an industry, trade associations are ideal tools for criminal collaboration. In electrical machinery and plumbing fixtures, the members met to fix prices. Others engage in "product-fixing." Thus, the 1969 case against the Automobile Manufacturers Association (settled by a consent decree) charged "the suppression of antipollution exhaust devices." And the Air Transport Association, in a situation which has not yet attracted an antitrust suit, arranged to have its members tell their respective states that they would not be able to attach antipollution devices except to one type of engine.

The basic problem is trade-association structure. Adam Smith long ago said, "People of the same trade seldom meet together, even for merriment and diversion, but the conversation ends in a conspiracy against the public, or in some contrivance to raise prices." Robert Cassner, a vice president of the Crane Company, one of the plumbing defendants, flatly stated that the only reason for a trade association is to fix prices. Fully 44% of all criminal antitrust cases filed in the history of the antitrust laws have involved trade associations.[34]

Given the actual frequency of trade-association dereliction, the structural likelihood that it will be so inclined, and continuous histories of trade-association criminality (40 years in plumbing, broken up by the 1940 convictions), strict punishment should be inflicted on them in criminal antitrust cases. Wherever the trade association is a vehicle for an illegal conspiracy, it should then be abolished. Professor Oppenheim's treatise *Federal Antitrust Laws* observes that "Unless trade associations promote competition, and except as they do so, there is little justification for their existence." For example, in the 1971 settlement to the Division's civil suit against the plumbing manufacturers, the Plumbing Fixtures Manufacturers Association was dissolved and its members barred for 10 years from belonging to any other trade group whose membership is solely plumbing-fixture producers. Such a penalty is especially appropriate for marketing-personnel trade associations, which lack the occasional benefits— exchange of technology and needed standardization—that can justify the existence of other associations.

"Competition has survived," Walter Lippmann has commented, "only where men have been unable to abolish it." [30] In these cases at least, especially the electrical and plumbing cases, those who were guilty did suffer. Some actually went to jail and all paid fines. In this respect these studies were misleading, for the overwhelmingly frequent situation is that antitrust violators do not go to jail, do pass go, and do collect $200—even when found guilty.

COSTS/BENEFITS—CRIME PAYS

Any system based on deterrence intends that when a potential transgressor contemplates a crime, the risk of getting caught and the punishment when caught will outweigh in his mind any anticipated benefits if not caught. If this balance is close or if the benefits exceed the costs, the deterrent is a failure. The system of antitrust sanctions is such a failure. The possible profits so outweigh the possible penalties that widespread noncompliance is inevitable.

The possible benefits are obvious: excessive profits. "According to the various empirical studies conducted in this area," writes one antitrust analyst, "[price-fixing] inflates prices by some 25% or more above the non-collusive or competitive level." [31] More spectacularly, as noted in the cases above, overcharges of 900% and 446% in the electrical cases and up to 600% in the quinine case were reported. In the recent antibiotic conspiracy (mentioned in Chapter 1), it was revealed that in 1953–61, the time covered by the indictment, the manufacturing cost of 100 capsules of 250-milligram dosages of tetracycline was about $1.52. The price to druggists, however, was $30.60, and the retail price was $51. Thus, there was a 3,350% mark-up on these medical necessities. A decade later, in 1971, post-conspiracy, the comparable amount of tetracycline was selling for about $5. Every time a consumer purchased a 100-capsule bottle, he paid about $46 extra to the druggist and producer because of an illegal conspiracy. In every illegal conspiracy such computations can be made, as corporations steal money from consumers.

Assuming what Justice Holmes termed the "bad man" theory of law, that there are individuals who scheme to break the law if it benefits them, what are the countervailing costs which could dissuade such business crime? There are four basic sanctions—imprisonment, criminal fines, treble damages, and loss of good will. Yet undermining the impact of *all* these sanctions are the no-contest (or *nolo contendere*) plea and the general judicial antipathy to antitrust.

By a no-contest plea a defendant admits without trial that he committed the alleged offense. Theoretically, it can subject the defendant to the same fines and sentences as if he had pleaded guilty. In fact, judges sentence far more leniently after a *nolo* plea than after a guilty plea or guilty conviction, and the press and public tend to treat a defendant entering a *nolo* plea as having technically violated the law, but not seriously. Most significantly, a *nolo* plea counts as a "consent decree" under Section 5(a) of the Clayton Act, which says that "consent judgments or decrees entered before any testimony has been taken" are not *prima facie* evidence in later civil proceedings. If later plaintiffs seeking damages from the defendants could refer to an earlier admission of criminal guilt by defendants as proof that they are liable for provable damages, the plaintiffs' case would be greatly benefited. This can be done with a guilty plea or an adjudication of guilty, but *not* a no-contest plea. This freedom from later liability is a key motive for the frequency with which defendants plead no contest. "Its value to defendants is incalculable," concludes a *Yale Law Journal* article on the subject.[32]

In the history of the antitrust laws, 73% of all convictions have been via *nolo contendere*.[33] (In the past decade it has been 79%.) Judges usually overrule government objections to disposing of a criminal case by such a mild rebuke. Between fiscal 1960 and fiscal 1970, courts accepted *nolo* pleas in 95% of the cases where the government opposed it.[34]

Aside from a disinclination to make lawless business and businessmen suffer, the basic reason cited by judges for accepting a *nolo* plea is that judicial resources are limited and court calendars are clogged, so a case should be disposed of without trial if possible. While it is true that courts are backlogged and that other cases are important, the court-resources argument cuts both ways. Refusing to simplify later treble-damage suits by giving them the right to cite the earlier conviction as precedent merely means that later civil cases will be more complicated and lengthy. Courts at times cite accompanying government civil suits as adequate protection for these later claimants; but some 80% of all civil cases are settled by consent decree, which *also* lack a *prima facie* effect for later bilked petitioners.

Judges should not be wary of refusing *nolo* offerings fearing lengthy trials, because the defendants may still choose to plead guilty (which *is* considered *prima facie* evidence). Of the 25 cases recorded between 1954 and 1964 where courts refused *nolo contendere* pleas, the defendants subsequently pleaded guilty in at least 15.[35] And when trials do occur, they may be an invaluable contribution to criminal enforcement. Legal philosopher Lon Fuller has argued that in relation to white-collar crimes, "there is a fairly respectable view, especially espoused by certain psychoanalysts, that the public trial and condemnation of the criminal serves the symbolic function of reinforcing the public sense that there are certain acts that are fundamentally wrong, that must not be done." [36] This view is especially applicable when many violate the law and few consider the action wrong. "In such a moral atmosphere," Fuller continues, "it may be argued, men need to have their sense of guilt restored."

At common law the equivalent of the *nolo contendere* plea was a plea of mercy to the sovereign, wholly a matter of court discretion. Traditionally, it was an admission of guilt, not an escape hatch from legal accountability. Now it has become a rubber-stamped right, as judges rarely refuse it.*

Even more subversive of antitrust enforcement than the judicial preference for *nolo contendere* pleas is the frequent judicial hostility toward any antitrust prosecution. District Court Judge Leon Yankwich undoubtedly reflected the views of many others on the bench when he said in one private antitrust case, "Antitrust laws are a part of America's romantic dream, which can never be realized in modern economics and [can never] actually maintain competition in a modern industrial system." [38]

The district court of Los Angeles, where many antitrust

---

* One of the very few district-court judges who will refuse a no-contest plea and insist on a guilty admission or trial is Judge Edward Weinfeld in New York City. One of his opinions refusing one deserves to be read by his colleagues: "Upon vigorous and constant enforcement depends the economic, political and social well-being of our nation. The concept that antitrust violations really are 'minor' and 'technical' infractions, involve no wrongdoing, and merely constitute 'white collar' offenses, has no place in the administration of justice."[37]

cases are heard, is among the nation's worst in this regard. Judge Charles Carr has greeted Antitrust Division attorneys as they enter the courtroom with a "Well, here come the drop-dead guys from Washington"—which, we're told, refers to his opinion that government lawyers act like big shots. The late Chief Judge Thurmond Clarke in the same district viewed antitrust crime with equanimity. The 1963 *United Fruit* indictment charged that firm and two of its officials with successfully monopolizing the importation of bananas into the Western states. *Nolo* pleas were accepted by Judge Clarke, who then fined United Fruit and the two individual defendants—who had reaped millions of dollars of illegal profits for years due to their criminal scheme—a grand total of $4,000. In the *GM–Los Angeles Dealers* case of the prior year, when GM coerced its dealers not to sell cars to discount houses, Judge Clarke quickly directed an acquittal in the original criminal suit. Judge Carr then did the same thing to the follow-up civil case. The Supreme Court reversed him on the latter and remanded for entry of a judgment against the defendants. Judge Carr initially refused even to sign the *negotiated* consent decree, since it admitted to a conspiracy which his brother judge had found did not exist. After much coaxing by Division attorneys, he acceded.

Judge Pierson Hall in the Los Angeles district "was not merely erroneous but outrageously wrong in the *ARMCO* case," according to a frustrated Antitrust Division attorney. In this case a grand jury returned a two-count indictment charging 11 defendants with fixing prices on subsurface gasoline pumps. Judge Hall severed the two counts for separate trials because he claimed that the violations alleged were so *different* it would be unfair to try the defendants on the two counts in a single trial. On February 16, 1966, he dismissed Count II for the government's failure to file a bill of particulars, "which, of course, we had done," said the Division attorney; then, two weeks later, he dismissed Count I since it was so *similar* to Count II that double jeopardy attached! Since a dismissal before trial can be reviewed by a later court, Judge Hall dismissed the case after one witness had taken the stand. This had the effect of a trial decision, which is *not* appealable.

Such performances are rarely reviewed by higher authorities, but when one was by the Supreme Court in the *El*

Paso case, Utah District Court Judge Willis Ritter found himself publicly chastised. Justice Douglas, expressing the High Court's impatience with lower-court delay over, and violation of, its earlier divestiture order, delivered the unusual rebuke:

The evil with which the proposed decree is permeated reflects the attitude or philosophy of the District Court. . . . The proposed decree in its various ramifications does . . . the opposite of what our prior opinion and mandate commanded. Once more, and nearly three years after we first spoke, we reverse and remand, with directions that there be divestiture without delay and that *the Chief Judge of the Circuit or the Judicial Council of the Circuit assign a different District Judge to hear the case.* [Emphasis supplied.] [39]

One top Division official, dejected about the low quality and hostility of many district-court judges, wished that many could be removed from the bench—which is a near impossibility, since the Constitution guarantees them lifetime tenure "during good behavior." Reform of the bench goes far beyond antitrust considerations, involving a reorientation away from patronage and fraternal appointments toward men of ability. More civil servants, law professors, and public-interest lawyers and fewer local law-firm titans should be chosen. In the antitrust area specifically, the special antitrust court recommended in Chapter IV would solve many problems. Yet perhaps one should be less surprised and more sanguine about the quality of judges. Ramsey Clark had no illusions about them. "I think judges are about as unstable as ordinary folks, on the average," he said. "That can be pretty unstable." [40] *

While the frequency of no-contest pleas and antagonis-

---

* There are some rare exceptions to this judicial softness. The late Judge Archibald Dawson in New York had a reputation for sternness with all defendants, businessmen included. In one case Lever Brothers was seeking crucial data on advertising expenditures from Procter & Gamble in an effort to show that Procter & Gamble was attempting to monopolize the market. Dawson ruled that Procter & Gamble had to produce the data. The president of the firm, Neil McElroy, met with the judge in chambers over his ruling. He said, in no logical order, that he was a busy man, a former Secretary of Defense, and that he would instruct his subordinate not to hand over the required data because it would give a competitor trade secrets. Judge Dawson said that if that were the case, "Tell your subordinate to come to court that day with his toothbrush and pajamas." McElroy flushed, sputtered, and left. Later in court, as the Procter & Gamble witness was asked for the data, a U.S. Marshal walked into the courtroom and sat near the witness stand. The employee gave over the required information.

tic judges reduces the deterrent potential of the four basic sanctions, each one is already perforated with exceptions and non-enforcement.

(1) Imprisonment

The likelihood of a white-collar antitrust criminal spending time in prison is near nil. Even in the 1940s, when a record number of criminal cases were filed, there was not one case where a defendant was actually incarcerated. Since 1890, 461 individual defendants have been sentenced to prison.[41] Most were labor racketeers or mixed violence with a labor or management scheme. In all but 26 criminal cases between 1890 and 1969, according to Richard Posner, the sentences were immediately suspended. Of these remaining 26, only *three* involved pure price-fixing by businessmen. The first prison sentence ever actually served for pure price-fixing by businessmen (*i.e.,* without the involvement of labor or violence) occurred in *1959.* From fiscal 1960 to fiscal 1970 there have been only two cases, out of 188 criminal cases brought (counting all the electrical-equipment cases as one), where some business defendants have served jail sentences of from one to 60 days: the electrical-equipment cases and the plumbing-fixtures case.

The reasons for the absence of prison terms are multiple. The Antitrust Division often reserves jail recommendations for big cases, and then gets them in neither the big nor the small since judges are unimpressed that sentences were not requested in earlier, smaller cases. The Division also prefers indicting corporations rather than individuals because (a) it is easier to prove institutional guilt than personal guilt, and because (b) juries are often loath to sentence a white-collar defendant to prison. Alan Dershowitz, professor of law at Harvard, taking note of the prior point, wrote that "because the corporation is a term on a very high level of abstraction, it frequently tends to conceal the real actors in a given situation." [42]

Point (b) is obvious to Division trial attorneys. It is difficult to convince 12 jurors that a mass of economic data, interspersed by some conduct by the defendants, equals criminal guilt beyond a reasonable doubt. Yet even when the evidence is strong, a form of jury nullification can occur where the jurors realize that a well-dressed,

white, wealthy, articulate father of three might actually go
to jail with unkempt, nonwhite, poor, uneducated street
criminals. At times, when a jury has been told that a corporation can only act through its agents, and that if the individual agents are innocent the corporation cannot be guilty,
the jury has *still* acquitted the individuals and convicted
the corporations. Such *non sequiturs* lead some courts to
rue, "We cannot understand how the jury could have acquitted all of the individual defendants. As a matter of
logic, reconciliation . . . is impossible"; [43] and, "How an
intelligent jury could have acquitted any of the defendants
we cannot conceive." [44]

If juries have difficulty convicting respectable businessmen, judges are overtly deferential. Judge George Hart of
the United States District Court in Washington, D.C., like
many of his colleagues, does not require indicted defendants in antitrust cases to be fingerprinted and photographed
as other criminal defendants would be. (Why? Are the rich
somehow different? "Yes. They have money," said Ernest
Hemingway.) When judges were asked, "Why do so few
convicted Sherman Act violators ever serve jail sentences?"
in the Judges' Questionnaire, some of the typical replies
were: "Recidivism is unlikely," "Violators are *not* hardened criminals," "Defendants are victims of economic
forces," and "Not clear in corporate case that guilty ones
are in court."* In the defendant's chair a judge sees someone who looks as he does, who may belong to the same
country-club milieu, or who, at the very least, is the kind
of client he represented in his former law practice. This
simpatico style has implications beyond the defendant. One
interviewee told us that "it is best to find the judge's friend
or law partner to defend an antitrust client—which we have
done."

Leniency toward corporate criminality contrasts with the
often sadistic sentences imposed on street criminals. A year
after seven electrical manufacturers were sent to jail for
30 days apiece, a man in Asbury Park, New Jersey, stole
a $2.98 pair of sunglasses and a $1 box of soap and was
sent to jail for four months. A George Jackson was sent

---

* In 1959 four manufacturers of garden tools were sent to jail for 90
days each. On the way to begin serving his sentence, one defendant shot
and killed himself. The well-publicized incident cooled any inclination
judges did retain toward prison sentences.

to prison for 10 years to life for stealing $70 from a gas station, his third minor offense; and in Dallas one Joseph Sills received a 1,000-year sentence for robbing $73.10. Many states send young students, who are marijuana first offenders, to jail for five to 10 years. But the *total* amount of time spent in jail by all businessmen who have violated the antitrust laws is a little under two years. Yet the electrical conspiracy alone robbed the public more than all other robberies and thefts in 1961 combined. This timidity toward antitrust violators is understood well by the violators themselves, for "recidivism" is not a word monopolized by preventive-detention advocates. Richard Posner found that at least 46 of 320 corporations convicted of a criminal violation between 1964 and 1968 had been previously convicted. But repeaters were punished no more severely than new defendants in the same case.[45]

When prison sentences are imposed, they require an unusual combination of circumstances. As in the electrical and plumbing-fixtures cases, defendants may go to jail if their actions are flagrant, willful, affect substantial commerce on a national scale, and involve businessmen sneaking around hotel rooms conversing in code. Even then it took personal pleas from an Assistant Attorney General and an Attorney General, as well as the happy coincidence of a strict, intelligent judge, to send the electrical executives to prison.

The Antitrust Division has occasionally fought judicial indifference to corporate crime. Sentencing conferences are held where Division officials deliver speeches on the dearth of criminal sentences and the resulting lack of deterrence. In May, 1966, AAG Turner himself went to Los Angeles to protest that the deterrence created by the electrical cases of five years past was wearing somewhat thin, and that antitrust enforcement was suffering. But such talks have had little effect.

(2) Criminal Fines

From 1890 to 1955 the maximum Sherman Act fine was $5,000 per violation; in 1955 it was increased to $50,000 per violation. It should be immediately apparent that both maxima are dwarfed by the average $48 million profit of the 500 top industrial firms in 1969.[46] Yet however inconsequential they are as compared to the size of the defendants, the *actual* fines levied are usually far below the maximum possible. Between 1946 and 1953, for example, the average Sherman Act fine was $2,600. The tenfold increase in possible penalties in 1955 did little to concern corporate boardrooms: between 1955 and 1965 corporate fines averaged $13,420 and individual fines $3,365.[47] *

From 1955 to 1962 the maximum fine was never imposed on an individual and was assessed against corporations in only four of the more than 130 Sherman Act cases where fines were imposed. (The frequency increased somewhat between July, 1966, and December, 1969, when nine criminal cases out of 44 had defendants who suffered the $50,000 fine.) But even in the very serious electrical cases the maximum $50,000 fine was imposed only once out of 159 total sentences. The average corporate fines per count in these cases was $16,500, although the commerce affected totaled some $7 billion (or an overcharge of approximately $840 million based on a modest 12% estimated inflated price); on one occasion the fine was one ten-millionth of the net profit aggregated during the period of the indictment.[48] While some court-imposed fines achieve compensation and others create deterrence, antitrust fines have the distinction of doing neither.

Although judges should sentence a defendant the same regardless of his plea, since both *nolo* and guilty pleas confess guilt, judges rarely fine *nolo* defendants as heavily. In 1953 Attorney General Herbert Brownell complained that "Uncontrolled use of the [*nolo*] plea has led to shockingly low sentences and insignificant fines which are no deterrent to crime." [49] The Antitrust Division then began a policy of opposing all *nolo* pleas—a policy which judges easily frustrated.

There is little disagreement on the inadequacy of these fines. Lee Loevinger, during his term in office, described GE's $437,500 total fine as "no more severe than a $3 ticket for overtime parking for a man with a $15,000 income." In the last three years alone, the President's Crime Commission, the 1969 Report of the Council of Economic Advisors, and the 1970 Economic Report of the President

---

* The $50,000 fine is small even by white-collar standards. The Nixon Environmental Program, if passed, would allow court-imposed fines as high as $50,000 *per day* for a second violation of water-quality standards.

all complained that the insignificant Sherman Act fines did not deter antitrust violations. Sixty-eight percent of the replies to the Businessmen's Questionnaire thought that the $50,000 should not be increased to $500,000; but when given a list of six possible reasons for obeying the antitrust laws, the fear of fines was considered the least significant of all. After nine years of various attempts, a bill to increase the maximum fine to $500,000 for corporations was introduced in 1970 by Senators Hart and Hruska. Except for the National Association of Manufacturers and the Chamber of Commerce, the bill had overwhelming bipartisan support and the blessings of both the Nixon administration and the American Bar Association. After getting through the Senate Antitrust Subcommittee, it died without fanfare in the full Judiciary Committee. Senator Hruska, one of the cosponsors, had changed his mind and blocked it.

(3) Treble-Damage Suits
Such actions under Section 4 of the Clayton Act could be a great deterrent to price-fixing. The theory is that any person who can prove damages from the illegal conspiracy can then recover three times his damages from the corporate defendant. The multifold return was intended to spur such private suits, which would both penalize the violator and indemnify the victim.

Again, neither goal has been attained. "Judicial reluctance to ease the path of treble-damage plaintiffs," Victor Kramer has written, "demonstrates that our courts are not prepared to emphasize the role of punishment in antitrust law enforcement." [50] For a number of reasons—the high rate of no-contest pleas, the difficulty of proving actual damage, the inhibitions of many harmed companies to sue a brother firm, and procedural obstacles—private treble-damage suits have never realized their potential and have not created a serious deterrence to antitrust crime. (These private actions will be considered in greater detail in the following chapter.) A recent *Yale Law Journal* article concluded that "in the overwhelming majority of all cases in which the government convinced a court that a violation of the antitrust laws had been committed, the convicted corporation paid nothing to private claimants in the form of damages or settlement." [51]

Until 1970, even if a successful suit was brought against

a price-fixing corporation, the pain was cushioned by the Internal Revenue Service. Revenue Ruling 64–224 in 1964 upheld the policy that treble-damage payments are tax deductible from income as an "ordinary and necessary [business] expense." Put another way, the ruling says: If you have to pay money for corporate criminality, the government in effect will subsidize one-half of the penalty, since corporations are taxed at 52% of net profits. (This deduction is only for treble damages, not the Sherman Act fines, which are far lower than damage payments.)

Although this controversial boondoggle was issued in 1964, it had been the informal IRS practice since at least 1948. Following the announcement of Ruling 64–224, Congressman Celler and Senator Hart sent a joint protest to IRS: "The ruling is likely to hamper effective antitrust enforcement both by mitigating the penalties which Congress has prescribed and by its tacit assumption that a hard-core criminal price-fixing conspiracy is 'ordinary and necessary' business." [52] Such protests, and later Congressional hearings, had little impact on either the IRS or Congress. By 1969, during the tax-reform battle on Capitol Hill, a code provision passed which partly undid the 1964 ruling. Two-thirds of any treble-damage payments would no longer be deductible if the corporation had been found guilty or pleaded no contest in a prior, government criminal action. If no such government case preceded the private action, then any damages paid out would still be deductible.

(4) Goodwill

A potentially powerful deterrent occurs when a corporation's goodwill is damaged by an antitrust conviction. "Who steals my purse steals trash," protested Iago, "but he that filches from me my good name . . . makes me poor indeed." So it is with corporations, who do not mind paying minor sums out of their coffers but do mind if their reputation is dimmed in consumers' minds. The disinterest of the news media, which underplay or ignore corporate crime, eases the burden of this informal stigma. And, as already stressed, "nolo" does not ring in people's minds as does "guilty." At times, however, business firms and law firms still contort to maintain the fiction that a *nolo* plea, while legally an admission of guilt, really concedes nothing at all, or even that a guilty plea doesn't mean quite that. Former Attorney General Herbert Brownell represented Westinghouse during the 1961 courtroom proceedings. Upon pleading his client guilty to seven counts, he had the pluck to assert that Westinghouse "does not admit the allegations of any of these indictments, but is simply changing its pleas for the purpose of promptly disposing of pending litigation." [53] *

In sum, the network of sanctions which aim to deter antitrust criminality do not outweigh the possible benefits to the violator. The meager fines imposed and even treble-damage payments become merely costs of doing business. This is the conclusion, among others, of H. N. McMenimen, Jr., consultant-analyst to the Law Department of the City of New York. He conducted a study for the City of New York, which is a huge purchaser of various commodities, to see if existing penalties discouraged antitrust violators. He found they did not, with one key element being the "interest-free borrowing" which indirectly occurs when one firm uses another's money (via an antitrust violation) for a long period of time. Based on six case studies, with some involving firms who had their damage payments trebled, McMenimen concluded:

Indictment by a federal grand jury, punishment inflicted through criminal action, the payment of trebled damages resulting from civil trials, all legal costs incurred in the process, *none of these nor any combination of them succeeds today in denying the price fixer a profit realization at least double a normal level.* [Emphasis supplied.] [54]

This view is corroborated by other interested authorities. Robert F. Lanzillotti and Joel Dirlam argued that for the rational businessmen interested in profit maximization, "antitrust involvement may even mean a sizable profit factor and reliable revenue stabilizer." [55] W. Bruce Erickson of the University of Minnesota conducted a careful study of the possible profitability of price-fixing based on four factors: the likelihood of getting caught; the proportion of sales involved in the treble-damage litigation; the length of time between discovery of the violation and the pay-

---

* The Businessmen's Questionnaire asked respondents to rank six factors in order of their significance in encouraging compliance with the antitrust laws. The six factors, from most important to least important as based on a consolidation of all of the replies, were: (1) Personal code/obligation to the law; (2) Fear of treble damages; (3) Adverse publicity; (4) Fear of imprisonment; (5) Competition essential to our economic system; (6) Fear of fines.

ment of damages; and the relationship between profits derived by the violator and the judge's or jury's evaluation of single damages. Even assuming that *all* antitrust violations are detected, Erickson concluded that "the typical violation may be profitable." When, more realistically, the probability of detection is assumed to be 50% or far less, "in all cases . . . antitrust violations are profitable, even after the possibility of treble damage payments is considered. . . . [T]he profitability of violations in high-return industries is impressive." [56]

The electrical-equipment and tetracycline cases, where the settlements to purchasers were among the largest in antitrust history, support these three studies. Manufacturers of electrical equipment paid out approximately $500 million to their overcharged victims; these were basically single damages or less, since all the private cases except four were settlements, not court-imposed treble damages. But a member of the GE antitrust-settlement unit told the Study Group that his firm overcharged customers by at least 12%. Based on the $7 billion of commerce affected, as charged by the criminal complaint (which covers only some of the years of the conspiracies), he estimated that excess profits due to the price-fixes were at least $840 million. An estimated $300 million-plus profit was therefore shared by all the defendants—even *after* damage payments and assessed fines. As a second example, drug houses selling certain broad-spectrum antibiotics have paid out about $29 million to individual consumers in settlement of private litigation. Using conservative estimates, Paul Scanlon, an attorney for some of the plaintiffs, estimates that a $630 million overcharge, not $29 million, was retained in the years at issue, 1954–61. Again, as always, collusion was highly profitable.

REMEDIES

Balancing the suspected prevalence of antitrust crime as against the infrequent cases brought, and balancing the costs as against the benefits, the system of criminal antitrust punishment requires drastic alteration at many levels. Initially, attitudinal changes on the part of judges and jurors are necessary, but such change will be slow and, by itself, not sufficient. Below is a brief list of remedies which can be implemented separately or together. They are predicated on an obvious fact about antitrust enforcement: violations are not spontaneous or *ad hoc,* but are carefully planned by intelligent people who balance the risks and benefits. It is with just such calculating individuals that strong and well-publicized penalties can be a successful deterrent.

—Corporate fines should be increased so that up to 10% of the corporation's sales receipts for the years of the indictment could be assessed. A minimum fine of 1% or $100,000, whichever is higher, would be levied, so as to strip judges of some of their historic abuse of discretion. The minimum would increase to 5% or $500,000 for a corporation convicted of a second offense within a five-year period. With serious financial penalties built into the fabric of enforcement, the profit motive itself should be adequate incentive to self-regulate the system into compliance. Studies should also be conducted on the success of the antitrust fine systems of the European Economic Community, which has a maximum of $1 million, and of Canada, which has no maximum whatsoever.

—Where an individual defendant is found guilty of (or pleads guilty or no contest to) a knowing and willful violation, there should be a mandatory minimum prison term of four months for the first offense and one year for the second. The awareness that, if caught, a prison term will be inevitable should discourage potential violators.

—Just as the Landrum-Griffin Act ousts labor leaders from their positions for criminal convictions, any member of management who obtains a criminal record relating to his corporate duties should be deprived of his position.*

—Some states, including the home of corporations, Delaware, permit indemnification by corporations where the firm assumes the burden of fines imposed on its agents

---

* Supporting this view is §3502 of the proposed new federal criminal code, drafted by the National Commission on Reform of Federal Criminal Laws and submitted to Congress this session:

An executive officer or other manager of an organization convicted of an offense committed in furtherance of the affairs of the organization may, as part of the sentence, be disqualified from exercising similar functions in the same or other organizations for a period not exceeding five years, if the court finds the scope or willfulness of his illegal actions make it dangerous [the final report deleted the words "or inadvisable" from the prior draft here] for such functions to be entrusted to him.

It should also be noted that in shaping relief, equity-antitrust courts have broad powers. In *Hartford–Empire Company v. United States,* in 1945, the offending officers and directors were removed from the Glass Container Association and their replacements had to get court approval.

or litigation expenses paid out by them. So that the individual should suffer the sting of liability for his personal wrongs, federal legislation should preempt state law to forbid indemnification of punitive fines for federal antitrust violations.

—A corporate agent in a supervisory capacity should be held criminally liable if he has specific knowledge of an antitrust violation occurring within his area of supervision and if he willfully defaults either to end it or report it. The willful disregard of a duty should give rise to legal accountability.

—Corporations should be compelled to advertise the fact of their criminal convictions as the only way to correct their massive publicity which falsely projects them as concerned and magnanimous citizens. The National Commission on the Reform of Federal Criminal Laws, chaired by ex-Governor Edmund Brown and with Senators Ervin, Hruska, and McClellan as members, has made the following recommendations:

Special Sanction for Organizations. When an organization is convicted of an offense, the court may require the organization to give notice of its conviction to the persons or class of persons ostensibly harmed by the offense, by mail or by advertising in designated media or otherwise.

The thinking behind this provision was spelled out in the Commission's working papers:

The main purpose would be to enhance the deterrent effect of the law. Since imprisonment is impossible and fines may be absorbed as a cost of business, adverse publicity in appropriate cases might be the most feared consequence of conviction in an era when public relations figure so largely among management concerns.

—*Nolo contendere* pleas should be *prima facie* evidence of legal liability in later private actions.*

—Consideration should be given to applying 15 U.S.C. §6, a forfeiture statute, to antitrust violations. It says that all goods used in any federal criminal conspiracy may be confiscated by the state and sold at auction. Instead of applying it to specific contraband, one should sell off divisions of a corporation which has been, say, thrice convicted of antitrust offenses within six years. Such sale would attempt

* A bill to this effect, S. 2512, was submitted by Senator Hart in September, 1965. Hearings were held in the summer of 1966, but the bill has languished in the Senate Antitrust & Monopoly Subcommittee ever since.

to restructure the firm and line up new management, in order to discourage future illegality. Given the obvious inadequacy of present criminal sanctions, Dr. Walter Erickson sees divestiture as the only remedy with a real deterrent effect.

—Consideration should also be given to the use and payment of informers to disclose antitrust illegality. Admittedly, informing for pay could be abused, but since enforcement agencies—like the Department of Justice—exploit the method for violent crimes, tax violations, political offenses, and pollution violations it should not be discounted for antitrust criminality; often an inside tip is the only way the Division can find out about an illegal scheme. For example, the informant could be guaranteed 10% of the fine, or $20,000, whichever is lower, for evidence directly leading to indictment and conviction.

—The Antitrust Division must employ more affirmative efforts to ferret out price-fixers. Most of the big cases of the decade—electrical machinery, antibiotics, quinine, and children's books—were initially triggered by Senate Hearings. The agency must cultivate its own detection devices. One idea is the use of computer analysis in a particular market to detect if there is significant excess pricing. High prices, especially if combined with an industry structure which makes price-fixing "inevitable," [57] could then generate a flurry of CIDs or a grand jury. Such a structure might be characterized by fixed market shares, stable prices over time, only regional price variation, and the exchange of price information among the firms. The Division must be willing to empanel more grand juries, and cut them off quicker, rather than being overly concerned that grand juries which do not return indictments give the appearance of a bad record. In fact, AAG Richard McLaren has recently announced that for the first time studies are under way into the pricing patterns of products in certain local areas in an attempt to detect price-fixing patterns.

The results of these studies and, more importantly, the chance of success of these suggested criminal penalties will decide the future of criminal antitrust enforcement. Four generations of the velvet glove are enough. Without more deterrent impact, antitrust law threatens to go the way of the Federal Corrupt Practices Act and the 1946 Lobbying-Registration Act—to disintegrate by desuetude, as the law is both unobserved and unenforced.

[T]he suit has been a futile exercise if the government proves a violation but fails to secure a remedy adequate to redress it. . . . [O]nce the government has successfully borne the considerable burden of establishing a violation of law, all doubts as to the remedy are to be resolved in its favor.
—U.S. Supreme Court,
United States v. DuPont (1944)

6

When Winning Is Losing: Civil Enforcement

CIVIL INJUNCTIVE DECREES

More than two-thirds of the cases that the Antitrust Division brought during the 1960s were civil suits seeking "to prevent and restrain" violations of the antitrust laws. Eighty-three percent of these were disposed of through "consent decrees"—voluntary settlements negotiated between defendants and the government and adopted by the court prior to trial. Counting consent decrees as victories, the Division's civil enforcement won/lost rate currently exceeds 90%. The figure is almost meaningless.

The Antitrust Division seeks to achieve effective relief through three basic types of provisions in its civil injunctive decrees.

(1) Relief by "Don't Do It Again" Decrees

The most common consent decrees, these are orders to cease anticompetitive *conduct,* such as price-fixing, reciprocity, or exclusive dealing contracts. As the name suggests, the most striking characteristic of this remedy is the absence of any deterrent effect. According to Richard Posner:

It is extremely common for the Department in price-fixing cases to obtain a decree that, stripped of the redundancies that are dear to lawyers, merely forbids further price-fixing. Since the illegality of price-fixing under the Sherman Act is well established, and directly punishable as a crime, the purpose of such an injunction is not immediately obvious. . . .[1]

The decree is usually by consent, which, like a no-contest plea, does *not* result in *prima facie* treble-damage liability. A no-contest plea and a light fine in the companion criminal prosecution (if any) complete the cycle of painless enforcement.

The Division defends "don't do it again" orders by arguing that if such an order is violated, the company could be convicted of criminal contempt and face fines and/or imprisonments in excess of the statutory maximum under the Sherman Act. This rationalization cannot withstand scrutiny. One judgments-section member frankly conceded that "in close cases the contempt route is not attractive to the front office" because new antitrust actions can be brought instead. Also, before the criminal contempt prosecution could serve as a deterrent, the Division would have to obtain detailed decrees against most corporations engaged in interstate commerce—otherwise there might be no outstanding decree upon which to base a contempt action. After the corporations were allowed one "free" detected violation of each antitrust prohibition, the recently revamped 15-member judgments section could begin the task of ensuring compliance. They would be overwhelmingly outmatched; as of August 1, 1970, there were approximately 1,200 outstanding decrees to monitor. A 1959 House Antitrust Subcommittee report assessed the task:

To a major extent the personnel of the judgments section deal with decree enforcement problems on an administrative basis. In this activity the Antitrust Division has undertaken a system of industry supervision and regulation. Since the primary responsibility of the Department of Justice is to serve as counsel for the Government in the conduct of litigation, the facilities of the Department are neither devised for, nor readily adaptable to, an administrative undertaking of this nature.[2]

Moreover, even now the criminal-contempt sanction is rarely used. Between 1890 and 1970 the Justice Department initiated only 42 criminal and civil contempt proceedings for violation of antitrust decrees.[3] In the Sixties the Division filed exactly *three* criminal-contempt motions. Finally, notwithstanding the initial thesis that judges *may* punish criminal contempt with fines and/or imprisonments in excess of the statutory maximums for original prosecutions, judges have simply not done so. Not once in this century has an antitrust criminal-contempt conviction sent anyone to prison.

Yet the contempt sanction is the only way to enforce compliance with "don't do it again" decrees. The toothlessness of civil relief was blamed, by the 1959 House Report, on "the complete absence of procedures to bring automatically to the attention of the Antitrust Division instances where defendants fail to comply with the requirements of a judgment. . . . The Antitrust Division relies upon the same surveillance procedures for an industry which is subject to the terms of an antitrust consent decree that it uses in an industry which has no history of antitrust litigation" —*i.e.,* the "mailbag"—and letters of complaint have proven very rare.

The only effort at systematic review of decrees by means of government-initiated compliance checks came on the heels of the 1959 House Report, when Lee Loevinger sent 56 carefully selected consent decrees to the FTC for a thorough investigation. As one member of the judgments section commented, "The whole affair was a public-relations gimmick to counter the still true charge that consent decrees are stored away and forgotten." The FTC subsequently reported that *one-third* of the decrees were being either violated or evaded, and it recommended as many contempt actions or decree modifications.[4] The Antitrust Division's reaction: *two* new antitrust suits and *one* contempt action.

The judgments section, if it is seriously interested in monitoring compliance with outstanding decrees, could benefit from the following approaches:

(a) The sole or even the primary responsibility for ensuring compliance with decrees should not rest upon the shoulders of a small unit whose members have no particular knowledge of industry practices. Attorneys in the litigating sections with expertise in certain industries should monitor compliance with outstanding decrees in those industries and prosecute contempt actions under the general supervision of the judgments section. It is typical of the Division's general approach to relief problems that litigating attorneys, having spent months and often years preparing for trial, ordinarily wash their hands of a case once the decree is entered.

(b) All future decrees should require, as part of the settlement, that the defendants bear the full expense of regular compliance checks conducted by the judgments section, the FTC, or court-appointed monitors.

(c) All future decrees should require defendants to submit regular and detailed reports to enable Division personnel to spot possible violations and to gauge whether the decree is accomplishing its purpose.

(d) The Division should insist upon a clause in each decree by which the defendant admits treble-damage liability to any person who can prove injury from a violation *of the terms of the decree*. Victims could allege and prove decree violations without having to await government contempt prosecutions. The Division opposes this recommendation, insisting that private plaintiffs would bring actions upon self-serving interpretations of decree provisions, which might not always coincide with what the Division had in mind in the decree.* The government would be forced to "waste" resources in opposing the decree interpretations of these plaintiffs. Otherwise, the argument goes, courts might render "wrong" decisions. Note first, however, that the Justice Department assigns itself *sole* responsibility for enforcing its decrees. Second, by refusing to facilitate the aid of

---

* A simple device could alleviate this hypothetical problem. Every consent decree could be accompanied by a written Antitrust Division "statement" setting forth its own view of the facts of the case, the purpose sought to be achieved by the decree, and a detailed interpretation of the important provisions. The 1959 House Report recommended this procedure. Nothing happened until 1967, when Chairman Celler reminded AAG Turner of the unexecuted recommendation. Turner replied that "It may well be we could and should supply more information than we have been accustomed to do, particularly in explaining the purposes of the decree and the expected impact of the relief obtained." [5] Still no action has been taken.

treble-damage plaintiffs injured by violations of decrees, which could invigorate the compliance program, the Division ignores that responsibility. Third, the self-interest of treble-damage plaintiffs would be bound to produce undiscovered decree violations. Division personnel cannot, should not, and, indeed, *have* not undertaken by themselves to gather the massive quantity of necessary compliance information.

It may seem strange that a law-enforcement agency would spend fully 40% of its time seeking "don't do it again" decrees which accomplish no more than the name implies. Yet the most casual glance at the array of other government agencies that purport to regulate corporate activities—from the Food and Drug Administration to the Federal Trade Commission—reveals the "don't do it again" decree or its equivalent to be the dominant enforcement technique. In light of its dubious enforcement value, the Antitrust Division should reserve "don't do it again" relief for those rare occasions when the government alleges for the first time that a type of conduct violates the antitrust laws—or for inclusion in litigated decrees which potential treble-damage plaintiffs could use as *prima facie* evidence of the defendant's violation.

(2) Relief by Regulatory Decrees

The second major form of civil relief is illustrated by the *Paramount* decrees—which also show its futility and its inconsistency with the competitive philosophy behind antitrust laws. In 1948 the Supreme Court ruled that the leading motion-picture producers had monopolized the market for first-run movie exhibitions in many cities, and ordered five vertically integrated defendants to divest their nationwide theater circuits. But further relief was necessary to prevent the divested theater chains from monopolizing the same market.

The ideal solution, therefore, would have been to break up the chains into small groups. But the government insisted merely on divestiture of enough theaters to provide "some" competition in most major cities. The divested theater chains remained the largest in the nation. As a substitute for the more drastic divestiture that was needed, the *Paramount* decrees inaugurated a full-scale regulatory system. Each time a defendant chain sought to acquire or construct a new theater, its application was first scrutinized by Division attorney Maurice Silverman. In the ensuing judicial proceeding, Silverman represented the government, opposing, favoring, or suggesting restrictions on proposed new theaters. In ruling upon the application, the court—Judge Edmund Palmieri of the Southern District of New York—functioned not unlike a regulatory commission. "What we have here," said one theater owner in a Supreme Court brief for review, "is a multibillion dollar industry being regulated not by a federal agency like the CAB or the FCC but by one man in the Department of Justice and one District Judge—and no one else." The last 15 years have seen 375 court hearings upon acquisition petitions under the *Paramount* decrees. Former Division attorney Phillip Marcus wrote in 1958 that "for one lengthy period, at least one-third of the entire correspondence of the Antitrust Division was in the motion picture field" [6]—certainly a poor way to deploy scarce enforcement resources.

Nor has this regulatory scheme achieved its objectives. Restrictions or prohibitions against chain expansion into the suburbs were anticompetitive, and a *Yale Law Review* article suggests that the scheme protects theater operators threatened with new competition.[7] Others, supported by strong circumstantial evidence, contend that "circuit bidding" and chain domination of first-run movie exhibition are widespread: movie producers receive 65% of their theater revenues from 13 chains, whose inherent economic power deadens competition.[8] Ten years after the *Paramount* decision, one study found true competitive bidding on films occurred only 3.2% of the time.[9]

Silverman claims to have opposed outright 18% of all new *theaters* applied for by the defendant chains in recent years, but he has opposed only 2% of the *applications*. He opposed several attempts to acquire whole theater *chains*. Silverman did not oppose one of the record 75 new-theater applications made in 1967; he explains that "they have learned the standards I use and only present me with acquisitions that I will and should approve." Yet Silverman concedes that he cannot thoroughly investigate the complaints of local theaters against the chain operations. "I get into them as best I can. I have handled as many as 54 by myself in one year." Whether Silverman

or his detractors are right is beside the point—which is
that the entire regulatory apparatus would have been unnecessary had the theater chains been broken up.

By Posner's count, there are 49 regulatory decrees in
force, plus 60 decrees that require defendants to license
patents at "reasonable royalties," a substitute for more
efficient and effective royalty-free licensing. Supervision of
regulatory decrees must be constant; an average of 13
years has passed between original entry of such decrees
and the most recent judicial proceedings under them. One
resulting problem is described by Dr. Kenneth Elzinga,
recently the resident economist at the Antitrust Division:

> In the complex Hartford-Empire decree, where marketing
> orders were substituted for structural relief, the Supreme Court
> installed a complex regulatory scheme of compulsory patent
> licensing, "reasonable rates," and complicated credit arrange-
> ments. The scheme was so complex, in fact, that all of the
> companies involved decided to form a committee to work out
> the difficulties among themselves! [10]

(3) Relief by Structural Decrees

The early 1960s witnessed an unbroken string of Antitrust Division antimerger victories in the Supreme Court.
Corporate antitrust counsel and dissenting Justices began
to say, "The government always wins." Does it, really?
The Supreme Court may declare that a merger is illegal,
but the Antitrust Division must then obtain a divestiture
remedy, by which is meant restoration of the *market structure* that would have existed *but for* the illegal acquisition.
Do Antitrust Division divestiture decrees achieve these
results? A study published in 1967 by Elzinga analyzed
the outcomes in Antitrust Division and FTC antimerger
decrees entered during 1955–64.[11] The relief actually obtained fell into four categories: (1) *Successful* relief was
obtained when the acquired firm was fully reestablished as
a viable entity under independent ownership. (2) *Sufficient*
relief was obtained when the acquired firm, though fully
reestablished as a viable entity, was sold to a somewhat less
than independent purchaser, such as a small vertical or
horizontal competitor. (3) Relief was *deficient* when the
divested entity, though viable, constituted only a partial
restoration of the illegally acquired assets, or where the
purchaser was an obvious potential competitor. (4) *Un-*

successful relief included (a) no relief at all, (b) no structural relief, only a ban on future acquisitions, (c) insignificant divestiture, (d) regulatory relief, (e) divestiture to a significant horizontal or vertical competitor, or (f) divestiture of a nonviable or failing firm.

Of the 39 cases in his sample, Elzinga found that 21 relief orders were unsuccessful and eight deficient. Approximately three-fourths of the cases, including 12 of 17 Antitrust Division cases, fell within the combined unsuccessful-deficient categories. Some typical examples follow:

—In 1954 Schenley Industries acquired Park & Tilford Distillers Corporation. By the time of the 1957 consent decree, many foreign suppliers of whiskey had canceled their distribution contracts with Park & Tilford, which had become a shadow of its former self. No divestiture at all was ordered—only a ban on future mergers. Schenley, with $358 million in assets, could and should have been ordered to create a new firm from scratch to take Park & Tilford's former market position. True, creation of a to-be-divested "going concern"—sometimes from scratch— may be expensive. But as the Supreme Court said long ago, "Those who violate the Act may not reap the benefit of their violations and avoid an undoing of their unlawful project on the plea of hardship and inconvenience."[12]

—In 1954 Hilton, the nation's largest hotel chain, acquired Statler, the second largest. Pursuant to a 1956 decree, Hilton kept all nine Statler hotels and divested three of its own slightly smaller, slightly inferior hotels. One was sold to the Sheraton chain, the others to the Hotel Corporation of America.

—The 1956 merger of the Continental Can Company and the Hazel-Atlas Glass Company was declared illegal by a heralded 1964 Supreme Court opinion. Yet Continental was allowed to keep the two most profitable of the 11 Hazel-Atlas plants. Eight other plants were sold to the Brockway Glass Company, which thereby became the second largest glass-container producer. In other words, the divestiture sale *itself* constituted a clearly illegal horizontal merger.

—The 1955 Brown Shoe–G. R. Kinney merger was overturned by the Supreme Court in 1962, in part because of the market shares involved, but also because of the powerful nationwide shoe-retailing chain that the merger would create. Kinney was sold to F. W. Woolworth, the seventh largest American merchandising firm.

—After Von's Grocery Co.'s 1960 acquisition of Shopping Bag, a competing chain, was voided by the Supreme Court in 1966, the relief decree required divestiture of a certain number of stores, but failed to specify which ones. Von's therefore divested those 40 of its 108 stores with the lowest profit margins—presumably ones lacking the market power (and excessive profits) with which the Supreme Court's decision had been concerned.

The Division's habit of seeking divestiture of specific assets, or of lines of commerce, rather than of a "going concern" is a fundamental cause of the failure of anti-merger relief. Who but an actual or potential competitor wants to buy assets that do not already function as part of a going business—especially if they are obsolete assets? Since there are few takers, and since many defendants claim they can find no buyers, they can often escape with no divestiture at all.

Of course, finding a buyer is no problem if the defendant must sell to the highest bidder. Yet the 1965 *Kaiser Aluminum & Chemical Corporation* decree provided for the dropping of the divestiture requirement if the assets could not be sold for at least their book values. Said Donald Turner, "Whether there were highly unusual circumstances making it reasonable to accept that clause in the particular case, I do not really know. But since that time we have uniformly refused to accept an upset price provision." [13] Instead, to avoid finding a buyer, defendants rely upon such divestiture clauses as "except at a price that is reasonable under all the circumstances" or simply "on reasonable terms and conditions." For example, the Lucky Lager Brewing Company was unable to divest the Fisher Brewing Company (39% of the Utah beer market) on "reasonable business terms" when ordered to do so in 1958. Five of the seven other divestiture decrees that were ultimately lifted for failure to locate a buyer contained "reasonable price" provisions.

According to Turner, the Division does not "desire to punish companies by unnecessarily forcing them to dispose of their assets at commercially unrealistic prices." But how can the highest bid, from a year or two of "good faith effort" to find a buyer, be "unreasonable"? The market is *assumed* to be "reasonable" and will pay what it will pay. It is clear that the failure to find a buyer, facilitated by the "reasonable price" loophole, is profitable and self-serving. According to Elzinga:

> Anyone who goes through the correspondence between a divesting firm (or its agent) and inquiring brokers and firms cannot help but be impressed at least by the sheer number of inquiries. Even as unlikely an asset as a salt plant in Utah drew 207 different inquiries. . . . It is in the divesting firm's interest to seek out or favor a buyer who will either be cooperative, phlegmatic in his rivalry, or destined to fail. It is in the public's interest that the buyer be independent, a business maverick, and destined to succeed. . . . Consequently, effective antimerger relief requires that the authorities not give the companies involved free rein in this selection.

It is natural that defendants have taken advantage of the initiative that the government has forfeited to them. An intensive study of antimerger relief by members of the *Yale Law Journal* remarks that "termination of ownership by the defendant seems to be the principal focus of Government enforcement efforts, rather than the restoration of a viable competitive market structure." Why? The authors' interviews revealed two key value judgments shared by Division personnel. First was the notion that the defendant continued to *own* the illegally acquired properties subject only to a broad obligation to divest at some future date. Second was the notion that the defendant should suffer no "penalty" as a consequence of divestiture —a notion closely associated with the use of such terms as "forced sale," "confiscation," "hardship," and "injury to stockholders." The requirements of structurally effective relief were systematically relegated to the prerogatives of "ownership" and the avoidance of "penalty" in the course of selecting the assets to be divested, the purchaser, and a price that was "reasonable." This enforcement philosophy, too, directly contravenes the Supreme Court's command: "Those who violate the Act may not reap the benefit of their violations and avoid an undoing of their unlawful project on the pleas of hardship and inconvenience." [14]

Several reforms are needed to upgrade merger relief. The divestiture of a "going concern" must be required with every decree, to assure that partial divestiture would produce a viable competitor. "Going concern" would be defined in terms of a market share that the divested entity must have the capacity to secure.* Next, each decree must set a fixed and unalterable deadline for the divested entity to begin operation. If the deadline passed, heavy escalating civil fines would automatically be levied upon the defendant. To ensure that the new competitor would have the necessary technological and managerial ability, the defendant would have to guarantee its creditors in bankruptcy for, say, five years. To help guard against defendants' circumventions or government's relaxations, the buyer of the to-be-created company should be selected quickly, so that he can help monitor compliance with the decree. Finally, to speed up finding an independent purchaser, the decree should place the choice in the hands of an appointed trustee, not the defendant.

If, after complying with the foregoing requirements, the defendant is still able to record a net profit on the divestiture sale, he should not keep these "fruits" of the illegal merger. Profiting from a divestiture sale is by no means a rare feat. Brown Shoe's 1963 Annual Report revealed a $14 million profit on the sale of Kinney. In the same year Owens-Illinois netted $15 million from divesting only six of 25 illegally acquired National Container Corporation properties, and sold them to a firm in which Owens owned a lot of stock. Divestiture decrees should require an accounting of the defendant's costs in assembling the new corporation and set a maximum sales price which will eliminate profit.

But there are also the interim profits of the acquired firm. In an FTC case, Procter & Gamble siphoned off $66,758,000 from Clorox in dividends during the 10-year period between the merger and divestiture. Section 7 will have little deterrent effect as long as corporations can keep profits earned by their illegal acquisitions throughout a period of protracted litigation with the government. Every divestiture decree, therefore, should require that the assets of the divested entity include all profits from its operations while under illegal ownership.

* Every divestiture decree should also specify a debt-equity ratio to be achieved before the new competitor can qualify as a "going concern." This would, first, guarantee that the new firm starts with the same financial strength and probability of survival as the illegally acquired competitor would have; and, second, would assure that the costs of organizing, equipping, and readying the new company for operation would come from the defendant's own pocket and not be passed on to some asset-purchasing new owner in the form of a heavy debt.

Elzinga noticed a high correlation between the failure of divestiture and the length of time between merger and decree. That should be anticipated under present methods of divestiture, for the longer a firm hangs on to illegally acquired assets, the more it profits and the more likely it becomes that the market will change and make divestiture "unreasonable." Under the suggested approach, the incentive to delay is broken, for the defendant must take whatever steps are necessary to restore a going concern. The longer he delays, the more expensive it will be to undo the damage. It will therefore be in the defendant's own financial interest to expedite the litigation and compliance.

New legislation could attack litigation delays directly. When a merger is planned involving a firm with over $5 million in assets, the merging firms should have to report their plans to the Division. Aided by the Economic Information Center proposed in Chapter IV and by the power to obtain prefiling depositions ("oral" CIDs), the Division would then have 60 days to decide whether to sue. During this time no merger could be consummated. If the Division did not file suit within 60 days, the merger would go through. If a complaint were filed, an automatic injunction would issue until a preliminary hearing were held within 60 days; if the government made a *prima facie* showing of illegality, the court would enjoin the merger pending a full trial. The preliminary injunction could not be denied unless the defendants first presented the court with a divestiture decree incorporating the "going concern" concepts set forth above. Moreover, there would be an automatic 30-day stay of any district-court denial of a preliminary injunction while the Division sought to appeal the decision*

The plan has the benefits of compelling expedition by both the Division and the defendants. The automatic injunction would also discourage the quick merger aimed at mixing assets to block Division attempts to divest. For example, the merger of the *Washington Post* and the old *Times-Herald* occurred literally overnight. It went unre-

---

* This plan is modeled on the Bank Merger Act of 1966, which gives the Division 30 days to decide whether or not to block a bank merger. If it does, the merger is enjoined. The Division staff are able to meet this 30-day deadline because the issues are relatively simple and because all the relevant data are available from banking-agency reporting requirements. Ideally, the Information Center can perform this function for other industries.

ported beforehand by, yes, the *Washington Post.* "Within a day there was almost nothing left of the *Herald,*" observed Robert Wright; "they obviously tried to sneak it by the Division because it's harder to overturn a *fait accompli.*"

The failure of structural relief is also evident when it comes to breaking up Sherman Act monopolies. Of 137 Section 2 charges filed against single firms during 1890–1969, only 24 resulted in significant divestiture of a national or large regional monopolist.[15] And the legal proceedings consumed almost eight years on the average. Even horizontal divestitures have seldom been structurally effective. Take the *Standard Oil* case of 1911. There, the dissolution of a national monopolist initially produced regional monopolists who were later demoted to regional oligopolists by market forces. In the famous 1945 *Alcoa* decision—which went a long way toward establishing the principle that market size alone may constitute an illegal monopoly—no divestiture at all was decreed. Instead, the Court relied upon postwar distribution of surplus aluminum, to be carried out in a manner that would create new competition for Alcoa. Kaiser and Reynolds did come into being this way, and Alcoa's market share of primary aluminum production capacity was reduced from 91% in 1941 to 38.4% in 1960. Replacing Alcoa's monopoly, however, was a vertically integrated three-firm oligopoly, which since 1945 has controlled around 90% of domestic primary and fabricated aluminum production.

The cigarette industry offers an even more salient example. By 1911 robber baron James B. Duke had gobbled up over 250 companies into the American Tobacco Trust. In that year the Supreme Court unanimously declared the monopoly illegal, but the ensuing tripartite dissolution did no more, again, than create a highly disciplined oligopoly. By 1930 R. J. Reynolds, American, and Liggett & Myers controlled 91% of the market. Various forms of inherently suspect conscious parallelism, including virtually identical prices after 1928, culminated in a criminal conviction of the tobacco oligopolists, affirmed by the Supreme Court in 1946. The government thus got a second chance to bust the tobacco trust with a follow-up civil suit.

Though a civil suit was not immediately filed, consent-decree negotiations commenced and lasted into 1949, when

Attorney General Tom Clark told a Congressional committee that a civil complaint had been prepared "and will be filed very shortly." We're still waiting.

Although the Division had intended to move, no one had been assigned to work on a theory of effective relief after Edwin H. Miller, who had headed the criminal prosecution, left for private practice in 1947. In the early 1950s an economist and a trial attorney began to tackle the relief issues. Then on June 3, 1953, section chief Victor Kramer approved a lengthy and detailed FBI investigation, which he called "a monumental piece of work." It was based on a relief scheme which included divesting the popular brands of the big four companies, with advertising limitations on the older firms to allow the new competitors time to entrench themselves. Antitrust chief Stanley Barnes was notified on June 25, 1953. Finally, one day in *1956,* shortly before Barnes was to leave the Division, he discovered a black binder in his office. It was the FBI investigation. Barnes claimed, to the attorney who had worked it up, that he had misplaced it in his desk in the intervening years!

Throughout 1969 Congressman John Dingell of Michigan pressed Richard McLaren to explain why the 23-year-old criminal conviction had never been followed up civilly. McLaren replied:

Although the possibility of civil action based on the facts presented in the criminal case was frequently discussed while the case was still fresh, neither the then available remedies nor the information at hand encouraged filing such a case. . . . Although the same companies continue to employ some of the business techniques exploited monopolistically by them in the 1930s we have no present reason to suppose that they are being consciously orchestrated to produce anticompetitive results.[16]

On February 6, 1970, Congressional testimony described the "delivered pricing" practice long employed by the tobacco oligopolists as a vehicle for eliminating price competition.[17] When Congressman Dingell asked McLaren about this practice—which exists largely because the three big firms were not broken up—the response was that "we continue of the view that we need more to go on than the bare fact that the practice is susceptible of abuse and of long standing." [18]

Another Section 2 debacle was the 1958 *United Fruit* decree. Some monopolists have relied at least in part upon modest production efficiencies and the high capital costs of new entry to ward off competitors. But bananas? All a new firm had to do was purchase a supply from tropical growers, transport it by refrigerated ships to the United States, and market it through regular food channels. Between 1899 and 1928 United Fruit acquired 22 of its competitors. By 1946 it owned 73% of the banana boats, had tied up most of the rest of the space with exclusive dealing contracts, and controlled the Central American railroads that transported bananas to ports; in 1954 it leased or controlled 85% of the land in the Western Hemisphere tropics suitable for banana cultivation and procured 10% of its supply through exclusive dealing contracts with independent growers; United's competitors had to buy their bananas from it. Former Antitrust Division attorney Milton Kallis concluded, after investigating the banana monopoly, that United Fruit had committed every antitrust violation on the books except those involving patents.

On the day that the trial was to start, four years after the Justice Department filed its monopolization complaint, United agreed to a consent decree. After 12 pages of "don't do it again" language, the decree ordered United to spin off a new competitor with sufficient land to grow nine million stems of "average" bananas per year, about 35% of the United States banana market at the time. That was apparently so severe that United was given eight years and five months to submit a "plan" for divestiture and four years to carry it out after it was approved. The divestiture deadline was set for July 28, 1971, 17 years after the suit was filed. The purchaser turned out to be Del Monte, the world's largest producer of canned fruits and vegetables, "a potential large-scale entrant into the banana business anyway," according to a Division attorney.

The reasons for the Division's antimonopoly and antimerger failures are identical. Following an effective trial presentation on the illegality of the United Shoe Machinery Company monopoly, the government made an unsuccessful plea to break up the single-plant firm into three competitors. It was, according to Judge Wyzanski's economist-clerk Carl Kaysen, "sketchy, poorly prepared, and failed to come to grips with any of the problems involved. . . . [What was needed was] a fairly detailed plan, well-supported by evidence, not ten pages of generalizations and citations from legal authorities, supported by ten minutes of oral presentation." [19] Elzinga agrees generally:

> The courts' shyness to order effective relief cannot be totally attributed to a recalcitrant conservatism on the part of the judiciary. At least an equal measure can be attributed, bluntly speaking, to ignorance. . . . When a judge tries a corporation for monopoly he is, in the first place, not so sure of rendering the correct verdict—and this uncertainty may cause him to hedge by formulating a weak relief decree. . . . The blame for this latter characteristic of the judiciary rests with the government's antitrust people. For their function should include the education of the courts on relief.

A dose of economic education from the Division would no doubt have prevented the Supreme Court's utterance in the 1947 *National Lead* case that "There is no showing that four major competing units would be preferable to two, or . . . that six would be better than four."

Even the hostile opinion that divestiture is a "harsh" remedy is confined, at the Supreme Court level, to a handful of statements more than two decades old. They hardly survive the Court's structurally based merger decisions in the Sixties. Moreover, in 1969 the Supreme Court ruled that the government could reopen the 1953 *United Shoe* decree —16 years after the case was decided—and ordered the district court to assess whether its remedies had been effective against the defendant's monopoly power. As a result, United Shoe has finally been required, through divestiture, to reduce its market share to no more than 33% within two years. The Division cannot continue in the future to under-utilize its legal authority to seek "drastic" structural relief in Section 2 monopolization cases.

COMPROMISE AND CONSENT

A leit-motif in our interviews was that "If we can get all we want with a consent decree, why bother litigating?" Yet no one has tried to compare the effectiveness of relief obtained by consent with relief granted after trial. The Division's insistence that there is no difference can neither be proved nor disproved. There are too few litigated cases to permit detailed predictions of how much relief a court *would* have granted if a case were litigated instead of settled. Hidden compromises in consent decrees cannot be uncovered. As the discussion of divestiture remedies suggested, even in litigated cases, the Division rarely presses for the maximum relief the law allows, so no one knows for sure how tough the courts really are.* At least, significant examples of consent decrees which claim to have obtained adequate relief, but in fact have not, can be cited. One, the 1956 *AT&T* decree, has already been described in Chapter II. Others include:

(1) United States v. Atlantic Refining Company (1941)

The original complaints had charged 22 major vertically integrated oil companies, 379 of their subsidiaries, and the American Petroleum Institute with combinations and attempts to monopolize and regulate crude-oil production, transportation, refining, and marketing. The defendants allegedly employed a full array of antitrust violations: price-fixing, predatory price wars, "basing point" delivered price schemes, exclusive dealing contracts, "full line forcing," tying arrangements, and a variety of other practices.

The complaint demanded sweeping divestiture of the oil companies' transportation and marketing facilities (pipelines, gas stations, etc.), plus injunctive relief against 15 separate categories of anticompetitive practices. But that was only the Sherman Act part. In addition, the defendants had controlling interests in the major oil pipelines that by statute were supposed to be regulated common carriers. The defendants had allegedly conspired to fix high pipeline rates to freeze out competitors, recouping their own pipeline expenses through dividends. It was charged that these dividends constituted illegal rebates under the Interstate Commerce Act and the Elkins Act. Successful litigation of all the government's Elkins Act claims would have saddled the petroleum industry with treble-damage penalties of $2.5 billion.

The consent decree waived the Elkins Act penalties and

---

* The *Yale Law Journal* divestiture study did observe that while seven Antitrust Division merger cases (and 13 FTC cases) resulted in consent decrees ordering no divestiture, only one litigated case in which the government prevailed ordered no divestiture. Also, only consent decrees granted divestiture relief which "appears to have little or no relation to the theory of the complaint." The two outstanding examples are (1) the LTV decree containing an option to divest both Braniff Airlines and the Okonite Company instead of Jones & Laughlin Steel, whose acquisition precipitated the government's suit, and (2) ITT's similar option to divest Avis, Levitt, and Hamilton Life instead of the Hartford Insurance Company.

contained *no antitrust relief*. The provisions dealt only with the pipeline rebates, the "relief" limiting dividend payments to shipper-owners to 7% of *total* pipeline assets. This they evaded by a bookkeeping trick.*

The root of this failure was the oil industry's power.[20] The provisions for divestiture of marketing and transportation facilities never even got into the complaint as filed. Before approving it, Attorney General Robert Jackson referred the complaint to the Council for National Defense, which passed it to an oil advisory committee, nine of whose 11 members were connected with either Standard Oil or Shell, both defendants. Although AAG Thurman Arnold pressed on with the case, the oil industry in effect threatened to withhold commitments to the war effort unless the Elkins Act claims were dropped, stiff controls on pipeline operations were abandoned, and the antitrust phases of the case were postponed until after the war—when the charges would have been too stale. The decree reflected this blackmail. Only Arnold signed it on the Antitrust Division's behalf. All the staffers on the case refused.

(2) United States v. El Paso Natural Gas Company (filed 1957—still pending) [21]

Until 1954 El Paso was the sole out-of-state supplier of natural gas to the California market. In that year the Pacific Northwest Pipeline Corporation received approval from the Federal Power Commission to build a pipeline from New Mexico to Washington State, enabling it to enter the California market. The mere threat of an alternative gas supplier forced El Paso to reduce its price to Southern California Edison from 40¢ to 30¢ per thousand cubic feet and to guarantee an uninterrupted supply. Desirous of acquiring its potential competitor, El Paso was informed by the first two law firms it approached that the merger would violate the antitrust laws. But when Arthur Dean of Sullivan & Cromwell "approved" the merger, El Paso acquired Pacific Northwest's stock in 1957. The Antitrust Division filed suit, but did not ask for a preliminary injunction.

---

* The pipelines shifted to financing their assets with debt instead of equity capital. This ploy enabled them to pay dividends in amounts reflecting enormous returns to owners on their stock investments, while at the same time not exceeding 7% of total pipeline assets (debt plus equity capital).

On December 23, 1958, the FPC, without the Division's participation, approved the transfer of Pacific Northwest's assets to El Paso. District Judge Ritter postponed the merger trial while William Bennett, representing California, appealed the FPC decision; in 1962 he obtained a Supreme Court reversal on the ground that the court should have ruled on the legality of the merger first. Thus, by 1963 when the trial began, the merger was already six years old. At the close of the three-week trial Judge Ritter announced from the bench that the government had lost and ordered *El Paso's lawyers* to prepare the findings of fact and conclusions of law, which he signed verbatim. "I shan't write an opinion in this case," he added. On appeal to the Supreme Court, Justice Douglas wrote, "We would have to wear blinders not to see" the illegality of the merger, which was so clear that the Supreme Court itself ordered immediate divestiture without remanding for further proceedings.

But the divestiture plan developed by the parties and Judge Ritter was inadequate. Justice Douglas, speaking for the Court, then accused the Division of "knuckling under" to El Paso. Worse, it did not even try; it merely objected to proposals formulated by El Paso. Due to the Division's passivity, the Supreme Court had no alternative relief plan by which to judge the district-court plan or to formulate detailed orders as to the type of divestiture to be ordered on remand. Finally, it was not the Division, but several states, gas consumers, and other private parties who appealed the decree.

On the next round of divestiture proceedings, the Division again refused to take the initiative in formulating the decree. It sent only one lawyer to the trial, while El Paso rented entire floors of hotels for dozens of lawyers, secretaries, engineers, and other specialists. In 1969 the divestiture decree was *again* reversed by the Supreme Court: the new company still had not been given enough gas reserves to compete in California; also, El Paso's ownership of New Company's nonvoting preferred stock and the decree provision requiring New Company to assume $170 million in El Paso debt did not accord with the "complete divestiture" the Court had ordered. The Court now required divestiture of such additional gas reserves as would be necessary to reinvigorate New Company's potential. Chief Justice Warren's decision to require a cash sale of New Company would increase El Paso's income taxes, but "the pinch on private interests is not relevant to fashioning an antitrust decree, as the public interest is our sole concern."

The Division hierarchy was furious at this decision, for the Court had taken the extraordinary step of acting after all parties had withdrawn their appeals, when two Utah law professors and William Bennett, now an independent "consumer spokesman," had warned that the Court's divestiture mandate was being dishonored. In fact, Colorado Interstate Gas Company, which had been named in the decree as the purchaser of New Company, bought up the appeals by promising Southern California Edison that it would build a pipeline to California to ensure Edison an additional source of supply, and by telling Utah's governor that it would put its headquarters in Salt Lake City, put a Utah man on its board, and buy Utah steel.

In the third round of divestiture proceedings now in progress, the Division is for the first time acting positively. Division attorney John Dougherty sought to discourage future delays by immediate attachment of the $25,000-per-day profits that El Paso is making on its Pacific Northwest operations. To counter El Paso's claim of a shortage of divestible gas reserves, Dougherty sought divestiture of pipeline facilities that would make New Company an actual, not just a potential, competitor. After 15 years and four trips to the Supreme Court, one would assume that competition was on the verge of being restored. Wrong! On June 25, 1971, Judge Chilson rejected the government's divestiture plan and accepted El Paso's—which was to grant New Company fewer reserves than the previous allocation that had been rejected by the Supreme Court as insufficient, a plan with essentially the same market division which Judge Ritter had proposed. "Consumer spokesman" Bennett, now at the height of frustration, filed a "Request . . . to educate the Court on the nature of this case and to the meaning of four decisions of the United States Supreme Court."

These findings represent a massive blunder, a complete misunderstanding of basic antitrust law, and an opinion at war with reality and significant portions of the record. The decision is so grossly in error as to escape understanding. . . . The only saving distinction . . . is that it is at least consistent with three previous District Court judgments including the last one rendered by Judge Chilson, which fortunately for the interest of the gas-consuming public was reversed.

Attached to Bennett's objections was a "Memorandum Brief" consisting primarily of dictionary definitions of the Supreme Court's original mandate—complete divestiture without delay.

One Division attorney ventured that "it would just be too embarrassing to the legal process to take this case to the Supreme Court a fifth time." Yet even that proposal was nearly mooted. Well in advance of Judge Chilson's ruling, El Paso had mobilized a powerful array of politicians, ex-governors, gas utilities, and business interests in the Northwest to back a bill sponsored by Senator Warren Magnusen (the Senate's "Mr. Consumer") to overrule the Supreme Court and allow El Paso to keep everything.[22]

(3) CIBA-Geigy (1970)

The merger of two Swiss firms, CIBA Limited and J. R. Geigy, S.A., combined worldwide chemical assets of $1.4 billion. The Division's complaint cited direct horizontal overlap in six separate lines of commerce in the United States. Although the complaint sought a complete halt to the merger of the American subsidiaries, McLaren's consent decree allowed the clearly illegal merger to go through. It required only that $93.8 million of assets be divested from the areas of horizontal overlap. The huge merged firm ended up with the *larger* of the former market shares of the merging companies in all areas of competitive overlap except one.

The decree, like several others, attempts to restructure the merger to appear to conform with Section 7. Structurally, however, it is a farce. There is no assurance that the new spin-off companies, like their parents, will have worldwide sales organizations, extensive research and development facilities, diversified product lines, and deep financial pockets. In some lines of commerce—especially technically sophisticated ones—these advantages are essential to compete.

Even the "carving out" aspect of the decree was incompletely engineered, for CIBA-Geigy was allowed to *keep* substantial manufacturing facilities, sales forces, and royalty-free patent licenses covering the lines of commerce to be "divested." In one line the merged company is permitted to keep illegally acquired patents and to saddle the divested firm with royalty payments. In another the new company must pay CIBA–Geigy for technical information and manufacturing know-how.

Gordon Spivack, here counsel for an intervenor in the decree proceedings, said that he could not recall a worse settlement in his 12 years of government antitrust work.

(4) Atlantic Richfield–Sinclair (1970)

Among domestic petroleum companies, Atlantic Richfield and Sinclair ranked tenth and eighth, respectively, in refining capacity and gasoline sales. The 15 largest oil companies account for 82% of domestic refinery runs, but regional concentration at the retail gasoline level is often substantially greater. Also, credit cards, billion-dollar assets, and national advertising make all major oil companies potential competitors in any market. The underlying cause of regional oligopolies is parallel vertical integration, by which the companies that "compete" in a market also control the pipelines, tankers, refineries, and crude-oil fields that supply it. Until the government seeks vertical divestiture throughout the entire oil industry (which is highly unlikely), the best hope of shaking up regional gasoline oligopolies lies in vigorous antimerger enforcement to head off further vertical integration and to force the major oil companies to expand internally into new geographic markets.

The Atlantic Richfield–Sinclair decree, negotiated in McLaren's regime, is the very antithesis of such a policy. After the government had obtained a preliminary injunction against the merger, Atlantic negotiated a sale of Sinclair's retail service stations, pipelines, and marketing facilities in 16 Eastern states, plus refining capacity of 200,000 barrels per day, to British Petroleum (BP).* A consent decree was then entered which allowed Atlantic to keep (a) 7,000 Sinclair service stations located in a 12-state area which included Chicago, Detroit, Houston, Dallas, Fort Worth, and Tulsa, (b) almost all of the remaining Sinclair refinery capacity, transportation and pipeline facilities, and

* That could hardly be considered a triumph for competition. BP, with 20% of the world's crude-oil reserves, was eagerly seeking marketing and refinery capacity with which to enter the American market. It should have been forced to enter through some route other than acquisition of a *major* competitor. That is supposed to be the primary function of antimerger law.

crude-oil reserves, including potentially important acreage in Indonesia, Alaska's North Slope, Venezuela, Libya, and Algeria, and (c) all of Sinclair's ships, oil shale, petro-chemicals, other mineral reserves, and oil-import quota allowance.

To be divested as a "going concern" are 2,500 Sinclair service stations in 14 sparsely populated mid-continent states. But Sinclair had *already* decided to sell these prop-erties because of their low rate of return. And Atlantic is required to divest only enough of the crude-oil production capacity and the refinery capacity to supply a small fraction of these service stations. How the new "going concern" will even survive, much less rival its former 42-state vertically integrated self, the consent decree does not say.

Atlantic had recently acquired substantial crude-oil re-serves on Alaska's North Slope and had announced its intention to market gasoline nationwide. It had acquired nine other petroleum companies since 1961. Thus, the Divi-sion had initially opposed Atlantic's acquisition of the 7,000 Sinclair stations in the Midwest because it was already a substantial competitor in three of the 12 states and because it was a potential competitor in the rest. Yet the Division instead allowed Sinclair to be eliminated by a potential com-petitor in the East (BP), absorbed by a near actual com-petitor in the Midwest, and disintegrated through dismem-berment in the mid-continent.

Wall Street Journal reporter Louis Kohlmeier, author of *The Regulators,* thinks that "McLaren's policies are those of big enforcement as far as the complaint is concerned, but the corporation can easily negotiate its way out of an illegal merger with a consent decree disposing of a relatively minor part of the acquired company." Robert Wright, who joined the Division under Thurman Arnold in 1949 and returned as Loevinger's and Orrick's top assistant in 1961–65, thinks that "all consent decrees combined have not given half the antitrust relief as the few cases that have been tried." The Antitrust Division still claims that consent decrees achieve all that the law allows. If so, we need new laws. As Wright points out, "Lawyers for major corporations that can afford protracted litigation will settle only when they have a bad defense; if they had a good defense, why should they settle? They'd win." Or perhaps the Division is catering to the hostility of most district-court judges. It is unlikely that the Supreme Court would limit the government to relief as ineffective as that which its consent decrees display. At least not a Supreme Court that has issued such declarations as "Divestiture has been called the most important of antitrust remedies. It is simple, relatively easy to administer, and sure. It should always be in the forefront of a court's mind when a violation of Section 7 has been found";[23] and "A public interest served by . . . civil suits is that they effectively pry open to competition a market that has been closed by defendant's illegal restraints. If this decree accomplishes less than that, the Government has won a lawsuit and lost a cause." [24] Despite such encouragement, the Division shies away from court cases and judgments. In all of 1969 there was only *one* litigated judgment secured by the Antitrust Division—from 316 lawyers.

PROCEDURAL PROBLEMS WITH CONSENT DECREES

The Division has a vested interest in the consent-decree method of enforcing antitrust laws. Jerry Wagshall, a Division attorney for eight years before joining the treble-damage plaintiff's bar, puts it bluntly: "The reason they like consent decrees is that they can run those operations." The entire consent-decree process is a private affair between the Division and the defendant in which the Division arrogates unto itself the exclusive role of protecting the public interest. The Division's zeal has been illustrated above. More general problems with the consent-decree process follow:

(1) Access

During the FTC's investigation of compliance with 56 Antitrust Division consent decrees, the issue of access arose: Did the decree clause granting the government "access" to the defendant's records mean unfettered access, or could the defendant disclose only material that *it* deemed "relevant"? The district court adopted the latter view in the 1962 *International Nickel* case. The Division decided not to appeal, for unfettered access might make consent decrees harder to get.

(2) "Prefiling" Negotiations

The Division presently attempts to negotiate a settlement before publicly filing a complaint. Supposedly, the consent decree can be obtained faster by giving the defendant a chance to avoid publicity. The complaint and the decree are then filed simultaneously. One of the obvious dangers of prefiling is that compromises may be hidden from public view by altering the complaint to conform with the decree. But the Division assures us that all complaints are approved by the Attorney General, and are unalterable, before prefiling negotiations commence.

On the other hand, certain tactical advantages are lost to Division attorneys through prefiling, such as the threat of public depositions, which led McLaren's Democratic predecessors to disapprove of the practice. The most severe disadvantage of prefiling is, according to *New York Times* reporter Eileen Shanahan, that it "insures that the story will be buried in the financial section rather than appearing on the front page where the consumer will be more likely to read it. This is true of all newspapers." "That," explains former AAG Edwin Zimmerman, "is why companies like it. They can then say to stockholders and the public that this was just a technical problem which was ironed out without difficulty." The Division should give wide publicity to its enforcement efforts, not to disgrace or pillory corporations, but to build an "antitrust constituency" among consumers and to communicate the message of vigilant enforcement to potential violators. Prefiling appears to be a deliberate underpublicizing of the Division's activities, which in the long run is highly detrimental to enforcement. It is the final devolution of the consent-decree process.

(3) Secrecy

Prefiling is symptomatic of the basic objection to the consent-decree process, which is the absolute secrecy of the proceedings and the Division's open disregard for the potential contributions of the public and interested third parties. By statute, none of the evidence gathered through the government's broad CID power can be made available to potential private plaintiffs (including state and local governments), to persons who may be injured by a weak decree, or to members of the public who simply want to evaluate the Division's performance. The negotiations themselves are secret. There is no transcript, not even for the Division's own files. After agreement is reached, there are no public hearings at which proposed decree provisions can be contested by, for example, the 2,500 gas-station operators who may have been "divested" from their livelihoods by the *Atlantic Richfield–Sinclair* decree. The only concession that the Division has ever granted to third parties is a 1961 regulation postponing the judicial rubber stamp for 30 days while they are allowed to submit "comments." Yet the Division need not make them public, nor respond to them.

The actions of most other federal agencies are circumscribed by the Administrative Procedure Act, which guarantees that all interested parties may participate in formal agency proceedings and may seek judicial review of the outcome. Consent-decree negotiations are essentially "administrative" proceedings. Yet the fiction persists that they are "judicial" proceedings—because the judge signs the decree. In most cases, says Professor John Flynn, the judicial role can at best "be analogized to the performance of a symbolic religious rite by a high priest, or, at worst, as the performance of an important public function with the machine-like logic of a chiclet dispenser." [25] Only once in history has a judge altogether refused to sign a consent decree.[26] (On at least three other occasions a district-court judge has forced modifications making the decree *weaker*).[27]

(4) Immunity

Frederick R. Kappel, Western Electric president, was pleased that the AT&T decree "generally makes legal an integrated Bell System—and, to that extent, it is my opinion we preserved the really important thing. In fact, we have good legal proof and a court order saying it is O.K. —a long-posed question settled!" [28] Donald Turner believes that this immunization argument is fallacious, that while the consent decree *itself* cannot be modified without consent of both parties, it cannot bar the government from a new antitrust suit. Nevertheless, all the efforts of Loevinger, Orrick, and Turner to file new suits against AT&T never got past the Attorney General. Another example concerns the exception-ridden 1960 oil-cartel settlement. When AAG Orrick suggested to Standard Oil attorneys in 1964 that this decree and the obligations it imposed on the defendants be dismissed outright, they refused. "They love that decree. It's a nice piece of protection," remarked a former Division official.

The Division may now be able to reopen the AT&T decree and scores of other weak settlements under the Su-

preme Court's 1968 *United Shoe* ruling. The Court held
that a decree can be modified if, after many years, it has
failed to achieve its original objective. But the Division
shows no signs of relieving consumers from the continuing
anticompetitive effects of past compromises by the creative
use of *United Shoe*'s suggestion. To head off weak consent
decrees in the future, Professor Flynn suggests that third
parties be allowed to present evidence and arguments in
the proceedings, as in *El Paso;* such continued prodding
can keep litigation-weary Division attorneys from caving
in on important relief issues. Since the 30-day comment
period was instituted, courts have denied intervention in
seven of the eight attempts involving Division consent decrees. The unsuccessful intervenors in those cases were severely handicapped, however, since they had no access to the
government's evidence, faced an insurmountable burden of
proving bad faith on the Division's part, and had no right
of appeal; it is not surprising that so few consent decrees
have been challenged.

The following recommendation is offered to overcome
these obstacles. Every proposed consent decree would be
sent to the FTC, which is presently authorized by Section
6(e) of the FTC Act "to investigate and make recommendation for the readjustment of the business of any corporation alleged to be violating the antitrust Acts in order
that the corporation may thereafter maintain its organization, management, and conduct of business in accordance
with law." The FTC would conduct an adversary proceeding in which interested parties who objected to the decree
could participate. The consent decree, together with an
FTC report suggesting modifications, would then be for-
warded to the court.

It is possible that these relief proceedings could turn into
the very trial that a consent decree seeks to avoid. However, a combination of strict deadlines and various "preliminary" burdens of proof could prevent any protracted
proceedings; only a few decrees can be expected to be
challenged in any event. Ideally, the Division, faced with
the embarrassing possibility of legal defeat, will itself become the prime preventer of such proceedings by not entering into any more weak consent decrees.

The Division gives one primary reason for seeking consent decrees: they conserve limited enforcement resources.

But that argument is hardly convincing in the light of how few cases are litigated each year and since the staff has already gathered most of its evidence prior to the complaint or decree. It is not necessary, however, for the Division to engage in litigation at all in order to promote treble-damage recoveries. There is a device called an "asphalt clause," so named after the first case in which it was employed, which gives a consent decree the effect of a litigated decree. It states that the defendant will not deny in any court that the consent decree holds him *prima facie* liable in treble damages to any person who can prove injury from the conduct alleged in the complaint.

The asphalt clause has a brief history. Only once has it been used successfully. The occasion was a group of 1960 Massachusetts cases alleging price-fixing and bid-rigging in the sale of asphalt and road-building materials.[29] After the defendants pleaded *nolo contendere* to criminal charges, Massachusetts Attorney General Edward McCormack protested to the Justice Department that "to accept a *nolo* plea in a criminal case and then a consent decree in a civil action completely destroys . . . the rights of the treble-damage litigant which, in this case, happens to be sister-governments, *i.e.,* the state of Massachusetts and the cities and towns therein. . . . The greatest deterrent to antitrust [violations] is being vitiated." [30] AAG Bicks agreed, supposedly initiating a new policy: the Division would seek asphalt clauses in cases in which a state or local government had been the primary victim of antitrust violations.

The new policy was given a jolt in the 1962 "gymnasium bleachers" case, when a Wisconsin federal district judge signed a "consent" decree without the asphalt clause the government had demanded.[31] Solicitor General Cox refused to appeal the district court's decision, and asphalt clauses never surfaced again. A few trial attorneys continued to seek them, but the Division did not support them. Loevinger told John Galgay, then head of the New York field office, that local governments had their own funds and that the Division did not need to spend its money to save them litigation costs. Turner and Zimmerman were even less enthusiastic. Indeed, Turner tended to view private treble-damage suits as potential nuisances to government antitrust policy. "Those corporations have very sophisticated antitrust counsel," he said, presuming that his honorable colleagues would instruct their clients to obey the law as laid down by Professor Turner.

McLaren is on record that "where the Division has determined to oppose the entry of *nolo* pleas in order to aid private litigants, but where the court nevertheless accepts the *nolo* pleas, it would seem to follow that in any companion civil case the Division should consider going to trial if the defendants will not agree to the inclusion of an 'asphalt clause' in the decree." [32] Yet he subsequently told the Study Group that "Congress wanted to encourage consent decrees" when it exempted them from the *prima facie* evidentiary-effect provisions of Section 5 of the Clayton Act. "The case [violation] must be so bad as to be outside the intent of Congress for us to ask for an asphalt clause." McLaren is apparently confused as to the purpose of asphalt clauses and the clear intent of Congress in passing Section 5—to promote treble-damage recoveries, not to grant defendants a "right" to a consent decree. The "badness" of the violation is not particularly relevant, since general deterrence, not compensation of particular victims, is the primary function of the treble-damage recoveries that asphalt clauses promote.

Another McLaren argument against asphalt clauses was that they "make it impossible to get a consent decree." That most defendants would refuse to accept asphalt clauses is highly speculative. McLaren's "evidence" was that "Bicks and Loevinger tried and failed many times to get them," and that *he* (McLaren) certainly would not counsel *his* clients to accept an asphalt clause. Bicks and Loevinger apparently did not press very hard for asphalt clauses. Only once, in the bleachers case, did they stand up to defendants who called their bluff. One former Division attorney said that "it's a bunch of bull that businesses won't accept an asphalt clause. They'll do whatever is necessary to avoid a trial. It's just a question of good bargaining."

The converse of McLaren's untested thesis is more plausible. The defendant who knows that he will lose in court will accept an asphalt clause if he also knows that otherwise the Division *will* take him to court. By accepting the asphalt clause the defendant can minimize publicity, save the time and expense of trial, and avoid a public record crammed with evidence useful to potential treble-damage plaintiffs.

How many defendants know that they would lose in court? Earl Jinkinson once wrote that "during the years that I have served as chief of the Southern and Midwest Offices of the Antitrust Division, I have seen about 150 civil cases initiated. *In over half of these cases* the facts and law were so clear that full-blown trial would have been futile."[33] In these cases, he added, "no one was surprised that the defendants asked for and received consent decrees." A highly significant analogy is that between 1954 and 1964 over 60% of the defendants whose *nolo* pleas were rejected subsequently chose to plead guilty, accepting both criminal sanctions and *prima facie* effect rather than enduring a public trial. An educated guess would be that 60–80% of all consent-decree defendants know they would lose at trial; the percentage is probably much higher for price-fixing cases, the staple of the treble-damage bar.

Finally, an asphalt clause does not mean automatic treble-damage liability. The *prima facie* presumption of liability is rebuttable, and the defendant would probably prefer doing battle with a private plaintiff rather than with the government. Moreover, the treble-damage suitor must prove the fact and amount of his damages in addition to the defendant's liability—a task that many private plaintiffs have been unable to accomplish.

There will nevertheless be cases, probably a handful per year, that will be forced into litigation by a mandatory asphalt-clause provision in consent decrees. But the Division resources consumed by these cases would by no means be wasted. If anything, an asphalt-clauseless "stop that" consent decree is itself the greatest waste of the Division's limited resources; since divestiture is not ordinarily applicable to many conduct-oriented antitrust abuses, the treble-damage deterrent is the *only* means of preventing them. The judicial precedent established through litigated decrees would be a valuable enforcement aid. Since the traditional enforcement theme has been "voluntary compliance," there must be some clear definition of what is to be complied with.

Reflection on why corporations violate the antitrust laws compels a tough enforcement philosophy precisely *because* the agency has limited resources. It is simply not true that corporations voluntarily comply with the antitrust laws and that violations are the result of inscrutable deviations that must be "fixed" by consent decrees. Excessive greed for profit is the ultimate cause of illegal conduct, to the point that many antitrust violators talk themselves into thinking they were doing the right or even the legal thing. Antitrust enforcement is too important to be voluntary. What Walton Hamilton and Irene Till said in their TNEC monograph 30 years ago still holds true: "[Antitrust enforcement] . . . must remain largely preventive. And prevention moves by example; it dangles before the many the fate of the few." [34]

TREBLE-DAMAGE SUITS: "PRIVATE" ATTORNEYS GENERAL

Given the gross failure of the government's criminal and civil antitrust programs, the treble-damage remedy may be the last hope for effective enforcement. But the treble-damage action's performance through the years has indeed been a saga of unmet potential. About 75% of private antitrust suits follow successfully litigated government judgments; yet of 136 such government antitrust victories from the passage of Section 5 of the Clayton Act in 1914 through June 30, 1959, only 29 were followed by treble-damage suits. Apparently the *prima facie* presumption of defendant liability arising from litigated government judgments (or guilty verdicts) is a necessary but not a sufficient aid to the treble-damage plaintiff. Professor John Guilfoil found that "from 1940 to 1963 . . . in price-fixing cases exclusive of electrical equipment suits, there exists *no* case where a Government judgment of guilty preceded court-awarded damages. But there were eight suits which plaintiffs lost that followed verdicts of guilty in Government suits." [35] These figures do not include the approximately one-fourth of private antitrust suits that are settled out of court.[36]

While treble damages seem like a substantial penalty, the already mentioned analyses of McMenimen, Erickson, Dirlam, and Lanzillotti demonstrate that price-fixing can be very profitable *even if* one unrealistically assumes a 100% probability that the violation will be detected and that plaintiffs will recover full treble damages. Three factors explain this phenomenon. First, because of the statute of limitations, a treble-damage action must be brought within four years of the plaintiffs' injury—unless the plaintiff can prove "fraudulent concealment," which is legally difficult to show. Second, not all of the defendant's victims will be willing, able, or knowledgeable enough to sue. And third, the defendant has interest-free use of the profits from his violation throughout both the statute-of-limitations period and the protracted litigation which precede the damage judgment.

While guilty defendants may profit in spite of treble-damage recoveries, plaintiffs with valid antitrust claims fare poorly. In 1969 the major manufacturers of plumbing fixtures were convicted of price-fixing. Plumbing fixtures are distributed through various chains of wholesalers, retailers, contractors, and subcontractors. These middlemen may have lost some profits on account of the manufacturers' conspiracy, for consumer demand can decline when middleman costs and prices rise. The primary victims, however, were the citizens, businesses, and government entities who paid more for homes and buildings containing plumbing fixtures. When they brought class actions to recover their damages, they were told that they did not have "standing" to sue, that because of the intervening middlemen their damages were too "remote" to be traced and attributed to the manufacturers.

Despite these formidable obstacles, increasing numbers of private antitrust suits have been brought in recent years. During the Sherman Act's first half-century there were only 175 reported decisions in private antitrust cases, with plaintiffs successful in only 13.[37] But during the 1965–69 period alone, 3,136 private antitrust suits were filed. Several factors underlie this upsurge. The liberalization of pretrial discovery procedures, beginning in 1939, has made it easier for plaintiffs' lawyers to gather evidence. In private actions following government criminal prosecutions which have ended in no-contest pleas, plaintiffs can now obtain access to certain grand-jury evidence. In the electrical-equipment and children's-book price-fixing cases, as well as in the smog conspiracy case, evidence presented to grand juries was impounded for appropriate use by later treble-damage suitors. The experience and the inspiration of the nationally coordinated electrical-conspiracy damage suits undoubtedly contributed to the burgeoning "treble-damage business." Much of the credit, however, belongs to a steady current of Supreme Court decisions extending the scope of litigated government victories to private suits, eliminating various defenses to treble-damage liability, and making it easier for plaintiffs to prove damages after establishing the defendant's liability.[38]

But impediments to effective treble-damage remedies persist: the settlement of claims for a fraction of treble damages, the defendant's retention of prejudgment interest on his illegal profits, the participation of treble-damage suits of less than all of the victims of an antitrust violation, the "remoteness" doctrine, and the protracted and expensive nature of antitrust litigation. Many of the legal doctrines behind these obstacles were created by a lower-court judiciary indifferent to antitrust violations and wary of adding protracted litigation to crowded court calendars. For example, the Supreme Court has never sanctioned the "remoteness" doctrine. Yet District Judge John Lord threw the plumbing-fixtures consumer plaintiffs out of his court on the basis of the Supreme Court's 1968 *Hanover Shoe* decision. This case allowed a shoe manufacturer to recover the entire amount of an illegal overcharge from a shoe-machinery manufacturing company, even though some portion of it may have been "passed on" to his own customers. The Supreme Court's stated objective in *Hanover Shoe* was to promote treble-damage recoveries by middlemen since ultimate "consumers would have little interest in bringing a class action." *Hanover Shoe* did *not* say that a middleman would not have to share his recovery with consumers if they *did* bring a class action. But Judge Lord assumed that consumers were to be prohibited from suing at all, and a federal appeals court cursorily affirmed Judge Lord's decision.* [39] The illogic of this interpretation, given *Hanover Shoe*'s professed purpose of encouraging plaintiffs by eliminating the "passing on" defense, is best illustrated by the middlemen-wholesalers' recovery in their suit against the plumbing-fixtures manufacturers—$2 million. This, plus $24.5 million that went to more remote purchasers in other settlements, amounted to about 10% of the $250 million

---

* In the antibiotic-drug price-fixing cases, the wholesalers and retailers, citing *Hanover Shoe,* held out for an $11 million share of the consumer settlement, even though they *profited* from the price-fixing conspiracy by adding their standard 65% mark-up to the already inflated manufacturer's price. District Judge Inzer B. Wyatt was not impressed by their argument.[40] Nor was Judge Manuel Real of Los Angeles impressed by the remoteness doctrine itself. He ruled that pollution victims were not too "remote" to sue the automobile industry for treble damages resulting from a conspiracy to retard the development and introduction of pollution-control devices.[41] (But he then threw out of court without explanation the class action brought in behalf of all individual pollution victims in the country.) The remoteness doctrine, created by district judges, can be abolished by them—or by a single Supreme Court decision.

in treble damages that should have been extracted from these convicted price-fixers.

Out-of-court settlements for single damages or less are the usual route that "successful" treble-damage cases take. "Those guys have hardly litigated a case since the electrical-equipment conspiracy trials," is how one disgruntled plaintiffs' lawyer characterized his peers. Why? Primarily because treble-damage litigation is enormously expensive and risky. While large defendant corporations can bear the heavy expenses of litigation, plaintiffs often cannot. Plaintiffs' lawyers interviewed by the Study Group all agreed that elimination of these difficulties would make treble-damage litigation worthy of its name and original purpose, but none were eager to jeopardize *their* cases to establish the requisite judicial precedents. It must also be stressed that the plaintiffs' lawyer lives in a highly uncertain environment. "He doesn't have a grand jury," says one; therefore, evidence must be gathered *after* filing suit. And plaintiffs' lawyers are often skeptical of any jury returning a verdict of, say, $500 million, no matter how strong the evidence.

For all these reasons, plaintiffs' lawyers prefer to settle their cases prior to a litigated trebled judgment. Why risk a guaranteed $5 million contingent fee from a $25 million settlement now, they ask themselves, by seeking a $25 million fee from a $100 million jury verdict five years later? Nor is the reason entirely financial. Litigating the protracted antitrust case is a difficult and painstaking task, and plaintiffs' lawyers share the natural human aversion to hard work.

Asphalt clauses are only one way of making treble-damage actions more viable. Senator Hart has proposed that the Small Business Administration make loans to small businessmen who lack funds to bring antitrust cases. The SBA's response has been that antitrust suits are too risky an investment—which may be true in the short run. Yet once a few judicial precedents are established which simplify the plaintiffs' burdens, the long-run benefits of effective deterrence of antitrust violations will accrue to small businessmen generally. A second possibility could be legislation creating a federal venture-capital corporation to lend money to treble-damage plaintiffs. A third would be to tap funds that have been recovered in prior antitrust class actions in behalf of damaged but unidentifiable consumers. In the antibiotics settlement, several million dollars of unclaimed monies have been placed in state trust funds to be used "for the benefit of consumers generally." Why not use these trust funds to make loans to support future antitrust litigation on behalf of consumers?

As a fourth possibility, entrepreneurs could sell stock in publicly held corporations which would make loans to antitrust plaintiffs in return for a percentage of the ultimate recovery. The lawyer, not "Treble Damages, Inc.," would decide when and whether to settle the case, but his professional judgment would no longer be distorted by a financial interest of his own in seeking a quick settlement. Moreover, unlike the wealthiest plaintiffs' attorneys, he could then afford to risk the large sums required to litigate protracted cases to a successful conclusion.

The most significant, and likely, corrective to the treble-damage failure is *class actions*. If the courts will solve the problems of remoteness, statute of limitations, and pre-judgment interest, and if the Antitrust Division will insist upon asphalt clauses in consent decrees, the class action can eliminate all other shortcomings of the treble-damage remedy. One of the most significant recent developments in antitrust enforcement has been a series of nationwide treble-damage actions, commonly brought in the name of state and local governments and consolidated before a single judge for pretrial discovery proceedings by the Judicial Panel on Multi-District Litigation. These cases are often brought as class actions in behalf of all governmental units—*e.g.*, hospitals, school districts—that purchased the price-fixed or bid-rigged items. Some of the products that this multidistrict litigation has involved are drugs, plumbing fixtures, burglary-protection devices, gasoline, gypsum wallboard, brass and copper tubing, children's books, and automobile-produced smog. In several cases the states have included as members of the plaintiff class all private consumers within their jurisdictions—pollution victims in the smog case and doctors' patients in the drug cases—and have sought to recover damages in their behalf.

A class action allows many similarly situated victims of antitrust violations to pool their claims in a single lawsuit. This aggregation of claims creates a contingent-fee potential large enough to attract a lawyer. Since all similar victims are automatically included in the class, except those who affirmatively opt out, the class action can confront the antitrust violator with claims for the entire amount of competitive harm that he has inflicted. The potential impact of class-action suits is illustrated by the following example:

In *West Virginia* v. *Charles R. Pfizer & Co.,* 49 states and several cities brought class actions against major drug firms charged with conspiring to fix the price of certain "broad spectrum" antibiotics. The complaints sought treble damages in behalf of various governmental units and private consumers who purchased the drugs through doctors' prescriptions. On February 6, 1969, the defendants offered to settle all of these claims for $100 million (plus a subsequent $32.5 million for another class action brought by private hospitals). After seven states and one city had rejected the offer as inadequate, a final settlement approximating $80 million was approved by the court. Although that sounds like a lot of money, consumers alone—who purchased 75% of the drugs during the 1954–66 conspiracy period but received only 37% of the settlement—might have recovered treble damages of $1.9 *billion* had the case been successfully litigated rather than settled. Arthur Galligan, one of the plaintiffs' lawyers, described the effect of the damage settlement upon the defendants as a "license fee to do business."

Although all state attorneys general and other class representatives were eventually united into a single "temporary national class," each class member still attempted to establish the amount of his damages—*i.e.,* who bought what from whom, when, how much, and at what price. Plaintiffs' lead counsel Dave Shapiro spent "one or two years" culling through New York City drug-purchase receipts in order to compile this "transaction data." Since the rules of the game forbid full treble damages until each class member produces documented evidence for every penny overcharged, instead of being allowed to claim a *pro rata* share of the statistically computed damages of the entire class, it is easy to understand why the pressure to settle for less than treble damages is on the plaintiffs. The reason that the defendants were willing to settle for as much as $100 million was that Shapiro, Galligan, and one other associate spent 30,000–40,000 man-hours, much of it collecting transaction data, for the 20 states and four cities they represented—at a cost of approximately $1 million. As they compiled more

and more transaction data, supplemented with statistical
surveys, the tables gradually turned on the defendants,
who settled.

In order for antitrust class actions, now in their infancy,
to transform the treble-damage remedy into an effective
deterrent, the courts must accept the "bifurcated trial" procedure. Suppose that the five manufacturers of "widgets"
have been engaged in a "fraudulently concealed" price-
fixing conspiracy for the last 10 years, during the course
of which one million widgets were sold annually at an average price of $2 each. Without a conspiracy the market
price of widgets would have been $1 each. The total over-
charge to the class of "all persons who have purchased
widgets in the last 10 years" would be $10 million, trebled
to $30 million. Upon proof *only* of the above facts, the
court should order the defendants to make a joint lump-
sum payment of $30 million to the plaintiff class *as an
entity*.

That would end the basic lawsuit between the plaintiffs and
the defendants. New proceedings would then commence,
perhaps partially under the supervision of a special court-
appointed master, to determine the share of the aggregate
damage fund to be contributed by each defendant and to
be received by each class member. Any controversies that
might arise over individual class members' shares would
be fought out among the class members themselves and
not between the class and the defendants. Since a speedy
resolution would be to everyone's advantage, the class
members would probably dispense with detailed transaction
data and fix upon some fair statistical formula to govern
the various amounts to be distributed. The bifurcated trial
would thus substantially alleviate the protractedness of
antitrust litigation, and the antitrust plaintiff would no
longer be so dependent upon financial ability for ultimate
victory. Most important, the bifurcated trial, with its threat
of aggregate damage liability, would force defendants to
settle sooner and for much larger amounts.* Finally, the

---

* It is probable that the level of treble-damage recoveries under a bifurcated-trial approach would force some defendants into bankruptcy. For
companies that were profitable and efficiently managed, bankruptcy would
usually mean only a change in ownership, not unemployment. The stockholders would suffer, but there is no more reason to protect them from
antitrust risks than from other types of management indiscretion which
may lead to bankruptcy. If a few major corporations were forced into
bankruptcy on account of antitrust criminality, other firms might finally
take note and be convinced that crime doesn't pay.

bifucated-trial technique has been recently approved, at least tentatively, in the antibiotic-drug litigation pressed by the seven states that had refused to accept the earlier settlement offer.[42]

While the bifurcated trial is the surest way to administer the deterrent function of the treble-damage remedy, it will not always be possible to identify the consumers who were actually victimized and to distribute the total damage fund to them alone. The notion that antitrust violators or consumer defrauders should be forced to pay damages to someone other than their actual victims is fundamentally opposed by the U.S. Chamber of Commerce, the ABA Antitrust Section, and AAG McLaren, all of whom have lobbied against legislation encouraging consumer class-action suits. McLaren assistant Bruce Wilson, who was recently appointed to head up a new Consumer Protection Unit within the Justice Department, states flatly that class actions are of little benefit to consumers. But if the treble-damage remedy is unable to achieve its *secondary* goal of compensation, that is certainly no reason to abandon its *primary* goal of deterrence. This primary purpose is achieved with equal effectiveness whether the damage payments are made to actual victims, victims' lawyers, or someone selected at random from the telephone book.

McLaren argues that raising the maximum criminal penalty under the Sherman Act to $500,000 would accomplish the same deterrent effect. Besides the fact that this legislative proposal failed in the last session of Congress, even that penalty would be small change to the defendants in the electrical-equipment and antibiotic-drug cases. In addition, the $500,000 fine would be a maximum, and judges are neither required nor likely to impose it. Finally, McLaren's alternative would provide no effective means of deterring *civil* antitrust violations.

Judges too are hostile to the "bounty hunting" aspects of bifurcated-trial class-action recoveries; the judicial euphemism is "unmanageability." When a class of 1.5 million bread consumers sued Philadelphia bakeries who had earlier pleaded no contest to price-fixing charges, Federal Judge Charles R. Weiner threw the case out because its "management" would prove "insuperable." [43] What he apparently had in mind was the difficulty of identifying each bread-purchaser class member and calculating how many loaves he had purchased and what damages he ought to recover.*

Since multidistrict class-action litigation is inordinately expensive, forcing the plaintiffs to duplicate the previous government investigation hardly makes sense. As Judge John P. Fullam told the ABA Subcommittee on Private Antitrust Litigation, "I wonder if anyone can rationally justify the concept of high-priced, highly skilled legal talent conducting file searches, for example, in preparation for a treble-damage claim, going through precisely the same files which the Justice Department has gone through, getting the same information all over again." Plaintiffs' attorney Dolores Korman gives an example. "On January 20, 1971, 34 lawyers representing the treble-damage plaintiffs and the defendants in over 200 plumbing-fixture antitrust cases . . . appeared in a Washington, D.C., courtroom to attend the beginning of the deposition of one witness which continued for 23 days. This deposition was scheduled to be followed by the depositions of at least 28 more witnesses called by the plaintiffs." [45] Certainly this situation calls for asphalt clauses, the opening up of government-collected evidence to private litigants, and perhaps new legislation spelling out acceptable formulas for proving damages. Such legislation could guarantee that plaintiffs who can prove liability and at least some damage are entitled to a minimum recovery of 10% of sales revenues.

The government could eliminate some of the duplication of effort by recouping the illegal profits of antitrust defendants it prosecutes civilly or criminally. The proceeds would then either be distributed directly to injured parties or held

* One remedy suggests itself: the defendant bakeries could be ordered to affix a coupon to all loaves of bread sold in the future. Substantially the same housewives who were previously victimized by illegally high bread prices, and who presumably would continue to purchase bread, could then redeem those coupons for cash at any grocery store. The grocery stores would be reimbursed upon surrendering their coupons to the administrator of the aggregate damage fund. The process would continue until the fund was exhausted. The defendants could not raise the price of bread to recoup their trust-fund payments without either (1) being prosecuted for price-fixing again or (2) losing substantial sales to new or nonconspiring competitors, who would also affix the coupons to their bread.[44]

Similar compensation schemes could be applied to most other consumer nondurables. Many durable goods, such as automobiles and appliances, are sold with warranties kept on file by the manufacturer. Banks, telephone companies, and electric utilities have records of transactions with their customers. If this bifurcated-trial class-action technique were adopted, new compensation schemes could probably be devised to fit the varying circumstances under which most price-fixed products are sold.

in trust for satisfaction of damage judgments in private suits. If the total amount of the proven damage claims exceeded the amount of the sequestered profits, recoveries would be limited to *pro rata* shares. Of course defendants would remain liable for the remainder in treble-damage suits. Since attaching illegal profits is simply a means of divesting the defendant of the "fruits" of his violation, no new legislation would be required for the Antitrust Division to obtain such civil relief.

It would be preferable, however, for new legislation to require the government to assess full treble damages against each civil and criminal antitrust violator.* [46] The government prosecution would be substituted for the first stage of the bifurcated treble-damage class action. Thereafter, injured parties would file claims for their shares against the government, just as they would against class damage funds in the second stage of a bifurcated trial. Private treble-damage suits filed prior to the government suit would not be destroyed. The government would be substituted for the defendants in the private action, and in addition to damages the claimants would be entitled to recover reasonable attorneys' fees from the government (which would be reimbursed by the defendants). To guard against government compromises in the damage-assessment proceedings, the government would be liable to injured parties for the full amount of their proven damages, even if the damage fund had been depleted. Administration of the treble-damage deterrent under the proposed system could not be prevented by a "gentlemen's agreement" between large industries not to sue "their fellow private corporations for treble damages unless pressed to do so by stockholders." [47] Of course, injured parties would remain free to bring treble-damage suits in the event that the government chose not to prosecute the defendant. The proposal is therefore a supplement, not a substitute, for strengthened private enforcement. But because of the threat of mandatory prison terms, the bifurcated class action, and automatic government treble-damage assessments, antitrust violations would be rare occurrences.

* Since the two-thirds "penalty" portion of the treble-damage recovery serves the same deterrent purpose as a criminal fine, fairness would dictate that the government remit criminal fines to a defendant who can establish *full* payment of all treble-damage claims that may have arisen from its antitrust violation.

Today we rank among the 150 world's leading corporations.
Between now and 2000 A.D. economists predict that this num-
ber of companies will be producing two-thirds of the free
world's goods. We intend to be among the leaders.
    —*Weyerhaeuser Company* Annual Report, *1968*

7

Antitrust Abroad

WORLD, INC.

On May 12, 1971, Chrysler Motors, the seventh largest
U.S. industrial corporation, entered into an agreement to
purchase 35% of Mitsubishi Motors, the wholly owned
subsidiary of Japan's fifth largest corporation. Chrysler is
already importing Mitsubishi compacts, which it markets
as Dodge Colts; in return Mitsubishi will begin importing
Valiants from Chrysler's Australian subsidiary. The merger
is just one step in Chrysler's aggressive worldwide acquisition of production and marketing facilities, an empire
that included over 40 subsidiaries in 20 countries by the
end of 1969. It is not surprising that General Motors and
Ford plan similar mergers with Japanese auto producers.
These are the most significant in a wave of international
mergers and acquisitions which began in the late 1950s
and continues unabated today. Some of the foreign firms

acquired by American corporations have been large: Reynolds Aluminum's 1959 acquisition of British Aluminum (Britain's largest aluminum producer), General Electric's mergers with France's Machines Bull and Italy's Olivetti, and Chrysler's acquisition of France's Simca and Britain's Rootes Motors, Ltd., in the 1960s. Most of the merger activity has escaped public notice; yet each year since 1968, American corporations have acquired interests in between 300 and 400 foreign companies, say unpublished Federal Trade Commission reports.

Merger is only one way to acquire facilities abroad; much American foreign investment results from setting up new branches and subsidiaries abroad. The book value of the direct investment by U.S. corporations was estimated by the Commerce Department to be some $77 billion at the end of 1970, 10 times what it was at the end of 1956. Although over 35,000 U.S. firms had foreign affiliates at last count (1966), some 200 giant corporations are believed to own at least 80% of U.S. direct investments abroad.[1] Trade (exports and imports) is no longer the most important link between the U.S. and foreign economies; the combined output of American foreign affiliates is estimated to be about five times the value of U.S. merchandise exports. It has become increasingly clear that our largest corporations are *multinational enterprises* which no longer plan production and marketing in terms of the domestic market alone.

Foreign corporations are playing the multinational merger and investment game with smaller stakes but no less vigor than their American counterparts. The Royal Dutch/ Shell group, Unilever (also British-Dutch), British Petroleum, and Nestlé (Swiss) have sizable investments in many countries, including the United States. Purchases of U.S. firms by foreign corporations include Olivetti's acquisition of Underwood in 1959, BASF's (Germany) acquisition of Wyandotte Chemical, Inc., and French Pechiney's purchase of 56% of Howmet, the fifth largest U.S. primary aluminum producer. Foreign direct investment in the United States is presently valued above $13 billion and is expected to grow 16% in 1971.[2]

As a consequence, concentration of power in world markets has grown. Steel mergers between two large German firms and a Dutch concern, between Japan's Yawata and

Fuji companies to form Nippon (now the world's largest steel producer), and mergers among France's largest steel companies have increased concentration in the world steel market. Britain's Dunlop recently merged with Italy's Pirelli to become the world's second largest producer of rubber products. Auto mergers have been numerous: besides the U.S.-Japanese mergers mentioned above, Volkswagen merged with Auto Union (DKW), British Motor Holdings and Leyland merged in 1968, Japan had four mergers of automobile companies in 1969, and Fiat and Citroën have recently announced collaboration in research and development. It is estimated that nine huge corporations account for four-fifths of global automobile production. Economic concentration in many other industries is likely to be on the increase, but it is difficult to make unequivocal statements because of the serious lack of data. The long-run trend, however, is apparent. As the quote from Weyerhaeuser indicates, continued consolidation of capital will result in monopolization of world markets by a few behemoths. This presents a challenge to antitrust enforcement paralleling that of the great American horizontal-merger movement of the late 19th Century. One hopes the present battle will be more successful.

PROTECTIONISM

A second international development with implications for antitrust is the deteriorating United States balance of trade, which is the difference between exports and imports of goods. Since 1893 the United States has annually sold more goods abroad than it has imported. The surplus averaged about $2.5 billion in the 1950s, grew to $5–$7 billion between 1960 and 1967, and fell to only $1–$2 billion since 1967. Not surprisingly, the recent shift in the trade balance coincided with the spurt in domestic inflation, fueled by military spending abroad and exacerbated by monopolistic prices at home. We are simply pricing our goods out of world markets. In July, 1971, Commerce Secretary Maurice Stans predicted that for the first time in this century the United States may have a trade deficit in 1971.

Various groups are blaming their economic woes, primarily a result of the domestic economic recession, on foreign competition. Businessmen who were once proponents of free international trade are now calling for protection from "unfair" foreign competition. While the original Henry Ford thought that "we need competition the world over to keep us on our toes," his grandson, Henry Ford II, complained to stockholders last year that "I frankly don't see how we're going to meet foreign competition. We've only seen the beginning." [3] American labor knows how Ford will meet the competition: by producing abroad. Labor is actively pushing for additional capital controls on American multinational corporations to prevent them from "exporting jobs" by expanding production in foreign subsidiaries as they cut back production at home. In addition, the AFL-CIO, which supported liberalization of trade restrictions throughout the 1950s, has joined the protectionist chorus. In testimony before a Senate subcommittee in May, 1970, AFL-CIO President George Meany recommended that the government promote "an orderly marketing mechanism . . . to regulate the flow of imports into the United States of those goods and product lines, in which sharply rising imports are displacing significant percentages of U.S. production and employment." [4]

A number of remedial steps to increase exports and limit imports have been advanced. Tax breaks for exporters, expansion of the amount of credit which the Export-Import Bank can extend for export transactions, subsidies for research and development, increased pressure on foreigners to take down trade barriers, and devaluation of the dollar are some of the frequently offered suggestions.* Since none of these proposals impinges directly on antitrust enforcement, we will not discuss them here. Two additional measures have been proposed, however, which would seriously damage competition in the domestic market: these are, first, relaxation of U.S. antitrust laws to remove alleged

* President Nixon hoped the measures he announced in his August 15 speech would shift the U.S. trade balance into the black and hence expand domestic production and employment. By refusing to sell any more gold at the old fixed price of $35 an ounce, the President forced foreign countries to revaluate their currencies upward against the dollar. This makes U.S. exports cheaper abroad and foreign products more expensive in the United States. The 10% surcharge on dutiable imports, and the 10% investment tax credit applying only to *domestic* firms, were further steps to make imports more expensive as well as a bargaining weapon to force recalcitrant countries (read Japan) to revalue their currencies. Finally, on December 14, 1971, President Nixon agreed to devalue the dollar by 8.5% and to drop the 10% surcharge.

hindrances to American companies' ability to compete with foreigners; and, second, the imposition of quota limits on various categories of imports which are felt to be injuring U.S. business.

RELAXING ANTITRUST

A suggestion long popular in business circles is the "liberalization" of the antitrust laws. In a hearty endorsement of Senator Javits' perennial bill to set up a commission to review the antitrust laws, W. F. Newton, a member of the board of the U.S. Chamber of Commerce, asserted that the antitrust laws seriously handicap U.S. producers in international competition. Why? Because our antitrust laws inhibit U.S. corporations from combining or cooperating in joint ventures, practices which are often allowed and sometimes even encouraged abroad. Newton claimed that "[t]his affects not only our ability to compete with foreign manufacturers in international markets, but is very seriously affecting our ability to resist penetration of many of our key domestic markets by foreign producers." [5]

Secretary of Commerce Stans, a long-time advocate for big business, testified on June 25, 1971, before a Congressional subcommittee that investigations were under way in the Executive Branch into the effect of the antitrust laws on international competition.

> We need also to examine our antitrust philosophies. These were developed in another era—when the United States was virtually isolated from foreign competition. They may no longer be appropriate for industries competing against foreign producers free of such restraints. [6]

Various other administration officials, including the President's principal economic spokesman, Treasury Secretary Connally, have endorsed this view. It has been repeated so often that it has become an article of faith among businessmen and their friends in government. Its proponents have rarely felt called upon to support it with evidence or logic.

In a series of hearings beginning in 1964, Senator Philip Hart asked for just such evidence. Only one witness came forward with specific examples of lost foreign sales. Mr. William Persen, editor of *Business International,* cited 20 such cases. [7] (All the cases were disguised to protect the identity of the firms involved, presumably to avoid leaking information to the Justice Department.) All but one of the cases involved U.S. firms setting up subsidiaries abroad, merging with a foreign company, or licensing production of its product abroad. Thus, Mr. Persen was really talking about foreign investment and not about exporting. Only one case involved a firm which was allegedly inhibited from exporting:

Case V: A U.S. electrical goods firm divested itself of its prewar network of companies in Europe under a consent decree, leaving only its export company. Due to fear of further action it refrained from any real export effort. Now it is starting a tentative return to these markets—but very late in the game.

How is it possible to evaluate these sketchy fragments? Certainly no company has been prosecuted for merely exporting merchandise through its export subsidiary. Perhaps the company was conspiring with another firm to "cross-license and hold patents for the purpose of keeping a Japanese company out of the United States . . . market" such as the firm cited in Case VI. In fact, most of the profitable business opportunities allegedly lost seemed, at least from the scant details given, to warrant prohibition anyway. For example, Case XVI states that "several U.S. firms are delaying joint ventures in Japan because they cannot find a legal way to prevent them from shipping back to the United States." Protecting the domestic markets from such cartels was the principal reason for the Sherman Act. Arrangements privately profitable for U.S. business, like monopolies and cartels, do not automatically promote the common good. At the close of the testimony Senator Hart remarked, "For us to understand the extent to which these laws do inhibit I think it is inevitable that we are going to have to get some concrete examples." [8] Seven years later we are still waiting.

The logic of the argument that our antitrust policy inhibits international trade is no more convincing than Persen's examples. By preventing mergers and joint ventures, so the argument runs, U.S. corporations are effectively kept smaller than they might otherwise be and unable to exploit economies of scale. But in most industries U.S. corporations are considerably larger than their foreign competitors. The 50 largest U.S. industrial corporations had larger sales, assets, net profits, and invested capital than the 200 largest non-U.S. corporations in 1969.[9] In each of several industries the story is the same. Table A gives the ratio of sales of U.S. corporations to sales of non-U.S. corporations in 1969 for five industries which figure prominently in foreign trade.

TABLE A:

Ratio of 1969 Sales of Largest U.S. Corporations to Sales of the Largest Non-U.S. Corporations by Industry

Rank of Company	Autos	Electrical Machinery & Electronics	Oil	Steel	Chemicals
1	6.9	2.3	1.5	1.7	1.1
2	6.3	2.5	1.9	1.3	1.2
3	3.0	2.0	3.6	0.8	0.9
4	0.3	1.6	3.0	0.8	0.8

Thus, in 1969 the sales of General Motors were 6.9 times as large as those of Volkswagen, the largest non-U.S. auto producer. Similarly, General Electric's sales were 2.3 times those of Philips (Dutch), Standard Oil dominated the Royal Dutch/Shell Group, United States Steel was over half again as large as British Steel, and DuPont's sales exceeded those of Britain's Imperial Chemical Industries (ICI). American airplane manufacturers have dominated world markets for years with virtually no competition. Rather than being overwhelmed by competition from gigantic foreign competitors, American corporations already reap the market power which large size confers. In fact, this point has been stressed by J.-J. Servan-Schreiber in his book *The American Challenge;* in it he argues that Europe should meet the challenge by creating its own giants. Mergers in both Europe and Japan, inspired by such arguments, have narrowed the size gap between U.S. and non-U.S. corporations in recent years.[10] Also, since 1969 U.S. corporations' sales and employment have declined somewhat relative to foreign corporations because of the domestic recession. But to say that U.S. companies have become too small to compete in world markets reverses reality.

Large size may not be the key to success anyway. A recent study of multinational corporations has uncovered evidence that, contrary to popular belief, the largest corporations have had slower rates of growth than their smaller competitors.[11]

What advantages might large size yield and how large must a corporation be to reap them? There is ample evidence, some cited in Chapter I, that the gigantic size of our largest firms is well beyond the size necessary for achieving the most efficient production. When it gives a firm market power, bigness is license for inefficiency. The most flagrant example of this phenomenon is the United States Steel Corporation. The following description of the company in the late 1930s was based on a report of a management-consulting firm hired by the company:

A big sprawling inert giant, whose production operations were improperly coordinated; suffering from a lack of a long-run planning agency; relying on an antiquated system of cost accounting; with an inadequate knowledge of costs or of the relative profitability of the many thousands of items it sold; with production and cost standards generally below those considered everyday practice in other industries; with inadequate knowledge of its domestic markets and no clear appreciation of its opportunities in foreign markets; with less efficient production facilities than its rivals had; slow in introducing new processes and new products.[12]

The situation in the steel industry may not be better today. A recent Presidential task-force report on steel pointed out that output per man-hour in the industry had remained virtually constant in recent years.[13] Past investment decisions in the industry have resulted in expensive idle capacity in finishing mills at times of normal production and the use of old and inefficient equipment in earlier production stages at peak periods. Furthermore, the report states that "although wage rates abroad are rising more rapidly than in the U.S., foreign productivity increases are also larger there." And economist Walter Adams told the House Ways and Means Committee that "the level of U.S. steel prices is uncompetitive not because of high labor costs, but because of our insensitive, monopolistic and suicidal pricing policy, on the one hand, and technological necessity on the other." Is it any wonder that steel is facing stiff foreign competition?

Steel is a concentrated industry, with U.S. Steel accounting for 25% and the four largest companies accounting for 54% of national raw-steel output. Professor Hendrik

Houthakker, chairman of the task force and a member of the President's Council of Economic Advisors, said that steel's disappointing productivity is a "result of the fact that competition isn't as much as it could be" in the industry.[14] Houthakker stated that he saw little justification for any mergers, since competition from foreign steel was strictly limited by quotas. Steel executives, however, are urging the Antitrust Division to take a "more flexible" position on mergers, alleging that it will enable them to compete more effectively with foreign producers. The Justice Department has reacted favorably to these appeals. The fourth largest producer, National Steel Corporation, was allowed to merge with Granite City Steel Corporation, the 11th largest, in August, 1971.

The most plausible case for relaxing antitrust laws to improve the balance of trade turns on the issue of technological progress. In recent years the United States has been most competitive in high-technology industries such as aircraft, electrical machinery, instruments, chemicals, and electronically controlled machine tools. High productivity in these industries, plus the fact that many of the products were not available elsewhere, seems to have accounted for our large export surplus. According to some observers such as Commerce Secretary Stans, Western Europe and Japan are narrowing the "technology gap," with disastrous results for our trade balance. One of his suggestions to a House subcommittee on science was that it might be time "to modernize antitrust laws . . . to permit the pooling of funds and risks that must accompany major technological advances." [15] He promised to produce a list of "50 different projects, major opportunities in technology in which the U.S. could take the lead." As examples he mentioned to a reporter the following: vertical-takeoff planes, ocean mining and ocean platforms, air-cushion land and water vehicles, high-speed ground transport, burnable plastics, solar power, oil from shale and tar sands, and fast-breeder nuclear reactors.[16]

The evidence relating firm size to the amount and effectiveness of research and development lends no support to Stans's case; the ratio of R&D to sales does not seem to increase with the size of the firm. It has been found that for a given amount of R&D expenditure, the inventive output tends to be *less* the larger the firm.[17] Major technological breakthroughs do not necessarily come out of large research projects anyway, as previously noted. Joint research efforts by corporations in the same industry would decrease the number of independent centers of innovation and hence might *lessen* the chances of major innovation.

So the only argument left for the proposal is that these projects are just too large and risky for one company to undertake profitably. But it is clearly absurd to contend that General Motors, with assets of $14 billion, needs Ford's help to develop an air-cushion vehicle, or that DuPont could not develop burnable plastics if it were profitable to do so. Available evidence on joint ventures indicates that although the 100 largest U.S. companies were the most frequent parents, only a handful of the 518 joint ventures surveyed had assets exceeding $80 million.[18] There may well be some projects comparable to the space program or producing a non-addicting substitute for heroin which are too big for one company. If it decided that the United States should have such a project, then either public funding or a tailored antitrust exemption would follow. At least in each case the Congress (and hopefully the public) can exercise some control and supervision over the direction of major technological change, and keep large companies from unnecessary collaboration.

Despite all the rhetorical puffing, then, there is no evidence that antitrust enforcement has placed American firms at a disadvantage in marketing abroad. Most of our large corporations, whether or not they produce abroad, have their own foreign sales networks; antitrust has not blocked this investment. Nor does antitrust discriminate against smaller companies who can reap advantages of large-scale marketing by setting up joint sales agencies exempted from antitrust laws by the 1918 Webb-Pomerene Act. Contrary to the expectations of the bill's authors, it has produced few favorable results in its 53 years. Only 35 Webb associations are presently registered with the FTC, and there have never been more than 42 at any one time. Exports reported by the associations account for about 2% of total exports.[19] A recent study showed that most of the *effective* associations—that is, those which actually functioned as joint selling agencies—were made up of the largest firms in the industry, many of which had considerable oligopolistic power in world markets anyway.[20] While it would be naive to believe that oligopolists could not coordinate their domestic prices and sales without the benefit of friendly Webb-association discussions about foreign sales, there is still wisdom in Judge Charles Wyzanski's opinion that cooperation in foreign markets may well affect the strength of competition in domestic markets.[21] So rather than strengthening Webb associations, as some government officials have recently urged, there seems to be a good case for abolishing them altogether. At the very least, membership should be restricted to small companies for whom the exemption was originally designed.

"PROTECTING" THE DOMESTIC MARKET

The second measure to cure the deteriorating balance of trade—restricting imports—affects antitrust laws only indirectly; nevertheless, its threat to domestic competition is real. If Congress can be convinced to impose quotas on imports, prices in the domestic market can more easily be maintained at monopolistic levels. Incentive for innovation declines. Giant domestic corporations retain their control of the domestic market, becoming even less responsive to the real needs of the consumer, who has no alternative but to "Buy American."

The pressure for protection from foreign competition comes from two organized groups: businessmen who feel their sales and profits are threatened and labor unions who fear for their members' jobs. In the spring of 1970 the House Ways and Means Committee heard 16 volumes of testimony from business and unions in such industries as textiles, apparel, shoes, glass, petroleum, steel, catfish, flowers, sardines, mink furs, and fishnets—all urging that strict quota limits be imposed to preserve their domestic markets.[22] The few witnesses testifying for the American consumer argued that imports resulted in lower prices and a greater variety of goods on the domestic market.* When the imports in question are coffee, bananas, or chromium, goods which we do not produce domestically, the benefit

---

* Disappointingly, the two agencies charged with enforcing the antitrust laws, the Antitrust Division and the FTC, did not appear to testify. The occasion, however, was extremely appropriate for a strong presentation. Given the difficulty of deconcentration suits in major shared monopolies, with which each agency is all too familiar, encouraging imports may be one way to revive competition in these markets.

of free trade is obvious. But economic gains are no less real when the imports compete directly with domestically produced goods. As long as American citizens can buy goods cheaper abroad than here, we gain economically by employing our resources in the production of goods we can produce *relatively more efficiently* and trading them for the cheaper foreign goods. Just as it is economically efficient for each individual in a community to specialize in tasks for which he has natural ability and training, so is it likewise rational for nations to specialize—which is the essence of the theory of *comparative advantage*. The inanity of the protectionists' arguments for quota limits was satirized by the French writer Bastiat in his imaginary petition by the French candlemakers to the Chamber of Deputies:

We are subjected to the intolerable competition of a foreign rival whose superior facilities for producing light enable him to flood the French market at so low a price as to take away all our customers the moment he appears, suddenly reducing an important branch of French industry to stagnation. This rival is the sun.

We request a law to shut up all windows, dormers, skylights, openings, holes, chinks, and fissures through which sunlight penetrates. Our industry provides such valuable manufactures that our country cannot, without ingratitude, leave us now to struggle unprotected through so unequal a contest.[23]

The United States has been negotiating reciprocal tariff cuts on imports since the imposition of the astronomically high Smoot-Hawley tariffs in 1930. In the last round of negotiations, the Kennedy Round completed in the summer of 1967, it was agreed that tariffs on non-agricultural goods traded by the United States, the European Economic Community (EEC), the United Kingdom, and Japan were to be cut by an average of 35%. By 1972, when all the negotiated tariff cuts are supposed to be fully effective, tariffs on dutiable non-agricultural imports will average only 9.9% in the U.S., 10.7% in Japan, 10.8% in U.K., and 8.6% in the EEC. But their liberalization of international trade was abruptly halted by President Nixon's imposition of a 10% surcharge on all dutiable imports. Termed "disturbing and unnecessary" by William M. Roth, the chief U.S. negotiator in the Kennedy Round, the surcharge predictably aroused hostility and threats of retaliation in foreign countries.

The movement toward freer international trade has also

been threatened by the increasing number of quota limits imposed on United States imports in recent years. From 1963 to 1970 the United States has imposed quotas on 60 items to bring the present total on industrial products to 67. Quotas are a more certain way of restricting imports than are tariffs. Once it has been filled, a quota limit works like an *infinite* tariff which foreign sellers cannot surmount no matter how much they lower their prices. Importers lucky enough to be granted licenses to import the restricted goods also like quotas because they reap as windfall profits the difference between the low world price at which they buy and the high domestic price at which they sell. Under a tariff system these profits go to the government as tax revenues, and thus to the public at large. So consumers lose two ways with quotas: they pay higher prices for the imported goods, and general government revenues are not increased by the amount of their loss.

How much more does the consuming public pay because of quotas? One careful estimate for petroleum was done by the Cabinet Task Force on Oil Import Control, which concluded the following: "In 1969, consumers paid about $5 billion more for oil products than they would have paid in the absence of such restrictions. By 1980, the annual cost to consumers would approximate $8.4 billion."[24] This staggering cost, most of which is a transfer of purchasing power from consumers to the oil companies, has traditionally been justified on the grounds that it is necessary for the national security. But even the Defense Department does not maintain that interruptions of our foreign oil supply would cripple our military. An Assistant Secretary of Defense recently testified:

Despite the vital importance of oil to our military forces, the risk to security from interruptions of oil supply do not, in the main, concern any danger to the functioning of the nation's armed forces. The military needs of the nation in an emergency, even if all requirements had to be produced in the United States, are such a small fraction of total domestic consumption that oil supply for the armed forces is very unlikely to be placed in jeopardy.[25]

But economic reality is not the same as political reality, especially where the powerful oil industry is concerned. Numerous recommendations to end the oil quota have gone exactly nowhere.

Some estimates of the cost of quotas on textiles and shoes, proposed in the Trade Bill of 1970, were made by Andrew F. Brimmer of the Board of Governors of the Federal Reserve System. He calculated that by 1975 consumers would be paying an extra $1.8 billion for textiles and $1.9 billion for shoes if the quotas had been enacted.[26] Quotas on these items, and the extra cost of clothes and shoes, would fall most heavily on the poor, who can least afford it. Fortunately, the Trade Bill did not pass before the 91st Congress adjourned, and it is unlikely that the two quotas will soon pass Congress. Why? Because Japanese and European producers have reportedly agreed "voluntarily" to limit their exports of textiles and shoes to the United States.

Unlike legislated quotas—where the relevant issues are publicly aired—voluntary quotas are arrived at in secret collaboration between private interests and government officials without publicity or procedural safeguards. One glaring example is the voluntary steel agreement which Japanese and European steel producers announced through the State Department in early 1969. In mid-December, 1968, the Japanese Iron and Steel Exporters' Association (JISEA) and members of the European Coal and Steel Community (ECSC) sent strikingly similar letters of intent to Secretary of State Rusk promising to limit steel exports to the United States to 5.75 million tons each in 1969 and to limit growth in exports to 5% each year through 1971. These letters were the final result of over two years of negotiation between representatives of the American steel industry, the State Department, and representatives of JISEA and ECSC. To avoid mandatory steel quotas, called for in a bill introduced in the Senate in 1967, the Japanese made offers in March and July, 1968, to limit exports here. Both these offers were rejected by American producers. Discussions aimed at making the voluntary quotas more restrictive continued between representatives of the American steel industry and the State Department, on the one hand, and the foreign producers, on the other.

Final agreement was reached in the late autumn of 1968. To avoid the appearance of violating the U.S. antitrust laws, the foreign producers were advised by the State Department to announce the agreement unilaterally in the letters of intent.[27] Secretary Rusk then sent word of the agreement to Congressman Mills and Senator Long, who made the official announcement in a joint press release. Thus, the agreement was "officially" announced by the Congress and had governmental backing. But does the Executive Branch have the authority to regulate foreign commerce, a power Constitutionally reserved for Congress? Furthermore, can the State Department unilaterally grant exemptions from the antitrust laws?

Although there was no written agreement between American steel producers and foreign steel producers, negotiations carried out via the State Department served the same purpose.[28] By limiting imports of steel into the United States, the arrangement is in effect a "conspiracy in restraint of trade among the several States [and] with foreign nations," which is illegal under Section 1 of the Sherman Act. The role of the Justice Department concerning the antitrust considerations in the arrangement is unclear. It is reported that the German steel representative requested that the State Department get Justice to endorse a draft of the letter of intent "as inoffensive to American antitrust laws. Apparently this was done." [29] Wilbur Fugate, chief of the Foreign Commerce Section of the Antitrust Division, denied in an interview that the Division had any part in the arrangement.*

The argument against import quotas is strong. Quotas misallocate economic resources and raise the price of goods to the consumer. But if the consumer as worker loses his job because of imports, the lower prices and greater variety of goods on the market will be of little comfort. There is no doubt that a great many workers have lost their jobs in the last two years. In May, 1971, the civilian unemployment rate (seasonally adjusted) rose to 6.2%; that corresponds

* Former AAG Zimmerman testified before Senator Hart's Antitrust and Monopoly Subcommittee in 1966 on the legality of voluntary trade restrictions: "I think that there have been some groups of producers who have hoped to substitute for the tariff protection that they have been receiving some understanding with foreign producers that the foreign producers would limit their exports to the United States. When we got indications of such hopes, we advised them very clearly that if they proceeded in this direction, we would regard it as a violation of the antitrust laws." [30]

Other aspects of the steel quota deserve more investigation. For example, by limiting the volume of imports, American producers can maintain the domestic price above the world price. Having to pay more for steel puts U.S. manufacturers of machinery, automobiles, and other finished steel products at a disadvantage relative to their foreign competitors. There are high-technology goods in which the United States has had a comparative advantage; quotas on steel may erode it.

to well over five million persons 16 years and older who were out of a job. And unemployment rates for minority groups and teenagers were over twice the national average. But the increase of 2.4 million in the ranks of the unemployed from May, 1969, to May, 1971, cannot be attributed primarily to imports. Imports of goods rose about $5.7 billion between the second quarter of 1969 and the second quarter of 1971. According to an unpublished Labor Department study, each $1 billion of increased imports displaced an average of 77,000 workers in 1969.[31] Therefore, the number of jobs lost to imports over these two years can be estimated to be in the neighborhood of 416,000 or 17% of the total loss. But this does not take into account extra jobs created by the $4.5 billion increase in exports over the same period. Contrary to protectionist rhetoric, international trade has not been the primary cause of job losses. Rising unemployment has been the inevitable result of the economic recession.

Belated recognition of the failure of his "steady-as-she-goes[-down] game plan" finally forced President Nixon to take measures to deal with the deteriorating economic situation. At this writing it is too early to tell whether employment will be stimulated by Nixon's new economic program. But even a return to reasonably full employment by the beginning of 1973 will not eliminate the structural adjustments inevitably occurring in a growing economy. Technological change, changes in the allocation of government expenditures, shifts in consumer tastes, as well as increases in foreign competition all require painful adjustment by workers facing a declining demand for their particular products. It is only natural—and necessary—that some firms will prosper and others will fail. The demise of the stagecoach industry did not spell economic disaster for the country, though it did considerable harm to stagecoach producers. Many foreign shoes and textiles will still undersell American products, despite the devaluation of the dollar. Loss of these industries will likewise not threaten the overall prosperity of the country. But the decline in the domestic textile and shoe industries will impose great hardship on the shoe worker in Brockton, Massachusetts, and the textile worker in Greensboro, North Carolina. Workers, particularly older ones, have difficulty changing jobs. A new job may mean a training period with lower pay and loss of seniority and pension rights. The unemployed worker may not be able to bear the expense of moving to another location where new jobs are being created.

Token recognition of the adjustment problem posed by foreign competition was embodied in the provision for adjustment assistance for firms and workers in the Trade Expansion Act of 1962. Unfortunately, the law and its strict interpretation by the Tariff Commission have made adjustment assistance difficult to obtain; in fact, no petitions for assistance were granted prior to November, 1969. According to the Act, the petitioner had to satisfy the Tariff Commissioners that he had suffered injury "in major part" from increased imports which had come into the country "in major part" because of tariff concessions negotiated under the Act—allegations difficult, if not impossible, to prove. But because imports have increased and the recession has raised unemployment, many more petitions have been filed in the past two years. Furthermore, some new members of the Tariff Commission adopted a more liberal interpretation of the language of the 1962 Act, so that 53 of the 98 petitions filed since 1969 have resulted in relief. Yet the relief has been inadequate. In fiscal year 1970 only 660 workers in four states got an average of $62.75 per week in unemployment benefits.[32] Although the law authorizes the Labor Department to grant travel allowances for retraining and relocation, no funds for these purposes were paid. An additional 5,897 workers in 13 states received an average compensation of $75.90 a week in fiscal year 1971, and 156 persons (almost all in Rhode Island) began retraining for new jobs. Should anyone be surprised that workers and unions have shown little enthusiasm for adjustment assistance, opting instead to preserve their jobs by limiting imports? To take the burden of maintaining relatively free trade off workers and a few domestic industries, it is essential that adequate adjustment assistance be enacted by Congress. The cost of not doing so may be protectionism and subsidization of inefficient industries.

And, finally, the argument that there are not enough jobs in the U.S. economy to employ *all* the labor force is foolishness. The needs of the country in rebuilding the cities, mass transit, pollution control, education, medical care for the poor, drug rehabilitation, and just feeding poor people here and abroad are enormous. The principal difficulty is that these activities have not been privately profitable, and were therefore not undertaken. A shift in federal government priorities from making armaments and war to building a decent society could create more than enough jobs to keep the labor force fully and usefully employed.

ENFORCEMENT AND THE ADVOCACY OF COMPETITION

What has been the position and effectiveness of the Antitrust Division in meeting the two major international challenges to competition outlined above: *viz.,* the rise of multinational oligopoly and the domestic groundswell of protectionism? In a recent speech AAG McLaren recognized the increasing necessity to view competition beyond the boundaries of the country as an important concern of the Division:

> The role that antitrust and competition policy play in American foreign commerce—exports as well as imports—is a necessary one. Antitrust enforcement cannot ignore foreign commerce, because national boundaries have lost much of their relevance to business reality. Our enforcement efforts must be extended to unduly restrictive activities outside our borders whenever—but only to the extent that—U.S. commerce is affected, whether immediately or prospectively.[33]

For a number of reasons, however, the effectiveness of the Division in this area has not been commensurate with the severity of the threat to competition. It is a failure traceable to three main sources: the nature and reach of American and foreign antitrust law, the lack of resources in the Division, and, finally, the inevitable intrusion of political impediments to effective enforcement.

Both the major pieces of U.S. antitrust legislation, the Sherman Act and the Clayton Act, expressly forbid restraints upon or monopolization of the commerce between the United States and foreign nations. The concern of Congress in promoting import competition was underscored by the Wilson Tariff Act (1894), forbidding certain restraints of import commerce. Early cases such as *American Tobacco* (1911) clearly established that international cartel agreements which divide international markets and restrict foreign competition are illegal; the *Quinine* case, mentioned previously, is a modern example of prosecution of this kind of cartel. Recently a few suits blocking acquisition of foreign firms by U.S. corporations were brought under Section 7 of the Clayton Act; for example, the District Court found in 1966 that the Schlitz Company's acquisition of 39.3% of John Labatt, Ltd., a large Canadian brewer, removed Labatt as an actual and potential competitor from the United States beer market. In such a case the government must show that the merger in question would *significantly decrease competition in the United States market.* But as former AAG Zimmerman remarked,

In the usual case of a merger or joint venture abroad, the primary impact would appear to be in the foreign country where the arrangement takes place. However, in some instances, there may also be sufficient impact on U.S. foreign trade for the Department to bring suit.[35]

Apparently the impact has seldom been found to be sufficient.

It has been argued that the large international mergers, such as Chrysler–Mitsubishi, Chrysler–Simca, Chrysler–Rootes, GM–Isuzu, Ford–Toyo Kogyo, Reynolds–British Aluminum, G.E.–Machines Bull, and G.E.–Olivetti did not (or will not) primarily affect competition in the U.S. market. This argument would be valid *a fortiori* for the 300–400 annual acquisitions by domestic corporations of smaller foreign companies. But the *long-run* anticompetitive effects on both the world and the U.S. markets of a whole series of such mergers, none of which alone is considered to pose a sufficient threat to domestic competition to warrant prosecution, may be greater than the sum of the parts. And once the threat of international oligopoly is fully perceived, the only real remedy would be dissolution suits. The discussion of such suits in a following chapter suggests that the chances that a dissolution suit against a multinational giant would be brought, much less won, are low. So more effective prophylactic measures are necessary.

Foreign antitrust enforcement, at least for the present, does not offer any real solution. Foreign antitrust law, or "competition policy," as the Europeans call it, is only a post-World War II phenomenon, which arose in some part because of the proselytizing of the United States. Although most developed countries—even Japan—have antitrust legislation, none has laws as strict as those of the United States. Moreover, the foreign laws emphasize behavior rather than structure. Thus, the approach is not preventive, like ours, and antimerger law is not highly developed.[36] In fact, a number of governments have actively encouraged mergers of domestic firms to compete with the U.S. giants. Some recent developments, however, point toward the possibility of a more procompetitive attitude abroad. Even though it could not be stopped, the recent Yawata-Fuji steel merger was at least held up by the Japanese Fair Trade Commission. And for the first time the European Economic Community Commission may successfully prosecute an international merger under Section 86 of the Treaty of Rome.[37] (This section prohibits any move "to take improper advantage of a dominant market position.") Not surprisingly, the major defendant in the suit is an American multinational company, Continental Can. This suit could establish precedents for future antimerger suits, perhaps with European corporate defendants.

What is really needed is some antitrust authority which is coterminous with the activities of multinational corporations. There were efforts to produce an international treaty on antitrust principles and enforcement as long ago as 1927 at the League of Nations World Economic Conference. Since then there were unsuccessful attempts in 1948 (Havana Charter) and 1951–55 (U.N.) to draft a treaty. In each case the difficulties of agreeing on what actions constituted restrictive business practices and the reluctance of the countries to surrender national sovereignty to an international organization doomed the effort. The present approach is to rely on consultation among nations on national enforcement. The major forum for this consultation is the Restrictive Business Practices Committee of the Organization for Economic Cooperation and Development (OECD). The Committee is composed of antitrust officials of the member nations (18 European countries, Japan, Canada, and the United States). They meet twice yearly to exchange information on antitrust developments in their countries. The exchange involves both information on general policies and bilateral exchanges of information and intentions in specific cases. For example, the countries involved in prosecuting the quinine cartel coordinated their investigation and litigation to some extent through the Committee.

One activity on which the OECD countries could cooperate is the collection and analysis of economic data similar to that collected in the United States on multinational and foreign corporations' sales, assets, profits, and market shares. Presently there is only the sketchiest of data available to the analyst interested in multinational corporate market power. In 1966 Senator Hart proposed that such a clearinghouse of economic information be established, observing:

I have a feeling that while we all have instinctive feelings about how international industry is composing, arranging, and structuring itself, really nobody can point to chapter and verse —certainly not in detail and with the assurance we can do domestically—with respect to structuring here.[38]

Although former AAG Zimmerman expressed mild interest in this enterprise at the time, very little has been done. Recently Wilbur Fugate said in an interview that the project was uneccessary; the Division's industry specialists, he thought, spotted the important changes in international markets by reading business publications and trade journals— a view which some of his staffers contested.

Responsibility for coordination of international antitrust cases in the Division falls on the Foreign Commerce Section, which is composed of Chief Fugate and nine other attorneys. The section was formed in 1962. Obviously, such a small group cannot handle all litigation with foreign aspects; most of the trial work is carried on by one of the litigating sections, which relies on the Foreign Commerce Section for expert advice and for liaison with the State Department. According to Fugate, about 15% of the Division's litigation involves foreign aspects. The number of "foreign" cases filed in recent years has been small: four in 1968, four in 1969, eight in 1970, and only one as of mid-1971. One staffer suggested that the number of foreign cases was small because the public gets more economic benefit per dollar of litigation from domestic cases. Another reason, suggested by author Richard J. Barber, former special counsel to Senator Hart's Antitrust Subcommittee, was that information on foreign cartels, restrictive trading agreements, and cross-licensing patent arrangements does not appear in the daily press. The Foreign Commerce Section might well put an investigator in London, Paris, or Tokyo if it is serious about prosecuting restrictions of international commerce affecting the United States.

Besides coordination of the foreign cases, the Foreign Commerce Section prepares reports for and sends a representative to the biannual OECD Committee on Restrictive Business Practices; its members also serve as the advocates for competition in many interagency matters which involve foreign commerce. It is in this second area, a relatively new one for the Section, that the lack of adequate resources seems most acute. The recent increases in imports and the dismal domestic economic situation has sent representatives of industries injured by "unfair" foreign competition scurrying to the Treasury and Tariff Commission seeking relief. Representatives of the Antitrust Division, from AAG McLaren on down, have sought to counter the anticompetitive, protectionist pleas of "dumping" made before the Tariff Commission.* The charge is almost impossible to prove or disprove, and the hearings have been called "farcical" by lawyers familiar with the procedure. The Foreign Commerce Section also has two representatives on the Oil Policy Committee administering the oil import-quota program. Some staffers are looking into anticompetitive effects of other quotas, such as the meat quota. When asked why the Section had not been more active in pushing for free trade and procompetitive policies in the last year, Fugate answered that they couldn't go sticking their noses in everywhere. Yet in an earlier interview he denied that the Section was hampered in its operations by lack of personnel and funds. While these two statements are not necessarily contradictory, they do betray a narrow view of the proper scope of competition advocacy.**

Foreign political considerations have also played a role in some of the Division's foreign cases. Each foreign case is cleared through the State Department, and the views of the foreign government or governments involved are solicited. Fugate said that no case had even been stopped because of foreign-policy considerations raised by the State Department, but that in touchy situations the Division "looks a bit harder at the facts of the case." As previously

---

* "Dumping" is the practice of selling in a foreign market at prices below what is charged in the domestic market; for example, the Japanese have been accused of dumping color TVs on the American market.

** Division timidity may be engendered by political problems. It is common knowledge that Treasury Secretary Connally did not exactly welcome representatives of the Antitrust Division at dumping hearings, and it would embarrass the Administration for the Antitrust Division to take a public position against the "voluntary" steel import quota negotiated, in part, by the State Department.

discussed, international politics played a major role in the oil-cartel cases and the recent exemption to permit American oil firms to bargain collectively with Middle Eastern countries. On the British Petroleum–Sohio merger, the chairman of BP, Eric Drake, personally visited Attorney General Mitchell and the State Department, getting assurances from each that some kind of compromise settlement would be reached—and it was. (One former antitrust AAG complained to the Study Group that McLaren had let himself be "outbluffed by the British and the State Department.") And when one of the Big Four U.S. aluminum companies, Reynolds Metals, acquired the biggest British aluminum producer just as it was about to enter the American aluminum market, politics seemed the determining factor. The explanation for the Division's inaction in this case is explained by Richard Barber as follows:

> The explanation is not very difficult: this merger involved substantial properties in two countries and the United States was hesitant to act for fear that the British would be chagrined. Conversely, the British also were reluctant to protest on the ground that this might anger their American friends.[39]

Thus, as so often happens, everybody's business becomes nobody's business.

8

Who Guards the Trusts/ Who Trusts the Guards?: Industry Case Studies

1. THE AUTOMOBILE INDUSTRY

An Industry Sketch

It is difficult to overstate the role of the automobile industry in the American economy. The Automobile Manufacturers Association boasts that one business out of six is automobile-related; in *Fortune*'s 1970 list of the 500 top industrials, General Motors was first, Ford third, and Chrysler seventh. The industry consumes one-fifth of the nation's steel production, two-fifths of its lead, one-half of its reclaimed rubber, and three-fourths of its upholstery leather. GM alone has 800,000 employees worldwide and over $20 bil-

lion each year in gross sales—more revenue than any
country's budget except that of the United States, the
Soviet Union, and Great Britain. But "with the possible
exception of the aluminum industry," Professor Robert
Lanzillotti has written, "the production of automobiles represents the nation's most highly concentrated industry." [1]
As a result, says a *Yale Law Journal* Note, "the industry is
said to exhibit the indicia of unsatisfactory market performance: inflated selling costs, product imitation, higher-
than-competitive prices, collusive suppression of technological innovation, and persistently high rates of return." [2]

Before discussing what the Antitrust Division has and
has not done in the auto industry, the structure and problems of this oligopoly should be sketched:

History and Structure

In 1904, 35 companies produced automobiles. The leaders
were the Olds Motor Works, Cadillac, and Ford. William
C. Durant founded General Motors in 1908, aiming to control all the principal manufacturers in the tradition of the
great trusts. By 1909 GM did control more than 20 automobile and accessory companies (including Olds and
Cadillac) and had narrowly missed out on the bid for Ford.
Between 1914 and the mid-Twenties Ford was the industry's leader, with approximately 50% of the market, due
largely to the success of its Model T: it was cheap and
efficient, with totally interchangeable parts between 1909
and 1926. By 1927, however, GM's sales had risen to 43%
of the market, due in large part to its acquisitions of
Chevrolet and the Fisher Body Company.

The peak number of firms in the industry was 88 in 1921.
Beginning in 1923, the number of automobile producers
rapidly declined. Various reasons for this increasing concentration have been offered: component integration, large-
scale advertising, franchised distribution, a huge increase
in capital requirements, and the poor product quality of
some firms. All but the last of these factors, argues one
critic, were in turn prompted by the annual model-style
change, inaugurated in 1923 (and discussed subsequently).[3]
The result: by 1926 there were 43 firms remaining; by 1935
only 10 firms were left; and today there are four domestic
manufacturers.[4]

Three of the present firms (GM, Ford, and Chrysler)

have accounted for 90% of all automobile sales in this country since 1935. The Big Three today have 97% of all domestic car sales and 83% of all sales; GM alone produces 54% of all American cars. The fourth American manufacturer—American Motors—comprises only 3% of the domestic market. GM's superior ability to put out a cheaper car, as well as its sale to American Motors of parts and financing, leads many observers to think that American exists only at GM's sufferance, since the auto giant is not eager to concentrate the industry further and invite antitrust retaliation.[5] Thurman Arnold has gone on to say, "It is my own belief that Ford and Chrysler, because of the failure of the Department of Justice to protect them, have become satellites of General Motors. General Motors will let them live as long as they do not grow too much at its expense." [6]

Economics of Scale/Entry Barriers

GM claims it is big because it is efficient, but industrial economists who have studied the industry disagree. Professor Joe Bain concluded that an automobile manufacturer could be efficient enough to compete if it produced only 300,000 to 600,000 cars per year. In 1958 George Romney, then president of American Motors, told a Senate committee that "all this talk about the disadvantage of lack of volume . . . is grossly exaggerated. . . . If you have 180,000 to 220,000 volume a year, you can compete effectively and efficiently in the automobile industry." Lawrence White, in *The American Automobile Industry in the Postwar Period* (1971), estimates that 400,000 cars exploit production efficiencies, while 800,000 cars (a two-model line) are the minimum diversity necessary in a risky market. Thus, GM's 1970 sales of 4.4 million cars are far higher than dictated by the inherent efficiencies of scale. Based on Bain's low figure of 300,000 units to White's top of 800,000, and based on a 10-million car market, there is room for 12 to 33 manufacturers.

Going further, a 1971 *Yale Law Journal* Note argues that only the annual style change necessitates economies even of this size. New styles every year mean new car dyes every year; since these dyes have a useful life of 250,000 cars, any production level less than this amount would lead to production costs substantially higher than those of larger-volume producers.[7] These styling changes, argue the *Journal* and Lanzillotti, doomed the smaller companies in the industry. Without these styling requirements, technical efficiencies could be achieved at any output greater than 60,000 units per year. Since the Big Three own 45 assembly plants which produce this amount or greater, there is room for 42 more auto manufacturers if all but one plant per firm were broken off from the Big Three.

Huge auto advertising also contributes to high entry barriers. The industry as a whole spends $400 to $600 million per year on advertising; in 1969 GM was second, Ford fifth, and Chrysler 11th among top national advertisers.[8] As a result of these "barriers," White estimates that it would cost the new entrant $1 billion alone at the manufacturing level; another $200 million would be necessary to set up a dealership network. This is nearly 12 times the amount considered by Bain as making entry highly improbable. White concludes: "Billion dollar corporations are not common phenomena, and forming one from scratch would be virtually impossible. . . . It is difficult to think of an industry with higher entry barriers." [9] There has not been a successful new domestic entrant into the automobile market since 1923.

Dealers

Almost all new cars are sold through independently owned, franchised dealerships. Lanzillotti observes that "the franchise requires that the dealer meet certain specified capital, character, and experience qualifications, and that he follow certain manufacturer-prescribed business and accounting practices." The manufacturer completely dominates this relationship; by a system called "forcing," the dealer must sell a quota of cars or be threatened with loss of franchise. A GM executive gave the following testimony in legislative hearings on the subject in the Fifties:

> It is the manufacturer who creates the franchise in the first place. . . . This ability to dispose [of it] cannot in any sense be shared by the dealer. The manufacturer must be in a position, based on his judgment and on his judgment alone, to retain a franchise, to grant it, or to withdraw it.[10]

Through World War II the franchise contract had a clause forbidding the dealer to sell cars of another make.

A 1949 Supreme Court case, *Standard Stations,* threw out such provisions; "still, the manufacturers have made clear their preference" notes White, "for exclusive dealing in cars and parts." The *de facto* policy has been nearly as successful as the earlier *de jure* one. In 1967 and 1968 only 2.48% of all dealers (mostly foreign) sold more than one car brand. Thus, interbrand retailing competition—with a local dealer selling several different makes—is severely restrained. These restrictions pose another serious entry barrier, since a new firm would be unable to sell its cars through established outlets.

Parts and Warranties

Planned obsolescence, which GM President Edward Cole is quoted as calling "synonymous with progress,"[11] prevails in the industry, causing rapid auto trade-in and a lucrative replacement-parts market. Under the franchise system, manufacturers can coerce their dealers to use their parts and accessories; this relationship forecloses an open market for replacement parts. The warranty system ensures this hegemony: usually only franchised dealers can perform warranty service, and use only parts authorized by the manufacturer. Economist Robert Crandell has written that 80% of all parts sold by auto dealers are sold to them by auto manufacturers,[12] even though dealers pay more for their manufacturer's parts than they pay independents for the same parts.[13] Crandell concluded his Ph.D. thesis on *Vertical Integration in the United States Automobile Industry* by stressing that GM's high return in replacement parts is a primary reason for its overall high profits.

Technology and Innovation

What Bain calls "product imitation," a defect common to tight oligopolies, prevails in the auto industry. Unwilling to risk the vagaries of consumer tastes, each firm offers models similar to its rivals' to reduce risks. Consequently, there is little performance competition, only frivolous style competition. It is not an atmosphere to nurture innovation —either in marketing (Detroit took 15 years to put out a car to compete with the imports) or in pollution technology (the smog story will follow). White observes that "Cars built in 1968 are not fundamentally different from cars built in 1946. A good 1946 auto mechanic would have little difficulty understanding a 1968 automobile." Former Ford Vice President Donald Frey told an engineering audience in 1964: "The automatic transmission [adapted in the 1930s] was the last major innovation of the industry."

Prices and Profits

Strict price leadership prevails, with GM in charge. An example is Ford's "double shift" on its 1957 models: in September, 1956, Ford announced suggested price increases, ranging from $1 to $104; two weeks later GM announced new Chevrolet prices, $50 to $166 higher than the year before; one week later Ford revised its prices upward, so that on 10 models the differences with Chevy were $1 to $2, while on two other models they were $10 to $11.

The profits of the industry, says White, are "clearly excessive"; economist William Shepherd adds that "the automobile industry has been *the* most profitable of major industries." Between 1946 and 1967, while manufacturing corporations were earning 9.02% return on net worth, the automobile industry was earning 16.67%; GM received a 20.67% return. Because of its oligopolistic structure, Shepherd says, as much as $½ billion per year in profits may represent redistribution from at least 10 million purchasers primarily to several hundred thousand significant shareowners, with a wealth impact of as much as $4 to $8 billion."

In sum, the automobile industry imposes classic oligopolistic costs on its consumers. The American Institute of Management ably summarized the problem: "One cannot study General Motors' massive operation without experiencing an inescapable feeling—General Motors is too big. It is too big for the good of American businessmen who must deal with it and too big for the good of the country."

Filed Successes/Filed Failures

GM is the keystone of the industry oligopoly; 18 antitrust actions have been brought against the firm through 1969. Eight were criminal indictments, of which six were convictions (a no-contest plea being legally tantamount to admission of guilt) and two dismissals. Ten were civil complaints; of them, there were two judgments against GM, five consent decrees, and three dismissals. Overall, if consent decrees are counted as "victories," as the Division claims, the Division won 13 cases and lost five.

Three of the more important successes were the *DuPont* case, the *Euclid Machinery* case, and the *L.A. Dealers* case. DuPont and Euclid have already been discussed. In 1962 DuPont was forced to sell its 23% stock interest in GM, obtained in 1917. It was an illegal, vertical acquisition under Section 7 of the Clayton Act. The case, however, had far more relevance to the auto paint-finish and interior-fabrics markets than the auto-manufacturing shared monopoly. *Euclid,* filed in 1959, sought to divest from GM its 1953 acquisition of the Euclid Road Machinery Company. The complaint alleged that the acquisition would tend to lessen competition in the manufacture and sale of off-highway earthmoving equipment. At the time of the suit GM made over 50% of all domestic highway trucks, 100% of passenger locomotives, 77% of all locomotives, and was a leading maker of off-highway earthmoving equipment (Euclid). A February 5, 1968, consent decree required GM to sell Euclid.

Finally, in California in the early Sixties, auto discount houses were underselling the established dealers. The Los Angeles Dealers Association and General Motors pressured the errant discount houses to cease undercutting their franchised brothers. The *Wall Street Journal* captured GM's concern:

> What auto men fear most of all is the possibility of huge auto discount houses in which side by side sit Chevys, Fords, Plymouths and other makes, each with the price clearly labeled. A single attendant at the door could collect the customers' money as they drive out with their new cars. Sales could be made without benefit of a sales pitch that one car is better than another and, worse from the manufacturers' view, without the discounter even caring what kind of car is sold. . . . One auto executive said: "It's a sales manager's nightmare."

The Division first proceeded criminally, charging a Sherman Act conspiracy in restraint of trade. Chief Judge Thurmond Clarke directed a verdict of not guilty after a trial in March, 1963. A companion civil suit, based on the same facts, was decided by Judge Charles Carr adversely to the government in June, 1964. On April 28, 1966, however, the Supreme Court reversed, calling the activity "a classic conspiracy in restraint of trade"; the later district-court judgment enjoined GM from conspiring with other dealers to ban sales to discount houses.

The Antitrust Division's successes have outnumbered, but not outweighed, its failures in auto-industry enforcement. The three biggest failures were the *GMAC*, the *GM Bus,* and the *GM Locomotive* cases.

The General Motors Acceptance Corporation (GMAC) was organized in 1919 as a wholly owned subsidiary of GM, to provide auto financing and to aid car sales. By the mid-Fifties it was the largest automobile-financing company in the world, with a third of the market, and averaged 18.7% net profit between 1950 and 1957.[14]

In 1939 GM, Ford, and Chrysler were each indicted for attempted monopolization of the auto-financing market by allegedly coercing their dealers to use their financing facilities. The indictments against Ford and Chrysler were dropped in return for two promises: if GM was convicted, they would stop coercing their dealers; if GMAC was divorced from GM, they would give up their own financing schemes (involving "factory preferred" companies rather than wholly owned subsidiaries). GM was convicted in 1941, which triggered the first promise, but a civil suit to spin off GMAC was not filed until 1949. During those eight years Ford and Chrysler kept their affiliations. In 1952 a consent decree settled the civil suit but did *not* divorce GMAC from GM. "The reasons all went to the difficulty of proving in 1952 facts and actions carried on in 1938," [15] complained Senator Joseph O'Mahoney. Since the problem was one of structure—GM's power over its dealers and its control of GMAC inevitably foreclosed much of the auto-financing market—O'Mahoney proposed legislation in 1959 to correct the Division's 1952 negligence, but Congress failed to act. Thurman Arnold was severely critical of this GM-GMAC relationship: "In my view the combination between General Motors and General Motors Acceptance Corporation violates every principle and policy embodied in the Sherman Act and particularly Section 7 of the Clayton Act." [16]

The *GM Bus* case was filed in 1956. It attacked GM's 85% monopoly of the new bus market, alleging that it was secured not by skill and foresight but by anticompetitive actions: GM influenced its principal competition by having a GM officer and director as Chairman of the Board and major stockholder of that company; GM entered into long-range requirement contracts with bus-operating companies; GM induced municipal transit systems to adopt bus specifications which could be met only by GM buses; and its financing subsidiary entrenched its dominance. The effect, said the complaint, was "to drive most of General Motors' competitors out of the bus manufacturing business." The suit sought to break up this bus monopoly.

A decade later, as five attorneys and an economist were preparing for trial in Detroit, Donald Turner drafted a consent decree which settled the case—without divestiture. There were various reasons for this omission. First, Judge Theodore Levin, the district-court judge in Detroit who presided over the action, personally called Attorney General Katzenbach to assert that the Justice Department was crazy if it thought he would break up GM's bus facilities. Although any such refusal by Judge Levin could have been appealed to the Supreme Court, his message cooled the Department's heels. In addition, Turner and his staff claim that it was impossible to split up GM's facilities since they were all in one plant complex. When the suit was filed in 1956, however, such a Solomonic riddle did not seem unsolvable to the antitrust enforcers. The eventual decree did have some novel clauses: GM bus patents must be freely available to any other bus maker; GM must sell parts, engines, and designs to other bus manufacturers; anytime from three to 10 years after settlement the government dealers and its control of GMAC inevitably foreclosed could reopen the decree if competition had not improved, and require GM to build and sell a new bus facility if the market could support it. But when the decree was formally entered in December, 1965, "there was no real expectation that any new entrants would soon be on the horizon," admitted a government signatory.

As a result of a 1959 grand-jury probe and investigations encouraged by Robert Bicks and Lee Loevinger, two cases were filed involving GM's 80% monopoly of new and rebuilt railroad locomotives. In April 1961 a criminal indictment accused GM of forcing most of the nation's railroads to buy locomotives made by GM's Electro-Motive Division; the case was dropped in December, 1964, by William Orrick. A similar fate met the civil suit. It charged

GM with monopolizing the locomotive market by its 1930 acquisition of two locomotive-manufacturing companies and by exploiting "reciprocity"—GM would ship its automobiles on Railroad X if X purchased GM's locomotives. Turner dismissed the case in June, 1967. In interviews he, Zimmerman, and some staff said that there was insufficient evidence to prove reciprocity. Two other staffers disagreed. One complained that "a judge would have taken judicial notice of reciprocity since it was so obvious. . . . At least we should have tried it out in court"; and a second lawyer thought the case was dropped because the evidence had grown stale and because the Division had mismanaged it. Just as it was Turner's honest judgment that GM's bus operations could not be separated, he also thought there was little evidence of reciprocity in locomotives. Another Division official who worked in both cases had a different view: "Bicks proposes; Turner disposes."

Cases under Wraps

(1) The saga of the Division's attempts to break up General Motors exemplifies the extreme in enforcement timidity. Suits are brought in the bus, locomotive, and earth-moving-machinery markets—but not in automobiles. A deconcentration suit was filed against Checker Cabs 20 years ago for monopolizing the taxicab market—but not against General Motors in automobiles.

In the mid-Fifties some Division staff studied a possible GM divestiture suit. Since Section 7 Clayton Act law had not yet developed and since the Supreme Court decision in *GM-DuPont* had not yet been reached, the inquiry aborted. In May of 1956, however, AAG Stanley Barnes did urge GM to surrender one of its divisions, like Oldsmobile, voluntarily, arguing that otherwise "somebody's going to do something." [17]

But by 1966 no one had done anything. In that year Division attorneys proposed to the upper staff a suit to break up GM. The 61-page fact memorandum and 106-page draft complaint—mostly the work of staffer Eugene Metzger and never released publicly—were based on both Section 2 of the Sherman Act and Section 7 of the Clayton Act. GM's monopoly was allegedly due to about 40 early and illegal mergers (like Chevrolet and Fisher Body) and to restrictive conduct (*e.g.,* dealership restraints, GMAC, and annual styling). Excerpts from the complaint follow:

The many acquisitions by General Motors of competing auto manufacturers were substantial factors leading to General Motors' dominance of automobiles. . . .

After General Motors had achieved a dominant position in the industry about 1919, it adopted the policy—in the early 1920s—of requiring its dealers to drop competitive lines and sell only General Motors' cars. . . .

Planned obsolescence introduced the practice of redesigning its automobiles annually. The practice superimposed on the normal effects of depreciation the added influence of a more rapid obsolescence.

The competitive impact of these vertical acquisitions [suppliers] was to heighten, by the adoption of General Motors[,] a policy of allocating a considerably higher rate of return to its parts manufacturing divisions than to its car assembly divisions. . . .

Based on these charges and supporting evidence, the complaint asked:

That in the resolution of the violation of the antitrust laws, General Motors be required to divest itself of said acquired companies and to reconstitute itself into a sufficiently large number of companies to accomplish a restoration of competitive conditions.

The case was never brought. A *Wall Street Journal* article a year and a half later strongly hinted that it had been suppressed by Lyndon Johnson's White House.[18] In fact, based on our own extensive interviewing, the case reached neither the Attorney General's office nor the White House. Turner and Zimmerman were simply not convinced, and reassigned the complaint for further staff study.

The result of additional study was unanimity: of 11 Division lawyers and economists who have looked at the problem to date, *all 11 urged that some antimonopoly action be brought against GM.* Ten of the succeeding staff to investigate the issue were either high Division staff, in the AAG's office, or in the Evaluation Section (Turner's doctrinal right hand). Some of the 11 suggested a Section 2 suit based on GM's alleged monopoly profits and monopoly market share; GM's approximate 50% of the market but nearly 70% of the profits, argued one official, were strong evidence of monopoly power. Others stressed GM's exclusionary behavior as a basis of either a horizontal-divestiture suit (breaking GM into a number of smaller firms) or a vertical-divestiture suit (ending the franchising and warranty systems). Finally, some of the 11 favored a shared-monopoly suit against the Big Three under Section 2, since, according to internal staff memoranda, (a) they collectively had a monopoly share, (b) they performed like a monopolist, and (c) they engaged in exclusionary conduct.

Included in this latter group was none other than Donald Turner. On July 24, 1968, after he had resigned as AAG but while a consultant to the Division, Turner proposed a suit to break up GM three ways and Ford two ways. His proposed complaint contained three counts: "(1) an individual monopolization charge against GM; (2) monopolization counts against GM, Ford, and Chrysler on a shared-monopoly theory; and (3) a direct attack on the franchise practices as unlawful attempts to monopolize and/or unlawful agreements in restraint of trade." Thus, Turner recommended a major deconcentration effort in 1959 (*Antitrust Policy*) and in 1968, but *not* during the three years when he had the means to achieve the results. When Zimmerman was asked about this recommendation in a September, 1971, Study Group interview, he claimed that he had never heard of it. "I can't believe such a recommendation would exist," he said, "and I don't know of it." Donald Turner confirmed its existence in an interview, adding, "Are you sure Ed didn't know about it?" And finally, when McLaren was asked by the Study Group if he was familiar with Turner's recommendation, he said no.

The doctrinal basis was clear, the potential return to consumers immense, yet no case even reached the Attorney General's desk. This failure can be traced to a blend of bureaucratic cowardice and anticipatory politics. When the Study Group asked Zimmerman why no suit was filed, he answered vaguely that they had many suits to study, and might have filed this one if they had had more time in office. (The combined three and a half years of the Turner-Zimmerman regime was the longest tenure since Thurman Arnold's.) Paul Owens, a senior trial attorney at the Division, said in an interview that "Resources were a genuine consideration." And no doubt comments such as the following one by a GM executive instilled some anxiety in the Division and Department: "If it tried to split off Chevrolet [the division usually mentioned], it would be ten years before the case even got to court." [19] But the oft-cited "resources" problem was an exaggeration. Much of the analytic work was already done, and surely five lawyers could be found out of 314 to prosecute the case—a case a thousandfold more significant than Turner's bull-semen suit. More simply, when given a choice to forge new law in a monumental area, official timidity smothered staff creativity, and a safe rather than a daring decision was rendered.

Peripheral bureaucratic excuses aside, there is the general political context of such a suit. Many interviewees mentioned the huge impact of such a case—on shareholders, unions, and the public; Turner predicted that "the UAW would scream." Any decision, they felt, would invite a political decision and interim political pressure. One of the 11 Division staff opted for vertical, not horizontal, divestiture, according to his memorandum to Turner, because "a Chevrolet case appears to me to be politically unacceptable."

AAG Richard McLaren shares the blame with Turner and Zimmerman for failing to file a GM suit. Two of his top aides have on file recommendations for antimonopoly auto complaints which he has ignored. Donald Baker, presently the Acting Director of Policy Planning, was one of the 11 reviewers, suggesting a shared-monopoly suit along the lines Turner urged. And Leonard Weiss, who was McLaren's first economic aide, agreed with the thesis. Weiss saw a huge economic benefit from the case. "If our actions resulted in cutting their profit rates to the average for all manufacturing (about 11%)," he speculated in a memorandum to McLaren, "we would save GM's customers $1.3 billion and Ford and Chrysler's $150 million each. . . . I doubt there is any other unregulated industry where increased competition would produce nearly so large a payoff." He predicted, of course, that the Big Three and auto dealers would be violently opposed, but added, in a memorable final flourish:

We would have lots of public opinion on our side. . . . In terms of winning votes, a big automobile case might be worth a hundred merger cases. Conceivably, it would make Nixon into another Teddy Roosevelt.

The perennial antitrust failure in the auto industry makes it increasingly difficult to file a successful deconcentration action. The Burger Court will be less receptive to such a dramatic request than the Warren Court would have been. And many feel, in a misdirection of sympathy, that as more years go by, it becomes less "equitable" to undo a long-existing situation.* Finally, GM itself has developed a defensive stratagem. In late 1971 GM announced that it was scrapping the "coordinated decentralization" plan of Alfred P. Sloan for a more centralized organization, probably to make antitrust enforcers more doubtful of the feasibility of any divestiture attempts. No longer would there be separate divisions like Chevrolet or Buick; instead a single engine division, for example, would supply engines to all car lines.[20]

(2) The 1969 suit and settlement in the so-called *Smog Conspiracy* case generated as much public controversy as any recent Justice Department antitrust action. Its vast impact on air pollution, industrial organization, and enforcement lassitude justify an extended discussion of the case.

"On October 12, 1964, Mr. Ralph Nader, then of the Department of Labor, met with Mr. William Orrick, Assistant Attorney General Antitrust Division, and others and charged that domestic automobile and truck manufacturers have been engaged in a concentrated effort not to compete with one another to improve automotive . . . pollution controls," reads the unreleased Antitrust Division History, now on file at the LBJ Library in Austin, Texas. The subsequent discussion is based on this Antitrust Division History, a Division memorandum summarizing the grand-jury investigation of the case, and Task Force interviewing.

The Division, responding to this complaint, sent out CIDs to all major domestic auto producers and the Automobile Manufacturers Association (AMA), investigating a 1955 cross-licensing agreement which allegedly restrained the development and installation of antipollution exhaust devices. The evidence collected led the staff to ask AAG Donald Turner to call a grand jury. He agreed, and in a May 12, 1966, memorandum to Attorney General Katzenbach, Turner explained that "if the grand jury investigation discloses an absence of justification for the agreement not to compete, *as seems quite likely, the agreement would be so plainly unlawful as to warrant a criminal proceeding.*"

---

* Less "equitable" to the firms, but what of the continuing consumer victims of illegal monopoly and oligopoly? The time-fairness argument, shorn of its legal doublethink, basically says that the longer the illegality, the more unjust to end it; if anything, justice demands the reverse.

(Emphasis added.) On May 23, 1966, Katzenbach approved the request; the grand jury was convened in June, 1966, and ran until December, 1967. During that time it uncovered extensive evidence of Detroit's indifference to, and suppression of, exhaust-control devices.

Why were the auto manufacturers uninterested in pollution abatement? As reported in *Unsafe at Any Speed* and later confirmed by Los Angeles Smog Supervisor Kenneth Hahn, when Hahn went to Detroit to press for exhaust controls, a senior official of one of the companies asked, "Well, Mr. Hahn, will that device sell more cars?" "No," said Hahn. "Will it look prettier," continued the official, "will it give us more horsepower? If not, we are not interested." A letter of November 17, 1958, from Lloyd Withrew of General Motors to Dr. L. R. Hafsted of that firm states that "the managements of Corporation Divisions are reluctant to undertake the engineering and development of devices, even though they appear to be based on sound principles." While the Big Four were not excited about pollution development, they *were* interested that "no one company should be in a position to capitalize upon or obtain competitive advantage over the other companies in the industry as a result of its solution to this problem" (Minutes of AMA Patent Committee Meeting, April 5, 1955).

Although a 1954 AMA document, authored by G. J. Gaudnon, recognized that "very serious legal problems might be involved in the cooperative acceptance and review of devices," Detroit nevertheless opted for a cross-licensing solution to their problem. The 1955 agreement provided for a royalty-free exchange of patents between the participants and a formula for sharing the costs of patent acquisition from third parties. The Division summary of the grand-jury investigation noted:

The cross-licensing agreement was merely a vehicle to accomplish the non-competitive and delaying activities of the signatories. . . . The evidence adduced before the Grand Jury clearly developed that the signatories to the cross-licensing agreement had the following understandings and agreements . . . : (A) not to publicize competitively any solution to the motor vehicle air pollution problem; (B) to adopt a uniform date for announcement of the discovery of any air pollution control device; and (C) to install devices only on an agreed date.

The result of the agreement was that between 1953 and 1967 there was no voluntary development and installation of antipollution control devices. In the early Sixties, Chrysler had developed an exhaust system but was shy about its introduction. In an October 5, 1961, memorandum D. C. Diggs of E. I. DuPont reported a talk with Charles Heinen, an assistant chief engineer of Chrysler:

> While admitting that favorable publicity would result, he was very forceful in telling me that if this was done Chrysler would be severely chastised by the rest of the industry. *He reminded me that the AMA agreement says that no one company will gain any competitive advantage because of smog,* and that Chrysler was a relatively small cog in the industry. *He indicated that Ford and GM were calling the shots. . . .* [Emphasis added.]

But a reluctant industry was being hurried along. By early 1964 the California Motor Vehicle Pollution Control Board was about to certify at least two exhaust-control devices produced by independent, non-automotive manufacturers, which would trigger a law compelling the Big Four to affix them to their 1966 models. A March 9, 1964, memorandum from William Sherman, manager of the Engineering and Technical Department of the AMA, to Harry Williams, managing director of the AMA, lucidly describes the laggard attitude of the trade association:

> While we certainly have the objective of holding the line until 1967 models . . . we would be exercising very poor judgment if we suggested or implied that we wanted them to hold off the triggering of the law. . . .
> *If they do* act in the near future to approve the catalytic devices, our companies would probably have to take the position, *anyhow,* that there is not enough engineering time to fit the catalytic converters under the frames and chassis of cars in time to meet the schedule of 1966 model production and there would be a strong likelihood of various delays until 1967 introductions.
> It would be very much to our advantage to avoid this topic —shrug it off or ignore it—for a month or two. In the interim a lot of things might change the picture, including even the withdrawal of the catalytic devices now on tests. . . . Thus the problem will have some tendency "to go away" if we don't aggravate discussion of it at this time. [Emphasis in original.]

This institutionalized obstruction of exhaust-device implementation resulted in a February 26, 1964, AMA resolution saying that devices should be ready for *1967* models, not 1966, and recommending that all companies make it the basis for their individual action. The resolution, however, was a lie, according to the Division's summary of the grand-jury probe: when the AMA statement asserted that the technology would not be ready by 1966, it *already* was available in the form of Chrysler's CAP system, GM's ManAirOx, Ford's Thermactor, and American Motors' Air-Guard. Internal memoranda expose the deceptions of the AMA resolution. "There is one disturbing element as far as GM and Ford are concerned in the position they have taken," wrote D. R. Diggs on July 8, 1964. "This is the fact that Chrysler *may* receive certification in California for their Clean Air Package; if so it is doubtful if Ford and GM can delay until 1967 the installation of comparable systems. . . ." Arjay Miller, president of Ford, complained in a handwritten note of February 18, 1964: "I think Chrysler is playing us as suckers. They get all the favorable publicity and the car sales, while giving up nothing." J. E. Yingst of the TRW Corporation, in a June 24, 1964, report, said that Chrysler had admitted "without reservation" that they could have put systems on *1965 cars*. The issue was resolved when California approved four exhaust devices in mid-1964, thereby requiring the auto companies to install *some* device on their 1966 models. Guilelessly the Big Four managed to develop their own devices almost immediately for the required model year, contrary to all their conspiratorially orchestrated protestations.*

The Division attorneys concluded their grand-jury probe as follows:

> We are convinced that we have shown the grand jury and are in possession of evidence to prove beyond a reasonable doubt the existence of an industry-wide agreement and conspiracy among the auto manufacturers, through AMA, not to compete in the research, development, manufacture and installation of motor vehicle air pollution control devices for the purpose of achieving interminable delays, or at least delays as long as possible. The cross-licensing agreement was used as a cover and focal point of the conspiracy.

---

* According to the grand-jury data, this pattern of the denial of technology *cum* its supression was repeated in the areas of evaporation losses, oxides of nitrogen, diesel engines, and crankcase ventilation systems—all of which affect pollution emissions.

Three of the four attorneys on the case recommended both civil and criminal actions. They urged that all the auto manufacturers and the AMA be indicted for a Sherman Act conspiracy in restraint of trade. In addition, they urged that 11 individuals, including some of the highest executives of the trade association and Big Four, be indicted as well.

Despite Turner's encouraging words when the investigation began, his eagerness to prosecute Detroit had waned. He asked Edwin Zimmerman to look at the case, who in turn asked Jonathan DuBois, in his second year with the Evaluation Section, to study it. DuBois recommended no indictments at all, which Turner accepted; thus the criminal case ended on December 15, 1967—but not without some final drama. Lacking Turner's permission, Division attorney Samuel Flatow could not ask the grand jury for indictments. *But* the grand jury, and especially its foreman, were eager to indict anyway, given the evidence they had heard. The threat of a "runaway" grand jury seemed real, but soon passed because, incredibly enough, the foreman did not realize that he and his co-jurors could have handed down an indictment unilaterally. Previously he had accepted Mr. Flatow's reluctant statement that the Division had instructed him not to ask for an indictment.

Turner felt that any charge of "product-fixing" was too novel to support a criminal indictment. In a later letter to Ralph Nader explaining his decision, Turner wrote that:

the joint research venture among the auto companies, though in my view unlawful (as the later civil suit charged), was not in the category of *"per se"* offenses and . . . most of the alleged restricted agreements were arguably ancillary to the joint undertaking. I will not pretend that a reasonable man, particularly if he had a more evangelical approach to antitrust than I have, could not have decided differently. . . .

Indeed, three of the four investigating Division attorneys and the grand jury *did* decide differently, although at least one section chief, Charles Mahaffie, disagreed. Turner also admitted in a Study Group interview that a Los Angeles jury would probably have convicted the recommended indictees.

The civil suit was finally filed by Zimmerman over a year later, on January 10, 1969. It alleged that the Big Four and the AMA, under the device of a cross-licensing agreement, had suppressed the research, development, and application of pollution-control devices. In addition to the agreement to be noncompetitive in the area of exhaust emission, the complaint charged that the defendants agreed on at least three occasions—1961, 1962, and 1964—to attempt to delay installation of control equipment. The auto firms lobbied strenuously to block the complaint, but were unsuccessful in their arguments to Attorney General Ramsey Clark. Commenting on their efforts, Clark told the Study Group of meetings with numerous auto representatives:

> Industry fought that tooth and nail. We had three separate meetings on it. Tom Mann still won't talk to me because he thought we had no moral right to bring the case. Cutler was at the meetings [AMA counsel] as was Ross Malone [GM's general counsel], whom I knew. It seemed that he was sent to make an *ad hominem* appeal.

By early September, 1969, rumors of a settlement by the Nixon Justice Department were widespread. Nineteen Congressmen protested to Attorney General Mitchell against any compromise consent decree:

> If these charges are true, the American people have a right to be fully informed of this outrageous corporate callousness by a full and open trial of the issues involved. . . . [But] we fear that the entire incident will be covered over by a legal deal arranged between the Department and the AMA's Washington counsel.

But on September 11 Mitchell and McLaren made public the Division's proposed consent decree with the defendants. The Department's press release stressed the adequacy of the relief obtained and the avoidance of years of court litigation which "would have delayed . . . efforts to end the alleged conspiracy and [would have delayed] its efforts to encourage immediate action by the automobile companies." The AMA press release acknowledged the required abolition of the cross-licensing agreement, but added that "the program substantially aided in providing workable and effective emission control devices throughout the nation much earlier than would have been possible without the cooperative program." (To comprehend the extent of this fabrication, it must be matched against the memoranda, quoted above at length, documenting the intentional industry retardation of antipollution effects.)

Basically, the decree said, "Don't do it again," which

of course permitted the industry to claim that it had never done anything wrong anyway. The major provisions were prohibitory—they could no longer join together to suppress antipollution development. But the inadequacies of the settlement were glaring:

(a) The consent decree could not be used as *prima facie* evidence by later litigants who claimed injury from the defendants' conspiracy. There was also no provision for release of the grand-jury transcript and other documents to later litigants, such as California, who would be compelled to duplicate much of the Division's substantial investigation. (The court, with the Division not objecting, did later impound the gathered evidence, for later plaintiffs' use where they could show need.) The way to have aided later plaintiffs (there are now 17 states filing on behalf of their citizens) was to have insisted on litigation and a court decision, or the inclusion of an asphalt clause, both of which would be tantamount to the defendants admitting their conspiracy in subsequent legal actions.

(b) The decree permitted the defendants a "grant back" patent provision guaranteeing them future rights growing out of any license they might grant. It could only aggravate the lockhold the big firms had on antipollution technology and give them a competitive advantage over other potential suppliers of motor-vehicle antipollution devices. Complaints about this provision by Ralph Nader and Robert Wright after the release of the decree, and prior to formal court approval, led to its elimination.

(c) There was no provision against the destruction of past evidence. And clauses prohibiting the exhange of confidential information and the filing of joint statements to regulatory agencies contained such loopholes that a skillful attorney could make the exception the rule.[21]

(d) There were few "affirmative" provisions. For example, the defendants could have been required to retrofit anti-emission exhaust devices onto cars in the California market, where the conspiracy was primarily aimed. The technology was available, and beyond a mere ban on future conspiracies, restitution for past failures seems equitable. (One Division attorney on the case balked at this notion: "Do you know how much that would have cost industry? Our purpose was to obtain competitive conditions; it would have been nice if we could have strained the atmosphere of air pollution too, but we couldn't.")

Also, there was no requirement that the AMA keep minutes of future meetings on the subject of pollution control and make them public. Given that the Plumbing Fixtures Trade Association was *dissolved* after their price-fix, and that culpable officers of the Glass Container Association were removed from their posts by a 1945 court order, such an affirmative requirement is well within reason. Finally, an affirmative provision which *was* present in the decree was inadequate: companies must give, to any who ask for them, technical reports prepared only within two years of the entry of the decree, although the alleged violations trace back *16* years to 1953.

(e) The deterrence and publicity benefits of an open, public trial were lost. Clearly, a function of public trials is to deter future violators, a point the government understands well in the arena of political "crime"—*e.g.,* the Spock and Chicago Eight prosecutions. In fact, such a trial is especially necessary in antitrust cases like *Smog Conspiracy*. "Consent settlement procedures," said the House Antitrust Subcommittee in 1959, "diminish the deterrent effect of the antitrust laws because they permit defenders to avoid much of the unfavorable publicity that usually attends antitrust litigation. . . .[22] It amounts to an invitation to . . . violate the law."

A public trial communicates a message not only to future violators but also to the inchoate antitrust constituency. In recent years nearly 90% of all cases have been settled before trial, and as the number of trials dwindles, the public is kept unaware of the extent and significance of antitrust illegality. A case connecting the major cause of air pollution in this country, automobiles, with an antitrust violation could have gone a long way toward educating the under-informed public.

(f) Finally, an opportunity to make new law was missed, for a consent decree is not court doctrine or precedent. The new doctrine could have dealt a clear blow to retardation of pollution development by joint industry "research." This general nexus between pollution/safety and antitrust— long ignored—has recently become a current topic of enforcement conversation. Recent speeches by Richard McLaren, Senator Philip Hart, and Washington antitrust lawyer Howard Adler, Jr., all caution against industry collaboration on problems better left to the competitive struggle.[23] But despite his general warnings, and despite the experience of the *Smog* case, McLaren still felt obliged to tell the annual meeting of the ABA's Antitrust Section that "Joint pooling of information and research, they say, will avoid needless duplication of efforts. I can make no categorical answer supporting or opposing these broad arguments because we simply don't know enough about the facts."

Bypassing these problems with the settlement, Judge Jesse W. Curtis denied the right of 21 public and private petitioners and 52 Congressmen to intervene in the proceedings and to modify the decree; it was approved on November 7, 1969. "It's apparent that the general public is aroused," said Judge Curtis, opening the court hearing, "and rightly so, but it may come as a shock that this isn't a hearing about smog. . . . Smog simply isn't a legal problem. It's a government problem. It's simply not a problem the courts can deal with." But smog *was* a legal problem merely because the auto firms had conspired to go slow on smog abatement.

In May, 1971, the problems of pollution concentration in the auto industry converged in one incident. Soon after the consent decree was formally entered, American Motors requested an exemption to purchase engineering services from GM for consultation on air-pollution emission-control devices. In a series of confidential letters uncovered by *Automotive News* reporter Helen Kahn, McLaren at first complained to AMC that

I am seriously troubled by the tone of this proposed agreement. . . . [I]t was never the purpose or intent of this Judgment to permit the wholesale purchase of technical services covering the entire field of emission control devices by a defendant from a competitor.

Nevertheless, after AMC made some slight changes in the proposal, McLaren approved of the year-long contract with GM, on March 10, 1970. AMC and GM requested permission to extend the agreement beyond the one-year period allowed. When the Division asked why, AMC replied in a May 11, 1971, letter that it lacked the money to undertake adequate research. "In the absence of an ability to meet these standards, the very survival of American Motors Corporation would be in jeopardy." It was obvious that AMC exploited market concentration to whipsaw the Division on the consent-decree pollution issue; the Division acquiesced to the retreat in June, 1971. Thus, a noncompetitive structure has the rippling effect of undercutting another important antitrust social issue—pollution abatement. A deconcentrated industry could serve both purposes.

(3) In 1969 two case situations were studied by Division trial staff, and their development depicts important aspects of Division decision-making.

Ford had done considerable pioneering in the auto industry on radial-ply tires, while in the tire industry Goodrich had taken a serious interest in the development of radial tires, which, though they give a less smooth ride, have much better road adhesion and last much longer than conventional tires. *Automotive News* reported that in mid-1966, Ford "was pretty strongly committed to them for future models." [24] But at about this time GM held its annual major meeting with its tire suppliers; they agreed that GM would use the poly-glass tires on its 1970 models. All four major car producers, including Ford, later announced they would use identical poly-glass bias-belted tires on their 1970 cars.

Such a uniformity could be easily explained without a conspiracy. GM's smaller competitors could have simply followed the lead of the auto giant. If all tire companies retooled to compete for GM's 25-million poly-glass-tire market, it would have been very expensive for Ford, Chrysler, and American Motors to choose different tire models. But there is another possibility. The tire manufacturers had a self-interest to " 'head off at the pass' the vaunted radial tire." [25] Substantial and costly retooling by tire firms would be necessary in order to go heavily into radials. Also, European radials already had an established reputation for excellence; therefore, even if domestic manufacturers purchased American-made radials, the market for replacement tires, which is double the original equipment market, would be wide open to imported radials. Therefore, said one Division memorandum, "the mutual interest of Detroit and Akron in preserving the *status quo* apparently provides a strong motive for an illegal agreement to delay or prevent serious development of the domestic market for radial ply tires." A Division attorney requested permission for a preliminary inquiry into the situation, with the concurrence of his section chief. Upper staff, however, refused, putting him off for over a year until the request was dropped. The attorney involved wrote a critical supplemental memorandum:

> Improved tires are probably the single most important components as far as automobile safety is concerned. More than 150,000,000 tires are sold each year in the United States. I cannot agree that the Antitrust Division should refuse to investigate a decision by Akron and Detroit to standardize a product that is so important to the safety of the automobile consuming public and the economy of the United States merely because we presently lack *direct* evidence of an illegal agreement.

In the second case, Ford announced in 1966 that it would build two $1.2 million "diagnostic service centers" in Chicago and Newark, using electronic equipment to diagnose a car's "ills" quickly and inexpensively. Distress over the decline of dealer servicing quality, and over its consequent bad image, led Ford into this experiment. Its dealers, however, were insulted by implications of their ineptness * and by the threat, as they viewed it, to the franchise system. Through 1968, after the centers had opened, New Jersey dealers met with Ford executives in an attempt to close them down. Despite surveys which showed consumers more satisfied with repairs at the centers than at dealers, Ford agreed with the dealers in late 1968 to close the two centers and to open no new ones.

Two Division attorneys in the New York field office recommended suit against Ford and the dealers for an illegal restraint of trade: Ford's servicing competition with their dealers was ended by agreement, they said, not market forces or independent decision. The internal memorandum suggesting a complaint concluded:

> This case would strike a meaningful blow for automobile owners. As the New Jersey Center was intended to test the feasibility of establishing highly automated diagnostic centers throughout the country, the amount of commerce affected is potentially much greater than the business handled by one facility. . . . Good service facilities are, of course, essential to highway safety. . . . At the very least the suit recommended herein would serve notice on the automobile industry that the Government will seriously scrutinize efforts to protect outmoded non-competitive elements of the industry.

The case got as high as the Deputy Director of Operations, Robert Hummel, who refused to recommend it up

---

* One Ford ad, promoting the centers, read: "Take the needless mumbo-jumbo, expense and inconvenience out of car servicing and . . . minimize the chances of fault, and unnecessary repairs."

the chain of command. In his judgment, the agreement was a reasonable part of the manufacturer-dealer relationship. But "Hummel viewed the reasonableness of the agreement from the perspective of the businessman who had to iron out differences with dealers," said a Division lawyer in an interview, "*not* from the perspective of the customer." If it is an illegal restraint for a manufacturer to limit a dealer's geographic marketing, it should also be an illegal restraint for a dealer to limit a manufacturer's "marketing" of a new competitive service. But with a chance to make some new law in a novel case, Hummel played it safe, as the Division hierarchy invariably does in borderline case situations, and as it has perennially done in the automobile industry.

2. THE PROFESSIONS

In most people's minds the word "profession" conjures up images of doctors and lawyers. Yet the word also implies a privilege of occupational monopoly—state licensing. "Professionalism" is widespread and growing. In 1968 the Council of State Governments reported 67 different occupations for which licensing was required by more than five states. In addition to lawyers, doctors, and pharmacists, the following occupations are licensed by more than 40 states: embalmers, funeral directors, accountants, architects, engineers, insurance brokers, real-estate brokers, teachers, surveyors, barbers, beauticians and cosmetologists. Over 75% of the state occupational licensing boards are composed *exclusively* of members of the licensed occupation.[1] As economist Milton Friedman has observed:

In the arguments that seek to persuade legislatures to enact such licensure provisions, the justification is always said to be the necessity of protecting the public interest. However, the pressure on the legislature to license an occupation rarely comes from the members of the public who have been abused by members of the occupation. On the contrary, the pressure invariably comes from members of the occupation itself.[2]

This section will focus on some of the problems caused by the medical and legal professional organizations, which under the guise of protecting the public from quacks and shysters raise prices and perpetuate the inefficient delivery of professional services. The recent trend is for consumers to spend a larger proportion of their disposable income on services instead of goods, and much of this increase goes to professional services. Consequently, consumer welfare demands that restrictive practices of professional organizations be made a high priority for antitrust enforcement.

The Medical Profession [3]

Doctors and other medical professionals dispensed $70 billion worth of health-care services in 1970—or at least that is the price that was paid. As early as 1938 the Antitrust Division filed suit against the American Medical Association, the District of Columbia Medical Association, and others for expelling doctors associated with a prepaid group health-care program. Stripped of medical-society membership, these doctors were denied access to hospitals and consultation with other doctors. In the 1943 *AMA* decision the Supreme Court unanimously upheld the government's antitrust charges.[4] During the late 1940s and early 1950s the Division staff recommended that cases be brought involving harassment of physicians working for prepaid group programs in Oregon, Washington, California, Arkansas, Oklahoma, Chicago, and New York. Only the Oregon case was brought, and it was decided against the government by an extremely hostile district judge. One of the defendant doctors testified, "I think that this is just an effort to smear the medical profession by the political coterie which is sitting at this table here, representing the Red wing of the Federal administration." [5] Chapter 3 noted that Attorney General Herbert Brownell declined to file the strongest case, involving the Health Insurance Plan of Greater New York (HIP), for fear of evoking "socialized medicine" cries from the American Medical Association. The Democrats have proven equally timid. A 1961 memorandum unsuccessfully urged AAG Loevinger to renew enforcement efforts against organized medicine. A veteran Division attorney demonstrated that their coercive actions against prepaid group practice were "as harmful and despicable as any [restraints of trade] that I have seen in a long association with the antitrust laws."

Like other professions, the practice of medicine requires a degree of expertise which the consumer is unable to match or evaluate. For the consumer of health services, free choice is illusory. As economist Elton Rayack observes:

It is the physician who makes the decision as to what kind of treatment is needed, and by his recommendations he can create a demand for his own product. It is the physician who decides whether or not drugs are required, whether or not hospitalization is desirable, whether or not surgery is necessary. The consumer has no way of knowing which alternative is best for him—he must rely upon his faith in the integrity and competence of the physician. Moreover, the consequences of a wrong choice on the part of the consumer can be disastrous.[6]

Granting such authority to a doctor—whose economic interest does not always coincide with the patient's interest—can encourage abuse. Worse, the task of channeling doctors' performances into efficient and inexpensive medical services has been delegated to the organized medical profession—the AMA and its affiliated state and local medical societies. They exercise an anticompetitive lockhold on the economics of the profession: state medical societies dominate state licensing and examination boards; county medical societies enforce the AMA "Principles of Medical Ethics"; the AMA's Council on Medical Education and Hospitals sets accreditation standards for medical schools and, through the Joint Committee on Hospital Accreditation, for hospitals; the Advisory Board for Medical Specialties coordinates 19 specialty boards which determine the qualifications for surgeons, obstetricians, and other specialists; and the American Medical Political Action Committee lobbies and funnels campaign contributions to candidates.

The AMA has exercised these enormous powers, first, to limit the supply of doctors. AMA President Dr. Walter L. Bierring stated in 1934: "One is forced to the conviction that more doctors are being turned out than society needs and can comfortably reward. . . . During the coming year the Association . . . will institute a resurvey of the medical schools of the country. . . . A fine piece of educational work could well be done if we were to use only half of the seventy-odd medical schools in the United States." [7] Threatened with loss of accreditation, the medical schools eagerly cut back the size of their student bodies and stabilized the growth of their physical facilities. After World War II the AMA lobbied vigorously against federal aid to medical schools, especially direct grants to medical students. It was 1958 before organized medicine conceded the existence of a serious doctor-shortage threat. One direct result of this now chronic shortage is that in 1969 the median net reported income for physicians was $40,550,[8] by far the highest income for any professional group.

As damaging as the shortage is the delivery of medical services. Since "ethics" forbids doctors (and most professionals) from advertising or soliciting patients, the consumer is helpless to decide when to visit a doctor, which type of specialist to seek out, and which doctor is competent or inexpensive. The most jealously guarded institution of medical practice is the fee-for-service charge—a separate bill for each service, as contrasted with a fixed payment by each patient to cover all illnesses during a stated period plus preventive check-ups. It is the fee-for-service arrangement which permits doctors to reap higher incomes than they would receive from fixed payments. Prepayments would be more susceptible to consumer evaluation and competitive pressures and would probably entail salaried positions with group health programs.

Nowhere else in America has such a lucrative calling been so disastrous for its consumers. While the United States spends more *per capita* on health—nearly $300 in 1969—than any other country in the world, America's health is steadily declining relative to that of other industrialized nations. The United States ranks 13th in infant mortality and 18th in male life expectancy, figures which have improved only slightly since 1954. The Nader Report on the quality of medical care, *One Life—One Physician,* reviewed evidence of startling incompetence among highly paid doctors—incompetence that is directly traceable to the fee-for-service approach to medical practice. Many doctors perform unnecessary surgery. A 1946 study by Dr. Norman F. Miller entitled "Hysterectomy: Therapeutic Necessity or Surgical Racket?" found that 30.8% of all women given hysterectomies had no pathology of the organs removed.[9] The fee-for-service arrangement provides a financial incentive for unnecessary operations. And because consumers are unable to separate the competent doctors from the incompetent, there is little inducement for doctors to keep abreast in their fields after they leave medical school.

Prepaid group practice can cure these consequences of medical self-regulation. Placing a team of doctors on fixed salaries would facilitate "peer review"—criticism and evaluation of each other's work. Peer review encourages dramatic improvements in the quality of medical care. In one experiment the introduction of peer review increased the number of "justifiable" operations from 30% to 80% in two years while the overall number of operations declined by 65%.[10] In addition, comprehensive prepaid group health programs offer preventive check-ups without additional charge, increase efficiency through the use of teams of specialists, and spread the lower cost of medical care evenly among consumers. Even greater efficiencies and innovations in the delivery of health care could be realized if there were vigorous price and quality competition among prepaid group health programs using *informational* advertising to educate consumers.

This type of program would largely remove control over the delivery of medical services from the hands of doctors and put it in the hands of consumers exercising free market choice—which is why organized medicine vehemently opposes it. When the profession began to realize the existence of this trend, it backed the Blue Shield plan, which simply reimburses doctors out of insurance premiums on a fee-for-service basis. In many states, legislatures have been pressured to pass "Blue Shield" statutes, of doubtful constitutionality, which generally require that all prepayment health programs preserve the fee-for-service concept and be controlled or operated by the medical society.[11] Blue Shield, like Blue Cross, has evolved into an inefficiency-inducing monopoly in most areas of the country.

Meanwhile, organized medicine has kept up its vigil against prepayment programs. The AMA deems it "unethical" (grounds for expulsion) for a doctor to participate in a profit-making program. It is also "unethical" for doctor-sponsored programs to advertise in any way—which means they cannot inform consumers of the existence and benefits of prepayment health plans.

By impeding a competing health-care delivery system, these "ethical" prohibitions violate the antitrust laws under the principles announced in the Supreme Court's 1943 *AMA* decision. The 75 prepaid group programs in existence throughout the nation serve only about 4% of the population. Coverage would be substantially greater, and the nation's health substantially better, had the Division enforced the antitrust laws against medical-society abuse after 1943. But the only judicial precedents established since that time have resulted from private suits brought when the Division declined to act.[12]

The Legal Profession

The delivery system for legal services in many respects resembles that for health services. The legal profession's attitude toward competition was summed up by the Ethics Committee of the Wisconsin Bar Association: "Efforts, direct or indirect, in any way to encroach upon the business of other lawyers are unworthy of those who should be brothers at the bar." [13] Bar Association fears over antitrust prosecution are reflected by the way it has openly fixed prices. It was "unethical" (grounds for disbarment) for lawyers to charge consistently less than the amount prescribed in published minimum-fee schedules. "The evils of fee-cutting ought to be apparent to all members of the bar," the American Bar Association's Committee on Professional Ethics said in 1961. "No lawyer should be put in the position of bidding competitively for clients. It is proper for the profession to combat such evils by suggesting . . . minimum fee schedules and other practices which have a tendency to discourage the rendering of services for inadequate compensation." [14]

If this attitude had been taken by the steel industry, the Division would have promptly filed a criminal price-fixing suit. The bar associations were approached on tiptoe. In June, 1966, as a response to Division murmurings, a statement appeared in the ABA-sponsored *Legal Economic News* entitled "Recommended Minimum Fee Schedules: Advisory or Mandatory?" It explained that one purpose of fee schedules was simply to help lawyers who might not know what to charge for a particular service by telling them what other lawyers were charging, and that a consideration of the totality of factors in a given case might or might not render fee-cutting unethical. The Division accepted this meaningless resolution, since it had in fact been drafted by Turner's legal assistant and then sent by Deputy AG Ramsey Clark to Cullen Smith, chairman of the ABA's Committee on the Economics of Law Practice. Subsequently the Division received complaints about the anticompetitive effects of minimum-fee schedules in the cities of Detroit, New Haven, and San Francisco, and the states of New York, Wisconsin, and Illinois. Finally, in 1970, ABA President Bernard Segal announced that, upon McLaren's advice, disciplinary actions would no longer be brought against fee-cutters.

The Division was completely satisfied. While the Supreme

Court had ruled in the *Container Corporation* case that even voluntary exchanges of price information were illegal if they facilitated conscious parallelism among oligopolists, the Division felt that the structure of the legal profession did not invoke that principle. Or did it? Sanctions against fee-cutters were exceedingly rare long before the ABA withdrew the threat in 1970. Nonetheless, lawyers had adhered to the fee schedules.[15] This quasi-oligopolistic behavior among thousands of lawyers is explainable by the prohibition on lawyer advertising, which eliminates price competition, forces lawyers to rely upon minimum-fee schedules as a pricing guide—whether mandatory or voluntary—and brings the legal profession within the *Container Corporation* principle.

Minimum-fee schedules are only one of the restrictions enforced by bar associations in the name of "professional ethics." The most important of these is that lawyers may neither advertise nor solicit clients. Indeed, with some exceptions, state bar associations prohibit lawyers from telling the public about their specialties—*e.g.,* John Doe, antitrust lawyer. Why should lawyers' skills remain secret? One reason is the fear that some lawyers' advertisements and solicitations would be deceptive, especially since potential clients are helpless to evaluate lawyers' claims. But deceptive advertising is a problem in any industry, and the fact that it may be more of a problem among professionals does not alter the solution: to impose sanctions against deceptive advertisers instead of banning advertising altogether.*

Curiously, most bar-association explanations for their rules against advertising and soliciting do not mention deception. Instead, advertising and soliciting are condemned because they "commercialize," "demean," lower the "dignity," and damage the "image" of the legal profession. (Ironically, many laymen view lawyers as shysters or crooks in spite of these prohibitions.) This effort to maintain a dignified image has at least two harmful consequences:

(1) The prohibitions against advertising and soliciting,

---

* There are several ways to prevent deceptive advertising by lawyers, among them (a) damage suits brought against soliciting attorneys by victimized clients; (b) a rule requiring attorneys to provide a solicited client with a list of other attorneys who specialize in similar cases; and (c) formation of a bar committee to review the substance of solicited cases with an eye toward informing the solicited client at an early date that his lawyer's legal theories are frivolous.[16]

by eliminating competition among lawyers for existing clients, discriminate in favor of established lawyers who already have clients and against lawyers entering the profession who have none. It is a form of illegal market-dividing based upon guild seniority concepts.

(2) In maintaining their "dignity," lawyers ensure that the legal profession and the legal system are virtually irrelevant to the vast majority of Americans unaware of their legal rights and uninformed about them by advertising. A survey conducted by the Missouri Bar Association discovered that 36% of that state's residents had never used a lawyer, 50% had not used a lawyer in the last five years, and 78% had used a lawyer no more than once in the last five years.[17] Most of those who went to lawyers wanted help with auto accidents, home purchases, wills, and other widely recognized problems. When less commonly recognized legal problems are involved, few people realize that legal remedies are available. Another survey found that only 3% of consumers would have sought a lawyer's aid after realizing that they had been defrauded.[18]

It is socially desirable for citizens to be informed of and to exercise their legal rights. Not only is it desirable that citizens be compensated for their injuries, but recovering damages through lawsuits also serves the public interest by deterring persons generally from violating the legal rights of others. Encouraging such a responsive legal system is apparently too burdensome for bar associations, which have long declared it "unethical" for lawyers to "stir up" lawsuits—meritorious as well as frivolous ones. To the organized legal profession, legal rights should be exercised primarily by the few who are already aware of them, not those who fail to comprehend them in the first place.

The bulk of the citizenry who never recognize their rights and who often do not even perceive their injuries are ignored by the legal profession. When groups of laymen, notably labor unions and civil-rights organizations, hired lawyers to inform injured workers and victims of discrimination of their legal rights, the organized bar brought solicitation charges. Fortunately, four times in the last eight years the Supreme Court has upheld the right of lay organizations to operate group legal-service programs, as an exercise of the First Amendment freedom to associate and to petition the government through the courts.[19] In one labor-union case, the ABA, 44 state bars, and the bars of four major cities unsuccessfully urged the Supreme Court to reconsider its decision. These group legal-service programs have drastically reduced the group members' attorney-fee costs. In a United Mine Workers program involved in one of the Supreme Court decisions, the union attorney was paid an annual salary of $12,400. Over a 30-month period he collected $2.5 million for injured workers. If these workers had been forced to hire outside counsel on a 20% contingent-fee basis, they would have paid out $500,000, not $12,400, for attorneys' fees.

Prepaid group legal-service programs have enormous potential to help citizens recognize and exercise their rights. They tap lawyers' special talents, spread costs, and eliminate the need for contingent fees in high-risk cases. Like prepaid group health-care programs, they eliminate the fee-for-service concept. Predictably, therefore, the organized bar prohibits most prepaid group programs, despite the Supreme Court decisions mentioned above and although disciplinary actions against lawyers participating in such programs would violate the Sherman Act in the same way that the AMA and the D.C. Medical Society were held by the Supreme Court to have violated it in 1943. Bar-association restrictions illegally attempt to exclude a competing method of delivering legal services.

3. THE OIL INDUSTRY

The International Oil Barons

"If it were not for the question of national security, we would be willing to face either a criminal or a civil suit. But this is the kind of information that the Kremlin would love to get its hands on." That argument was made in 1952 by Arthur Dean, attorney for Standard Oil of New Jersey, urging that documents be withheld from a grand jury investigating the international oil cartel.[1] The documents had already been screened by an interdepartmental committee representing the CIA and the Departments of Justice, State, and Defense. One document this committee kept from the grand jury was the FTC's *International Petroleum Cartel Report,* which, after careful editing, had already been released to the public. This report had formed the basis for the Antitrust Division's attempt to indict Jersey Standard, California Standard, Gulf, Texaco, and Socony-Vacuum (now Mobil) for conspiring since 1928 to divide world markets, fix oil prices, and limit imports of cheap foreign oil.

"National security" has come to mean whatever the oil industry wants it to mean. Its argument against public release of the FTC report, as related by Jersey Standard to its stockholders, was that Middle Eastern capitols would raise cries of economic imperialism—not on account of the cartel itself, but because "attempts by the United States to enforce its antitrust laws" would tell the Arabs that the American oil companies did not enjoy the full backing of their government. In fact, our government did give its full backing, including a promise of antitrust immunity, to the cartel's boycott of Iranian oil when it was nationalized by Premier Mossadegh in 1951. This boycott, CIA activities, and Defense Department aid to Mossadegh's opponents contributed to his ouster in August of 1953. The State Department then dispatched oilman Herbert Hoover, Jr., to engineer a "consortium" (read "cartel") of oil companies, including the five defendants, to operate the Iranian concessions on a joint basis. Thus the State and Defense Departments were aiding the cartel while the Justice Department was theoretically attacking it.

"The only way to bring an oil case is if the President is not running for reelection," said Ken Harkins, the Division's number-two man on the case. "Thus, we initially [empaneled the grand jury] when Truman decided not to run in '52." Even Truman, just before he left office, offered to dismiss the grand jury and substitute a civil suit if the defendants would pledge to give over subpoenaed documents. That condition was refused by the oil companies, who knew they would fare well when their traditional political allies, the Republicans, came to power in January. (The incoming Secretary of State, John Foster Dulles, was Arthur Dean's law partner.) The Eisenhower administration hastily dismissed the grand-jury investigation into what the FTC report considered a multibillion-dollar theft, again citing "national security." A civil suit was substituted, but without an advance commitment by the defendants to turn over the documents they had fought to keep from the grand jury. At that point Leonard Emmerglick, the Division's chief prosecutor, resigned. As the civil case "progressed," the interdepartmental screening committee continued its work. One of the Division's trial attorneys on the case told the Study

Group, "How can you try a case when your adversary keeps claiming that to reveal what you seek would violate the national security, especially when the court and the Executive Branch go along?"

The 1952 FTC report emphasized that the structure of the international oil industry had enabled the five defendants and two foreign companies to maintain and police explicit cartel agreements. Complex agreements were required, for oil production is potentially one of the most competitive industries in the world. The seven cartel members had to limit supply and keep it out of the hands of competitors. Outside of the United States and Soviet-bloc territories these seven companies in 1949 controlled nearly 90% of world crude-oil reserves, 88% of crude-oil production, 77% of refining capacity, 85% of cracking capacity, two-thirds of the privately owned tanker fleet, and "every important pipeline in existence or even proposed," according to the FTC. At some point along the line between the oil well and the ultimate consumer, any smaller competitor had to buy from, sell to, or use the transportation facilities of the majors. And to cement their own alliance, the seven engaged in many joint ventures in exploration, production, pipelines, joint patents, etc. Indeed, interlocking joint ventures were the rule:

The directors of the Standard of New Jersey and Socony-Vacuum, who determine the policies of the Arabian-American Oil Co. [Saudi Arabia], are the same men who help shape the behavior of the Iraq Petroleum Company. The directors of Anglo-Iranian Company [now British Petroleum], who assist in making high oil policy for Iraq and Iran, participate, along with the directors of Gulf, in planning the price and production policies in Kuwait.[2]

This interlocking, horizontally concentrated, and vertically integrated structure enabled the cartel's explicit price-fixing agreements to succeed. As one Senate staffer put it: "The closest analogy to the way oil production and pricing decisions were made is the Soviet economy, where bureaucrats determine in advance how much will be needed."

The National Security Council forbade any attempt to dismantle the cartel's structure. By 1960 rumors of a "sell-out" consent-decree settlement had reached Senator Joseph C. O'Mahoney (D.-Wyo.). He was reassured by the Justice Department that no settlement was imminent—the day before consent decrees with Gulf and Jersey Standard were announced. The relief consisted primarily of vague bans on future agreements to fix prices, divide markets, restrict output, or exclude competitors. Even these provisions were riddled with loopholes. O'Mahoney was so furious over the decree provisions, according to his former aide, that he briefly considered bringing suit against the settlement. By 1963 another consent decree, similar to the earlier ones, was entered against Texaco. In 1967 the cases against California Standard and Mobil were dismissed "without prejudice," a legal formalism which means that the Division can reopen the case and spend another 13 years seeking another meaningless decree.

Since the oil-cartel cases, 10 oil-producing nations have formed the Organization of Petroleum Exporting Countries (OPEC), a sellers' cartel of their own, to raise the level of royalty revenues exacted from all oil companies. In this setting, on January 15, 1971, the Antitrust Division issued a secret business-review letter authorizing the oil companies to bargain jointly with the OPEC countries. McLaren defended this promised immunity as a form of "countervailing power" to protect smaller companies from being discriminated against by the OPEC countries. Actually, the agreement was announced by the Big Eight and seven other large, integrated companies. The smaller independents were "invited" to join and were advised that their interests would be represented at the bargaining table by Jersey Standard and British Petroleum.

The anticompetitive consequences of this arrangement are not yet clear. McLaren conceded that no other business-review letter in Division history had authorized buyers to bargain jointly with sellers. But while the oil companies' united front might hold down the amount of royalty increases *this* time, the long-run effect may be to strengthen *both* cartels. With joint oil-company bargaining, there are fewer opportunities for individual companies to seek special royalty discounts from individual nations. Likewise, the majors can employ the joint-bargaining device to lure the more aggressive independents into their fold, reducing the likelihood of beneficial price-cutting. Finally, the majors may actually have benefited from a royalty increase, since it afforded them an opportunity to pass on to European and Japanese consumers *more* in higher prices than the amount of their own cost increases. Royalties paid to foreign governments are considered "taxes" on profits from crude-oil production, and the U.S. companies are allowed a federal tax credit for foreign "taxes." Thus, the U.S. companies can profit by a royalty increase if they can pass on any of the foreign government's increased take.

The largest royalty increases came not from the Persian Gulf countries, where the majors have staked out their most lucrative claims, but from Libya, where some of the majors and Occidental Petroleum had procured a source of high-quality, low-polluting oil close to the European market. Another McLaren business-review letter authorized a pooling agreement: the signatory companies would share their own oil with Occidental if the Libyan regime chose to press its demands by stopping all production. Senator William Proxmire protested to McLaren that this was a production-allocation agreement in violation of the 1960 consent decrees. He branded McLaren's denial as "Orwellian double-think at its most blatant." A Division attorney conceded in an interview that the pooling arrangement was a "technical violation" of the consent decrees. "But you have to understand," he said, "that we didn't have much choice in the matter."

Which was true—for the business-review letter was presented to the Division as a *fait accompli* quite unrelated to antitrust policy. Arthur Dean had marched into Attorney General Mitchell's office with the Defense Department under one arm and the State Department under the other. Antitrust immunity was necessary to head off a threat by Arab nations to cut off oil supplies to Europe, which would endanger NATO preparedness, he said; moreover, the Europeans would appreciate help from the united bargaining power of U.S. oil giants.

The Arabs would of course be angry, but "they're going to nationalize their oil sooner or later anyway," said the Division attorney. In short, antitrust non-enforcement was used to further geopolitical objectives. A similar grant of antitrust immunity was made in 1956 when Europe was threatened by Nasser's takeover of the Suez Canal. Immunity was granted then under the Defense Production Act, now expired, which provided for government participation in oil-company decisions and required approval of both the Justice Department and the chairman of the FTC. This time, when oil-company representatives met in London to work out their bargaining arrangements, State Department officials were excluded. When Senator Proxmire asked why, he was told that their presence might inhibit free discussion. If the Executive Branch thinks that U.S. foreign-policy interests are coincident with U.S. oil-company economic interests abroad, it should ask Congress for legislation saying so. But whether American, European, or Arab interests should exploit Middle Eastern oil is not an issue which should be decided by distorting antitrust policy.

The Domestic Cartel: Government as Promoter

Within the United States the oil industry does not need a cartel to limit output and raise prices. The government does —again under the pretext of "national security"—in the form of import quotas, depletion allowances, and prorationing. The capstone of the government's largess is the oil import quota, which, by excluding cheaper foreign oil, costs American consumers $5–$7 billion per year, and may cost $8.4 billion by 1980.[3]

Why is American oil so much more expensive than foreign oil? In fact a large portion of domestically produced oil comes from relatively high-volume wells which could compete with Middle Eastern wells because transportation is cheaper. However, the oil depletion allowance and the intangible drilling-expense tax write-off, by increasing the profits from oil production to promote increased domestic exploration, have made it profitable to continue pumping oil out of high-cost "stripper" wells. These comprise 70% of the nation's 550,000 oil wells, but account for only 16% of domestic oil production.

The lowest-cost wells, which in 1965 produced .4 billion of a total 2.7 billion barrels, could have expanded their production sixfold except that state "prorationing" commissions limited their production in the name of conservation.[4] Since many separately owned wells ordinarily draw from the same underground reservoir, some type of conservation is indeed necessary to prevent a costly race in which each well operator seeks to get "his" oil out of the ground before the others. Moreover, the amount of natural pressure under which oil flows out of a reservoir, and the extra pressure needed to pump it out, are directly related to the number, location, and withdrawal rates of the wells lifting from that reservoir. Inefficient operations can deplete the underground pressure and make it much more expensive to extract the oil in future years. Two remedies are possible. The best is "unitization," by which all parties drawing from a single reservoir designate a single authority to control the entire operation. This usually results in fewer wells, lower drilling costs, and more efficient well spacing in order to conserve pressure. The other is "maximum efficient rate prorationing," by which a state commission calculates the most efficient withdrawal rate and prorates the total among the individual wells. But notably in Texas and Louisiana, where three-fourths of the oil is produced, the state commissions, captives of the oil industry, have used their power to (1) restrict output of high-capability wells more than low-capability wells, and (2) restrict output generally, thereby keeping the price of oil high.

Economist Joel Dirlam sums up the situation created by the import quota, depletion allowance, and prorationing: "The major purpose of our present policy is to increase the profits of domestic producers and royalty payments to landowners in the Southwest at the expense of consumers everywhere." [5] An analogous assessment could be made of farm price supports and agricultural marketing cooperatives, merchant-marine subsidies, union featherbedding, and "voluntary" import restrictions on textiles and steel. When a competition-"plagued" industry finds itself short on profits and progress but long on numbers of employees and political clout, it turns to government to do for it what unenforceable price-fixing or oligopolistic interdependence cannot.

Of course, the "national security" basis for this government-promoted oil cartel is a sham. If bolstering our own oil reserves is the objective, then the government should long ago have initiated a crash program to make it commercially feasible to develop our two trillion barrels of oil shale or to convert our centuries-long supply of coal into oil. Instead, all the years of propping up the domestic oil industry have depleted our own oil reserves. Our offshore oil wells and tankers plying between the Gulf Coast crude-producing and refinery complex and the Eastern Seaboard are more susceptible to Cuban-based submarines than are tankers from Venezuela. Even overland imports from Canada are restricted in the name of national security. At perhaps a single year's installment of the $5–$7 billion annual cost of keeping the entire domestic oil-production industry ready for a national emergency, the government could simply purchase a number of already drilled wells, cap them, and construct pipelines linking them with refineries.[6] Once constructed, the system could be maintained at minimal cost and activated almost immediately to meet any oil shortage. President Nixon's Cabinet Task Force on Oil Import Control estimated that even if import quotas were scrapped with no contingency plans at all, the U.S. would continue to produce enough oil so that domestic reserves, plus Canadian and Venezuelan imports, could supply *all* of our 1980 needs for a year.[7]

Government favoritism to the oil industry affects its structure as well as practice. For example, the depletion allowance is more than just a tax giveaway; * it also fosters vertical integration of refining and production. The allowance provides for a tax deduction of 22% of the *gross* income up to 50% of *net* income from *oil production,* not refining. It therefore encourages an integrated company to inflate the accounting value of its oil at the wellhead and minimize it at the refinery, thus maximizing the tax benefit of the depletion allowance. The integrated companies accomplish this artifice by posting a high price on crude oil that they produce themselves and "sell" to their own refineries. So lucrative is the depletion allowance that it is actually profitable for the integrated companies to pay high prices for crude oil. Economists Alfred Kahn and Melvin de Chazeau calculated that if an integrated company can supply at least 77% of its refinery requirements with its own crude-oil production, it will be better off purchasing the remainder of its crude at an inflated price—even without raising retail prices.[8]

But note that the high crude-oil prices which the refineries of integrated companies pay—primarily to themselves—become the prices which non-integrated refiners must pay to independent crude producers. This severely squeezes the profit margins of independent refineries. Consequently, they either suffer competitively, go out of business, are force to merge with crude-oil producers, or are acquired by the major integrated companies which dominate the in-

---

* In 1969 tax favors to the oil industry depleted the U.S. treasury by $1.125 billion. In light of the avowed purpose of these tax loopholes to promote domestic oil exploration in the interest of national security, it is curious that U.S. oil companies are given a full tax credit on "taxes" (royalties) paid to foreign governments. The result is to encourage foreign oil exploration instead of domestic. During 1963–67, Jersey Standard, Gulf, Texaco, Mobil, and California Standard paid $1 billion in taxes on total net income of $21 billion—a 4.9% rate. Atlantic Richfield paid no income taxes at all from 1962 to 1967.

dustry. Acquisitions of independent refiners accounted for 40.7% of the increase in refining capacity among the top 20 oil companies between 1959 and 1966.[9] During 1951–63, 27 of the larger independent refiners disappeared.[10]

While there has been a definite trend toward greater vertical integration and horizontal concentration, it is difficult to paint a precise and accurate picture of the oil industry's structure.* State gasoline-tax payment records are often relied upon. But the company that sells the gasoline often is not the one that pays the tax on it. In one Antitrust Division investigation, state tax records indicated a combined market share for the companies involved of 34%; their responses to CIDs placed it at 92%. At the least, horizontal concentration is substantial in regional markets, which are served either by pipelines jointly owned by the integrated companies themselves or by tankers which they control through ownership or long-term charters. Thus, to the extent that the dominant firms are vertically integrated, the only level other than retail or wholesale distribution at which a competitive market can occur is production, where the government hands the oil companies a cartel price on a gold platter.

Even at the marketing levels "the general abhorrence of price competition by the majors," say marketing professors Allvine and Patterson, "is supported by a variety of sources including statements of oil executives and field personnel, the findings of the 1965 FTC study, and independent studies of pricing practices." [11] Kahn adds, "The $100 million to $1 billion companies dominating individual market areas . . . recognize their mutual interdependence. . . . They expect to be in business for decades, and have a strong interest in avoiding hasty pursuit of the short-run advantage." [12] There are about 20 oil companies operating in the United States with assets of over $1 billion, and nine of the 20 largest industrial corporations in the United States are oil companies.

* There is probably less publicly available economic data concerning the oil industry than about any other major industry. A former Antitrust Division trial attorney told the Study Group of extreme difficulty in securing elementary data from the Oil and Gas Division of the Interior Department—"a retirement haven for ex-oil-industry operatives." "It's not by accident," he said, "that lack of elementary data cripples the ability of the Division and the FTC to spot oil-industry antitrust violations." For example, short of subpoena or CID, there is no way for federal antitrust agencies to determine a particular company's share of the gasoline market in a given state or region.

What competition exists at the marketing level is channeled into nonprice areas. Two brands of gasoline of similar octane rating are as approximately alike as two glasses of water or two different kilowatts. But an artificial customer brand preference is created by psychological manipulation of "symbolic words, colors, station design, cleanliness, pump shape, signs, displays, lighting, general appearance of apron and personnel." And to induce the customer to come back again and again there are credit cards, trading stamps, games of chance, continuity premiums, glasses, dishware, and the like. These marketing inefficiencies highlight the importance of the "private branders"—mass-merchandising specialists who buy from independent refineries and terminal operators or obtain surplus stocks from the majors. The difference between the majors and the private branders is that between the "service station" and the "gas station." The private branders do not employ games, stamps, or similar promotional devices; they are able to undercut the majors by 2¢ to 5¢ per gallon. "In the process," Allvine and Patterson conclude, "they serve an extremely useful function for the gasoline consumer—even those consumers who never patronize the private brander. Specifically, they keep a downward pressure on the retail price of gasoline." If consumers were aware that all gasoline brands are virtually identical, and if the majors were forced by consumer demand to switch to private-brander-type marketing methods at 3¢ less per gallon, the consumer savings would exceed $2.5 billion.[13] Like it or not, the majors must live with the private branders if only because the majors often refine more gasoline than their own dealers can sell. Due to high start-up costs, their refineries cannot simply be shut down in time of oversupply. They must keep their gasoline moving into the market as soon as it comes out of the refinery, even if it has to be sold at low prices. But the private branders and the franchised dealers must also live with the majors. For these "independent businessmen" (the Supreme Court's appellation) it is truly a closed enterprise system. When they try to cut prices below levels acceptable to their majors, or when branded dealers refuse to carry their major's tires, batteries, and accessories, they are disciplined through a price war or destroyed through supply or dealership cut-offs.

The majors also employ a variety of sophisticated devices to keep gasoline out of the hands of private branders. One is an intricate system of "barter" by which an integrated company with a temporary oil surplus will trade it to another integrated company with a temporary shortage in exchange for a future trade moving in the other direction; this move avoids a distress sale to a private brander and avoids its own dealers having to cut their prices to sell off excesses. A practice such as barter which closes off entire markets could reasonably be viewed as either an unfair trade practice under Section Five of the FTC Act or a combination in restraint of trade under Section 1 of the Sherman Act (the combination consisting of a pattern or series of barters; the restraint of trade their cumulative effect).

Enforcement Against Oil

The considerable number of government antitrust prosecutions against the oil industry have had negligible impact upon its structure and performance. The 1941 case against Atlantic Refining, discussed in Chapter VI, was perhaps the most ambitious ever undertaken by the Antitrust Division—and certainly one of its biggest failures. After World War II there was an attempt to revive the Atlantic program on a piecemeal basis. In the *West Coast Petroleum* case, filed in 1950, the Division sought to divest California Standard and six other companies of their service-station operations. But when the district judge made it plain that he would not order divestiture even if the government proved its allegations, the Division meekly accepted a consent decree banning future price-fixing and other illegal conduct.

The Division has even had difficulty securing convictions in straightforward price-fixing cases. During the mid-1950s veteran trial attorneys persuaded AAG Stanley Barnes to call a broad grand-jury inquiry into patterns of regional gasoline-price leadership that had persisted, at least in some areas, since the 1911 break-up of the Standard Oil Trust. Brownell's office finally permitted a nationwide investigation, but only if a grand jury empaneled at Alexandria, Virginia, first found evidence of a local price conspiracy. Then, in 1957 during the Suez crisis, 29 oil companies issued price increases shortly after their executives had talked to one another by telephone, after several executives had publicly invited price hikes, and when crude oil was in ample supply. The Alexandria grand jury returned an indictment for the price increase, with the case later transferred to Judge Royce H. Savage in Tulsa over the Division's objection.

At the close of the government's 11-day presentation of its case, the defendants moved for a dismissal due to lack of evidence. Although an Atlantic executive's diary contained a January 2 notation of Humble's January 3 price increase, and although the defendants had presented no rebuttal evidence of their own, Judge Savage promptly stated his "absolute conviction, personally" that the defendants had done nothing wrong and dismissed the case. The entire oil industry rejoiced. Headlines in the *Oil and Gas Journal* read "Oil is Acquitted, But the Government Now Stands Indicted." The editorial columns of some major newspapers echoed that theme; said the *Chicago Tribune,* "To accuse the companies of conspiracy under these conditions was as senseless as it would be to accuse a class of first graders of cheating because they all agreed that two plus two equals four." It was rather embarrassing when, a year later, Judge Savage resigned from the bench to become a vice president of Gulf, one of the defendants.

The Colonial Pipeline, which runs from the Gulf Coast refineries through Virginia, Washington, and into New Jersey, illustrates the advantage of joint control to its nine owners. Colonial is by far the largest petroleum-products pipeline in the country. Except for the smaller, 30-year-old Plantation Pipeline, it is the only pipeline transporting gasoline and heating oil from the Gulf Coast refineries to the Southeast markets. The majors that own Colonial, together with Shell, Jersey Standard, and California Standard, which jointly own Plantation, market 79% of the gasoline sold in the entire Southeast.

ICC regulations require pipelines to serve all shippers on reasonable and nondiscriminatory terms. Since Colonial began operation in 1963, however, nearly all shipments through it have been made by its owners. Indeed, in planning the pipeline's dimensions, the owners limited its capacity to the quantity of petroleum products which they expected to market in the areas through which it would travel, leaving no room for independent competing refineries. Few companies would be willing to invest hundreds of thousands of dollars to lay gathering lines to a pipeline which is already 100% in use.

The Antitrust Division contemplated a suit to divest all

of the majors except one of ownership of Colonial. This remedy would not deter future pipeline construction since Colonial's billionaire owners had together invested only $40 million in their $400 million venture, with insurance companies financing the remainder. The Division issued CIDs, and by 1965 a proposed complaint had been drafted. Nothing happened. A former Division attorney told the Study Group, "Every three months or so the guys below would ask whether the case was going to be filed or officially rejected. They never got an answer." There was much talk of political influence, and a favorite staff greeting became "Whatever happened to Colonial Pipeline?"

What had happened was that Donald Turner had found himself a very complex, sophisticated, "big" case. One theory, apart from the exclusion of others from access to the pipeline, was that Colonial's owners intended to use the pipeline as a device to stabilize their own market shares within the regional cartel. The pipeline could control cheating by forcing any user who sold more than his share to buy his extra supplies from other members. On the other hand, the pipeline could facilitate a system of barter to stabilize the supplies of companies that adhered to their pre-existing market shares. Economists William Comanor of Harvard and Paul MacAvoy of M.I.T. were retained to resolve this complex behavioral issue. New CIDs were dispatched; in reply, most of the companies claimed that they lacked data of the kinds requested. Instead, they sent what they had, which in one case was 400 pounds of documents. Since it was too expensive to put these massive materials through a computer analysis—and since meaningful results were not guaranteed in any event—that inquiry was abandoned.

Turner was, as usual, looking for a better case than he needed. In 1968 Gordon Spivack argued that competing refiners would be excluded from the pipeline through the joint-ownership arrangement. There were staff expectations under McLaren that the simmering case would finally be filed, but he proved no more eager than Turner to tackle these oil giants. By now the Division has been looking at Colonial Pipeline for nine years.

Far more strategically important than Colonial will be the Trans-Alaska Pipeline. The present controversy surrounding this 800-mile project has thus far focused upon adverse environmental consequences, yet competitive problems also abound. The proven oil reserves on Alaska's North Slope, where the pipeline will originate, are presently 15 billion barrels. The proven reserves for the entire rest of the United States are only 29 billion barrels. Thus the Alaska pipeline will serve as a bottleneck to one-third of the total domestic supply of oil. Three companies—British Petroleum, ARCO, and Jersey Standard—own about two-thirds of these Alaskan reserves. They plan to combine their production of it through a joint venture. The same three companies hold an 87.5% interest in the Trans-Alaska Pipeline. Together with their other U.S. reserves, they will then control half of U.S. oil production.

With these market shares, the Antitrust Division would be hard pressed to find a more illegal joint venture. The staff, therefore, prepared CIDs for what would ordinarily be a routine preliminary investigation. Although CIDs are not even regularly scrutinized by the AAG, this time Attorney General Mitchell himself vetoed the CIDs. He said that an investigation would not be appropriate in light of the current sensitive situation surrounding the proposed pipelines, meaning the pollution imbroglio.

In 1967 FTC Chief Economist Willard Mueller told the Senate Antitrust Subcommittee of an impending threat to perhaps the one redeeming feature of the oil industry's structure:

Traditionally, the industry has consisted of refiners and distributors of varying sizes and of differing degrees of crude self-sufficiency, integration into distribution, and geographic coverage. This asymmetrical organizational structure has been a major factor stimulating competitive rivalry. Small refiners often expanded to achieve economies of larger scale operations; refiners lacking self-sufficiency in crude integrated backward into crude production; other refiners integrated forward into distribution; some distributors developed chains of private brand stations; and both fully integrated and partially integrated concerns expanded into new geographic areas. Each of these moves, particularly when achieved by internal expansion, tended to disturb the status quo by introducing new competitive elements at one or more stages in the processing-distributing channel. *An ultimate coalescence of the petroleum industry in the hands of a few very large, fully integrated petroleum companies would put an end to this important source of rivalry.*[14]

The danger to which Mueller alluded—a merger trend among the majors—is now in full swing. By 1971 eight firms that were among the 25 top oil companies in 1960 had been taken over through mergers—Standard of Kentucky, Pure, Tidewater, Richfield, Sunray DX, Sinclair, Standard of Ohio, and Amerada. This trend was triggered by Donald Turner's decision not to challenge the $1¾ billion Union-Pure merger, which joined the 15th and 16th largest oil companies to form the ninth largest. Although the two firms did not compete in the same geographic market—Union was fourth in the West, Pure 10th in the Midwest and eighth in the Southeast—the entire Division staff urged that the case be brought except for Turner's assistant Steve Breyer, who said in a memorandum that "Section 7 should not be used to prevent concentration of wealth unaccompanied by significant anticompetitive effects."

But there *were* "significant anticompetitive effects." Union and Pure were direct competitors in exploration for crude oil and natural gas and in marketing automotive oil and petrochemicals. More important was their potential competition in gasoline marketing. Turner was told that Union had recently shown an interest in expanding toward the Midwest and had increased its reserves in the Gulf Coast area. In addition, Gordon Spivack told Turner that the movement toward credit cards and nationwide advertising would produce a trend toward nationwide marketing by geographically based firms. It was logical that firms of this size could be potential entrants into any market. Because entry barriers were high and the oil industry was already substantially concentrated, geographic expansion via merger rather than internal expansion was likely unless the Division took action. If the Division let *this* merger pass, staff advised Turner, other oil mergers might be encouraged. Nevertheless, Turner wrote Senator Wayne Morse, "We . . . were unable to say that the acquisition by eliminating . . . potential competition could lessen competition substantially." This decision, coming three weeks after he had arrived at the Division, surprised and infuriated many of his staff, as Turner admitted in an interview.

Turner did challenge the Phillips-Tidewater merger, on the strength of greater evidence of Phillips's *actual intent* to expand into Tidewater's market. He thought that it was a "close" case, but that his oath of office imposed upon him a duty to file the "close" cases and let the Supreme

Court decide. But when his staff had told Turner that the
Union-Pure merger was a big one and the Supreme Court
would void it, he replied that he did not care what the
Supreme Court would do. Later Turner overruled his staff
and allowed the merger between Sun Oil and Sunray DX,
the 13th and 17th largest oil companies in the nation. Sun
was strong in the Northeast and very strong in the Middle
Atlantic states, ranking third in Pennsylvania, for example.
Sunray DX was strong in the Midwest. Their adjacent markets actually overlapped in four states. The merger meshed
excess gasoline supplies and marketing outlets so as to
facilitate a cut-off of some private branders.

In 1966 Turner permitted Atlantic, the 14th largest oil
company, to acquire Richfield, ranked 23rd nationally in
assets (but seventh in gasoline sales on the West Coast),
as a means of settling a prior suit seeking to divest Richfield from Cities Service and Sinclair. Turner reasoned
that Cities Service and Sinclair were much more likely to
enter the West Coast market than Atlantic. But as it turned
out, by the time of its later merger with Sinclair, Atlantic
had made nine acquisitions since 1961, making it one of
the 25 most active acquiring companies among the nation's
200 largest corporations. Even if Turner's assumption had
been correct, however, he should have forced the purchase
of Richfield by a company less likely to enter the West
Coast market than Cities Service, Sinclair, *or* Atlantic.

Similarly, Humble, the domestic subsidiary of Jersey
Standard with 1.5% of the West Coast market, acquired
California Standard's Signal stations, which held 2.5% of
the West Coast market. Since Signal was owned by California Standard, which dominated that market with a
23.5% share, Turner wrote Senator Morse that "this acquisition has the procompetitive effect of increasing the
market share of a small competitor at the expense of the
largest one." Again it would have been even more procompetitive if Signal had been purchased by an entirely new
entrant to the West Coast or by another company with a
1.5% share of that market rather than Humble, a recent
entrant whose parent, Jersey Standard, was by far the largest oil company in the world (assets: $18 billion). Turner
also allowed Gulf, the nation's third largest oil company
(assets: $8.5 billion) to acquire Cities Service's marketing
and refining assets in the Midwest where Gulf, a recent entrant, had already captured 1.4% of the market.

The Turner approach to oil mergers was based on economic theories which he refused to alter when they failed to conform with economic realities. McLaren has not done much better, especially in light of the Atlantic Richfield–Sinclair settlements discussed in Chapter 6 and the similarly inadequate partial divestiture of service stations that ended the BP–Sohio case. When the Study Group asked him whether any companies within the 500 largest had been allowed to merge notwithstanding Attorney General Mitchell's stern warnings against such mergers, McLaren mentioned that Amerada-Hess merger had been approved because "it was not anticompetitive." Actually, the Division trial attorney assigned to the case *had* recommended suit. True, Amerada was primarily a crude-producing company, ranking 17th, and Hess a refiner, ranking 20th. But Hess was a very innovative and aggressive marketer—it had to be, since it lacked its own crude supply, saw its refining margin squeezed by the depletion allowance, and had to make a profit, if at all, in marketing. Thus, by acquiring its own crude, Hess could join the club and cease its aggressive competition.

In sum, the Division's oil-merger policy has been to focus mechanically on existing market shares in particular geographical areas. This approach failed to assess adequately the vital role that potential competition must play in an industry remarkably noncompetitive in spite of a relatively large number of firms.* While the Division has at least paid lip service to potential competition at the *marketing* level, it has ignored the elimination of competing refinery capacity caused by most of these mergers. The number of separately owned refineries that can serve a given area is more important to the industry's ability to discipline price-cutters by supply cut-offs than the existing market shares of merging companies.

Petroleum products, which are only one type of energy fuel, account for 44% of total U.S. energy consumption.

---

* Of course, one way the Division could avoid having to wait for potential competition to become actual competition would be to seek divestiture of refineries or crude-oil production firms on the basis of past mergers, using the *GM-DuPont* theory. For example, in 1919 Jersey Standard acquired 50% of the stock of Texas Humble, a substantial crude producer. Divestiture of the former Texas Humble properties would force Jersey Standard to compete for more crude reserves and tempt Texas Humble to integrate forward as a new competitor in refining and marketing. In fact, the Division trial staff unsuccessfully recommended that this very case be brought in 1957.

Natural gas, which is found in the ground and extracted along with oil, accounts for another 30%. Control over two or more competing fuels (*e.g.*, coal and oil) poses serious dangers. The supply or technological development of the fuel in which the owner has a smaller investment could be held back to raise the price of the other. A case in point is natural gas. In 1970 the oil companies successfully threatened to withhold natural-gas production unless the FPC raised price ceilings by 30%. The prevailing FPC rates were probably too low for many producers—but not for *all* of them who threatened to withhold production. An FTC economist recommended an investigation into a tacit conspiracy to withhold production on the following theory: Costs varied greatly among the producers, and many admitted not even being able to estimate their own costs accurately; yet *each* was somehow able to conclude that the FPC rates were too low to permit *his own* profitable gas production.

In 1965 Continental, the nation's ninth largest oil company in assets, announced that it would merge with the largest coal producer, Consolidation, which held 11% of that market. Turner knew that coal, fuel oil, and natural gas competed directly as fuels, especially in sales to utilities. Also, new technology was developing to convert coal into oil, gasoline, and gas at competitive costs. But Continental and Consolidation marketed in different regions. Competition between the two companies, Turner told the Study Group, "was as remote as you can get." The coal industry, he thought, was still relatively unconcentrated—although much coal production was effectively "captured," through ownership or long-term contracts with steel and electric-power companies; although the four largest non-captive coal companies produced 36% of the noncaptive total in 1969; and although regional concentration in coal is often substantially higher than national concentration.

As in the Union-Pure merger, Turner was warned (by the FPC no less) that Continental-Consolidation was a test case—that if the Division did not challenge this oil-coal merger, others would follow. Turner's response was to issue a business-review letter approving the merger. One Division trial lawyer (one of the very few whom Turner has described as "excellent") later commented that Turner had "immunized the oil industry from antitrust" by non-action on both Union-Pure and Consolidation-Continental. Soon thereafter Occidental Petroleum acquired Island Creek Coal, the second largest noncaptive producer. At present 29 of the 50 top coal companies, accounting for 28% of total production, are oil-industry subsidiaries. By early 1970 oil companies held at least 31% of coal reserves, with thousands of acres left unmined. Coal production has remained stable even though the demand by utilities for coal has soared and fuel shortages have arisen. Consequently, coal prices rose 72% in two years.[15]

With many utilities and fuel users shifting to low-pollution natural gas and fuel oil, the petroleum industry, under the guise of diversification, is systematically buying up its competition. This includes not only coal—which will be convertible into oil and gas and which will last for centuries, given present supplies—but also the huge stocks of potentially convertible tar sands and oil shale, where a pattern of joint ventures has already developed.[16] In addition, oil companies produced 14% of domestic uranium in 1969 and now control 45% of known uranium reserves. The oil industry is thus in a position to control the price and technological development of competing fuels.

The domestic oil cartel can be dismantled with remarkable ease. The solution requires the immediate elimination of (1) the oil import quota, (2) the oil depletion allowance, (3) prorationing output restrictions, (4) barter exchanges, plus (5) vertical divestiture of marketing, pipelines, refining, and production, so that only independent, non-integrated companies compete at each level.

Which, admittedly, is far easier said than done. Oil's political power is legendary. The list of high government officials from key oil states includes the Speaker of the House (Carl Albert of Oklahoma), the House Majority Leader (Hale Boggs of Louisiana), the Chairman of the House Appropriations Committee (George Mahon of Texas), the Chairman of the House Democratic Caucus (Olin Teague of Texas), the Chairman of the House Armed Services Committee (F. Edward Hebert of Louisiana), the Chairman of the House Interior Subcommittee, which deals with mineral policy (Ed Edmondson of Oklahoma), the President Pro-Tempore of the Senate (Allen Ellender of Louisiana), the Chairman of the Senate Finance Committee (Russell Long of Louisiana), and the Secretary of the Treasury (John Connally of Texas).

Most of these officials have been eager political advocates for oil interests. Some have had close economic ties to oil. Louisiana Senator Russell Long, for example, inherited valuable oil property and has himself participated in drilling 30 or 40 wells. For Long, being pro-oil is being pro-Louisiana. "I've never heard anyone complaining about someone from a state that produced cotton being interested in cotton," he has said.[17] His allegiance to Louisiana's economic interests dictated Long's successful opposition to severe reductions in the depletion allowance in the 1969 Tax "Reform" Act. The allowance was cut from 27.5% to 22%, but 22% was about the average depletion deduction which was being taken by oil companies anyway.

There are many Senator Longs in the Southwest. The economies of their political constituents would indeed be temporarily disrupted if government action broke up their domestic cartel and removed from the rest of society the burden of subsidizing their economic security. These constituents are the so-called "Texas Independents"—the smaller, independent producers; the stripper-well operators; the Southwestern landowners who receive their royalties. The most cherished items for them on the oil giveaway list are import quotas, prorationing, and the intangible drilling expense.

The other oil is big oil, the integrated majors, highly sophisticated industrial statesmen with highly sophisticated lawyers and advisors. Their favorite items on the oil agenda are the depletion allowance and the foreign tax credit. The majors are not concentrated in particular political districts. But they have wealth—enormous wealth—and they extend it eagerly. During the 1968 Presidential campaign, oil millionaires at the Houston Petroleum Club promised heavy contributions to Hubert Humphrey if he would pledge to oppose cuts in the depletion allowance. He refused. But Richard Nixon said yes. He received $215,000 from the Mellons, $84,000 from the Pews (Sun Oil), and $60,000 from Robert O. Anderson (Atlantic Richfield). Franklin D. Roosevelt best capsulized the oil phenomenon: "The trouble with this country is that you can't win an election without the oil bloc and you can't govern with it."

9

Deconcentration: Antitrust on Ice

NEED FOR ACTIVISM

Economic concentration in America is prevalent, persistent, and tolerated. As described in Chapter I, the costs of overall concentration and monopoly/oligopoly are clear, as is its extent—despite the self-serving ministrations of the business community and press. Even if concentration is not on the rise (which it is), we are *already* at the level of superconcentration.

Nevertheless, the Antitrust Division remains soft on concentration. "We are accustomed," Eugene Rostow wrote in 1947, "to a Sherman Act which occasionally sends forth a thunderbolt, but normally slumbers in the law libraries while the concentration of economic power continues to increase." The Division does sue some firms who bring you kosher hotdog rolls and chrysanthemums, but ignores opportunities to attack GM and Anaconda Copper. By focusing on the transgressions of the less powerful, the enforcement agencies aid and abet the real economic royalists. "Much of what the law forbids today," one enforcement attorney summarized, "the modern would-be monopolist doesn't *need* to practice anyway. And what he *does* need in order to ply his trade, the law often allows." [1]

There is a growing consensus favoring these views among industrial economists. Simon N. Whitney, distinguished attorney and author, has written that "most economists writing on antitrust appear to favor a campaign against oligopoly." [2] *The Antitrust Law & Economics Review* asked 10 leading economists their views on a range of antitrust issues; six of the eight who addressed themselves to concentration problems favored large-scale dissolution suits in American industries. The industries they most frequently mentioned included tobacco, steel, television networks, pharmaceuticals, aluminum, petroleum refining, tires, automobiles, electrical machinery, cereals, soaps and detergents, copper, beer, bread, and AT&T. [3]

Yet many who agree that anti-oligopoly suits are economically valuable still get apprehensive at the thought. A restructuring is considered too heady a venture. They fear, first, widespread disruption in American industry—to which even Donald Turner answered, "The disruptive effects are usually exaggerated anyway." [4] Breaking up bloated corporations does not mean that firms are put out of business or that workers are laid off. Rather, separate firms result, jobs remain, and, according to the competitive model, more jobs are created as competition increases. Others fear that deconcentration suits are a harsh penalty even for monopolistic firms, but conservative economist George Stigler reminds us that "inadequate remedies for monopoly are 'harsh' treatment for the public interest." [5] Third, inadequate agency resources are cited. The inadequacy is real, but, based on any cost-benefit analysis, resources should be spent on deconcentration suits, since they bring the biggest return. Fourth, would such suits inhibit growth by penalizing firms for success? The chance that long-term success may result in an antitrust case will not deter profit-minded corporations. They will always seek profit, especially interim monopoly profits earned prior to dissolution suits.

Fifth, many wonder if the public—much of which is dependent on giant business—would support such serious moves. Does a constituency exist here? It did in 1906; it did in 1950. The potential for such a constituency exists today, but it needs significant lawsuits to nourish it. Inaction is a certain guarantee of the absence of public discussion and interest.

The final *caveat* is as self-fulfilling as the prior one: Can cases against oligopolies be won? There is only one way to find out.

THE DOCTRINAL BASES

Edward Levi, later president of the University of Chicago, said in 1947 that "We are not sure whether we are against monopoly or the abuses of monopoly." [6] While Section 1 of the Sherman Act clearly aimed at conspiratorial behavior, a Section 2 "monopolization" charge is a different animal. It aims at monopoly *power* (the power to control price and exclude competitors) rather than evil *conduct,* although the two may overlap. Levi answered his own uncertainty by asserting:

The truth is, of course, that in most monopoly cases, if the court has a mind to do so, it can find abuses. As Mr. Brandeis stated in testifying before a Senate Committee in 1912, he had not dealt with a monopoly situation where there was not also abuses.[7]

Indeed, except in the rare instances of a patent monopoly or natural monopoly, virtually all monopoly is obtained by anticompetitive practices.

Based on this assumption that monopoly and oligopoly are costly and not inevitable, there are three approaches to a deconcentration strategy. The first concerns what level of common conduct in an oligopoly triggers a monopolization charge under Section 2. As the evidence of such conduct becomes more indirect, the first approach leads into the second: At what point does monopoly or oligopoly power *per se* become illegal? Third, how can the law get at *past* monopolizing situations, those where the allegedly anticompetitive act occurred years or decades before? The "New Sherman Act" cases of the late 1940s—*American Tobacco, Alcoa, Paramount,* and *Cement Institute*—support these two approaches. The *General Motors–DuPont* case of 1957 supports the third.

Legal support for approaches one and two (conduct

creating a "shared monopoly" and monopoly *per se*) begins with the *Standard Oil* and *American Tobacco* prosecutions of 1911. In the *Standard Oil* case the trust had been involved in espionage, local price-cutting, secret rebates, and huge profits; in *American Tobacco* the United States successfully argued that "if duress, and wicked and unfair methods are essential, they all appear." [8] The decisions pronounced the "rule of reason," that not *all* restraints of trade were illegal, only unreasonable ones, and that not *all* trusts were illegal, only the bad ones. The first Justice Harlan in his dissent complained that the Court, "by mere interpretation, modified the act of Congress, and deprived it of practical value as a defensive measure against the evils to be remedied." [9] Ignoring such warnings, the majority opinion by Justice Edward White set a tone which was to dominate antitrust thinking for decades: Venality, not power, was the nub of the offense.

Thus, in the 1920 *U.S. Steel* case the Supreme Court intoned that "the law does not make mere size an offense or the existence of unexerted power an offense." And in 1927 this approach was reaffirmed in *United States* v. *International Harvester Company:* "The law . . . does not make the mere size of a corporation, however impressive, or the existence of unexerted power on its part, an offense, when unaccompanied by unlawful conduct. . . ." [10]

Two decisions in the 1930s slightly affected this doctrine. Justice Benjamin Cardozo stated in 1932:

> Mere size, according to the holding of this court, is not an offense against the Sherman Act *unless* magnified to the point at which it amounts to a monopoly, but size carries with it an *opportunity for abuse* that is not to be ignored when the opportunity is proved to have been utilized in the past.[11] [Emphasis added.]

There are two hints here: monopoly size alone may be illegal; large size *plus* some past abuse can generate a Section 2 complaint. Seven years later the Supreme Court decided the *Interstate Circuit* case. Here a movie distributing chain wrote its distributors and asked that specific prices be charged at first-run movies, specific different prices at second-run movies, and that no "double features" be shown at first-run theatres. All distributors went along, without specifically conspiring, yet aware that the cooperation of all was necessary for the scheme to work. The

Court held that under Section 1 no formal agreement was necessary; the parallel action of all sufficed for a violation. "It was enough that, knowing that concerted action was contemplated and invited, the distributors gave their adherence to the scheme and participated in it." [12]

The strains from these two cases—that both monopoly *per se* and shared-monopoly behavior may be illegal—came together in the late Forties. First came the *Alcoa* case in 1945, where Judge Learned Hand of the Second Circuit Court held Alcoa's 90% control of the virgin-aluminum ingot market an illegal monopoly. Unless a monopoly had been "thrust" upon a company due purely to skill, foresight, and industry, it was illegal. Judge Hand found that Alcoa's retention of monopoly over time was not an inevitable, ordained occurrence. His written opinion contained many novel arguments:

> Size was not only evidence of violation, or of potential violation, it was the essence of the offense. . . . [I]t is doubtful whether sixty or sixty-four percent would be enough [for a monopoly]; and certainly thirty-three percent is not. . . . Congress did not condone "good trusts" and condemn "bad" ones; it forbade all. . . . Nothing compelled it [Alcoa] to keep doubling and redoubling its capacity before others entered the field. It insists that it never excluded competitors, but we can think of no more effective exclusion than progressively to embrace each new opportunity as it opened, and to face every new corner with new capacity already geared into a great organization. . . . No monopolist monopolizes unconscious of what he is doing.[13]

Alcoa stands for the proposition that monopoly size over time, unless the result of unexpired patent or efficiencies of scale, is illegal. Evil conduct and evil intent are not required; monopoly power, whether or not exercised, is the offense.

The second *American Tobacco* decision in 1946 supports the shared-monopoly approach. For the 12 years prior to suit in 1940, the Big Three in the industry—American Tobacco, Liggett & Meyers, and R. J. Reynolds—together controlled 68% to 90% of all cigarette production. With no overt collusion, they maintained their dominance by heavy advertising, periodic price increases (seven identical increases from 1928 to 1940, all within days of each other), and an auction-market practice that led none to buy unless all did. In the Depression they twice flexed their muscles in like ways: All the three majors, marketing 15¢ brands, purchased much 10¢ leaf to choke off their cheaper competitors; in 1931, with leaf costs very low and in a time of plunging consumer demand, all *raised* cigarette prices. The Supreme Court affirmed a district-court jury view that these acts were an illegal attempt to monopolize the cigarette trade:

> This particular conspiracy . . . was established, not through the presentation of a formal written agreement, but through the evidence of widespread and effective conduct on the part of petitioners in relation to their existing or potential competitors.
>
> The material consideration in determining whether a monopoly exists is not that prices are raised and that competition actually is excluded but that power exists to raise prices or to exclude competition when it is desired to do so.[14]

Although Section 1 conspiracy charges were interspersed with Section 2 "attempts to monopolize," Eugene Rostow observed at that time that "the major evidence of combination in the *Tobacco* case was inference from parallel action—evidence which should not be hard to match in any of a dozen industrial situations."[15]

Reinforcing the *Alcoa* and *American Tobacco* breakthroughs were the 1948 motion-picture cases and *Cement Institute* case. In the former (*Paramount, Schine,* and *Griffin* in the Supreme Court) the Court did not search for evil intent. Typical of the three, *Schine* said:

> It is, however, not always necessary to find a specific intent to restrain trade or to build a monopoly in order to find that the antitrust laws have been violated. It is sufficient that a restraint of trade or monopoly results as the consequence of a defendant's conduct of business arrangements. . . . To require a greater showing would cripple the Act.[16]

And the *Cement Institute* case, although brought under Section 5 of the FTC Act, made headway on the issue of evidentiary requirements to establish a violation of the law against independent producers in a common course of action—*i.e.,* shared monopoly. The Supreme Court found various practices, especially the "basing-point system" of computing delivered prices, to be sufficient indirect evidence of a conspiracy to restrain trade.[17] A subsequent FTC staff memorandum asserted that parallel pricing should be open to attack: "When a number of enterprises follow a parallel course of action in the knowledge and contemplation that all are acting alike, they have, in effect, formed an agreement. . . ."

These cases, taken together, reveal a developing doctrine that (a) monopoly power, (b) shared-monopoly behavior, and (c) shared monopoly *per se* may violate the antitrust laws. *Alcoa* supports (a); *American Tobacco* and the 1948 cases underpin (b); and combining *Alcoa* with *American Tobacco* leads to (c).*

The shared-monopoly thesis has attracted the most recent attention, since problems of industrial concentration focus mainly on oligopoly, not monopoly. Donald Turner actively supports this theory. If United Shoe Machinery is declared an illegal monopoly, he argues, why not three shoe-machinery firms whose parallel acts and social costs are identical to the acts and costs of United Shoe? "It is appropriate to put a time limit," Turner writes, "on continuing monopoly power that rests in part on earlier success, regardless of how the early success was achieved. . . . [T]here is not enough difference between individual and shared monopoly to warrant different treatment." [20]

Richard Posner agrees. He also anticipates the arguments that oligopolists behave as market structure compels them to behave (Ford *has* to look at GM's prices and raise its own equally), and that any court decree forbidding such behavior will therefore be irrational. Posner responds that oligopoly pricing is *voluntary,* not inevitable. He lists the following practices as justifying a Sherman Act shared-monopoly case: systematic price discrimination, prolonged excess capacity, refusal to offer discounts during substantial excess capacity, infrequent and identical price changes, abnormally high profits, announcement of price increases far in advance, public statements concerning the "correct price," fixed market shares for a long period of time, and identical sealed bids on nonstandard items. [21] Posner, too, urges dissolving existing oligopoly structures to help a return to competition. A similar view of shared monopoly, representing a different "interest group," is held by Paul

* Language from two other Supreme Court cases, focusing on parallel oligopoly action rather than monopoly power, lend additional support to the shared-monopoly theory: *Standard Oil Company* (1948)—"their effect has been . . . collectively, even though not collusively, to prevent a later arrival from wresting away more than an insignificant portion of the market"; [18] *FTC* v. *Motion Picture Service*—"respondent and the three other major companies have foreclosed to competitors 75 percent of all available outlets for this business throughout the United States." [19]

Scanlon, plaintiffs' attorney and associate editor of the
Antitrust Law and Economics Review:

> There is little doubt today that oligopoly ("shared monop-
> oly") is already illegal, *provided* it is accompanied by poor
> "performance," particularly *prices* that exceed competitive
> levels by substantial amounts. Few knowledgeable analysts
> would be prepared to predict, for example, that the Supreme
> Court would really decline to order the restructuring of an
> industry in which the (1) four largest firms held, say 50%
> or more of its total sales, *and* (2) it could be shown by com-
> petent economic evidence that those four largest firms were
> charging the consuming public a price that exceeded by, say,
> 20% the price that would be expected to prevail if it was
> more competitively structured.[22]

The third approach to deconcentration—attacking past
monopolization retroactively—rests on the *General Mo-
tors-DuPont* case. A 1949 complaint charged that Du-
Pont's 1917 acquisition of 23% of GM's stock violated
the Sherman Act's antimonopolization section. The Supreme
Court upheld the government in 1957, arguing that Du-
Pont's stock purchase was an anticompetitive vertical
acquisition under Section 7 of the original Clayton Act
because it insulated the GM market for auto finishes and
fabrics from free competition. At the time of the acquisition, given GM's small size, it was not illegal; however, it
grew to be illegal. The defendants claimed that the acquisition had to be judged on its merits when it occurred, in
1917; the government claimed that it should be judged at
the time of suit, 1949. The Court found that the philosophy of Section 7—"to arrest monopolies in their incipiency and before consummation"—required action against
a merger any time it threatened to become anticompetitive.
Justice Harold Burton, dissenting, understood the great
potential now created to "reach back" to undo many other
past consolidations:

> Thus after 40 years . . . it now becomes apparent that
> Section 7 has been a sleeping giant all along. Every corpora-
> tion which has acquired a stock interest in another corpora-
> tion after the enactment of the Clayton Act in 1914, and
> which has had business dealings with that corporation, is
> exposed, retroactively, to the bite of newly discovered Sec-
> tion 7.[23]

Although the case dealt with a stock acquisition, not an
asset acquisition, its logic encompasses the latter. Com-

plaints by business that to disassemble such long-standing entities is inequitable have little foundation. DuPont's shareholders were not hurt; they had received for years, and could keep, illegal profits, and would now simply receive a capital gain in lieu of future dividends. In addition, it is normal for any form of economic regulation to affect existing relationships. If it were otherwise, no economic policy could succeed.

In 1937 the eminent economist E. S. Mason complained that legal and economic meanings of monopoly were diverging. In the legal sense it meant restrictive or abusive practices, while in an economic sense, he noted, it meant market power. The dissimilarity was due to the lawyer's need for tests which would stand up in court. By the late 1940s, however, the two approaches seemed to be converging on an emphasis of market power, whether monopoly or oligopoly. There was widespread anticipation of a modern, more relevant and energetic antitrust enforcement. Eugene Rostow coined the phrase "The New Sherman Act," and he heralded: "Recent decisions have given the Department of Justice its greatest opportunity since the act was passed to seek the enforcement of the law on a grand scale. . . ." [24]

A similar sense was in the air after the dramatic *GM-DuPont* decision a decade later. One sympathetic writer observed that "it is wishful thinking to hope that the government will not make use of it." [25] He thought the case "would seem to require that both government and industry examine the current effects of all acquisitions made since the passage of the original Act in 1914." This tall prediction was worriedly repeated by business magazines. *Business Week* thought that "the antitrust attorneys in the Department of Justice will have a power that comes very close to being the power to say just how much—and how —big business can grow." [26]

The stage was set for follow-up test suits by the Antitrust Division—whether a 65% monopoly was *per se* illegal, what conduct justified a shared-monopoly suit, whether a shared-monopoly structure *per se* was illegal, and whether past *asset* acquisitions could be dissolved. The line of doctrinal development was clear, the potential for enforcement power evident, and the composition of the Supreme Court, especially after 1953, opportune. But nothing happened.

THE FAILURE OF FOLLOW-UP

The failure became apparent in the 15 years following the *Alcoa* and *American Tobacco* decisions. The Truman and Eisenhower administrations were not prepared to attack Big Business. For the Truman years the cooperative, collusive relationships encouraged by New Deal legislation and the war were of recent memory. During the postwar prosperity the public paid little attention to economic concentration. Three different and important antimonopoly suits were attempted—*AT&T–Western Electric, GM-DuPont,* and *DuPont-Cellophane*—and a high percentage of all cases brought were regular Section 2 cases; but suits growing from the 1946 decisions were not pursued. The difficulty of liberal economists and policy-makers in translating doctrine into action, as well as Democratic deference to the power of big labor unions, restrained such filings.

Eisenhower, a patron of business, was far from eager to challenge his constituency. Some antimonopoly cases were hindered or dismissed (*e.g.,* the oil-cartel and *AT&T–Western Electric* situations), and the Celler-Kefauver Act was under-enforced. One critic said, "So far at least [1961], delays which can be characterized only as incredible have been the sole serious problem for 'new' section 7." [27] AAG Stanley Barnes almost ignored the deconcentration issue, while Robert Bicks in the late 1950s argued, "Absolute size is absolutely irrelevant." Bicks also objected to the difficulty and length of big antimonopoly cases—thereby choosing easy over significant enforcement and forgetting that sometimes it's hard cases which make good law.

Victor Hansen, the antitrust chief between Barnes and Bicks, was somewhat more ambivalent. At one point Hansen seemed tempted toward big anti-oligopoly cases. One Justice Department official described it as "dice 'em and slice 'em policy. . . . They want us to pay more attention to redesigning basic industries and less to simple violations of law." [28] A *Wall Street Journal* headline of June 27, 1958, asked, "Will Hansen Go Whole Hog?" The *Journal* answered itself five months later in another headline: "Merger-Monopoly Targets Are Passed Up. . . ." The demise actually began earlier. By 1955–57 only 19% of cases filed —down from 46% in 1946–48—fell within the Section 2 monopolization proviso. The slowdown was noticed and criticized by a Special House Subcommittee in 1960:

This declining number of cases brought by the Department of Justice under section 2 of the Sherman Antitrust Act against monopolization and attempts to monopolize is a manifestation of the policy apparently inaugurated 4 or 5 years ago, when it was made clear that the Department would try to avoid bringing big cases against big business in the antitrust field. . . .

Of the 63 antitrust cases filed with the Department of Justice in 1959, only 6 in any way involved Section 2, the antimonopoly section of the Sherman Act. Only two of those involved substantial antimonopoly problems, and they did not touch any significant part of our economy.[29]

Democrat Lee Loevinger followed in the same vein as his Republican predecessors. Splashy Section 2 cases were kept under wraps, with Loevinger weakly explaining that "it just doesn't seem like the time to file any breathtaking, world-shaking cases—even if we were ready to." [30] He was, however, presented with the deconcentration issue in a lengthy internal memorandum by a top staff assistant. The aide urged complaints against parallel oligopoly behavior based on the *American Tobacco* and *Paramount* cases, as well as antimonopoly suits expanding on the *Alcoa* doctrine:

Nevertheless, to the best of the writer's knowledge, little use has been made by the Division to test this principle. In the last five or six years, the whole current of our efforts to stem the increase in dominant or monopoly power has been through use of Section 7 of the Clayton Act, namely, to prevent acquisitions which are likely to have that effect. Section 2 cases that have been brought have relied almost entirely upon proof of orthodox monopoly practices, namely, a combination of predatory and pricing practices.

Loevinger received this advice his first week in office and ignored it thereafter. Although he increased the *rate* of general Section 2 cases, test cases against the giants were not forthcoming.

Yet one monopolization suit Loevinger filed became something of a classic due to a creative judge. District Judge Charles Wyzanski found in *United States* v. *Grinnell* that the defendant's 87% of the national market for fire-station fire alarms was an illegal monopoly. It was not his finding but his legal analysis which was startling:

It is the highly exceptional case, a *rara avis* more often found in academic groves than in the thickets of business, where monopoly power was thrust upon an enterprise by the economic character of the industry and by what Judge L. Hand in *Aluminum* called "superior skill, foresight and industry." More than 7 decades of Sherman Act enforcement leave the informed observer with the abiding conviction that durable non-statutory monopolies (ones created without patents or licenses or lasting beyond their term) are, to a moral certainty, due to acquisitions of competitors or restraints of trade prohibited by § 1. They are the achievement of the quiet life after the enemy's capitulation or his defeat in inglorious battle.[31]

Judge Wyzanski then formulated a rule that once the government has proven a firm has a predominance of the relevant market, there is a "rebuttable presumption" that it has illegally acquired its monopoly. Unless the defendant can prove "superior skill, superior products, natural advantages, technological or economic efficiency"—all *rarae avii,* according to Wyzanski—the firm would be broken up. The Supreme Court did not consider Judge Wyzanski's new test, upholding his decision on other grounds. His wording and formulation thus remain intact, with obvious and important implications for shared-monopoly theory. If a monopoly can be rebuttably presumed illegal, why not a shared monopoly, one with such precise parallelism that it is virtually identical to a monopolistic firm?

Antitrust chief William Orrick (1963–65) was more interested in deconcentration cases than Loevinger, but ultimately disappointed the expectation he excited. As briefly mentioned in Chapter III, Orrick had the Economic Section of the Division develop a list of the most appropriate targets for an antimonopoly/oligopoly attack. (Among others, they suggested automobiles, steel, copper, computers, soaps and detergents, and petroleum refining.) More extensive studies on the automobile and soap-and-detergent industries (centering on GM and Procter & Gamble) were prepared urging further antitrust action. At about this time Orrick unleashed a thunderbolt, being the first, and to this day the only, Assistant Attorney General to even *threaten* to use the *GM-DuPont* precedent to attack past mergers.

I see no reason why, in selected cases, we could not or should not proceed against previously accomplished mergers or acquisitions, even in the absence of a current merger. . . . I think my duty to enforce the antitrust laws also requires equal sensitivity to the instances of concentration and oligopoly which produce essentially the same end result as price-fixing.[32]

Presumably, Orrick afterward did see reasons why *not*. No such cases were filed. The economist who had developed the earlier studies for Orrick was hard-pressed to explain the reversal. "My own guess is that the primary cause was bureaucratic caution and inertia," he said.

If disappointment can be defined as the gap between expectation and reality, then Donald Turner was the most disappointing of all Antitrust chiefs on the oligopoly issue. His 1959 book with Carl Kaysen, *Antitrust Policy*, discussed the extent of concentration in industry and proposed radical restructuring as the long-range solution. One cannot assume, as tempting as it is, that Turner simply left his ideological baggage behind when he entered public office. In April, 1966, he appointed a team of evaluators to study shared-monopoly suits. Eight specific standards were established to test whether an actionable shared monopoly existed: Is the market share of the top four 60% and rising; are the shares of the top four similar and long-standing; are annual shipments over $250 million; do multiple plants of economic scale exist; are prices "administered"; what is the technological performance; how excessive are net profits; has there been a merger history or anticompetitive behavior?

Based on these criteria, the staff produced the following list of potential cases, quoted in full:

Promising Shared-Monopoly Cases

Electric lamps—GE, Westinghouse, General Telephone & Electric
Tires and tubes—Goodyear, Firestone, Uniroyal
Flat Glass—Pittsburgh, Libby-Owens-Ford
Steel ingots—U.S. Steel, Bethlehem, Republic
Automobiles—GM, Ford, Chrysler
Metal Containers—American Can, Continental Can
Explosives—DuPont, Hercules
Sulphur—Texas Gulf Sulphur, Freeport
Primary Batteries—Union Carbide, ESB (Ray-O-Vac)
Carbon & Graphite—Union Carbide, Air Reduction
Cereals—General Mills, Kellogg, Quaker Oats
Auto Rentals—Hertz, Avis, National

Marginals

Transformers—GE, Westinghouse (declining concentrations)
Copper—Anaconda, Kennecott, Asurco (byzantine complexity)

Trucks—GM, Ford, International Harvester
Gypsum—U.S. Gypsum, National Gypsum

A supplemental memorandum from William Shepherd,
Turner's chief economic aide, noted that the Council of
Economic Advisors also favored suits against electric lamps,
tires, copper, cereals, sulphur, steel, gypsum, and automobiles. An accompanying staff memorandum concluded: "We
note that the 'promising' list may indicate fairly accurately
the potential reach of a successful shared-monopoly case.
This reach appears to be a happy medium: large enough
to have real significance but not so large as to be truly
alarming (although this may be a matter of opinion!)."

Although Turner served nine months after receiving this
list, and although his hand-picked successor, Edwin Zimmerman, served eight months more, none of these cases
was filed. A theory which was Turner's, based on standards
which he developed, had produced the case possibilities.
Translating thought into action, however, was not Professor Turner's forte.

This conclusion became painfully evident in yet another
shared-monopoly investigation, involving Procter & Gamble,
Lever Brothers, and Colgate-Palmolive in the soap-and-
detergent industry. Led by Procter & Gamble, the three
dominated all lines of household cleaners. Huge advertising
expenditure (Procter & Gamble was the nation's biggest
advertiser in 1969) created "product differentiation" and
high entry barriers. William Comaner, Turner's top economist preceding Shepherd, concluded that Procter & Gamble
had the power, although temporarily unexercised, to exclude
all competition by advertising. He wanted to restrict this
giant to "reasonable" levels of promotion. Turner and most
of the staff reviewing the case rejected any formal complaint. Some staffers disagreed, stressing that advertising
expenditures were lowest in the highly concentrated sub-
markets, thereby indicating an exclusionary intent in the
less concentrated markets. They urged additional study,
but no additional CIDs were sent out, and this potentially
precedential case expired. "Turner just hated the big case,"
one of his evaluators later complained.

Turner had the worst record of any AAG in the 1960s
on Section 2 cases, filing an average of only five per year,
and they were as small in impact as they were in number.
Upon leaving the Division, however, and while a "con-

sultant" to Zimmerman, his concern over oligopoly power was rekindled: as noted, he recommended a case to break up General Motors. (When a 106-page complaint urging the identical case was drawn up in 1966, Turner had disregarded it.) Six months after retirement, he published a *Harvard Law Review* article emphasizing how necessary shared-monopoly suits were to "any effective competitive policy." It was Monday-morning quarterbacking at its best, a move which incumbent officials at the Division deeply resented.

Zimmerman was in office too briefly for his views and moves against concentration to be assessed—other than to say that he *did* file the IBM case, two days before the Republican administration took over. It was a case which Turner had reservations about and which ex-Attorney General Katzenbach (who became IBM's general counsel) thought should not have been brought because of insufficient evidence. IBM, at the time of the suit, controlled 74% of the $3 billion market for digital computers. The Section 2 civil complaint was a combination of anticompetitive conduct and structure. IBM's dominance was not "thrust" upon it, but was due, according to the allegation, to three practices: a one-price system whereby "hardware" (the computer system) and "software" (programming know-how) were sold together; oddly low pricing in markets where competitors had footholds; and "exceptional discriminatory allowances" favoring universities, which led to dominance in the educational market for digital computers. The relief sought was any "divorcement, divestiture and reorganization" necessary to restore competition. The computer industry is considered the fastest-growing in the world, perhaps to become the world's largest industry in the near future. Thus, although it is doubtful that new law will be made if the Division wins, the potential economic impact of the IBM case is mammoth.

Unlike Orrick and Turner, Richard McLaren at least has the virtue of consistency. Upon taking office he stated that existing concentration would be adequately eroded by new technology and entrants (the longevity of GM, U.S. Steel, R. J. Reynolds, Texas Gulf Sulphur, Kennecott Copper, Goodyear notwithstanding). And in July, 1970, he repeated his conviction: "One thing that is not feasible under present law is the wholesale dissolution of oligopolistic firms." [33] Antimerger policy, to stop new concentrations of economic

power, rather than antimonopoly policy, would be emphasized in enforcement. Strangely, however, his budget request
for fiscal 1970 sounded militantly antimonopoly:

> Most of our resources in this subcategory [monopoly] must
> be committed to what could be termed responsive as opposed
> to affirmative action. . . . We have not been able to under-
> take, in the scope that would appear indicated, a sufficient
> number of the broad-scale investigations and studies of the
> kind that lead to Section 2 cases against firms in monopolistic
> or tightly oligopolistic industries. The potential gains to com-
> petition in the economy and to the public interest in this area
> are enormous.[34]

To be sure, McLaren has had many opportunities to
make new anti-oligopoly law. A staff memorandum in late
1969 urged a shared-monopoly case against two banks which
together controlled nearly all commercial banking in Oregon. The suggested suit would be based on a combination
of *Grinnell* and *Alcoa*: shared monopoly power, willfully
acquired and retained, is illegal. The factual proof of "willfulness" is simple. The two banks—First National Bank of
Oregon and the U.S. National Bank of Oregon—together
assembled more than one-half their market monopoly by
acquiring other banks; they got Bank Americard franchises
on the same day; and they opened branches far in advance
of demand which directly excluded potential competitors.
It was a perfect test case, but Richard McLaren's (and
Richard Nixon's) regime was uninterested in molding new
anti-oligopoly law.

Thus, due to a combination of inadequate staffing, official
timidity, and political pressures, anti-oligopoly doctrine was
never exploited or developed. *Alcoa, American Tobacco,
GM-DuPont,* and *Grinnell* remain aberrations, stuff for
taxidermists, not enforcement officials. A generation of eight
Assistant Attorneys General all found reasons to be cautious rather than creative. And their vacillations might
prove critical, as the conservative Burger Court replaces
the more populist Warren Court.

LEGISLATIVE PROPOSALS

Consequently, the hand of oligopoly grips us all. Not only
has the law not been developed, it has not been given a
chance to fail. It was after the Supreme Court's disappointing *Columbia Steel* decision of 1948 that the country, and

Congress, realized that new legislation was needed. Similar test cases have not been forthcoming. The resulting irony was noted by professor Louis Schwartz: "The great combines in steel, motors, and banking have their dominance confirmed by anti-merger acts which inhibit the amalgamation of smaller units but fail to provide for dissolution of the very amalgamations whose formation stimulated enactment of the laws." [35] To cure that anomaly, we recommend new legislation to break up dominant firms in oligopolistic industries. Enactment of such legislation is the most important single step that can be taken to reduce the cost of oligopoly.

The first widely discussed proposal for oligopoly-dissolution legislation was contained in Kaysen's and Turner's *Antitrust Policy*. This proposed statute makes "market power," defined as the oligopolist's ability to restrict output and raise prices without losing profits or decreasing its market share, illegal. Market power is "conclusively presumed where, for five years or more, one company has accounted for 50 percent or more of annual sales in the market, or four or fewer companies have accounted for 80 percent of sales." Only those industries whose annual sales exceed $250 million would be affected. Divestiture of firms possessing market power could be ordered, "if feasible," by a special Economic Court, but some concentrated oligopolies could avoid that remedy by proving that the minimum efficient scale of operations for a single competitor is too large to be attainable after divestiture. Other defenses, in addition to this "natural oligopoly" defense, include (a) market power achieved by "low prices or superior products attributable to the introduction of new processes, product improvements or marketing methods, or to extraordinary efficiency"; (b) the to-be-divested assets are contained within a single plant; and (c) other means of achieving deconcentration short of divestiture exist, such as patent licensing.

The impact of the Kaysen-Turner proposal was confined largely to academic circles. In 1962 Representative Celler did introduce a bill to authorize divestiture whenever four firms controlled as much as 50% of their market (also subject to various "efficiency" defenses), but held no hearings on it. The Congressional indifference was best captured by Senator Russell Long: "But as far as moving against one of these major companies goes, I agree that there is no prospect of it until the public becomes upset, enraged and aroused about it—and then you cannot justify voting any other way." [36]

Yet deconcentration legislation is not, as many contend, politically impossible. In June, 1968, a 12-man White House Task Force on Antitrust Policy, chaired by Dean Phil C. Neal of the University of Chicago Law School, recommended a "Concentrated Industries Act" similar to the Kaysen-Turner proposal. A former White House assistant close to President Johnson told the Study Group that, had LBJ sought and won reelection in 1968, one of the legislative priorities of the new Democratic administration would have been the Neal Report deconcentration statute. "It was good public policy, cheap to pass, and would help out the consumer," he reasoned.

Like the Kaysen-Turner proposal, the Neal Report recommendation is essentially an explicit statutory authorization for the Antitrust Division and the FTC to bring shared-monopoly divestiture suits against the most concentrated oligopolies. It would apply only to an industry with annual sales of over $500 million and a stable four-firm concentration ratio of at least 70% during four of the last five and seven of the last 10 years. Also, like the Kaysen-Turner proposal, the Act's objective of reducing the market shares of oligopoly firms to below 12% is subject to a natural-oligopoly defense and need not be achieved by immediate divestiture if other relief proved adequate. These deconcentration statutes have been cautiously limited to the most highly concentrated and important industries; they permit "natural oligopoly" and other defenses to avoid dismemberment of possibly "good" oligopolies. But, as Chapter I makes clear, even "good" oligopolies produce harms: inefficiency, laggard innovation, pollution, inflation, the exclusion of price and quality factors as the primary basis of consumer choice, unequal distribution of wealth and income, and concentration of political power. It is easier to produce statistical correlations between oligopoly and excessive profits than to relate market power to these latter evils. But all of them would be substantially alleviated by decentralization of oligopolistic market structures —no defenses, no discretion excusing executive non-enforcement, and mandatory timetables for completion of divestiture.

Based on these assumptions, the scope of deconcentration legislation should not be limited to the largest and most highly concentrated industries in the face of strong evidence that oligopolistic behavior generally occurs when an industry's four-firm concentration ratio exceeds 50% *or* when its eight-firm ratio exceeds 70%.[37] A more effective statute would presume the existence of illegal market power in industries characterized by these concentration ratios. Less concentrated industries would still be open to prosecution upon direct proof of oligopolistic behavior. Market-power illegality in smaller industries would depend upon the persistence of excessive concentration—*e.g.*, nine of the last ten years for industries with $50–100 million in annual sales, or four of the last five years for industries with more than $250 million in annual sales.

Any government deconcentration plan or proceeding must also achieve its objective within a reasonable time. The average length of divestiture proceedings in monopolization cases brought under Section 2 of the Sherman Act has been 93 months—nearly eight years—and that does not include time spent researching and drafting the complaint or carrying out a divestiture order. The availability of the natural-oligopoly defense, plus the defendants' opportunity to argue that less drastic remedies than divestiture may suffice, would convert deconcentration proceedings under the proposed legislation into endless litigation battles. The Concentrated Industries Act provides for a one-year stay of the proceedings for "voluntary" industry deconcentration efforts after the initial judicial finding of illegal market power. Then it allows defendants four years to carry out a final deconcentration decree after the exhaustion of all appeals. After that, the industry structure would be reviewed every four or five years to examine whether the relief ordered had in fact brought about deconcentration—a procedure which will surely induce judges to postpone actual divestiture until the ineffectiveness of all other remedies has been empirically demonstrated.

To eliminate the possibility of delay, the natural-oligopoly defense should be abolished,* with a court ruling re-

* A presumption against "efficiencies" defenses is neither new nor radical. Derek Bok, now president of Harvard University, argued in a 1961 *Harvard Law Review* article against the acceptance of an economies defense; although they may occasionally exist, he reasoned, the cost in delayed and complex proceedings was simply not worth the infrequent benefit. The Antitrust Division has generally followed this advice in their antimerger cases and in their Merger Guidelines.

In fact, there are very few "natural oligopolies." A seemingly mono-

quired on the existence of illegal market power within one year after the suit is filed; automatic divestiture within two more years would follow. Upon a clear showing of special hardship, the court could extend the divestiture deadline by six to 24 months, depending upon the size of the industry involved.

Deconcentration proceedings must not only be completed promptly; the legislation must also eliminate any government discretion not to file suit against an oligopolistic industry which the statute declares illegal *per se*. To achieve this objective, the enforcement agency—the Antitrust Division, the FTC, or a new antitrust agency as proposed in Chapter XV—should be required to publish each year a list of all concentrated industries that it could move against under the Act. Then, after expiration of a three-year grace period from the date of the Act's passage, if the agency does not file suit against an industry on the list within one year, any citizen would be empowered to seek a writ of *mandamus* directing the agency to sue. In case the agency does not act within six more months, perhaps because of budgetary limitations, the citizen may proceed against the industry himself. He would have at his disposal the full array of government discovery powers, and if his suit were successful, the citizen-plaintiff would be entitled to recover from the government his litigation costs, attorney's fees, and a "reward" ranging from $10,000 to $100,000, depending upon the size of the industry.

In conclusion, a deconcentration statute is needed which adopts the basic approach of the Neal and Kaysen-Turner proposals and incorporates these suggestions: an irrebuttable presumption of illegal market power if an industry's four-firm concentration ratio exceeds 50% or its eight-firm concentration ratio exceeds 70%; horizontal and vertical divestiture as the mandatory remedy for presumptively illegal market power; fixed timetables for the completion

---

lithic corporation often operates through a number of plants, each of which could be split off and operated as an independent corporate entity. The Neal Report cited the conclusion of conservative economist George Stigler: "In the manufacturing sector there are few industries in which the minimum efficient size of firm is as much as 5 percent of the industry's output, and concentration must be explained on other grounds." Furthermore, defenses for natural oligopoly and single-plant indivisibility would no doubt become self-fulfilling prophecies as oligopolistic firms rushed to combine scattered production facilities into single plants of super-optimal size that would be difficult to break up.

of judicial proceedings and the carrying out of remedies; and citizen checks on executive non-enforcement.*

While a strong deconcentration law is essential to restore workable competition to much of our manufacturing sector, supplemental legislation is needed to correct the economic mischief that leads to market concentration and bigness initially.

(1) *Delivered Pricing* enables competitors to quote a single price for a product delivered to any point in the entire nation, regardless of differences in transportation costs. A similar scheme is "basing-point pricing," by which competitors add on to the basic price the freight rate from an arbitrarily selected location to the point of destination. In either case, the effect is to facilitate oligopolistic pricing by eliminating differences in transportation costs that would otherwise result from the varying geographic locations of competitors' plants.

A series of FTC cases in the late 1940s adopted the view that the mere practice of delivered pricing, when adhered to by an entire industry, was a *per se* unfair trade practice under Section Five of the FTC Act; but the FTC soon retreated from that position.[38] Today the tobacco and other industries employ the device to orchestrate conscious parallelism. Either judicial precedent or affirmative legislation is needed to stop this anticompetitive practice.

(2) *Interlocking Directorates* between two or more competing corporations were banned by Section 8 of the Clayton Act, but the Act did not cover interlocking *managers;* nor did it prohibit interlocks with banks, customers, or suppliers that were not competitors, or indirect corporate links through agents, brokers, or other representatives. Moreover, the various regulatory agencies empowered to pass on interlocks within their fields have generally not ruled consistently with antitrust strictures.

A bill introduced in the 92nd Congress by Representative Celler would close most of the interlock loopholes.

---

* This proposal deals only with market concentration, not absolute size or conglomerate firms. To the extent that our deconcentration legislation is successful, formerly oligopolistic firms may be encouraged to diversify into many different industries. Oligopolist X, which had controlled 50% of one large market, may now control 10% of 20 different markets. To avoid this result, we propose an additional statute, requiring that when any of the 500 top corporations acquired another firm, it would have to divest an equal amount of assets.

Equally pressing is the need for a new enforcement mechanism. Between 1914 and 1965 the Antitrust Division filed only 10 cases (and the FTC only 13) to enforce Section 8 of the Clayton Act. The Division has merely filed civil suits of the cease-and-desist type, asking defendants to abandon interlocks before trial—the height of pettiness for an enforcement agency that should be devoting its resources to restructuring entire industries. What is needed is a new statutory provision authorizing any citizen to file suit for injunctive relief against illegal interlocks. If successful, the citizen-plaintiff could recover from the defendant litigation costs, attorneys' fees, and civil damages ranging from $1,000 to $10,000. This approach would deter violations while freeing the Justice Department and the FTC for more substantial duties.

(3) *Joint Ventures* not only enhance opportunities for collusion but may eliminate potential competitors from concentrated markets. Here again, while many joint ventures exist among the largest corporations in the nation, the Division has been indifferent. A critical test of legality—whether one of the ventures would have entered the market alone —has often led to a search for documents showing a "subjective" willingness to enter independently. A better test is whether the venturer *could* have entered independently— *i.e.,* is it as large, in terms of access to capital, as other corporations that have entered and survived? Legislation must be passed, or a judicial precedent set, which bans all joint ventures that cannot meet this test.

(4) *The Corporate Income Tax* (48% on net income) encourages expansion for expansion's sake; such artificial growth is often the genesis of market power. Since payment of dividends invokes two tax bites—one on corporate income, another on shareholder personal income—shareholders are generally better off if corporations plow back their earnings into expansion. Because the retained earnings increase the market value of the stock to offset the loss of immediate dividends, the shareholder can defer payment of his accrued taxes until he sell his shares and then avail himself of lower capital-gain rates. Milton Friedman's critique is shared by many economists:

This tax structure encourages retention of corporate earnings. Even if the return that can be earned internally is appreciably less than the return that the stockholder himself could earn by investing the funds externally, it may pay to invest internally because of the tax savings. This leads to a waste of capital, to its use for less productive rather than more productive purposes. It has been a major reason for the post-World War II tendency toward horizontal diversification as firms have sought outlets for their earnings. It is also a great source of strength for established corporations relative to new enterprises. The established corporations can be less productive than new enterprises, yet their stockholders have an incentive to invest in them rather than . . . in new enterprises. . . .[39]

To the extent that corporations can pass their taxes on to consumers in the form of higher prices, the corporate income tax is regressive; and corporations that have attained market power are better able to pass their taxes on to consumers than corporations that face effective competition. Thus the corporate tax structure encourages the quest for market power by firms that do not possess it, both to improve the shareholder's tax position during expansion and to increase the corporation's after-tax profits if the quest is successful. The remedy is to abolish the corporate income tax entirely and to tax corporations as partnerships. Each stockholder would be taxed on the basis of his full *pro rata* share of the corporation's earnings, regardless of what portion of those earnings was actually paid in dividends.

(5) *The Miller-Tydings* and *McGuire Acts,* which legalize vertical price-fixing, must be abolished. Political benefits aside, the economic costs of resale-price maintenance ("fair trade" laws) are severe and undeniable. In 1945 the *FTC Report on Resale Price Maintenance* concluded that "The consumer is . . . entitled . . . to competition between dealers handling the same branded products." A decade later the *Attorney General's Report* found that "fair" trade "is at odds with the most elementary principles of a dynamic free enterprise system." One study found that retail prices for electrical housewares were 35–40% higher in Baltimore and Richmond (fair-trade areas) than in Washington (a nonfair-trade area). By 1967 Attorney General Ramsey Clark formally proposed to President Johnson that legislation be submitted to end this practice. Clark's memorandum of January 4, 1967, estimated that resale-price maintenance raised the prices of fair-trade items 15–25%, at an overall annual cost to the economy of $2 billion. Clark went on to assess the prevailing political climate for such a move:

While resale price maintenance may be both undesirable and expensive for the country to maintain, strong political forces favor it. We would be supported in an attempt to eliminate resale price maintenance by the unions, consumer groups, farm groups, senior citizens and retirees, state and local purchasing agents, virtually unanimous legal and economic professions, and all departments in the Executive Branch.

Antitrust Division officials and Clark expected Johnson to propose the reforms in his annual economic message. The message was delivered, but no mention was made of fair-trade laws, and the reform died by omission. The arguments against resale-price maintenance are equally valid today.

(6) Finally, *Barriers to Entry* must be reduced to encourage the break-up of an oligopoly by the entry of new competitors. A variety of legislative approaches are possible:

(a) Removing all tariffs and import quotas (including "voluntary" quotas on steel and other products) would save billions of consumer dollars. Foreign competition would have the same effect as new entry into concentrated markets by domestic corporations. Second, we would be free to allocate our productive resources, including labor, to goods and services that we can produce more efficiently than any other nation, instead of wasting resources on goods and services that other nations can produce more cheaply. This is the "law of comparative advantage," which supports the benefits of free trade even if unilaterally declared by the United States.[40] As a back-up alternative, legislation should permit the President to lower tariffs on any commodity which the Tariff Commission or the FTC found to be produced by a domestic oligopolist—defined again by a four-firm concentration ratio of 50% or an eight-firm concentration ratio of 70%.

(b) Another entry barrier, the high cost of capital for new ventures, results in part from state and federal laws which limit entry into banking. The rationale for this policy is to prevent bank failures, but depositors can be just as well protected by extending Federal Deposit Insurance to all bank deposits.

(c) The present patent system grants an inventor a monopoly not only over his idea, but over the production and marketing of the product as well. No doubt invention should be encouraged by reward. But the patentee's rights should be limited to fixing a royalty rate at which he must license all competitors. Because royalty revenues would afford a patentee corporation an edge over equally efficient competitors in production and marketing, it should be required to spin off another corporation to its own stockholders, the assets of which would consist of the patent and all royalties. New technologies could then be fully exploited through vigorous competition while the inventor is rewarded with a percentage of the gross revenues of those who use his idea. Indeed, since output is not restricted under a compulsory licensing system, the inventor's royalty revenues should be greater than under the present system of exclusive licensing.

(d) "Refusal to deal" is another monopolistic practice that raises entry barriers. Producers of automobiles, gasoline, television programs, and a host of other products select a single retail dealer in each area and refuse to sell to any others. Although the dealers are legally free to sell products of competing manufacturers, in practice most are unwilling to risk having their dealership contracts terminated. Consequently, the manufacturer maintains its own nationwide network of exclusive dealers, forcing a new entrant to set up his own dealership system as well as manufacturing plant. Geographic exclusivity eliminates *intra*-brand competition (*e.g.,* between GM dealers), while the higher entry barriers wards off new *inter*-brand competition. Moreover, the duplication of retail outlets by a new competitor who surmounts the entry barrier is a waste of economic resources.

Legislation amending Section 2 of the Sherman Act (or a Supreme Court decision overruling the 1912 *Colgate* case) should make it illegal for any corporation possessing "incipient market power" to refuse to sell its product or service to all would-be purchasers on equal terms. A firm would possess "incipient market power" if it controls more than 10% of a market in which four firms control 40% or eight firms control 60% of industry sales, or if its branded product commands a market price 10% higher than other brands clearly of like kind and quality that have been on the market for at least three years.

(e) The increase in concentration among consumer-goods industries due to artificial product-differentiation calls for an attack upon its chief cause: excessive non-informational advertising. Some recent studies shed light on the direct relationship between advertising and concentration.*

The legitimate economic function of advertising is to supply consumers with information; it should not become a substitute for competition in price and quality. When advertising expenditures exceed a certain percentage of sales revenues, "product information" tends to give way to "sales manipulation." And even if all advertising were informational, it is not consistent with notions of "equal time" that large firms, solely on account of their greater sales volume, can out-advertise their competitors. The Study Group recommends that a 100% tax be levied on all advertising expenditures of firms possessing "incipient market power" in excess of a percent of sales revenues, to be determined by the FTC after a major study of the link between advertising and concentration. The tax funds would then be disbursed among consumer organizations to finance "counter-advertisements." Giving consumers "equal time" should at least ensure "informational" content for excessive advertising that is not deterred by the tax.

Taken together, these proposals and others in this book go a long way toward achieving a competitive economic system, one with maximum production at the cheapest prices. No doubt many will balk at such a marked departure from the industrial *status quo*. On the contrary, what is radical is the distance between the rhetoric of our "free enterprise system" and the fact of our closed enterprise system. Snatching competition from the jaws of monopoly avoids the hypocrisy of the present marketplace. And these reforms can be implemented at a cost remarkably lower than generally assumed. It is the continuing cost of *not* implementing these proposals—unrealized production, economic injustice, restrained technology, and centralized political power—that is truly staggering. Matching up America's rhetoric with oligopoly's costs, critics who ask of these proposals, "Why?" should be made to answer, "Why not?"

* Consumer goods account for about 44% of total manufacturing shipments. "Differentiated" products (which can command consumer brand-name loyalty due to large advertising expenditures) account for 75% of the total value of consumer goods marketed annually. During 1947–63 the four-firm concentration ratios increased for industries accounting for 60% of the value of "differentiated" consumer products, while concentration dropped in industries accounting for 67% of "undifferentiated" consumer products.[41] One study found that 86% of the increase in concentration was related to increases in advertising.[42]

PART III

The Federal Trade Commission

The Commission is rudderless; poorly managed and poorly staffed; obsessed with trivia; politicized; all in all inefficient and incompetent. And—the persistence of these criticisms would seem to indicate—largely impervious to criticism.[1]

—*Richard Posner*

10

Looking Backward

THE AGENCY

In a triangular building three blocks from the Justice Department is the second major agency enforcing the antitrust laws, the Federal Trade Commission. By government standards the FTC is tiny. In fiscal 1971 the total Agency budget was about $21 million. Although this appropriation is about 250% larger than it was 10 years earlier, the Commission is still spread thinly. Since its birth in 1914, the FTC has been laden with responsibility. Regulating mergers, rooting out unfair trade practices, checking the authenticity of wool and fur products, uncovering price discrimination, and studying industrial economic trends are all within its province. In addition, the FTC must handle lesser tasks, ranging from the Packers and Stockyard Act to the Federal Cigarette Labeling and Advertising Act to the Webb-Pomerene Export Trade Act. Antitrust enforcement at the

FTC is allocated only $8,389,000 of the 1970 budget, or 40.5% of the total; the Antitrust Division, by comparison, gets $11.5 million.

The FTC is in theory an independent agency, which means in fact that it has historically been sensitive to the whims of Congress. Its five Commissioners are appointed by the President and confirmed by the Senate for staggered seven-year terms. No more than three members of the Commission can belong to the same political party. The President designates the Chairman from among the Commissioners. The Chairman is responsible for administering the Agency; the other Commissioners have essentially deliberative roles. Formal complaints are issued by a vote of the Commission acting on staff recommendations. If the complaint is not settled, a hearing examiner then decides the case, but his findings can be overturned by the Commissioners. Once a violation is established, the FTC issues a cease-and-desist order, which, if violated, can result in fines of up to $5,000 per day. Such sanctions are rare.

Since 1924 the Commission has been the target of biting criticism—and it is usually the same from decade to decade. By 1934 the Commission had earned the dubious honor of being the most studied and criticized agency in Washington.[2] The most recent critiques have focused on the consumer-protection side of the Commission. In 1968 a team of students guided by Ralph Nader criticized Chairman Paul Rand Dixon's administration of the Agency's deceptive-practices section. President Nixon requested the American Bar Association to evaluate the FTC in light of the Nader group's charges. The ABA group concluded, "The FTC has mismanaged its own resources," [3] and recommended a major overhaul. The Nader group report did not deal with the antitrust-enforcement activities of the FTC, and the ABA group gave it secondary consideration.

It is appropriate, then, to examine in detail the past anti-trust policies of the FTC and the prospects for the future. Most of the Commission's antitrust functions have been lodged in the old Bureau of Restraint of Trade, with separate divisions focusing on mergers, discriminatory pricing, and general trade restraints. During the recent reorganization of the FTC the operating divisions of the Bureau of Restraint of Trade were consolidated into one new Bureau of Competition. It is easier, and still functionally accurate, to use the old division breakdown in the following chapters.

THE PAST AS PROLOGUE

The FTC was born in confusion. In 1911 Chief Supreme Court Justice White declared that Standard Oil had an illegal monopoly and then went on to announce an amorphous antitrust doctrine known as "the rule of reason." According to White, the Sherman Act could only be used to attack unreasonable conduct, but the Justice never defined "unreasonable." By 1912, therefore, an intense debate over antitrust enforcement had been sparked in the private sector and among the major political parties. Big business wanted clearly articulated standards to guide its activities. It felt that the day of the natural monopoly had arrived, that government officials only needed to be advised about the necessary scales and practices of American industry, and that the Sherman Act was a blunt and dangerous instrument, attacking corporate structure rather than any specific problem that might exist. On the other hand, critics of the Justice Department wanted vigorous enforcement, believing that a commission of experts could frame better remedies than the courts, and fearing that the rule of reason would give the courts an excuse to be lax in their treatment of the trusts. In 1914 both sides—those advocating a kind of business advisor and those seeking a more energetic trustbuster—compromised to produce the Federal Trade Commission. From the beginning, therefore, its goals, powers, and constituency were quite ambivalent.[4]

Woodrow Wilson certainly did not see the FTC wielding a big stick. Speaking of the FTC, he proudly asserted, "It has transformed the government of the United States from being an antagonist of business into being a friend of business." [5] During its early years the FTC was more involved in mobilizing the economy for the war effort than in trustbusting. By 1925, the Republicans had attained a majority of the Commission with Calvin Coolidge's appointment of William E. Humphrey. Humphrey, a lame-duck Congressman who had voted against the Clayton Act, was decidedly of the FTC-as-business-advisor school. Talking about the FTC before he arrived, Humphrey said, "Under the old policy of litigation, it became an instrument of oppression and disturbance and injury instead of a help to business." [6] Humphrey and the Commission majority were such good friends of business that one Senator was prodded to say: "A Federal Trade Commission that is blind to trusts and combinations and monopolies and unfair methods of competition in commerce and misinterprets the law is not only a useless appendage but a real menace." [7]

Humphrey capped his career with the adoption of his Trade Practice Conference approach to business problems. Seeing little reason to go around suing responsible businessmen, Humphrey urged the Commission to have the major companies from various industries come together and talk about the voluntary establishment of antitrust standards under FTC guidance. The sessions "ironically but logically degenerated into price-fixing conferences. . . . In 1929, indeed, things went so far that the Department of Justice had to step in and hint strongly that the FTC was coming very close to encouraging violations of the Sherman Act." [8]

When President Roosevelt took office, he tried to revamp the FTC by asking for Humphrey's resignation; finally, he fired him, but the Supreme Court declared that the President could not remove a Commissioner except for misconduct.[9] The case sealed the fate of the New Deal FTC, for Roosevelt soon lost interest in it as a reform vehicle. Politician that he was, Roosevelt paid off his political debts by giving control over the FTC to Senator Kenneth McKellar of Tennessee, who in turn ran it through Commissioner Ewin C. Davis. Until Davis's tenure ended in 1949, the FTC was essentially an extension of "Boss" Crump's Memphis machine.[10]

The tenor of the pre-Eisenhower FTC is evident by examining the background of the Commissioners in 1952. The Chairman was ex-New York Senator James M. Mead. The other Commissioners were also politicos. William A. Ayres, 84 in 1952, was a Kansas Democrat elected to Congress for 20 years and then appointed to the FTC in 1934. John Carson was a former aide to Senator Couzens of Michigan. Stephen J. Spingarn was a White House aide when Truman appointed him in 1950. The most colorful Commissioner was former lobbyist Lowell Mason, whose portrait in *Fortune* was illuminating:

He promptly applied a running hotfoot to the Commission. Addressing businessmen in a convention as "fellow law violators," he ridiculed his FTC colleagues for their "gobble-good" and gaily punctured their tautologies. He dissents from nearly all the Commission's decisions as unrealistic and legalistic. . . . "My sympathies are with the defendants in all cases before this agency." [11]

The Republicans pledged a new FTC, but under Chairman Edward Howrey they didn't get one. Howrey's exploits reminded the staff that politics was still king at the FTC. Although Chairman for only two years, Howrey cast a shadow over the Agency that remains to this day. Throughout the Eisenhower years his cronies remained in power, and even today his private firm wields a disproportionate influence. Before becoming Chairman of the FTC, Howrey was a partner in the politically potent Washington firm of Sanders, Gravelle, Whitlock & Howrey. Whitlock was the acting GOP chairman in charge of the National Committee, and the other partners' political connections were also excellent. The firm represented some 25–30 corporations, many of whom had dealings with the FTC. Among Howrey's biggest clients was the Firestone Rubber Company, which had a case pending before the Commission. Howrey's nomination to the Commission by Eisenhower, therefore, created a stir. At Howrey's confirmation hearing, Senator Magnuson grilled him about possible conflicts of interest. In such cases Howrey said, "I should disqualify myself in every respect. . . ." Magnuson retorted, "I am afraid that you might be on a vacation almost permanently down there." [12]

Howrey began with a wholesale purge. Democrats and men who had opposed him in previous Commission cases were quickly dropped. Commissioner Stephen J. Spingarn claimed that the firings were politically motivated. He pointed especially to the dismissal of three top economists who had prepared a report charging five major oil companies with illegal conspiracies to restrain trade since 1928.[13] Congressman Evins charged that although Howrey's displacement of many FTC employees was supposedly an economy move, after the Chairman's reorganization was complete there was little net savings.[14] Howrey stacked the Commission with his own men, often, as he admitted to a House committee, recommended by the White House patronage office.

After restaffing the FTC, Howrey tried his hand at a new antitrust philosophy. Rather than relying on market shares as evidence of trade restraints, Howrey wanted showings of actual anticompetitive effects. His version of a "multiple factors" test led *Business Week* to write, "Some observers say that as a practical matter, the FTC is setting standards of proof that will make the lawyer's job almost impossible." [15]

In 1955 Howrey was attacked for a sharp conflict of interest. During his confirmation hearings Howrey had explicitly promised to disqualify himself from every aspect of the FTC price-discrimination case against Firestone Tire. In routine Congressional questioning a hesitant FTC General Counsel, Earl W. Kintner, revealed that Howrey had secretly consulted with the Solicitor General about the Supreme Court appeal on the case. Howrey's critics howled. Congressman Evins challenged the FTC Chairman:

> Mr. Howrey, you disqualified yourself before the Commission in its vote, you disqualified yourself in statements before the bar associations and in public speeches, you disqualified yourself by statements before this committee, but when it came to seeking *certiorari* you went to the Department of Justice and talked with the Solicitor General.[16]

Howrey, however, contended that he was *seeking certiorari,* not trying to get it denied. This denial was greeted with some skepticism,[17] although our research indicates that his explanation was accurate. But the overall questioning and acrimonious attacks that bombarded the controversial Howrey during his term had their toll; Howrey resigned on September 12, 1955, to enter private practice, claiming he had accomplished his intended goal of reorienting the FTC.

Three years later the story of Howrey's regime was capped by the Sherman Adams scandal. Industrialist Bernard Goldfine had paid some hotel bills for and given gifts to top Presidential aide Sherman Adams. Adams, in turn, helped Goldfine with problems before two regulatory agencies, the SEC and the FTC. Howrey had a major role in this process. In response to Adams's questioning, he sent a 1953 secret memorandum describing the progress of the FTC case against Goldfine-controlled Northfield Mills. After the memo was sent, the FTC settled the case, which charged deliberate mislabeling of fabrics, on Northfield Mills' written promise to describe the content of its products accurately thereafter. The FTC continued to receive complaints about the Northfield products, however, and in 1955 Goldfine asked Adams to make an appointment for him to see Howrey. Although the staff recommended that the Commission issue a formal complaint and that the case also be sent over to the Justice Department for a criminal prosecution, there was in 1957 another settlement.[18]

At hearings on the incident, Harvey Hannah, chief of the FTC's Textile Division, testified that he had been in Howrey's office during a conference with Goldfine. Hannah said he had heard Goldfine ask as the conference ended "for a secretary or someone" to get Adams at the White House on the phone. Goldfine then told Adams "something to the effect he was well treated here." [19] Goldfine apparently felt his time was well spent. According to Boston lawyer John Fox, he went around boasting that Adams would take care of his FTC troubles.[20] Later, in Howrey's testimony before Congress, there were indications that the Goldfine incident was not isolated. He admitted sending four other memos to Adams, identifying them only as "the merger case, insurance and coffee matters" and a case relating to a West Coast labor union.[21]

When Howrey left the FTC in 1955, he remained largely in control. As *Business Week* pointed out, "Howrey, who left his post last week after serving only a little over two years of his seven-year term, leaves a group of hand-picked lieutenants who can pretty much shape the activities of the Commission." [22] He hand-picked the new Chairman, John W. Gwynne, 65, a former Republican Congressman. As *Fortune* described Gwynne, "His record in the House was consistently conservative (against public power, rent control, the Marshall Plan, etc.)." [23] Gwynne did turn out to be more aggressive than his mentor, but antitrust enforcement at the FTC still languished.

The only break in the bleak record of the Eisenhower FTC was the short chairmanship of Earl Kintner after Gwynne left in May, 1959. During his nearly two years in office, former General Counsel Kintner managed to boost staff morale to the point where the lawyers began to think of the Commission as an enforcement agency rather than as a repository for unemployed politicians. In 1960, for example, Kintner instituted six times the annual average of Robinson-Patman complaints from 1935 to 1956. Although many of the complaints were frivolous, the statistics were misleading, and the economic effect was questionable (see Chapter 14), and although Kintner's critics argue that he overemphasized the protection of small business at the expense of cases of wider consumer interest, a spirit of vitality did filter down to the staff, an elusive *esprit de corps* which is prerequisite for an effective agency.

But when the Democrats came back into power, there was naturally another reorganization and most of Kintner's protégés left. The new Chairman was Paul Rand Dixon, who had achieved fame at the FTC before for his adroit ability to raise Democratic campaign funds in the late Forties. Dixon was sponsored by fellow Tennessean Senator Estes Kefauver, and the new Chairman promptly made sure that the FTC was stocked with men from his state. He also managed to open an unpublicized branch office in Oak Ridge, Tennessee, to spread the patronage around. The Nader Report which examined the consumer-protection side of the FTC described in detail the web of cronyism woven by Dixon; [24] its findings were confirmed by the ABA study, which wrote:

We believe that the FTC has serious problems in this area [personnel] and that it will be impossible for it to implement present programs effectively . . . unless it attracts new personnel of high quality. We are informed by a majority of the present Commissioners that the FTC's task in this respect is made particularly difficult by pressure from Congressmen to hire or promote particular individuals.[25]

Dixon had joined the FTC as a trial attorney in 1938 and stayed with the Commission, except for a tour in the Navy, until 1957, when he was named Staff Director of Kefauver's Senate Antitrust and Monopoly Subcommittee. With the gloss of the Kefauver crusading experience, Dixon was first labeled by the business press as a "wild man," but after taking office Dixon changed his image. Perhaps because of the administration's desire not to appear to be antibusiness, or because of the deaths of his sponsors, President Kennedy and Senator Kefauver, Dixon innovated a new strategy. "Shortly after I became Chairman of the Federal Trade Commission," he said, "the Commission turned from its general policy of emphasizing case-by-case adjudication to one seeking broader compliance with the law through new procedures. Experience had taught me that the case-by-case approach standing alone was not appropriate to the 1960s."[26]

In theory this approach was fine. Certainly Kintner had gone overboard playing the "numbers game" of meaningless litigation statistics. But the Dixon tragedy was that his concept was only implemented halfway; the litigation began to grind to a halt, but the promised broad regulatory policies barely emerged. For example, in the merger area, during his first two years in office from March 21, 1961, to March 21, 1963, only *one* complaint was issued. Significantly, the 1963 annual report did not even have a chapter about merger enforcement, although it has ones on "The Industry Guidance Program" and "The Fight to Protect Small Business." Exactly what Dixon was substituting for action in the merger area is unclear. The few merger guidelines that eventually began to emerge must be considered to some degree a tribute to Dixon; however, they do not compensate for the deterioration in the rest of the Commission's program. Generally, soft consent orders and voluntary assurances replaced hard cases. Dixon's program, which had much promise, ultimately created a result worse than the pre-existing situation.

Commissioner Dixon refused to grant us an interview, but from talking to his aides, fellow Commissioners, and staff, the picture emerges of a man with conflicting threads of populist and politician. Although some critics have castigated Dixon for his political machinations, he proudly considered them a necessity to increase the FTC budget. As rival-agency personnel can attest, Dixon had the knack of dealing with Congress. He knew who held the purse strings. Thus, to Dixon's mind, soliciting campaign contributions from top FTC personnel, hiring men from the states of key Congressmen, and opening up an office in Oak Ridge were all part of his job. Under his aegis the FTC budget skyrocketed from $8,009,500 in 1961 to $20,889,213 in 1970—although most of the increase was due to statutory pay raises.

The Dixon approach caused a sharp division among the other Commissioners. His closest supporter was A. Everett MacIntyre, a zealous advocate for the controversial Robinson-Patman Act. Before being appointed a Commissioner in September, 1961, MacIntyre was General Counsel to the House Select Committee on Small Business, which helps to account for his emphasis on the small businessman rather than the consumer.

Dixon's chief adversary was Philip Elman. Although originally Elman was on the best of terms with Dixon, a split gradually evolved and escalated into bitterness. Elman, a former editor of the *Harvard Law Review,* clerk to Justice Frankfurter, and top assistant to the Solicitor General, was politically "independent"; thus, President

Kennedy was able to appoint him to a Commissionership although there were already three Democrats serving. Much of the breakthrough analysis in the FTC merger cases can be attributed to Elman. Yet he was constantly a critic of Robinson-Patman enforcement, often provoking barbed comments from staffers because of his criticisms of the Act and the Commission's enforcement of it. His emphasis on economic analysis rather than blind support of small business antagonized both MacIntyre and Dixon.

Aside from policy differences, the first explosive issue to emerge was political contributions. Dixon would call in the higher staff and personally ask for contributions to the Democratic party; these chiefs in turn would put the bite on their men. Many staffers received letters at home from the Democratic National Committee. A list of those who contributed was sent to Dixon, and, as one former top staffer put it, "Those who didn't got remembered." Dixon openly boasted about the amount of money he raised. One reluctant contributor remembers him saying, "You don't run parties on air. Who knows the need for Democrats more than the public servants at the FTC?"

When Mary Gardiner Jones was appointed a Commissioner in 1964, Elman, who had apparently been receiving frequent complaints from disgruntled staffers, attempted to refer the issue of Hatch Act violations to the Attorney General. Elman saw Jones, a graduate of Yale Law School, where she was managing editor of the *Law Journal*, as an ally in the attempt to limit the flagrantly illegal solicitations.

Elman finally complained to the Attorney General's office, and the word was passed to Dixon to damper the fund-raising activities. Although the on-premises solicitation did subside, the home mail letters continued. Interestingly, when the Republicans came into power, lawyers at the FTC found that their letters from Democratic committees stopped and solicitations for GOP candidates commenced. Some lawyers have had mailings sent to them at the office—a clear Hatch Act violation. Although there is absolutely no indication that the Republican Commissioners have any connection with these appeals, some staffers reported that they had changed their donation patterns "just for insurance."

The next serious controversy concerned *ex parte* communications. Critics of the FTC have pointed out that historically the Agency was susceptible to political influence. Part of the problem was the Agency's closed-door decision-making process. As Commissioner Elman wrote to Senator Edward Kennedy's Subcommittee on Administrative Practice:

> *Ex parte* communications by outside parties with individual commissioners are not forbidden or limited as they are in adjudicative proceedings. By their nature, then, these activities of the Commission provide a fertile breeding ground for dark rumors and ugly suspicions. At the very least they permit the appearance of impropriety to cast a cloud over whatever action is taken and to this extent reduce public confidence in the *bona fide* integrity and wisdom of the Commission's action.[27]

Elman provoked much antagonism by his attempts to limit the scope of his fellow Commissioners' actions. When he did propose a ban on *ex parte* contact, the motion failed for want of a second. Elman thereafter imposed a voluntary ban on himself—which was not too strenuous an ordeal because, as he himself admitted, few people sought to contact him, knowing it would not do any good.

Antagonism between Dixon and Elman climaxed when Elman made a motion that some 65 appointments at the FTC should be subject to the approval of the whole Commission. This move gravely threatened the power and patronage of Dixon, who considered only about eight positions subject to the endorsement of the other Commissioners. On January 31, 1969, Elman received the support of Commissioners Jones and Nicholson in his motion. Chairman Dixon voted in the negative, declaring for the minutes that he would not abide by the Commission vote. On May 2 Elman discovered Dixon had secretly written to the Civil Service Commission requesting approval of FTC appointments without seeking the approval of the rest of the Commission. Although the General Counsel in a May 29 memorandum affirmed the position of the majority, Dixon on June 12 sent a letter to Attorney General John Mitchell pleading his case. While this fight was unfolding, there was an angry stand-off on appointments. The Dixon view seems to have prevailed, although Elman made his last days in the Chairmanship very uncomfortable. In the July 21, 1969, minutes for example, Commissioner Elman requested that his position be shown in the request to the Bureau of the Budget as follows:

Commissioner Elman does not support an increase in the Commission's budget so long as it remains under present management. In his view, the manifest failures and deficiencies in the Commission's performance would not be removed by increasing its appropriations; indeed, they would only be magnified. Doubling the Commission's budget, in itself, would only double the Commission's problems. More money, in itself, would mean more waste, more inefficiency, more aimlessness, more delays, more dissipation of resources on relatively insignificant matters, more jobs (especially in the higher pay brackets) filled by incompetent personnel.[28]

By the end of Elman's term as a Commissioner, he had moved from being a lone dissenter to having attained a majority of the Commission for his point of view. Despite his more generalized criticisms of the FTC, both of the new reform Republican Chairmen, Caspar Weinberger and later Miles Kirkpatrick, heavily relied on his perspective. How long Elman's ideological triumph will persist is uncertain. When he retired, the replacement for the brilliant maverick was another rural, former Republican Congressman who had no particular background in antitrust, David Dennison. One FTC official told the Study Group, "Considering that Nixon nominated Carswell to the Supreme Court, we think it's a pretty good appointment."

Dixon was obviously unnerved by the internal and public criticism of his regime. Some sense of his attitude is derived from the following transcript of his testimony before the Kennedy Subcommittee:

DIXON: Now I see you smiling up there, sir, and I want to tell you I don't know what the smiling is about—

KENNEDY: Who are you referring to?

DIXON: This is one of them here, and I don't know what it means, but I am very proud of this program [recruiting] and the hundreds of young men who have come to the Commission under that program.

KENNEDY: Isn't it all right for them to smile?

DIXON: Yes, sir; they can smile, but not laugh at me.

KENNEDY: I don't think anyone is in any way affording any disrespect here. We are listening at some length to your comments.[29]

Thus concluded Dixon's career as Chairman. (He still remains a Commissioner filling out his term of office.) In the end, he triumphed neither as a populist nor as a politician.

Critics have always chastised the Commission, and the FTC has regularly reorganized to meet them. Yet as ABA Commission member Richard Posner pointed out, "the most remarkable thing about the criticisms is their consistency." [30] Gerard Henderson pointed out in 1924 that the Commission had no coherent method of planning policy, and that its procedure, "which requires that it be the formal complainant in the very litigation in which it is also the judge," [31] was unfair. In 1935 E. Pendleton Herring provided the lasting insight that "the control of business remains too controversial and too vital a political issue to be relegated successfully to a commission independent of close control by the policy-formulating agencies of the government. Administrators cannot assume the responsibilities of statesmen without incurring likewise the tribulations of politicians." [32] The Hoover Commission Report of 1949, the Heller Report of 1954, the Landis Report of 1960, and the various Bureau of the Budget studies and others all present the same picture.

Professor Carl Auerbach made the poignant observation that the FTC's effectiveness, or lack thereof, was not altered by reorganizations.[33] The Hoover Commission wanted an organization along program lines; the Heller Report wanted process lines with one attorney investigating and one litigating. Then Landis argued for going back to program lines. In an agency the size of the FTC it all made little difference. Each time a new organization came about, the next report criticized it for increasing paperwork and recommended a new panacea. Successive Chairmen simply used reorganizations as excuses to juggle staff to fit their wishes.

The "friends of business," the political back-slappers, the small-business partisans, and the bitterly quarreling Commissioners described in this chapter set the context of our study. But it is also important to understand that the failings of the FTC go beyond its people. The murky objectives, the lack of any coherent strategy of enforcement, the procedural infirmities of the administrative process, and the lack of a national commitment to antitrust are equally important. The FTC cannot be seriously reformed unless all these problems are attacked and resolved—and exposed.

The Commission thundered in the complaint and cheeped in the order.

> —*Commissioner John Reilly, commenting on Procter & Gamble–Folger Coffee merger*

11

The Merger Game

The staff of the merger division has always been the FTC's crack unit. Its morale and skill have been the highest in the Commission, so much so that one implicit goal of the recent Weinberger reorganization was for the shine of the merger division to spread to the rest of the lackluster FTC antitrust staff. In our interviews with FTC merger attorneys, lawyer after lawyer chided the rest of the Commission and then proudly declared, "Well, you know, the ABA report couldn't find fault with us." Indeed, compared to the attacks on other FTC enforcement activities, the ABA comments were quite favorable: "In this area . . . the FTC has contributed to the adoption of original and important theories of antitrust enforcement. The principal difficulty . . . is that the FTC has not committed enough of its resources to the divisions charged with responsibilities in the merger area." [1] The 1970 Bureau of the Budget study of the FTC reinforced the ABA view. After identifying problem areas in the rest of the Commission, the BOB report pointed out in a footnote, "Not applicable to Mergers Division; no significant management problem identified." [2] Despite these tributes to the staff, serious problems with the Commission's enforcement policies surface in the areas of consent orders, litigation, procedural obstacles, and strategy formulation.

AN EARLY SKETCH

Until 1950 the FTC merger experience was a systematic disaster. The FTC's basic antimerger weapon, Section 7 of the Clayton Act, did not cover asset acquisitions; corporations easily avoided the FTC by purchasing assets rather than stock. Moreover, the conservative courts of the 1920s castrated the Act in a series of decisions. The FTC's first antimerger order was issued in 1921 against Alcoa for acquiring control of the stock of Aluminum Rolling Mills. The Commission's order to divest was upheld, but the decree was completely undermined when an appeals court allowed Alcoa to purchase the assets at a later sheriff's sale. In 1926 the Supreme Court held the FTC had no jurisdiction if two merging companies exchanged stock and dissolved the subsidiary before a complaint was filed.[3] This doctrine was expanded, first with a ruling that only courts had the power to undo a consummated merger,[4] then with a decision that even if a complaint had been issued by the FTC before the merger, the Commission lost jurisdiction if its final cease-and-desist order came afterward.[5]

The courts generally interpreted the Clayton Act, which was designed to cover *potential* monopolies, so strictly that its scope did not go much beyond the Sherman Act.[6] From 1927 to 1950 the FTC filed 31 antimerger complaints and obtained only five successful orders. Finally, in reaction to a rising merger wave, the Celler-Kefauver Amendment of 1950 plugged up the major loopholes in the old Section 7, and a new era in FTC enforcement commenced. But the scars of the Twenties remain; not until 1963 did the Supreme Court give the FTC broad remedial powers,[7] and the Commissioners still come in for some rude surprises. For example, the rule-making power of the Commission is still questionable; it has recently been stripped of its right to enforce subpoenas.[8]

Part of the problem is that the FTC was created before modern administrative law was firmly settled, so that its legal foundations are shaky; Commissioners frankly admit that anxiety over the FTC's procedural and enforcement powers is one reason they do not push as hard as some critics suggest they should.

The modern era of merger enforcement at the FTC began with a whimper. In June, 1952, the Commission filed a complaint against Pillsbury Mills for its acquisition of some flour companies. Fourteen years later the FTC issued an order dismissing the complaint. The case record filled some 40,000 pages, and the series of remands, Congressional hearings, and bungling is a caricature of the FTC in action.

By the mid-Fifties Chairman Edward Howrey seemed to be sitting on Section 7 cases, so a frustrated Senator Estes Kefauver summoned him before the Antitrust Subcommittee to explain. Kefauver criticized Howrey for adhering to the conservative "balancing the factors" standard for gauging mergers rather than a market-share test, and cited *Pillsbury* as an example. Howrey replied that as a quasi-judicial officer he should not talk about pending cases. Kefauver badgered Howrey to the point where he said he would have to remove himself from the case.[9] Pillsbury then charged that Kefauver's hearings had poisoned the Commission's determination of the case, and in 1966 a Court of Appeals agreed:

> To subject an administrator to a searching examination as to how and why he reached his decision in a case still pending before him and to criticize him for reaching the "wrong" decision as the Senate Subcommittee did in this case sacrifices the appearance of impartiality—the *sine qua non* of American judicial justice. . . .[10]

Yet while the olympian judges rightfully cleansed the administrative process of the contaminating influence of politics, covert political pressure on behalf of private parties was still quite common. Kefauver could not interfere with the FTC process, but Sherman Adams did. Indeed, the contrast between the "appearance of impartiality" and the reality of the FTC in both procedure and implementation is sharp.

Eighteen months after its first complaint, the FTC in 1954 filed a suit against Luria Brothers for acquiring a number of scrap-metal companies. This case outlived even *Pillsbury;* a final remedy was achieved 15 years later. This time there was a divestiture, and the price of scrap metal dropped significantly.

The third complaint issued by the FTC took "only" 10 years. The defense counsel in the case against Crown Zellerbach for its acquisition of St. Helens Pulp and Paper Company knew their craft. There are more than 1,500 pages of pretrial procedural maneuverings in the record. Once the Commission finally issued an order to divest in 1957, the attorneys dragged out court appeals for another five years. The divestiture order stood up, but there is some question about the success of the FTC's efforts. Economist Kenneth Elzinga studied the case in depth and concluded that the relief obtained was "deficient."

The sale by Crown of St. Helens to Boise-Cascade could hardly be classified a rousing choice of buyer. Boise-Cascade had substantial timber holdings in the Pacific Northwest and was committed to entering the paper industry on a large scale. Part of its growth had been via the merger route; by 1963 it advertised: "Paper is now our biggest business." [11]

Elzinga charges that Crown pursued only Boise as the buyer for these assets, ignoring other potential buyers. Citing the sales agreement, Elzinga also notes that "The terms of the sale so closely tie Crown and Boise together in reciprocal sales, pulp, and facilities agreements that one can justifiably question the degree of rivalry that will be found between the two companies." [12]

A STATISTICAL OVERVIEW

Our examination will focus on merger policy at the FTC since Paul Rand Dixon became Chairman in March, 1961. In this time the merger division had a staff averaging 25 lawyers. By fiscal 1970 enough men were added to merger work to raise the total before the July 1, 1970, reorganization to 33 attorneys. From the time Dixon became Chairman in March, 1961, until January, 1970, when Caspar Weinberger was sworn in as Chairman, the performance of the merger division could be summarized as follows: [13]

—There were 56 complaints, of which the Commission issued an initial order in 46. The other 10 have not yet reached the Commission decision-making level. In these nine years the FTC averaged 6.2 complaints a year. In the first two years of Dixon's tenure only one complaint was issued.

—Of the 46 complaints on which the Commission has acted, 34 (74%) were terminated by consent orders without formal litigation.

—Of these 34 consent orders, 10 (29.4%) involved no divestiture of assets, 17 (50%) required partial divestiture, and seven (20.6%) ordered total divestiture.

—Sixteen of the 56 cases reached the hearing-examiner level, although four of them as of September, 1970, had not yet been acted on by the Commission. Of these 16, the hearing examiners ruled for the FTC in 10 cases (62.4%) and ruled for the defendants in six.

—In five cases a hearing examiner decided against the government and the case reached the Commission; in *all* five the hearing examiner was reversed. Hearing examiners were reversed in only two of the seven decisions where they ruled in favor of the FTC. Overall, hearing examiners were reversed in seven of their 12 decisions reaching the Commission (58.3%).

—The mean time for a hearing examiner to issue his decision after a complaint has been issued is 18.7 months. The mean time for the Commission to act on a decision given by the hearing examiner is another 13.9 months. The combined mean is 32.6 months to achieve an initial Commission order, before any court appeals.

—On complaints filed after March, 1961, the Commission issued only 10 litigated divestiture orders. This is a stunning average of 1.1 per year.

Although the merger division expected some 58 attorneys in fiscal 1971 and 1972, they were obviously dreaming. The desired increase of $321,000 for fiscal 1971, which would support 26 new attorney positions, was transformed by the Bureau of the Budget into a request for two additional lawyers. Thus, despite the alarming increase in corporate mergers, the size of the division only rose from 22 to 33 lawyers during the 1960s.

The Commission is subject to important constraints when it seeks to increase its emphasis on merger enforcement. Its overall funds are limited, and, naturally, no FTC division wants to see its interests traded off for an increase in merger enforcement. The merger division—certainly one of the most important activities of the Commission—has been relegated to the role of the budgetary stepchild. The ABA report makes this point well:

> In 1959, the FTC spent a little over $1 million, about 16.9% of its total budget in that year, on enforcement directly related to Section 7 of the Clayton Act. Although total dollars spent rose slowly to a high of a little more than $1.5 million in 1967, the percentage of the budget decreased fairly steadily . . . to about $1.35 million in 1968 and $1.4 million in 1969, representing 8.8% and then approximately 9% of the total FTC budget. Thus, in terms of a percentage of its total budget, the FTC was spending in 1968 and 1969 about one half as much on merger enforcement as it had been spending in 1959. This reduction took place during a period when the United States . . . was undergoing the greatest surge of merger activity in its history. . . .
>
> By comparison, in 1959 the FTC spent a little over $600,000 (about 9.3% of its total budget) on the enforcement work of the Bureau of Textiles and Furs. Thereafter, the amount of money devoted to textile and fur enforcement rose steadily year by year until 1968, when the expenditure was over $1.6 million, and 1969, when about $1.7 million was spent. In terms of percentage of available resources, the FTC spent 10.5% in 1968 and approximately 11% in 1969. Thus, the FTC was actually spending more dollars and a greater percentage of its budget in 1968 and 1969 on Bureau of Textile and Fur Enforcement than it was to support its division of mergers.[14]

CONSENT ORDERS—"LET'S DECLARE VICTORY AND GO HOME"

(1) No Divestiture

President Nixon should have hired some of the FTC staff as his foreign-policy advisors; they would have solved our Viet Nam puzzle, as Senator George Aiken once suggested, by declaring victory and withdrawing. In the last nine years the FTC managed to achieve 10 consent-order settlements without *any* divestiture. As with the Department of Justice, the government always wins and the defendant corporation never loses. The consent orders in the department-store cases are particularly illustrative of the Commission's approach.

Federated Department Stores acquired Bullock's Stores in 1965. Federated was then the fourth largest chain in the U.S., with sales of $933 million from such famous stores as Bloomingdale's, Filene's, and Abraham & Straus; Bullock's, then the 17th largest chain in the country, had sales of about $200 million. Concentration had been increasing in the department-store industry, and by 1961 the five largest chains had a 41% market share. The case was complicated, however, because the two chains served different geographical markets—Federated the East and Midwest and Bullock's the West Coast. Since the Commissioners considered the case difficult, they settled for a consent order that prohibited future acquisitions by Federated for five years without prior FTC approval, but did *not* require any divestiture. Yet certainly a strong case could have been made that Federated's swift expansion across the country had made it at least a potential competitor of Bullock's. The argument seems easier than the 1963 FTC decision, later accepted by the Supreme Court in the *Clorox* case, where Procter & Gamble had to divest Clorox because it was a potential competitor in the bleach market. Lyndon Johnson's intimate Abe Fortas represented Federated in this case. Given the FTC's reputation, and particularly the weaker position of Chairman Dixon after the death of Estes Kefauver, a political deal was suspected by many agency staff and Washington lawyers. The suspicions were encouraged by the decision-making process in the *Federated* cases as explained by Commissioner MacIntyre:

> In the *Federated* case, the crucial decisions were made in the course of and pursuant to oral presentations to the Commission by respondents on an off the record basis. A vital part of the decision-making process in that proceeding, as a practical matter, was simply unreviewable. . . . Moreover, while the Commission agreed to listen to an informal presentation, by Federated, it refused over my objection to extend a similar opportunity to one of the parties most directly concerned, the Chief Executive of Bullocks, the acquired concern, who opposed the merger. . . .[15]

The rumors that Fortas had swayed the FTC to his client's side put the FTC in a dilemma in the next department-store case. West Coast-based Broadway-Hale was in 1966 the nation's 16th largest department-store chain. It had acquired some 30% of the stock of Emporium Capwell, a $166 million-in-sales chain with 10 stores in the San Francisco Bay area. The critical difference between this acquisition and *Federated* was that the geographical market for both chains was the West Coast; given this strong case, FTC attorneys recommended that any settlement without divestiture be rejected. Covington & Burling partner H. Thomas Austern, counsel for Broadway-Hale, argued to the Commissioners, however, that if they did not settle the case it would appear to prove political favoritism in the earlier one. Meanwhile, Edward Carter, the president of Broadway-Hale and a man with considerable political clout, told the Commissioners that the stock interest in Emporium Capwell was merely an investment rather than an attempt at further market control. Between the investment story, the political pressure, and the problem of being attacked as being singularly easy on Fortas, the FTC permitted the merger over the intense objections of the staff.

A few months after the Broadway-Hale decree, May Department Stores managed to obtain another sweetheart settlement.[16] In the words of an FTC attorney, May was able to get "two bites of the apple." Not only was the nation's sixth largest chain store allowed to acquire the Meier and Frank Stores in Portland, Oregon, but it was also permitted to buy G. Fox in Hartford, Connecticut. The combined acquisitions had sales of some $136 million. May's lawyer also adopted the Austern tactic of arguing treat-me-the-same-way-as-you-treated-Fortas. And so the Commission did. After all, it was by now a matter of precedent.

The department-store saga was yet to be capped. Rebounding from the FTC's first legal action, Broadway-Hale asked permission under the consent decree to acquire Neiman-Marcus of Texas. On December 17, 1968, a majority consisting of Commissioners Elman, Jones, and Nicholson voted to deny the acquisition. The next day Miss Jones withdrew her vote and asked for further study. She was given the job of supervising the staff study on the case, but on January 17 withdrew from that responsibility; the task was reassigned to Commissioner Elman. On January 23 the Commissioners voted again, but the result was a 2–2 tie since Miss Jones declined to participate in the vote. Before the merging companies could be formally notified about the tie vote, which had the effect of vetoing their merger, Broadway-Hale president Edward Carter asked Chairman Dixon for an informal conference. Miss Jones broke a speaking engagement to hear the arguments and cast the deciding vote in favor of the merger.

As Miss Jones said to the *Wall Street Journal*, "I flip-flopped all over the place and at one time I tried to duck." [17] While the case seemed a clear Section 7 violation, the usually vigilant Miss Jones went against her past voting record. Some Washington cynics attributed her vote to her desire to become the FTC Chairman. As the sole Republican on the Commission, she was being pushed by a number of prominent sponsors, including Broadway-Hale lawyer H. Thomas Austern. According to the *Wall Street Journal* report, Miss Jones argued that propriety did not prohibit her from discussing her ambitions with lawyer friends who happen to be involved in FTC cases. But she admitted, "Tommy has been helpful and encouraging."

Mary Jones did not get the job she wanted, and most of the people we interviewed who know her doubted that politics swayed her vote. The case, however, became a *cause célèbre* at the FTC. Commissioner Elman pointed out that in this case, "no investigation was made by the Commission, no document subpoenaed. The Commission's findings generally . . . are predicated solely on materials submitted by the parties in an *ex parte* non-adversary proceeding, with no opportunity for cross-examination." [18] And the staff had been unanimous in recommending that the acquisition be disapproved.

In April, 1971, Broadway-Hale announced its intention to acquire, if it could get FTC permission, the luxury department stores of Bergdorf-Goodman in New York. *Business Week* described Broadway-Hale's plans regarding FTC approval:

. . . Broadway-Hale is encouraged. In 1969, the agency approved the purchase of Neiman-Marcus, which then did more than twice Bergdorf's current volume (about $33 million) because the acquisition was outside Broadway-Hale's operating territory. Carter and Goodman hope that the same view will prevail this time. Still, FTC approval has Bergdorf's lawyers so touchy that they had the public relations people rewrite the merger announcement 45 times. [19]

Ironically, Broadway-Hale's own activities disprove its contention that it is not a potential competitor outside limited geographical markets. Broadway-Hale spends about $40 million a year on new store construction and, as *Business Week* points out, "Carter predicts that spending will approach $50 million if the Bergdorf-Goodman merger is consummated." Some of this spending is decidedly outside traditional markets. For example, since the takeover,

Broadway-Hale-owned Neiman-Marcus opened its first store outside Texas this year—in Bal Harbour, Florida. Another store is under construction in Atlanta, and the company is investigating sites in Washington and Chicago. Only at the FTC could a company win a cushy order by claiming that internal market extension doesn't occur in the department-store field—and then turn around with the approved acquisition to disprove the argument. But more incredible is the same company coming back to pull the same trick again. When will the Commission start acting like an antitrust enforcer? The least the FTC could do is deny the Bergdorf acquisition.

The department-store cases are not isolated examples of settlements with no divestiture whatsoever. A case like *Federated Department Stores* was the acquisition by American Bakeries, the third largest bakery-products company in 1963, of Langendorf United Bakeries, the seventh largest. The two companies had historically had different geographical markets. Again the FTC accepted an order prohibiting further acquisitions without permission for 10 years rather than litigate the case or require any divestiture.

Various FTC officials told us that Chairman Dixon's vote on this case was influenced by the presence of Edward McCormick, the nephew of the then House Speaker, as the lawyer for American Bakeries. In an April, 1971, interview, McCormick admitted that the Commission had originally voted a substantial divestiture of assets but later reversed itself. He believed they changed their minds because he argued that the suggested remedy—sale of the divested assets to another baking company—might be more anticompetitive than leaving them in the hands of American. McCormick added, "At the FTC there is a lot of politicking, but few political decisions. It's too visible." Asked why he was hired for this case when his legal specialty is state administrative law, he said, "Well, in general, businessmen always want an edge."

A classic FTC horizontal consent order is the *Burlington Mills* case.[20] Burlington, the world's largest textile company, with net sales in 1967 (the time of the order) of $1.36 billion, had in the early Sixties acquired Erwin Mills and Fabrex Corporation with combined sales of $103.5 million. In 1968, while the Commission was negotiating with Burlington, it was at the same time formulating guidelines for the industry to indicate which mergers it would challenge. Burlington made sure it presented a convincing case. In the private conference with the Commissioners, Burlington's antitrust lawyer was flanked by two distinguished attorneys: former FDR confidant Tommy "the Cork" Corcoran and James Rowe, a co-chairman of the then Citizens for Johnson. They convinced the FTC to permit the acquisitions as long as Burlington asked FTC permission for future mergers in the next 10 years.

Then the Commission issued guidelines to the textile industry which *specifically prohibited* such mergers as this one. As Commissioner Jones pointed out, "Burlington's 1962 acquisition of Fabrex Corporation, a textile fabric converter, 'violated' the $10 million acquired-firm guideline as Fabrex had 1961 sales of $35.5 million." [21] Jones dissented in both the issuance of the decree and the subsequent guidelines. As she put it, "The Commission here accepts a consent order which forecloses the possibility of definitely determining this anticompetitive issue and at the same time issues guidelines which foreclose comparable acquisitions on the part of Burlington's competitors." While her aim was right, her target was wrong. The problem was not the guidelines but the Burlington case itself. All the staff on the case had refused the consent order. Even after the Commission told them to approve the case, the chief investigating lawyer refused. So the Commission got one white-haired gentleman—who said to us that his main function as a $23,573 attorney was to answer mail and "look like a judge" at pretrial hearings—to sign the decree.

As *Fortune* pointed out, the Burlington case was "a notable instance of Washington lawyers practicing their profession without using words at all, much less writing briefs. . . ." [22] *Fortune* went on to quote one FTC official's reaction to the Burlington presentation:

Bergson made his argument for more than an hour. Neither Corcoran nor Rowe said a single word throughout the hearing. But there they were. L.B.J. was still President. Rowe was one of his closest advisors. . . . You had to feel their presence was a signal of some kind.

The staff interviewed believed that Herbert Bergson, the antitrust specialist who was arguing for Burlington, had hired Corcoran and Rowe for their political impact. In fact Corcoran and Rowe had been Burlington's lawyers for many years and they had hired Bergson to work on this particular case with them. Burlington had hired the right people a long time before the crisis.

The actions of the Commission in this consent-order area demonstrate how an "innovation" can become counter-productive when it is not fully understood. Under Robert Hammond (prior to his Antitrust Division tenure), the merger enforcement activity of the Commission had pro-gressed from its low point during the first two years of the Dixon administration. Hammond's strategy involved focus-ing on a few industries in which the FTC had expertise—such as cement, foods, and department stores—and attack-ing anticompetitive trends. The no-divestiture consent order was an important part of Hammond's implementa-tion program. It was designed as a signal to an industry that from then on mergers would be carefully scrutinized By requiring FTC permission for future mergers over a period of years, it also slowed down the more aggressive acquiring companies. In Commissioner Nicholson's words, the agency "was willing to grant respondents one bite at the apple in return for containment of a demonstrated trend toward concentration." [23]

Unfortunately, no-divestiture orders were taken as green lights rather than yellow or red ones. Given the political image of the Agency, these orders on their face also became an obvious target for rumors of political dealing. And the Commission itself undermined the Hammond "signal" con-cept by using these decrees as forms of tokenism. If a case was rotten or stale or politically hot, a no-divestiture decree was used. The public could not tell with any particular case whether the Commission was on the move or the make.

Also because of its complex image problem, the Agency had trouble distinguishing one case, where no-divestiture order might be appropriate, from another in the same in-dustry where the facts dictated a different remedy. In addi-tion, when a company was under FTC order, the Commis-sion bound itself tacitly to approve or disapprove a merger at its inception; it was not allowed the luxury of examining the impact any time after consummation.

Furthermore, there was no clear standard for giving or withholding FTC permission before making another acqui-sition. Commissioner Nicholson believed that "It is incor-rect in my opinion to say that we will judge future acquisi-tions by those already under order solely under the criteria as to whether the new acquisition violates Section 7. The standard is less." [24] Some other Commissioners, however, disagree and apply conventional Section 7 standards to acquisitions of a company under an outstanding order. But if all the FTC gets for allowing a questionable merger is the ability to judge any subsequent merger under the standards it would have judged it by anyway, the consent program is a sham.

In hindsight, Hammond admits that his consent-order program "has problems in it I didn't fully appreciate at the time." Nevertheless, he is rightfully proud of the flurry of litigation he did bring. Essentially, however, the no-divestiture decree is a story of a strategy that was misunderstood and abused.

(2) Partial Divestiture

While no-divestiture consent orders account for 10 of the 36 consent orders negotiated in the Sixties, about half the orders are partial divestitures—a far more subtle remedy. A no-divestiture order naturally raises eyebrows. But when a company divests itself of some of its acquisition, the record looks far more impressive. Beyond appearances, however, serious questions arise. Some partial divestitures begin to look like a more sophisticated version of the philosophy of everybody wins and nobody loses so evident in the no-divestiture cases.

For example, when a complaint was issued in the *Campbell-Taggart Associated Bakeries* case, in June of 1960, Campbell was the second largest commercial baker in the United States. Six years later the opinion of the hearing examiner was filed, urging a divestiture of nine acquired bakeries. The Commission vacated the hearing examiner's decision and accepted a consent order requiring the sale of only four bakeries.* [25] But the divestitures involved were minimal. As Commissioner Reilly pointed out, "The divestitures as ordered will do little to remedy the harms caused by respondent's action. The plants involved are only token representatives of group acquisitions." [26] Commissioner Jones made a more piercing point. It turned out that Campbell had dropped the brand name of the bakeries it had acquired for several years. Consequently, when the individ-

---

* Why the Commission accepted a consent order at all—after six years of litigation—is a serious question. According to some Washington attorneys, the extraordinary decision resulted because the record was stale and the hearing examiner's opinion was highly confused.

ual plants were sold, they would have no immediate market. The old competition was dead, and the FTC was satisfied to have a plant divestiture with Campbell keeping the business—an exercise, at best, in nominalism.

The Campbell case particularly stirred staff sensibilities. Originally Fred Rowe, a leading Washington antitrust lawyer, represented Campbell-Taggart in unsuccessful attempts to achieve a soft consent order. Rowe then traveled the litigation route, and again Campbell did not seem to be faring well. Just before the hearing examiner handed down his decision against the company, Frazor Edmondson, Chairman of the Executive Committee of Campbell-Taggart, called up a lawyer in Chattanooga, Tennessee: William Spears of Spears, Moore, Rebman & Williams. Mr. Spears, whose specialty had been the Federal Power Commission, told us in a telephone interview that he was specifically hired to work out a settlement. Although the skilled Rowe had not been able to obtain a settlement from the Commission, Spears was suddenly able to get a lenient consent order, with Rand Dixon a vigorous proponent of accepting the Campbell-Taggart offer. The political context of these events is suspect. Edmondson was on the Alumni Board of Directors of Vanderbilt University; Spears was a trustee of Vanderbilt; and Chairman Dixon was also on the Alumni Board.[*]

Partial divestiture can take even more bizarre forms, as in the *Textron* case.[27] With 1968 sales of $1.7 billion, Textron had gotten a foothold in the ball-bearing business with its acquisition of Aetna in 1963. By 1967 the Aetna ball-bearing division had $7.8 million in sales, 1.6% of total industry shipments. The industry as a whole, however, was highly concentrated, with the four largest producers accounting for 63.4% of total shipments in 1967. Then, in 1968, Textron paid $184 million in stock to acquire Fafnir, which had ball-bearing sales of $77 million and a 17.1% market share. The FTC challenged the Fafnir acquisition, but then, in spring of 1970, proposed to accept a consent order that allowed Textron to keep Fafnir, the second

---

[*] Political pressure, according to some firms, can cut the other way. In a May, 1971, submission to the FTC, the Kennecott Copper Corporation charged that influential members of Congress had convinced the Commission to make Kennecott give up its control of Peabody Coal. In another case, with the Hearst chain accused of misleading sales tactics, Hearst countercharged that Representative Fred Rooney (D.-Pa.) spurred the FTC to bring the charges.

largest company in the industry, and divest itself of the
relatively small Aetna. This settlement triggered a string of
angry communications to the Agency from the FTC's
former chief economist, Willard F. Mueller. He wrote,
"Unless antitrust authorities require meaningful relief in
matters such as this, they provide substance to Professor
Galbraith's charge that antitrust is merely a 'charade.' "

Washington lawyer Worth Rowley added his voice to
Mueller's: "Illusory measures that can only put a façade
of propriety upon an unlawful transaction tend to discredit
the Commission." Despite those protests, and more, the
FTC held to its acceptance of the proposed consent order.
The Commission reasoned that if Fafnir had been acquired
first, it would not have been challenged, so in effect the
same result was achieved by allowing the spin-off of Aetna.

Mueller was not convinced, and dashed off a letter to
Commissioner Philip Elman, author of the seminal *Bendix*
case on conglomerate mergers and a member of the majority in Textron. The letter read simply, "Bendix yes! Textron
no! Although 500 is a good batting average in baseball, it
isn't good enough in antitrust." Commissioner Elman has
let it be known that he was not pleased with the letter, which
has become a Washington classic. His essential contention
is that, even given Mueller's perspective, considering Elman's innovative cases such as *Clorox, Consolidated Foods,*
and *Beatrice,* the former Chief Economist can't add.

The *Textron* decision is extremely dangerous. First, it
creates a façade of action when it entails considered inaction. Second, it can be used by analogy in other situations
where a company with a position in an industry gobbles up
a leading firm and sacrifices a small firm to make it pass
FTC scrutiny. The FTC seemed to be concerned more with
fairness to Textron than with allegiance to competition.
Textron could have used its huge resources to help develop
tiny Aetna into a major competitor, and help break up an
oligopolistic industry. The FTC allowed anticompetitive
activity if the acquiring company was willing to sacrifice
its pawn to capture a queen.

When Procter & Gamble acquired Folger Coffee, the
largest independent coffee company with 15% of national
grocery coffee sales, the FTC lost a chance to make significant antimerger law by falling back on a partial-divestiture
order. The Commission required a divestiture of one coffee
plant out of Folger's five largest facilities and required that

Procter & Gamble get permission for future acquisitions. Commissioner Reilly ridiculed the decision, saying, "The Commission thundered in the complaint and cheeped in the order." [28] Commissioner Jones complained that a full divestiture was the only way to restore the competitive situation. Unlike *Textron,* which did not involve innovative legal concepts, the *Folger* case was predicated on the emerging notion that a conglomerate merger can have anticompetitive effects. The FTC in the *Clorox* case had begun to explore the conglomerate area, although there was little follow-through until the *Bendix-Fram* decision in June, 1970. By settling a token consent order, the FTC neither aided the development of new precedent nor substantially changed the economic effects of the merger.

On March 27, 1969, the Bureau of Economics sent a memorandum to the Commission which discussed the problems with FTC consent orders:

> Over the past three years . . . most Commission consent settlements have required little or no divestiture; 35% required no divestiture and 45% required only partial divestiture. Additionally, several partial divestitures involved the disposition of only a small part of acquired assets—particularly, *Foremost, Proctor & Gamble,* and *Bohack.* Finally, all four full divestiture cases involved rather minor operations—three cement companies and a key blank manufacturer.[29]

The legal staff replied by citing their limited resources. The argument does not hold. If the reason for these giveaway orders was that the FTC wished to concentrate on the innovative suits dealing with "larger, contemporary conglomerate mergers," the result in the *Folger* case is clearly contradictory to this policy. The underlying problem is that the FTC has never clearly articulated its antitrust strategy.

(3) Consent Orders as a Process

Essentially, a consent order involves negotiations beyond the public eye. Under the current rules, before the Commission formally issues a complaint, it notifies the prospective defendant of its intent; he then has 10 days to tell the Commission whether he is interested in having a proceeding disposed of by a consent order. If the reply is positive, which it generally is, the party is allowed up to 30 days to submit a suggested order to the Commission. Up to this point, the defendant has achieved delay and has not compromised his position. Since 1967 the Commission only accepts consent orders provisionally, putting the orders on the public record for 30 days for comment, but despite this gesture at public participation, a comment on an order is in fact quite rare, except in a case like *Textron* where a sophisticated, interested party has organized support.

The crux of the consent-order process is the private maneuvering of attorneys seeking deals not subject to the light of the public record. The *Federated* case, previously discussed, where an agile Abe Fortas managed to convince the Commissioners to hear his client's viewpoint privately but not allow the chief executive of the acquired chain to speak, is a prime illustration. Whatever conversations Commissioner Jones might have had with Broadway-Hale counsel H. Thomas Austern prior to her surprise switch in the *Neiman-Marcus* case will remain a mystery. Yet the pressures of the process were more visible in Occidental Petroleum Company's acquisition of Maust Coal.

There was little doubt that a merger between Occidental and Maust Coal was anticompetitive; the majority of the Commission, which allowed the merger, admitted to itself: "The Commission, on the basis of its present information, is inclined to believe that there may be an adverse effect from the combination of Island Creek [an Occidental subsidiary] and Maust properties and assets. . . ." [30] Occidental, whose president, Dr. Armand Hammer, made his first fortune delivering art treasures from Russia before the Bolsheviks could get them shortly after World War I, is a company well aware of its political environment. The major oil companies were stunned when Occidental got major Libyan oil concessions because of its ability to pander to the tastes of the country's then royal family. Now the same skill was applied in Washington. The argument Occidental made for its Maust acquisition was that the coal company was a failing business and therefore the situation should be exempted from normal antitrust standards. (Yet, buried in the public record was a report by Occidental consultant R. H. Neilson which said that if the company were bought at book value, more than Occidental was paying, there would be a hefty 16% rate of return.[31]) Occidental mobilized its resources. Letter after letter streamed in from mayors in West Virginia saying that if the merger were not approved, disaster would strike. Jennings Randolph, the Senator from that state, sent telegrams such as "After careful review of the Maust situation, I believe early and favorable action without resort to quote 'tentative approval' is necessary." Yet, as one Commissioner told the Study Group, "All the telegrams don't mean a thing. It's the meetings and the phone calls, and that never goes on the public record."

As long as *ex parte* communication is an integral part of the consent-order process, it will continue to taint the FTC. Commissioner Elman, whose motion for banning *ex parte* communications was defeated by his fellow Commissioners, articulated the problems with the process quite clearly before the Kennedy Subcommittee on Administrative Procedures:

> There is an atmosphere created, an appearance created which does nobody any good. There may, in fact, be absolutely no impropriety, but if there are such interventions, particularly if the intervention comes on behalf of a company that people suspect may have made a campaign contribution to a particular Senator or Member of Congress, the wrong inferences will be drawn. . . . I think they usually are telephone conversations. But there are merger matters particularly, where millions of dollars may be at stake where there are private interests at stake that are substantial. . . .[32]

In theory, the Commission has begun to apply itself to some of these problems. There is allegedly less leniency in allowing defense counsel to delay cases by protracted consent-order negotiations; the Commissioners have also agreed to send each other memoranda concerning relevant *ex parte* contacts. But these measures are only faltering steps. As long as the Commission is willing to settle for token remedies, defense counsel still makes substantial progress in negotiations by offering nothing. And if a Commissioner were injudiciously influenced by *ex parte* contacts, he would certainly not write his colleagues about it.

In the meantime, until the FTC does some *bona fide* housecleaning, the prudent executive hires President Nixon's old law firm, former Commissioners, the nephew of the Speaker of the House, Tommy "the Cork," and fellow alumni of Rand Dixon—just for insurance. In these million-dollar cases, as Edward McCormick pointed out, "Businessmen always want an edge."

THE FAILURE OF LITIGATION

Settlements, however, are not always consent orders. Sometimes the FTC litigates. One of the most striking aspects of the Commission's litigation program is the number of cases dismissed or settled by the Commission without explanation although litigation was already fully under way.

In the *Crown Cork and Seal* case the Commission vacated the hearing examiner's decision and dismissed the complaint. Here, Crown Cork, the largest producer of metal crowns for bottles, acquired the sixth largest producer, Mundet; the hearing examiner found that the acquisition violated Section 7 of the Clayton Act. At the hearing-examiner level, the controversy focused on whether Mundet was a failing corporation, and therefore possibly eligible for an exemption from standard antitrust doctrine. In their opinion, however, the Commissioners merely said that "the complaint should be dismissed because of the special circumstances surrounding the acquisition of Mundet Cork Corporation by respondent and that it is therefore unnecessary to determine whether Mundet Cork Corporation was a failing company within the meaning of the precedents." [33] The "special circumstances" were never described. One Commissioner, asked to describe those "circumstances," said "I don't remember," even after looking at the files on the case. Another responded in an interview that it was all very simple:

> The Commission just couldn't agree on their reasoning and that is why the opinion is so curt. In my view this was a case of a failing estate rather than a failing company. The estate had to sell the company, but there was only one potential purchaser. Either we had to say that the property couldn't be sold at all, or allow the acquisition.

While such an argument is possible, it was not explicitly made before the hearing examiner, and the Commission itself never mentioned it. So vague an opinion, dropping a complaint after it has already gone through litigation, always raises questions about the decision-making process at the FTC. As another Commissioner put it, "Whenever you go against the staff, they suspect you of a fix." This staff attitude is hardly surprising when the Commissioners fail to articulate the basis for their decisions.

A similar obscurity shrouded the decision in the *Kroger* case. A complaint issued by the FTC in 1959 charged Kroger, then the third largest food chain, with past illegal acquisition of more than 40 companies. Kroger fought vigorously, checkmating the Commission for eight years.

It filed a motion in 1967 that the case be dismissed; the hearing examiner bucked the motion up to the Commission. The Commission remanded the motion back to the hearing examiner "with directions that he explore the possibilities of a settlement." The examiner reported back that the parties had "fundamental differences and that no useful purpose would be served in further discussions." So the FTC neatly resolved its problem by dropping the case— after *eight years* of work on it. Their announcement stated:

The Commission has determined that the public interest does not warrant further proceedings. This determination is based on the longevity of the case, the fact that evidentiary hearings would have to be further delayed as a result of an additional acquisition challenged in the complaint and the fact that the Commission had announced its enforcement policy with respect to mergers in the food distribution industries.[34]

If the additional acquisition, Market Basket, a Los Angeles-based chain, was illegal, as charged by the FTC in the amended complaint, the need for more evidence is not a persuasive basis for dismissal. As far as the trumpeted arrival of the enforcement policy statement, all that says is that the FTC will look carefully at acquisitions by companies with over $500 million in sales. The promulgation of such a rule seems little reason for terminating a case that is covered by its terms.

The FTC rules specifically state, "After a complaint has been issued, the consent order procedure . . . will not be available. However, in exceptional and unusual circumstances, the Commission may . . . withdraw a matter from adjudication for the purpose of negotiating a settlement." [35] But there have been a series of complaints settled during litigation, and the "exceptional" circumstances are usually unclear or unarticulated. The *Campbell-Taggart Bakery* case, which resulted in a token consent order after six years of litigation, has already been discussed. Another prime example of this practice was the *Beatrice Foods* case.

In *Beatrice Foods* a 1955 complaint challenged the acquisition by Beatrice, the fourth largest dairy, of some 174 companies in similar product lines. Eight years later the hearing examiner judged a portion of those acquisitions to be illegal, and his judgment was sustained by the Commission in 1965. Then in 1967, while the case was still pending for review before the Ninth Circuit Court of Appeals, the Commission, by a 2–1 vote, abruptly decided to terminate the proceeding and accept a consent order. In his dissent Commissioner Elman pointed out some of the peculiarities in the decision: "Today's settlement does not come in advance of trial before the allegations of the complaint have been tested, but after the case has already been fully tried and adjudicated by the Commission." [36] Calling the case "one of the most important ever brought in the merger field," Elman pointed out that the relief given in the consent order "falls substantially short of the relief which the Commission . . . determined to be necessary. There is no reason to anticipate that the Commission's decision and order would not be sustained on review." The Commission never explained the "extraordinary" circumstances that justified accepting a decree under its rules. The trial attorneys on the FTC staff were known to be enraged by the decision, and many Washington antitrust lawyers were puzzled. Eleven years of litigation, a clear legal precedent within grasp, and the FTC knuckled under. At the very least, the Commission owed the taxpayer an explanation of its actions.[37] But again a veil of mystery enshrouds the public record.

A chief reason for this receptivity toward settlements is the FTC's inability to enforce its own civil penalty suits. Rather, it must go through a uninterested Justice Department, which farms the cases out to the United States Attorneys, who could not care less about the FTC's problems. As one high FTC official pointed out to the Study Group, "Not only does the U.S. Attorney not know what you're talking about, but he doesn't care to learn. Face it. In an office like the Southern District of New York you have a lot of bright young guys with high grades who are trying to make a name for themselves. Our cases don't get anywhere, and we're forced to settle for minimal compliance." The net effect is a delayed enforcement of Commission orders.

An illustrative case study is the *ABC Consolidated* case. The FTC issued a final order in October, 1964, asking for divestiture by ABC theater concessions having some $4 million in sales. By 1967, however, ABC had only sold assets with sales of $1,186,000. So the FTC finally decided in 1967 to seek its first civil penalty proceeding against a company violating an outstanding Section 7 order. The suit sought damages of $321,000 and injunctive relief. Three years later, in August of 1970, the FTC was still pressing its civil penalty suit. Finally, it accepted a stipulation with ABC which terminated the suit by requiring ABC to divest the assets it was supposed to sell six years before and to pay a fine of $200,000. Although $200,000 seems like a lot, it merely indicates what Washington lawyers already know: delay pays. Assuming ABC earned 5% on the $3 million in sales not divested, its financial reward more than doubles the cost of the civil penalty suit over the six-year period.

PROCEDURAL PITFALLS

Bargained decrees reflect the relative power of the parties. Although the FTC has a strong substantive legal position, due to an antitrust-minded Supreme Court, its procedure is so anachronistic that overall its strength is limited. Regarding the substantive law, as Justice Stewart pointed out in *Von's,* "The sole consistency that I can find is that under Section 7, the Government always wins." [38] But the procedural hurdles to a victory on the merits are so substantial that this advantage is usually offset. These problems are particularly evident in the merger area, although they affect all areas of litigation. Among the most pressing problems are the costs of delay, the lack of effective preliminary injunction power, the failure of the hearing-examiner process, and outmoded rules of procedure.

(1) Delay

Although administrative agencies were supposed to be faster and more efficient than the judicial process, most of the lawyers we interviewed believed that bringing a case through the FTC was as slow as or slower than bringing a suit through the court. As indicated above, for complaints issued during Dixon's chairmanship the mean time for the issuance of the complaint to the Commission's cease-and-desist order was 32.6 months. It took 18.7 months on the average to reach the hearing examiner and 13.9 months to reach the Commission. And even these statistics show faster action than actually exists, because complaints not yet acted on are not reflected even if they have already taken longer than the mean times.

Economist Kenneth Elzinga found that for FTC cases which resulted in some form of divestiture the average time from acquisition to divestiture was 67.5 months. The Justice Department secured structural relief in an average of 63.8 months.[39] This is not to praise the Antitrust Division—over five years is still a long time—but it points out the myth of administrative agencies cutting through the morass of judicial precedent and procedural anachronisms to achieve an expeditious and just result.

(2) Preliminary Injunctions

One of the basic problems with the FTC's merger program is its general inability to block a merger before consummation. This inability generates the incentive for corporate lawyers to exploit dilatory tactics. As mentioned previously, every day a case is delayed is another day the acquiring company can reap profits from its acquisition. Furthermore, as occurred in the *Pillsbury* case and *CBS*,[40] the record becomes so stale that a court remands the case back to the Commission for fresher evidence, thereby triggering even more delay.

The merger notification program innovated by the Commission in March of 1969 is a minimal step in the right direction. Within 10 days after an agreement in principle is reached to merge, an acquiring company with $250 million or more in assets must notify the FTC of its merger plans if the acquired company had at least $10 million in assets. Also, if a corporation with $250 million in assets purchases more than 10% of the voting stock of a company with $10 million in assets, it must file a report with the FTC within 10 days after the transaction. The mergers cannot be consummated for at least 60 days after the date of notification. This program, while helpful, does not fundamentally alter the problem; it just gives the FTC two months more to investigate.

Another attempt to achieve some binding jurisdiction on forthcoming mergers has been the FTC consent-order program. By challenging mergers in certain industries and accepting lenient decrees with provisions that the company must seek FTC permission for future mergers, the Commission accomplishes two purposes. First, if a proposed merger does violate Section 7, the FTC can so rule and bypass the cumbersome administrative process. Second, delay in this situation works against the corporation. The effect of an FTC decision is immediate. Even in litigated cases, the hearing examiners are now putting provisions into their orders that require the company to seek FTC permission for mergers in the future. The long-term result of this strategy will be that a substantial fraction of American industry will be unable to merge without explicit permission from the FTC. However, as was pointed out in the discussion of FTC consent decrees, this program has a high cost in allowing many acquisitions of dubious legality to take place with token spin-offs, if any.

Use of the preliminary injunction offers the obvious solution to the problem of attacking mergers after consummation. But the FTC's experience with this remedy has been tortured, explaining much about the preference for the consent-decree approach. Before 1966 it was unclear if the FTC had the right to petition a court for a preliminary injunction, although the Justice Department did. As pointed out in the 1956 denial of such power for the FTC in the *International Papers* case,[41] there was no specific statutory authorization for the FTC, while there was one for the Justice Department in Section 15 of the Clayton Act. Some young FTC lawyers still felt that they could successfully argue for a preliminary-injunctive power under the vague "All Writs" Act which allows courts to issue necessary orders.

In the 1966 *Dean Foods* case, a sharply divided Supreme Court upheld this contention in a 5–4 decision.[42] The case involved an imminent sale of property in an acquisition that had a very high probability of violating Section 7. Since *Dean* the FTC has sought a preliminary injunction only *once* in a Section 7 situation, in the *OKC* case, which also involved an imminent sale. The staff, however, has asked for Commission approval to seek preliminary injunctions a number of times. Although on its face the injunction seems to solve many of the FTC's problems, its scope as a remedy has been conservatively self-limited by the FTC. As one Commissioner pointed out in an interview:

After *Dean* there was no enthusiasm for preliminary injunctions despite our victory there. In order to get an order there, we had to argue the case on its merits before the court of appeals. Our case was based around the idea that the likelihood of an order was so great. Then the court gave us only four months to try the case. The case was then before a hearing examiner. The staff of Commissioner Jones, knowing the time pressures for their opinion, were writing why the acquisition was illegal before the case was argued before the Commission. We had prejudgment in spades. The Commission says the acquisition is illegal in order to get an injunction and then the case comes up from the hearing examiner and we are supposed to act as a judicial body. After *Dean,* Dixon said, "We don't want to go through that again." . . . So *Dean* is really a paper victory.

(3) The Hearing Examiners

In theory, an administrative agency is preferable to a court as a forum for economic regulation litigation because of its expertise and tailored procedure. The hearing-examiner process represents in many ways the guts of this assumption, for he is the administrative agency's "expert." Statistics give an interesting picture of hearing-examiner performance. In the merger area, the decisions of the hearing examiners in cases initiated during Dixon's reign as Chairman were reversed by the Commission in 58.3% of the cases. This high reversal rate reflects the lack of confidence the Commission has in its own examiners. Surveying the opinions, it is clear that the reversals are not only on questions of law but also a critical analysis of the examiner's analysis of the facts of the cases.

This lack of confidence is also evident in the decreasing role of litigation in the Agency, which is partially attributable to the failure of the hearing-examiner process. A dramatic indication of the change of emphasis at the Commission is the drop in the number of hearing examiners from 22 in 1964 to 12 in 1970. Furthermore, as Chief Hearing Examiner Edward Creel pointed out in an interview, the examiners now spend a sizable proportion of their time doing work for other agencies. In fiscal 1970, at the FTC itself, the 12 examiners spent a total of 278 days at hearings and prehearings adjudicating a total of 38 cases ranging from complex merger litigation to simple deceptive-advertising suits. On the average, each examiner at the FTC handled three cases and spent a total of 23 days at hearings and prehearings in fiscal 1970. Clearly, the examining staff is not overburdened.

Most FTC staff we interviewed had no regard for the caliber of the examiners. On the other hand, many examiners did not think highly of the trial skills of FTC attorneys. Perhaps both are correct. Because so few cases are litigated at the Commission, trial experience is meager. Although lawyers call a hearing examiner "Judge" when addressing him, the reality is that the occupation of hearing examiner just does not attract people of the quality of federal district-court judges. The Administrative Conference of the United States, a body charged by statute with recommending improvements in the administrative process, considered changing the title of the hearing examiner as a solution to this problem.

The FTC was among the agencies opposing the use of the term "judge" for the examiners. Given the present selection procedure, that opposition was probably justified. Although in theory the Civil Service system works to get the best men as examiners, the selection process as it now operates often has the opposite result. Wilson Mathews, the Director of the Office of Hearing Examiners of the Civil Service Commission, explained in an interview what at first seemed like a fairly rigorous selection process:

In the last six years, there have been some 2,500 applicants of which 450 people got to an oral-interview stage after taking a written examination. The exam consists of writing up an opinion on a case within 6 hours as a test of analytic and writing ability. The interview panels, which consist of a career civil servant, an ABA-supplied attorney, and a ranking agency officer, reviews the files and sustains the initial grade in about 50% of the cases. . . .

However fair this system is in theory, it is ineffective in practice. The foremost problem is that of the veterans' preference. Ninety-five percent of the list, according to Mathews, are veterans, who are awarded five extra "points," or 10 if they were injured. On a recent list seven of the top 10 names were men who got a 10-point bonus. A non-veteran, unless he is truly remarkable, stands little chance under this point system, and even a veteran who is not eligible for the 10-point bonus has difficulties. Thus, the merit system of the Civil Service results in the appointment of the least competent. The Administrative Conference in January, 1970, submitted their recommendation that veterans' preference be abolished, but so far there has been no change in the procedures.

One possible method of reforming the hearing-examiner system would be to divide the FTC examiners into two classes. One group would try the routine deceptive-practices

cases and have a GS-15 standing. They would be subject
to the same selection criteria as, for example, examiners in
HEW hearing social-security cases. The other half of the
examiners would be GS-17s and called "administrative
judges." They would deal with complex cases, and have
access to a supporting staff including economists. Perhaps
the expert opinions of examiners in merger cases might
then materialize.

(4) Commission Rules

Many of the procedural problems can be attributed to the
Commission's rules. Rather than being looked on as mere
technicalities fit only for discussion by lawyers, the rules
must be considered as important reflections of implicit policy positions. The following are a few of the most important rules that have stifled the effectiveness of the Commission's program:

EX PARTE COMMUNICATIONS. Presently there is no rule
banning *ex parte* communication at any precomplaint stage
in the Commission process. The problems with *ex parte*
contact have already been discussed, and on the balance we
feel it should be banned. If there is a great advantage in
mutual understanding when Commissioners meet directly
with the attorneys for the defendants, these meetings
should be formally structured to include the Commission
staff. Although there are arguments against making these
conferences public records because of the "confidential"
information exchanged, the rules applicable to such knowledge should be similar to those of "confidential" information obtained in the discovery process. The burden to make
any part of the process nondisclosable should be on the
defendants. No single Commissioner should be able to meet
with a party without an offer extended to the other Commissioners to do likewise. The FTC has traditionally excited a crisis of confidence, which can be cured only if it
purges itself of this secretive process.

THE EXTENT OF POST-COMPLAINT DISCOVERY. Following
from the requirement to have a *prima facie* case before a
complaint is issued, the FTC lawyer is circumscribed in the
scope of his postcomplaint discovery. Basically, any discovery he makes must be only minor and supplemental to the
points already established. This requirement guarantees out-
dated cases, such as *Columbia Broadcasting System,* where

the Court of Appeals felt obliged to remand an FTC case because a 1967 cease-and-desist order was based on a 1959 investigation. Allowing post-complaint discovery seems essential to modernizing the FTC process.

INTERLOCUTORY APPEALS. In the abortive *Koppers* case, to be discussed later, there were some 25 interlocutory appeals from the hearing examiner to the Commission while the trial was taking place. The Commission must give permission for an appeal to be filed, and even this process takes time. After *Koppers* the trend has rightly been toward tightening up the permissions process and dealing with the appeals more rapidly. The risk, however, is that when the Commission refuses to hear important points on an interlocutory basis, the whole trial will be wasted if the Commission subsequently reverses the hearing examiner's findings. The only solution would seem to be to get hearing examiners who are right more often, a solution tied to our earlier hearing-examiner proposals.

THE COMMISSION'S DUAL ROLE. An underlying assumption of the FTC rule system is that the Commission must act both as prosecutor and as judge. In some other agencies, such as the NLRB, these functions are sharply separated. Commissioner Elman is particularly sensitive about this point, claiming that it causes confusion of the Commissioner's role. As he pointed out in an interview, "It's not all right to talk to a judge about a pending case, but you can talk to the district attorney. Who are we supposed to be?"

This particular difficulty could be alleviated without any major legislative overhaul of the Agency. For example, the Commission could still formally issue the complaint, but they could bind themselves to always follow the recommendation of, say, the General Counsel. In essence, their prosecutorial discretion would be absolutely delegated to the staff. Such a system would solve the "prejudgment" problem experienced by Commissioners who vote to issue a complaint and then have to vote later on whether to issue a cease-and-desist order. But this delegation would undermine the role of the Chairman, who is supposedly responsible for the administration of the Agency. A hybrid system might be easier to implement, if not more effective. Under one alternative, the Chairman would remain as the chief administrative officer, but would also not vote on initiation of investigation, complaints, etc. Another possibility is for the Chairman to remove himself from the judicial role by not voting on the cease-and-desist orders, and being the sole determinant of investigations, complaints, and also chief administrator. All these concepts have their difficulties, but the present structure seems worse.

SUCCESSFUL LITIGATION

Of the 56 complaints issued since March, 1961, 10 had resulted in a successful Commission order by January, 1970. Three of these cases—*Diamond Alkali, United States Steel,* and *Mississippi River Fuel*—dealt with the vertical-integration problem in the portland-cement industry. Generally, the FTC's strategy in the cement industry seems commendable and will be described in the following chapter's discussion of guidelines.

Five of the remaining seven successful prosecutions since 1961 were the following Commission orders:

—In a straight horizontal-merger suit, Swingline was divested of two acquisitions in the stapler-fastener industry. The two companies combined had cost Swingline a total of $5,600,000 in stock.[43]

—In another horizontal case, Seeburg, with some $22,575,000 sales in the vending-machine business, was forced to divest Cavalier, which had 1963 sales of $8,408,823 in the bottle vending-machine industry. Cavalier had been purchased for $11.8 million and raised Seeburg's market share to 18.9%.[44]

—American Brake Shoe was divested of S. K. Wellman, another friction metal producer, in a horizontal suit. Wellman had sales of $12,421,240 in 1962 in the industry, while Brake Shoe itself had $2,743,000 sales in this market. These friction metal units were used in automotive and industrial energy-conversion devices.[45]

—Allied Chemical had to divest itself of all assets used in the manufacture of webbing for automotive-safety seat belts. Allied was selling about $3.8 million worth of yarn to the webbing-producing industry, and had acquired seat-belt manufacturing assets which had sales of $34.5 million. This vertical integration was held by the Commission to foreclose markets to other webbing-yarn manufacturers.[46]

—In Dean Foods, the Commission ordered divestiture

of certain horizontal dairy acquisitions. However, when the case was being appealed, the Commission agreed to a consent order that stipulated less divestitures. The dairy-industry litigations are described in more detail in the discussion of guidelines.

Aside from the cement cases, the FTC's record is disappointing: 10 complaints followed through to a Commission order in nine years is a very meager success story. Furthermore, the importance of some of the cases, involving small industries or companies with small sales, is obvious from their description.

Some of the Commission's successes—especially in the area of conglomerate mergers and potential competition—are based on cases filed prior to March, 1961, although decisions came down in the mid-Sixties. Much of this doctrinal development is due to Commissioner Elman's insightful opinions; and Elman, in turn, points out his debt to Willard Mueller, chief of the Bureau of Economics. This tribute raises an obvious question: If the Bureau was so helpful to Elman as a Commissioner, why wasn't it helpful to the legal staff and Commissioners generally?

The most famous of Elman's opinions is the 1963 *Procter & Gamble* decision (P&G) in which the acquisition of Clorox, the leading manufacturer of household bleach, by the $1 billion sales P&G was held to violate Section 7 of the Clayton Act.[47] P&G in 1957 was the nation's largest advertiser, having used its marketing expertise to capture 54% of the packaged-detergent market. Clorox had 49% of the liquid-bleach market. Its nearest competitor was Purex with a 16% market share; the top six firms had 80% of the market, with most of the other producers quite small. Elman found that the substitution of P&G for Clorox would discourage potential and existing competitors fearful of possible P&G retaliation. Furthermore, Clorox might increase its market share by P&G exploiting its leverage to get more supermarket shelf space and by predatory pricing financed out of P&G's other profits. The opinion also developed the concept of "potential competition." Elman believed that P&G was a potential entrant into the industry, thereby restraining Clorox's action as an oligopolist; if it had ever entered, of course, Clorox's market share would have been reduced. For these reasons the Commission concluded that the acquisition was anti-competitive. Although the Court of Appeals reversed the Commission's decision, finding it based on "treacherous conjecture," [48] the Supreme Court affirmed the FTC in 1966.[49]

The *S.O.S.* case illustrates the fertile possibilities for the expansion of *Clorox*. General Foods had acquired S.O.S. in 1957 when the company had about $15 million in steel-wool soap-pad sales. By 1962 S.O.S. achieved a 56% share of the $34 million market, with most of the rest going to arch-competitor Brillo. Although General Foods was not regarded as a potential entrant into the soap-pad industry, the majority of the Commissioners held that S.O.S. should be divested because General Food's marketing prowess would result in there eventually being less competition in the industry. The Court of Appeals upheld the *S.O.S.* decision, which greatly expanded anticonglomerate law: "the . . . case is an example of a mixed conglomerate merger in that the acquired product line, S.O.S. soap pads, 'fits' quite closely into the overall marketing program utilized by G.F. [General Foods]." [50] Such logic would have been extremely useful in the Procter & Gamble–Folger Coffee case if the FTC had not settled it.

This time Elman dissented, evidently wary of economic analysis being lost in a wave of undisciplined populist sentiment. To him, the analysis of harm in *Clorox* had rigor; in *S.O.S.* it did not. But seven years after the FTC decision in *Clorox,* Elman decided that the time had come for extending that case. In the *Bendix-Fram* decision the "potential competition" doctrine developed new scope.[51] Fram was the third-ranking producer of automotive filters in 1966. Bendix, the acquiring company, was the 61st largest company in the nation with 1966 sales of $1.05 billion, of which auto parts totaled about $229 million. The top six firms in the passenger market accounted for some 89% of sales. On its facts, the case extends the *P&G* doctrine considerably. Unlike the bleach market, the "deep pocket" argument (a big firm can subsidize losses of a small one) and advertising advantages are inapplicable. The leading firm in the industry is the AC Division of General Motors, a company certainly able to resist any attempt at predatory action by Bendix. Furthermore, Fram had only a 12% market share, while Clorox was the leading firm with a 49% share. Also, the evidence of planned entry into the market seemed stronger in *Clorox,* and certainly the restraining influence of P&G was greater than that of Bendix on the relevant markets. Nevertheless, *Bendix* quite logically flows from the principles in *Clorox,* assuming there was a desire to expand its doctrines. The real issue which emerges is why cases such as *Clorox, S.O.S.,* and *Bendix* are the exception at the FTC rather than the rule.

THE NEED FOR STRATEGIC ENFORCEMENT

Aside from these problems of light caseload, lenient orders, under-budgeting, archaic procedures, uncreative cases, and political input—there is a final flaw in merger enforcement within the FTC administrative context: the lack of strategy. To have a strategy, an agency must also understand its objectives, resources, and means of measuring performance. The FTC does not. A statement of overall objectives of its merger unit is non-existent. Projections into the future are mechanical, without any policy examination, and performance measures are nearly meaningless, with no attempt made to distinguish significant cases from insignificant ones.

Should the FTC be taking stock enforcement cases, or should it concentrate only on cases developing new doctrines or involving economic complexity? What of the vaunted economic expertise of the Commission? Why are there so few economists? The success or failure of the Commission cannot be measured unless one assumes some standard of performance. If one assumes that the FTC should merely enforce the laws, it is at best mediocre, at worst bad. But if a higher standard is set, demanding that the FTC should be an innovating force in merger theory, its performance rates far lower.

Many of the cases of the last nine years were decided without regard for the doctrines that the FTC prides itself on developing. For example, in the department-store cases Commissioners settled for consent orders because they thought that chains in different geographical markets did not represent potential competitors through internal expansion or toehold acquisitions. But, as Commissioner Elman demonstrated in his dissent in the *Broadway-Hale–Neiman-Marcus* case, the jumping of geographical areas even through internal expansion was not uncommon. Cases like *Textron* are especially disappointing from the "potential competition" viewpoint. After the Supreme Court decision in *Clorox,* which contained very flexible language, and the Appeals Court ruling in *S.O.S.,* the decisions to accept consent orders in *Textron* and *Folger Coffee* are indefensible. Historically then, doctrinal innovations have been obviated by the sluggish follow-up by the Commission. The FTC wins battles and loses wars.

Willard Mueller and Robert Hammond both seemed to realize that the doctrinal pattern rather than individual litigation was of primary significance. Their concept, as manifested in cases such as *Federated,* involved giving a signal to an industry that new standards were being set, articulated, and amplified. As it turned out, the FTC simply failed to use the strategy. Acceptance of the consent order in the *Beatrice* case, which squelched what could have been a seminal Supreme Court opinion, is also indicative of a thoughtless enforcement philosophy. *Clorox* and *Bendix* prove that the FTC or its Commissioners are capable of occasional flashes of brilliance; but the difference between a flash that fades away and one that sparks a fire is some intricate strategic planning. The fundamental fact, more important than any perceived political "fix," is that people can work very hard and still be ineffective if they do not know what they are trying to accomplish.

The first imperative for effective management of the FTC's merger program requires a determination of its objective. This question in turn involves two major elements. First, within the general constraints of the administrative process and of the FTC budget, what are its distinctive institutional strengths? What is the rationale for its existence? Can it indeed do anything more competently than the alternative allocation of funds to the Justice Department? The classic defense of the FTC asserts that it is a body of economic expertise useful for developing broad policy. If that is the institutional goal of the FTC, it should focus on developing that ability. It implies more economists, less attention to *per se* enforcement in areas such as the Robinson-Patman Act, an industry-wide approach, and a selection of cases for their innovative impact.

Secondly, given institutional objectives, there must be policy goals. Does the FTC have an overall vision of the economic structure it seeks to create? If it did, it could then determine how close a given action came to accomplishing those ends. For example, it is easily arguable that most of the FTC's horizontal suits in the last nine years contradicted the Commission's basic mandate of trying only innovative cases with complex economic issues. The *Economic Report on Corporate Mergers* seems to indicate that overall industrial concentration is the prime worry of the economists at the Commission; perhaps the FTC should concentrate only on this difficult problem, and leave the easier cases to the Justice Department. Obviously, if a comprehensive economic scheme is desired, enforcement will have to go beyond merely prospective Section 7 cases. Mergers in the past may have to be undone, and the latent power of Section Five of the FTC Act should be employed to attack oligopolistic patterns.

The new policy-planning unit at the FTC now boasts that it is developing a system that will tell them the number of men on a case, the case name, the unit responsible, the type of violation, and the cumulative hours already spent. If this pedestrian compilation is considered a breakthrough, imagine the way the system operated in the past. The type of data being accumulated is information of actions taken, which is of some importance; but more critical would be general data on the array of alternative actions in the future and their potential impact. It should be stressed that even now, under the supposedly reform-minded Kirkpatrick regime, the resources of the policy-planning group are quite limited, involving only four to five professionals.

The FTC's merger enforcement program is said to represent the best aspect of the agency. The present regime has found little to overhaul in basic strategy here because observers, such as the ABA Commission, had found little to criticize in the past. We believe these conclusions are misfounded. The glories of *Clorox* cannot excuse a record of only 10 successfully initiated and litigated cases in nine years. Reveling in that 1963 victory does not excuse the lack of strategy, the inconsistent doctrine, the lack of experimentation, the weak orders, and the lost potential of applying Section 7 to new enforcement areas.

To me oligopoly just sounds like an immoral sex act.
                    —Basil Mezines, Executive Director, FTC

12

Economists and Economics

THE CONFINES OF POLITICS

The FTC's original mission was to uncover the underlying
realities of our economy, performing as an industrial think
tank for the federal government. However disparaging
critics have been about the rest of the Agency, no other
government department has a similar capacity for corporate economic analysis. But budgetary, political, and workload restrictions have stunted the FTC's Bureau of Economics from its beginning. It remains, however, a symbol
of the FTC that might have been.

The political story begins with the meat-packing investigation conducted by Chief Economist Francis Walker. An
original report, biting, innovative, and informative, was
published in six parts in 1919 and led to antitrust prosecutions of the five big packers. The 1921 Packers and
Stockyards Act also flowed from this crucial study. Unfortunately, politically powerful Senator Watson of the

FTC's appropriations committee was perturbed. A Swift Company partisan, he commenced a witch-hunting investigation of the Commission's employees, charging some with "socialist tendencies." Although those charged were exonerated, some were dropped from the Commission as a result.

Despite such intimidation, FTC economists continued to make valuable studies. Extensive inquiry into holding-company operations (1927) was an important factor in bringing about the Securities Act of 1933, the Public Utility Holding Company Act, the Federal Power Act, and the Natural Gas Act. The Commission's chain-store investigation (1930) was vital in the fight for the Robinson-Patman Act. And in an extended line of reports—from one on agricultural implements and machinery (1938) to the *Report of the Federal Trade Commission on the Merger Movement* (1948)—the Commission's economic staff supplied the basic arguments leading to the Celler-Kefauver amendment to Section 7 of the Clayton Act.[1]

Yet political restrictions remained important. During World War II a Federal Reports Act was passed which required that questionnaires sent to 10 or more persons or firms must have Bureau of the Budget approval. The Budget Bureau (now the Office of Management and Budget —OMB) has a Business Advisory Council on Federal Reports which in theory merely advises on technical problems in obtaining data; in fact, it has a large policy-making input. Chapter II briefly described the attempt by Willard Mueller, head of the FTC Economics Bureau from 1961 to 1969, to conduct an intensive study of the 1,000 leading American industrial firms. The Business Advisory Council's subcommittee on the FTC study was composed of many executives of the very companies the FTC was seeking to investigate—and, not surprisingly, they received the proposal coldly. The Council leaked information about the proposed study to the Chamber of Commerce, who in turn contacted Congressional adherents. When the FTC went before its House Appropriations Committee, Chairman Albert Thomas of Texas and Charles Jonas of North Carolina jumped on the request. They argued that such questionnaires were "harassing the business community to death" and helping to squeeze "the profit margin of all businesses . . . to practically nothing."[2] This, of course, was nonsense. An almost identical study done in 1950 had proved of little immediate cost to either businessmen or taxpayers.

Further exemplifying the FTC's political straitjacket was the role of the Council of Economic Advisors (CEA) during this episode. The CEA favored the study. Chairman Walter Heller had promised to make his support known to Warren Magnuson, Chairman of the FTC's appropriations committee in the Senate, as a counterweight to extensive lobbying by the paper and electronics industries. But Heller was overruled by a White House advisor, and the CEA never took an official position on the FTC proposal.

To make certain the proposed study was dead, Congress attached a rider to the FTC appropriation forbidding any such investigation. As a result, the FTC must often use data based on economic studies done in the Fifties or before. These political restrictions combine with the lack of useful product-line reporting to limit the economic data immediately available to the antitrust agencies.

A recent attempt at more precise product-line reporting has again been discouraged by OMB's Business Advisory Council. As of January, 1971, the SEC's and FTC's Quarterly Financial Reports (Q.F.R.) were consolidated within the FTC; the Commission's penalties for noncompliance made it a far better data collector than the gentler SEC. An effort was made to include some product-line reporting requirements in the Q.F.R. surveys, to be used for statistical purposes only and not for enforcement. Even this antagonized the Business Advisory Council. On January 21, 1971, it met with OMB, SEC, and FTC officials and denounced the scheme as unconstitutional, as an invasion of confidential material, and as futile, since firms did not keep the data anyway. Thirty-seven of manufacturing's 200 top firms were in attendance, as were five corporate chairmen, the National Association of Manufacturers, the American Petroleum Institute, and the Automobile Manufacturers' Association, but no consumers and no government officials outside OMB, SEC, and FTC.

THE OPERATIONS OF THE BUREAU

Staffing the Bureau of Economics has been a major problem. In 1928 the FTC had 28 economists and 86 attorneys.

By 1960 there were still only 28 economists, while the legal staff had grown to 320. By 1969 the situation somewhat improved: there were 46 economists and 470 attorneys. Still, economists—the basis for the FTC's vaunted economic expertise—have a second-class status in the budget and in operations. Only one staff member of one Commissioner is an economist. Although notables such as Corwin Edwards, John Blair, Jesse Markham, and Willard Mueller have held top economic posts at the Commission, the relative unattractiveness of the FTC is indicated by the extreme difficulty Chairman Weinberger had in finding an adequate replacement for Mueller.

Under the guidance of Willard Mueller in the Sixties, the Bureau of Economics' budget ballooned from $305,000 in 1960 to $1,261,000 in 1968. Yet even under Mueller only about six economists in the Bureau were of top quality. Of the approximately 40 "economists" at the Commission, only about eight have Ph.Ds.

The Bureau of Economics is divided into three units, with about 20 economists in Economic Evidence, 20 in Industry Analysis, and a handful in Financial Statistics. The divisions are flexible. Any major project is directed by a senior person who draws his staff from all three.

(1) Casework

The division of Economic Evidence assists on casework. Some 90% of the division's time is spent on Section 7 merger cases. Here economists are readily accepted by the attorneys, and they sometimes send their own recommendations on cases to the Commission.

The economists could have much to contribute to the Section Five area, but they have been sparingly utilized here by the Commission. Until recently the attorneys were not receptive to their help. Yet if the Commission keeps only 20 men in the division of Economic Evidence, economists cannot be involved in every matter; given the high rate of merger activity, their concentration in the Section 7 area seems sensible.

Unlike Section 7 of the Clayton and Section Five of the FTC Act, which require proof of some threat to competition, the test for Robinson-Patman violations is largely through the application of *per se* rules. Because economic analysis is not necessary for proving unlawful behavior, the economist has been virtually excluded from Robinson-Patman activity. But rational administration of the Robinson-Patman Act cannot be accomplished unless viewed from an economic setting, which perhaps explains the FTC's erratic performance in this area. The scarcity of economic talent at the FTC argues against allocating such talent to run-of-the-mill Robinson-Patman cases—but this in turn argues for an industry-wide approach to enforcement. A coordinated effort using economic studies and all the statutory implementation devices available to the FTC assures more rational enforcement, even if the statute is *per se* by its terms.

(2) Reports

A principal function of the FTC is to serve as a fact-finding body, studying the economy and exposing corporate practices harmful to competition. Some ground-breaking efforts of the 1920s–1940s have been mentioned. The economic reports from the Industry Analysis Group are of varying quality. Considering that many of the staff could not be considered academic economists of the highest caliber, the reports are often surprisingly expert and informative, usually because the best staff men are put on the studies.

The 1969 *Economic Report on Corporate Mergers* (also called the *Conglomerate I Report*), however, has been severely criticized. Commissioner Jones found the recommendations and many of the conclusions "premature, and not supported by the type of hard empirical data which is potentially available to the Commission" and "the empirical data respecting performance which is referred to in the report for the most part was already in existence before the Commission's study." [3] A critique of the *Conglomerate I Report* by M.I.T. economics professor Paul MacAvoy supports Commissioner Jones's complaint:

The staff went away with Commission resources and brought back "new research" that cannot meet minimum economists' standards for constructing analytical arguments and testing those arguments against statistical materials. The Federal Trade Commission and the Senate Committee now have a book that would certainly be rejected for publication on grounds of insufficient art as a treatise and insufficient science as a research report. [4]

Other economists have jumped to the defense of the *Report* and its authors. Professor Joel Dirlam of the University of Rhode Island states that "as a preliminary but encyclopaedic compendium the Report is a highly useful document. . . . The analysis of reciprocity is definitive." Former Berkeley Professor Lee Preston writes that the FTC staff "is to be congratulated on assembling a document of this caliber within the time and resources available. . . . I do not know where else in the literature one would turn for a collection of factual material and analysis comparable to that provided by the Merger Report." [5]

Much of the new information for the *Report* was expected to come from an in-depth study of conglomerates such as Gulf & Western, LTV, ITT. The data, however, was unattainable, demonstrating that the Commission's fabled inquiry power under the FTC Act is not as potent in fact as it is on paper. But Willard Mueller emphasizes that the Commission can get the facts once business knows it has the will to fight if challenged. "The threshold question," he said in an interview, "is whether the Commission is really willing to exert its will."

The economics staff is back at work on a "Conglomerate II Report." There was still a problem with getting data, but Commissioner Jones intervened and arranged the "voluntary" cooperation of many of the companies involved. This solution, some staff members point out, raises questions about the reliability and depth of the information received. "Conglomerate II" still will not be what *Conglomerate I* was supposed to be—a fresh look at the economic problems of conglomerates, with new data obtained by the Agency's investigating power. Rather, it will be mostly based on the replies of companies fully aware that anything they reveal may be used against them by a Bureau noted for strong views on conglomerates. Commissioner Jones herself summed up the problem: "Not only can firms be notoriously ambiguous or uncooperative in their answers to even the simplest questions concerning the competitive aspects of their acquired assets, but the answers once yielded may be very difficult to interpret unambiguously." [6]

A number of staff economists believe that the FTC's economic manpower can be better utilized in other studies. It is true that in the Industry Analysis section, as in the rest of the Commission, priorities are not set systematically. In Industry Analysis, in fact, one-third to one-half of the tiny $400,000 budget is annually set aside for "*ad hoc* assignments at the direction of the Commission," [7] assignments often deriving from Congressional requests. Due to this arbitrary method of policy planning, and the inadequacy of resources, important areas are being neglected. Currently a study of concentrated industries is languishing because of inadequate manpower. Numerous other aspects of our economy, such as the possible anticompetitive effects of tertiary corporate interlocks, or the spread of joint ventures, have not been scrutinized.

(3) Guidelines

To commissioner Elman, case-by-case merger enforcement is "an excessively slow, expensive, clumsy, and inadequate process for resolving technical and complex issues." [8] To avoid these pitfalls, the FTC has inched into a broader attack on problems using its relatively competent economic staff. Industries rather than companies are intensively analyzed, and guidelines are issued that indicate which mergers will be carefully scrutinized by the FTC. Although the guidelines are merely advisory, the thought is that no company will make an acquisition if it thinks the FTC will probably issue a complaint. Although they do not provide a blanket exemption for mergers falling outside the standards, attention is focused on mergers from which no significant benefits can be expected. To date the Commission has issued merger guidelines for five industries: dairies, cement, food distribution, grocery-products manufacturing, and textile-mill products. All of these were promulgated in the latter half of the 1960s, after the FTC already had significant experience in attempting to litigate on a case-by-case basis in these industries. The first two industries will be considered.

DAIRIES. Since 1920 large national dairies had been acquiring their competitors at a rapid rate. In 1956 the FTC issued complaints against the four largest dairy concerns, which together had acquired several hundred dairies between 1951 and 1956. Foremost Dairies had acquired 52 dairy and other firms with combined annual sales of some $342 million. Beatrice Foods made 175 acquisitions with $147.5 million combined sales. The Commission issued its first dairy decision in 1962,[9] requiring Foremost Dairies to divest certain properties with sales in excess of $100 million. Cases involving Borden and National Dairy were settled by consent decrees, also requiring partial divestiture. The *Beatrice Foods* [10] decision in 1965 ordered some divestiture and, like all three previous orders, placed a 10-year ban on future dairy acquisitions without prior Commission approval. In addition, it attempted to establish "clear and concrete legal standards for mergers for the guidance of businessmen." [11]

The Commission actions and guidelines were not designed to stop merger activity in the industry. Technical developments have dictated an increasing scale of operations and the demise of many of the small firms. But while market and technological forces have led to a fundamental reorganization of the dairy industry, "they did not dictate the rise of vast, national, multimarket dairy enterprises," [12] according to Willard Mueller.

The guides promulgated in the *Beatrice* decision were designed for the control of market-extension mergers. Recognizing the considerable forces encouraging large-scale enterprise, the guidelines sought the preservation of *potential* competition—the maintenance of a large number of medium-sized firms capable of entering various local markets if conditions should warrant. The idea was to re-channel merger activity away from the large firms capable of "repulsing new competition in markets where they have become strongly entrenched" [13] and toward combinations of small or medium and small companies. While antitrust enforcement in the dairy industry was late in coming, since 1962, the available evidence suggests the FTC's efforts have paid off.

Between 1950 and 1955 the eight largest dairies made an average of 71 acquisitions per year. From the time the first complaint was issued in 1956 until the hearing examiners' initial decision in the *Foremost* case in December, 1960, the merger activity of the top eight slowed appreciably to 28 acquisitions per year. Since the Commission's *Foremost* decision in April, 1962, these companies averaged only five small dairy acquisitions per year. On the other hand, the number of mergers by dairies other than the top eight continued at the same relative pace throughout (totaling some 100 per year).[14]

The guidelines announced in the *Beatrice* case helped coordinate and harmonize the various Commission orders in the cases involving the four leading dairies. Yet the earlier *Foremost* decision, rather than the guidelines, seems most responsible for the Commission's success in curbing large-firm acquisitions. Furthermore, since 1965 the original *Foremost* divestiture requirements were loosened, and, as has been previously discussed, the *Beatrice* order was substantially modified in a controversial consent settlement prior to a Court of Appeals decision. *Beatrice* should have capped the Commission's dairy enforcement pattern established through its guidelines, but the unexplainable settlement of the case—what Mueller has called "a serious administrative error" to the Study Group—considerably detracts from an otherwise commendable industry enforcement strategy.

CEMENT. Between 1960 and 1967 the FTC issued 11 complaints challenging 17 ready-mix concrete acquisitions. Commission activity in the cement field represented the most extensive merger-enforcement effort ever undertaken in a single industry. Although the Commission issued complaints in 1960, 1961, 1963, and 1964, the forward integration by merger of cement into the concrete industry continued unabated. From 1965 to 1967 another seven complaints were issued.

In 1964 the Commission recognized the urgency and industry-wide nature of the merger movement. A Bureau of Economics study resulted in the 1966 staff economic report on mergers and vertical integration in the cement industry. Public hearings were subsequently held, and in January, 1967, the guidelines were released. The Commission action has apparently retarded this merger movement. In the first seven years of the 1960s cement manufacturers acquired 72 cement users, while in the three years following the issuance of the guides only 12 were acquired. Only one of these mergers conflicted with the enforcement policy statement, and it was challenged by the FTC.[15]

The Commission's enforcement policy [16] has been criticized by some as being too stringent,[17] preventing the achievement of possible economies. Willard Mueller replies: "To date, cement companies have not entered ready-mix by the internal-growth route. This suggests that there were no compelling real economies of integrated operations underlying the vertical mergers occurring in this industry." [18] This was also the conclusion of the Commission staff study and of the preponderance of industry testimony. Mueller generally believes that it is better to err on the side of a too strict rather than a too lenient antimerger policy. As Professor M. A. Adelman has stated, "Even a right decision to break up a going concern has costs; a wrong decision is much worse. But the worst that a wrong merger decision can do is to force the company to build rather than buy." [19]

The Commission's merger enforcement policy in the cement industries is regarded by many as one of its major successes. Yet it is interesting to observe the adaptability of business behavior, its remarkable ability to skirt the law. Currently, for example, unable to acquire concrete firms, some cement manufacturers are tying up ready-mixers through various financial devices, such as extending large amounts of credit on extremely liberal terms to cement purchasers, or guaranteeing ready-mixers' bank loans. There are fears that this may trigger another merger chain reaction. To achieve its purpose of preventing market foreclosure, the FTC will itself have to show a similar adaptiveness.

GUIDELINES AS AN ENFORCEMENT TOOL. Antitrust must be viewed from the perspective of competition in an industry, not on an *ad hoc* company-by-company basis. Of all the activities we examined at the FTC, the tactics used in combating concentration in the cement industry seemed the most impressive. The in-depth study, coupled with the public hearing and followed by the promulgation of guidelines, seems a definite step toward sanity in economic regulation. Unfortunately, the other guidelines did not involve public hearings, and some of them, particularly the guidelines for textile-mills products, may lack the depth of research exemplified in the cement study. (The study of the textile-mill industry was never published by the Commission.) Clear evidence, however, is lacking that the guidelines had a causal impact on the decline of mergers in the covered industries. The industries were in general under heavy litigation when the guidelines were issued, and most of them did not articulate any startling findings.

Guidelines are most useful if they come before the case-by-case adjudication begins, not after. To argue that the guidelines should be issued in industries where the FTC already is highly active is to say that the Agency should find out what it should be doing after it has already performed its task. Future mergers may be blocked, but a needless increase in concentration has probably already occurred. Guidelines would be more helpful if they went beyond the simplistic statement that a merger beyond a certain sales figure will be challenged. There should be a demarcation of gray area with the highlights of factors to be considered in challenging an acquisition—a move which would make screening of cases much easier for the staff. Additionally, guidelines should not be restricted to horizontal mergers. The FTC should explore new possible areas for their use, such as franchising or patent licensing. Finally, the procedural implementation of the guidelines must be standardized and democratized so that the industries involved and public-interest groups, as well as the government position, would be fairly represented.

(4) Rule-making

The term "rule-making" is confusing because of its myriad meanings. Here we are referring to the creation of legal precedent through general pronouncements rather than case-by-case litigation. The difference between a "guideline" and a "rule" is that a "guideline" is advisory while a "rule" is law, assuming valid promulgation. Rules have several advantages over guidelines. The Commission's guidelines merely indicate who the Commission will challenge; once that party is challenged, the guide has no precedential effect, except as embodied in prior case law. On the other hand, a "rule" is a binding principle that can streamline the detailed inquiry in case-by-case litigation. For example, if an industry guideline stipulates that no $100 million firm can acquire any firm with sales of more than $10 million, and a given acquisition violated those terms, the litigation would involve proving whether the result was anticompetitive regardless of what the guidelines said. But if the "guideline" were a "rule," the only relevant facts would be that the rule was validly promulgated and the rule was broken.

Rule-making could create "procedural" innovations. For example, a "rule" could stipulate that the 500 largest corporations must get FTC approval before any further mergers. Or, there could be a rule, in an industry which the FTC had studied, saying that any acquisition by a company with more than $50 million in sales of a company with more than $5 million in sales needs FTC approval. These "procedural" rules would be based on an analysis of the substance of the economic situation, which dictated that although not all mergers covered by these numbers should be banned, they deserve careful scrutiny. If such "rules" can be made, much of what Robert Hammond sought to accomplish in his no-divestiture decrees will be attained.

Rules could also clarify the law in fields such as price discrimination, where doctrine is *ad hoc* and ambiguous. New doctrine, of course, would be announced through case law, but, as the Supreme Court pointed out in *National Labor Relations Board* v. *Wyman-Gordon Company*,[20] rule-making sharpens both the scope and doctrine of new principles. A similar use of rules is in setting principles in an area not already replete with case law: *e.g.,* the franchising field, which is currently under study by the FTC.

Although rule-making has many advantages, the FTC's authority to issue rules is unclear. While Commissioner Elman, in the *Statement of Basis* for the 1964 trade regulation on advertising, argues that Section 6(g) of the FTC Act does give it the authority, critics disagree. They argue that 6(g)— which says that the Commission shall have the power, "to make rules and regulations for the purpose of carrying out the provisions of this Act"— is not a delegation of legislative rule-making; it only enables the Agency to make up rules for its internal administration, not those dealing with substantive doctrine.

One result of this debate has been that the FTC is reluctant to attempt new approaches in economic regulation, fearing that the courts will overturn its exercise of power. There has been no concerted attempt on the part of the Agency to build up gradual precedents leading to a general acceptance of rule-making powers. Right now the FTC finds itself in a rather peculiar situation. After trumpeting its rule-making power and hardly ever using it, a number of bills have been introduced in Congress granting the Commission rule-making power. Of course, if the FTC already has such power, the bills would be superfluous; yet if the FTC does not support them, it may be without authoritative rule-making power. The General Counsel's office made sure that the Commission had it both ways. For example, when Section 105 of Title I of S.3201 was reported out of the Senate Commerce Committee in August, 1970, the report said the bill would "make explicit the implicit authority" of the Commission to make rules.

Despite this confusion, the fact remains that an administrative agency without rule-making authority is a eunuch. What is so perplexing about the Commission's historical abstention in furthering its rule-making powers is that the process is so uniquely suited to the FTC's theoretical expertise. Formal hearings based on economic data should be the ideal process for the Commission—not the litigation route. Although some men at the FTC, now most notably General Counsel Joseph Martin, appear to understand the benefits of rule-making, their voices seem lost in the inertia of continuing to do things the way they have been done in the past. The underlying problem remains: what is the trade-off in enforcement value between general standards promulgated in rules and guidelines and specific analysis in individual litigation?

Derek Bok notes that the agonizing economic appraisal of each case may be self-defeating because delays inflicted in all cases would not be worth possible benefits in some: "In striving to be flexible we may simply be obscure . . . in seeking expertness we may only end in extravagance." [21] Donald Turner sounds a similar theme:

In theory, the ideal regulatory policy would be one that discriminated carefully on a case-by-case basis between those mergers that threaten substantial anticompetitive consequences and those that do not. In fact, it seems almost impossible to carry out any such policy and still have an effective merger statute.[22]

If the FTC evolves into a body of experts, the issue remains how that limited pool of expertise can be utilized. We think that guidelines and rule-making represent the Agency's most effective institutional approach. The argument for this approach, even recognizing its margin of individual case error, is reinforced by realizing that litigation—even with consent orders—at the FTC is an expensive process; resources are quite limited, and the impact of broader guidelines will greatly increase the impact of the Commission's dollars. Money spent on some of the small cases the Commission has litigated seems essentially wasted, when those funds could have been spent on alternative procedures for whole industries.

ECONOMISTS AND POLICY PLANNING

As an undirected, underbudgeted agency, the FTC faces serious decisions concerning its objectives and methods. The Commission could, for example, spend all its resources in the Robinson-Patman fresh fruit and vegetable field alone. Since there are many complaints here, the lawyers could work very hard, yet little of national benefit would result. Only when Agency objectives are clearly defined can rational plans for achieving them be made. Yet the FTC has never effectively defined its objectives, nor given the economist, trained to understand resource optimization, more than a minor role in any planning efforts.

Throughout the history of the Commission there have been transient "program-review councils" or offices. Under Paul Rand Dixon's Chairmanship the office was basically a box on an organization chart. Most of the staff positions were left vacant for months, and when they were filled the actual impact was minimal. The reorganized FTC has now a revamped program-review office, but again staffing is very limited. Rather than being pivotal to the FTC, it is acting as an adjunct specialist emphasizing cases which—for either political or doctrinal reasons—are particularly difficult. Yet almost every careful study of the Commission from Henderson to Nader [23] has stressed the need of establishing sensible planning procedures. Staff comments on this subject, quoted in the impressive Nicholson Report [24] of 1969, are illustrative of the sentiments the Study Group found in its interviewing:

During the six years in which I have been on the staff I cannot recall anything coming to my attention which would indicate that the Commission has defined the broad objectives of the agency in terms of policy and set priorities for such objectives.

At the present time investigations are sometimes opened because an applicant bears down and complains long enough and loudly enough. . . . If Commission priorities were more clearly formulated, it would be correspondingly simpler to tell an applicant that we do not have sufficient resources to investigate this kind of problem at the present time.

As far as I know, the Commission and the bureau division heads do not generally care which sector of the economy or which kind of substantive case the staff pays attention to first.

The fact is I have no idea what the Commission wants or expects of those in my division; and I would expect if there has been any program, or policy, for us over the past years, I would have heard about it. The only policy could be characterized as one of lie low and don't make waves, and we have done that fairly well.

These comments by staff attorneys illuminate the mammoth problems created by the FTC's failure to establish priorities. This failure is both a cause and a result of the "mailbag approach," the determining of the areas of Commission activity largely by the complaint letters arriving in the daily mail. The loudest complainers—often individual Congressmen—direct the Commission's energies. The mailbag approach also provides an incentive to stay away from the innovative or difficult case.

Over-reliance on the mailbag for case selection has been a particular problem in Robinson-Patman and Section Five enforcement. In 1962, 90% of restraint-of-trade investigations arose from random "applications for complaint." Nor has the situation improved. In 1969 Commissioner Nicholson wrote that, "declarations to the contrary notwithstanding, I know from one year's experience that we still let the mailbag plan just about all our operations." [25] Commissioner Elman agrees: "If anything, the Commission has in recent years relied even more on outside complaints instead of developing its own program, selecting those areas that are most important and should command its attention." [26]

And so the FTC is obsessed with trivia. Last things come first. A complete monopolist cannot be accused of unfair practices by competitors. In oligopolistic industries the small are understandably hesitant about lodging complaints against the industry giants, while the dominant firms tolerate their unimportant rivals and forgive their sister oligopolists, since they behave the same way. In competitive industries, however, there is usually an abundance of producers all too eager to complain of a rival's slightest transgression.

Other reasons exist for the Commission's preoccupation with trivia. The continuing pressure to present a good caseload record to the Budget Bureau and Appropriations Committees encourages quick and easy cases, which are usually insignificant. Second, it is safer to bring little actions than big ones, especially when respectable businessmen inspire the action. Third, staff quantity and quality discourage big cases, especially against wealthy and clever adversaries. Still, the principal cause of the FTC's failure to give first attention to the most serious areas of concentration remains the mailbag approach. "[T]he Federal Trade Commission operates as a kind of court handling complaints, big and little, as they come to them, and processes them as they are received." [27] That was written by a House Small Business Subcommittee in 1946, and it remains true a quarter of a century later.

As a new starting point, the Commission needs to be able to assess its own effectiveness. But the Commission, except to a small extent in the merger area, has not tried to evaluate its performance. Until such an evaluation is made and results are measured against the effort required to attain them, the FTC will drift rudderless in a wave of mergers.

Measuring input, or effort, should not be difficult. It is merely the number of hours times the value of those hours. The real problem with "input" analysis is that it is difficult to estimate before a case goes through litigation how much time it will take. After all, it could be settled, be dismissed at the hearing-examiner stage, or involve a prolonged procedural appeal. Modern statistical decision theory can solve many of these problems. First, an analysis of past results can be made. Second, estimates on the margin of error can be made and a running tabulation can be kept. In the future, analysis will be sensitive to that error factor. Third, it should be possible to effectively separate out estimated time consumed for various types and strengths of decrees. For example, a lawyer could estimate the investigation time and negotiation effort involved in getting a partial-divestiture consent order as compared to going through litigation. The probabilities of the corporate adversary accepting various types of orders could then be brought into the analysis so that strategic alternatives could be mapped out.

The real problem is computing results or output. One measure might be "consumer dollars saved." Another might be the change in the concentration ratios in an industry, with weight given to the importance of the industry. The difficulty comes when the FTC argues that it should litigate a small case for deterrence purposes, because otherwise many smaller firms feel that the government is not screening their activities. But this problem, too, can be solved, if the Commission begins to think explicitly about the value of such deterrence suits. One possible way to *begin* thinking—real thought has hardly commenced in this area, either at the Antitrust Division, where policy planning turned out to be glorified brief writing, or at the FTC—is to call a conference of economists, lawyers, and business-management theorists to articulate the problems of priority planning. A special task force of economists would then follow up on the suggestions and produce within a reasonable period of time a management system applicable to antitrust enforcement.

Whether the use of economists and policy planning will increase is far from clear. For an agency dealing largely with economic law, the FTC's Bureau of Economics is pitifully understaffed. Moreover, the economist staff needs to be greatly upgraded in quality. The May, 1971, relocation of the economists from the main FTC building, however, to a site two miles away (and without a library) races in the opposite direction. The economists will now be even more remote. The staff of the Bureau of Economics is severely demoralized by the purge, with a prominent member of the Bureau staff explaining the cause: "Mezines [the Executive Director of the FTC] just doesn't like economists or economic complexity. Hell, he could have moved Textiles and Furs out; why us?"

The conflict between the legal condemnation of monopoly and its de facto acceptance in slightly imperfect form as oligopoly is stark.

—*John Kenneth Galbraith*

13

The Broken Trust: Section Five

Section Five of the Federal Trade Commission Act forbids "unfair methods of competition"—obviously quite a flexible statutory phrase. The courts have recognized that the scope of the statute goes beyond the Sherman Act in prohibiting anticompetitive conduct. As the *Motion Picture Advertising Service* case stated, "The Federal Trade Commission Act was designed to supplement and bolster the Sherman Act and the Clayton Act . . . to stop in their incipiency acts and practices which, when full blown, would violate those Acts." [1] Section Five thus gives the Commission a unique potential for innovating new doctrine and remedies for competitive problems. This potential, however, has not been realized, and Section Five remains the FTC's great missed opportunity.

THE RECORD

Although some 25 attorneys usually work in this area, in the last five years the FTC has averaged only five case dispositions per year, the majority of which led to consent decrees. Moreover, the cases have not been directed at major problem areas in our economy. Instead the Commission in the 1960s has been content to litigate against such insignificant corporations as Topps Chewing Gum, Inc., a giant in the bubble-gum industry, and Carvel Corporation, a Northeast ice-cream retailer with some $5 million in sales.[2]

The minuscule size of the Commission's Section Five caseload must in part be blamed on poor management. The LP Gas investigation is a case in point. For three successive years the FTC proudly reported to Congress on its investigations of alleged price-fixing, attempts to monopolize, and refusals to deal by the major firms in this industry.[3] When the reorganization of the FTC occurred, the new management discovered boxes upon boxes of unopened materials concerning this investigation. The attorney in charge of the probe had left the Commission, and apparently no one was assigned to take his place. The investigation is now formally closed. Badly organized and poorly directed, thousands of man-hours were poured into it, with no results. John Ferguson, an assistant to the Director of the Bureau of Competition, called it a "tragic situation" in an interview.

The Commission officially defends its slim Section Five enforcement by emphasizing instead its increase in informal corrective measures. Such measures, however, are often not an adequate substitute for adjudication or rule-making, since informal procedures should generally be used only for minor violations. Furthermore, the Commission has virtually no idea how effective are its informal procedures, such as the Assurance of Voluntary Compliance (AVC). An AVC is a promise by a firm, not legally enforceable, not to do the complained-of act again. It is not an admission of fault and can be revoked by the Commission, although it seldom is. In issuing an AVC the Commission is supposed to consider (1) the nature and gravity of the alleged violations, (2) the prior record and good faith of the parties involved, and (3) other factors, in-

The Broken Trust: Section Five

cluding, where appropriate, adequate assurance of compliance.[4]

In the Section Five area, problems with the AVC come up clearly in conjunction with reciprocal dealings between corporations, which are illegal and which amount, according to Harry A. Garfield, an assistant director of the Bureau of Competition, to "billions of dollars per year." The FTC has not issued a formal reciprocity complaint in over three decades; the six most recent reciprocity cases were settled by AVCs. One of them involved American Standard on illegal-reciprocity charges. The AVC was issued just as American Standard was getting involved in the plumbing-fixtures price-fixing litigation. With a long list of antitrust violations, American Standard hardly has the prior good record required by the Commission's own standards for AVCs. In September, 1970, the new Kirkpatrick regime announced that it would no longer accept AVCs in reciprocity cases.

Section Five investigations arise principally from complaints, and complaints are received at the rate of some 1,000 per year. Reliance on the mailbag has a direct causal relation to the abundance of trivia in the Agency, as described in the preceding chapter. Moreover, as a random *ad hoc* method of enforcement, rewarding the persistent complainers encourages political pressure. When it becomes apparent that an agency's priorities are shaped by outside forces, such pressure becomes inevitable. For example, complaints by independent garage owners against the major auto manufacturers' distribution system for sheet-metal body parts lay dormant in the FTC until the spring of 1966, when the Independent Garage Owners Association set up a committee to lobby Congressmen to complain to the Commission. An important meeting followed with Chairman Dixon, who then ordered an eight-man whirlwind investigation; a complaint was soon filed.

Compounding the problem of a small and trivial caseload is the slowness with which Section Five actions proceed. Often enforcement takes so long that FTC intervention is meaningless. This difficulty is especially important in cases such as refusals to deal and predatory pricing, where quick FTC action is essential to preserve competition. The *Curtiss-Wright* case,[5] for example, was an alleged attempt to monopolize parts for piston-driven aircraft engines. The defendant supposedly refused to see repair parts needed for the overhaul of these engines. The case, concerning the 1960–63 actions, was brought in the summer of 1966. In 1969 the Commission dismissed it since jet engines had replaced prop planes to such an extent as to make the case inconsequential. Another situation where the market changed before the FTC was capable of acting involved rebuilt TV tubes, where the advent of color drastically diminished the demand for rebuilt black-and-whites. The *Columbia Broadcasting System* [6] case provides an example of Commission delay causing the courts to remand a case for more current evidence. The case was a complicated one on the issue of licensing agreements in the record industry; at one time or another, seven FTC attorneys were involved, and over 10,000 pages of hearings were printed. The complaint was served in 1962, the hearing examiner's opinion came in 1964, and the Commission finally decided the case in 1967. Reviewing the case in 1969, the Seventh Circuit Court found that the Section Five evidence of injury to competition was based on a *1959* investigation and remanded the case back to the Commission. On remand, the FTC finally and quickly settled the case by consent order.

KOPPERS: A CASE STUDY [7]

The *Koppers* case, a clear instance of an illegal attempt to monopolize, is described at length here because it illustrates many of the problems of Section Five enforcement: delay, political pressure, overdependence on the mailbag, and, more generally, the administrative process itself.

Pittsburgh-based Koppers Company is a diversified manufacturer of chemicals, plastics, and forest products with 1965 sales of $371 million. For 16 years Koppers had a monopoly on the manufacture of resorcinol, a synthetic chemical which has great adhesive power. Although Koppers had monopoly initially thrust upon it when the plant of its chief competitor, Heyden Company, exploded in the early 1950s, the firm managed to retain its position through highly questionable tactics. To prevent Heyden from rebuilding its plant, Koppers made a deal: Koppers packaged resorcinol in bags with Heyden's distinctive markings and used Heyden's former plant as a base for freight shipments; Heyden then sold the resorcinol to its customers at Koppers' list prices and received a reseller's discount of 10%. In 1963 Koppers stopped packaging resorcinol in Heyden bags and discontinued the use of the former Heyden plant as a basing point. Heyden's sales decreased. By 1965 Heyden was no longer considered a threat, and the seller arrangement was terminated.

Meanwhile Koppers's profits and prices boomed. In 1948 the price of resorcinol, with three producers, was 63¢ per pound. By 1954 a monopolistic Koppers had raised the price to 77.5¢ where it stayed until 1963 although costs of production decreased. Even with a reduction in price to 65.5¢ in 1964 Koppers sold $8.8 million worth of resorcinol and made monopoly profit of $4.7 million. Throughout the period a tariff of 22.9¢ per pound protected Koppers from foreign competition. By the 1960s Koppers was well entrenched in the United States and on its way toward extending that position overseas. During this period its own marketing report argued that by slashing prices in Europe 35¢–40¢ per pound it could destroy most of the competition there—a move Koppers successfully executed.

In 1964 United States Pipe & Foundry announced its intention of entering the resorcinol market. Koppers reacted swiftly. It tied up its customers with long-term requirement contracts, cut back the domestic price to 50¢ a pound, and threatened to cut prices further. U.S. Pipe complained to the FTC. The FTC did not use the complaint as a bridgehead to attacking Koppers' monopoly, but contented itself with acting as the proxy for U.S. Pipe in a personal war.

Koppers' counsel was the law firm of Howrey, Simon, Baker & Murchison, a firm with many former FTC lawyers, including several who were high in the hierarchy, most notably Former Chairman Edward Howrey. Aside from its reputed political influence, the Howrey, Simon specialty is delay. If attempts to obtain a soft consent order fail, they defend the case on procedure rather than on substance. Koppers illustrates both tactics of politics and procedure.

First, Howrey, Simon sought a consent order via personal contact. Retaining his good relations with Rufus "Duke" Wilson, the Section Five chief at the FTC, William Simon was busy drinking with Mr. Wilson at the elegant Metropolitan Club in Washington. In *Koppers,* Wilson recommended a consent order with which the staff on the case bitterly disagreed; the Commission turned down his suggested order and the litigation phase continued. Second, Simon set up *Koppers* as a due-process problem rather than a case of monopolization. In March, 1968, Howrey, Simon began asking for discovery from U.S. Pipe. Their overall tactic was to shift the focus of the case away from Koppers's action toward whether U.S. Pipe was efficient enough to compete in the resorcinol market. U.S. Pipe balked at the relevance of these requests, but the Commission supported Koppers. Since the FTC was unable to enforce its own subpoenas, the case was delayed while the discovery battle was fought in the D.C. District Court. From January 12, 1968, when the complaint was issued, until January 12, 1970, the date the formal hearings began, there were some 25 interlocutory appeals taken by all parties from the hearing examiner to the Commission.

The situation was comic. The counsel for U.S. Pipe lost control over his client and was unable to get its co-operation even in small matters. Walter Bennett, the hearing examiner in the case, was furious at the dilatory tactics of defense, and was in turn charged with bias by defense counsel. Bennett, reportedly disgusted, finally withdrew from the case, refusing to discuss the situation with us, although his anger was well known at the Agency. Dan Kane, the FTC lawyer on the case, refused to sign the consent settlement written up by his boss, Duke Wilson, because of its inadequate relief. As for the Howrey brief, he called that "wildly emotional," and complained about the "ad hominem" attacks on complaint counsel. Howrey, Simon then accused Kane of distorting the record in his presentations.

Although Koppers's request that the hearings be held in Pittsburgh, its corporate headquarters, was granted, no one from Koppers even testified. Counsel for Koppers produced no evidence whatsoever, except by way of cross-examination. The thrust of the case for the defense was lack of due process because of limited discovery and the lack of public interest. While the new hearing examiner backed these contentions, the Commission reversed and remanded that opinion.

It is now seven years since U.S. Pipe announced its intention to enter the resorcinol business, and the FTC case is far from over. But it tells a great deal about the FTC's process. At the Commission level the *Koppers* case points out the undesirable effect of undue reliance on the mailbag. As usual, the Commission's concern was with competitors and not with competition. It is significant that the Commission attacked Koppers when it cut its price to the lowest point in history, rather than in the 1950s when prices were exorbitant. Complete reliance on the mailbag leads the Commission to miss important events, such as the takeover of the European market by Koppers; the continental companies have no Congressmen to write to.

Koppers also highlights a recurrent problem—political pressure. The Koppers Company attempted to get the Secretary of Commerce to intervene on its behalf in the proceedings, claiming that FTC action would hurt the balance of payments. If Koppers were embroiled in a dispute before a district court, such an attempt would undoubtedly not have been made. Most important, *Koppers* exposes defects in the administrative process. Whatever the substantive merits of the FTC case, the litigation zoo in this case is unacceptable as a process. The trivial interlocutory appeals and the inability of the Commission to enforce its own subpoenas play into the hands of delay-minded counsel.

In antitrust, procedure often is more important than substance. A procedurally impotent agency can rarely achieve success despite the work of its staff and the availability of substantive precedents. In the final analysis, *Koppers* points more to the failure of a process than a staff, more to the failure of an agency than any individual.

THE POTENTIAL

While Section Five enforcement has been largely unproductive, the FTC has been able to document a few instances where its action was of considerable benefit to the consuming public. One example is the Seattle bread conspiracy mentioned in the opening chapter. The FTC's complaint was issued in March, 1961; its final decision was in December, 1964. One month after that date the Bureau of Labor Statistics reported that bread prices in

Seattle had begun to fall, and in April, 1965, open price competition broke out; prices ultimately dropped below the national average.[8] Section Five also broke up the tetracycline patent fraud conspiracy. Exposure of the unenforceability of the patent, plus fear of treble-damage suits, caused prices for the antibiotic to plunge from about $51 per 100 tablets to about $5, and consumers saved tens of millions of dollars per year.[9]

There have been at least two innovations in terms of Section Five remedies. In the Nashua Company assurance of voluntary compliance, for example, Nashua not only agreed to stop granting rebates to dealers who sold at a stipulated price, but also agreed to reimburse dealers who lost the rebate for past sales at other than that price; the next step, of course, is restitution to the consumer. The *L. G. Balfour* case,[10] now on appeal, is the first and only Section Five case with an order requiring divestiture. *Balfour,* however, is a somewhat different Section Five case, since it involved an *acquisition* by this dominant company in high-school and college rings. Balfour had secretly acquired its major competitor some years before (a fact which makes suspect the claims by the FTC and Antitrust Division that they detect all important mergers by simply reading the trade press and the *Wall Street Journal*).

These successes and innovations are minimal when compared with the major economic problems in our society inflicted by the parallel pricing and product behavior of oligopolistic firms. Section Five is so broadly drafted as to enable the Commission to combat virtually all "unfair methods of competition." Section Five therefore gives the Commission a unique tool, a mandate to move with the times. Despite this broad statute and the adequacy of case law, the FTC has *never* lodged a monopolization charge against a major American industry. If it is found that antitrust law is inadequate to cope with this crucial antitrust issue, then the Commission's responsibility is to determine whether new legislation is desirable. But a problem which goes unraised goes unanswered.

In an attempt to improve on this record, the Commission has in the past two years made some attempt to focus on industries and business practices where action is most warranted. Aside from the cereal investigation to be discussed later, the Commission has, for example, instituted a plan to study important, highly concentrated industries such as drugs, automobiles, and steel. In its budget request for fiscal year 1971 the Commission stated:

> The existence of discretionary market power in the hands of a few industry leaders sufficient to control and administer prices and the extent of production is a matter of serious antitrust concern. Additionally, product differentiation, and other means by which barriers are raised against the entry of new competition, are being examined, looking to the possibility of corrective action under the existing statutes. . . . Further definition of the law, particularly the reaches of Section Five of the FTC Act, is anticipated in the Bureau's planning.[12]

Unfortunately, there is some question about the Commission's complete commitment in this effort to become a more relevant agency. Chairman Weinberger, when asked about "further definitions of the law," responded: "I think it is more or less in . . . the possibility of reaching anti-competitive activity by defining it as a deceptive practice."[13] At least the Chairman of the Commission, then, did not seem to be thinking of extending Section Five to reach important hard-core areas of oligopoly/monopoly. Further, the Commission, instead of increasing the staff of the Industrial Analysis group in the Bureau of Economics, had frozen their numbers at a very low level, approximately 22; reportedly, at the April, 1971, closed-door budget hearings on Capitol Hill, there were requests for about four more economists here. Considering the other work piled on the economists by the Commission, such as the conglomerate-merger study, it was predictable that by the end of the 1970 summer the heralded concentrated-industry studies would not have begun. Only in the drug industry had even the most preliminary research been accomplished. By April, 1971, the studies had progressed only slightly, although the new head of the Bureau, Michael Mann, seemed eager to push them along. And in May, 1971, the Commission finally announced it was beginning its study of concentration in the energy field—a promising development, if the study is followed through.

Undoubtedly a major impetus for the announced reordering of priorities has been the economic literature and analysis that have finally crept into the Section Five area of the Commission. This awareness by a number of attorneys has led to a visible split within the FTC concerning the proper approach to antitrust enforcement. The "structuralists" emphasize the documented connection between market structure and economic performance, and argue that the market structure of an industry—the concentration, degree of product differentiation, and entry barriers— must often be changed if marked improvements are to be noted in terms of price, progressiveness, or product quality. The structuralists thus seek to focus attention on those large oligopolistic industries where economists have indicated that performance is clearly inadequate. On the other hand, the old conservative core of the division favors the traditional "conduct" approach to antitrust. Like most lawyers, they think primarily in terms of behavior, harm, investigation, and remedy, essentially believing that prevention of clearly illegal business practices can lead to acceptable performance levels.

The dangers of a narrow, conduct-oriented approach are evident in the following example. In the Minneapolis–St. Paul milk market, competition reigns. There are a large number of firms with none clearly dominant. There is a real threat of vertical integration into milk processing by the larger grocery chains. Justice Department antitrust action in the 1950s dissolved interlocking directorates and trade associations here, a move which has discouraged price leadership and coordination in this market. Prices are very flexible and responsive to movement in raw-milk prices; they are also low. In Duluth-Superior, on the other hand, three firms sell over 90% of the area's milk; all recognize their mutual interdependence. Because this market is smaller, the threat of vertical integration by major grocery chains is much lower. Prices here are less responsive, the producers' margin is much higher, and prices are some 30% more.

A local statute, the Minnesota Dairy Industry Unfair Trade Practices Act of 1957, defines some 17 unfair practices. In the competitive Minneapolis–St. Paul market, all 17, including price discrimination, loans to customers, advertising allowances, free labor, secret rebates, and sales below cost, were found to exist. In the oligopolistic Duluth-Superior market, however, none of the 17 "unfair practices" was anywhere in evidence. The firms engaged neither in price nor in nonprice competition. A conduct-dominated approach to antitrust in the milk market would, with disastrous results, focus on the competitive market while ignoring the oligopolistic one nearby.[13]

The connection between market structure and economic performance has been long understood by economists, and offers vast potential for Section Five activity. One industry where market structure has led to an unacceptable level of market performance, and where the FTC is presently investigating, is the breakfast-cereals industry. Six producers account for 97% of the $650 million yearly sales of the ready-to-eat cereals; the three largest (Kellogg, General Mills, and General Foods) comprise over 82% of the market. Massive advertising, product differentiation, and product proliferation have raised entry barriers, permitting an excessive 20% rate of return on investment. Expenditures on advertising, often appealing to youngsters and containing virtually no informational content, amounted to 15% of sales, compared with 5% for all food products. FTC experts indicate that restoration of effective competition in the industry could lower cereal prices some 20%, with annual savings to consumers of close to $150 million.

Despite the publicity the FTC has given the investigation, there is great doubt whether the remedy chosen will set a meaningful pattern for other oligopolistic situations. The cereals case has become a symbol of the split between the structural and purely conduct-oriented approaches to antitrust enforcement. Only in the spring of 1971, with the investigation well under way, did the Commission assign a full-time economist to the case. The attorney who inaugurated and developed the cereals case, Charles Mueller, was removed from the case by Basil Mezines. The staff interpreted the transfer as the Commission's not-so-subtle way of rewarding innovative thinking.

To have any real effect on the industry, a cereals case must be a sophisticated shared-monopoly case, with a remedy of divestiture. Yet except for the *Balfour* case, which involved a recent acquisition, Section Five has never been used to break up a monopoly or shared monopoly. Also significant in this industry is the staff consideration to limit excessive advertising by showing it to be an "unfair trade practice." Excessive advertising in the cereals industry, and others such as tobacco, soap, and cosmetics, raises

entry barriers and raises prices also—without adding information or improving product quality. It seems quite appropriate for the Commission to regard excessive advertising
by the dominant firms in concentrated industries as an
unfair method of competition. The Courts have clearly
established, in such cases as *Alcoa* and *United Shoe,* that
business practices which are "honestly industrial" in competitive industries may nonetheless be illegal when used
by corporations with substantial market power. Moreover,
Judges Hand and Wyzanski were discussing Section 2
violations of the Sherman Act; the FTC's own Section Five
at once encompasses Sherman violations and goes further.

A related method by which concentrated industries raise
entry barriers and thus limit competition, while at the same
time providing little real benefit, is the steady turnover in
practically identical brands. The cereal industry provides
a fair example of this practice, while the case of the auto
industry can be considered classic. The yearly restyling by
the domestic auto companies, for example, adds about
$195 in tooling costs per new car, and two to three times
that amount at retail,[14] while bringing little real product
improvement.[15] More important, it raises the entry costs
to potential new firms, who must not only have a superior
product in the initial year, but may feel compelled to
spend the enormous cost of retooling and advertising each
year to match the "new" products of the domestic rivals.
On April 16, 1971, Ralph Nader and the editors of the
Yale Law Journal petitioned Miles Kirkpatrick to launch
an FTC study of the automobile annual style change as
an unfair method of competition under Section Five of the
FTC Act. An internal FTC memorandum in June, 1971,
from the Director of the Bureau of Competition, rejected
this request, considering annual restyling merely a symp-
tom of (and not the cause of) the oligopolistic nature of
the industry. But the request may have an unintended
spinoff. After dismissing the purpose of the request, the
memo spent 34 pages urging that the FTC bring Section
Five cases to decentralize some of our worst shared monopolies.

Surely, a "first-of-its-kind" challenge to oligopoly presents
a "difficult and complex antitrust question" uniquely appropriate to the Commission's talents. The oligopoly problem is,
perhaps beyond question, the most important issue to which
the Commission could address its efforts. . . .

If incipient practices can be reached, there is no reason why more mature non-competitive forms such as oligopolies themselves, demonstrably non-competitive, could not be attacked under Section 5. .. . . An analogy, though approximate, would be a penal code proscribing attempts but not consummated crimes.

The paper, by its analysis and its aim, stands as a model of what the FTC was intended to be and of what—depending on how such suggestions are received—it may yet become.

14

Robinson-Patman Roulette

THE ACT

What can you say about a 35-year-old law that is dying? That it has outlived its purpose, if it ever had one? That it reduces competition in the name of competitors; that it consumes a third of the Agency's budget, yet resulted in *one* litigated case in 1969? All three. Yet the Robinson-Patman Act is as much a part of the antitrust scene as the Sherman and Clayton Acts.

Why? Along with apple pie, Mom, and flag decals, small businessmen inspire national respect. These "noble savages" of the business community are supposed to possess much of the virtue and independence of the American entrepreneur. Aside from being so highly regarded, they also have political clout. Upset at the growth of large chain firms in the Thirties, which could underprice low-volume stores, small businessmen managed to get the 1936 Robin-

son-Patman Act passed. It was an amendment to the Clayton Act, making discriminations in price and other practices
unlawful [1] and designed to afford "protection against these
practices to *individual competitors* at all levels of competition to preserve competition generally and protect small
business in particular." [2] The Act contains six sections
dealing with unlawful practices plus a rarely enforced
criminal section:

—2(a) prohibits price discrimination which injures compe-
        tition;
—2(b) allows a defense of meeting competitor's prices;
—2(c) prohibits the seller paying the brokerage fee for the
        buyer;
—2(d) prohibits discriminatory promotional grants by the
        seller to a buyer;
—2(e) requires similar terms for promotional services to
        all customers;
—2(f) prohibits a buyer from knowingly inducing or re-
        ceiving a discriminatory price;
—3   [the criminal section] prohibits predatory pricing and
        price discrimination for the purpose of destroying
        competition.

If discussion could kill, the Robinson-Patman Act would
have been dead years ago. Joseph Sheehy of the FTC began
a 1966 talk before the antitrust section of the American
Bar Association as follows: "This morning we find our-
selves again discussing the Robinson-Patman Amendment
to the Clayton Act. It's been discussed and cussed for thirty
years. I doubt that any piece of legislation, unless possibly
the prohibition laws, has stimulated so much oral and
written comment." [3] And the last speaker that morning
noted: "Anyone approaching this statute shared the difficulty of a mosquito in a nudist camp; the field is vast, and
one is not quite sure where to begin." [4] So much discussion
reflects the fact that the Act is notoriously unclear. "Given
its purpose of protecting a special class of businessmen
from the rigors of price competition," Louis Kohlmeier
of the *Wall Street Journal* has written, "the Robinson-
Patman Act . . . could not have been a model of clarity.
It was not and still is not." [5] The text has proven painfully
obscure to the businessmen, lawyers, and judges who strain
to decipher it.

Although the purpose of the Act was to protect small

businessmen, it has been used more often against them. The Act has consistently been invoked in competitive (food, apparel, publications, etc.) rather than noncompetitive industries. From 1936 to 1963, Section 2(c), the brokerage section, was used against only 10 major firms out of a total of 344 2(c) complaints.[7] The R-P Act was aimed at the power buyer to help small sellers, but from 1937 to 1969 a total of only 28 orders under 2(f), the inducing discrimination section, were issued by the Commission.

Robinson-Patman has been criticized for three other reasons. First, it attacks the symptoms, not the causes, of antitrust problems. Since "some degree of market power is always necessary for a firm to practice price discrimination,"[8] according to Kaysen and Turner, price discrimination is more often a result of market power than a cause of it. Second, R-P enforcement can raise or rigidify prices by making it legally hazardous for a seller to vary his price. And third, the Act can disrupt distribution methods; according to the Neal Report (President Johnson's Task Force on Antitrust):

> By discouraging sellers from passing on cost savings to buyers, [the Robinson-Patman Act] has impaired experimentation with possibly more efficient methods of distribution integrating wholesale and retail function; by requiring proportionally equal treatment in certain promotional practices, it has discouraged experimentation with price-cutting methods which are equivalent to desirable types of price differentials; by prohibiting sellers from paying brokerage to customers of their agents, it has erected an artificial protective barrier around independent brokers and inhibited integration of brokerage functions.[9]

The proponents of Robinson-Patman—such groups as retail druggists, retail grocers, and National Farmers Union —tend to ignore the critics, successfully relying on the inertia of Congress to preserve the Act. Whatever their numbers, the arguments offered by R-P partisans are hardly overwhelming. The members of the House Small Business Committee, through their general counsel, defend the Act as follows: "If somebody had shown a little more concern for Hudson, if someone had shown a little more concern for Pierce Arrow, if someone had shown a little more concern for Packard, would we today just have the Big Three? Obviously not."[10] By nurturing small firms, advocates of

R-P continue, potential competitors in product markets are developed. Essentially, even if the Act does bend to protect "inefficient" firms, in the long run that nurturing process will result in increased competition. A variation on this theme is that, regardless of efficiency, small firms are worth preserving for their social value. A nation of entrepreneurs running their own businesses is preferable to giant industrial complexes, even if the consumer must pay a higher price.

Robert Brooks, one of the few professors of law who are also proponents of the Robinson-Patman Act, has studied the litigated Section 2(a) cases from 1936 to 1969, dividing them into three categories. The first category contains cases where, but for R-P enforcement, there would have been true injury to competition; the second category contains those cases where competition would not have suffered; and the third group is made up of cases whose effects are unclear.

	Cases	Valid Basis	Invalid Basis	"Type III"
1936 to 6/30/58	51	21	12	18
1/1/62 to mid–69	22	4	0	18

Professor Brooks concludes: "[T]his is not a picture of myopic roughshod enforcement where there is no awareness of the possibility that price differences may not be hurtful, or may even be helpful to competition. . . ."

Yet Brooks seems more of an apologist of the Robinson-Patman Act than a proponent. His chart applies only to Section 2(a), the R-P section least frequently attacked, and it applies only to litigated cases—73 out of approximately 2,000 investigations of Section 2(a) violations since 1934.

While the arguments continue, one theme runs throughout the R-P literature: observers cannot really *document* its harmful or beneficial effects. Due partly to haphazard enforcement of the Act, the difficulty of documentation is mainly attributable to Commission failure to review and analyze the effects of R-P on competition in the American economy. Practically every study on the antitrust laws and on the FTC in the last 15 years has stated that the Act must be reevaluated and reformed. The Attorney General's Report on the antitrust laws in 1955, the ABA report on the Federal Trade Commission of 1969, and the Johnson and Nixon antitrust task forces—all have urged the study and revision of Robinson-Patman law. Equally monotonous and liturgical has been the response of FTC chairmen during the last 10 years, all of whom have publicly declared that R-P should be studied by the Commission. Despite all the pronouncements, the FTC has never conducted a thorough study of the Act. After some young lawyers at the FTC criticized R-P enforcement in a memorandum that leaked to the press, pressure built up for a study in 1970. But a prominent Weinberger aide described to the Study Group the aborted attempt which followed:

> That study was never destined to get off the ground. There were some suggestions for an outside study, but the Commission members wanted a patsy. They knew what the economists or the ABA types like Rowe would say. MacIntyre suggested Sherman Hill, who was a good staff-director type if he weren't so old. Weinberger was pleased because it was so easy a solution to a hell of a problem. Then after two weeks Hill said that he couldn't do the study. He thought he could do all the work away from Washington, but found that he could not. [Other FTC sources cited the lack of an adequate staff and budget as the prime factors.] Hill wrote a letter resigning, and Weinberger was furious. But for now the study is dead.

As criticism about the FTC's role in R-P enforcement continued to mount, the House Committee on Small Business appointed a subcommittee to hold hearings on the subject. Its Chairman is Joe L. Evins of Tennessee, a fervent R-P supporter who has also been the Chairman of the House Appropriations Subcommittee on Independent Offices. The connection between his two positions has always been historically clear to FTC enforcers: if the Commission wanted generous funding, R-P enforcement was mandatory. The three volumes of testimony and documentation resulting from the Small Business Committee's hearings in 1969 and 1970 merely reaffirm the general confusion about the role of R-P: strong feelings, little data, and substantial vested interests. The Subcommittee, however, did denounce critics for their "theoretical" premises, which supposedly lacked a sense of the realities of business:

> The subcommittee finds that the most recurring of all these premises is the economic assumption that price discrimination is generally procompetitive and only exceptionally anticom-

petitive. Legislative and judicial history concretely show that both Congress and the courts have found the opposite to be true. . . . The subcommittee finds that the existing evidence and cases support the Robinson-Patman Act, and that the burden of persuasion is on the critics to develop hard evidence to support their denunciation of the Act.

Yet the Subcommittee itself and the FTC, for all their resources, did not themselves have the evidence to support the supposed benefits of the Act. Instead, they asked their opponents to bring in data they should have been collecting. The Subcommittee rejected the economists' analysis of the situation because it was too "hypothetical"; "realistic" information was substituted to offset criticisms based on theory. Not surprisingly, the Subcommittee recommended a study. The study was premised on the assumption that the research project promised by Chairman Weinberger was already under way. But, as previously explained, it was not.

In November, 1970, the Committee reaffirmed its interest in the non-existent R-P report. And the FTC, now under Miles Kirkpatrick, has finally begun to inch toward action. Again, an in-house study was the method of inquiry adopted. But problems arose. The new director of the Bureau of Economics, Michael Mann, explained to the Commission that he thought the valuable economic resources of the Agency could be better used by studying oligopoly than by mulling over old R-P orders. By March, 1971, a "protocol" of the study was prepared which mapped out the key areas of interest. Finally, in late May, 1971, the Commission announced that it would study 24 R-P orders since 1960 taken randomly from various industries. Unfortunately, this approach focuses on the individual order rather than the economic context of the industry as a whole. And regardless of its findings, the study will undoubtedly trigger accusations of bias because it is an in-house study which is being sent to a Congressional committee strongly in favor of the Act.

R-P CASE ILLUSTRATIONS

1. AMC: 23 Years = 0

In 1945 the FTC issued an order to Associated Merchandise Corporation (AMC), barring it from continuing to solicit and receive from manufacturers preferential quantity discounts and rebates in violation of the Robinson-Patman Act. In 1949 the Commission received information that AMC was violating that order, and investigated. Nineteen years later, while the case was still in negotiation, the defendants offered to settle. The Commission was so deadlocked on the Act's enforcement philosophy that the Commission decided, rather than litigate or settle the case, to drop it. It did so on the condition that none of the Commissioners would file a dissent—which was to avoid public embarrassment. To reach this end, the FTC had expended some 22,000 man-hours. The case is a paradigm of R-P enforcement, which has been controversial, confused, and wasteful.

2. The Case of the Dominant Toothpick Manufacturer

In the late 1950s Forster Manufacturing Company was the dominant American seller of woodenware products like toothpicks, clothespins, eating utensils, ice-cream sticks, and skewers. Forster was more than a tough competitor; it was a monopolist and enjoyed punishing its rivals. In 1956 Forster told its chief competitor in the skewer industry, Farmington Dowel, to give up its distributors of skewers. When Farmington refused, Forster lowered its prices on skewers and drove Farmington out of business. The Commission, notified by the rapidly sinking Farmington, attempted to rescue it by a Robinson-Patman suit against Forster.

The Commission is rather tenacious when one of its constituents is actually driven out of business. It issued an R-P complaint against Forster (a) alleging a price discrimination in the sale of wooden spoons to Sealtest and Pet, (b) alleging a price discrimination in the sale of skewers to Armour & Company, and (c) attacking a special promotional sale on clothespins in Philadelphia. Forster argued that the lower prices were cost justified, and that the special deal on clothespins was an attempt to meet competition in Philadelphia. The full Commission heard the case in 1962, deciding that Forster's discriminatory practices violated the R-P Act. Forster appealed to the First Circuit Court of Appeals, which reversed the FTC's holding and remanded the case for a reconsideration of Forster's defenses.[11] On remand, the Commission held, now in more legalistic language, that Forster had violated R-P. Forster again appealed. This time the First Circuit begrudgingly upheld the Commission's opinion, but still attacked the FTC for "blackening an opponent by general accusations that one fails to support. It is particularly inappropriate for this to be done by an agency of the government." [12]

About seven years were spent investigating and litigating *Forster Manufacturing Co., Inc.* The total amount of resources spent is unknown; the total effect was nugatory. The Commission issued an unintelligible order against future price discriminations by Forster, which in effect merely says that the Robinson-Patman Act should be followed. But the case raises some questions about Commission enforcement of the Act. First, although *Forster* is a clear example of predatory pricing, Robinson-Patman was barely able to attack it. Second, *Forster* presents a simple case of successful monopolization. It had a lion's share (70%) of the skewer market, and it intended to, and did, destroy its strongest (22%) competitor. *Forster* would have been far simpler to try, and far more amenable to relief, under Section Five of the Federal Trade Commission Act. By the use of R-P, however, the First Circuit Court was clearly unnerved: "These facts are complex; they are embodied in numerous exhibits consisting of orders, vouchers and the like. . . ." [13] Third, *Forster* points out the use of R-P against a seller, when power buyers obviously induced the lower prices they received. In a letter to Forster by Armour & Company, Armour stated: "competition is becoming very keen and in view of interesting offers made by your competition, we feel that the volume of orders from Armour & Company will be considerably reduced." [14] Immediately thereafter Forster lowered its price to Armour & Company. Finally, one must ask: is this the kind of case a government agency, with a limited amount of resources, should undertake? While there may be those who love toothpicks and ice-cream spoons, protection of the woodenware industry requires the channeling of resources away from more important industries.

3. Toilets

The plumbing-fixtures industry had been fixing prices since 1926, with two major interruptions. The first was a result of an antitrust suit in 1940; the second occurred in 1957, when business was so bad that the conspirators could not keep together. When competition broke out in 1957, Universal Rundle began discriminating in price; so the FTC issued an order for them to cease and desist from such practices.[15] The FTC was totally unaware of the price-fix before 1957 and the one after 1961. It is revealing, however, that during the only time of actual competition in the plumbing-fixtures industry, the FTC attacked with R-P.

Prices from 1957 to 1961 in the plumbing-fixtures industry were markedly lower than after 1961. Preconspiracy toilets sold for $11–$13; the postconspiracy fixed price was $17. The preconspiracy differential between white and colored toilets was 10%; after the fix the differential was 25%. But the FTC does no price follow-up on its orders, so that the increase would pass unnoticed. And since the Commission thinks in terms of price cuts rather than price increases, the rise in prices, even if detected, would not alarm the FTC.

4. Auto Parts: The Pyrrhic Victory

The auto-parts market is a $6 billion industry which the antitrust agencies have been contending with for the past 35 years; indeed, auto parts seem to have consumed about one-third of the R-P budget over the last 20 years. Highly concentrated at the manufacturers' level and representing a significant consumer expenditure, the industry was ripe for FTC concern. Unfortunately, the FTC did not know what it was doing.

The harm created by some of the Agency's orders is clearly shown in the ignition-parts submarket. General Motors, the dominant supplier, has long controlled about half the market; Electric Auto-Lite has been its principal competitor. In the Forties and Fifties smaller suppliers entered the market, trying to attract new customers by offering lower prices than those given to other clients. The FTC jumped on this form of "price discrimination," charging 2(a) violations in its complaint. So in the 1950s we have the bewildering situation of the FTC successfully protecting General Motors against such evil predators as C. E. Neihoff, Guaranteed Parts, and P. Sorenson, each with a market share ranging from 1% to 5%.

Robinson-Patman at the same time was preventing the

smaller businessmen in the industry from achieving an efficient distribution system. Steven Nelson, now an FTC staff economist, argued in his doctoral dissertation that if the FTC had not attacked buying groups formed by small businessmen, there would have been both "increased competition among manufacturers and lower prices charged. . . ." [16] Yet, curiously, while R-P litigation was unfolding here, little was done about structural problems in the auto-parts industry. The irony of auto-parts enforcement is that R-P, heralded as the protector of the small businessman, has at best been ineffective in helping him and at worst has helped maintain the dominant position of the large corporations.

Meanwhile, Basil Mezines, executive director of the FTC, articulated the Commission's position on Robinson-Patman enforcement in general quite clearly: "There will be no moratorium on enforcement of this Act pending completion of the studies." So the Commission will again start bringing wasteful, ineffective, and sometimes harmful suits, when its highest officials privately admit that they do not know the impact of their actions. Considering that it took more than a year for the "protocol" of the R-P study to be hammered out, it appears that the wait for the results could be a long one.

THE IMPACT OF R-P ON THE FTC

Whether and how to enforce R-P has been a controversial topic at the Commission for the last 10 years. Certainly the difference in attitude toward the Act has to a large degree caused the bitter split between Elman and Dixon. To MacIntyre and Dixon the Act is sacrosanct. "I think it compares favorably with the Magna Carta or the Sherman Act," Dixon said of it in a 1969 speech. Commissioner Elman disagrees:

if the Commission really agrees with me as it sometimes says it does, that antitrust enforcement should focus on market structure rather than conduct, why does it have 46 people in the Division of Discriminatory Practices—most of them investigating trivial violations of the Robinson-Patman Act, investigations many of which will eventually be closed for lack of evidence, staleness or lack of public interest—and only 35 in the Division of Mergers which is attempting to deal with the current merger wave? [18]

Former Commissioner Nicholson, in hearings before the
Senate, said, "It seems to me that the Robinson-Patman
Act has a significant role to play in the body of antitrust
laws, but I do not think that the mechanical directions that
the Commission has taken, without considering whether in
a particular case there has been real damage to competition, is the proper direction." [19] Former Commissioner
Reilly, when asked about R-P in an interview, said simply:
"I think it is worthless."

The staff is also split on the importance and effectiveness
of the Act. Lack of direction at the top has caused inertia
to set in in Robinson-Patman enforcement. Two hundred
and twenty-one complaints were issued in 1963; six were
issued in 1967, eight in 1968, and nine in 1969. Most of
these are settled by consent orders; in 1969, as noted,
only *one* final R-P order was litigated.

Before the reorganization, the despair among the R-P
staff was deep. Greg Potvin, former Counsel to the Special
Subcommittee on Small Business and the Robinson-Patman
Act, pointed out in his hearings that the R-P staff had "just
the highest degree of discouragement, that morale had
really reached abysmal depths. They felt that they were
floundering about, and more importantly, perhaps, that
they were being rejected by those they sought to serve."
Basil Mezines, a former R-P attorney, and Lewis Parker
seem to be among the few lawyers in the R-P division who
were doing work. Mezines's interest in enforcement, however, has come under frequent criticism from other staffers.
"Hell, all the cases he tried were in California or in
Florida," one said; "he'd just jump on a case if it was from
there." Mezines admits this geographical bias, but points
out, "At least, I was trying cases." In fact, there were two
basic strategies among most R-P people. Either you litigated easy *per se* violations in Florida to win kudos, or
you simply slacked off. Doing nothing never hurt.

A partisan of Robinson-Patman, such as the House Subcommittee, is undoubtedly bitter that so little litigation has
emanated from the Commission. From the consumer's perspective, there is an obvious waste of funds on R-P, given
other, more productive uses. Thus, regardless of one's
views of R-P, the Commission's enforcement pattern over
the past 10 years gives grounds for complaint. A few, from
the "consumer" perspective, follow: First, despite the pro-

testations of the Act's supporters, there is little evidence to suggest that the consumer benefits, and much to say he does not, from literal enforcement of the statute. It is true that historically the Act has given the FTC a recognized constituency, the small businessman. This in itself has misdirected the Commission away from the man who is to benefit most from competition and a free enterprise economy—the consumer. By focusing on price cuts rather than price rises, the Commission has favored the welfare of a small class of businessmen. The behavioralists at the Commission are so concerned about predatory pricing that they can only think of stabilizing prices, which benefits no one but the most inefficient firms. And there is very little question at the FTC that R-P enforcement has stabilized prices in the retail petroleum industry, the garment industry, and to some degree in the citrus industry.

Second, by forcing it to rely on complaints prior to investigation, R-P has misdirected the Commission away from monopoly aspects of the American economy. The Koppers Company had a monopoly on resorcinol for 16 years, but only after a new competitor complained about being undercut did the Commission investigate Koppers, and then not for its monopoly prices but for its price cuts. Who is going to complain to the FTC in the automobile industry, the steel industry, or the tobacco industry?

Third, the statute is so complicated that businessmen can be caught in its intricacies unintentionally, even with the advice of counsel, to the delight of the Robinson-Patman personnel at the Commission. As Frank Mayer, former head of the Bureau of Discriminatory Practices and "Mr. R-P" at the Commission, said to the Study Group:

> Big Corporations have sophisticated house counsel who spend probably 40 percent of their time on Robinson-Patman work. You know why? Because of all the grey areas. No one really knows, unless you set it up in the market place, whether you can give a customer a better deal than another. That's the exciting part of Robinson-Patman work.

Fourth, the Act has fostered in the Commission a narrow, legalistic approach to antitrust. For lawyers who think in terms of behavior, individual blame, and remedy, Robinson-Patman is a gold mine. Not only does it pinpoint the behavior and the "harm" to a particular competitor, it even aids the less energetic FTC enforcer by placing the burden of proof on the defendant. By fostering the legalistic outlook on antitrust matters, R-P has turned the Commission away from its original goal—to be expert in the field of antitrust, to be innovative and original—toward its present role as an enforcer of triviality and irrelevancies.

R-P, therefore, has taken the Commission as far away from its goal as possible. Originally created with 30 economists and 80 lawyers, the Commission has become an enforcement agency with 470 lawyers and 46 economists. In the past, with one full section devoted to R-P, as well as half of the compliance section, three-fourths of the accounting section, and a substantial amount of fieldwork time, the Commission has forsaken its goal of expertise for a statute of questionable value. In the process, the Commission has lost its direction and its ability to plan policy; it has succumbed to the mailbag. It has been split from the inside and attacked from without for its lack of direction, haphazard enforcement, and confusing decisions. All of this for a constituency that is vocal and organized— the small businessman—and to the detriment of a constituency that is not—the consumer.

The costs inflicted by R-P enforcement on the FTC was perhaps best summed up in an internal memorandum by two Commissioners:

A substantial amount of solid, empirical data is readily available on the effects of mergers, price fixing, exclusive dealing, high concentration, high entry barriers, high degrees of product differentiation, excessive advertising and other types of vertical and horizontal restraints. When the researcher turns to price discrimination, however, there is virtually no data available. The unmistakable inference, unfortunately, is that this dearth of research on price discrimination reflects a substantial consensus in the scholarly community that any such effort would be unproductive, i.e., that the potential gains to be realized from even the most rationally-conceived antidiscrimination program would be more than offset by the cost of devising and administering it. The largest of these costs, of course, is what the economist calls the "opportunity cost"; a thousand man-hours spent on a Robinson-Patman Act case necessarily means, given a fixed budget, a thousand man-hours withdrawn from an enticingly high-yield case in one of the three areas known to be most productive, namely, merger, price fixing, and deconcentration cases.

THE FUTURE OF ROBINSON-PATMAN

What solution is there for the R-P dilemma? As described subsequently, Weinberger's reorganization merged the R-P division into a general Bureau of Competition. Thus, there will be fewer lawyers who do only R-P work. While the projection is that fewer man-hours will be spent on its enforcement, the policy dilemma still remains.

Full enforcement as desired by the Congressmen on the Small Business Committee is impossible. It would not only require the Commission to monitor the prices of every business in the country, but would also drain all of the FTC's resources. Furthermore, literal enforcement of the law might very well bring about anticompetitive results that other programs at the FTC and Antitrust Division are combating.

The opposite alternative would repeal the Act or not enforce it at all. The basic argument here, aside from all the costs of enforcement described above, is that any anticompetitive activities could be attacked by means of Section Five of the FTC Act ("unfair practices") or Section 2 of the Sherman Act ("attempt to monopolize"). If there is predatory pricing or unfair discrimination in price, it would still be illegal. After digesting thousands of pages which explain the complexities of the Act, and exploring the distorting effect of R-P on the Commission, this idea seems at first attractive. The problem is that the competitive harms the Act was designed to cover are real and the burden of proof in Section Five litigation, showing in Court an actual injury to competition, may make enforcement difficult and expensive. At this point the alternative of Section Five enforcement should be attempted in some trial cases to assess whether it can be substituted for R-P.

The third alternative, which we for the time being endorse, is to make an attempt at rational enforcement. Here too there are basic alternatives. The Commission could receive complaints very much as it does now, but agree .to enforce them after doing some preliminary economic analysis of the situation. Or the Commission could completely abandon the mailbag philosophy of enforcement, making R-P an available tool if prior economic analysis revealed a substantial competitive problem in the industry. The difference is whether the Commission should proceed inductively or deductively in enforcing the Act. Should R-P spring an economic investigation, or should an economic investigation bring about the possible use of R-P? We opt for integrating R-P into general antitrust enforcement as just another device in the arsenal of procedural remedies which may, or may not, be useful. Its controversial *per se* sections would therefore be used only in cases where there is deemed to be an anticompetitive effect but proof of it in court would either be difficult or too expensive.

We believe that rational antitrust enforcement must begin with economic analysis, not with the motivation to enforce certain statutory sections. Data must be accumulated industry-wide, not on the isolated actions of any individual firms. To have the FTC oriented toward prosecuting R-P for R-P's sake would negate this vision of the Agency. Furthermore, if R-P is of value, the Department of Justice should be enforcing it also. But historically, as a former Director of Operations at the Antitrust Division explained in an interview, "Robinson-Patman was felt to be incompatible with the purpose of the Sherman Act." The problem, however, with our suggestion is that it assumes the ability to use wisely discretionary power. In the past, the record of the FTC has not supported this assumption. If this tendency of blind enforcement continues, then the Robinson-Patman Act should be repealed.

A program whose basic thesis is not that the system of free private enterprise has failed . . . but that it has not yet been tried.

> —*President Franklin D. Roosevelt,*
> *Message on Concentration of*
> *Economic Power, 1938*

15

Looking Forward

ENTER AND EXIT CASPAR WEINBERGER

In response to the criticisms by the ABA Report, President Nixon chose Caspar Weinberger—California Finance Director under Ronald Reagan and a moderate Republican —as the man to invigorate the FTC. Weinberger spent much of his brief six months in office consulting with the White House on matters other than the Commission, a versatility rewarded by his appointment as the number-two man in the Office of Management and Budget (OMB). But he did manage to lay the groundwork for change while at the FTC. In a letter to Senator Edward Kennedy, Weinberger outlined what he considered his greatest accomplishments: (1) improving internal procedures through a reorganization which speeded up the review process and created more effective policy planning; (2) creating more contact between the Commission and the public; (3) more probing of the "frontiers of our statutes." [1]

Looking at the statistical record, however, the months Weinberger was in office were unproductive. Even including the whole fiscal year 1970, only one complaint was docketed in general trade restraints, four in mergers, and seven in discriminatory practices. But in order to clear the FTC for more effective action, the cost of some slowdown, although not as severe as actually occurred, probably had to be tolerated.

As a basic component of his "reorganization" plans, Weinberger ended the formal divisional breakdown by statutory responsibility. There are no longer separate Robinson-Patman, Section 7, or Section Five divisions. But the assistant directors of the present Bureau of Competition each still specializes in a given statutory area. Although these directors and the older staff continue to do the same kind of work, there is wider exposure for the younger staff, who can work in more than one area at the same time. The fact that Weinberger not only consulted with the younger staff in making the changes, but also tried to integrate their suggestions in his proposals, boosted morale, although the staff was understandably suspicious:

They stuck a pitchfork in a pile of manure and gave it a flip.

Great.

You just have to realize that all these reports and reorganizations coincide with changeovers in Administrations. And when the new lines are drawn, the old division chiefs of the other political party drop out.

It's a way of satisfying the Civil Service Commission so that staff people can be appointed who agree with the Chairman.

Makes it look like something's happening.

In one respect, the reorganization was extremely shrewd. Given the unproductive Robinson-Patman division, the quickest way to change the pace was to eliminate it. As Basil Mezines, Executive Director of the FTC, indicated, "The R-P statistics are so bad, we'll do better with less manpower. We might even triple, well, not triple, but we'll do better." Unfortunately, but perhaps inevitably, the Weinberger administration treated the R-P Act as gently as possible to avoid a confrontation with its staunch loyalists in Congress. Rather than confront the Act's failure directly, the FTC gradually scaled down its commitment in the area. The reorganization helps obfuscate the trend toward a lower manpower commitment to R-P, since there are no longer separate figures given for lawyers enforcing R-P.

Politics figured in Weinberger's personnel selection, too. The man he originally wanted to be head of the Public Relations Department was blackballed by White House patronage specialist Harry Fleming, who then dug up a suitable replacement. And the bright young man whom Weinberger picked to direct Policy Planning happened to be an assistant to Republican Senator Robert Griffin. Moreover, as an assistant to Fleming admitted in a Study Group interview, the Commission sent a monthly list to the White House with information about the political affiliations of top employees. The surprising resignation of Joe O'Malley as an assistant director of the Bureau of Deceptive Practices, shortly after he was appointed, raises questions about the impact of these lists, for O'Malley, considered by fellow staffers as one of the best FTC merger trial attorneys, is a Democrat.*

But Weinberger was willing to bend only so far. His predecessor, Paul Rand Dixon, in an attempt to remain Chairman under the Nixon administration by throwing the GOP a patronage bone, nominated the FTC's most prominent Republican, "Tennessee" Charlie Moore, to a top position. Commissioners Nicholson, Jones, and Elman refused to approve the appointment because of Moore's uninspiring reputation, thereby stymieing Dixon. When Weinberger was appointed, the pressure descended from Moore's friends on Capitol Hill, including Tennessee Democrat Joe Evins, the chairman of the House Appropriations Subcommittee, which had overseen the FTC's budget. According to Weinberger aides, Evins hinted that he would cut off $1 million if Moore were not appointed.

---

* O'Malley is said to have resigned because of a "misunderstanding" about his salary. The merger staff openly accuse the White House of intervention, although their contention cannot be proved.

Weinberger stood firm and, in fact, once threw Moore out of his office. The budget was slashed by $875,000, although Evins denies that the Moore incident had any causal relationship.

One of the most important appointments was that of Basil Mezines as Acting Executive Director. At the Agency since 1950, he was Acting Executive Director under the Republicans in 1958 and spent the 1960s prosecuting R-P cases—mostly in Florida or California. Some in-house critics point to the naming of Mezines to such a high position as an extrapolation of the FTC tradition of cronyism. After all, as one of the few Republicans left at the FTC after eight years of Democratic reign, Mezines was destined for a top spot; furthermore, Mezines was both politically adept and well connected. But what apparently impressed Weinberger (and Miles Kirkpatrick after him, who named Mezines Executive Director) was his thorough knowledge of the Agency's institutional failings. During his eight years out of a top position Mezines had developed biting critiques of his own Agency: he saw law firms drop their relationships with friendly staffers who had lost power, lawyers demoralized by trivial work, and an Agency whose enforcement policies had become a joke to Washington insiders. And his views could at times translate into policy: The recommendation to have the R-P staff do its own field investigations, for example, was based on Mezines's own experiences.

In sum, Weinberger did not conceptualize a new vision of the FTC; he was neither a crusading prosecutor nor an innovative economic theorist. He was simply an administrator who halted the steady deterioration of an agency: the FTC's fat was trimmed and its muscles toned up.

THE KIRKPATRICK REGIME

On September 15, 1970, Miles W. Kirkpatrick, 52, became the Chairman of the FTC. Kirkpatrick is almost a caricature of the legal patrician: tall, thin, silvery hair, inactive Republican, Princeton undergraduate, University of Pennsylvania Law School, partner in the prestigious law firm of Morgan, Lewis & Bockius in Philadelphia. As chairman of the Antitrust Section of the American Bar Association, he headed the ABA Commission that severely criticized the management of the FTC. Even that report had the touch of the gentleman. A detailed analysis of the work performed by FTC lawyers was deliberately omitted for fear that it was "unfair"—even though researchers had spent considerable effort conducting this "biopsy" of the Agency. Kirkpatrick was reluctant at first to be Chairman, but finally, under considerable pressure from ABA colleagues, he accepted.

Kirkpatrick's lack of political background is a refreshing break with tradition, but many staffers felt it could turn into a problem. Their theory was that Kirkpatrick could not shield the FTC from the White House and the Congress. Confidants of Kirkpatrick replied that before he was appointed Kirkpatrick was guaranteed no outside political meddling, but the appointment of the new Commissioner to replace outgoing Philip Elman scuttles that hope.

The man Richard Nixon named to replace an antitrust innovator was David Dennison, a former Republican Congressman from Ohio, who readily admits to no special antitrust background. President Nixon first wanted to nominate him to the Maritime Commission, but key Congressional powers balked at the prospect.[2] Dennison was elected to Congress in 1956 and narrowly lost bids for reelection in 1958 and 1960. A graduate of Western Reserve Law School, most of his legal career was spent in a small-town practice in Warren, Ohio. When rumors of Dennison's forthcoming nomination swept Washington in summer 1970, one New York friend of Kirkpatrick brushed the speculation aside. "They couldn't. If Miles knew, he wouldn't take the job. In fact, if Dennison is nominated, I'll shoot my foot." Kirkpatrick did speak to Dennison before his confirmation, and indicated that he had no objection to the nomination.

In an interview six months after he had taken office, Dennison seemed generally open-minded but unknowledgeable. He had not yet judged the virtues of Robinson-Patman enforcement, although he felt it was the Commission's obligation to enforce the law even if it hurt competition. He could not comment on the FTC's economic study on mergers because he had not read it; he was unfamiliar with the consent-order program in mergers and therefore declined to analyze it. The one subject he had a vigorous opinion on was *ex parte* communication. According to

Dennison, "You never talk privately *ex parte* to a judge. It would be presumptuous." For this reason, the Commissioner promised strict limits on his own accessibility.

To condemn Commissioner Dennison merely for being an ex-Congressman would be unfair.* Aides of the other Commissioners have been impressed by his able grasp of new issues. Yet his lack of experience in antitrust and consumer protection was confirmation that the vision of the new FTC, free from political appointees, would be short-lived. To replace an Elman with a Dennison is not revitalizing the Agency. The working majority for substantial innovation, formed by the Elman-Jones-Nicholson coalition, and later by Weinberger taking over for Nicholson, is no longer. When important issues surface, such as the appropriate remedies to use in concentrated markets like the cereal industry, it is unclear that the "new" FTC will be an improvement.

Despite the Dennison setback, Kirkpatrick went on with his program to reform the administration of the Commission. His first step was to upgrade personnel. Among his key appointments were:

—Basil Mezines, 46, as Executive Director of the Commission, thus assuring continuity with the Weinberger program;

—Alan S. Ward, 40, a Washington antitrust lawyer, as director of the FTC's Bureau of Competition. Ward is a veteran of the Antitrust Division at Justice and a highly regarded partner in a Washington law firm, Hollabaugh, Jacobs & Ward.

—Robert Pitofsy, 41, as the director of the Bureau of Consumer Protection. Pitofsky, a professor teaching trade regulation at New York University Law School, chaired the consumer-protection committee of the ABA's Antitrust Section, and worked closely with Kirkpatrick in preparing the ABA report.

—H. Michael Mann, 37, as Director of the Bureau of Economics. Mann, a Democrat with a Ph.D. from Cornell, was chairman of the economics department at Boston College and had worked as a special economic assistant to the Antitrust Division.

* Former Commissioner Nicholson was also a defeated Congressional candidate, and he turned out to be one of the FTC's most insightful officials.

The Ward-Pitofsky-Mann triumvirate is probably the most impressive group of Bureau leaders the FTC has had in recent history. Each has a distinguished reputation, is relatively young, and is anxious to make a mark during his tenure at the Commission. Pitofsky has already inspired admiration from his staff for his innovative ideas in the consumer area. Our attention, however, is focused basically on the efforts of Ward to resuscitate his Bureau. Since Mann was named director of the Bureau of Economics on January 20, 1971, and worked part time at the Commission until the end of the academic year, it is too early to judge his impact. However, it is known that he feels economists are increasingly being pushed into a secondary role at the Commission. He resents moving the economists out of the main building and the pressure to hire men whom top staffers believe unqualified.

Ward is looking forward to a recalibration of his Bureau's efforts. In the merger area, less emphasis will be put on cement and more on the energy and drug industries. This shift in priorities was somewhat forced on the FTC: the energy examination was pushed by Congress after the winter's fuel-shortage crisis, and the drug cases fell into the Commission's lap after Justice passed on the politically hot Warner-Lambert case. But the new emphasis does conform with Ward's concept of the Commission. As he pointed out in a February, 1971, interview, the FTC is especially interested in industries which directly affect the consumer—foods, drugs, heating are all obvious targets. By this approach, Ward hopes to build up a new constituency for the FTC. Although the specific industries studied will change, essentially the FTC will continue to act parallel to the Justice Department. "Actually, we're not very different from Justice," Ward pointed out. "Everyone assumes that we are better set up procedurally for certain new areas of law, but that may be a myth. The Commission also seems to have the edge with Section Five, but the Sherman Act has flexibility."

The more important cases filed by Ward's Bureau of Competition have been the following: *

—Seven large soft-drink manufacturers have been charged with imposing territorial restrictions on licensee

---

* All these proposed complaints are still subject to the possibility of consent orders.

bottlers in a way which restricts competition at the consumer level. The case seems a first step into the franchising and licensed-dealer field.

—In its first action challenging a merger between insurance companies, the FTC issued a proposed complaint against the merger of American General Insurance Company, with total assets over $1.5 billion, and the Fidelity and Deposit Company, with assets of about $160 million. Allegedly, the merger will have anticompetitive effects in the business of underwriting fidelity and surety bonds.

—A proposed complaint was issued against the Parke-Davis merger with Warner-Lambert. According to the FTC, the merger had an adverse effect on the markets for both ethical and hospital drugs, as well as increasing aggregate concentration in the industry as a whole. This case was a *cause célèbre* at the Justice Department. Assistant Attorney General Richard McLaren has sought to issue a complaint, but it was blocked by Richard Kleindienst, as has been described in detail in Chapter 2.

—Finally, a potentially precedential shared-monopoly case was filed charging five tire companies with pursuing a parallel course of action which forced bus operators to lease rather than buy their tires. The complaint did not allege collusion or conspiracy, emphasizing structure rather than conduct. Although the case had been semidormant in the Division of General Trade Restraints for some time (it was sent from an uninterested Justice Department in 1965), Ward realized its importance and had it filed. However, the case was settled by a consent order rather than litigation in April, 1971. Innovative case law was not made, although the FTC staff claim that litigation was not possible since all their requested relief was agreed to by the defendants.

Perhaps the boldest step of the Kirkpatrick administration has been its personnel policy. Reviewing the performance of the Commission, Kirkpatrick and his staff decided that the only way to achieve a dramatic improvement was to get rid of 30–50 unproductive lawyers. This "purge" or "personnel revitalization," depending on your perspective, is quite controversial because of the "due process' problems involved. According to Civil Service regulations, attorneys who are not veterans can be dismissed without cause on 30 days' notice. To dismiss veterans, "cause" must be shown. Basil Mezines, now known around the Commission as "the hatchet man," has a list of people he considers expendable; he amiably discusses with them the alternatives: retire or be fired. Not surprisingly, many of the less productive FTC personnel eligible for retirement are now leaving. Reactions to this "personnel revitalization" program have been mixed. At first, the younger staff was enthusiastic. As one Kirkpatrick partisan stated, "It shows that we're going somewhere, and loosens up higher-paying jobs. The FTC isn't a retirement home. Lawyers should produce or get out." The older staff are less than excited.

On the other hand, the heavy-handedness of Mezines with FTC attorney Jim Wood reveals the dangers inherent in such a process. Wood, regarded as one of the Commission's better trial attorneys, was called into Mezines's office in April, 1971, and informed that if he did not resign, "charges" would be brought against him. When Wood inquired into the nature of the charges, Mezines refused to specify unless and until Wood first resigned. Wood asked if he could at least transfer to the Wool and Fur Division of the FTC, but Mezines refused. Mezines now claims that Wood's performance at the Sterling Drug hearing in the Commission was so poor that the FTC hierarchy lost confidence in him. But the legal staff at the Bureau of Competition is convinced the dismissal is due to Wood's advocacy of innovative economic concepts in his drug-merger cases. Whatever the accuracy of this perception, the firing of this experienced trial attorney has chilled the present staff from attempting similar new arguments. Complaints to Kirkpatrick and Mezines from outside the Commission helped reverse the dismissal decision, permitting Wood to go to Wool and Fur. The incident reflects badly not only on the grossly harsh tactics of Mezines but on Kirkpatrick's leadership as well, since he was both uninformed about, and uninterested in, the details of such personnel problems. The gentlemanly Chairman must realize that the FTC is not an ABA convention, and that politics and personnel play a decisive role in the performance of an agency.

It remains true that "deadwood," accustomed to the relaxed atmosphere of the Dixon days, has to be removed to get the FTC into high gear. Without increasing the

Agency's budget at all, its litigating power can be significantly strengthened by the turnover from senior to junior personnel. But there is clearly a morale cost if the dismissal process is abused. In the long run, then, devising adequate due-process protection for attorneys in Civil Service positions seems essential. The incompetent must be removed, but they must be removed equitably.

While there is some progress in the area of staff size and efficiency, there are contrary hints of retreat in other policy areas. The rapid rejection of the *Yale Law Journal* petition on annual styling change in the automobile industry is one example. In the *Georgia Pacific* case, which was bottled up in Policy Planning for longer than it took to research and draft the complaint, the FTC wanted to charge Georgia Pacific with injuring plywood competition because it cut off potential sources of competition by limiting the available sources of lumber. In other words, by integrating backward, Georgia Pacific was injuring competition at the horizontal level. The novel case bobbed back and forth at the FTC, up to the Commission, over to Policy Planning, to Ward's desk, and around again. Policy Planning delayed the filing of the case nine months, playing the same brief-writing game its parallel section traditionally performed at Justice.

Finally, Dennison's antitrust conservatism is beginning to surface. General Counsel Joseph Martin and some associates wanted to send a letter to all the major bakeries in the Seattle area, informing them that they were liable to civil penalties, under the order obtained in the *Bakers of Washington* case, if they attempted to fix prices. The bakers were already on legal notice of the terms of the court order, the idea went, even though they specifically were not covered. Commissioner Dennison balked at the letter, convincing the Commission to sustain his viewpoint. What was especially irritating to staff men was Dennison's suggestion that it was unclear that the industry was prone to price-fixing, even though the economics staff had done extensive research indicating that it was.

At this point the Kirkpatrick administration is very much of a question mark. Despite all the impressive publicity, the statistical record so far has been disappointing. In the first half of fiscal 1971, only *one* merger case, *no* Robinson-Patman cases, and *one* Section Five case had been docketed; and only three formal new merger investigations were requested. Two cases in six months with a staff of 92 lawyers is a dismal performance. Although five more proposed complaints have been issued in the merger field since January, 1971, the FTC has a long way to go before its actual record matches the image of its public-relations releases. There are dangers in only playing numbers games, and there is some justification in that much of the FTC's effort has focused on restructuring itself and that the cases will come later. But this was also the argument of the Weinberger era. At some point such explanations turn into rationalizations.

ALTERNATIVE MODELS FOR THE FUTURE

On August 11, 1970, outgoing Commissioner Philip Elman stunned an ABA Antitrust Section meeting by stating:

> While I have long held to the opposite view, I am now convinced that we will lose nothing, and gain much, by eliminating from agencies like the Federal Trade Commission the function of case-by-case adjudication of alleged violations of law.[3]

In a broad indictment he charged, "The most fundamental deficiency has been found to be the agencies' chronic failure to fulfill their unique quasi-legislative function of developing and implementing regulatory policies. . . ." The current conception and structure of antitrust enforcement does inherently disregard the importance of a broad economic regulatory pattern, a point at which the prior five chapters were aimed. Various alternative models, all seeking more rational policy and enforcement, follow:

(1) The Trade Court

Elman made these specific points on the traits of independent, multimember agencies:

> Contrary to the original theory, independence is a source of institutional weakness, not strength, and tends to discourage creative and courageous regulation in the public interest. Independence means that an agency lacks a constituency, a power base, and the backing of the President.
> Turning now to its multi-member structure, experience shows that this produces a dangerous depersonalization and invisibility of agency activity.

As a device for developing regulatory policy, case-by-case adjudication of alleged violations of law has proved to be inefficient and ineffective, and in many cases, unfair.

We should relieve agency members of the impossible duty of determining whether the allegations of their own complaint have been proved by the evidence in the record of a proceeding in which the agency itself is an adversary party.[4]

As a remedy for all these problems, Elman proposed a new model for antitrust enforcement. First, the FTC would be stripped of its adjudicative role. This function would be transferred to the courts, or preferably to a new Trade Court, which would have jurisdiction over Commission actions and the private suits related to them.* Second, the remaining functions of the FTC would be vested in a single Commissioner, "serving at the pleasure of *both* the President and Congress, and removable by either." The high visibility of this man would make him more responsive to public desires and would also attract men of greater talent to the position. Free from the burden of adjudicating, this official could pursue the broad sweep of formulating regulatory policy.

The concept of a trade court is not new. The unfortunate experience of the ICC Trade Court was discussed in Chapter 4. Our primary recommendation in that chapter was for a "trade court" of rotating district-court judges, each handling his normal responsibilities and occasionally being assigned a difficult antitrust case. One of the FTC-type trade courts might be no more expert than the current set of hearing examiners. The rotation system avoids the danger of one set of judges becoming hostile to vigorous antitrust actions, the kind of developed allegiance to business defendants which toppled the ICC Trade Court 50 years ago. In addition, the judges selected, or the court as a whole, must be appropriated money for economist clerks

---

* A variation on the trade-court concept was proposed by John D. French.[5] In his concurring statement to the ABA Report, he suggested that the FTC abandon its prosecutorial role and become a trade court itself. The novel cases which the Justice Department filed would be brought to it, while pedestrian factual litigations would be relegated to the courts. The advantage of the French proposal is that it encompasses the present jurisdiction of both Justice and the FTC; Elman makes no mention of Antitrust Division litigation. A remaining problem is: what happens to the economic study and rule-making function of the Agency? French seems to indicate that these would be retained; but, as Elman pointed out in his speech, it is awkward for a traditional judicial body to be involved in such endeavors.

to help in the framing of issues and relief. The use by Judge Wyzanski of economist Carl Kaysen in the *United Shoe* case is a model of the fusion of judicial and economic expertise.

(2) The Ash Report

The most recent suggestion about the future role for FTC enforcement has come from the President's Advisory Council on Executive Organization—better known as the Ash Report.[6] Curiously, this section on the FTC was the work of only three of the Council's six members, since for various reasons the other three did not, or could not, participate. Thus, we have the recommendations of Treasury Secretary John Connally, former ATT Chairman Frederick Kappel, and management consultant Richard M. Paget. Since Kappel dissented from the views of the majority, the conclusions on the FTC cannot be said to have an overwhelming mandate. *New York Times* reporter Eileen Shanahan has accused it generally of being "something less than a work of great depth." [7] According to Miss Shanahan, who is regarded as one of the best regulatory reporters in Washington, "It reads as though its authors had decided what to say after a discussion of a day or so and then left the staff to give the thing some tone of scholarship by looking up some citations and writing the footnotes. Indeed, the dissenting opinion by Frederick R. Kappel . . . hints that this is precisely the way the study was done." [8]

Despite these problems, the Ash Report does contain some interesting recommendations. Its basic proposal: "That the Federal Trade Commission be abolished and its consumer protection responsibilities vested in a new Federal Trade Practices Agency headed by a single administrator. That antitrust enforcement responsibilities of the FTC be transferred to a new Federal Antitrust Board." [9] Basically, the Ash group felt that the consumer-deception cases were incompatible with antitrust enforcement, a viewpoint discussed below.

This Federal Antitrust Board would seem to perform functions similar to those performed now by the FTC, except that it would make greater use of its economic expertise. The Board would consist of a Chairman and two economic administrators; the Chairman would administer the agency. One of the economists would be the director of the agency's economic research and the other would be a member of the President's Council of Economic Advisors. Apparently the Board might do some litigating, but the scope of its role is left unclear. The rationale for continued bifurcation of antitrust responsibilities in the report is also quite bewildering:

> We propose establishment of the separate Federal Antitrust Board only after carefully considering the alternative of vesting all authority for antitrust enforcement in the Department of Justice. Although this alternative would probably result in increased consistency of policy, elimination of overlapping efforts, and possible cost reductions, we have concluded that the advantages of dual enforcement and the intensive economic analysis available through the Antitrust Board should be maintained and developed still further.[10]

The only problem with this assertion is that the report fails to mention exactly what the advantages are.

The Report's idea of having two economists as administrators seems commendable as a vehicle for shifting priorities and assuring that economic analysis will predominate. The use of a member of the Council of Economic Advisors, encouraging some integration with national economic policy, is particularly valuable. Although the Report does talk about the unimportance of case-by-case adjudication under the new Board, it forgoes any mention of rule-making. In summary, the Ash Report is somewhat provoking, but mostly unenlightening. It splits the FTC in two, and lessens the number of Commissioners. Not really revolutionary, but perhaps constructive. What is disappointing about the Report is the lack of detail about its suggested scheme and the lack of explanation about implicit assumptions.

(3) Dual Enforcement: Justice and FTC

Why does the FTC, supposedly the refuge of economic expertise, bring the *per se* Robinson-Patman cases while the Justice Department, which has the authority to do so, brings none? The whole merger area is divided between the agencies by industry—not by the difficulty of the case or the economic complexity of the problem. Is the FTC just another enforcement agency in the merger area? Is it parallel to the Antitrust Division, or is it supposed to be doing something different? If the Commission ignores the standard cases, it will not be fulfilling its task as an enforcer; but if it concentrates its energies on enforcement, it will not be the broad economic innovator. It is, therefore, predictable that an agency will lack a clear concept of itself when it possesses an unrelated grab-bag of responsibilities. Nor is it surprising that the idea of two agencies enforcing the same laws seems nonsensical and confusing to the layman.

Thus, beyond the question of the rational use of the FTC's particular capabilities, there is the crucial organizational problem of having two government agencies with overlapping responsibilities. At present the Antitrust Division and the FTC have concurrent jurisdiction to enforce Sections 2, 3, 7, and 8 of the Clayton Act; and Section Five of the FTC Act gives that Agency power to attack activities also prohibited by the Sherman Act, which the Division alone enforces. All the prior sections of this Report have assumed the existence of and continuance of two agencies, each with many failings but each capable of improvement, given legislative and internal reforms. A second level of remedial analysis focuses around the question of whether there should be a merger of these two agencies or whether they should continue to function in their parallel but separate ways.

The 1960 Landis Report to President-elect Kennedy advised that this bureaucratic "overlap calls for correction." Stating its view without supporting evidence, Dean Landis concluded that "a sensible arrangement would be to transfer the antitrust activities of the Federal Trade Commission (not including its Robinson-Patman jurisdiction) to the Department of Justice." As is true with many illustrious commissions, this advice went unheeded. Nine years later another report, this time from the ABA Commission, came to the opposite conclusion, although again little support was offered:

We have been advised by personnel who have recently been discharging coordination responsibilities in the FTC and the Department of Justice, that the arrangements are stable and reasonably effective in avoiding conflicting investigations by the two agencies. We accept that judgment. . . .[11]

It therefore concluded that the agencies should remain separate. Based on our interviewing, we do not so blithely accept that judgment. Robert Wright, former number-two

man at the Antitrust Division, called communication between the two agencies "purely *ad hoc*. We'd get on the
phone and say, 'Well, who's got this one?' And then we'd
argue about it. Crazy." One Division attorney was asked
how cases are divided up between the two bodies. "Finders
keepers" he replied. An attorney in the office of the
Director of Operations at the Antitrust Division, which
handles liaison matters with the FTC, ridiculed the relationship:

> Every proposed investigation is cleared with the other
> agency. There it's a fight-to-the-death for the good investiga-
> tion. We officially claim that we never swap or trade off cases,
> that the most logical agency to handle the case does, but
> actually we do end up bartering, with the FTC eventually
> complaining, "Hey! You got the last four good ones."

Another former number-two man at the Antitrust Division
told the Study Group:

> We sent over the cats and dogs which we didn't want,
> keeping the good stuff. Generally relations were remote
> and competitive. At one point during the merger wave, the
> FTC offices opened at 8:30 and the Division's at 9:00. We
> found that they were calling up by 9:00 saying which mergers
> they wanted. So we arranged to have our FTC liaison woman
> get the *Wall Street Journal* delivered before 8:30 to spot the
> good mergers first.

In June, 1948, the modern liaison relationship between
the Antitrust Division and the FTC was formulated.
Basically, the two governmental bodies agreed to "a systematic mutual exchange of information regarding pending antimonopoly investigations. . . . The exchange of
information proposed would include the following for
each investigation: the file number, the title, specification
of product or products involved, and statement of
charges." [12] By 1962 some confusion in the relationship
was apparent. Lee Loevinger, then Assistant Attorney General for Antitrust, wrote a curt note to Chairman Dixon
explaining that the Division went a week to 10 days without receiving an answer to its clearance requests. This was
unacceptable, according to Loevinger, because he wanted
to respond to matters referred by Congressmen within 48
hours. He charged that "a delay of a week or more in
securing a response from FTC substantially impedes the

operation of this Division." Loevinger therefore established a presumption that Division investigations were cleared, unless advised to the contrary, by "one day after reference"; the FTC then established a similar policy.[13] Loevinger also sought to redefine more clearly the differentiation between the two bodies, but Chairman Dixon, in an April 11, 1963, letter, indicated that he liked the existing arrangement.

Misunderstandings about the liaison flared up again in 1966. Chairman Dixon wrote to Assistant Attorney General Donald Turner in October to complain that "recent developments . . . indicate that the basic procedures of the liaison arrangement are not being followed in a substantial number of instances by the Antitrust Division." [14] Dixon cited specific cases to support his allegations:

—In the RCA-Whirlpool acquisition of the Norge Division of Borg-Warner, the FTC commenced an investigation in July, 1966, being informed that the Division had no action pending. Seven days later the FTC was told by the Division that in January, 1966, it had orally advised counsel for Borg-Warner that there would be no antitrust action against that company for the merger. No information about this oral premerger clearance was given to the FTC at that time.

—In the 1966 case of a joint venture by Imperial Chemical Industries and the Ethyl Corporation, the Division gave an oral clearance although it knew the FTC intended to investigate the arrangement.

—In the Fannie May Candy acquisition of Andes Candy, the Division gave clearance without notifying the FTC. Again the FTC found out about its sister agency's action only after it had itself decided to investigate the merger.

—In the Whirlpool acquisition of Warwick from Sears Roebuck, the Division again gave clearance without notifying the FTC. The FTC was seeking clearance a week later to investigate, when it found out about the Division action.

—In the Hoerner Box Company merger with Waldorf Paper Product, the FTC notified the Division on November 1, 1966, that it intended to investigate and then found out that the Antitrust Division also wished to investigate. Rather than resolving the impasse, the Division went ahead and commenced its investigation.

Donald Turner replied to Dixon's complaints by point-ing out that the FTC was requesting clearances in hun-dreds of cases. "I should make it clear that we cannot consider technical clearances on this scale as a basis for clearing to the Commission future mergers in which the Antitrust Division has a substantial interest." [15]

There is another equally important level of inter-agency conflict: when one agency seeks aid from the other. In 1962 Robert Kennedy and Lee Loevinger sent 56 consent decrees over to the FTC for a compliance study, pursuant to that section of the FTC Act which makes the FTC a research arm of Justice. Loevinger later complained to the Study Group that very few contempt cases ever resulted because the Commission had done a poor job on the decrees. "The study didn't turn up much, mostly because the FTC didn't want to work for the Department of Justice. Just natural bureaucratic jealousy." But Charles Bangert, who headed the FTC study and who is now General Counsel of Senator Hart's Antitrust Subcommittee, hotly disagrees. "We put our best people on it," he said, stressing that Justice simply would not file the many good contempt cases which the FTC referred.* More recently Basil Mezines of the FTC sketched out in an interview the bureaucratic battleground with surprising candor:

The Attorney General under the FTCA can ask us to con-duct an investigation. Now you know that I'd just put my worst men on that when I got the request. Well, it's the same thing when we want something from them. . . .

You know most outsiders think that when an order is out-standing it means something significant. But Justice won't enforce the orders, especially in the consumer-protection field. The orders are really meaningless.

A flagrant instance of FTC-Justice quarreling took place in the *Guignon* case.[16] Here the Justice Department actually filed a brief opposing the right of the FTC to enforce its own subpoenas. The FTC, which traditionally thought it had this power and had exercised it, was dis-mayed. And when the Court of Appeals accepted the argument of the Justice Department, the Solicitor Gen-eral's office refused to seek *certiorari* for the FTC with

---

* When we asked each agency to see the FTC report, we were told it was not available because the recommendations were still under "investi-gation" at Justice.

the Supreme Court. The FTC is particularly embittered about *Guignon* because it places subpoena enforcement in the hands of an agency notably unenthusiastic about following through with FTC business. Although publicly relations are cordial, there is in fact much rancor beneath the veil of civility.

Internal FTC memoranda have revealed some examples of the problem: [17]

—On August 1, 1968, the FTC accused the National Electrical Manufacturers Association of violating an order against price-fixing and recommended $6.9 million in penalties. A year later the Justice Department finally advised the FTC that there was "insufficient evidence" in its case. The FTC balked. Talks were held, and now again the case is being reconsidered by Justice.

—In April, 1966, the FTC asked Justice to seek $140,000 in civil penalties for price-fixing from P. H. Haynes, a large underwear manufacturer. Justice sought but failed to get a criminal indictment, and then also dropped the civil-penalty suit. The FTC charges the price-fix has continued since the Justice inaction, and the Commission is still investigating Haynes.

The FTC, seeking to have a whole panoply of enforcement remedies available to it, is presently negotiating with the Justice Department. It desires to be able to enforce its own subpoenas, get civil penalties, and more easily obtain preliminary injunctions. Justice wants to limit the FTC's role for two reasons. As Richard McLaren points out, "Our position on the FTC going to courts is that since 1870 it has been the general policy, frequently affirmed by Congress, that the Justice Department is the agency through which the government goes to court." [18] But beyond this desire to retain its traditional procedural role, Justice is also attempting to keep a control over the substantive policies of the FTC—an agency it mistrusts. In the overwhelming majority of interviews conducted by the Study Group at the Justice Department, attorneys expressed disdain for the ability and productivity of their FTC counterparts. And although formally the Antitrust Division has little to do with actions of either the Solicitor General or other divisions of Justice, in fact Antitrust does seem to influence their posture toward the FTC. By its proximity to the rest of Justice's procedural powers, the Division becomes the senior partner in antitrust policy-making.

Even given these wasteful quarrels, and although admitting that the FTC's general antitrust record was one of "missed opportunity," [19] the ABA group specifically recommended the continuation of dual enforcement. According to the ABA Report, the FTC had a wide range of powers beyond those of the Justice Department, including the ability to investigate, and had an expertise unavailable in the judicial system. The ABA was particularly enthusiastic about Section 7 enforcement at the FTC, believing that the Commission showed promise in this area. It also urged increasing specialization of the two agencies:

> Cases of *per se* illegality, such as price fixing, market allocation, and boycotts designed to enforce price fixing cartels should thus be left to the Department of Justice. For the trial of these cases which usually involve nothing more than controversies over whether alleged conduct in fact occurred, the criminal sanctions, where appropriate, and litigation procedures of the district courts are better suited than the FTC's administrative procedures.
>
> On the other hand, where issues of anticompetitive effects turn essentially on complicated economic analysis, and where decided cases have not yet succeeded in fashioning a clear line marking the boundary between legal and illegal conduct, such matters should generally be assigned to the FTC.[20]

This kind of theoretical division has much appeal, yet there are basic difficulties with its implementation.

Why should the Antitrust Division willingly relegate itself to the role of the *per se* enforcer? Assistant Attorneys General win praise by prosecuting the occasional difficult case, not by handing it over to the FTC. To the degree the ABA model depends on the subordination of the Antitrust Division, its attainment will prove elusive. Considering the consensus that the Division has a more enviable enforcement record, it also seems illogical to reduce the scope of one agency to accomodate one which is not performing as well.

Such a step could be rationalized if the structural and procedural possibilities of one agency were so inherently superior that historical performance could be excused. But this raises a second difficulty. Is the ABA's implicit assumption as to the power of the administrative process valid? The "experts" of the administrative process—the hearing examiners—are nothing of the sort. The procedures, as we have seen, are not swifter, more just, or more sophisticated than the judicial process. The FTC's vaunted economic staff turns out, in fact, to consume only 10% of its budget. Its heralded 6(b) investigatory powers are easily stalled; the Commissioners can be as political as officers of the executive branch.

Finally, conflict is structural as well as emotional. There are built-in discrepancies between the Division's Merger Guidelines and the FTC's Industry Guides, both of which can apply to the same company. And having two agencies doing the same thing also encourages agency-shopping, where a firm will present its preliminary intent to that agency with which it thinks it can work best.

But what about the possibility of a new version of the administrative process, one where guidelines and rules are preeminent and economists take a leading role? Conceivably an FTC with a full range of power and the will to use it could evolve the following pattern: There could be a general ordering of priorities to determine which factors in industrial structure need examination first. Economists would focus on a specific area; guidelines and rules would be promulgated after formal hearings; lawyers at the agency would bring test cases. In a few years analysis would have coalesced to the point where the problem could be turned over to Justice for methodical enforcement. The Justice Department could still file its own innovative cases. But essentially the FTC would act as the broad economic regulator, seeking the economic facts and setting standards, while basically Justice would be the enforcer. Conceivably, all this is possible, but nearly 60 years of contrary FTC performance and a battery of periodic critiques carrying similar messages make one wonder whether reality will ever catch up to theory at the FTC.

We conclude that a consolidation of the antitrust functions of the FTC and the Antitrust Division into a unified new administrative agency—the Competition Protection Agency—would serve both good government and good antitrust enforcement. If responsibilities are more rationally allocated by the approach of the FTC as "brain" and the Antitrust Division as "body," there seems little reason why the head and the body should be severed. Yet there are obvious costs to its separation:

First, "bureaucratic jealousy," in Loevinger's words, creates continuous friction between the two, reducing effectiveness and crippling a coordinated antitrust policy.

Second, some argue that two agencies are beneficial, since if one is performing badly, the other can take up the slack. If true, then why not two ICCs, two FCCs, or two CABs? Rather than complement each other, we think dual enforcement in antitrust unwittingly divides and conquers itself. The whole here is *less* than the sum of its parts. How many people think of antitrust when the FTC is mentioned? Or when the Department of Justice is mentioned? Antitrust enforcement is submerged, actually and in people's minds, to other ascendant areas. Unification of antitrust enforcement would cement its importance in the public consciousness, as a separate and substantial agency promotes the importance of competition in our society. The new Environmental Protection Agency, by consolidating the separated environmental responsibilities in the federal government, has served precisely this function in the pollution domain.

Third, each separate agency is now so small that a critical mass of bodies and planners is lacking for the big or innovative case—an antimonopoly GM suit, a shared-monopoly case, an advertising-as-entry-barrier suit—the kind of case which usually elicited the official response, "But we just lack the resources for it." One large agency could more easily devote adequate staff to a big case, or a creative idea, exploiting uncharted possibilities. Now, however, each agency dedicates its slim resources to overlapping and often trivial cases. Also, a combination of the two would automatically save some resources, as duplicate supervisory and staff personnel (two heads of policy planning, operations, liaison, etc.) would be eliminated.

Fourth, some understandably fear that no future Congress will again pass legislation like Section 6(b) of the FTC Act, giving the Commission wide investigatory powers, or Section Five of that Act, giving it a wide mandate to move against "unfair practices." As a mandatory condition of any reorganization of these agencies, such powers must be secured for the new agency.

Finally, it should not prove difficult to separate out the

antitrust sections of the FTC and the Justice Department. They are each largely autonomous within their agency, and each has, in effect, a separate budget.

One difficult problem concerns whether or not to integrate consumer enforcement responsibilities into the new agency. A reasonable argument can be made that antitrust must be closely connected to classic consumer areas, in order to reinforce the importance of antitrust and generate an antitrust constituency through the back door of consumerism. Yet inclusion of standard consumer enforcement would entail serious costs. Truth-in-lending, flammable fabrics, etc., are really the targets of *per se* enforcement rather than complicated economic litigation. Integrating them into the Competition Protection Agency would have the effect of distorting the priority system, of trivializing overall enforcement, much as Robinson-Patman has done historically at the FTC. When the Ash Commission recommended a spin-off of the consumer-protection activities from the FTC, officials at the Commission responded that a vital interplay between structural and behavioral enforcement would be lost. The historical fact, however, is that there has been little coordination in Commission policies in these two areas, and there is little reason to suspect that under a Department of Competition the situation would be substantially altered. On balance, we therefore suggest the allocation of the non-antitrust consumer responsibilities to a separate independent agency, as has been urged in the pending Rosenthal-Eckhardt bill before Congress.

Specifically, the new Competition Protection Agency would contain the powers recommended throughout this book. Allocated a budget of $100 million, it would possess the ability to conduct wide-ranging investigations and to impose automatic temporary injunctions on mergers. Criminal penalties would be significant, not invisible; and civil decrees would contain meaningful remedies, to be followed up by compliance studies. The Department would be divided into two parts: an Economics Bureau, for industry studies, rules, and guidelines, and an Enforcement Bureau. At least one-quarter of the staff would be economists. The quality of personnel would increase as staff "deadwood" was trimmed by due-process proceedings. Competent judges sitting on a rotating antitrust court would handle the difficult and important structural cases. There would be a single head of the Agency, a Presidential appointment for a four-year term, able to be reappointed and removable only for "cause" or malfeasance in office.

This construct retains the best of each agency—the Division's injunctive powers and greater prosecutorial clout, and the FTC's investigatory, economic, and rule-making powers—and it projects a synergistic payoff. Presently, however, each agency has atrophied at an extremely low level. At the Division, manpower has not appreciably grown in 20 years, and the number of cases has slightly decreased in a 30-year period; at the FTC, statutory powers like Section 6(b) and Section Five have continued in a state of permanent pregnancy, unborn. A Competition Protection Agency could hardly do worse; in design and aim, it should clearly do better. Justice Hugo Black's dictum on Washington agencies generally contributes a final impetus to a single agency. He thought that all agencies should be abolished and recreated every 10 years. Beyond that first decade of life, an agency loses its enthusiasm and drive, existing for its own sake and not for the originally intended purpose. Eight decades after the birth of the Sherman Act, we agree.

Independent of whether or not such an agency comes into existence, there is an important complementary role for citizen professionals. Antitrust lawyers can become "public-interest lawyers," working on a flat salary basis and representing consumers generally in the antitrust arena. When only businessmen, business periodicals, and defense counsel make known their views on antitrust, the result is politically predictable: timid or nonexistent legislation and enforcement. The legal system, with its opposing counsel, and the political system, with its "factions," both assume that a continuing contest of views will produce the distilled "truth." Lacking a persistent consumer-antitrust presence in Washington, the interests of industry prevail by default. What is needed is a corporate counterweight—identifying the sell-out settlements when the political-industrial complex sees no problem, lobbying for new antitrust legislation and higher budgets, arguing *for* innovative cases when defense counsel lobby *against* them, generating ideas and approaches which the conventional wisdom declares unthinkable, exposing political tampering with the administration of justice, and, finally, mutually interacting with an emergent consumer-antitrust constituency.

With the support of these new professionals and constituents, enforcers may finally test the waters of anti-oligopoly and judges may finally dispense justice evenhandedly—not according to the color of defendants' collars. Until the existing anti-antitrust consensus is reversed, we grope about in economic darkness toward efficiency and equity; until our government fulfills its promise to watch what they *do* and not what they *say,* we mock our lofty and reiterated commitments to free enterprise and equal justice. If business and Washington shun the question, aroused citizens and lawyers and economists must raise it: Whatever happened to antitrust?

NOTES

CHAPTER 1

1. Subcommittee on Antitrust and Monopoly, *Report on Prices of Quinine and Quinidine,* 89th Cong., 2nd Sess. 2 (1967).
2. Kuhlman, "Nature and Significance of Price Fixing Rings," 2 *Antitrust Law and Economics Review* (Spring, 1969).
3. See Knutson, "Public Policy and Unfair Competition: Structure, Conduct and Performance in the Milk Industry," 2 *Antitrust Law and Economics Review* 97 (1968).
4. Lobel, "Red, White, Blue and Gold: The Oil Import Quotas," *Washington Monthly,* June, 1970, at 8.
5. Kroll, "Oil Lobby," *N.Y. Times Magazine,* March 8, 1970.
6. *Wall Street Journal,* March 7, 1967, at 1.
7. *Standard Oil Company* v. *United States,* 221 U.S. 1, 52 (1911).
8. *United States* v. *Dupont,* 351 U.S. 377, 426 (Warren, C.J., dissenting) (1956).
9. *Washington Post,* Feb. 24, 1963, at E-1 (Statement of Victor Hansen).
10. *See* Kaysen and Turner, *Antitrust Policy* (1959).
11. W. Shepherd, *Market Power and Economic Welfare,* 106 (1970); R. Barber, *The American Corporation* (1969). The 1969 Cabinet Committee on Price Stability reported that the average four-firm concentration ratio was 42%, *Studies by the Staff of the Cabinet Committee on Price Stability* 58, Government Printing Office, 1969, [hereinafter *Cabinet Committee Report*]; using more refined

Notes 439

economic date, Shepherd has put the figure as high as 60% (*op. cit.*, at 106).

12. See F. M. Scherer, *Industrial Market Structure and Economic Performance* 63 (1970).
13. *Cabinet Committee Report* at 60; *cf.* Brozen, "The Antitrust Task Force Deconcentration Recommendation," XIII *J. of Law & Econ.* 279 (1970).
14. Dr. Willard Mueller, Chief of the Bureau of Economics at the Federal Trade Commission, "Statement before Senate Committee on Small Business" 50 (March 15, 1967).
15. *Cabinet Committee Report* at 51.
16. Boyle, "An Estimate of the Number and Size Distribution of Domestic Joint Ventures," *Antitrust Law and Economics Review* (Spring, 1968).
17. *Cabinet Committee Report* at 61–2. Twenty-four of the corporations with which GM interlocks had combined 1962 assets of $65 billion; 27 of the 89 U.S. Steel interlocks had combined 1962 assets of over $100 billion.
18. *Ibid.* at 52–3.
19. A. Berle, *Power Without Property* 52–3 (1959).
20. Hearings before the Subcommittee on Antitrust and Monopoly, Senate Judiciary Committee, "Economic Concentration," 91st Cong., 2nd Sess. 4551 (Nov. 4, 1969) [hereinafter cited as *Economic Concentration Hearings*].
21. S. Reid, *Mergers, Managers and the Economy* 38 (1968). Much of the following data on successive merger waves is taken from this source.
22. H. Seager and C. Gulick, Jr., *Trust and Corporation Problems* 61 (1929).
23. Study by Dr. Johan Bjorksten, economic consultant, *cited in* J. Cohen and M. Mintz, *America, Inc.* (1971) [hereinafter cited as Mintz-Cohen].
24. Federal Trade Commission, *Economic Report on Corporate Mergers* 143 (1970).
25. *Cited in* G. Kolko, *Wealth and Power* (1957).
26. *Supra* note 12 at 33.
27. Bossons, Cohen and Reid, "Mergers for Whom—Managers or Stockholders?" Carnegie Institute of Technology, Working Paper #14; Cohen and Reid, "The Benefits and Costs of Bank Mergers," *Journal of Finance and Quantitative Analysis,* December, 1967.
28. *Wall Street Journal,* September 28, 1968, at 1.
29. Rostow, "The New Sherman Act: A Positive Instrument of Progress," 14 *U. of Chicago L. Rev.* 567–8 (1947).
30. Speech of Donald Turner, "Advertising and Competition," before the Briefing Conference on Federal Controls of Advertising and Promotion (June 2, 1966).
31. Weiss, "Econometric Studies of Industrial Organization," (paper done while resident economist at Antitrust Division).
32. Kamerschen, "An Estimation of the 'Welfare Losses' from Monopoly in the American Economy," 4 *Western Economic Journal* 221 (1966). Estimate based on discrepancy between price and marginal cost in a variety of industries. Thus, his 6% does

not include substantial losses from monopoly inefficiency—having high costs because incentive is lacking to keep them down—and from planned obsolescence, which is, effectively, a plot to waste resources.

33. F. M. Scherer, *Industrial Market Structure and Economic Performance* 408 (1970). Final estimate based on wasteful promotional efforts, operations at less than optimal scale, pricing distortions in regulated sectors, monopoly inefficiencies due to insulation from competition, excess capacity due to cartelization and the stimulus of collusive profits, and transportation costs associated with distorted locational decisions.
34. W. Shepherd, *Market Power and Economic Welfa*re 212 (1970).
35. Cited in M. Harrington, *The Accidental Century* 81 (1966).
36. R. Heilbroner, *The Worldly Philosophers* 2 (1953).
37. Cited in Mintz-Cohen.
38. J. Blair, *Economic Concentration* (to be published in late 1971). For a contrary view of oligopoly pricing and inflation, see the study presented by Antitrust Division economist Leonard Weiss to the Joint Economic Comittee of Congress, July 10, 1970.
39. Hart, "Emerging Paradoxes in Antitrust," 30 *ABA Antitrust Section* 80 (1966).
40. Cited in Mintz-Cohen.
41. Cited in E. Kefauver, *In a Few Hands* 168–78 (1965).
42. Shepherd, "Conglomerate Mergers in Perspective," 2 *Antitrust L. & Eco. Rev.* 20–21 (Fall, 1968).
43. Speech to the Lawyers Club in Ann Arbor, Michigan, April 8, 1969.
44. *N.Y. Times,* March 28, 1970.
45. See, *e.g., Standard Oil Company of California et al.* v. *United States,* 337 U.S. 243 (1949).
46. *United States* v. *Aluminum Company of America,* 148 F. 2d 416 (2d Cir. 1945).
47. *Economic Concentration Hearings,* at 810.
48. Williamson, "Managerial Discretion and Business Behavior, 52 *American Economic Review* (December, 1963).
49. J. Bain, *Barriers to New Competition* 111 (1957). A study by William Comanor and T. A. Wilson similarly concluded, in 24 of 29 industries studied, "the average size of the four largest firms exceeds the size which exhausts all economies of scale" (Comanor and Wilson, "Advertising the Advantages of Size," *American Economic Review,* May, 1969, at 91). The Cabinet Committee on Price Stability agreed: "existing concentration levels in many industries are greater than necessary to achieve economies of scale in production, research and innovation" (*Cabinet Committee Report* at 81); see also Saving, "Estimation of Optimum Size of plant by the Survivor Technique," 75 *Quarterly Journal of Economics* 569 (1961).
50. Weiss, *supra* note 31, at 48.
51. Scherer, "Firm Size, Market Structure, Opportunity and the Output of Potential Inventions," *American Economic Review,* December, 1964, at 1121–22.
52. Mansfield, "Size of Firm, Market Structure and Innovation," *Journal of Political Economy,* December, 1963. See also Adams

and Dirlam, "Big Steel, Invention and Innovation," *Quarterly Journal of Economics,* May, 1966.
53. T. K. Quinn, *Giant Business* 116–17 (1953).
54. "Chrysler Solves Two Big Barriers to Gas Turbine," *Automotive News,* March, 1964.
55. Esposito and Silverman, *Vanishing Air* 19–20 (1970).
56. FTC, *Statistical Report No. 6, Current Trends in Merger Activity,* 1969, March, 1970, at 19.
57. Quoted in *Washington Post,* March 16, 1969, at B6.
58. *Ibid.*
59. *Economic Concentration Hearings* at 4766, referring to studies by Professors Reid, Kelly, Fogarty, Eslick, and Arnold.
60. House Antitrust Subcommittee, Report, *Investigation of Conglomerate Corporations,* June, 1971.
61. Zimmerman, "Introduction to Conglomerate Symposium," 44 *St. John's L. Rev.* 3,5 (1970).
62. Letter of Senator William Proxmire to Senator Frank Moss, Chairman, Consumer Subcommittee of the Senate Commerce Committee, quoted in "The Making of the FTC: Organization in Search of a Constituency?" 3 *Antitrust Law and Economics Review* 31, 40 (Spring, 1970).
63. Harrington, *op. cit.,* at 80–1.

CHAPTER 2

1. *Wall Street Journal,* June 16, 1965, at 1.
2. *Ibid.*
3. C. Edwards, *Maintaining Competition* 14 (1964).
4. *Chicago Daily News,* July 11, 1969.
5. Sherrill, "We Can't Depend on Congress to Keep Congress Honest," *N.Y. Times Magazine,* July 19, 1970, at 20.
6. *Business Week,* February 4, 1956, at 26.
7. Goulden, *Monopoly* 102–3 (1968).
8. *Time,* January 26, 1968, at 71-A.
9. *FDA Reports,* November 16, 1970, Vol. 32, No. 46, p. 35.
10. Anderson, "FTC, SEC May Take Up Merger Case Justice Shied From," *Washington Post,* December 28, 1970.
11. *Supra,* note 9.
12. R. Hofstadter, *The Age of Reform* 245 (1955).
13. *Ibid.*
14. Joseph P. McKenna, *quoted in* S. R. Reed, *Mergers Managers and the Economy* 99 (1968).
15. Federal Trade Commission, *Report on the Present Trend of Corporate Mergers and Acquisitions,* 23 (1947).
16. 96 *Cong. Rec.* 16452 (1950).
17. *Brown Shoe Co.* v. *United States,* 370 U.S. 294, 315 (1962).
18. H. R. Rep. No. 1191, 81st Cong., 1st Sess. (1949).
19. *Ibid.,* at 11.
20. C. Edwards, *Maintaining Competition* 64–5 (1964).
21. *Quoted in* Fellmeth, *The Interstate Commerce Omission* 137 (1970).
22. K. Elzinga, *The Effectiveness of Relief Decrees in Merger Cases*

(dissertation, Department of Economics, Michigan State University, 1967).
23. Lea, "Lobbying Overwhelms Opponents of Newspaper Preservation Act," *National Journal,* July 7, 1970, at 1606.
24. *Ibid.*
25. *Ibid.*
26. Lea, "Senate's Antitrust Watchdog Moves Into Environment, Consumer Areas," *National Journal,* August 22, 1970, at 1828.
27. *Quoted in* S. R. Reed, *Mergers, Managers and the Economy* 97 (1968).
28. A. Hacker (ed.). *The Corporation Takeover* 7 (1965).

CHAPTER 3

1. L. Huston, *The Department of Justice* 98 (1967).
2. R. Hofstadter, *The Age of Reform* 246 (1956).
3. *Ibid.,* at 246, n. 4.
4. Arnold, "Antitrust Law Enforcement, Past and Future," 7 *Law and Contemporary Problems* 5, 12 (1940).
5. Engler, *The Politics of Oil* 216 (1961).
6. Smith, "What Antitrust Means under Mr. Bicks," *Fortune,* March, 1960, at 120.
7. *Ibid.*
8. *N.Y. Times,* March 12, 1960, at 20.
9. *N.Y. Times,* December 24, 1961, at 61.
10. Bookman, "Loevinger vs. Big Business," *Fortune,* January, 1962, at 93.
11. *Wall Street Journal,* June 4, 1963, at 18.
12. *Supra,* note 10.
13. *N.Y. Times,* June 24, 1962, at 38.
14. "Antitrust Boss Takes New Swipe at ATT," *Business Week,* August 12, 1961, at 31, 35.
15. The statistic is based on an internal Justice Department study of antitrust enforcement in 1962–63.
16. Speech of William Orrick, "Profile of an Antitrust Enforcement Program," January 30, 1964 (on file at Antitrust Division library).
17. Posner, "A Program for the Antitrust Division," 38 *U. of Chicago L. Rev.* 500, 533 (1971).
18. *N.Y. Times,* May 9, 1965, at 36.
19. Meyers, "Professor Turner's Turn at Antitrust," *Fortune,* September, 1965, at 168.
20. Address of Donald Turner before the American Bar Association, August 10, 1965.
21. Posner, "A Statistical Study of Antitrust Enforcement," XIII *The Journal of Law & Economics* 365, 419 (1970).
22. 374 U.S. 321, 371 (1963).
23. Note, "Section 5 of the Clayton Act and the Nolo Contendere Plea," 75 *Yale L. J.* 845 (1966).
24. *N.Y. Times,* June 29, 1966, at 65.
25. FTC Statistical Report No. 6, *Current Trends in Merger Activity 1969,* March, 1970.

26. Lawrence, "Must Competitors Be Equalized in Money and Skills?" *U.S. News & World Report,* November 28, 1966, at 112.
27. "How McDonnell Won Douglas," *Fortune,* March, 1967, at 155.
28. *Wall Street Journal,* February 10, 1967, at 1.
29. Lehrman, "Antitrust: A Hard Look at the Guidelines," *Dun's Review,* September, 1968, at 65.
30. *F.T.C.* v. *Waugh Equipment Co.,* 15 F.T.C. 232 (1931); *F.T.C.* v. *Mechanical Manufacturing Co.,* 16 F.T.C. 67 (1932); *F.T.C.* v. *California Packing Corp.,* 25 F.T.C. 379 (1957).
31. *Wall Street Journal,* June 20, 1969, at 40.
32. *Wall Street Journal,* March 25, 1969, at 1.
33. *Quoted in* Stelzer, "Antitrust Policy and the Conglomerates," Remarks at McDonnell & Co., Institutional Research Conference, New York, June 20, 1969.
34. *N.Y. Times,* June 13, 1969, at 67.
35. *N.Y. Times,* February 19, 1970.
36. *Supra* note 33, *quoting* "Why Leasco Failed to Net Chemical," *Business Week,* April 26, 1969, at 144.
37. "The Multicompanies: Conglomerate, Agglomerate and Inbetween," *Forbes,* January 1, 1969, at 77.
38. *Washington Evening Star,* February 19, 1969.
39. "Interview with Richard McLaren," *Dun's Review,* October, 1969, at 12.
40. Testimony before the Joint Economic Committee, July 10, 1970.
41. "Honeywell Tries to Make Its Merger Work," *Business Week,* September 26, 1970, at 93.
42. Silberman, "The Coming Assault on Bigness," *Fortune,* June, 1957, at 57.
43. Posner, *supra* note 21 at 411–12.

CHAPTER 4

1. Hearings before a Subcommittee of the House Appropriations Committee, Part 1—The Judiciary, Department of Justice, 91st Cong., 2nd Sess. 529, March 4, 1970.
2. Hearings before a Subcommittee of the House Appropriations Committee, the Department of Justice, 82nd Cong., 2d Sess. 241, February 16, 1951.
3. *N.Y. Times,* January 7, 1971, at 18.
4. Smith, "Antitrust and the Monopoly Problem: Toward a More Relevant Legal Analysis," 2 *Antitrust Law and Economics Review* 19, 32 (Summer, 1969).
5. Havighurst, "Prosecutorial Discretion of the Antitrust Division," unpublished memorandum concerning his summer experience in Washington, 1966.
6. Note, "Congress Enacts Antitrust Civil Process Act," 111 *U. of Pa. L. Rev.* 1021, 1022 (1963).
7. *N.Y. Times,* April 24, 1961, at 20.
8. *Wall Street Journal,* September 11, 1962, at 1.
9. *Wall Street Journal,* February 2, 1971, at 1.
10. *Ibid.,* and "Next: Divisional Reporting by Public Corporations," *Forbes,* July 15, 1966.

444 NOTES

11. Smith, "Antitrust and the Monopoly Problem: Toward a More Relevant Legal Analysis," 2 *Antitrust Law and Economics Review* 19, 37–38 (Summer, 1969).
12. Posner, "A Statistical Study of Antitrust Enforcement," XIII *The Journal of Law and Economics* 365, 377 (1970).
13. Based on data supplied the Study Groups by the Antitrust Division.
14. Bromley, "Judicial Control of Antitrust Cases," 23 F.R.D. 417 (1959).
15. Kramer, "The Trial of a Protracted Antitrust Case: A Proposal," 18 *ABA Antitrust Section* 41 (1961).
16. *Ibid.*
17. *Quoted in* "The Effectiveness of the Federal Antitrust Laws: A Symposium," *American Economic Review,* June, 1949.
18. This data was compiled from statistics supplied by the Antitrust Division entitled *Comparative Analysis of Antitrust Cases Filed by Fiscal Years.*
19. The excess profits rank is based on a statistical measure developed by Dr. D. R. Kamerschen. This Table is the product of unpublished research conducted by Dr. Richard Schramm of Cornell.

CHAPTER 5

1. E. Sutherland, *White Collar Crime* 61 (1949).
2. Baumhart, "How Ethical Are Businessmen?" *in* Geis, *White Collar Criminal* 119 (1968).
3. *Quoted in* Cook "The Corrupt Society," *Nation,* June 1, 1963 at 453.
4. *The Histories of Polybius* 393 (1923).
5. Jacobs, "Statistical Standardization and Research Activities," 6 *ABA Antitrust Section* 80, 81 (1955).
6. Cook, "The Corrupt Society," *Nation,* June 1, 1963, at 453.
7. *Wall Street Journal,* June 9, 1959, at 1.
8. Chatfield and Mathias, *Profitable Oil Jobbing* 28 (1968).
9. *Supra* note 7.
10. Note, "The Frequency of Price Fixing: An Indication," 57 *Nw. L. Rev.* 151 (1962).
11. *Ibid.*
12. Hearings before the Subcommittee on Antitrust and Monopoly of the Senate Judiciary Committee, "Increasing Sherman Act Criminal Penalties," 91st Cong., 2d Sess. 49, March 5, 1970.
13. Cahill, "Must We Brand Business by Indictment as Criminal?" 1 *ABA Antitrust Section* 26 (1952).
14. Address of Daniel Peterkin, President of Morton Salt Company, at the Commonwealth Club of California, May 22, 1964.
15. For expanded version of points 1–4, *see* Flynn, "Criminal Sanctions Under State and Federal Antitrust Laws," 45 *Texas L. Rev.* 1301 (1967).
16. Loevinger, "The New Frontier in Antitrust," 39 *Texas L. Rev.* 865, 866 (1961).
17. *New Republic,* February 20, 1961, at 7.

18. Note, "Increasing Community Control over Corporate Crime—A Problem in the Law of Sanctions," 71 *Yale L. J.* 280 (1961).
19. Quoted in *ibid.*
20. *Wall Street Journal,* February 8, 1961 at 12.
21. Posner, "A Statistical Study of Antitrust Enforcement," XIII *Journal of Law & Economics* 365, 385, 390 (1970). (Hereinafter cited as Posner).
22. Smith, "The Incredible Electrical Conspiracy," *Fortune,* April, 1961, at 132.
23. *Ibid.*
24. *N.Y. Times,* February 7, 1961, at 1.
25. *Quoted in* Cook, "The Corrupt Society," *Nation,* June 1, 1963, at 453.
26. Demaree, "Judgment Comes for the Plumbing Manufacturers," *Fortune,* December, 1969, at 96.
27. *Ibid.*
28. *Ibid.*
29. Posner at 400.
30. *Quoted in* Kramer, "Criminal Prosecutions for Violations of the Sherman Act: In Search of a Policy," 48 *Georg. L. J.* 530, 536 (1960).
31. Smith, "Antitrust and the Monopoly Problem: Toward a More Relevant Legal Analysis," 2 *Antitrust Law & Economics Review* 19, 33 (Spring, 1969).
32. Note, "Section 5 of the Clayton Act and the Nolo Contendere Plea," 75 *Yale L. J.* 845, 846 (1966).
33. Hearings before the Senate Subcommittee on Antitrust and Monopoly, "Increasing Sherman Act Criminal Penalties," 91st Cong., 2d Sess., March 7, 1970.
34. Of 97 government objections to the entry of *nolo* pleas, 92 were overruled by judges. This data is based on tables supplied the Study Group by the Antitrust Division.
35. *Ibid.*
36. Fuller, *The Anatomy of Law* 28 (1968).
37. *United States* v. *Standard Ultramarine & Color Co.,* 137 F. Supp. 167, 170 (S.D.N.Y. 1955).
38. *Quoted in* Hardy, "Section 5 of the Clayton Act," 49 *Georg. L. J.* 44, 69 (1960).
39. *Cascade National Case Corp.* v. *El Paso Natural Gas Co., et al.,* 386 U.S. 129 (1967).
40. Sherrill, "Justice in a Torn Nation," *Nation,* December 7, 1970, at 590.
41. Speech by Robert L. Wright, First Assistant of the Antitrust Division, October 21, 1964, *and* statistics supplied by the Antitrust Division as to sentences imposed and served fiscal 1963–70.
42. Note, "Increasing Community Control over Corporate Crime—A Problem in the Law of Sanctions," 71 *Yale L. J.* 280 (1961).
43. *United States* v. *General Motors,* 121 F. 2d 376, 411 (7th Cir. 1941).
44. *United States* v. *Austin-Bagley Corp.,* 31 F. 2d 229, 233 (2d Cir. 1929).
45. Posner at 395.
46. *Supra* note 33.

47. Clabault and Burton, *Sherman Act Indictments* 40 (Supp. 1967).
48. *Supra* note 42 at 287.
49. Note, "Section 5 of the Clayton Act and the Nolo Contendere Plea," 75 *Yale L. J.* 845 (1966).
50. *Supra* note 30.
51. *Supra* note 42.
52. Barber, "Windfall for Conspiracy," *Nation,* November 9, 1964, at 332.
53. *N.Y. Times,* December 9, 1960, at 22.
54. H. N. McMenimen, Jr., *High Profitability–The Reward for Price Fixing* 1 (1969). (These statistics do not take account of the 1969 Tax Reform Act, which permitted only one-third of the treble damages to be deductible.)
55. Lanzillotti and Dirlam, *Optimum Engagement in Antitrust Risks* unpublished manuscript, p. 2.
56. Erickson, *Dissolution and Treble Damages in Private Antitrust,* unpublished manuscript, p. 11.
57. Erickson, *Price-fixing Under the Sherman Act: Case Studies in Conspiracy* (dissertation, Michigan State University, 1965).

CHAPTER 6

1. Posner, "A Statistical Study of Antitrust Enforcement," XIII *Journal of Law & Economics* 365, 385–8 (1970).
2. "Consent Decree Program of the Department of Justice," H. R. Rep. (H. Res. 27), 86th Cong., 1st Sess. at 302–3 (1959).
3. *See* Posner, *supra* note 1, at 387.
4. Hearings before the Subcommittee on Independent Offices of the House Appropriations Committee, 88th Cong., 1st Sess., pt. 1 at 108 (1967).
5. 297 *BNA Antitrust & Trade Regulation Report* X-2 (March 21, 1967).
6. Marcus, "The Impact on Business of Antitrust Decrees," 11 *Vanderbilt L. Rev.* 303, 323 (1958).
7. Comment, "An Experiment in Preventive Antitrust: Judicial Regulation of the Motion Picture Exhibition Market under the *Paramount* Decrees," 74 *Yale L. J.* 1040 (1964).
8. Address of Gordon Stulberg, Center Cinema Films, to symposium at the University of Southern California, February 5, 1971.
9. Cassady, "Impact of the *Paramount* Decision on Motion Picture Distribution and Price Making," 31 *S. Cal. L. Rev.* 150, 161 n. 77 (1958).
10. K. Elzinga, The Effectiveness of Relief Decrees in Antimerger Cases (unpublished doctoral thesis, Michigan State University, Department of Economics) 114 (1967).
11. *Ibid.,* Elzinga, "The Antimerger Law: Pyrrhic Victories?" 12 *Journal of Law & Economics* 43 (1969). See also Note, "Divestiture of Illegally Held Assets: Observations on its Scope, Objective, and Limitations," 64 *Michigan L. Rev.* 1574 (1966).
12. *United States* v. *Crescent Amusement Co.,* 323 U.S. 173, 189 (1944).

13. Turner, "Antitrust Consent Decrees: Some Basic Policy Questions" 11 (December 13, 1967) (speech to the Association of the Bar of the City of New York).
14. *United States* v. *Crescent Amusement Co.,* 323 U.S. 173, 189 (1944).
15. Posner, *supra* note 1, at 406.
16. Letter from Assistant Attorney General Richard McLaren to Rep. John D. Dingell, September 2, 1969.
17. Hearings on H. Res. 66 before the Special Subcommittee on Small Business and the Robinson-Patman Act of the Select Committee on Small Business, 91st Cong., 2d Sess., at 641–4 (Testimony of Stewart W. Pierce).
18. Letter from Assistant Attorney General Richard McLaren to Rep. John D. Dingell, June 8, 1970.
19. C. Kaysen, *United States* v. *United Shoe Machinery Corporation* (Harvard Economic Studies No. 99) 343 (1956).
20. See generally "Consent Decree Program of the Department of Justice," *supra* note 2, at 149–76.
21. The four Supreme Court decisions in this case are: *California* v. *Federal Power Comm'n,* 369 U.S. 482 (1962); *United States* v. *El Paso Gas Co.,* 376 U.S. 651 (1964); *Cascade Natural Gas Co.* v. *El Paso Natural Gas Co.,* 386 U.S. 129 (1967); *Utah Public Service Comm'n* v. *El Paso Natural Gas Co.,* 395 U.S. 464 (1969).
22. *N.Y. Times,* February 25, 1971, at 34; *ibid.,* April 21, 1971, at 75.
23. *United States* v. *E. I. duPont de Nemours & Co.,* 366 U.S. 316, 331 (1961).
24. *International Salt Co.* v. *United States* 332 U.S. 392, 401 (1947).
25. Flynn, "Consent Decrees in Antitrust Enforcement: Some Thoughts and Proposals," 53 *Iowa L. Rev.* 983, 989–90 (1968).
26. *United States* v. *Pan Am World Airlines, Inc.,* 1959 Trade Cas. ¶75,138 (S.D.N.Y.).
27. *United States* v. *Brunswick-Balke-Collender Co.,* 203 F. Supp. 657 (E.D. Wis., 1962); *United States* v. *Ward Baking Co.,* 1963 Trade Cas. ¶70,609 (M. D. Fla.), *rev'd* 376 U.S. 327 (1964); *United States* v. *Blue Chip Stamp Co.,* 1967 Trade Cas. ¶72,239 (N.D. Cal.), *aff'd mem,* 389 U.S. 580 (1968).
28. M. Goldberg, *supra* note 3, at 44.
29. *United States* v. *Lake Asphalt & Petroleum Co.,* 1960 Trade Cas. ¶69,835, (D. Mass.); *United States* v. *Allied Chemical Corp.,* 1961 Trade Cas. ¶69,923 (D. Mass.); *United States* v. *Bituminous Concrete Ass'n,* 1960 Trade Cas. ¶69,878 (D. Mass.).
30. Letter from Massachusetts Attorney General Edward J. McCormack, Jr., to United States Attorney General William P. Rogers, February 13, 1960; *cited in* Kaplan, "The Asphalt Clause—a New Weapon in Antitrust Enforcement," 3 *Boston College Industrial and Commercial L. Rev.* 355, 358 (1962).
31. *United States* v. *Brunswick-Balke-Collender Co.,* 203 F. Supp. 657 (E.D. Wis., 1962).
32. McLaren, "The Government and the Private Antitrust Suit" 13 (Address to the Antitrust Committees of the Federal Bar Association and the Philadelphia Bar Association, December 11, 1969).

33. Jinkinson, "Negotiation of Consent Decrees," 9 *Antitrust Bulletin* 673, 674 (1964).
34. W. Hamilton & I. Till, "Antitrust in Action" (TNEC Monograph No. 16, 1940), at 81.
35. *Ibid.*
36. Comment, "Antitrust Enforcement by Private Parties: Analysis of Developments in the Treble Damage Suit," 61 *Yale L. J.* 1010, 1060 (1952).
37. Comment, 18 *U. of Chicago L. Rev.* 130, 138 (1950).
38. *E.g., Bigelow* v. *RKO Radio Pictures, Inc.,* 327 U.S. 251 (1946); *Minnesota Mining & Mfg. Co.* v. *New Jersey Wood Finishing Co.,* 381 U.S. 311 (1965); *Leh* v. *General Petroleum Corp.* 382 U.S. 54 (1965); *Perma Life Mufflers Inc.* v. *International Parts Corp.,* 392 U.S. 135 (1968); *Hanover Shoe* v. *United Shoe Machinery Corp.,* 392 U.S. 481 (1968); *Zenith Radio Corp.* v. *Hazeltine Research, Inc.,* 395 U.S. 100 (1969).
39. *Mangano* v. *American Radiator & Standard Sanitary Corp.,* 5 CCH Trade Reg. Rep. (1971 Trade Cases, ¶73,447) 3d Cir. Feb. 18, 1971 (*per curiam*), *affirming* 309 F. Supp., 1057 (E.D. Pa. 1970).
40. See *West Virginia* v. *Charles R. Pfizer & Co., Inc.,* 1970 CCH Trade Cases ¶73,240 at 88,925 (S.D.N.Y. 1970), *affirmed* 5 CCH Trade Reg. Rep. (1971 Trade Cases ¶73,540) 2d Cir. March 29, 1971).
41. In Re Multidistrict Private Civil Treble Damage Antitrust Litigation Involving Motor Vehicle Air Pollution Control Equipment, 1970 CCH Trade Cases ¶73,518 (C.D. Cal. Sept. 4, 1970).
42. In Re Coordinated Pretrial Proceedings in Antibiotic Antitrust Actions, 5 CCH Trade Reg. Rep. (1961 Trade Cases) ¶73,482 S.D.N.Y. Feb. 17, 1971).
43. *Hackett* v. *General Host Corp.,* 476 *BNA Antitrust & Trade Reg. Rep.* A-6 (E. D. Pa. July 30, 1970).
44. This type of recovery has already been sanctioned by courts in cases involving fare overcharges by streetcars, buses, and taxicabs, with an aggregate damage fund established to subsidize fares or improve service for future passengers on the theory that a substantial portion of the formerly overcharged patrons would thereby be compensated. (*Market St. Ry. Co.* v. *Railroad Comm.,* 171 P. 2d 875 (Cal. 1946); *Bebchick* v. *Public Utilities Comm.,* 318 F. 2d 187, 203–204 (D.C. Cir. 1963) (*en banc*), *cert. denied,* 373 U.S. 913; *Daar* v. *Yellow Cab Co.,* 433 P. 2d 732 (Cal. 1967). And in a recent antitrust case, *Eisen* v. *Carlisle & Jacquelin,* brought on behalf of four million "odd-lot" stock purchasers (an odd lot is less than 100 shares), alleging that two dominant brokerage houses had monopolistically inflated the odd-lot brokerage commission, a district court ruled that aggregate damages could be distributed through a fund which reduced the commission in the future. (52 F.R.D. 253 [S.D.N.Y.]). The lone setback thus far has been the district-court ruling in *Philadelphia* v. *American Oil Company* (1971 Trade Cases, ¶73,625 [D.N.J.]). This case held that a class of at least six million motorists could not seek damages inflicted through price-fixing because included among the beneficiaries of gasoline prices sub-

sidized by an aggregate damage fund would be motorists who, for example, had not resided in the area when the overcharges were in effect. But to argue that an inevitable windfall to a few should vitiate compensation for many of the actual victims is to forget that price-fixers would be equally deterred, and the true function of compensation served, if the undistributed damage recovery were simply placed in a trust fund "for the benefit of consumers generally." That is precisely what was done with the residual consumer recovery in the antibiotic-drug settlement after 42,000 consumers had submitted individual damage claims in response to newspaper and television announcements.

45. Korman, "The Antitrust Plaintiff Following in the Government's Footsteps," 16 *Villanova L. Rev.* 57, 78 (1970).
46. See Note, "Increasing Community Control Over Corporate Crime—A Problem in the Law of Sanctions," 71 *Yale L. J.* 280, 298–301 (1961).
47. Lewis, "Trust Case Raises Big Questions," *N.Y. Times,* February 12, 1961, at 6-E.

CHAPTER 7

1. Speech by Assistant Secretary of State Philip Trezise printed in the State Department *Bulletin,* May 24, 1971, at 670.
2. *Fortune,* August, 1971, at 118.
3. *Ibid.,* at 109.
4. U.S. Senate, Subcommittee on International Trade, Committee on Finance, *Foreign Trade,* 92nd Cong., 1st Sess. 74 (1971).
5. *Journal of Commerce,* July 9, 1971, at 10.
6. Testimony before the Joint Economic Committee Subcommittee on Foreign Economic Policy, June 25, 1971.
7. U.S. Senate, Subcommittee on Antitrust and Monopoly, *Foreign Trade and the Antitrust Laws,* 88th Cong., 2nd Sess. 52–3 (1964).
8. *Ibid.,* at 61.
9. *Fortune,* Aug., 1970, at 142.
10. For comparisons with 1967 ratios see Stephen Hymer and Robert Rowthorn, "Multinational Corporations and International Oligopoly: The Non-American Challenge," in C. Kindleberger (ed.), *The International Corporation* 59–65 (1970).
11. *Ibid.,* at 66–70.
12. House of Representatives, Judiciary Committee Subcommittee on the Study of Monopoly Power, *Steel,* Serial 14, Part 4-A at 967 (1950).
13. Report to the President on the Economic Position of the Steel Industry, July 6, 1971.
14. *Wall Street Journal,* May 18, 1971, at 13.
15. Statement before the House Subcommittee on Science, Research and Development, July 27, 1971.
16. *Washington Post,* July 28, 1971, at 42.
17. E. Mansfield, *The Economics of Technological Change,* at 216.
18. *Studies by the Staff of the Cabinet Committee on Price Stability* 50–1 (1969).

450   NOTES

19. W. Mueller, "The Nature and Scope of Webb-Pomerene Associations," in *International Aspects of Antitrust,* Subcommittee on Antitrust and Monopoly, 90th Cong., 1st Sess. 34 (1967).
20. David A. Larson, "An Economic Analysis of the Webb-Pomerene Act," *Journal of Law and Economics,* October 1970, at 461–500.
21. *United States* vs. *Minnesota Mining and Manufacturing Company,* 92 F. Supp. 947 at 963 (D. Mass. 1950).
22. House of Representatives, Committee on Ways and Means, *Tariff and Trade Proposals,* 91st Cong., 2nd Sess. (1970).
23. Frederic Bastiat, *Sophismes Economiques,* quoted from L. B. Yeager and D. G. Tuerck, *Trade Policy and the Price System* 141 (1966).
24. Cabinet Task Force on Oil Import Control, *The Oil Import Question,* at 22, 207.
25. Statement of Barry J. Shillito, Assistant Secretary of Defense, before House Committee on Interior and Insular Affairs, 91st Cong., 2nd Sess. 4–5 (1970).
26. Andrew F. Brimmer, *Import Controls and Domestic Inflation,* November 11, 1970 (unpublished).
27. Dutlef G. Lehnardt, "Executive Authority and Antitrust Considerations in 'Voluntary' Limits on Steel Imports," 118 *Penn. L. Rev.* 105.
28. A legal argument for establishing that a conspiracy existed is developed in the article cited in *ibid.*
29. *Ibid.,* at 110.
30. U.S. Senate, Subcommittee on Antitrust and Monopoly, *International Aspects of Antitrust,* 88th Cong., 2nd Sess., at 499 (1963).
31. Bureau of Labor Statistics, *Foreign Trade and Employment,* 1970 (unpublished).
32. U.S. Department of Labor, unpublished statistics, June 27, 1971.
33. Address by Richard W. McLaren, "Competition in the Foreign Commerce of the United States," before the Symposium on Antitrust and Related Issues and Their Solutions in International Trade and Productive Investment, The American Society of International Law and the Marshall-Wythe School of Law, College of William and Mary, Williamsburg, Virginia, October 16, 1970.
34. *U.S.* vs *Jos. Schlitz Brewing Co.,* 253 F. Supp. 129 (1966).
35. U.S. Senate, Subcommittee on Antitrust and Monopoly, *International Aspects of Antitrust,* 89th Cong., 2nd Sess., 491 (1965).
36. O.E.C.D., *Market Power and the Law* 65–96 (Paris, 1970).
37. *Fortune,* September, 1970, at 81.
38. U.S. Senate, Subcommittee on Antitrust and Monopoly, *International Aspects of Antitrust,* 89th Cong., 2nd Sess. 497 (1965).
39. Richard J. Barber, *The American Corporation* 282 (1970).

CHAPTER 8

1. THE AUTOMOBILE INDUSTRY

1 Lanzillotti, "The Automobile Industry," in W. Adams (ed.), *The Structure of American Industry* 311 (1961).

2. "Annual Style Change in the Automobile Industry as an Unfair Method of Competition," 80 *Yale L. J.* 567, 571 (1971) (hereinafter *Yale Law Journal Note*), which cites, among others: L. Weiss, *Economics and the American Industry* 350–368 (1966); Lanzillotti, *supra* note 1; J. Bain, *Industrial Organization* (1968); J. Esposito, L. Silverman, *Vanishing Air* (1970). Loescher in Hearings before Select Committee on Small Business on Planning, "Regulation and Competition in the American Industry," 90th Cong., 2d Sess., 907, 920 (hereinafter cited as *1968 Hearings*).

3. *Yale Law Journal Note* at 577.

4. Checker Motors Corporation, which produces .15% of the auto market, and a handful of firms making under 500 cars a year are not considered viable competitors and are therefore excluded.

5. This historical sketch is derived from: Lanzillotti, *supra* note 1; *Yale Law Journal Note; 1968 Hearings;* Moore, "What's Good for the Country Is Good for GM," *Washington Monthly,* December, 1970, at 10; Subcommittee on Antitrust and Monopoly, "Administered Prices Automobiles," 85th Cong., 2d Sess. (November, 1968).

6. Hearings before Senate Subcommittee on Antitrust and Monopoly, "Auto Financing Legislation," 86th Cong., 1st Sess. 263 (1959).

7. *Yale Law Journal Note.*

8. *Advertising Age,* July 13, 1970, at 37.

9. L. White, *The American Automobile Industry in the Postwar Period* (1971) (taken from final manuscript prior to printing).

10. Quoted in *Ibid.*

11. Moore, "What's Good for the Country Is Good for GM," *Washington Monthly,* December, 1970, at 14.

12. Crandell, "The Decline of the Franchise Dealer in the Automotive Repair Market," *Journal of Business,* Fall, 1969; See also Davidson, *The Marketing of Automotive Parts,* Michigan Business Studies, Vol. XII, No. 1 (1954).

13. *Ibid.*

14. W. Shepherd, *Market Power & Economic Welfare* 242 (1970).

15. *Wall Street Journal,* November 20, 1962, at 1.

16. *1968 Hearings,* at 147–54.

17. *N.Y. Times,* May 9, 1956.

18. *Wall Street Journal,* October 31, 1967, at 1.

19. *Wall Street Journal,* April 18, 1962, at 1.

20. *Automotive News,* Sept. 20, 1971, at 1, 36.

21. For details of these exemptions, see *Cong. Record,* September 16, 1969, letter of Ralph Nader to Richard McLaren.

22. House Subcommittee on Antitrust, "The Consent Decree Program," 85th Cong., 2d Sess. (1959).

23. Speeches of Richard McLaren, before the Spring Meeting of the Antitrust Section, American Bar Association, Washington, D.C., April 1, 1971; Speech of Howard Adler, Jr., Remarks Prepared for Delivery at the Tenth Antitrust Conference of the National Industry Conference Board, March 11, 1971.

24. *Automotive News,* February 26, 1968, at 16.

25. *Ibid.*

2. THE PROFESSIONS

1. Council of State Governments, *Occupations and Professions Licensed by the States, Puerto Rico and the Virgin Islands* (1968).
2. M. Friedman, *Capitalism and Freedom* 140 (1962).
3. See generally Comment, "The American Medical Association: Power, Purpose, and Politics in Organized Medicine," 63 *Yale L. J.* 943 (1953).
4. *American Medical Association* v. *United States,* 317 U.S. 519 (1943).
5. *Portland Oregonian,* February 2, 1950, at 1.
6. Rayack, "Restrictive Practices of Organized Medicine," 13 *Antitrust Bulletin* 659, 662 (1968).
7. Bierring, "The Family Doctor and the Changing Order," *Journal of the American Medical Association,* June 16, 1934, at 1997.
8. *Medical Economics,* December 21, 1970, at 70.
9. Miller, "Hysterectomy: Therapeutic Necessity or Surgical Racket?" 51 *American Journal of Obstetrics and Gynecology* 804 (1946).
10. Lembcke, "Medical Auditing by Scientific Methods: Illustrated by Major Female Pelvic Surgery," 162 *Journal of the American Medical Association* 646 (1956).
11. See Note, "The Role of Prepaid Group Practice in Relieving the Medical Care Crisis," 84 *Harvard L. Rev.* 887, 962–9 (1971).
12. See Rayack, *supra* note 6, at 677–97.
13. Ethics Committee of the Wisconsin Bar Association, "Opinion No. 8," 29 *Wisconsin Bar Bulletin* 66 (1956).
14. ABA Committee on Professional Ethics, *Opinions,* No. 302 (1961).
15. See Comment, "Controlling Lawyers through Bar Associations and Courts," 5 *Harvard Civil Rights–Civil Liberties Law Review* 301, 334, 344 n. 20 (1970).
16. *Ibid.,* at 370–4.
17. Missouri Bar, *A Motivational Study of Public Attitudes and Law Office Management* 35 (Prentice-Hall, 1963), discussed in standing Committee of the California State Bar on Group Services, "Report on Group Legal Services," 39 *California State Bar Journal,* 639, 652 (1964).
18. D. Caplovitz, *The Poor Pay More* 175 (1963).
19. *NAACP* v. *Button,* 371 U.S. 415 (1963); *Brotherhood of Railway Trainmen* v. *Virginia State Bar,* 377 U.S. 1 (1964); *United Mine Workers* v. *Illinois State Bar Association,* 389 U.S. 217 (1967); *United Transportation Union* v. *State Bar of Michigan,* 39 U.S.L.W. 4428 (April 5, 1971). See generally, Comment, *supra* note 16, at 348–76.

3. THE OIL INDUSTRY

1. R. Engler, *The Politics of Oil* 215 (1961). Certain other aspects of the cartel case, as discussed subsequently in the text, are drawn from Dr. Engler's book.
2. Abstract of the Report on the International Petroleum Cartel by the Federal Trade Commission, in *Hearings Before the Subcommittee on Antitrust and Monopoly of the Senate Judiciary Com-*

mittee, "Governmental Intervention in the Market Mechanism— The Petroleum Industry," 91st Cong., 1st Sess., pt. 1, at 553 (1969).

3. Cabinet Task Force on Oil Import Control, *The Oil Import Question* 262 (1970).

4. *Hearings, supra* note 2, at 208–33, 221, 223 (testimony of Dr. Henry Steele).

5. Dirlam, "The Petroleum Industry," in W. Adams (ed.), *The Structure of American Industry* 277, 299 (3rd ed. 1961).

6. Mead & Sorensen, "A National Defense Petroleum Reserve Alternative to Oil Import Quotas" (paper presented before the Annual Meeting of the Western Economic Association at Davis, California, August 27–28, 1970; to be published in the August, 1971, issue of *Land Economics*).

7. Cabinet Task Force, *supra* note 3, at 65, Table K.

8. A. Kahn & M. DeChazeau, *Integration and Competition in the Petroleum Industry* 222 n. 48–9 (1959).

9. "Structure of the Petroleum Industry and Its Relation to Oil Shale and Other Energy Sources," in Bureau of Economics, Federal Trade Commission, *Economic Papers* 1966–69, 184, 188 (1967).

10. Hearings before the Subcommittee on Antitrust and Monopoly of the Senate Judiciary Committee, "Economic Concentration," 89th Congress, 1st Session, pt. 2, at 591, 593 (1965) (testimony of Dr. Alfred E. Kahn).

11. *Hearings, supra* note 2, pt. 3, at 1289, 1287–95.

12. *Hearings, supra* note 10, at 597.

13. 87 billion gallons consumed annually times 3¢ savings per gallon = $2.61 billion.

14. "Structure of the Petroleum Industry," *supra* note 9, at 190.

15. See generally Beck & Rawlings, "Coal: The Captive Giant" (1971) (obtainable from Stuart Rawlings, 2125 Observatory Place, N.W., Washington, D.C. 20007).

16. See Mead, "The Structure of the Buyer Market for Oil Shale Resources," 8 *Natural Resources Journal* 604 (1968). See also Mead, "The Competitive Significance of Joint Ventures," 12 *Antitrust Bulletin* 819 (1967) for an analysis of the remarkable pattern of joint ventures in offshore oil leases among the largest companies. In 1969 the Division's Los Angeles office investigated the Santa Inez offshore joint venture involving Standard (Cal.), Arco, Standard (N.J.), and probably two billion barrels of oil. The recommended suit was quashed "by those who for some reason couldn't understand that companies that big don't need to merge to do anything," recalled a Division attorney. "The Gulf Coast offshore venturers are at least as bad."

17. Dugger, "Oil and Politics," *Atlantic,* September, 1969, at 66, 73.

CHAPTER 9

1. Smith, "Antitrust and the Monopoly Problem: Toward a More Relevant Legal Analysis," 2 *Antitrust Law and Economic Review* 19, 48 (Summer, 1969).

2. Whitney, "The Economic Impact of Antitrust: An Overview," 9 *Antitrust Bulletin* 509, 519 (1964).

3. "Priorities in Antitrust: Some Communications," 1 *Antitrust Law and Economic Review* 11 (Spring, 1968).

4. Turner, "The Scope of Antitrust and Other Economic Regulatory Policies," 82 *Harvard L. Rev.* 1207 (1969).

5. Stigler, "The Case Against Bigness," *in* Mansfield (ed.) *Monopoly Power and Economic Performance* 3, 11 (1964).

6. Levi, "The Antitrust Laws and Monopoly," 14 *U. of Chicago L. Rev.* 153 (1947).

7. *Ibid.*, at 158.

8. *Ibid.*

9. 221 U.S. 1 (1911).

10. 274 U.S. 613, 708 (1927).

11. *United States v. Swift & Co.*, 286 U.S. 106, 116 (1932).

12. *Interstate Circuit, Inc.* v. *United States*, 306 U.S. 208 (1939).

13. *United States* v. *Aluminum Co. of America*, 148 F. 2d 416, 424, 427, 431 (2d Cir. 1945).

14. *American Tobacco Co.* v. *United States*, 328 U.S. 781, 789 (1946).

15. Rostow, "The New Sherman Act: A Positive Instrument of Progress," 14 *U. of Chicago L. Rev.* 567, 586 (1947).

16. *United States* v. *Schine*, 334 U.S. 110 (1948).

17. *Federal Trade Commission* v. *Cement Institute*, 333 U.S. 683 (1948).

18. *Standard Oil Co.* v. *United States*, 337 U.S. 293, 304 (1948).

19. *Federal Trade Commission* v. *Motion Picture Advertising Services Co., Inc.*, 344 U.S. 392, 395 (1952).

20. Turner, "The Scope of Antitrust and Other Regulatory Policies," 82 *Harvard L. Rev.* 1207, 1219 (1969).

21. Posner, "Oligopoly and the Antitrust Laws: A Suggested Approach," 21 *Stanford L. Rev.* 1562 (1969).

22. Scanlon, "Economics in the Courtroom: The Technology of Antitrust Litigation," 3 *Antitrust Law and Economic Review* 43, 49 (Fall, 1969).

23. *United States* v. *E. I. duPont de Nemours & Co.*, 353 U.S. 586 (1957) (Burton, J., dissenting).

24. Rostow, "The New Sherman Act: A Positive Instrument of Progress," 14 *U. of Chicago L. Rev.* 567, 576 (1947).

25. Baldridge, "The Present Status of Large Corporations, Under Section 7 of the Clayton Act," 3 *Antitrust Bulletin* 25 (1958).

26. "The Bite of the GM Decision," *Business Week*, June 8, 1957, at 41.

27. Steele, "A Decade of the Celler-Kefauver Anti-merger Act," 14 *Vanderbilt L. Rev.* 1049 (1961).

28. *Wall Street Journal*, June 27, 1958, at 1.

29. Subcommittee No. 5 of the Select Committee on Small Business, House of Representatives, 86th Congress, 2d Session 109 (December 27, 1960).

30. *New York Times*, June 24, 1962, at 38.

31. 236 F. Supp. 244, 248 (D.R.I. 1964).

32. Speech by William Orrick, April 17, 1964 (located in Antitrust Division Library, Department of Justice).

33. Statement of Richard W. McLaren, before the Joint Economic Committee, July 10, 1970, at 12.

34. Hearings before the House Appropriations Subcommittee, 90th Congress, 2d Session, 757 (February, 1969).

35. Schwartz, "New Approaches to the Control of Oligopoly," 109 *U. Pa. L. Rev.* 31, 42 (1960).

36. Hearings before the Senate Select Committee on Small Business, "Planning, Regulation, and Competition," 90th Congress, 1st Session 38 (1967).

37. *E.g.,* J. Bain, *Barriers to New Competition* 195, 197 (1956); Mann, "Seller Concentration, Barriers to Entry, and Rates of Return in Thirty Industries," 48 *Rev. Econ. & Stat.* 296–307 (1966).

38. Compare *Triangle Conduit & Cable Co.* v. *F.T.C.,* 168 F. 2d 175 (7th Cir. 1948), *aff'd* by an equally divided Court *sub. nom. Clayton Mark & Co.* v. *F.T.C.,* 336 U.S. 956 (1949) with *Crouse-Hinds Co.,* 46 F.T.C. 1114 (1950).

39. M. Friedman, *Capitalism & Freedom* 130 (1962).

40. *Ibid.,* at 73; P. Samuelson, *Economics* 673 (7th ed. 1967).

41. Mueller, "Sources of Monopoly Power: A Phenomenon Called 'Product Differentiation,'" 2 *Antitrust Law & Economics Review* 59, 66–8 (Summer, 1969).

42. Yang, "Industrial Concentration and Advertising," in Hearings before Senate Subcommittee on Antitrust and Monopoly, Economic Concentration, 89th Congress, 2d Session at 2153 (1966).

CHAPTER 10

1. Among the leading books and articles and studies of the Federal Trade Commission are the following, in historical order: T. Blaisdell, *The FTC: An Experiment in the Control of Business* (1924); G. Henderson, *The Federal Trade Commission* (1924); Herring, "Politics, Personalities and the Federal Trade Commission," 28 *Am. Pol. Sci. Rev.* 1016 (1934); "The Federal Trade Commission Silver Anniversary Issue," 8 *Georg. Wash. L. Rev.* 249 (1940); Simon, "The Case Against the Federal Trade Commission," 19 *U. Chic. L. Rev.* 297 (1952); Kintner, "The Revitalized Federal Trade Commission: A Two Year Evaluation," 30 *N.Y.U. L. Rev.* 1143 (1955); Comment, "The New Federal Trade Commission and the Enforcement of the Antitrust Laws," 65 *Yale L. J.* 34 (1955); Auerbach, "The Federal Trade Commission," 48 *Minn. L. Rev.* 393 (1964); "The Fiftieth Anniversary of the Federal Trade Commission," 64 *Colum. L. Rev.* 385 (1964); Blair, "Planning for Competition," 64 *Colum. L. Rev.* 524 (1964); Posner, "The Federal Trade Commission," 37 *U. Chic. L. Rev.* 47 (1969); E. Cox, R. Fellmeth, J. Schultz, *The Nader Report on the Federal Trade Commission* (1969) [hereinafter cited as *Nader Report*].

2. Herring, "Politics, Personalities and the Federal Trade Commission," 28 *Am. Pol. Sci. Rev.,* 1016 at 1016 (1934) (hereinafter cited as Herring I).

3. *Report of the ABA Commission to Study the Federal Trade Commission* 1 (1969) (hereinafter *ABA Report*).

4. Herring I at 1016; see also Henderson, *supra* note 1, at 17.
5. *Ibid.*, at 1018.
6. Herring, "Politics, Personalities and the Federal Trade Commission," 29 *Am. Pol. Sci. Rev.* 21 at 21 (1935) (hereinafter cited as Herring II).
7. Herring I at 1022 (Remarks of Senator King).
8. "The Zealous Men of the FTC," *Fortune,* February, 1952, 107 at 108.
9. *Humphrey's Executor* v. *United States,* 295 U.S. 602 (1935).
10. See *Nader Report* at 132–141.
11. *Fortune, supra* note 12, at 108.
12. "Behind the Committee Doors: The Appointees Refute the Promises," *New Republic,* May 4, 1953, 12 at 13.
13. *New York Times,* September 3, 1953, at 31.
14. The reduction in force is discussed in detail at Hearings Pursuant to H. Res. 114 before Subcommittee No. 1 of the Select Committee on Small Business, 84th Congress, 1st Session, pt. 1 at 272–80 (1955).
15. "Republicans Reshape the FTC," *Business Week,* June 5, 1954, at 43.
16. Hearings *supra* note 14, at 114.
17. "And So Is Mr. Howrey," *New Republic,* August 1, 1955, at 6.
18. *New York Times,* June 17, 1958, at 13. *See also* L. Kohlmeier, *The Regulators* 44–5 (1969).
19. *New York Times,* June 17, 1958, at 13.
20. *New York Times,* June 27, 1958, at 10.
21. *New York Times,* June 17, 1958, at 13.
22. "New Chairman of FTC Will Have Easier Role," *Business Week,* August 20, 1955, at 74.
23. "New Chairman for FTC," *Fortune,* September, 1955, at 46.
24. *Nader Report* at 140–154.
25. *ABA Report* at 33.
26. *Nader Report* at 183.
27. Senate Subcommittee on Administrative Practice and Procedure of the Committee on the Judiciary, "Responses to Questionnaire on Citizen Involvement and Responsive Agency Decision Making," 91st Cong., 1st Sess. 133 (1969).
28. *Ibid.*, at 822.
29. Senate Subcommittee on Administrative Practice and Procedure of the Committee on the Judiciary, "Federal Agency Responsiveness to Public Needs," 91st Cong., 1st Sess. 17 (1969).
30. Posner, *supra* note 1, at 47.
31. Henderson, *supra* note 1, at 327.
32. Herring II at 35.
33. Auerbach, *supra* note 1.

CHAPTER 11

1. *ABA Report* at 69.
2. Bureau of the Budget, Management Review of the Federal Trade Commission, "Bureau of Restraint of Trade," at n. 1. (1970).

3. *Thatcher Mfg. Co.* v. *FTC*, 272 U.S. 554 (1926).

4. *FTC* v. *Eastman Kodak Co.*, 274 U.S. 619 (1927).

5. *Arrow-Hart & Hegeman Electric Co.* v. *FTC*, 291 U.S. 587 (1934).

6. *See* D. Martin, *Mergers and the Clayton Act,* Chapter 2 (1959) at 135–46.

7. "Congress in 1950 clearly intended to remove all question concerning the FTC's remedial power over corporate acquisitions." *U.S.* v. *Philadelphia National Bank*, 374 U.S. 321 at 348 (1963).

8. *FTC* v. *Guignon*, 390 F. 2d 323 (8th Cir. 1968).

9. Hearings pursuant to S. Res. 61 before the Subcommittee on Antitrust and Monopoly of the Senate Committee on the Judiciary, 84th Cong., 1st Sess., pt. 1 (1955).

10. *Pillsbury Co.* v. *FTC* (1966 Trade Cases) *Trade Reg. Rep.* ¶ 71646 at 81,900 (5th Cir., January 7, 1966).

11. K. G. Elzinga, *The Effectiveness of Relief Decrees in Antimerger Cases* (1967) (unpublished doctoral thesis) (hereinafter cited as *Elzinga*), at 107.

12. *Ibid.*, at 240.

13. These statistics are based on our own analysis and computations. It should be pointed out that they only refer to complaints issued after March, 1961. Therefore, litigation commenced prior to that date is not included. The figures are actually conservative because they only estimate the time taken to a Commission order. This obviously does not include the lengthy appeal process and the further time required for an actual divestiture of acquired assets. Moreover, it does not take into account the cases which have truly become bogged down, since they have not yet reached the hearing examiner or the Commission.

14. *ABA Report* at 27.

15. *Broadway-Hale Stores, Inc.* (1967–1970 Transfer Binder), *Trade Reg. Rep.* ¶18,692 at 21,064 (FTC 1969).

16. *May Department Stores Co.* (1965–1967 Transfer Binder), *Trade Reg. Rep.* ¶17,684 (FTC 1966).

17. *Wall Street Journal*, February 5, 1969, at 8.

18. *Broadway-Hale*, ¶18,692 at 21,067.

19. "Broadway-Hale Makes It to Fifth Avenue," *Business Week*, April 3, 1971, at 68, 72.

20. *Burlington Industries, Inc.* (1967–1970 Transfer Binder), *Trade Reg. Rep.* ¶18,635 (FTC 1969).

21. *Ibid.*, at 21,001–21,002, n. 2.

22. "The Small World of Big Washington Lawyers," *Fortune,* September, 1969, at 197.

23. Broadway-Hale Stores, Inc. (1967–1970 Transfer Binder), *Trade Reg. Rep.* ¶18,692 at 21,070 (FTC 1969).

24. *Ibid.*, at 21,070.

25. *Campbell-Taggart Associated Bakeries, Inc.* 1967–1970 Transfer Binder), *Trade Reg. Rep.* ¶17,912 (FTC 1967).

26. *Ibid.*, at 20,304.

27. *Textron Inc.* (1967–1970 Transfer Binder), *Trade Reg. Rep.* ¶19,260.

28. Procter & Gamble Co. (1965–1967 Transfer Binder), *Trade Reg. Rep.* ¶17,858 at 23,216 (FTC 1967).

29. Subcommittee on Administrative Practice and Procedure of the Committee on the Judiciary, "Responses to Questionnaire on Citizen Involvement and Responsive Agency Decision-Making," 91st Cong., 1st Sess. 284–85 (1969) (hereinafter cited as *Responses*).

30. Occidental Petroleum Corp. (1967–1970 Transfer Binder), *Trade Reg. Rep.* ¶18,797 (tentative approval), ¶18,864 (final approval) (FTC 1969).

31. Mr. Neilson's calculations are found in the FTC File, Occidental Petroleum Corp., Docket C–1450.

32. FTC Procedures Before Senate Subcommittee on Administrative Practice and Procedure of the Committee on the Judiciary, 91st Cong., 1st Sess. 44 (1969) (hereinafter cited as *Kennedy Hearings*).

33. *Crown Cork & Seal Co.* (1967–1970 Transfer Binder), *Trade Reg. Rep.* ¶18,456 at 20,805 (FTC 1968).

34. *Kroger Co.* (1967–1970 Transfer Binder), *Trade Reg. Rep.* ¶18,582 at 20,922 (FTC 1968).

35. 16 C. F. R. §2.34(d) (1971).

36. *Beatrice Foods Co.* (1967–1970 Transfer Binder), *Trade Reg. Rep.* ¶17,949 at 20,327 (FTC 1967).

37. Perhaps the most devastating aspect of the *Beatrice* settlement is that it obliterated the possibiliy of a clear Supreme Court precedent in the market-extension area. Ironically, it is in the market-extension area that many of the Commission's consent orders seem particularly lax—*e.g.*, the department-store cases.

38. *United States* v. *Von's Grocery Co.*, 384 U.S. 270 at 301 (1966).

39. *Elzinga* at 73.

40. *Columbia Broadcasting System Co.* (1969 Trade Cases), *Trade Reg. Rep.* ¶72,835 (7th Cir., June 26, 1969).

41. *FTC* v. *International Paper Co.*, 241 F. 2d 372 (1956).

42. *FTC* v. *Dean Foods Co.*, 384 U.S. 597 (1966).

43. The Commission's order is found at *Swingline, Inc.* (1967–1970 Transfer Binder), *Trade Reg. Rep.* ¶18,948 (FTC 1969).

44. *Seeburg Corp.* (1967–1970 Transfer Binder), *Trade Reg. Rep.*, ¶18,748 (FTC 1969).

45. *American Brake Shoe Co.* (1967–1970 Transfer Binder), *Trade Reg. Rep.* ¶18,339 (FTC 1968).

46. *Allied Chemical Corp.* (1967–1970 Transfer Binder), *Trade Reg. Rep.* ¶19,237 (FTC 1970).

47. *Procter & Gamble Co.* (1963–1965 Transfer Binder), *Trade Reg. Rep.* ¶16,673 (FTC 1963).

48. *Procter & Gamble* v. *FTC*, 258 F. 2d 74 at 83 (6th Cir. 1966).

49. *FTC* v. *Procter & Gamble Co.* (Clorox), 386 U.S. 568 (1967).

50. *General Foods Corp.* v. *FTC* (1967 Trade Cases) *Trade Reg. Rep.* ¶72,269 at 84,636 (3d Cir., November 9, 1967).

51. *The Bendix Corp.*, 3 *Trade Reg. Rep.* ¶19,288 FTC (1970).

CHAPTER 12

1. Markham, "The Federal Trade Commission's Use of Economics," 64 *Columbia L. Rev.* at 405–408; refer also to *FTC, Here Is Your Federal Trade Commission* (pamphlet) at 20.

2. House Appropriations Hearings for Independent Offices, 1963, at 85, 168.

3. *FTC, Economic Report on Corporate Mergers,* 1969, at 13, 15.

4. MacAvoy, "The Federal Trade Commission: Staff Economic Report on Corporate Merger," *N.Y. St. Bar Ass'n Antitrust Law Symposium* 1970 at 55.

5. Letter from Dirlam to FTC, February 24, 1970; letter from Preston to FTC, May 3, 1970.

6. *FTC, Economic Report, supra* note 3, at 16.

7. 1971 FTC Budget Hearings, at 1470.

8. Elman, "The Regulatory Process: A Personal View," *ABA Antitrust Section Convention,* St. Louis, August 11, 1970.

9. *Foremost Dairies,* Docket No. 6495.

10. *Beatrice Foods,* Docket No. 6653.

11. *Ibid.,* opinion of the Commission, at 51; refer also to Mueller, "Public Policy Toward Mergers in the Dairy Industry," in *FTC Economic Papers* 1966–1969, Chapter 7.

12 W. Mueller, *The Celler-Kefauver Act: 16 Years of Enforcement* 18 (1967).

13. *In the Matter of Beatrice Foods,* at 43–44.

14. W. Mueller, *supra* note 12, at 54.

15. Boyd, "Vertical Integration in the Cement and Concrete Industries," Address before National Sand & Gravel Association, National Ready-Mix Concrete Association, January 28, 1970.

16. *FTC, Economic Report on Mergers and Vertical Integration in Cement Industry* 14 (1966).

17. *E.g., Report of the Stigler Task Force to President Nixon; see also* Bork & Bowman (a member of the Stigler team), "The Crisis in Antitrust," *Fortune,* December, 1963; Whalen, "Vertical Mergers in the Cement Industry," 3 *Antitrust Law & Economics Review* (Fall, 1969), who dislikes the FTC enforcement policy because it condemns the concrete industry to a "perpetually disadvantaged existence, one in which the economic power of both its major suppliers and its major customers far exceeds any it can claim."

18. Mueller, "Vertical Integration and Public Policy Toward Vertical Mergers," *FTC Economic Papers* at 113.

19. Adelman, "Market Issues: An Economist's View," *National Industrial Conference Board, The Impact of Antitrust on Economic Growth,* March 5, 1964, at 30.

20. *National Labor Relations Board* v. *Wyman-Gordon Co.,* 394 U.S. 759 (1969).

21. Bok, "Section 7 of the Clayton Act and the Merging of Law and Economics," 74 *Harvard L. Rev.* 226 (1960).

22. Turner, "Conglomerate Mergers and Section 7 of the Clayton Act," 78 *Harvard L. Rev.* 1313, at 1318 (1965).

23. *See* note 1 in Chapter X.

24. Responses cited of various unidentified staff attorneys, in the *Nicholson Report.*

25. James Nicholson memorandum, January 17, 1969, published as Attachment A to "Nicholson Memo."

26. Elman response to the Subcommittee on Administrative Practice, May 12, 1969, *supra* note 30 at 139.

27. Staff of Monopoly Subcommittee, House Committee on Small

Business, 79th Congress, 1st Sess. 22 "United States Versus Economic Concentration and Monopoly," 1946.

CHAPTER 13

1. 344 U.S. 394–5 (1953).
2. *Re Topps Chewing Gum, Inc.*, FTC Docket 8755; *Carvel Corporation*, FTC Docket 8574.
3. Hearings on Independent Offices Appropriations for 1971 before a Subcommittee of the House Appropriations Committee, 91st Congress, 2d Session 1373 (1970); Appropriations for 1970, 91st Congress, 1st Session 433 (1969); Appropriations for 1969, 90th Congress, 2d Session 100 (1968).
4. 16 CFR §2.21 (1970).
5. *Re Curtiss-Wright Corp., Inc.*, FTC Docket 8703.
6. *Re Columbia Broadcasting System*, FTC Docket 8512.
7. The information for this section comes largely through interviews, plus the Proposed Findings of Fact, the Findings of Complaint Counsel, and the Initial Decision in *Re Koppers Co., Inc.*, FTC Docket 8755.
8. Parker, "The Baking Industry," 2 *Antitrust & Economics Review* 118–120 (Summer, 1967). *See also* W. Mueller, "The Effects of Antitrust Enforcement in the Food Industry," reprinted in the Commission staff report *Economic Papers* (1966–1969).
9. Costello, "The Tetracycline Conspiracy," 1 *Antitrust Law & Economic Review* (Summer, 1968); *also* interviews with Thomas Athridge and Ernest Barnes *et al.*, at the Commission. *See also Re American Cyanamid Co.*, FTC Docket 7211.
10. *Re L. G. Balfour*, FTC Docket 8435.
11. *See* note 3 *supra*, Appropriations for 1971, 91st Congress, 2d Session 1365 (1970).
12. *Ibid.* at 1360–61.
13. Knutson, "Public Policy and Unfair Competition: Structure, Conduct and Performance in the Milk Industry," 2 *Antitrust Law & Economics Review* (Winter, 1968–69).
14. Hearings before Subcommittees of the Select Committee on Small Business, "Planning, Regulation and Competition: Automobile Industry–1968," U.S. Senate, 90th Congress, 2d Session 1075–91 (July 23, 1968) ("The Costs of Automobile Model Changes Since 1949" by Gurliches & Kaysen).
15. *See* Note, "Annual Style Change in the Automobile Industry as an Unfair Method of Competition," 80 *Yale L.J.* 567 (1971).

CHAPTER 14

1. 38 Stat. 730, 15 U.S.C. §13 (1964).
2. C. Austin, *Price Discrimination and Related Problems Under the Robinson-Patman Act* 1 (3rd ed. 1959).
3. Sheehy, "Like Grade and Quality," 30 *ABA Antitrust Section* 2 (1966).

4. Austern, "Isn't Thirty Years Enough?" 30 *ABA Antitrust Section* 18 (1966).

5. L. Kohlmeier, *The Regulators* 88 (1969).

6. Rowe, "The Federal Trade Commission's Administration of the Anti-Price Discrimination Law," 64 *Colum. L. Rev.* 415, 430 (1964).

7. *Ibid.* at 431.

8. C. Kaysen, D. Turner, *Antitrust Policy* 180 (1965).

9. *White House Task Force Report on Antitrust Policy* 33 (1969).

10. Hearings on Small Business and the Robinson-Patman Act before the Select Committee on Small Business, House of Representatives, 91st Cong., 1st Sess., vol. 1, at 123 (1969) (hereinafter cited as *House Small Business Hearings*).

11. *Forster Mfg. Co., Inc.* v. *F.T.C.*, 335 F. 2d 47 (1st Cir. 1964).

12. *Forster Mfg. Co., Inc.* v. *F.T.C.* 361 F. 2d 340, 342 (1st Cir. 1966).

13. *Supra* note 11 at 51.

14. *Forster Mfg. Co., Inc.*, CCH *Trade Reg. Rep.* ¶13,304 (FTC 1965).

15. *Universal Rundle Corp.*, CCH *Trade Reg. Rep.* ¶16,948 (FTC 1963).

16. S. Nelson, *An Economic Analysis of Industry Practices and Antitrust Policy in the Automotive Parts Industry* 58 (1970) (published by the Motor Equipment Manufacturers Association).

17. Address by Paul Rand Dixon before the National Association of Chain Drug Stores, April 16, 1969.

18. Responses to Questionnaire on Citizen Involvement and Responsive Agency Decision-Making, Submitted to the Subcommittee on Administrative Practice and Procedure to the Senate Committee on the Judiciary, 91st Cong., 1st Sess. 185 (1969).

19. Hearings on Federal Trade Commission Procedures before the Subcommittee on Administrative Practice and Procedures of the Senate Committee on the Judiciary, 91st Cong., 1st Sess. 102 (1969).

CHAPTER 15

1. Letter from Caspar Weinberger to Senator Edward Kennedy, July 22, 1970.

2. *Advertising Age,* Sept. 28, 1970, at 4.

3. Address by Commissioner Elman, "The Regulatory Process: A Personal View," ABA Convention, St. Louis, August 11, 1970, at 17.

4. *Ibid.* at 11–17.

5. *ABA Report* at 91.

6. See *Ash Report* at 140–4 for a summary of the various studies and bills supporting an administrative court.

7. *N.Y. Times,* Feb. 21, 1971, §3 (Business and Finance) at 7.

8. *Ibid.,* at 7.

9. *Ash Report* at 87.

10. *Ash Report* at 94.

11. *ABA Report* at 65.

12. *Supra* note 10, Chapter 14, pt. 3 at 586.

13. *Ibid.*, at 586.
14. *Ibid.*, at 578.
15. *Ibid.*, at 578.
16. *FTC* v. *Guignon*, 390 F. 2d 323 (8th Cir. 1968).
17. These were leaked to the press. *See Washington Post*, Oct. 5, 1970, at A–8.
18. *Ibid.*
19. *ABA Report* at 65.
20. *ABA Report* at 192.

APPENDICES

APPENDIX A

I*
Period in Which Case Was Instituted

	1890 to 1894	1895 to 1899	1900 to 1904	1905 to 1909	1910 to 1914	1915 to 1919	1920 to 1924	1925 to 1929	1930 to 1934	1935 to 1939	1940 to 1944	1945 to 1949	1950 to 1954	1955 to 1959	1960 to 1964	1965 to 1969	Total
Horizontal Conspiracy	3	7	5	28	62	29	50	36	19	34	179	114	122	122	104	75	989
Monopolizing	3	1		9	25	3	7	8	9	14	65	60	62	45	40	19	370
Acquisitions Short of Monopoly			1	2	3	1	1	5	1	3	2	5	3	26	61	80	194
Boycott		1	2	15	9	10	20	5	8		43	20	44	38	18	12	245
Resale Price Maintenance				2			2	1	2	1	1		4	4	8	2	27
Vertical Integration				2	3	4				7	6	11	6	6	7	1	53
Tying Arrangements					3	2		1	1	4	8	23	12	5	4	2	65
Exclusive Dealing	1		1		9	1	3	1		4	16	24	29	23	22	6	140
Territorial and Customer Limitations						5							4	28	24	13	74
Violence	4	1			6		8	3	10		7	2		4		2	47
Price Discrimination	1		3	6		2	1	4	1	5	29	20	16	15	14	6	123
Other Predatory or Unfair Conduct	1		3	2		3	1	2	1	5	27	17	7	4	11	4	88
Interlocking Directorates								2			1	5	4	2	2		16
Clayton Act, sec. 10													1		2		3
Labor Cases	3		2				16	6	7	18	35	2	17	7	5	1	125
Patent and Copyright Cases				6	6	1	8		2	3	36	45	22	15	13	11	165
Total Cases in Period	9	1	6	39	91	43	66	69	30	57	223	157	159	195	215	195	1551

Source: Computed from the Bluebook, as reported in Posner, "A Statistical Study of Antitrust Enforcement," XIII *The Journal of Law and Economics*, 365 (1970).

* Table shows distribution of allegations, not of cases.

II*

Period in Which Case Was Instituted	Number Won	Number Lost	Percentage Won	Number Won in Supreme Court	Number Lost in Supreme Court	Percentage Won in Supreme Court
1890–1894	3	5	38	1	1	50
1895–1899	4	3	57	2	2	50
1900–1904	5	1	83	2	0	100
1905–1909	21	17	55	6	1	86
1910–1914	61	30	67	8	8	50
1915–1919	31	12	72	2	2	50
1920–1924	42	24	64	6	6	50
1925–1929	53	4	93	6	0	100
1930–1934	23	6	79	2	1	67
1935–1939	45	12	79	12	6	67
1940–1944	173	50	78	12	9	57
1945–1949	131	28	82	20	6	77
1950–1954	135	22	86	12	4	75
1955–1959	176	18	91	19	5	79
1960–1964	180	31	85	32	3	91
1965–1967	78	3	96	6	0	100

Source: Computed from the Bluebook, as reported in Posner, *ibid.*

III*

ANTITRUST CASES INSTITUTED BY THE DEPARTMENT OF JUSTICE

Year	Cases	Year	Cases	Year	Cases
1890	1	1918	10	1945	20
1891	0	1919	3	1946	37
1892	5	1915–1919	43	1947	25
1893	1	1920	8	1948	44
1894	2	1921	20	1949	31
1890–1894	9	1922	17	1945–1949	157
1895	1	1923	8	1950	48
1896	3	1924	13	1951	42
1897	2	1920–1924	66	1952	27
1898	0	1925	12	1953	18
1899	1	1926	9	1954	24
1895–1899	7	1927	13	1950–1954	159
1900	0	1928	17	1955	34
1901	0	1929	8	1956	30
1902	3	1925–1929	59	1957	38
1903	2	1930	7	1958	47
1904	1	1931	3	1959	46
1900–1904	6	1932	5	1955–1959	195
1905	5	1933	9	1960	35

Source: Computed from the Bluebook, as reported in Posner, *ibid.*

III (*Continued*)

Year	Count	Year	Count	Year	Count
1906	14	1934	6	1961	47
1907	10	1930–1934	30	1962	56
1908	7	1935	4	1963	26
1909	3	1936	5	1964	51
1905–1909	39	1937	7	1960–1964	215
1910	15	1938	10	1965	35
1911	23	1939	31	1966	36
1912	20	1935–1939	57	1967	34
1913	22	1940	65	1968	47
1914	11	1941	71	1969	43
1910–1914	91	1942	46	1965–1969	195
1915	7	1943	22		
1916	2	1944	19	Total	1551
1917	21	1940–1944	223		

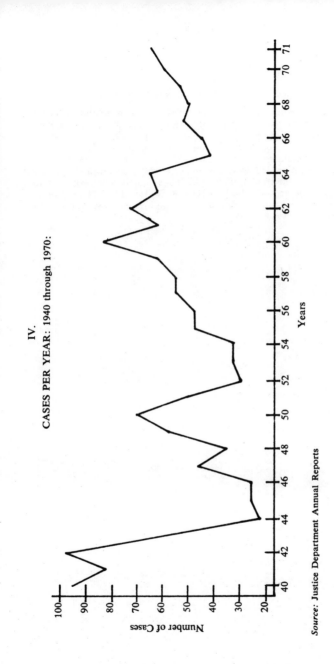

IV.

CASES PER YEAR: 1940 through 1970:

Number of Cases

Years

Source: Justice Department Annual Reports

APPENDIX B

Survey of Businessmen's Attitudes Toward the Antitrust Laws

The Study Group dispatched the questions below to the presidents of *Fortune's* 1,000 largest manufacturing corporations. Anonymous replies were solicited, and 11.0% responded. There was a relatively even distribution of responses among corporations of various sizes. Of 110 respondants, 108 indicated which 100th of the *Fortune* 1,000 their corporation fell within. Compared with the mean of 10.8 responses per 100-firm grouping, the actual number of responses for each group was: 1–12; 2–13; 3–11; 4–8; 5–11; 6–13; 7–10; 8–9; 9–11; 10–10. The responses to each question are broken down into top 500 and second 500 firms.

QUESTION	RESPONSE		NUMBER OF RESPONSES AS % OF TOTAL POPULATION (500 CORPORATIONS)
1. Are you a diversified, multiproduct firm, or do you produce mostly one product?	*ONE PRODUCT* (Top 500) 16.6% (2nd 500) 41.5%	*MULTIPRODUCT* (Top 500) 83.4% (2nd 500) 58.5%	(Top 500) 10.8% (2nd 500) 10.6%
2. Have you been involved in the last five years in antitrust litigation?	*YES* (Top 500) 49.1% (2nd 500) 13.2%	*NO* (Top 500) 50.9% (2nd 500) 86.8%	(Top 500) 10.6% (2nd 500) 10.6%
3. Do you think American industry is too concentrated?	(Top 500) 13.5% (2nd 500) 26.4%	(Top 500) 86.5% (2nd 500) 73.6%	(Top 500) 10.4% (2nd 500) 10.6%
4. Do you think that conglomerates pose a threat to the American economy?	(Top 500) 12.2% (2nd 500) 22.2%	(Top 500) 87.8% (2nd 500) 77.8%	(Top 500) 9.8% (2nd 500) 10.8%
5. Do you think that conglomerates pose a threat to the American society or political system?	(Top 500) 3.9% (2nd 500) 14.0%	(Top 500) 96.1% (2nd 500) 86.0%	(Top 500) 10.2% (2nd 500) 10.0%
6. Should there be any law limiting the absolute size of conglomerates?	(Top 500) 0.0% (2nd 500) 21.6%	(Top 500) 100.0% (2nd 500) 78.4%	(Top 500) 10.0% (2nd 500) 10.2%
7. Should there be any law limiting the absolute size of oligopolists?	(Top 500) 4.8% (2nd 500) 23.3%	(Top 500) 95.2% (2nd 500) 76.7%	(Top 500) 8.4% (2nd 500) 8.6%
8. Do you think there is a political motivation behind the current suits against conglomerates?	(Top 500) 38.1% (2nd 500) 55.3%	(Top 500) 61.9% (2nd 500) 44.7%	(Top 500) 8.4% (2nd 500) 9.4%
9. Do you think political considerations are ever involved when the government decides whom to sue and whom not to sue?	*YES* (Top 500) 62.0% (2nd 500) 91.8%	*NO* (Top 500) 38.0% (2nd 500) 8.2%	(Top 500) 10.0% (2nd 500) 9.8%

QUESTION	RESPONSE		NUMBER OF RESPONSES AS % OF TOTAL POPULATION (500 CORPORATIONS)	
10. One defendant in the Electrical Manufacturing Price-fixing Cases said that he had acted illegally but not immorally. Do you agree?	(Top 500) 15.4% (2nd 500) 39.6%	(Top 500) 84.6% (2nd 500) 60.4%	(Top 500) 10.4% (2nd 500) 9.6%	
11. In addition, this defendant said that many others also price-fix. Do you agree?	(Top 500) 46.8% (2nd 500) 70.5%	(Top 500) 53.2% (2nd 500) 29.5%	(Top 500) 9.4% (2nd 500) 8.8%	
12. Would you favor raising the Sherman Act ceiling for criminal violations from $50,000 to $500,000?	(Top 500) 39.2% (2nd 500) 27.3%	(Top 500) 60.8% (2nd 500) 72.7%	(Top 500) 10.2% (2nd 500) 8.8%	
13. Would you favor a fine which was proportional to the asset size or sales receipts of the defendant company, rather than an absolute maximum amount?	(Top 500) 23.5% (2nd 500) 48.9%	(Top 500) 76.5% (2nd 500) 51.1%	(Top 500) 10.2% (2nd 500) 9.8%	
	LAX	*VIGOROUS*		
14. How do you rate the Antitrust Division in terms of the vigor of its enforcement efforts?	(Top 500) 19.6% (2nd 500) 30.4%	(Top 500) 80.4% (2nd 500) 69.6%	(Top 500) 10.2% (2nd 500) 9.2%	
15. How do you rate the FTC in this same area?	(Top 500) 43.1% (2nd 500) 39.1%	(Top 500) 56.9% (2nd 500) 60.9%	(Top 500) 10.2% (2nd 500) 9.2%	
	JOHNSON	*NIXON* / *NEITHER*		
16. Which administration has been more active in its antitrust enforcement: the Johnson administration or the Nixon administration?	(Top 500) 20.9% (2nd 500) 31.8%	(Top 500) 53.5% 25.6% (2nd 500) 40.9% 27.3%	(Top 500) 8.6% (2nd 500) 8.8%	
	YES	*NO*		
17. Have you ever felt harassed by the antitrust agencies?	(Top 500) 49.1% (2nd 500) 29.6%	(Top 500) 50.9% (2nd 500) 70.4%	(Top 500) 11.0% (2nd 500) 10.8%	

QUESTION	RESPONSE		NUMBER OF RESPONSES AS % OF TOTAL POPULATION (500 CORPORATIONS)
18. Have you ever been specifically helped by the antitrust laws?	(Top 500) 26.5% (2nd 500) 18.4%	(Top 500) 73.5% (2nd 500) 81.6%	(Top 500) 9.8% (2nd 500) 9.8%
19. Do you think vigorous antitrust enforcement is probusiness or antibusiness?	*PRO* (Top 500) 66.6% (2nd 500) 28.9%	*ANTI* (Top 500) 33.4% (2nd 500) 71.1%	(Top 500) 9.6% (2nd 500) 7.6%
20. Do you think American industry would function better without any antitrust laws?	*YES* (Top 500) 11.1% (2nd 500) 9.5%	*NO* (Top 500) 88.9% (2nd 500) 90.5%	(Top 500) 10.8% (2nd 500) 8.4%
21. Does your company have an antitrust compliance program for its officers and employees?	(Top 500) 84.3% (2nd 500) 44.4%	(Top 500) 15.7% (2nd 500) 55.6%	(Top 500) 10.2% (2nd 500) 10.8%

22. In order to assess what types of antitrust deterrents have the greatest impact, businessmen were asked to rank several considerations by assigning each a number from one to six, corresponding to its importance in enforcing compliance with the antitrust laws. The resulting scores, for the Top 500 corporations, were:

258—Personal code/obligation to obey the law
188—Fear of treble damages
153—Competition essential to our economic system
140—Adverse publicity
140—Fear of fines
136—Fear of imprisonment

For the second 500 corporations:

269—Personal code/obligation to obey the law
166—Adverse publicity
159—Fear of imprisonment
158—Fear of treble damages
145—Competition essential to our economic system
144—Fear of fines

APPENDIX C

Survey of Federal District Judges' Attitudes Toward the Antitrust Laws

The Study Group sent questionnaires to 335 federal district-court judges and received anonymous responses from 43, or 13%.

QUESTION	RESPONSE YES	NO	NUMBER OF RESPONSES AS % OF TOTAL POPULATION (335 JUDGES)
1. Have you handled any antitrust cases in the past two years?	34.5%	65.5%	8.7%
2. Did you have any background in economics before your appointment to the bench?	(college major 19.0%) (college courses 11.9%) 33.8%	66.2%	12.5%
3. Judges rarely reject proffered consent decrees. Do you think it *possible* for judges to exercise a more independent role toward acceptance of consent decrees?	85.7%	14.3%	10.4%
4. Do you think it *desirable?*	77.8%	22.2%	8.4%
5. Do you think the trend toward increasing third-party intervention into consent-decree proceedings in court is a good one?	67.6%	32.4%	11.0%
6. Would you favor an increase in the number of class-action treble-damage antitrust actions?	50.0%	50.0%	11.3%
7. Given the complexity and size of some antitrust cases, do you ever find yourself ill-equipped to deal with a large antitrust case?	42.9%	57.1%	10.4%

QUESTION	RESPONSE YES	NO	NUMBER RESPONSES AS % OF TOTAL POPULATION (335 JUDGES)
8. To facilitate disposition of antitrust cases, would you favor:			
a) A special, Article III, Antitrust/Trade Court?	32.4%	67.6%	11.0%
b) Different discovery rules for antitrust cases?	33.3%	66.7%	10.7%
c) Mandatory pretrial timetables laid down by street judges?	77.8%	22.2%	10.7%
d) Greater use of special masters?	58.8%	41.2%	10.1%

9. The length of time an antitrust case takes has been criticized by many observers. Would you rank the following considerations 1–5 in degree of responsibility for delays involved in antitrust cases, with 1 being the factor most responsible for delay and with 5 being the least:

	Total points	7.5%
1) inherent in the case	47	
2) defense counsel	49	
3) plaintiff counsel	67	
4) Antitrust Division	83	
5) judges	90	

QUESTION	YES	NO	%
10. Would you favor a Congressional proposal to increase the maximum Sherman Act fine to $500,000 for corporations?	75%	25%	9.6%
11. Do you think this will considerably increase the fines imposed, since already they fell far short of the present $50,000 maximum?	65.4%	34.6%	8.1%

QUESTION	RESPONSE		NUMBER RESPONSES AS % OF TOTAL POPULATION (335 JUDGES)
	YES	NO	
12. Would you favor making the fine a percentage of a firm's assets or sales rather than a fixed amount?	35.5%	64.5%	9.3%
13. Would you favor having more jail sentences actually served by convicted offenders?	38.7%	25.8%	(Depends on circumstances) 44.5% 9.3%
14. Do you accept *nolo contendere* pleas over government objections?	58.9%	23.5%	(Sometimes) 17.6% 10.1%

INDEX

478   *Index*